D1710416

ENCYCLOPEDIA OF

FOLK HEROES

ENCYCLOPEDIA OF

FOLK HEROES

Graham Seal

A B C ☰ C L I O

Santa Barbara, California   Denver, Colorado   Oxford, England

"Billy the Kid"
Words and Music by Andrew Jenkins
© Copyright Universal - Duchess Music Corporation (BMI)
Inernational Copyright Secured   All Rights Reserved

Library of Congress Cataloging-in-Publication Data

    Seal, Graham, 1950–
    Encyclopedia of folk heroes / Graham Seal.
       p. cm.
       Includes bibliographical references and index.
       ISBN 1-57607-216-9 (hardcover: alk. paper); 1-57607-718-7 (e-book)
       1. Folklore—Encyclopedias. 2. Heroes—Folklore—Encyclopedias. I. Title.
    GR35 .S4 2001
    398'.03—dc21
    2001004423

06 05 04 03 02 01   10 9 8 7 6 5 4 3 2 1

This book is also available on the World Wide Web as an e-book. Visit abc-clio.com for details.

ABC-CLIO, Inc.
130 Cremona Drive, P.O. Box 1911
Santa Barbara, California 93116-1911

This book is printed on acid-free paper ♾.

Manufactured in the United States of America

CONTENTS

Introduction   xi

Encyclopedia of Folk Heroes

INTRODUCTION

The first thing to say about folk heroes is that the world has a great number of them. Our ability to produce stories about heroism, actual or imagined, is remarkable and is one of the defining characteristics of humanity. It seems there has not been a culture, language, time, or place since recorded history, and presumably before, that has not generated stories or ballads about outstanding individuals. Thus, even a book of this size cannot hope to include more than a tiny selection of all possible candidates, and even these need to be described concisely. Those few hundreds of folk heroes who fight, love, play tricks, and doggedly pursue their various quests and fates through the following pages are representative of many traditions and cultures. The main aim of the selection assembled here is to present an overview of heroism as it exists in folklore—that is, in the informal expressions and practices of social collectivities that exhibit a strong sense of identity and communality, usually called "folk groups." This overview involves looking at both legendary and historical figures who appear in folktales, folk songs, and other forms of folk expression and practice, including customs, beliefs, and speech, as well as "fairy tales," the modern reworking of that genre of folktale usually called "wonder tales" or "magic tales."

Criteria for Inclusion and Exclusion

Readers of this encyclopedia will find a representative selection of legendary, historical, and magical heroes from many of the world's extensive folklores, past and present. Almost entirely these figures have been selected from authenticated folk traditions—tales, legends, songs, verse, and occasionally other folkloric forms, as represented in published anthologies and other works in English and in translation from a great many other languages. In some instances the results of primary source research are incorporated into the relevant entries.

Not included, as a rule, are gods and other characters of mythology, such as those of Greece, Rome, or Scandinavia, nor heroes of literary epics like Gilgamesh and Beowulf. There are already many dictionaries and anthologies of these figures, and relatively few of them appear in folklore, although the themes and motifs of their stories often do, as discussed later. Where mythic figures do make significant appearances in folk songs, tales, or other folkloric expressions and activities, as, for example, in the case of King Arthur and a number of Jewish figures, they have been included.

Many of the hero traditions of the world fall into certain generally well-defined categories: outlaw heroes, culture heroes, warriors, tricksters, lovers, occupational heroes, fantasy/supernatural figures, magicians, some "fairy" tale characters, heroes of political and trade union struggles, frontier pioneers, and so on. While this book is a work of synthesis rather than analysis, it tries to suggest something of the cultural, social, or historical significance of individual heroes. In addition to entries for individual figures, the reader will encounter a number of generic entries, two thematic indexes (one for heroic types and one for country/culture), and a chronology of heroes. Some readers should find these signposts especially useful.

Politicians, sport stars, and popular icons such as aviators, explorers, and celebrities are generally avoided, not because they do not deserve acclamation, but because such figures often do not persist much beyond the generation that salutes them, other than in sporting record and history books. Even more importantly for the purpose of this book, they tend not to appear as significant figures of the folkloric expressions mentioned below. Of course, as any folklorist will be quick to point out, nothing in folklore is ever cut and dried, and the relationship between folk expression and other cultural forms such as literature, art, film, television, popular music, and, increasingly, the Internet is a vital one that cannot be ignored in trying to understand the complex processes through which folk heroes are generated and perpetuated.

Religious heroes such as saints, saviors, or prophets are touched upon only lightly. There are far too many of these figures to deal with in a book of this size, or even in a number of such books. It is also often the case that religious figures are largely the creation of the organizations they represent rather than of the people who follow such faiths. A selection of religious heroes with a popular appeal (officially recognized or otherwise) that is reinforced by some folkloric expression has been included. Readers interested in hagiography, a substantial field of its own with ample displays of heroic behavior, are referred to the many available studies of saints, some of which are included in the relevant entries and in the bibliography.

The folkloric genre that is the main vehicle for hero traditions is the folktale, particularly in its forms of legend, wonder tale, migratory tale, anecdote, and yarn. Following in close second place are the extensive traditions of folk song, ballad, and verse, including nursery rhymes and some children's folk expressions. Heroic figures also appear in genres such as puppetry and folk drama, for example, the characters of the English mummers' play (in its hero-combat version especially) and Karagiozis, the comic hero of the Greek shadow puppet theater. Heroic figures may also be the focus of certain folk customs, such as the English Jack-in-the-Green or the Japanese Kobo Daishi (Kukai). Furthermore, folk heroes may be referred to in jokes and colloquial sayings, especially those of a proverbial nature. In the entries, attention has been given to the appearance of folk heroes in different genres. Where relevant, the text of songs and verse—sometimes in full, sometimes in excerpt—may be given, as may information about the appearance of heroes in folk speech, custom, dance, or drama.

Of course, folk heroes do not need to be fictions. Many of the figures who appear in folklore are historical characters, even though the deeds attributed to them in story, song, or verse may or may not be historically accurate. Inaccuracies can generally be traced in folklore. In entries on historical heroes readers will usually find, as far as knowledge allows, some indications of the historicity of the deeds recounted in tradition.

In recent times, and to a lesser degree in earlier periods, folk heroes are the product of interaction between informal oral traditions and other cultural forms. As many of the entries in this encyclopedia demonstrate, there is a continual two-way traffic between oral tradition and literature, the mass media, and cultural forms such as cinema, television, and the Internet. The processes involved in these interactions vary from place to place and time to time, though they tend to emphasize a relatively limited number of favored heroic types or categories. Readers will find considerable, if diverse, discussion about these categories, both in the entries on individual heroes and in entries of a generic nature.

The Qualities of Folk Heroism
The question of what constitutes heroism, whether demonstrated by women or men, is obviously a pressing one for the compiler of a work such as this. In the case of folk heroes— that is, individuals who have some purchase in folklore and, possibly, in literature and popular culture—this question often presents some intriguing difficulties.

The heroes of folklore are often more ambiguous figures than their literary or popular equivalents. The qualities of the protagonist(s) highlighted in tales and songs are not always unreservedly or even significantly positive. Many folk heroes walk a thin and fuzzy line between the admirable and the reprehensible.

This line is seen most clearly, perhaps, in the ubiquitous figure of the outlaw hero, where the practicalities of defying the law are continually balanced by the injustices—real or otherwise—inflicted by those who control that law, as discussed in further detail below.

This moral uncertainty is also found in other traditions, including those of hunting and poaching, of warriors, and even in "fairy" tales where heroes frequently do rather questionable or otherwise unheroic things. When the Russian hero Dobrynya Nikitich goes away, another hero, the part trickster Aloisha Popovich, tells Dobrynya's wife, Princess Nastasya, that her husband is dead in order to win her for himself. The motives of the Chinese Uygar hero Aniz the Shepherd are hatred for and revenge upon the landlord who once insulted and fired him. As readers will discover in the following pages, so it goes throughout the heroic traditions of the world's folklore.

Even those characteristics of a more positive kind associated with heroism are not always as straightforward as we might think. Those activities that generally confer heroism upon individuals may, singly or in various combinations, include the following:

- physical strength
- cleverness
- persistence
- luck
- magic
- wisdom
- helping others
- righteousness
- cunning
- prowess
- power
- lying
- stupidity

We may admire cunning in the form of the trickster's ability to shape-shift, outwit, disguise, and escape, but there is a distinctly uncomfortable aspect to his (far less frequently her) abilities. We are never sure whether the trickster will be using those abilities for us or against us. The Turkish and eastern European trickster, the Hodja, for instance, is admired for his cleverness but is often hard on his neighbors. The tricksters of other cultures can sometimes be reckless, cruel, even stupid, and are frequently subversive of social norms and taboos.

Other wellsprings of heroism involve the magnification or exaggeration of everyday activities, attributes, or skills. Foolishness is one example, with most cultures having an enduring affection for the heroically stupid, it seems, judging by the number and variety of "numskulls," simpletons, noodles, and suchlike figures that people the world's folklores. Another example of ordinariness amplified can be found in relation to occupational heroes who are generally celebrated for their superior, sometimes supernaturally so, work skills and abilities. Such figures, again primarily male, are found in many of the world's folk traditions and include the different but surprisingly similar Paul Bunyan of North American logging fame; Crooked Mick, the outback Australian hero of shearers; and Mikula, the Russian ploughman, to name only some.

On the other hand, a good number of folk heroes employ magic and/or supernatural abilities to achieve their ends and to protect themselves from various forms of villainy. The traditions of China, Japan, Korea, and other eastern countries are especially rich in magical heroes, though such figures also play significant roles in many other cultures. Like most other attributes of heroism, magic may be deployed ambiguously for good or evil purposes. Thus the widely dispersed figure of the witch or female wizard is counterpointed by the human or animal character who uses magical or supernatural power in a positive way, usually to assist the hero. The "Fairy Godmother" is the fairy tale expression of this folkloric feature, which is found almost wherever heroes are talked of or sung about.

Some Interpretations of Folk Heroism

While this book is not primarily an interpretative one, it nevertheless seems necessary to observe that the failings, strengths, and more than occasional moral ambiguities in folk heroes are an aspect of their continuing appeal to people across often considerable time spans and distances. It is not simply their heroism we relate to, but also their human foibles. Heroes are at once those things that almost none of us can ever be, yet they are still like us in so many ways—ways various enough to ensure that some or another hero will appeal to one or more groups of people and so come to be featured in their folk expressions.

These considerations are also relevant to an understanding of the recurrence of heroes, plots, and motifs or story elements throughout the world's cultures, creeds, and languages. In many cases, these recurrences involve cultural groups that had no known historical contact with each other. How did such similar stories come to be told at different times, in different places, by different people without—as far as we know—knowledge of each other's existence?

This difficult, and still unanswered, question was one of the mainsprings behind the great nineteenth- and early twentieth-century upsurge of interest in tales, legends, myths, and other folklore. This interest was spurred on if not initiated by publication of the Grimm brothers *Kinder- und Hausmärchen* ("Children's and Household Tales") in 1812 and its subsequent translations into other languages. Scholars like Andrew Lang, Max Müller, Joseph Jacobs, and Sir James Frazer, to name only some of the better known figures, scoured the world's mythologies, literatures, and folklores, as far as information about them was then available, in search of answers to the conundrum of origins and dispersion. Their conclusions and contentions, now mostly forgotten or debunked, were of thunderous importance in their time, occupying center stage in contemporary intellectual, artistic, and philosophical debates.

Subsequent and current thinking about these matters has tended to slip them quietly into "the too-hard basket" in favor of a more manageable "cultural" approach. This approach acknowledges the diversity and differences of cultures and peoples and generally contents itself with studying folklore in its specificities of time, place, and circumstance. This focused mini- and mono-study has been the predominant approach of folklore scholarship for decades, an approach that eschews the grand global theorizings of Lang, Müller, Frazer, and, specifically in relation to the themes of this encyclopedia, Otto Rank and Lord Raglan. While we now, rightly in many cases, smile at the attempts of the past masters (as in folklore, the culture heroes of this intellectual tradition were almost all male) to make sense of what appeared to them to be a momentous dimension of the human experience, the question is still a nagging one that must lie behind any consideration of the meaning and purpose of folk heroes. There have been, and are, many schools of interpretation, some of which are complementary, more of which are mutually exclusive.

Some solutions for these enigmas move toward the metaphysical. The Jungian emphasis on archetypes in global myths and folktales, deriving from Freud's initial interest in such matters, is perhaps the best known of these approaches. Jungians generally see the recurrence of characters, plots, and motifs as evidence of a supraorganic "race memory" (or, less offensively, "collective memory") and argue that the ultimate meaning of such echoes is the same for all people at all times. Folklorists and other scholars point out that such an approach neglects the cultural, historical, and social specifics that form these expressions in the first place, not to mention their continued development and adaptation according to changing cultural circumstances.

A similar approach to that of Jung and his disciples has been taken more recently by followers of Joseph Campbell, whose works appearing under the general title *The Masks of God*, together with a stream of subsequent works by Campbell and others, reinvented myth and hero studies in ways that at once have continued the grand global arguments of the earlier scholarship on myth and legend mentioned above and have been congenial to the "new age" emphasis on the self. Again, folklorists and others will generally observe that whatever meanings we might ultimately make for folk heroes, their songs and stories are fundamentally rooted in the imperatives of communal expression and communication rather than in the needs, legitimate or otherwise, of the individual. It is this shared meaning that gives the kinds of heroes contained in this book their continuing significance, both for social groups and for our personal hopes and perceptions.

Some psychologists, again taking their lead from Freud, have sought to use folktales as a form of therapy. One of the best-known exponents and proponents of this approach was Bruno Bettelheim, whose *The Uses of Enchantment* (1976) was a best-selling and highly influential work in this field. Many people have followed Bettelheim's lead, and today myths, fairy tales, and heroes are often included in the medicine bag of therapists of all kinds and are even used in such apparently pragmatic fields as management theory and corporate relations. The recent reissuing of Bettelheim's work, together with the many other approaches that espouse similar interpretations of folk heroism, suggests that there is a continuing interest in such applied aspects of folk and fairy tales.

Other scholars have tackled heroism from a structural perspective. An early approach of this kind, building on the previous scholarship of Rank, was that of Lord Raglan, whose work was published comprehensively in his 1936 book *The Hero*. Raglan analyzed mainly mythical figures from a number of traditions and concluded that there were a possible twenty-two elements or "archetypes" that a hero story could possibly encompass. These elements included the unusual circumstances of the hero's birth; his royal parentage; attempts to kill him at birth; his victory over a king, dragon, giant, or wild beast; his assumption of leadership; his mysterious death; the existence of one or more sacred burial sites; and so on. When this approach was applied to the traditions of various heroes, their stories could be "scored" in accordance with Raglan's elements. Thus Oedipus scored 20, King Arthur scored 16, and Nyikang, a hero of the Shilluk culture of the White Nile, scored 12. While this approach was useful in highlighting the similarities between traditions, the recurrence of certain themes and motifs, thus enabling comparison, it did not in the end say a great deal about the meanings that such stories, and the heroes who peopled

them, might have for those who told and retold them. This limitation applies to other such morphological and structural analyses, although Claude Lévi-Strauss and his followers have attempted to discern the deep structures of cultural meaning that underlie myths collected in the field.

One approach that does attempt to relate analysis to lived experience, past and present, is that of Jack Zipes, who interprets fairy tales as ways of rationalizing and so colluding with the darker aspects of modern life. In a number of deeply researched and closely argued books, Zipes has presented an increasingly persuasive case for this view, especially in relation to the uses and abuses of the fairy tale in literature, education, and popular media such as film. A number of other scholars, especially those approaching these matters from a feminist perspective, have made similar observations and arguments, as discussed briefly below and in various entries throughout this encyclopedia.

The folkloric approach to folktales and to other forms of human expression and activity is based upon materials collected in the field. Collecting folktales and songs involves eliciting material from individuals or groups of performers in, as closely as possible, the normal context in which such expressions are communicated. Folklorists consider these versions of songs or stories to be primary sources and all other versions—literary, filmic, and so on—to be of secondary interest. This is not to say that no attention is paid to secondary manifestations of folklore. Instead, modern folklorists usually wish to emphasize the fact that literary and other secondary forms tend to "freeze" a folklore text, whereas in the mouths and, increasingly, in the electrons of the "folk," such texts are constantly being adapted to new cultural circumstances and needs. Alan Dundes provides a forthright and still accurate description of the folkloric approach, as applied to fairy tales, in his "Fairy Tales from a Folkloristic Perspective," in Ruth Bottigheimer's 1986 *Fairy Tales and Society: Illusion, Allusion, and Paradigm*. Dundes has also published extensive examples of his own and others' work in this field. An encyclopedia intended for a general readership cannot hope to provide such ethnographic detail for such a wide range of traditional heroes, even if it were available, which, in many cases it is not. Wherever possible, however, such materials have been preferred for inclusion.

One approach that many scholars of folktale find useful is that of the great folklorists Antii Aarne and Stith Thompson. (In addition to his collaboration with Aarne, Thompson is the author of the classic work *The Folktale*.) Basing their work on what is often called the "Historic-Geographic" method of research, Aarne and Thompson compiled *The Types of the Folktale: A Classification and Bibliography*, a massively learned compendium that collated a good many of the world's folktales and broke them down according to the motifs—the discrete plot elements—of which they were constituted. Their work also identified recurrent "types" or categories of tales to which they assigned an alphanumeric code, usually called a "tale type number." While this approach is very much a generalizing one that takes no account of the cultural and historical contexts within which the stories are told and retold, many researchers, especially those with a classificatory purpose such as educationalists and librarians, still find the Aarne-Thompson approach—and its occasional more specialized successor—useful for the categorization and comparison of texts from a wide variety of cultures and languages. The strengths of motif indexing and tale type numbering are most apparent in the European and North American sources best-known to the compilers. The method has also been the subject of considerable criticism in relation to its gender biases. Motif and tale type numbers are rarely found in anthropological studies dealing with similar spoken materials and, significantly, with the cultural contexts in which they are enunciated.

While necessarily noting the recurrence of motifs and tale types, this encyclopedia makes little use of the Aarne-Thompson approach, because, first, of the limitations just mentioned, but also because such considerations are of more interest to the specialist than to the general reader, and because the heroes peopling these pages pursue their various, though usually similar, ends in a number of expressive forms other than tales, including songs, verse, customs, proverbs, and even jokes. The Aarne-Thompson approach is based almost totally on folktales and so loses a good deal of its comparative and categorizing value when a diversity of folklore genres is examined.

Despite the presence of heroes in a number of folk genres, the folktale is undoubtedly the major bearer of heroic traditions, and it is the genre that has been the subject of most analytic interest. The structural studies initiated by Vladimir Propp, for instance, tend to emphasize the various roles or "functions" of characters in the plots of folk tales. The anthropologist Claude Lévi-Strauss championed a similar structuralist approach to tales and, especially, myths in his numerous and influential works. Again, these works were more concerned with relating the structure of the narratives to the cultural experiences and perceptions that, it was argued, underpinned them and of which they were essentially verbal projections. In these and related approaches the importance of the individual hero, as such, is generally subsumed by larger concerns about the deeper cultural and social significance of the story.

Whatever the interpretative approach taken and whatever the exact circumstances of the hero, though, a constant factor in heroism is struggle. This struggle takes many forms but usually involves heroes overcoming obstacles and difficulties and confronting enemies, monsters, fears, or powers greater than themselves. Sometimes the hero wins. In many cases, he or she loses. But it is not necessarily the winning or the losing that produces stories of heroes; it is their willingness to struggle, to try and overcome or escape forces greater than themselves and, indeed, greater than all our selves.

Here is one important reason why there are so many heroes: they represent our own fears and insecurities and provide a vicarious expression of how we would like to be able to handle our own problems, both personal and communal. It matters not whether folk heroes are portrayed as lords and ladies or as humble peasants, or whether their victories are against serpents, ogres, or other monsters. Beneath the superficialities of character, plot, and story are the deep, global structures of tale and ballad, the recurring motifs of conflict and confrontation. Tellers of tales and singers of songs select from these ancient motif menus to combine and recombine them into stories that are ever-changing in response to new and different circumstances, yet that remain powerfully consistent across centuries, continents, and cultures.

Heroines, Villains, and Fairy Tales

Heroines

Another inescapable conclusion reached from studying folk heroism is the preponderance of heroes over heroines. When there are heroines, they are often in a subservient or subsidiary role as part of a hero story, especially as constant, often unnamed, lovers. Consider the many versions of the ballad "Geordie," where the wife of the main character who vows to "fight for the life of Geordie" is clearly the hero. Yet the ballad is named after her husband or lover, whose principal action in the song is to be hung. In many other narratives sung, recited, or told, women are in marginal, subservient, dependent, or otherwise minor roles. The heroic rescue of the "damsel in distress" is the most blatant example, perhaps, though readers will find other examples in the following pages, which recount numerous stories in which women provide useful help that allows a hero to triumph or in which a portion of the hero's reward is the hand of the beautiful princess in marriage. Such portrayals are especially typical of the modern "fairy" tale. Although they are less cloyingly apparent in the earthier traditions of the told tale and the ballad, here too the heroes are decidedly in the ascendant.

This marginalization and minimization of the feminine seems to hold true, to a greater or lesser degree, almost universally and reflects the male domination and male orientation of most cultures at most times. Observations of this kind have been made by female scholars and writers for well over a century. Since the Victorian era, in the work of Anne Thackeray Ritchie, and more so in recent years through the work of Angela Carter, Margaret Atwood, and others noted in relevant entries and the bibliography, feminist scholars and writers have observed this evidence of patriarchy reflected in folklore and have tried to do something about it. These actions have involved rewriting traditional tales from a feminist point of view or reviewing previous scholarship—mostly by men—with a view to better articulating heroines and/or reinterpreting tales from a feminist perspective.

There has also been a related interest in collecting the versions of tales told by women, and often for women, many of which restructure the gender balance in the narrative. An example of this restructuring is provided in Herbert Halpert and John Widdowson's recent monumental work of folktale scholarship, the two-volume *Folktales of Newfoundland*, in which it is observed that the tales told by a female informant were more likely to contain heroines and that the vast majority of the tales and variants in the collection featured a hero rather than a heroine. The feminist perspective provides another and necessary dimension to an already multifaceted and fascinating form of human expression.

Villains

Without villains there would be few heroes. Villains provide the forces against which heroes strive. Like heroes, villains come in a variety of forms, including male, female, animal, monsters, sorcerers, and so forth. They are variously outwitted, outfought, escaped, or dispatched. No consideration of folk heroism would be complete without some reference to its evil oppositions. Accordingly, a select number of noted villains are included here, such as Bluebeard and a few notorious pirates, along with some discussion of the various types into which villains, or the usually evil oppositional principles they embody, typically coalesce. These types include dragons, ogres, monsters, and some varieties of ill-disposed fairies.

Villains, like the heroes they oppose, may also have ambiguous roles in folklore. As in the case of supernatural beings like fairies, they may be unpredictably helpful or harmful, like the Russian Baba-Yaga. And, again as with many heroes, one folk group's villain may be another folk group's hero. This ambiguity is especially marked in relation to outlaws and other criminal heroes, such as pirates like Blackbeard and Captain Kidd. How many people have not felt at least a glimmer of sympathy for characters like the ogre in "Jack and the Beanstalk," whose villainy is no more than the product of his nature. That his villainy involves eating little boys is unfortunate, but the mostly hapless, opportunistic, and thieving Jack is not exactly a totally admirable hero either.

Fairy Tales

The unhappy prefixing of "fairy" to "tale" is, from most scholarly positions, a nuisance. So widespread is the use and abuse of the term, though, that it cannot be avoided here, especially since stories called "fairy tales" are significant bearers of hero traditions throughout the world. The term "fairy tale" is usually associated with Charles Perrault, the French author whose *Histoires du temps passé: Avec des Moralitez* was published in 1697. However, fairy tale as a generic term for tales of wonder and magic, many of which have nothing to do with fairies, seems to have been invented by a woman contemporary, Mme d'Aulnoy (1655–1705) who used the term for her collection of rewritten folk stories, *Contes des fées*, also first published in 1697. Some of these stories were translated into English in 1699, and the term has been used continually since then.

When the Grimms' collection of folktales—or "household tales," as they were more accurately described in the original German title *Kinder- und Hausmärchen*—was translated into English, the term "fairy tales" was employed. The tremendous and continuing success of the Grimms' work and its never-ending spin-offs and inspirations, from Walt Disney films to the envelopes of folktales available in vending machines at Austrian freeway rest stops, have ensured the continued use of this inaccurate but now unavoidable term. Readers will find a reasonably detailed entry on this enormous field of cultural production and the scholarship that surrounds it. Fairy tales are an important vehicle for folk heroes, but they are far from being the only means of transport, as the diverse entries in this encyclopedia demonstrate.

Why Folk Heroes?

Folk heroes come from many sources—from mythology, from history, from religion. And folk heroes often do not inhabit only folklore. They are also found, in varying presentations, in literature, art, and, in recent times, the media. This diversity of origins and dispersion is a complicating factor. Where do we draw the line between a hero of mythology or a hero of history and a hero of folklore?

The answer is that we do not. Instead, we seek individuals—real and fictional—who have received celebration in one or more forms of folkloric expression and practice—in folktales, folk songs, folk customs, folk speech, and the other informal genres of everyday life. In those genres, we will identify narrative elements or motifs drawn from ancient mythologies, recycled in literature, art, and the mass media. These motifs are not only found in folklore but are part of a much larger pool of common narrative elements that exist in most traditions of the world and that are available for use and reuse by anyone who cares to deploy them—artists, writers, journalists, politicians, and other professionals with a vested interest. When such motifs are used by groups of people in the informal exchanges of everyday life, they are then "folklore." Folklorists take these informal expressions and practices as their object of study and seek to understand and explain their significance, often utilizing the slippery but still useful concept of "tradition" to indicate the extent and spread of such coherent narrative complexes over time and space.

These processes apply not only to fictional characters of legend, wonder tale, and ballad. Historical figures—warriors, jokers, bandits, and the like—may also become folk heroes. The stories that are told about these figures in folklore will relate to their historical activities insofar as those activities are seen to fit into an existing traditional stereotype or narrative structure. In English-language tradition the archetypal narrative for outlaw heroes is provided by Robin Hood, who is, as far as anyone has been able to discover, a fiction. Nevertheless, dozens, if not hundreds, of historical criminals in Britain, America, Australia, and elsewhere have become outlaw heroes in the mold of Robin Hood. This tradition has persisted, as far as we know, for almost a millennium and is one version of a narrative complex known around the world and in considerably older forms in other languages. The historical Dick Turpin, Jesse James, and Ned Kelly did not (at least as far as is recorded, which comes to the same thing) rob back a poor widow's rent from a grasping and heartless landlord—but they all do so in their folklore. For such traditions to become attached to historical characters their actual deeds must be susceptible to such interpretation and, thus, to folkloric celebration in the manner of the outlaw hero. That this is so becomes clear when we consider that out of all the highwaymen, badmen, bushrangers, and others who have operated outside the law, only a select few become the objects of folkloric heroization.

A similar hazy relationship between fact and fantasy can be detected in the many cases where fictional folk heroes are based on historical personages. Tricksters like Till Eulenspiegel, Pedro de Urdemalas, Herschel Ostropolier, and the Hodja are thought to have their origins in the pranks and witticisms of identifiable individuals. Nevertheless, the deeds credited to them in folklore are often the same as those purportedly carried out by other folk tricksters at different times and places. It is not the historical personage who is the folk hero, but the image or representation of that person in folklore. Emperor Napoleon Bonaparte, whatever his achievements as a "great man" of history, is not a folk hero. But the figure "Boney" appears in folklore in a particularly heroic light for some folk groups, notably malcontents among the nineteenth-century British underclass and sailors.

In the popular celebration of selected historical individuals, the relationship between history and folklore is one in which folklore always gets the upper hand, regardless of the historical facts. Nevertheless, to understand how some historical figures become folk heroes we need to know something of their time, their place, and their circumstances. As with literature, art media, and the myriad other forms of human activity, folklore cannot be quarantined from history.

The approach of this encyclopedia of folk heroes—of whom outlaws and tricksters are but two of many types—understands this complex cultural and historical process in the terms outlined above and seeks to explain the necessarily few heroes presented here as representative examples of this widespread and important form of human expression.

Whatever types of heroes we care to mention and whatever attributes, positive or negative, they may display, most have in common a greater or lesser degree of ambiguity, anomaly, and often downright contradiction. This contradiction arises from the fact that heroes frequently straddle the chasms and the conflicts between social groups, between notions of good and evil, right and wrong, power and lack of it, the legal and the illegal. In other words, heroes are liminal figures, forever caught betwixt and between competing and usually conflicting aspects of culture. In their lore, they inhabit anomalous and ambiguous cultural spaces in which the "normal" rules of behavior are suspended, thus allowing heroes to be heroic—that is like us, but better—at least in story and song.

Folk heroes often transgress the normal margins, borders, boundaries, and "rules" of everyday behavior and expectation in the societies where they are celebrated. They are produced by the tensions that define and buttress such margins, tensions that may be the product of political and economic power or other relations. Thus the female warrior figure straddles the gender divide, and the outlaw mediates the line between the legal and the illegal, at least insofar as that line is determined by those who are running things. Other heroes of the people may negotiate boundaries of class and status, as "Princes Di" does for the very British boundary between royalty and commoners.

Of course, the late Lady Diana Spencer's popularity goes far beyond the shores of the British Isles and its peculiar class history. The folk image or persona of "Princes Di" (as opposed to the real Lady Diana Spencer) has sometimes complementary, sometimes quite different, meanings to many people in many different countries, as evidenced by the extraordinary outpourings of grief and other emotions at her death, and since. Her image as a victimized hero of a fairy tale romance, wedding, and, apparently, marriage had much in common with the Cinderella folk narratives. She had come suddenly to prominence from nowhere, just like Cinderella marrying her real-life prince. Then it had all gone horribly wrong and, like Rapunzel, she was banished to the wilderness where she performed good works. Finally, those good works and sacrifices were rewarded by her liaison with a new prince. Not a prince of birth like the old-world nobility, but a prince of new-world wealth. Their death as lovers entwined in the mangled metal of a Paris car wreck was easily interpreted as the "died for love" scenario of Barbara Allen and a thousand other such narratives. The real events of Diana Spencer's life were easily interpreted in terms of a number of folkloric motifs. Thus the folkloric "Lady Di" lived and died the plots of a number of venerable and widespread folk narratives, creating a story that was intelligible and meaningful to millions of people, especially women, on a global scale that far transcended the insularities of the British class system.

The story of Lady Di is an example of the two-way process that typifies the creation of a folk hero. On the one hand, significant communities must have some vested interest in celebrating an individual, real or fictional. But on the other hand, that individual must perform, or be seen to perform, acts congruent with the existing cultural stereotype for such figures. Thus Lady Di fits the late twentieth-century cultural category of "fairy tale princess." Whether her image will persist over generations remains to be seen. More likely, she belongs to the category of celebrity hero, and the imperatives that focused the attention of a generation on her life and death will fade. However, the tradition into which she has been inserted, the cultural category she fits, will continue as long as significant groups of people have need of it. Other figures may take their place within it, but only those who are perceived to be appropriate.

Other folk heroes, from the unpromising bits of boys named Jack, Hans, or Muhammad to the Japanese warrior hero Yuriwaka, are also creations of this two-way process. Their legends arise because they have, inadvertently or otherwise, performed acts, real or imagined, that allow at least one sympathetic group to perceive them as heroic and so reconstruct them as one of the type—or types—of hero that produces meanings essential to this group's view of and place within the world.

The ability of heroes to inhabit a number of different heroic roles is another significant element of folk heroism. Trickster heroes around the world are frequently both "good" and "bad," breaking strong taboos but also affirming the essentials of everyday life in their traditions. The transgressions of the Native American Coyote, for example, include rape, incest, cannibalism, and other lesser but definitely unheroic misdemeanors. Similar contradictions can be observed in trickster and some other hero traditions of many cultures. While these acts of violence and social vandalism may not be held up in the tradition as positive, the figures that carry them out are nevertheless considered "heroic" by the cultures that support them, and their tales, songs, and other folkloric representations persist.

These contradictions are at the base of the tendency of some heroes to take on different, even antagonistic, meanings for various social groups. As noted, the folk hero of one social group is often the villain of another. Outlaws and criminals are obvious examples, but such contradictions are also common in occupational, industrial, and political spheres, where competing views of the world are in a constant state of struggle.

Many folk heroes can also be seen inhabiting a number of apparently antagonistic roles, such as warrior, religious figure, lover, and healer, as is the case of the complex figure of the English hero, Guy of Warwick. Saints and otherwise celebrated religious types may, like St. Patrick of Ireland, also be portrayed in folklore as fearsome and decidedly unsaintly magicians. Many such ostensibly contradictory heroes will be found in this book.

Nor are folk heroes necessarily "heroic" in the sense of being immensely brave, strong, clever, or otherwise empowered. Often their heroism proceeds from the opposite position, from their low social status, as in the case of Cinderella-style traditions, or from a most unpromising start as a good-for-nothing, layabout dreamer, like the young protagonist of Jack and the Beanstalk and the many other such characters that fill the world's traditions.

Stunning success and the overcoming of all obstacles to attain the golden end of the quest is not a necessary component of folk heroism, either. Plenty of those real and mythic figures celebrated in folklore are heroic failures. This is certainly the case with outlaw heroes, with most heroes of struggle, and with national and culture heroes like Arthur who met their earthly end and are now sleeping, waiting to come again. Just winning is not enough to make anyone a folk hero, there must be other factors involved.

One important factor, perhaps the most important one in the modern era, is the multirole suitability of many types of hero to the demands of mass media, especially the entertainment industries. Such suitability has certainly been fundamental to the continued presence of outlaw heroes like Robin Hood, Billy the Kid, and Jesse James, all of whom have been extensively heroized in film, TV, and popular literature. The meanings made in each of these representations differ; nevertheless, the character and many of his or her central attributes continue to be placed before audiences. In these roles, heroes perform certain necessary mediations and negotiations essential to the continued cultural equilibrium(s) of their communities.

The Meanings of Folk Heroes

As mentioned above, there are few approaches to the understanding of the human condition that have not been applied to the explanation of heroism. All of these approaches have something, often much, to offer in enlightening us about our stories of heroic men and women. In the end, though, the celebration of heroes in folklore is mostly about balance.

Through the hero narratives told and retold time and again, tellers and hearers negotiate the imbalances implicit in the stories, which are themselves a reflection of imbalances in the societies from which they spring and to which they continue to speak. Hero narratives mediate such imbalances. Sometimes they ameliorate imbalance and restore equilibrium; sometimes they destroy equilibrium by irritating imbalance. Here we see the necessity of the duality inherent in heroes that enables them to carry out such an important cultural function. Folk heroes, and their stories, songs, and other expressions, allow us continually—if vicariously—to renegotiate the conditions of our culture, to question what is right and what is wrong, to challenge what is legal and what is illegal, to deal with who has power and who does not. Fundamentally, folk heroes allow us to manage the contradictions and conflicts inherent in all cultures.

Ultimately, the aim of hero narratives of all kinds is to restore order, to symbolically create or re-create the everyday equilibrium that must lie at the base of all functioning societies—in short, to make everything all right again. We need folk heroes, and they need us. Depending on our position in time and place, we have various needs to fulfill, tensions to mediate, dreams to dream. We articulate these needs in the form of the folk hero narratives we construct and share. But those figures, real or not, who we choose to celebrate (even if in problematic ways) require our willingness to glamorize them as much as we need them to negotiate for us. In this two-way cultural process, we give something to our folk heroes, and they give something—often something more—to us.

This is what folk heroes have always meant. It is what they will continue to mean as long as human beings aspire to better things.

Using This Book

The entries are arranged alphabetically by surname. Where a hero has a nickname by which he or she is generally known, that name is listed alphabetically with directions to the full entry under that person's real or proper name.

Spelling of proper, and improper, names varies wildly in the sources, both primary and secondary. In most cases, I have used the most common spelling or, failing that, the spelling that makes the most sense in English. Similarly, with the exception of the diacritical marks familiar to readers of French and German, many of the sometimes exotic diacritics necessitated by the pronunciation of languages such as Korean, African, and some South American dialects are not included. Generally, all non-English proper names have been anglicized.

Most entries have a "References and further reading" list appended, as well as a "Related entries" section directing the reader to related entries. The "References and further readings" listings provide the source or sources of the information in the entry and may also include references to other versions of a hero narrative and to critical, contextual, or other works relevant to the subject. Some entries have bibliographical pointers to other reference works, such as encyclopedias or anthologies, which themselves usually provide additional bibliographical resources for further research.

Additional tools for the use of readers have also been provided. These are:

Index of Heroic Types

Here the headwords are arranged in accordance with the variety of heroism that they exemplify, such as outlaws, tricksters, helpers, warriors, and so on.

Please note that in both these indexes the same hero may appear in more than one category, since a common feature of folk heroism is its multifaceted nature.

Country/Culture Index

This index provides a rudimentary guide to the geographical and cultural occurrence of folk heroes. Since the same heroes may appear in different countries and cultures and/or their characteristic exploits may occur in different traditions attached to different heroes, this is a necessarily imperfect tool. It does, however, provide some assistance for readers seeking heroes from particular national, cultural, and ethnic groupings.

Chronology of Folk Heroes

In this chronology the earliest known occurrence of a hero in a tradition, and/or the works that refer to him or her, are presented century by century. This is also a necessarily imperfect aid. In many cases it is simply not possible to date the age of a tradition. Rather than attempt the impossible—and so to mislead—I have included here only those heroes for whom there is a reasonably reliable date of origin or initial recording available.

Bibliography

A lengthy, though necessarily selective, bibliography has been provided. It includes a reasonably comprehensive listing of the major sources for the entries in the encyclopedia and for other works relevant to the folklore of heroes. Most of these works contain extensive bibliographies for further research. There is a large literature on folktales and associated topics in other languages, especially in German and French. Where English translations of these are known to exist they are noted. In addition to scholarly and reference works from the field of folklore, readers will also find some works from other specialties, including history, anthropology, and literature. The aim here, as in many of the bibliographical references appended to the entries, is to give readers access to a wide range of approaches to, and uses of, folk heroes.

Despite massive scholarly efforts over almost two centuries, knowledge of folktale and other folklore forms around the world remains partial. This situation is reflected in the entries and in the bibliography. The limitations of knowledge and of the author are unavoidable. One instance highlights the situation. China has many massive archives of the vast and enduring folklores of its numerous peoples, only a tiny proportion of which has been published in a great number of frequently multivolume books. Most of this collection and scholarship is unknown in the West, since relatively little has been translated into English or other European languages (with the partial exception of German). Readers interested in further serious world folktale scholarship will find ample signposts to published research in many of the works listed in the bibliography.

General Index

This index presents all significant topics, names, and so on alphabetically and by page number. A good many individual heroes who do not have their own entry in the encyclopedia but are mentioned in relation to those who do, or who appear in the generic entries, are included here. Readers should consult this index if they do not find an individual entry for the hero they seek in the body of the encyclopedia.

Acknowledgments

The members of the editorial board have provided oversight and guidance in a number of areas as this work has developed. Staff and readers at ABC-CLIO have been critically constructive throughout a long research, writing, and publishing project. Colleagues at Curtin University of Technology have provided the opportunity for a significant portion of the research necessary for this project, together with a continually stimulating occupational environment. Finally, having survived the obstacles of this particular quest, I would like to thank my personal heroines, Maureen, Kylie, and Jenna.

Select references

Aarne, A. and Thompson, S., *The Types of the Folktale: A Classification and Bibliography*, Folklore Fellows Communication 184, Helsinki: Academia Scientiarum Fennica, 1961. Translated and enlarged from the 1928 edition written by S. Thompson.

Bettelheim, B., *The Uses of Enchantment: The Meaning and Importance of Fairy Tales*, New York: Knopf, 1976.

Bottigheimer, R. (ed.), *Fairy Tales and Society: Illusion, Allusion, and Paradigm*, Philadelphia: University of Pennsylvania Press, 1986.

Campbell, J., *The Hero with a Thousand Faces*, Princeton, NJ: Princeton University Press, 1968.

Ellis, J., *One Fairy Story Too Many: The Brothers Grimm and Their Tales*, Chicago: University of Chicago Press, 1983.

Halpert, H. and Widdowson, J., *Folktales of Newfoundland: The Resilience of the Oral Tradition*, 2 vols., New York: Garland, 1996.

Hearne, B., *Beauty and the Beast: Visions and Revisions of an Old Tale*, Chicago: University of Chicago Press, 1989.

Jurich, M., *Scheherazade's Sisters: Trickster Heroines and Their Stories in World Literature*, Westport and London: Greenwood Press, 1998.

Klapp, O., "The Folk Hero," *Journal of American Folklore* 62, 1949.

Lundell, T., "Folktale Heroines and the Type and Motif Indexes," *Folklore* 94, no. 2 (1983): 240–246.

Luthi, M. (trans. Erickson, J.), *The Fairytale as Art Form and Portrait of Man*, Bloomington: Indiana University Press, 1984 (1975).

Minard, R., *Womenfolk and Fairy Tales*, Boston: Houghton Mifflin, 1975.

Propp, V., *The Morphology of the Folktale*, Austin: University of Texas Press, 1968.

Raglan, Lord, *The Hero: A Study in Tradition, Myth, and Drama*, London: Methuen & Co., Ltd., 1936.

Rank, O., *The Myth of the Birth of the Hero*, New York: 1914.

Simpson, J., "'Be bold, but not too bold': Female Courage in Some British and Scandinavian Legends," *Folklore* 102, no. 1 (1991): 16–30.

Stone, K., "Things Walt Disney Never Told Us," *Journal of American Folklore* 88, 1975.

Tatar, M., *The Hard Facts of the Grimms' Fairy Tales*, Princeton, NJ: Princeton University Press, 1987.

Thompson, S., *The Folktale*, New York: Holt, Rinehart, and Winston, 1946.

Warner, M., *From the Beast to the Blonde: On Fairy Tales and Their Tellers*, London: Chatto and Windus, 1994.

Zipes, J., *Fairy Tales and the Art of Subversion*, New York: Wildman Press, 1983.

Zipes, J., *Happily Ever After: Fairy Tales, Children, and the Culture Industry*, New York and London: Routledge, 1997.

Zipes, J., *When Dreams Came True: Classical Fairy Tales and Their Tradition*, New York and London: Routledge, 1999.

Zipes, J. (ed.), *The Trials and Tribulations of Little Red Riding Hood*, New York: Routledge, 1993.

ENCYCLOPEDIA OF

FOLK HEROES

A

Abunuwas

Also called Kibunwas, Abunuwas is the trickster hero of East Africa, Zanzibar, Madagascar, and Mauritius, and also appears in Egyptian tradition as "Abu-Nawwass." Abunuwas is believed to be based on the eighth-century Arabic poet Abu Nuwas, who was depicted in Arabic literature as cunning, intelligent, and decidedly amoral. These characteristic features made the poet an ideal focus for the accretion of many stories from both Arabic and non-Arabic sources, including those told of Hodja and other tricksters.

In a Mauritian story, Abunuwas borrows a copper saucepan from his neighbor. He keeps it for three days and on the fourth day returns it with a smaller saucepan nesting inside. The neighbor says that the small saucepan is not his, but Abunuwas insists that the larger saucepan has given birth to the smaller saucepan and so the new implement is rightfully the property of his neighbor. Gratefully, the neighbor accepts. Three days later Abunuwas borrows the large saucepan again, but this time he does not return it. Eventually the neighbor asks him for it, but Abunuwas tells the neighbor that the saucepan has died. Incredulous, the neighbor asks if it is possible for copper to die. Abunuwas then asks him if the saucepan did not give birth to a smaller one. The neighbor, having already accepted the smaller saucepan on this assumption, has to agree, and Abunuwas points out that if it is possible for a saucepan to give birth, then it is also possible for it to die. Reluctantly, the neighbor has to agree with this reasoning, especially as it is backed up by the learned elders. The neighbor is poorer but wiser, and Abunuwas gains a saucepan. Much the same story is attached to the Turkish Hodja and to other tricksters.

Related entries: Anansi; Coyote; Ero; Eulenspiegel, Till; Gearoidh, Iarla; Gizo; Hare; Hlakanyana; Hodja, The; Jack o' Kent; Jones, Galloping; Kabajan; Magicians; Maui; Nanabozho; O'Connell, Daniel; Ostropolier, Hershel; Popovich, Aloisha; Quevedo; Rabbit; Ramalingadu, Tenali; Shape-Shifters; Shine; Skorobogaty, Kuzma; Spider; Tortoise; Tricksters; Urdemalas, Pedro de

References and further reading

Arnott, K. (ed.), *African Myths and Legends*, London: Oxford University Press, 1962.

Bushnaq, I. (trans. and ed.), *Arab Folktales*, New York: Pantheon Books, 1986, pp. 273–276.

Courlander, H., *A Treasury of African Folklore*, New York: Crown, 1975, pp. 574–587.

El-Shamy, H. (coll., trans., ed.), *Folktales of Egypt*, Chicago: University of Chicago Press, 1980, pp. 219–226.

Achikar

Assyrian (Iraq) wise man of legend who in old age, being childless, adopts his nephew, Nadan. Nadan is a villain who soon manages to get the king of Assyria to condemn Achikar to death. Achikar escapes and is presumed dead. The king of Assyria then receives a demand from the Egyptian pharaoh to build a fantastic tower or castle in the air. If he succeeds, the pharaoh will reward the king with great wealth. If he fails, the pharaoh will confiscate the same amount from the king. This impossible task is magically carried out when Achikar returns, claiming the prize and being admitted back into the king's favor.

Achikar is also known as Ahikar, Achhiacarus, Ahiqar, and, in Burton's supplement to *The 1,001 Nights*, Haykar the Sage. His tale was probably old when it was included in a fifth-century B.C. papyrus. It is known in ancient Arabic, Syriac, Ethiopic, Armenian, and Slavonic sources, and in Jewish, Turkish, and Rumanian versions, though it is thought to be of Macedonian origin. Whatever its source, this tale, with its castle-in-the-air motif, is extremely widespread in folklore.

The impossible task accomplished and the reinstatement of the previously despised hero to good standing after he applies his wisdom to save the kingdom and its people is also found in variants of this tradition, including stories in which a king orders all elderly men to be executed because they are unable to till the fields. One such man is sheltered from death by his son and is eventually the only person in the land with the necessary wisdom to save the kingdom from one catastrophe or another.

Related entries: Adam, Rabbi; Ahmed; Culture Heroes; Dog-Nyong, General Gim; Eight Immortals, The; Fereyel; Gim; Habermani; Helpers; Loew, Rabbi Judah; Magicians; Marendenboni; Merlin; Molo; Nue the Hunter; Pied Piper, The; Wirreenun the Rainmaker; Wise Men and Women
References and further reading
Burton, R., *The Arabian Nights' Entertainments*, 13 vols., London: H. Nichols, 1894–1897.
Christensen, A. (ed.), Kurti, A. (trans.), *Persian Folktales*, London: Bell and Sons, 1971.
Leach, M. (ed.), *Funk and Wagnall's Standard Dictionary of Folklore, Mythology, and Legend*, London: New English Library, 1975, p. 6. Abridged one-volume edition of *Funk and Wagnall's Standard Dictionary of Folklore, Mythology, and Legend*, 2 vols., New York: Funk and Wagnall, 1972.

Adam, Rabbi

A medieval Jewish magician and illusionist. A sorcerer often referred to as "the master of all mysteries." Rabbi Adam is said to be the possessor of the Book of Adam, also called the Book of Mysteries, given to the first man and containing many secrets. The book has been entrusted to only six humans before him and is given into his care because of the great spiritual learning he has achieved. Throughout his life Rabbi Adam watches over the book and its secrets. But as he grows older, he begins to worry about entrusting the book to a suitable successor. He asks God to give him a son to whom he can teach all the wisdom he himself has attained.

God obliges, and the Rabbi is blessed with an intelligent and willing son to whom he teaches everything he knows, which is a great deal indeed. The son learns the Torah and then the Cabbala. But then he asks no more questions, content with the great wisdom he has already absorbed. Rabbi Adam knows now that his son is not the one to take the book. The rabbi is old and tired and wishes only to die, and there are numerous stories about his efforts to find a person worthy to hold the Book of Mysteries after his death.

The figure of the rabbi is featured extensively in Jewish folklore throughout the world, often in the role of the wise man or magician and as the target of the trickster, and even in the series of Aladdin-like sea adventures experienced by the Talmudic sage Rabbah Bar Bar Hannah.

Related entries: Baal-Shem-Tov; Loew, Rabbi Judah; Magicians; Religious Heroes
References and further reading
Ausubel, N. (ed.), *A Treasury of Jewish Folklore*, London: Vallentine, Mitchell, 1972 (1948).
Bin Gorion, M. (coll.), Ben-Amos, D. (trans.), *Mimekor Yisrael: Classical Jewish Folktales*, 3 vols., Bloomington: Indiana University Press, 1976.
Cavendish, R. (ed.), *Legends of the World*, London: Orbis, 1982, pp. 107–109.
Ginzberg, L. (trans. Szold, H.), *The Legends of the Jews*, 7 vols., Philadelphia: The Jewish Publication Society of America, 1900.
Schwartz, H., *Elijah's Violin and Other Jewish Fairy Tales*, New York: Harper and Row, 1983, pp. 152–158.

Admiral Benbow

See Benbow, Admiral

Ahay

Brother of legendary Chinese Sani heroine, Ashma. Ahay goes to rescue Ashma from the dungeon where a wicked landlord has imprisoned her to be his son's bride. Ahay wins archery contests organized by the bridegroom and gains a promise of his and Ashma's release. But the landlord and his son betray the brother and sister by sending three tigers into Ahay's room. He survives the tigers' attack, causing the landlord and his son to admit they have been bested. They then release Ahay and Ashma.

But as the brother and sister go on their way through the mountains, the landlord has his men breach a lake. Despite Ahay's attempts to save his sister, Ashma is drowned in the resulting flood, becoming a local heroine of the Sani people around the Stone Forest of Yunnan Province.

Related entries: Ashma; Hood, Robin; Hou Yi; Ivanovich, Dunai; Local Heroes; Tametomo; Yuriwaka

References and further reading
Ding Wangdao, *Chinese Myths and Fantasies*, Beijing: China Translation Publishing Company, 1991.
Li, N., *Old Tales of China*, Singapore: Graham Brash, 1983 (1981), pp. 2–4.

Ahmed

Possessor of a magic tent and a magic apple, Ahmed appears in *The Arabian (1,001) Nights* (and elsewhere, such as Lang's *Blue Fairy Book*) as hero of the story of Prince Ahmed and Periebanou, a fairy. Ahmed comes into possession of many magical objects, including a tent that can be carried in a pocket, but when pitched can hold an army, and an apple that cures any illness. Although he possesses and uses magical objects, Ahmed is not himself a magician. In this respect he is similar to many folk heroes, such as Aladdin, Sindbad, and others, who are also able to make use of magical implements but do not have the power to create or destroy such things. These powers are reserved for a more exalted and more powerful form of folk hero, the wizard or magician. Ahmed is thus similar to characters from other traditions, such as the hero of medieval folktales named Fortunatus, who had a collection of useful magical possessions, including a purse that provided an inexhaustible supply of money. The magical object that provides a never-ending supply of food, money, or other necessities is a common feature of folk traditions.

Related entries: Achikar; Adam, Rabbi; Aladdin; Arabian Nights, The; Baba, Ali; Dog-Nyong, General Gim; Eight Immortals, The; Fereyel; Gim; Habermani; Loew, Rabbi Judah; Magicians; Marendenboni; Merlin; Molo; Nue the Hunter; Pied Piper, The; Scheherazade; Väinämöinen; Wirreenun the Rainmaker

References and further reading
Burton, R., *The Arabian Nights' Entertainments*, 13 vols., London: H. Nichols, 1894–1897.
Bushnaq, I. (trans. and ed.), *Arab Folktales*, New York: Pantheon Books, 1986.
Irwin, R., *The Arabian Nights: A Companion*, London: Allen Lane, 1994, p. 47.

Aladdin

Son of a poor Chinese tailor's widow, the legendary Aladdin is one of the best-known characters of *The 1,001 Nights*. Like many other heroes, he has an unpromising beginning as a lazy good-for-nothing who is one day sought out by a magician to enter a cave of treasure. In particular, the magician wants Aladdin to bring him a copper lamp that lies within the cave. The magician gives Aladdin his signet ring as protection, and the boy enters the cave, eventually coming back to the entrance with handfuls of treasure. He asks the magician to help him out, but the magician fears Aladdin is trying to trick him and closes the boy into the cave. Here, Aladdin accidentally rubs the magician's signet ring, and a jinni ("genie") appears and helps him return to his mother. Aladdin returns as a much more useful member of society, still carrying the copper lamp. He discovers that there is a jinni in the lamp, who comes to his aid later in the story. One day when cleaning the lamp, Aladdin's mother releases the jinni within and their wishes are granted, allowing them to escape their life of poverty.

With the help of a jinni, Aladdin accomplishes numerous impossible tasks set by the sultan and marries the sultan's daughter, Princess Badr al-Budur. One day the magician, having heard about the lamp and wanting it for himself, cleverly pretends to be giving away new lamps for old. The princess unwittingly hands over the magic lamp, and the magician is able to command the jinni of the lamp to abduct the princess and transport her to Africa. Assisted by the jinni of the ring, Aladdin pursues them and is able to rescue the princess and kill the magician.

This is the basic story familiar in one version or another to most people as "Aladdin and the Lamp," staple fare of pantomimes, storybooks,

Aladdin receiving the Princess (Bettmann/Corbis)

and animated movies, the majority of which portray Aladdin as Middle Eastern rather than as Chinese. Scholars have determined that the Aladdin story is a mixture of Asian and European elements.

The poor boy, often as initially worthless as Aladdin, unexpectedly developing into a hero is a near-universal theme of folktale. Many of the other motifs in the story are also widespread, including the discovery of a magic object beneath the ground, a magical lamp that grants wishes, magical transportation by air, and, of course, the happy ending. These elements have contributed to the longevity and popularity of Aladdin in many forms of cultural expression, including folklore, literature, theater, and film.

Related entries: Ahmed; Arabian Nights, The; Baba, Ali; Fairy Tale Heroes; Jack; Magicians; Scheherazade

References and further reading

Burton, R., *The Arabian Nights' Entertainments*, 13 vols., London: H. Nichols, 1894–1897, chap. 31.

Clouston, W., *Popular Tales and Fictions: Their Migrations and Transformations*, 2 vols., Edinburgh and London: William Blackwood, 1887, pp. 407–482.

Irwin, R., *The Arabian Nights: A Companion*, London: Allen Lane, 1994, pp. 2, 17–18, 27, 30, 47–48, 57–58, 101, 159, 185–186, 191, 197, 201, 236–237, 242, 267–268, 281, 289.

Alexander the Great

King of Macedonia (356–323 B.C.) and the focus of a considerable body of folklore in many cultures. Alexander conquered much of the known world, including the extensive Persian Empire, between his ascension to the Macedonian throne in 336 B.C. and his death at the age of only thirty-three. Generally considered to be one of the finest military geniuses of all time, Alexander persists as a great hero in the folk songs and tales of the many lands and people his conquests traversed, from Macedonia to India. The remarkable facts of Alexander's brief but eventful life, together with his far-flung military adventures, have produced a large body of folklore. He appears in Christian, Jewish, and Muslim traditions. In the latter, he is usually named "Iskander" and is often linked with El Khidre, another widespread hero. As well as having perhaps the widest geographical distribution of any named folk hero, Alexander is also an unusually multifaceted hero, having attracted to his image a great many of the legends told of other notables.

One of the most powerful aspects of Alexander's legend is, not surprisingly, his stature as a warrior. Iranian tradition, for example, often refers to the hero as "King Alexander" and recounts his brilliant, ruthless, and sometimes bloodthirsty victories and accomplishments. Medieval Christian stories have Alexander fighting female cannibals, six-headed giants, and other monsters in the best traditions of the giant-slayer. In both Jewish and Christian tradition, Alexander is said to have reached the gates of paradise.

One tradition has it that Alexander, passing through Phrygia in 334, cut the Gordian Knot. In Greek myth, the Gordian Knot is tied by a commoner, Gordius, who becomes king of Phrygia through an oracle decreeing that the first person to drive a wagon into the public square should become ruler of the country. Gordius is the lucky wagoner who does this. He then dedicates his wagon to the god Zeus, leaving it within a temple with the pole of the wagon tied by a bark rope to its yoke. So complex is this knot that no one is able to untie it, and the belief arises that whoever can untie the knot will be ruler of the entire Asian continent. The legend goes that Alexander tried to untie the knot but, failing, characteristically sliced it apart with his sword, going on to become lord of Asia. The folk saying to "cut the Gordian Knot," meaning to resolve a difficult problem, persists today.

Alexander's imperious nature is also the implicit subject of one of the tales most commonly told of him. In the middle of a dusty desert, Alexander comes upon a small river. The tranquillity and beauty of the river tempt Alexander to forgo the world of violence, greed, and treachery and to live by the river in peace. However, Alexander rejects this possibility and marches on. Eventually he and his army must rest by the banks of the river, from which a fish is caught for the great man's supper. So fine does the fish taste that Alexander concludes that the river must flow from a rich country. He follows the river and comes to the gates of paradise. Alexander announces himself as the great conqueror and lord of all the earth and demands to be allowed into paradise. But the gates remain locked, and a voice from the other side says that this is the home of the just and the peaceful and that only those who have conquered their passions may enter. "Nations may have paid homage to thee, but thy soul is not worthy to be admitted within the gates of the abode of the just. Go thy ways, endeavor to cure thy soul, and learn more wisdom than thou hast done hitherto," says an Israeli version of the tale given by Rappoport.

No matter how Alexander asks to enter, he is refused. Eventually he asks for a gift that will prove that he has traveled to the gates of paradise. The guardian of the gates gives him a human skull, saying that it can teach Alexander more wisdom than he has acquired in all his conquests. Angrily, Alexander throws the skull down. However, a learned man among his retinue suggests to Alexander that the skull be weighed with gold. To Alexander's surprise, the skull outweighs all the gold brought to the scales. Alexander asks if there is anything that could outweigh his skull from the gates of paradise. "Yes," says the learned man, pointing to an eye socket. "This fragment, great king, is the socket of a human eye that, though small in compass, is unbounded in desire. The more gold it has the more it craves for and is never satisfied. But once it is laid in the grave, there is an end to its lust and ambition." The wise man then asks Alexander to have the eye socket covered in dirt. As soon as this is done, the gold outweighs the skull. The moral of the story is the futility of human endeavor, even endeavors as great as those of Alexander.

The range and variety of traditions about Alexander have led at least one authority, writing in Funk and Wagnall's Standard Dictionary of Folklore, Mythology, and Legend, to claim Alexander is the greatest folk hero of all. In addition to his extensive folklore, and as a consequence of his historical deeds, Alexander is also revered as a Macedonian culture and national hero.

Related entries: Culture Heroes; Khidre, El; National Heroes; Warriors

References and further reading
Abbott, G., Macedonian Folklore, Cambridge: Cambridge University Press, 1903, pp. 279–289.
Alexander the Great on the Web, www.isidore-of-seville.com/Alexanderama.html.
Cavendish, R. (ed.), Legends of the World, London: Orbis, 1982, pp. 106–107, 230–234, 283–284.
Christensen, A. (ed.), Kurti, A. (trans.), Persian Folktales, London: Bell and Sons, 1971.
Eberhard, W. (ed.), Parsons, D. (trans.), Folktales of China, Chicago: University of Chicago Press, 1965 (1937), pp. 91, 219.
Leach, M. (ed.), Funk and Wagnall's Standard Dictionary of Folklore, Mythology, and Legend, 2 vols., New York: Funk and Wagnall, 1972, vol. 1, pp. 34–35.
Ranelagh, E., The Past We Share: The Near Eastern Ancestry of Western Folk Literature, London: Quartet Books, 1979, pp. 45–80.
Rappoport, A., Myth and Legend of Ancient Israel, 2 vols., London: Gresham Publishing Co., 1928, vol. 1, pp. 126–129.
Stoneman, R. (trans. and ed.), Legends of Alexander the Great, London: J. M. Dent, 1994.

Alfred the Great

Alfred the Great (849–899) was king of Wessex between 871 and 899. His historical fame is primarily that of a statesman, leader, and successful resister of Danish incursions, but he appears most famously in folklore in the story of the king who burned the cakes. The tradition is that during one of his campaigns against the marauding Danes, Alfred sought shelter and rest in a cowherd's hut. Not announcing himself as king, and not recognized as such by his humble hosts, Alfred is left to mind the cakes (or bread) that the cowherd's wife is baking. With his mind on loftier matters, Alfred fails to notice that the cakes are burning and is roundly chastised by the baker when she returns to find her work ruined. The sign of Alfred's true greatness as a leader of his people is that he allows even the lowliest of his subjects to scold him for an oversight trivial to a king but significant to a poor commoner. This tale, perhaps from as early as the eleventh century, is still told in England.

However, not all versions of the story say that Alfred burned the cakes, so it is perhaps dangerous to speculate about its significance, except insofar as this story and other traditions about Alfred reflect his status as a culture and national hero of the English. Alfred's activities eventually lead him to be recognized as king of England.

Another tradition about Alfred is that he disguised himself as a harper to penetrate the camp of the Danes in order to learn their battle plans, a story told of many other heroes of folklore and literature, including Hereward the Wake.

Related entries: Culture Heroes; Hereward the Wake; National Heroes

References and further reading

Briggs, K. and Tongue, R. (eds.), *Folktales of England*, London: Routledge and Kegan Paul, 1965.

Westwood, J., *Albion: A Guide to Legendary Britain*, London: Granada, 1985, pp. 3–4, 71, 181, 281.

Ali Baba

See Baba, Ali

Allen, Barbara

Heroine of a ballad composed or adapted from tradition by Allan Ramsey, perhaps as early as 1724 (Oliver Goldsmith [1730–1774] recalled it being sung to him by "our old dairy-maid"). The basic Barbara Allen story, of which numerous variations exist, is of a beautiful woman who scorns the affections of a young man. Unable to bear his rejection, the young man suicides. Barbara Allen is overcome with remorse and dies from grief; she usually requests to be buried beside the unrequited lover. The last verse often revolves around the motif of entwined roses growing from the graves of Barbara Allen and her disappointed suitor, a motif also found in other ballads on similar themes. However, tradition supports less clichéd conclusions to the story, as in the version from Percy's *Reliques* (1765), given by Child (1965):

> So this maid she then did dye,
> And desired to be buried by him,
> And repented herself before she dy'd,
> That ever she did deny him.

The apparent oversentimentality of the basic story disappears in the often powerful renditions of good ballad singers. The "died for love" motif is one found in many hero and heroine traditions and is especially favored in ballads. Barbara Allen is still sung widely in Britain, America, and Australia.

Related entries: Ataba; Bernèz; E-ttool, Zarief; Little Goose Girl, The; Morevna, Marya; Nastasya, Princess; Nou Plai; Rapunzel; Rose-Red; Sahin; Spiewna; Vasilisa; Xishi; Zeej Choj Kim

References and further reading

Belden, H. (ed.), *Ballads and Songs Collected by the Missouri Folklore Society*, University of Missouri Studies 15, no. 1, 1940, pp. 60–65.

Botkin, B. (ed.), *A Treasury of American Folklore: Stories, Ballads, and Traditions of the People*, New York: Crown Publishers, 1944, pp. 820–822.

Chappell, W., *Popular Music of the Olden Time*, 2 vols., New York: Dover Publications, 1965 (1859), pp. 538–539.

Child, F. J., *The English and Scottish Popular Ballads*, 5 vols., New York: Dover Publications, 1965 (1882–1898), vol. 2, pp. 276–279, no. 84.

Lloyd, A., *Folksong in England*, New York: International Publishers, 1970 (1967), pp. 31, 154.

Amala

Legendary Native American Tsimshian, Nass, Skidegate, Kaigani, Massett, and Tlingit culture hero. Amala or "Very Dirty" (the name literally means "smoke hole") is usually said to be a lazy, weakling youngest brother who, like Cinderella, sleeps in the ashes and is generally mistreated by all. In many versions of these stories, the hero is marked out from the rest of the group because he sleeps in his own urine. Secretly, though, he gains supernatural strength, becoming handsome, strong, powerful, saving relatives from enemies, and generally performing many feats of strength. His final task is to take over the support of the world from a dying chief on an island in the Southwest sea. Hearing of Amala's deeds, the dying chief sends for the hero and transfers the long pole holding up the flat world revolving on it from his chest to Amala's. Assisted by a large spoonful of duck grease and annual bodily anointments of wild-duck oil, Amala keeps the world spinning. When he dies, the world will end.

It is likely that the cycle of stories featuring Amala may have been influenced by European-introduced Cinderella and Atlas traditions. In the case of Amala and other similar Native American heroes, these traditions of the outcast hero and the chthonic or underworld-dwelling hero have been combined in a variety of stories in which the despised hero triumphs over various difficulties despite the hostility of his tribal group. Studies indicate that while the same or similar themes and motifs may be present in the hero traditions of different cultural groups, the exact forms they take and the meanings they have will depend upon the belief systems, needs, and other aspects of each group.

Related entries: Assipattle; Cap o' Rushes; Catskin; Cinderella; Cinder-Mary; Culture Heroes; Fairy Tale Heroes; Ye Xian

References and further reading

Boaz, F. (ed.), *Folk-Tales of Salishan and Sahaptin Tribes*, Lancaster, PA: American Folklore Society, 1917.
Leach, M. (ed.), *Funk and Wagnall's Standard Dictionary of Folklore, Mythology, and Legend*, London: New English Library, 1975, p. 41. Abridged one-volume edition of *Funk and Wagnall's Standard Dictionary of Folklore, Mythology, and Legend*, 2 vols., New York: Funk and Wagnall, 1972.
Randall, B., "The Cinderella Theme in North-West Indian Folklore," in Smith, M. (ed.), *Indians of the Urban North-West*, New York: Columbia University Press, 1949.
Segal, D., "The Connections between the Semantics and the Formal Structure of a Text," in Maranda, P. (ed.), *Mythology*, Harmondsworth, Middlesex: Penguin, 1972, pp. 215–249. Translated from Italian by R. Vitello. Originally published in Russian in *Peotika II*, Varsovie, 1966, pp. 15–44.

Amaradevi

Legendary Kampuchean (Cambodia) princess who outwits the king's four grand ministers, who plot to marry her so that they can control her wealth. They spread false rumors about Amaradevi's husband, Mahoseth Pandide, and the king banishes him from the country, allowing the ministers to court the princess. Being clever as well as beautiful, Amaradevi is well aware of the ministers' real intentions and has a pit dug beneath her room, covered with a trapdoor. Her servants fill the pit with mud, sticky rice, and hot water. As each minister comes to her room, professing his false love for her while he steals her jewels, he is tipped into the pit. All four ministers are left in the sticky pit for the night, thrashing around and becoming increasingly glued to the stolen jewels each carries. In the morning, Amaradevi has them taken to her father the king, and she triumphantly reveals the ministers' treachery by drawing forth a precious royal jewel from each of their pockets. The ministers are dragged through the streets on elephants, and Amaradevi bows to the king and returns to her rooms in the palace, her duty done. The theme of the clever woman outwitting those powerful male forces that would coerce her into unacceptable situations, including death, is found throughout folk tradition, for example, in the stories of Scheherazade and Fatima, the last wife of the monstrous Bluebeard, among others. Also widespread is the essential theme of this story, the revelation of wrongdoing by the trusted servants of a greater power, usually a king.

This story of Amaradevi, together with many other Cambodian tales, is contained in the *Gatiloke*, a collection of the tales and traditions of the Cambodian people compiled in the nineteenth century. One of the main reasons for compiling the tales, and one of the main reasons such tales were and are told in Cambodia, is that they taught children—and reminded adults—of Cambodian morals and values. *Gati* is usually translated as "the path of morality" and *loke* means "the world." Thus *Gatiloke* can be understood as "the correct way to live in the world." The tales and other traditions of most cultures may also function as such moral guides, whether the moral is formally drawn or not, as it is in the story of Amaradevi.

Related entries: Fairy Tale Heroes; Scheherazade; Wise Men and Women

References and further reading

Carrison, M. and Chhean, K., *Cambodian Folk Stories from the Gatiloke*, Rutland, VT and Tokyo: C. E. Tuttle Co., 1987, pp. 23–30.

Faurot, J. (ed.), *Asian-Pacific Folktales and Legends*, New York: Simon and Schuster, 1995.

Anansi

Spider trickster of West and Central Africa and of the African diaspora in the Caribbean, northern South America, and the United States of America. Anansi (also spelled Ananse, Anancy, or Nansi) goes by numerous localized names, including "Ti Malice" in Haiti, "Boy Nasty" or "B'Rabby" in the Bahamas, "Nancy" in Curacao, and "Aunt Nancy" or "Miss Nancy" along the Carolina and Georgia coast. Wherever he is found, Anansi is a cunning trickster, making full use of his insect abilities, such as eight feet and a sticky web, along with his magical powers to attain his usually greedy, self-centered ends. Anansi is able to transform into a hare, a fox, or even a human and is usually thought to be the origin of Brer Rabbit, as popularized by Joel Chandler Harris in his Uncle Remus stories from 1880. Like many trickster figures, Anansi is amoral, duplicitous, and greedy and is sometimes shown being outwitted by other animals, or even by humans.

Among the most frequently encountered Anansi tales are those that tell of his tricking Tiger into letting him ride on his back and of how Anansi stole the sun. Also typical of Anansi tales are those that show him being bested, as in the story of the farmer who, fed up with Anansi's thieving of his property, places a tar or gum baby in his field. When Anansi comes to the field he greets the tar baby and, receiving no response, slaps the sticky figure with his hand, which immediately sticks to the doll. Anansi tries to kick the tar baby with the same result. The farmer arrives, finds Anansi struggling to escape the tar baby, and, gleefully, beats Anansi flat, thus explaining how spiders came to be such flattened-out creatures.

As well as explanatory legends of this kind, trickster tales often point to a moral, a characteristic well illustrated by a Jamaican Anansi story in which the trickster is living in a country where the queen is also a witch. Her secret name is the word "five," and she decrees that anyone who speaks the word will die on the spot. Scheming Anansi, known as "Buh Anansi" in Jamaica, is hungry because there is a famine. He has an idea. He decides to build a house on the river where people come to get their water, and he makes a pile of yam hills. Whenever anyone comes for water, he calls out to them, saying that he cannot count and so will they help him out by counting the yam hills. They count "one, two, three, four, five" and, according to the witch-queen's curse, drop dead. Then Anansi plans to preserve all the bodies so he will have plenty to eat, whether there is a famine or not. A guinea fowl comes down to the river, and Anansi calls out for her to count how many yam hills he has. The guinea fowl sits on one of the yam hills and counts: "one, two, three, four, and the one I'm standing on." "No," Anansi says, thwarted, "you can't count." So the guinea fowl moves to another yam hill and counts again the same way. "You don't count right at all," says the frustrated Anansi. "How do you count then?" asks the guinea fowl. Like this, replies Anansi: "one, two, three, four, five." At the last word, he drops dead, and the guinea fowl eats him up. The moral of the story is: "being greedy chokes the puppy."

Among the Ashanti and related Akan peoples of Africa, Anansi the spider, often called "Uncle Anansi," is a major figure, appearing in many tales. These tales often portray him as a fool trying, usually without much success, to outwit animals, humans, and even the gods. Although sometimes shown as wise, Anansi is also greedy, cunning, and ruthless, though his occasional victories over bullies are often used as moral examples. As well as these cultural roles, Anansi may take on the functions of a creator hero in Ashanti and Akanese tradition, where he is credited with the creation of the moon and the founding of customary and other traditional activities. Less positively, he is also blamed for bringing debt and greed into the world.

Significantly, Anansi is also said to own all the tales ever told, as recounted in an Ashanti legend in which Anansi displays some of his most heroic and cunning traits. In the beginning, all stories were owned by the sky-god Nyame, but Anansi wants them and so asks the god if he will sell them to him. The price Nyame demands is that Anansi bring him the hornets (Mmoboro), the great python (Onini), and the leopard (Osebo). Using his skill, cunning, and bravery, Anansi succeeds in capturing all three and delivers them to Nyame, who, astonished at Anansi's success where great warriors had tried and failed, decrees that from then on all stories shall belong to Anansi the spider.

Anansi also features in West African proverbs that reflect well his ambivalent importance, including: "Woe to him who would put his trust in Anansi—a sly, selfish, and greedy fellow"; and "The wisdom of the spider is greater than that of all the world put together." Anansi and his doings have been the raw material of much children's fiction and of numerous popular folktale anthologies.

Related entries: Abunuwas; Ero; Gearoidh, Iarla; Gizo; Hare; Hlakanyana; Hodja, The; Jones, Galloping; Kabajan; Magicians; Maui; Nanabozho; O'Connell, Daniel; Ostropolier, Hershel; Popovich, Aloisha; Quevedo; Rabbit; Ramalingadu, Tenali; Shape-Shifters; Shine; Skorobogaty, Kuzma; Spider; Tortoise; Tricksters; Urdemalas, Pedro de

References and further reading

Abrahams, R., *Afro-American Folktales*, New York: Pantheon Books, 1985.
Arnott, K. (ed.), *African Myths and Legends*, London: Oxford University Press, 1962, pp. 64–67, 74–77.
Bascom, W., *African Folktales in the New World*, Bloomington: Indiana University Press, 1992.
Bennett, M., *West African Trickster Tales*, Oxford: Oxford University Press, 1994, pp. 61–69, 89–101.
Courlander, H. (comp.), *A Treasury of African Folklore*, New York: Crown, 1975, pp. 118–140.
Dadié, B. (trans. Hatch, C.), *The Black Cloth: A Collection of African Folktales*, Amherst: University of Massachusetts Press, 1987 (1955).
Dorson, R. (ed.), *African Folklore*, Bloomington: Indiana University Press, 1972, 1979.
Evans-Pritchard, E. (ed.), *The Zande Trickster*, Oxford: Oxford University Press, 1967.
Jekyll, W. (coll. and ed.), *Jamaican Song and Story*, New York: Dover, 1966 (1907), pp. 7–156.
Sherlock, P. (ed.), *West Indian Folk-Tales*, Oxford: Oxford University Press, 1966, pp. 45–64, 71–85, 97–111, 118–124.

Androcles

Escaped Roman slave of legend who rids a lion of a painful thorn in its paw. Later Androcles is recaptured and, literally, thrown to a lion. The lion turns out to be the very same lion that Androcles helped, and the noble animal refuses to harm Androcles, who is subsequently released. Long a Sunday School favorite, this basic folktale type in which a human is later helped by an animal after doing the animal a good turn is found in many versions, including one attached to the figure of St. Jerome (c. 341–420), translator of the Vulgate Bible. The story also appears in *Aesop's Fables* as "The Slave and the Lion" and in a fourteenth-century compilation of legends, the *Gesta Romanorum*, or "Deeds of the Romans."

Ancient as the theme is, it is still active in modern times. Estonian folklorists have documented a strong tradition of a boy soldier in the Afghanistan war of the mid-late 1980s who is saved by a snake. The story goes that since the boy is not much use for fighting, he is given the job of cook. He feeds the scraps and leftovers to the snakes that gather in a ravine near the army camp. One night as he feeds the snakes, a large one coils itself around him and holds him tight. The snake holds the boy all night, during which ordeal his hair turns white with fear. In the morning, the snake uncoils and allows the terrified boy to leave. When he gets back to his camp, he finds that all his comrades' throats have been cut in an enemy attack. The snake had saved his life.

Related entries: Aniz; Berni, Cesarino Di; Frog Prince, The; Gellert; Goose Girl, The; Habermani; Helpers; Yao Wang
References and further reading
Jones, V. (trans.), *Aesop's Fables*, London: Heinemann, 1912, pp. 31–32.
Kalmre, E., "Legends of the Afghanistan War: The Boy Saved by the Snake," *Folklore* 1, June 1996, http://haldjas.folklore.ee/folklore/nr1/vol1.htm.

Aniz

Legendary hero of the Uygar nationality of China, Aniz is a poor young man hired by a wealthy landlord to watch over his flocks. Aniz has a simple bamboo flute that he plays exquisitely and that almost everyone who hears his music enjoys—except the landlord who feels that Aniz should spend more time doing what he is paid for and less time entertaining the people. One day the landlord pretends that Aniz has done something wrong. He beats the boy and deliberately breaks his flute, turning him out into the street for good measure. Tearful and hurt, Aniz wanders through the streets of the town until he comes across a kindly old man who, on hearing Aniz's story, shows him how to have revenge on the landlord. The old man makes Aniz a new and better bamboo flute and teaches him how to play it so well that not only humans but also the beasts of the forest are entranced by his music.

One day the landlord has a dream featuring a white rabbit with a black spot on its head. He calls his three sons to him and asks them to go and find the rabbit and bring it to him. The eldest son, sensing that he must ensure his inheritance, volunteers to search for the rabbit. On the way, he bumps into a kindly old man who asks him where he is going. When the son tells him, the old man directs him to the forest where Aniz is tending the sheep and tells him to ask Aniz for help. After listening to the eldest son, Aniz agrees to help him in return for a good sum of money. When the eldest son returns to the forest that evening, he finds Aniz playing his flute with all the animals gathered round him, listening. Among them is the white rabbit with the black spot. Aniz picks up the rabbit and gives it to the eldest son in exchange for the money. The eldest son thanks Aniz and makes his way out of the forest to bring the rabbit to his father. At the edge of the forest, he suddenly hears the flute again, and the rabbit jumps out of his hands and escapes. The eldest son returns to Aniz and asks him to get the rabbit back. But Aniz says he cannot help. So the eldest son returns to his father without the rabbit.

The second son then says that he will go and catch the rabbit. Exactly the same things happen to him, and he returns home without the rabbit and considerably poorer. Then the third son goes, with exactly the same result, or lack of one. Their father the landlord is furious and berates them for being fools and incompetents. "I will go and catch the rabbit myself," he says. The next day, the landlord goes into the forest. When Aniz sees him, he plays his flute, bringing all the rabbits, bears, snakes, wolves, birds, and other animals out of the forest to surround the terrified landlord. He begs Aniz for mercy, entreating him not to be as cruel to him as he once was to Aniz. He promises to do anything in return for his life.

Aniz agrees to spare his life as long as the landlord promises never to bully poor people again and as long as he gives half his worldly goods to the poor villagers. The landlord agrees and is allowed to leave the forest. He keeps the bargain, making Aniz even more popular with the people than he was before.

This story is similar in many respects to justified revenge tales told around the world, in particular to a story known as "The Rabbit Herd." It is also part of a large body of tales in which the hero or heroine is able to communicate with animals and benefits from this relationship.

Related entries: Androcles; Berni, Cesarino Di; Fox Maiden, The; Frog Prince, The; Gellert; Goose Girl, The; Habermani; Shape-Shifters; Yao Wang
References and further reading
Ding Wangdao, *Chinese Myths and Fantasies*, Beijing: China Translation Publishing Company, 1991.

Eberhard, W. (ed.), Parsons, D. (trans.), *Folktales of China*, Chicago: University of Chicago Press, 1965.

Minford, J., *Favourite Folktales of China*, Beijing: New World Press, 1983, pp. 95–100.

Apekura (Apakura)

Mythical heroine of Samoan, Marquesan, and, in the variant name Apekua, of New Zealand legend. Apekura's son is slain in his quest for a bride, the daughter of Hatea-motua. Apekura seeks revenge and, helped by one of her brothers, tries to carve a canoe from a tree. But the tree will not allow itself to be cut down. Another brother knows where to find the secret axe that will cut the tree down. Apekura's forces then slay the destructive vines, seaweed, and killer octopus defending Hatea-motua, thus gaining revenge. In another version of the story, Apekura's husband is treacherously murdered by her own brothers and her revenge is carried out by her youngest son. In this version, Apekura is said to be constantly weeping and singing a lament that can still be heard in the waves of the sea.

Related entries: Aniz; Maui; Victims

References and further reading

Alpers, A., *Legends of the South Sea*, London: John Murray, 1970, pp. 171–182, 377, 405.

Leach, M. (ed.), *Funk and Wagnall's Standard Dictionary of Folklore, Mythology, and Legend*, London: New English Library, 1975, p. 66. Abridged one-volume edition of *Funk and Wagnall's Standard Dictionary of Folklore, Mythology, and Legend*, 2 vols., New York: Funk and Wagnall, 1972.

Orbell, M., *The Illustrated Encyclopedia of Maori Myth and Legend*, Christchurch, New Zealand: Canterbury University Press, 1995.

Appleseed, Johnny

See Chapman, John

Arabian Nights, The

Also widely known as *1001 Nights*, this is a collection of folktales and fables common to Indian, Arabic, and Eastern traditions. A Persian collection compiled between 988 and 1011 is thought to be the inspiration for the first European translation of 1704–1715, made by Antoine Galland (1646–1715). Different versions of the early compilations include different stories, though all versions use the device of the frame narrative in which Scheherazade tells unfinished stories to her murderous husband, King Schariar, for 1,001 nights, eventually curing him of his hatred for women and saving herself from execution. Scheherazade tells many stories, including that of the lovers Camaralzan and Badoura, who is said to be the world's most beautiful woman. Widely translated, the best-known and perhaps most controversial—though by no means the only—English version is by Sir Richard Burton, made between 1885 and 1888 and published as *The Arabian Nights' Entertainments*.

One of the most popular and well-known of the stories in *The Arabian Nights* is that of the seafaring hero, Sindbad the Sailor. Originally a wealthy merchant, Sindbad squanders his wealth and has to go to sea as a merchant adventurer. He makes seven wondrous sea voyages and has many fantastic encounters with an island that turns out to be, variously, the back of a whale, dwarves, one-eyed monsters, fabulous birds called "rocs," cannibals, pirates, slavers, and Caliphs. On his last voyage, he is captured by pirates and sold into a form of slavery that involves hunting elephants. Fortunately, Sindbad finds out the whereabouts of the elephants' graveyard, which is mounded high with valuable ivory tusks. He purchases his freedom from slavery and returns to his home.

While the materials of *The Arabian Nights* are in many cases of considerable age, like all such compilations, these stories have been reworked so often over the centuries that later material has crept in, as in the story of Ali Baba, an eighteenth-century addition. Hasan of Bassorah is another of the numerous ne'er-do-well heroes of *The Arabian Nights*. Hasan has many adventures, overcomes many obstacles, and ultimately achieves the object of his quest, a princess. The late appearance of this story in *The Arabian Nights*, together with its rather forced and overdone motifs of seven princesses, ten swan maidens, and so on, strongly suggests that it, too, is a literary fabrication, a deliberate synthesis of various folkloric elements, rather than an originally oral tale. These stories highlight the fact that, while *The Arabian Nights* contains a great deal of folkloric material, it is essentially a work of literature, one of the world's finest.

Such fine points have not interfered with the continuing popularity of *The Arabian Nights*, especially the stories of Aladdin, Sindbad, Ali Baba and the Forty Thieves, and, of course, the brave and wily Scheherazade herself, epitome of the clever woman found in many folk traditions. These and other characters from the rich resources of this work have filled children's books and delighted moviegoers for generations, thus, for example, Walt Disney's 1992 reworking of the Aladdin story.

Related entries: Ahmed; Aladdin; Baba, Ali; Fairy Tale Heroes; Magicians; Sadko; Scheherazade
References and further reading
Burton, R., *The Arabian Nights' Entertainments,* 13 vols., London: H. Nichols, 1894–1897, chaps. 18–25.
Irwin, R., *The Arabian Nights: A Companion,* London: Allen Lane, 1994.
Ranelagh, E., *The Past We Share: The Near Eastern Ancestry of Western Folk Literature,* London: Quartet Books, London, pp. 195–242.
Zipes, J., *When Dreams Came True: Classical Fairy Tales and Their Tradition,* New York and London: Routledge, 1999, pp. 49–60.

Armstrong, Johnnie

Johnnie Armstrong appears in sixteenth-century Scots ballad-lore as a betrayed rebel leader. Believing he will be pardoned by James V of Scotland (1512–1542), Armstrong and his men attend at court, only to be condemned to death:

But when John came the king before,
With his eight score men so gallant to see,
The king he moved his bonnet to him
he thought he had been a king as well as
    he . . .
Away with thee thou false traitor!
No pardon I will grant thee,
but tomorrow before eight of the clock,
I will hang thy eight score men and thee.

In the ballad, though not in fact, Armstrong then cuts off the king's head and he and his men fight a fearsome battle against the king's guards.

Then they fought on like mad men all,
Till many a man lay dead on the plain;
For they were resolved before they would
    yield,
That every man would there be slain.

In the end, only "little Musgrave," Armstrong's foot-page, escapes, and he carries the dreadful news to the dead outlaw's family, whereupon Armstrong's young son swears:

If ever I live to be a man,
My fathers [sic] blood revenged shall be.

Johnnie Armstrong is a Scots national hero and a hero of struggle.

Related entries: Heroes of Struggle; National Heroes; Victims
References and further reading
Chappell, W., *Popular Music of the Olden Time,* 2 vols., New York: Dover Publications, 1965 (1859), pp. 260, 538.
Child, F. J., *The English and Scottish Popular Ballads,* 5 vols., New York: Dover, 1965 (1882–1898), vol. 3, pp. 362–372, no. 169.

Arthur

Pivotal figure of an extensive Celtic and medieval mythology, Arthur, "the once and future king," also turns up occasionally in folk song, ballad, and folktale, though usually in subsidiary roles rather than in the regal or heroic ones with which he is now widely identified. Probably based on legends about a fifth- or sixth-century British chieftain, Arthur has much in common with folktale heroes. He hunts and kills mythic creatures such as the Cat of Lossanne, and in Welsh and other writings dating from the ninth century, he is the focal point of numerous wonders. Around the twelfth century, the various written and oral traditions about Arthur, cross-fertilized with elements from continental romance, Celtic mythology, and Christianity, began to be drawn together into the canon that we are familiar with today, assisted by the later writings of Thomas Malory, Walter Scott, and a host of greater and lesser poets. Since then, King Arthur and his considerable legendry have continued to cast a powerful glamour in English-speaking cultures, all of which seem to have produced at least one, usually many, Arthurian works, in an incessant flow of learned and popular literature, film, television, music, stage, and all other imaginable forms of human expression.

While King Arthur is the object of considerable literary, scholarly, and popular entertainment interest, these facets of his mythology have comparatively little presence in twentieth-century folk expression, although many of the elements of the Arthurian cycle are to be found in folk tradition, including the unusual circumstances of the hero's conception, birth, and ultimate recognition as a hero (pulling the sword from the stone); a supernaturally powerful weapon (the sword Excalibur); the helpful elemental (the Lady of the Lake); the alternatively helping and hindering sorcerer (Merlin); the forces of evil (Mordred, Morgan le Fay, and the temptation of Guineviere and Lancelot); the quest (the Holy Grail); the companions of the quest (the Knights of the Round Table); the last great battle and the subsequent journey to the afterlife (Avalon).

However, there are alternative "apocryphal" stories and beliefs about Arthur that give different locations for such matters as his death and burial. These stories are found in Welsh traditions that claim that the great king was killed at *Bwlch y Seathau* (the Pass of Arrows) in Snowdonia, that he is buried at *Carnedd* (Cairn), and that his army is sleeping in *Ogof Llanciau Eryri* (the Cave of the Young Men of Snowdonia). Other folklore about Arthur includes his role as leader of the Wild Hunt, a supernatural company of riders known in Britain, Brittany, and elsewhere in France until at least the nineteenth century. There is also a belief that Arthur lives on in the form of a bird. Britain and areas with strong Celtic connections, including Brittany, contain numerous examples of place-names and local legends associated with Arthur and his enduring narratives.

Arthur's main folkloric presence is in the continued British belief—or at least the continued articulation of the story—that, like many culture heroes, Arthur is not dead but only sleeping until the hour of his country's need. In this element of his mythology, Arthur is in the company of numerous other sleeping folk heroes.

Related entries: Barbarossa; Batradz; Culture Heroes; Danske, Holger; Jack the Giant-Killer; Merlin; National Heroes; Sleepers; Warriors

References and further reading

Barber, R., *Myths and Legends of the British Isles*, Rochester, NY: Boydell Press, 1999, pp. 159–183.
Cavendish, R. (ed.), *Legends of the World*, London: Orbis, 1982, pp. 195–197.
Goetinck, G., *Peredur: A Study of Welsh Traditions in the Grail Legends*, Cardiff: University of Wales Press, 1975.
Jones, G., *Welsh Legends and Folk Tales*, London: Oxford University Press, 1955, pp. 169–174.
Littleton, C. and Thomas, A., "The Sarmatian Connection: New Light on the Origin of the Arthurian and Holy Grail Legends," *Journal of American Folklore* 91 (1978): 513–527.
Loomis, R. (ed.), *The Grail: From Celtic Myth to Christian Symbol*, London: Constable, 1993.
Topsfield, L., *Chrétien de Troyes: A Study of the Arthurian Romances*, Cambridge: Cambridge University Press, 1981.
Wadge, R., "King Arthur: A British or Sarmatian Tradition?" *Folklore* 98, no. 2 (1987): 204–215.

Aryg, Altyn

Legendary heroine of Siberian tradition. Daughter and only child of Kara Khan, who badly desires a son and heir, Altyn Aryg offers to take over the running of her father's flocks, but he spurns her offer on the grounds that a woman cannot do a man's job. Angry, Altyn Aryg leaves her father's tent and goes in search of the fearsome Snake Prince that eats human beings and frightens even the greatest of heroes. Calmly, she walks into the monster's belly, finding imprisoned there everyone the Snake Prince has previously devoured. They tell Altyn Aryg that all the prisoners have tried to escape by stabbing the monster's heart with their weapons, but the heart is so hard that none has succeeded, and nor will she. But Altyn Aryg is able to pierce the Snake Prince's heart, killing the monster and freeing the heroes trapped inside. Refusing their offers of great rewards, she returns home, tells her father of her deeds, and is given control of his peoples and flocks. Eventually she marries a man who owns nothing but a horse and who becomes the caretaker of her considerable estates.

Related entries: Dragon-Slayers; Warriors; Women Dressed as Men
References and further reading
Baumann, H., *Hero Legends of the World*, London: Dent and Sons, 1975 (1972), pp. 43–46.
Riordan, J. (coll. and trans.), *The Sun Maiden and the Crescent Moon: Siberian Folk Tales*, New York: Interlink Books, 1991.

Ashblower, Ivan

Son of a wealthy peasant, Ivan is a legendary Russian hero who grows into a handsome man only a day after his birth. He is, however, born with the considerable impediment of chicken's feet. Wishing to court the czar's daughter, he is given impossible tasks by the czar, eventually winning the daughter's hand in marriage. Unhappy with being married to a peasant with chicken's feet, Ivan's new wife cuts them off while he sleeps. Ivan then wanders widely through the world having adventures and encounters of various kinds, including one with Torok, a man who has no hands. Together they encounter the devil. Ivan beats up the devil and forces him to take himself and Torok to a spring, the waters of which grow human feet at the end of his legs and hands at the end of Torok's arms. Ivan and Torok then kill the devil. Ivan returns home to find his wife about to marry another man. She recognizes Ivan from a finger ring he wears and, full of remorse, embraces him gladly. Upon discovering who Ivan is, the czar has the unlucky bridegroom killed, and Ivan is reinstated as husband of the czar's daughter.

It is not clear why Ivan is named "Ashblower," unless it derives from the many candles his father burned, asking God to give him a son. The hero who grows to manhood almost immediately after his birth is a theme echoed in a number of other hero traditions in Europe and Africa, while the besting of the devil, the last-moment return as the beloved is about to marry another, the recognition device of the finger ring, and the happy ending—for Ivan, at least—are all commonplaces of folktale and ballad.

Related entries: Fereyel; Jack Tales
References and further reading
Afanas'ev, A. (comp.), Guterman, N. (trans.), *Russian Fairy Tales*, New York: Pantheon Books, 1945.
Elstob, E. and Barber, R. (trans.), *Russian Folktales*, London: Bell and Sons, 1971, pp. 65–67. First published as Von Lowis of Menar, A. (trans.) and Olesch, R. (ed.), *Russische Volksmärchen*, 1959.

Ashma

Legendary poor heroine of a Sani (Yi nationality, People's Republic of China) tradition. Ashma is forced into marriage with the feckless son of the wealthy landowner, Rabubalor. Her brother Ahay attempts to rescue her from the dungeon where the wicked landlord keeps his son's reluctant bride. Ahay is faced with contests organized by the bridegroom and wins them all, eventually shooting three arrows into the landlord's house. These magic arrows mean bad luck for the landlord and his son and can be removed only by a good person. Rabubalor and his son try to pull the arrows from their lodgments in various parts of the house but fail. Rabubalor promises to release both Ashma and Ahay if they can remove the arrows, which Ashma does with ease. After inviting the brother and sister to stay in the house for one more night, the landlord releases three tigers into Ahay's room. In the morning all three animals are dead and skinned, but Ahay is alive and well. Accepting defeat, Rabubalor lets the brother and sister free, but as they pass beneath a high lake in the mountains he has his men break down the walls and flood the pass through which Ashma and Ahay are making their escape. Ahay's desperate attempts to save Ashma from the floodwaters fail, and she is washed away. When the waters go down, Ashma reappears transformed into the beautiful rock bearing her name in the Stone Forest of Lunan county in the Province of Yunnan.

This tradition combines a local legend of China's colorful Sani people with a form of magical contest often encountered in hero tales and ballads.

Related entries: Dojrana; Local Heroes; Magicians
References and further reading
Anon., *The Peacock Maiden: Folk Tales from China* (3d series), Beijing: Foreign Languages Press, 1981 (1958).
Li, N., *Old Tales of China*, Singapore: Graham Brash, 1983 (1981), pp. 2–4.
Loewe, M., "Heroes in Chinese Tradition," in Davidson, H. (ed.), *The Hero in Tradition and Folklore*, London: Mistletoe Books, 1985, pp. 142–155.

Assipattle

Central legendary figure of a number of Orkney Islands tales. He is, like many "Jack" characters, a bit of a dreamer and lazy with it. He is a seventh son, usually said to be lucky, but his brothers make him sleep in the ashes. In spite of his lowly status, Assipattle continually tells stories about the wonderful deeds of heroism he will one day perform. His brothers scornfully ignore him, but his sister listens to the stories and believes them. Eventually, Assipattle proves himself to be a great hero when he rescues the beautiful princess Gemdelovely from a dragon, slaying the monster in the process. The name "Assipattle" is said to be cognate with that of "Ashenputtle," heroine of a Scots version of Cinderella in which the familiar gender roles are also reversed.

Related entries: Cinderella; Cinder-Mary; Dragon-Slayers; Fairy Tale Heroes; Jack; Jack Tales; Jack the Giant-Killer; Rashin' Coatie; Rose-Red
References and further reading
Briggs, K. (ed.), *A Dictionary of British Folk-Tales in the English Language*, 4 vols., London: Routledge and Kegan Paul, 1970–1971, vol. 1, pp. 138–140, 144–147.
Hallett, M. and Karasek, B. (eds.), *Folk and Fairy Tales*, Ontario: Broadview Press, 1996, pp. 59–65.

Ataba

Representing the Palestinian ideal of womanly love, the legendary Ataba is pursued in marriage by the young, handsome, and strong Zarief E-ttool, also a legendary symbol of ideal Palestinian manhood. These characters appear in many songs, stories, and folk dances popular among Palestinians and are also celebrated elsewhere in Arabic tradition in the countries of Jordan, Syria, Iraq, and Lebanon. The basic story is that Zarief E-ttool is the employee of Ataba's wealthy trader father. Ataba and Zarief E-ttool fall in love, but the father rejects Zarief E-ttool as a suitor because he is too poor. The young man argues his case, and eventually the father agrees, on the condition that Zarief E-ttool brings to him the best grapes in the country. Zarief E-ttool travels to the city of Khalil where the best grapes are to be had. He spends all his money on grapes and takes them back to Ataba's father. The father had hoped that Zarief E-ttool would not survive his journey and now demands that the young man go to the city of Yafa and bring him the best oranges.

This pattern goes on and on. Every time Zarief E-ttool returns with the object of his quest, Ataba's father comes up with a new impossible task for the young hero. In this way, Zarief E-ttool eventually travels all over the country, letting all the people know of his problem in the process. Finally, Zarief E-ttool goes to Egypt to consult with a powerful friend of Ataba's father, a Mukhtar. Zarief E-ttool tells the Mukhtar of his plight, and the Mukhtar agrees to accompany him back to Palestine and to Ataba's heartless father. When they arrive, Ataba's father is honored and flattered to receive his powerful friend, and the Mukhtar tells him that he will be the guarantor for Zarief E-ttool's marriage to Ataba. The faithful heroine and the persevering hero are married at an enormous wedding attended by people from all across the land, who sing, dance, and wish the couple well.

The impossible task or tasks set the unsuitable suitor by the would-be bride's father, sometimes mother, is a standard feature of hero and heroine lore the world around. Also common are the roles of the helper, in this case a Mukhtar, who is the means by which the young hero's perseverance is finally rewarded.

Related entries: E-ttool, Zarief; Helpers
References and further reading
Abdelhady, T., *Palestinian Folk-Tales*, Beirut: n.d., vol. 3, p. 136.
Muhawi, I. and Kanaana, S. (eds.), *Speak, Bird, Speak Again: Palestinian Arab Folktales*, Berkeley: University of California Press, 1989.

Avdotya

A fictional woman in Russian tradition who dies and is brought back to life by the bravery of her husband, Mikhail Potyk. Mikhail travels to the underworld after Avdotya's death. Finding her body, he is then attacked by a fiery dragon. He slays the monster and rubs its severed head against his wife's corpse, thus reviving her. They return together to the world of life above ground, where they live happily together for many more years.

Related entries: Dragon-Slayers; Ivan the Mare's Son; Mu Lian; Mu-Monto; Nakali; Potyk, Mikhail; Saburo, Koga; Sadko; Tam Lin; Thomas the Rhymer

References and further reading

Dixon-Kennedy, M., *European Myths and Legends,* London: Blandford, 1997, p. 28.

Elstob, E. and Barber, R. (trans.), *Russian Folktales,* London: Bell and Sons, 1971. First published as Von Lowis of Menar, A. (trans.) and Olesch, R. (ed.), *Russische Volksmärchen,* 1959.

B

Baal-Shem-Tov

Israel ben Eliezer, known as Israel Baal-Shem or Baal-Shem-Tov was an eastern European Jewish cultural-religious hero and founder of Hasidism, the popular mystical sect of Judaism. His assumed name means "Master of the Good Name." He was born in 1700 and was noted for his sympathy with nature, his good works, and his spirituality. The spread of Hasidism among eastern European Jewry during the eighteenth century was a result of its down-to-earth, folksy nature and also of the fact that the movement was almost immediately banned by the religious authorities. Rabbi Israel became the focus of a body of legendary anecdotes, many emphasizing the rabbi's common touch, as in the oft-told story of why he laughed three times.

One night the Baal-Shem-Tov, surrounded by disciples after performing his religious duties, is heard to laugh three times for no apparent reason. The disciples question the rabbi about his odd behavior, and he promises to tell them the reason for it. That Sabbath night, the rabbi takes his disciples on a long journey to the town of Kozenitz, where, to the great excitement of the locals, the rabbi holds the morning service. After the service, he asks to see Reb Shabsi, the town bookbinder. Puzzled as to why the great rabbi wishes to speak to such a worthy but lowly individual as the bookbinder, the leader of the town nevertheless acquiesces to the rabbi's wish. The bookbinder is brought to the great man, who asks him to tell the whole community assembled there exactly what he did the previous night. Reb Shabsi, fearing that he has committed some sin, nevertheless describes how he and his wife have grown so old and poor that they are unable to purchase the necessary Sabbath offer-

ings. Nonetheless, Reb Shabsi keeps up his religious obligation as well as he can and attends the synagogue with nothing. Reb Shabsi then explains that on the night in question, while he was away at the synagogue, his wife found a long-lost old jacket with gold-plated silver buttons. She was able to sell these and so purchase the necessities for the Sabbath meal. He thus returned from the synagogue, disconsolate, to find the table set with all the necessities and some money left over. He was so overjoyed that he danced and laughed with his wife three times during and after the meal.

When the bookbinder finishes recounting these events, he asks the rabbi if he has sinned by dancing on the Sabbath. The rabbi turns to his disciples and says that when Reb Shabsi and his old wife laughed and danced with joy, all the angels in heaven likewise laughed and danced. And he then asks, if the angels of heaven were moved to such mirth, how could I not be also? Turning to the bookbinder and his wife, the rabbi asks them what their greatest wish may be. They tell the rabbi that they do not want riches but, having been childless, desire a son, despite their advanced years. The rabbi tells them that they will have a son within one year and that they must name him Israel. The rabbi himself will be his godfather. Sure enough, one year later, it happened as the rabbi said it would, and the boy grew into the honored Preacher of Kozenitz, a noted wise man and saint.

In another story about the Baal-Shem-Tov a young woman dies on the day of her wedding. Naturally the family of bride and groom and the whole community is distressed. The Baal-Shem-Tov had foreseen these things and knew what to do. He instructed the people to put the corpse into the grave and to have two young men get in, one on either side. They were on no account to be frightened of anything they saw and were not to take their eyes off the dead bride's face. All was done as the Baal-Shem-Tov commanded, and after a while the bride opened her eyes. She was taken from the grave, and the wedding proceeded as if nothing untoward had occurred. The explanation for the Baal-Shem-Tov's ability to raise the dead was that a *gilgl* (the spirit of someone who has died) had occupied the young woman's body, forcing out her own soul. This had been revealed to the holy man in his vision, and when the Baal-Shem-Tov had ordered the *gilgl* to leave, it had no choice but to obey immediately, allowing the girl's own soul to return to her body.

The rabbi was also believed to be able to destroy things, to discover secrets, and to do almost anything else. But great and holy though he was, the Baal-Shem-Tov could not travel to the Holy Land. Such a trip, it is said, would bring about the destruction of all things.

Related entries: Adam, Rabbi; Loew, Rabbi Judah; Religious Heroes; Wise Men and Women

References and further reading

Ausubel, N. (ed.), *A Treasury of Jewish Folklore*, London: Vallentine, Mitchell, 1972 (1948), pp. 176, 179, 182, 186, 188, 191–192, 287.

Bin Gorion, M. (coll.), Ben-Amos, D. (trans.), *Mimekor Yisrael: Classical Jewish Folktales*, 3 vols., Bloomington: Indiana University Press, 1976.

Cavendish, R. (ed.), *Legends of the World*, London: Orbis, 1982, pp. 111–112.

Weinreich, B. (ed.), *Yiddish Folktales*, New York: Pantheon, 1988, 267–269, 342–343.

Baba, Ali

Next to Aladdin, Ali Baba is probably the best-known character of *The Arabian Nights*. He is a poor woodchopper who stumbles across a magic cave full of robber treasure. He learns the secret formula that opens the cave—"open sesame"—and becomes instantly wealthy. However, the robbers pursue him, and he is saved from a brutal end only by the wit and bravery of his servant girl, Morgiana. A grateful Ali Baba marries Morgiana to his nephew or, in some versions, to his son.

Ali Baba is usually considered to be representative of the widespread master-thief type of folk

Ali Baba showing bags of treasure to his wife (North Wind Picture Archives)

hero. Related to the trickster, the master thief is one who thieves with great cleverness and cunning. However, rather than planning a heist, Ali Baba stumbles upon the booty, and in his attempts to retain it he displays little of the ingenuity of the master thief. It is the servant girl, Morgiana, who is the real heroine of the story.

Although exhibiting many of the familiar motifs of folktale, including hidden treasure, magic caves, disguises, and escapes, this tale did not appear in any edition of *The Arabian Nights* until the eighteenth century, when it was reportedly collected from an Arab in Paris. It has since become one of the most popular stories of *The Arabian Nights*, often retold in children's books, on stage, and in the cinema.

Related entries: Aladdin; *Arabian Nights, The*; Fairy Tale Heroes

References and further reading

Burton, R., *The Arabian Nights' Entertainments*, 13 vols., London: H. Nichols, 1894–1897, chap. 32.

Dawkins, R. (comp. and trans.), *Modern Greek Folktales*, Oxford: Clarendon Press, 1953, pp. 344–345; reprint Westport, CT: Greenwood Press, 1974.

Irwin, R., *The Arabian Nights: A Companion*, London: Allen Lane, 1994, pp. 2, 17–18, 47, 52, 58, 62, 101, 159, 168, 179, 197, 225, 237, 269–270, 274, 280, 281.

Baba-Yaga

The archvillainess of Russian and Slavic lore. Usually portrayed as a witch, she is often said to live in a revolving house that rests on chicken's legs and is located deep in a gloomy forest. Baba-Yaga, often called the Baba-Yaga, an indication of her central place as a folk villain, has great powers over time, nature, and life itself. She frequently abducts children, killing and eating them, though in some tales she may also be helpful to heroes and heroines, if usually only in return for something she wants.

Some scholars suggest that Baba-Yaga symbolizes the interface between the world of the living and the world of the dead, her function being to send those whose time has come into the afterlife. This may explain why she sometimes helps humans, as in some versions of the tale of Vasilisa, where the heroine completes all the impossible tasks set for her by Baba-Yaga and is rewarded with a magic skull that allows her to escape the clutches of her wicked stepmother and stepsisters. In other versions of the same story, though, including the one in this encyclopedia, it is the Baba-Yaga's maidservant who helps Vasilisa escape.

A similar figure, variously named Frau Berchtam, Berkta, Brechta, and other variations, exists in German folklore, and many other traditions harbor similarly monstrous types.

Related entries: Hansel; Helpers; Magicians; Morevna, Marya; Ogres; Vasilisa; Villains
References and further reading
Ivanits, L., Russian Folk Belief, Armonk and London: M. E. Sharpe Inc., 1989, pp. 99, 100, 227.

The Baba-Yaga chases the girl in a mortar. Scene from a Russian nursery tale titled "The Hut of Baba Yaga" (Mary Evans Picture Library)

Badikan

Legendary Armenian giant-slayer. Badikan is the youngest of a king's forty sons and in his search for a suitable bride overcomes demons, beasts, and strong men. He eventually takes up with a giant named Khan Bogu. The giant is besotted with a princess, and Badikan undertakes to abduct the princess on the giant's behalf. But Badikan and the princess fall in love and have to find a way to escape from the giant. The princess wheedles from the giant the secret source of his strength—a magical white ox filled with many other animals. She tells Badikan the secret, and he locates and kills the ox, thus killing Khan Bogu in the nick of time as he seeks to take revenge on the princess who is still within his power and whose betrayal he realizes. Badikan and the princess marry and live happily ever after.

Related entries: Dragon-Slayers; Fairy Tale Heroes; George, Saint; Giant-Killers; Jack the Giant-Killer
References and further reading
Downing, C. (trans. and ed.), Armenian Folk-Tales and Fables, London: Oxford University Press, 1972, pp. 91–96.

Bahram

See Helpers

Bai Suzhen

In Chinese tradition a white snake, also known as "The White Lady," who marries a human shopkeeper called Xu Xian but runs into trouble with the evil abbot of Jinshan Monastery, Fahai. The abbot is determined to destroy the marriage and stops at nothing to bring this about, eventually imprisoning Bai Suzhen by magic in Leifeng Pagoda near West Lake. Bai Suzhen has a faithful maidservant, Xiaoqing, who returns to the pagoda many years later, burns it down, and releases her mistress.

Related entries: Habermani; Helpers; White Lady; Xiaoqing
References and further reading
Li, N., Old Tales of China, Singapore: Graham Brash, 1983 (1981), pp. 12–14.

Baldpate

Hero of a Gypsy tale who undertakes to locate a beautiful young dervish's daughter, desired by the king's son. Baldpate and the king's son sail away for seven years in search of the beauty. They find her and bring her back. One night, Baldpate protects the lovers from a dragon, but they mistake his drawn sword for a plot against them, and the king sentences Baldpate to death. Baldpate tells the king that three birds have given him secret information about threats to the king's son and the dervish's daughter. It is on this information that he has been acting to protect the young lovers. However, the birds conveyed the information to Baldpate with the stipulation that if he revealed the secrets, he would be turned to stone. As he tells each of his three secrets, Baldpate is gradually turned to stone. They bury him, and the king's son takes to the road in penance for Baldpate's service to him. On his wanderings he has a dream in which Baldpate tells him to take some earth and sprinkle it on his tomb. He does so, and Baldpate is resurrected and taken to the palace where the king makes him a great one.

This tale twines a number of familiar motifs, including the faithful servant and helper, the quest, being turned to stone, and the dragon-slayer.

Related entries: Dragon-Slayers; Faithful Henry; Faithful John; Giant-Killers; Helpers; Peterkin; Yannakis

References and further reading

Groome, F. H., *Gypsy Folk Tales*, London: Hutchinson, 1899.

Lee, F. H. (comp.), *Folk Tales of All Nations*, London: Harrap, 1931, pp. 533–537.

Tong, D., *Gypsy Folktales*, New York: Harcourt Brace Jovanovich, 1989.

Ballila

See Local Heroes

Bamapana

See Tricksters

Barbarossa

Frederick I (c. 1123–1190), known colloquially to the Italians and more widely as Bar-

barossa (Redbeard). Frederick was Holy Roman Emperor and is considered a German national hero. Like King Arthur and other great leaders, he is said to be only sleeping in the Kyffhäuser Mountains until his country needs him once again. In some folktales, his beard is said to be still growing around a large marble table. When his red whiskers have wrapped themselves around the table three times, he will awaken and return to his people. Related legends tell of dwarves leading peasants into the mountains, where they are privileged with a sighting of the sleeping monarch.

Related entries: Arthur; Batradz; Culture Heroes; Danske, Holger; Gearoidh, Iarla; National Heroes; Sleepers

References and further reading

Grimm, J. and W. (trans. Ashliman, D.), *Deutsche Sagen* (1816–1818), Folklore and Mythology Electronic Texts, Pittsburgh, PA: University of Pittsburgh, 2000, www.pitt.edu/~dash/folktexts.html#a.

Ranke, K. (ed.), (trans. Baumann, L.), *Folktales of Germany*, Chicago: University of Chicago Press, 1966.

Barleycorn, John

Legendary figure in a famous English and Scottish folk song, being an anthropomorphized representation of the plants, processes, and results of brewing beer. In the song, most versions of which are related to Robert Burns's lyric of 1786, John Barleycorn is cut down, rolled into hay, threshed, and brewed into beer. Ultimately, as some renditions of the song put it, the drunkard "pissed him against the wall" and that was the end of John Barleycorn. Usually John Barleycorn is depicted as winning, because he grows again the following year. The ritualized nature of the song and its humanization of nature has led many scholars to argue that John Barleycorn is a modernized pagan corn god. There is little evidence to support such assertions, also commonly made about many aspects of allegedly "ancient" folklore.

In the various transformations undergone by John Barleycorn, we can see more than a little of the shape-shifter, while in his ultimate triumph over his tormentors he moves from victim to hero.

Related entries: Shape-shifters; Victims

References and further reading

Hamer, F. (comp.), *Garner's Gay*, London: EFDS Publications, 1967, pp. 8–9.

Lloyd, A., *Folksong in England*, New York: International Publishers, 1970 (1967), p. 80.

Vaughan Williams, R. and Lloyd, A. (eds.), *The Penguin Book of English Folk Songs*, Harmondsworth, Middlesex: 1959, pp. 56–57.

Bass, Sam

Born in Indiana in 1851, Bass was one of ten children on a small but comfortable farm. His parents died before he reached his teens, and he was raised by an uncle until 1869, when he left home to make his own way in the world. In 1875, after various jobs in a mill, a hotel, and as a cowboy, Bass suddenly, it seems, took to gambling and fast living, followed by horse stealing. Various crimes, including stealing, stagecoach holdups, and train robberies, occupied Bass and his companions in Nebraska and Texas. Closely pursued, Bass escaped to rob a number of trains in the Dallas and Fort Worth area in 1878. Some of his companions were killed and captured by Texas Rangers, and one of the survivors was persuaded to return to the gang and inform on their movements. In July 1878, Bass's attempt to rob the bank in Round Rock was foiled by the informer, and in the ensuing gunfight Bass was wounded, dying two days later on his birthday.

There seems little in the bare facts of Bass's brief life to justify his distinction as an outlaw hero. Bass managed to avoid killing anyone, until the end of his career, and seems to have been regarded in Texas, at least, as something of a mild-mannered hero, or so his folklore asserts. The opening verse of his ballad, as given by Lingenfelter, runs:

Sam Bass was born in Indiana—it was his
    native home—
And at the age of seventeen, young Sam
    began to roam.
He first went down to Texas, a cowboy
    bold to be;
A kinder-hearted fellow, you'd scarcely ever
    see.

In folk song, story, and belief Sam Bass is presented as kindhearted and generous: he tips the porters and brakemen on the trains he robs; he gives cripples silver dollars; he pays for simple country generosity and sustenance with two twenty-dollar gold pieces; and he forgoes robbing a naive young store clerk, warning him of the dangers of leaving too much cash in view. He also performs feats of pistol shooting, such as tattooing his initials into a tree, and he foils hoaxes, escapes a deputy sheriff, and is almost everyone's popular hero. The story of Sam paying the mortgage of a poor widow and then robbing it back from the landlord is also told of many, if not most, other outlaw heroes. He is betrayed, as he was in reality, and there is at least one legend that Sam Bass is not the man inside the grave bearing his headstone. It is said that Bass's lost treasure can still be found—somewhere—in the Round Rock country.

Related entries: Bonney, William; Fisk, Jim; James, Jesse; Outlaws; Parker, Robert Leroy; Quantrill, William Clarke

References and further reading

Dobie, F. J., *Tales of Old Time Texas* (1928), London: Hammond, 1959, pp. 78–90.

Lingenfelter, R. et al. (eds.) *Songs of the American West*, Los Angeles: University of California Press, 1968, pp. 316–317.

Lomax, J. and A. (colls. and comps.), *American Ballads and Folk Songs*, New York: Macmillan, 1934, p. 126.

Martin, Charles L., *A Sketch of Sam Bass, the Bandit*, Dallas, TX: Worley & Co., 1880.

Batradz

Legendary Russian warrior hero. Receiving a mortal wound in battle, Batradz begs his two remaining soldiers to throw his sword into the water. Unwilling to perform this symbolic act of defeat, the soldiers twice pretend that they have carried out Batradz's wishes, but he discovers they have not. At the third attempt, they do as they are bidden, and the water is blown by strong winds and turns blood-red in color.

The obvious similarity between this story, originating with the Alans and Sarmatian peoples of Russia, and that of King Arthur has led some scholars to suggest that it is the pre-

Christian origin of the Excalibur and Lady of the Lake legends.

Related entries: Arthur; Warriors
References and further reading
Curtin, J. (ed.), *Myths and Folktales of the Russians, Western Slavs, and Magyars*, Boston: Little, Brown, 1890.
Dixon-Kennedy, M., *European Myth and Legend*, London: Blandford, 1997, p. 43.
Littleton, C. and Thomas, A., "The Sarmatian Connection: New Light on the Origin of the Arthurian and Holy Grail Legends," *Journal of American Folklore* 91, 1978, pp. 513–527.
Wadge, R., "King Arthur: A British or Sarmatian Tradition?" *Folklore* 98, no. 2, 1987, pp. 204–215.

Bean, Roy

Roy Bean (1825[?]–1903) assumed the role of unofficial justice of the peace and became by default the "law west of the Pecos" during the 1880s. "Judge" Bean was famous for holding court in saloons, mainly his own, in the town of Langtry, named after the entertainer Lily Langtry, a woman idolized by the judge. Stories about Bean dispensing frontier justice with whiskey, six-guns, shrewdness, and sentiment are many. They include those about his beer-drinking bear, his practice of fining all dead bodies the amount found on their persons (in his capacity as coroner), and his freeing of a man who murdered a Chinese in 1884 because, the story goes, Bean could find no law that said it was illegal to kill a Chinaman.

Related entries: Frontier Heroes
References and further reading
Botkin, B. (ed.), *A Treasury of American Folklore: Stories, Ballads, and Traditions of the People*, New York: Crown Publishers, 1944, pp. 131–132, 134–150.
Greenway, J. (ed.), *Folklore of the Great West*, Palo Alto, CA: American West Publishing Company, 1969.
Lomax, J. and A. (colls. and comps.), *American Ballads and Folk Songs*, New York: Macmillan, 1934, p. 413.

Beauty and the Beast

Best-known fairy tale version of a widespread tale type usually called "beast marriage." The youngest of three daughters asks nothing more of her poor father than to bring her home a rose, grape, or other apparently trivial item from his travels, while the other two selfish daughters ask for expensive fripperies. The father's travels, usually on business, are not blessed with success and, disconsolately returning home, he recalls his promise to his youngest daughter. He then goes into a castle or other place, such as a garden, and obtains the requested item, only to be confronted with an angry beast. Fearfully explaining why he has stolen the item, the beast allows the father to go on the condition that he returns with one of his daughters, or he will be killed. Returning home, the father tells the daughters of his predicament, and the loyal youngest daughter, the beauty, volunteers to go and live with the beast.

They live together for some time, the beast treating beauty with kindness and consideration. But she becomes increasingly depressed, missing her family. She asks to be allowed to visit her home, and the beast, giving her a ring, sometimes a mirror, consents to her going for one week. Once home with her lonely father, beauty cannot bear to leave him and so outstays the allotted week. One night she has a dream (or sees in the magic mirror) of the beast near death. She rushes back to the castle and agrees to become his wife. This breaks the spell, and the beast is immediately revealed as a handsome prince. The selfish sisters are turned into statues, in which form they are condemned to view the happiness of their selfless younger sister until they change their jealous characters.

This version of the tale, the one that has become canonized through literary and Disney recyclings, was recorded in 1756 by Mme Leprince de Beaumont in her *Magasin des Enfants*. Like other such literary reworkers of folktales, the author considerably reshaped the traditional elements in this retelling. In the many other versions of this story found around the world, the beast may take various forms, including a white wolf in Lithuania, a pig in Magyar lore, a snake in Basque tradition, or a crocodile in Africa. In an English version, known as "The Small-Tooth Dog," the heroine has to humor an unpleasant dog who turns into "the handsomest young man in the world" after the usual incidents. In Switzerland, the beast ap-

Illustration by M. Brock showing the Beast talking to a frightened Beauty (Leonard de Selva/Corbis)

pears as a "Bear Prince," and an Italian version involves a heroic younger daughter named Zelinda or Belinda and a dragon. Portuguese versions of the story exist in Brazil, and the element of the handsome young man, often a prince, having been bewitched into his monstrous shape is found in many other folktale traditions, including that of "The Frog Prince," "Bearskin," and "Cinderella." There is considerable interaction between these similar, though distinctive, traditions.

Related entries: Cinderella; Cinder-Mary; Fairy Tale Heroes; Faithful Henry; Frog Prince, The; Woodencloak, Katie; Zelinda

References and further reading

Addy, S., *Household Tales and Other Traditional Remains*, London and Sheffield: 1895, pp. 1–4.

Calvino, I. (trans. Martin, G.), *Italian Folk Tales: Selected and Retold by Italo Calvino*, New York: Harcourt Brace Jovanovich, Penguin, 1980 (1956), 197–202.

Falassi, A., *Folklore by the Fireside: Text and Context in the Tuscan Veglia*, London: Scolar Press, 1980, p. 58.

Hallett, M. and Karasek, B. (eds.), *Folk and Fairy Tales*, Ontario: Broadview Press, 1996, pp. 124–135.

Hearne, B., *Beauty and the Beast: Visions and Revisions of an Old Tale*, Chicago: University of Chicago Press, 1989.

Bell, Adam

Main character of a sixteenth-century English outlaw hero ballad. Together with his companions Clym of the Clough and William of Cloudesly, Adam Bell is a skilled archer and an outlaw. William is captured and about to be executed when Adam and Clym rescue him. They ride to London and secure the favor of the king and his queen, whereupon they are all pardoned, demonstrating outstanding archery skills that ensure the continuation of the royal favor. While such myths about the monarch's propensity to pardon outlaws feature strongly in folklore, history shows that such benevolence rarely occurs. Adam Bell is one of many archer heroes who appear in the world's folklores.

Related entries: Ahay; Clym of the Clough; Hood, Robin; Ivanovich, Dunai; Outlaws; Tametomo; Tell, William; William of Cloudesly; Yuriwaka

References and further reading

Briggs, K., *A Dictionary of British Folk-Tales in the English Language*, 2 vols., London: Routledge and Kegan Paul, 1970, pp. 369–374.

Child, F. J., *The English and Scottish Popular Ballads*, 5 vols., New York: Dover, 1965 (1882–1898), no. 116, vol. 3, pp. 14–39.

Knight, S., *Robin Hood: A Complete Study of the English Outlaw*, Oxford: Blackwell, 1994.

Belle Starr

See Women Dressed as Men

Benbow, Admiral

English naval officer Admiral John Benbow (1653–1702). His celebration as a hero of British seamen is based mainly on his final encounter against the French. Due to a mutiny of his officers, this encounter was a failure, and Benbow died from wounds sustained in battle, as the best known of his ballads recounts in the version given by Whall:

O come all you seaman bold, lend an ear, lend an ear,
O come all you seaman bold, lend an ear,

It's of an admiral's fame,
Brave Benbow was his name,
And how he fought upon the main
You shall hear, you shall hear. . .

Despite being mortally wounded, Benbow refuses to retire or to resign. Instead, he variously asks to be taken away from sight of his men in case his death should weaken their fighting spirit or to be propped up facing the enemy until the last.

When the surgeon dressed his wound, then he cried:
"Let my cradle now in haste
On my quarter-deck be placed
That my enemies I may face till I'm dead.

Benbow's valiant defiance is usually contrasted to that of his mutinous officers who, in the view of the sailors, display conspicuous cowardice in the face of the enemy. This verse from another Benbow ballad also given by Whall gives the general flavor:

And there Captain Kirby proved a coward at last,
And with Wade played at bo-peep behind the main-mast;
And there they did stand boys, and shiver and shake,
For fear that those French dogs their lives they should take.

As well as a military hero, Benbow is in some senses an occupational hero of Royal Navy sailors, and, in his day and for some time after, he was a more widely known national hero. In the modern era, Benbow might have been a "celebrity," though that concept had not been developed in the seventeenth century.

Related entries: Benkei; Bonaparte, Napoleon; Celebrity Heroes; Franklin, Lord; Gam-Czan, Marshall Gang; McCaffery; Military Heroes; National Heroes; Nautical Heroes; Occupational Heroes; Santa Anna, General Antonio López de; Wolfe, General James

References and further reading

Copper, B., *A Song for Every Season*, Frogmore, UK: Paladin, 1975 (1971), pp. 266–267.

Doerflinger, W. (coll. and ed.), *Songs of the Sailor and Lumberman*, New York: Macmillan, 1972 (1951).
Lloyd, A., *Folksong in England*, New York: International Publishers, 1970 (1967), pp. 275–276.
Whall, W. (coll. and ed.), *Sea Songs and Shanties*, London: Brown, Son, and Ferguson, 1910, pp. 79–81.

Benkei

Legendary Japanese warrior hero. Son of a priest, his nickname was Oniwaka or "young demon," a reference to his fighting abilities. He was eight feet tall and stronger than 100 men. He is said to have learned many tricks from the *tengu* (spirits or fairies), to have carried the massive mortar-shaped stones of Ishiusu, and to have fought alongside the warrior hero Yoshitsune with the Minamoto clan against the Taira in the civil wars of the twelfth century.

The considerable legend cycles of Benkei and Yoshitsune are intertwined in ways reminiscent of the English outlaw Robin Hood. Benkei and Yoshitsune meet for the first time on Kyoto's Gojo Bridge, where the bulky and boisterous Benkei has arranged his magnificent collection of swords with the intention of stealing the sword of the next traveler to cross the bridge. Yoshitsune and Benkei fight a mythic sword battle on the bridge. Eventually Yoshitsune, with the help of the *tengu*, prevails, and Benkei is forced to yield. The two then become firm friends and comrades, frequently appearing in each other's martial legends. In the end, pursued by the Shogun, Yoshitsune and Benkei are cornered. Benkei holds off the samurai long enough for Yoshitsune to suicide and then fights on, remaining upright and giving his assailants the impression that he is invincible. Indeed, it is only by accident that they discover that he is already dead. In common with much hero lore, one version of Benkei's legend has it that he escaped this last battle and joined the Mongols, taking the name Genghis Khan.

As well as being a hero of various legends, Benkei also appears in traditional Japanese drama, the Noh plays.

Related entries: Tametomo; Warriors; Yamato; Yoshitsune; Yuriwaka

References and further reading

Cavendish, R. (ed.), *Legends of the World*, London: Orbis, 1982, pp. 64–66.

Davis, F., *Myths and Legends of Japan*, London: Harrap, 1913, pp. xvi, 39–44, 142–143, 351–352.

Dorson, R., *Folk Legends of Japan*, Rutland, VT, and Tokyo: Charles E. Tuttle, 1962.

Seki, K. (ed.), Adams, R. (trans.), *Folktales of Japan*, London: Routledge and Kegan Paul, 1963. First published in Japanese in 1956–1957.

Bernèz

Legendary hero of a Breton tradition about the moving stones of Plouhinec. According to the story, Bernèz (or Bernet) works for a farmer and falls in love with the farmer's beautiful sister, Rozennik, who also loves Bernèz. But the farmer will not allow the pair to marry, as Bernèz is too poor. Come Christmas Eve, a strange old beggar arrives at the farm of Rozennik's brother and asks to be accommodated for the night. He is put up in the barn with the animals. While he rests there, he overhears a conversation between the donkey and the ox in which they reveal the whereabouts of a vast treasure trove beneath the stones of Plouhinec. Once every 100 years, the animals say, on New Year's Eve, the stones move themselves down to the river for a drink. The treasure that is usually concealed beneath their great mass can then be taken. But there is a catch. Whoever takes the treasure needs three things: some crow's-foot, a five-leafed trefoil, and a Christian soul willing to be offered in exchange for the treasure. Without these things, the stones will crush anyone who seeks to steal their treasure.

The next morning, the old beggar begins his search for crow's-foot and a five-leafed trefoil. He eventually finds these and arrives back at Plouhinec on the last day of the year. He goes out onto the moor where the stones are and there finds young Bernèz dreaming gloomily of the lovely but unattainable Rozennik and carving a cross into the large stone on which he is sitting. The beggar recognizes Bernèz from his Christmas Eve accommodation at the farm and, being a cunning and sharp-eyed rogue, recalls that he had noticed the boy's love for the farmer's lovely sister. Cleverly, the beggar tells Bernèz all about the treasure, except for the se-cret three things needed to obtain it. He asks if Bernèz would like a share of the gold, and, of course, Bernèz is only too happy to agree to return that night, New Year's Eve, to help the beggar and make himself rich enough to marry Rozennik. The beggar is pleased at how easy it has been to trick a Christian soul into dying for the treasure he plans to steal.

That midnight the beggar and Bernèz are hiding in the darkness, watching the stones. As soon as the hour arrives, the earth shakes and the giant stones begin to roll down to the river, just as the animals had said they would. The beggar and Bernèz rush to look at the now-uncovered earth beneath the stones and see great treasure everywhere. Greedily, the beggar scoops up all he can while Bernèz, overawed by it all, manages only to fill his pockets with gold. Then the ground shakes again, and the stones begin to move back to their accustomed places. Bernèz shouts out to the beggar that they must go or be crushed. The beggar laughs and tells Bernèz that he has the magic crow's-foot and five-leafed trefoil and that Bernèz, a Christian soul, will be the one to die. Horrified, Bernèz watches the stones move back to their places, all avoiding the beggar holding up the magic plants. The largest stone then looms up in front of Bernèz, about to crush him into the ground. But suddenly, the stone stops, just hovering over him and seemingly protecting him from all the other stones rolling past on their way back to their locations. When Bernèz looks up fearfully at the teetering stone, he sees that it is the same one on which he had carved the cross earlier in the day. As soon as all the other stones were back in their places, the stone with the cross on it rolled toward the beggar, weighed down with all the sacks of gold he was trying to carry. The beggar heard it coming, stopped, turned, and held the crow's-foot and five-leafed trefoil aloft, laughing. But the cross on the stone made the power of the magic plants ineffective, and the stone crushed the beggar to death, settling back into the ground for another century. A relieved and grateful Bernèz ran back to the farm with his pockets full of gold and was allowed to marry his beloved Rozennik.

This elaborate tale contains a number of common themes and motifs, including the poor youth who must carry out some impossible task in order to win the hand of a beautiful young woman. The greedy, scheming villain gets what he deserves, and, through the piety of Bernèz, the young couple is able to achieve their hearts' desire in the familiar manner of the fairy tale ending.

Related entries: Ataba; E-ttool, Zarief; Fairy Tale Heroes; Religious Heroes
References and further reading
Delarue, P. (ed.), Fife, A. (trans.), *The Borzoi Book of French Folk Tales*, New York: Knopf, 1956.
Lee, F. H. (comp.), *Folk Tales of All Nations*, London: Harrap, 1931, pp. 196–203.
Massignon, G. (ed.), Hyland, J. (trans.), *Folktales of France*, Chicago: University of Chicago Press, 1968.
Picard, B. (ed.), *French Legends, Tales, and Fairy Stories*, Oxford: Oxford University Press, 1955.

Berni, Cesarino Di

A legendary hero of Calabria, Italy, who had a mysterious ability to bond and communicate with animals, especially the bear, wolf, and lion who accompanied him on his travels. Cesarino kills a dragon that has captured a king's daughter, Dorothea, and wins the monarch's favor and the damsel's hand. But Cesarino's mother and sisters, traveling to Cesarino's new home, soon become envious of him and poison him. Cesarino's three animal friends magically resurrect him, and he is restored to his wife and position. His mother and sisters' guilt is soon discovered, whereupon the king has them tortured to confession, then burned to death. Cesarino and Dorothea live long and happy lives and have many children, and Cesarino's lion, bear, and wolf live out their days as the objects of great affection and tenderness.

Heroes' ability to communicate with animals in words or music, always to their ultimate benefit, is a widespread folktale motif found in folk traditions throughout Europe, Asia, Africa, India, and the Americas. Huathicuri, for example, is a Peruvian hero able to speak with animals, who communicate information to help him on his various quests and adventures. Huathicuri wins the hand of the chief's daughter when a fox tells him the cause of the chief's mysterious sickness, enabling the chief to be cured. As in many folk traditions, the implied lesson seems to be that our ends are best achieved through a balanced and harmonious relationship with the natural world.

Related entries: Androcles; Aniz; Dragon-Slayers; Helpers; Yao Wang
References and further reading
Arnott, K. (ed.), *African Myths and Legends*, London: Oxford University Press, pp. 5–12.
Crane, T., *Italian Popular Tales*, Boston and New York: Houghton Mifflin and Co., 1885; reprint, Detroit: Singing Tree Press, 1968.
Robe, S. (ed.), *Hispanic Folktales from New Mexico: Narratives from the R. D. Jameson Collection*, Mythology and Folktale Studies 30, Berkeley and Los Angeles: University of California Press, 1976, pp. 102–111.
Waters, G. W., *The Nights of Straparola*, 2 vols., London: Lawrence and Bullen, 1894.

Bertoldo

Peasant jester, antihero, and trickster-like creation of Bolognese street singer Guilio Cesare Croce (1550–1609). Croce drew heavily on existing literary and oral traditions to present a popular figure who represents the peasant view of the world, full of humor, homespun wisdom, proverbs, pranks, and witticisms in the manner of the Commedia dell' arte. Croce also created a son, Bertoldino, who takes the role of the fool. Both characters faded from view for several hundred years, undergoing revivals in the eighteenth century, from which time they became theatrical figures and spread throughout Europe.

Related entries: Numskulls and Noodles; Tricksters
References and further reading
Croce, G. (ed. Camporesi; trans. Di Guilio, P.), *Bertoldo*, New York: Vantage, 1958.
Del Guidice, L., "Bertoldo," in Brown, M. and Rosenberg, B. (eds.), *Encyclopedia of Folklore and Literature*, Santa Barbara: ABC-CLIO, 1998, pp. 148–150, 487–489.

Billy the Kid

See Bonney, William

Bindieye, Jacky

Australian Aboriginal character (also Jacky Bindi-I), usually a stockman, sometimes a station roustabout, sometimes a layabout, who appears in a number of bush yarns common in the north of Australia, probably originating in the late nineteenth century. In these stories, Jacky's exaggerated stupidity usually has the effect of undercutting the assumed superiority of white authority figures, including the boss, policemen, and magistrates.

On one occasion Jacky and the boss need to cross a flooded river, but the only boat is on the far bank. The boss tells Jacky to swim across and bring the boat back. Jacky protests, saying that there may be crocodiles in the river. The boss says that he need not worry, as crocodiles never touch blackfellas. Jacky replies that the crocodiles might be color-blind and that it would be better to wait until the flood subsides. On another occasion, when Jacky is in a distant part of the property minding a mob of sheep, he needs his rations and other necessities delivered to him by the boss each week. One week the boss forgets to bring Jacky's food. Jacky is not too happy and tells the boss that he has only a bone left from last week's rations and that it will be another week before any more meat comes. The boss laughs and tells him not to worry, saying, "The nearer the bone the sweeter the meat." When the boss returns the next week, the sheep are in a terrible condition, as Jacky had kept them where there was no grass to eat. The boss turns on Jacky and angrily asks him what he thinks he is doing. Jacky just laughs and says, "The nearer the ground, the sweeter the grass."

Jacky Bindieye's other main activity is stealing sheep, for which he is frequently brought before the courts. At one of his hearings, the judge gives Jacky three years in prison and asks him if he has anything to say. "Yes," says Jacky angrily, "You're bloody free with other peoples' time." In another court, this time for being drunk and disorderly, the magistrate fines Jacky and gives him twenty days in prison. "I'll tell you what I'll do, boss," says Jacky. "I'll toss you—forty days or nothing."

This form of humorous passive resistance is found in the traditions of many other occupied or colonized groups. The American "Marster John" stories, featuring a slave named John who uses the white stereotype of the slave to outwit the master, is one example. Other examples abound in Jewish and Yugoslavian tradition.

> **Related entries:** Heroes of Struggle; Numskulls and Noodles; Occupational Heroes; Victims
> **References and further reading**
> Wannan, W., *Come in Spinner: A Treasury of Popular Australian Humour*, Melbourne: John Currey, O'Neill Publishers, 1976 (1964), pp. 142–146.

Black Whirlwind, The

See Li Kui

Blackbeard

See Teach, Edward

Blondel

See Helpers

Bluebeard

Legendary French nobleman who kills his wives for disobeying his orders not to look inside a locked room in his castle. The seventh wife, Fatima, does the same, finding inside the bodies of the wives previously murdered by Bluebeard. As in many folktales of this widespread type, the heroine's brothers arrive in the nick of time and kill Bluebeard. This character has been linked with the historical French wife-killer, Gilles de Rais (1404–1440), but it accords with similar folktales told in many traditions. A well-known English version is usually called "Mr. Fox." Obviously Bluebeard is a villain rather than a hero. However, his murderous villainy provides the opportunity for the heroine to "right the wrong." Bluebeard-like traditions are found throughout Europe, especially in Germany and Italy, in Africa and India, and in African-American versions. Although, the name Bluebeard only became attached to this tradition in the 1820s, such tales are considerably older.

> **Related entries:** Fatima; Ogres; Reynard the Fox; Scheherazade; Villains

References and further reading

Briggs, K., *British Folktales*, New York: Pantheon Books, 1977, pp. 87–89.

Brown, M. and Rosenberg, B. (eds.), *Encyclopedia of Folklore and Literature*, Santa Barbara: ABC-CLIO, 1998, pp. 98, 503.

Delarue, P. (ed.), Fife, A. (trans.), *The Borzoi Book of French Folk Tales*, New York: Knopf, 1956.

Hallett, M. and Karasek, B. (eds.), *Folk and Fairy Tales*, Ontario: Broadview Press, 1996, pp. 117–121.

Klipple, M., *African Folktales with Foreign Analogues*, New York: Garland, 1992, 134–135.

Tatar, M., *The Hard Facts of the Grimms' Fairy Tales*, Princeton, NJ: Princeton University Press, 1987, pp. 156–178.

Bonaparte, Napoleon

"Boney," the folk name for Napoleon Bonaparte (1769–1821), French emperor and conqueror, is the heroic focus of various folklores. He appears in a number of sailor chanteys and songs as "Boney." In one such song, usually titled "Boney" or "Boney Was a Warrior," he "beat the Prussians / And then he licked the Russians." In other British folk ballads of the Napoleonic period, Bonaparte generally appears as a great hero, even as a savior. Popular discontent and hardship in Britain at this time led many people to conclude that they might be better ruled by Napoleon than by their own government.

With some hero types, notably outlaws and many warrior heroes, political conflict may be the source of their celebration in ballad and tale. Boney is an interesting example of a hybrid folk hero, having the combined characteristics of a warrior, a military leader, and, for some people at least, a hero of struggle and a national hero.

Related entries: Benbow, Admiral; Dog-Nyong, General Gim; Franklin, Lord; Gam-Czan, Marshall Gang; Heroes of Struggle; McCaffery; McDonald, Flora; Military Heroes; National Heroes; Santa Anna, General Antonio López de; Stuart, Prince Charles Edward; Warriors; Wolfe, General James

References and further reading

Ashton, J., *Modern Street Ballads*, New York and London: Benjamin Blom, 1968 (1888), pp. 303–304.

Broadwood, L., *English Traditional Songs and Carols*, London: E. P. Publishing, Rowman and Littlefield, 1974 (1908), pp. 34–35.

Engraved portrait of Napoleon Bonaparte (Library of Congress)

Haswell, G. (coll.), *Ten Shanties Sung on the Australian Run, 1879*, Perth: The Antipodes Press, 1992, n.p., no. 6.

Hugill, S., *Shanties from the Seven Seas*, London: Routledge & Kegan Paul, 1984 (1961), p. 445.

Lloyd, A., *Folksong in England*, New York: International Publishers, 1970 (1967), p. 47.

Boney

See Bonaparte, Napoleon

Bonney, William

Historical American outlaw. Known to legend as "Billy the Kid," the historical William Bonney also went by a number of other names in his short life. Probably born in New York City on November 23, 1859, he was known as Henry McCarty and Henry Antrim at various times. He shot dead a blacksmith at Fort Grant, Arizona Territory, in August 1877. On the run, he was hired by the English rancher John Tun-

Movie poster: "MGM presents Robert Taylor as Billy the Kid," c. 1955 (Library of Congress)

stall and became deeply involved in the Lincoln County range war in the New Mexico of the late 1870s. Bonney was either responsible for or deeply implicated in the killing of numerous men working for the "Santa Fe Ring," a group of ranchers and traders apparently colluding with the authorities and desperate to protect their interests against the threat from the ambitious Tunstall.

In 1878, the Lincoln range war subsided somewhat. After the killing of Tunstall, the now-secure business-official combine took its revenge on the losers. Bonney became a fugitive and later negotiated an amnesty that saw him taken into protective custody. Due to further political machinations, Bonney decided,

after a few months of custody, that he would be safer outside jail. He escaped but was recaptured late in 1880 by the new sheriff, Pat Garrett, an old acquaintance. In April 1881, Bonney was found guilty of murder and sentenced to death. But, probably with the aid of a sympathizer, he escaped again, killing two prison guards and disappearing. After some delay, Garrett formed a posse and pursued Bonney to Fort Sumner where, on July 14, 1881, he shot Billy the Kid dead.

As this summary of his short but violent life suggests, Bonney was an unlikely hero, but there were some facets of his life that could be transmuted into legend. He was young when he died. His killings, while hardly brave, were at least in line with the implicit machismo of the outlaw hero. He did perform a sensational, if bloody, jailbreak, and the man who killed him was a onetime friend, so Billy the Kid could be seen as the victim of treachery. He has been referred to as "the darling of the common people," and Bonney's popularity among Mexican-Americans is well-documented, though there is little evidence that he did perform a Robin Hood role to this particular group. More likely, he was seen as something of an avenging demon, spreading terror among the hated Americans, rather than as a bandit hero like Murieta or Gregorio Cortez, who were admired by their peers. As is common with outlaw heroes, many people refused to believe that Billy the Kid was dead, and stories about his survival or even resurrection were rife in New Mexico and elsewhere. Tradition has Billy driven to crime by persecution, and the stock outlaw story in which the hero first pays a poor widow's mortgage to the greedy landlord and then robs it back again is often attached to the legend of Billy the Kid.

Billy the Kid's ballad, written in 1927 and here given by Lomax, is a particularly good example of the balancing of tradition and history to produce an outlaw hero out of an unlikely set of events and personalities:

Song of Billy the Kid
I'll sing you a true song of Billy the Kid,
I'll sing of the desperate deeds that he did
Way out in New Mexico long, long ago,
When a man's only chance was his own
    forty four.

When Billy the Kid was a very young lad,
In old Silver City he went to the bad;
Way out in the West with a gun in his hand
At the age of twelve years he first killed his
    man.

Fair Mexican maidens play guitars and sing
A song about Billy, their boy bandit king,
How ere his young manhood had reached
    its dead end
He'd a notch on his pistol for twenty-one
    men.

'Twas on the same night when poor Billy
    died
He said to his friends: "I am not satisfied;
There are twenty-one men I have put bullets through
And sheriff Pat Garrett must make twenty-two."

Now, this is how Billy the Kid met his fate:
The bright moon was shining, the hour
    was late.
Shot down by Pat Garrett, who once was
    his friend,
The young outlaw's life had now come to
    its end.

There's many a man with a face fine and
    fair
Who starts out in life with a chance to be
    square,
But just like poor Billy he wanders astray
And loses his life in the very same way.

After his violent end, Billy the Kid was rapidly appropriated by the popular media of the day, his real and imagined deeds being widely reported (and plagiarized) in newspapers and given fictional representation in dime novels and "biographies." The man who killed Bonney was one of the first to establish the outlaw's legendary characteristics. Pat Garrett published a ghost-written book in 1882 titled *The Authentic Life of Billy the Kid*, in which he described the outlaw as brave, loyal, generous, resourceful, and gallant, and also as the equal of "any fabled brigand."

There were—and continue to be—many popular treatments of the life and legend of Billy the Kid, beginning with the 1903 melodrama "Billy the Kid" by Walter Woods and continuing through Hollywood adaptations of inaccurate but best-selling journalistic treatments of the story that began to appear in the mid-1920s. The first of these was W. Burns's *Saga of Billy the Kid* (1926), upon which the first Hollywood feature film, *Billy the Kid* (MGM) was based. This film appeared in 1930 and has been followed by at least thirty other feature films about Billy the Kid, as well as by a 1960s television series, *The Tall Man*. In most of these representations, the Kid appears as the wronged, often innocent, youth of somewhat ambiguous morality who nevertheless displays virtues of manliness, generosity, and likability.

The second film of the Kid's saga, *The Gamblin' Man*, was released in 1934, and Aaron Copland created a ballet based on the legend in 1938. Most recently, Bonney has been featured in the movies *Young Guns* (1988) and *Young Guns II* (1990), mostly though not totally in accord with the romantic aspects of his legend. As well, numerous persons have claimed to be Billy the Kid, and there is also a thriving "Kid" tourist industry in the region where he was active.

Related entries: Bass, Sam; Cortez, Gregorio; Fisk, Jim; Hood, Robin; James, Jesse; Outlaws; Parker, Robert Leroy; Quantrill, William Clarke; Slater, Morris; Turpin, Richard

References and further reading
Botkin, B. (ed.), *A Treasury of American Folklore*, New York: Crown, 1944.
Kooistra, P., *Criminals as Heroes: Structure, Power, and Identity*, Bowling Green, OH: Bowling Green State University Press, 1989.
Lomax, J. and A. (colls. and comps.), *American Ballads and Folk Songs*, New York: Macmillan, 1934, p. 136.
Steckmesser, K. L., *The Western Hero in History and Legend*, Norman: University of Oklahoma Press, 1965.
Tatum, S., *Inventing Billy the Kid: Visions of the Outlaw in America, 1881–1981*, Albuquerque: University of New Mexico Press, 1982.

Bonnie Prince Charlie
See Stuart, Prince Charles Edward

Boone, Daniel
See Frontier Heroes

Boots
Boots is a name given to the youngest son in many Norwegian folktales, in the same way that "Jack" is almost indiscriminately applied in English-language tradition. In the tale of "Boots and His Brothers," Boots is the youngest of three brothers in a poor family. Not far from the small cottage where Boots and his brothers live is the king's palace. A large oak tree has grown over the

palace window, cutting off the light, and the king offers a reward for anyone who can cut it down. The oak is no ordinary tree though; it is so potent that whenever anyone cuts it, the chips that fall from it cause new trees to spring up, compounding the king's light problem. The king also lacks a well that can hold sufficient water for a year, and he offers riches to anyone who can dig it, but the ground around the castle is so hard and rocky that no one succeeds. The king lets it be known throughout his kingdom that whoever is able to cut down the tree and dig the well will wed the princess and be given half of the kingdom. Many people try to accomplish these tasks, but all fail. One day, the two elder brothers decide that they will try their luck at the king's tasks and set off for the castle. Reluctantly, they take Boots along with them.

Along the way Boots investigates unusual sights and sounds that interest him, much to the scorn of the older brothers. First he comes across a magic axe that cuts by itself and that also talks. Later he obtains a magic spade that digs by itself and that, like the axe, talks. Later still, he discovers a walnut from which a river runs. He stops up the hole in the walnut where the water runs and puts the walnut in his pocket. When they reach the castle, the two elder brothers try to cut down the oak tree. They fail, and Boots says he would like to try. The brothers ridicule him but eventually allow him to try. He gets out the magic ax and tells it to "hew away." Soon the oak has been felled, and Boots then takes out the shovel and starts on the well, telling the tool to "dig away." The shovel magically digs a deep well, into one corner of which Boots places the walnut. He removes the plug and says "trickle and run," and the well quickly fills. Boots weds the princess and is given half the kingdom as promised. The brothers have to admit that Boots's curiosity was not so silly after all.

To some extent, the Boots character is a male Cinderella: usually found at the bottom of the pecking order, despised, ridiculed, and given the most menial tasks to perform. Unlike those who consider themselves his betters, though, Boots is usually kind, generous, honest, and competent. He is ultimately rewarded for these virtues with success: conquering trolls, over-coming all kinds of obstacles, and, inevitably, winning the hand of the princess and gaining a share, or more, of the kingdom. In some Boots stories, the young hero kills some giants, saving his brothers and their brides from death. Eventually, Boots wins the most beautiful bride of all for himself, a scenario that may be familiar to many people as the basis of the musical *Seven Brides for Seven Brothers*. In Sweden, the Boots role is often taken by a character called "Pinkel," and in Germany by a youth named "Dummling."

In another Scandinavian story, a character named Osborn Boots is the lazy youngest son of a poor farming family. Osborn helps out an old woman who gives him a magic pipe as thanks. The pipe has the power to disperse and reassemble anything at all, after which feats Osborn pronounces in amazement: "Now, that's a pipe!" Osborn deploys the pipe in a series of events controlled by a greedy king and queen. Eventually Osborn cleverly escapes a death sentence decreed by the king and is granted the hand of the princess and half the kingdom. "Now, that's a pipe!" says Osborn Boots.

The Boots character is representative of the extensive tradition of the unpromising hero who makes good in the end. In many such stories, the hero is a layabout younger son, like Osborn Boots. In others, he may be marked by small stature, as in the tale of Kihuo; by physical or unnatural deformity, as in the case of Ivanko the Bear's Son; or simply by poverty and apparent stupidity, as in the case of Jack and the Beanstalk.

Related entries: Dragon-Slayers; Fairy Tale Heroes; Ivanko the Bear's Son; Jack; Jack and the Beanstalk; Jack Tales; Jack the Giant-Killer; Kihuo; Marendenboni; Tardanak

References and further reading
Booss, C., *Scandinavian Folk and Fairy Tales*, New York: Crown Publishers, Avenel Books, 1984.
Clarkson, A. and Cross, B. (eds.), *World Folktales: A Scribner Resource Collection*, New York: Charles Scribner's Sons, 1980, pp. 277–282.
Dasent, G. (comp.), *Popular Tales from the Norse*, Edinburgh: David Douglas, 1888; reprint, Detroit: Grand River Books, 1971; and also as *East o' the Sun and West o' the Moon*, New York: Dover Publications, 1970, pp. 36–8, 48–50, 215–221, 330–336.
Kvideland, R. and Sehmsdorf, H. (eds.), *Scandinavian Folk Belief and Legend*, Minneapolis: University of Minnesota Press, 1988.
Lee, F. H. (comp.), *Folk Tales of All Nations*, London: Harrap, 1931, pp. 781–786.

Boots, Osborn
See Boots

Boru, Brian
See Culture Heroes

Bowie, Jim
See Crockett, Davy; Frontier Heroes

Brennan, William
Also known as "Captain Brennan," William Brennan was hanged in Cork in 1804. He was a farm laborer who, according to tradition, was forced to take to the road when a hoax on a British officer backfired. After Brennan's execution a tradition of a treasure that he had concealed persisted for many years, but this was never found. The numerous versions of the ballad "Brennan on the Moor" show Willie to be fearless, to rob only the wealthy, and to divide his spoils with the poor, usually represented by "widows in distress." Brennan's capture occurs only after a fierce fight in which he is severely wounded.

Brennan's encounter with the packman, or itinerant peddler, is described in "Brennan on the Moor," which is a loud echo of the Robin Hood ballad "Robin Hood and the Peddler." The following version was sung by Mr. Tom Sprachlan, Hambridge, Somerset, in 1903 and was collected by the English folk song collector Cecil Sharp. This ballad is typical of the celebration of the outlaw hero in folklore, not only of the British Isles but also of many other cultures.

It's of a fearless highwayman a story I will tell,
His name was William Brennan and in Ireland he did dwell,
And up on the Libbery mountains he commenced his wild career
Where many a wealthy gentleman before him shook with fear.

Chorus:
Bold and undaunted stood bold Brennan
on the moor,
Brennan on the moor,
Brennan on the moor,
Bold and undaunted stood Brennan on the
moor.

A brace of loaded pistols he carried night
and day,
He never robbed a poor man all on the
King's highway,
But what he'd taken from the rich, like
Turpin and Black Bess,
He always did divide between the widows
in distress.

One day he robbed a packman and his
name was Peddler Bawn,
They travelled on together till the day
began to dawn.
The peddler found his money gone, likewise his watch and chain,
He at once surrounded Brennan and he
robbed him back again.

When Brennan saw the peddler was as
good a man as he,
He took him on the highway his companion to be.
The peddler threw away his pack without
any more delay,
And proved a faithful comrade until his
dying day.

One day upon the highway as Willie he sat
down,
He met the Mayor of Cashel a mile outside
the town;
The mayor knew his features, "I think
you're my man," said he,
"I think you're William Brennan, you must
come along o' me."

Willie's wife had been to town provisions
for to buy.
When she saw her Willie she began to sob
and cry.

He said: "Give me tenpence." As quick as
Willie spoke,
She handed him a blunderbuss from un-
derneath her cloak.
Now with this loaded blunderbuss, the
truth I will unfold,
He made the mayor to tremble and robbed
him of his gold.
A hundred pounds was offered for his ap-
prehension there,
But with his horse and saddle to the moun-
tains did repair.

He lay among the fern all day, it was thick
upon the field,
And nine wounds he had received before
that he would yield.
He was captured and found guilty and the
judge made his reply:
"For robbing on the King's highway you're
both condemned to die."

Besides this well-known song, many folktales are still told about Brennan in Irish communities. Some of these tales are prose renditions of the events described in "Brennan on
the Moor," namely, the encounter with the Bold
Peddler Bawn and the incident of robbing back
the poor woman's rent. This common motif of
outlaw hero traditions is also part of the legendry of a white South African outlaw hero
named Scotty Smith, active during the 1870s
and 1880s; of the Scots Rob Roy MacGregor; of
Captain James Hind (1616–1652), a highwayman who was hanged and quartered for treason; of Jesse James, and of many others.

Related entries: Hood, Robin; MacGregor, Robert;
Outlaws; Swift Nicks; Turpin, Richard

References and further reading
Glassie, H. (ed.), Irish Folk Tales, New York: Pantheon,
1985.
Karpeles, M. (ed.), Cecil Sharp's Collection of English Folk
Songs, London: Oxford University Press, 1974,
vol. 2, pp. 166–167, no. 245.
O'Sullivan, S. (ed.), Legends from Ireland, London:
Batsford, 1977, p. 139.
Seal, G., The Outlaw Legend: A Cultural Tradition in Britain,
America, and Australia, Cambridge: Cambridge
University Press, 1996, pp. 74–76.

Brigid (Brigit), Saint

Also known as St. Bride (pronounced "breed") or "Mary of the Gaels," Brigid (453–523) is the one female among Ireland's three patron saints, the others being St. Patrick and St. Columcille. As with many early Christian figures, Brigid's folklore is a mixture of Celtic belief, Christianity, and superstition. In her youth, the lowborn Brigid was renowned for her charity, her firmness in refusing the suitors to whom her father sought to marry her, and her sincere piety. Eventually she obtained her father's permission to become a nun and founded her order and church at Kildare.

There is a considerable body of folklore surrounding Brigid, including calendar customs associated with her day, February 1, which is also the traditional beginning of the Irish spring. She is said to have been the first to weave cloth in Ireland, and so this day is also the feast day of weavers and spinners. A rush worn around the head on St. Brigid's Eve is said to cure headaches, and St. Brigid's Bow, a cross made of straw, is said to protect a house from harm. A well sacred to St. Brigid is said to have magical curative powers.

Lady Gregory (1906) gives one of many stories told of Brigid. This one, collected in Galway, exemplifies the saint's sanctity, her pity, and her characteristic blending of the spiritual and the practical. While at her father's house in Munster, Brigid was cooking bacon for some honored guests of her father. A hungry dog came to the house, and Brigid took pity on the beast, giving it one of the pieces of bacon reserved for the guests. The dog was still hungry, and so she gave it another piece. When her father came to inquire where the bacon was, all five pieces had been miraculously restored. The high priest who had been present through all this, although Brigid thought him asleep, saw what had happened and informed her father. None of the guests would eat the bacon, saying that they were not worthy of it, and so "it was given to the poor and the wretched."

Related entries: Helpers; Religious Heroes; Wise Men and Women

References and further reading
Glassie, H., *Irish Folk Tales*, Philadelphia: University of Pennsylvania Press, 1985, pp. 58–60.
O'Sullivan, S. (ed.), *Legends from Ireland*, London: Batsford, 1977, pp. 150–151.

Brown, John

John Brown (1800–1859) was an American abolitionist who attacked and occupied a federal arsenal at Harper's Ferry in October 1859. He was executed for treason and became a martyr to the abolitionist cause and a hero of the song "John Brown's Body," later sung as an anthem by the Union forces in the U.S. Civil War. Since then the song has become widely known and almost as widely parodied, especially by military bodies for paeans of tongue-in-cheek self-glorification, as in the World War II paratrooper's song, with its mock heroic chorus "Glory, glory, what a hell of a way to die." This song has generated countless parodies, many of which retain John Brown in one form or another, especially the line "his soul goes marching on."

Related entries: Heroes of Struggle; National Heroes
References and further reading
Lomax, J. and A. (colls. and comps.), *American Ballads and Folk Songs*, New York: Macmillan, 1934, p. 528.

Buffalo Bill

See Frontier Heroes

Bunyan, Paul

Occupational hero of American and Canadian lumbermen. Although a possible French-Canadian origin in a similarly named giant fighter of the 1837 Papineau Rebellion has been suggested, the character of Paul Bunyan first appears in print, obscurely, in 1910. Between 1914 and 1922 a number of advertising booklets were produced by the Red River Lumber Company featuring Bunyan anecdotes compiled and written by a former lumberjack-turned-advertising man, W. B. Laughead. The 1922 edition was extremely popular and established Bunyan well beyond the narrow circle of lumber workers. Bunyan was portrayed as a larger-than-life superman figure who was the first logger in the west and who dug Puget Sound with the help of his fabulously large and strong blue Ox, Babe. Babe's footprints were so big that men drowned in them, and the ox had to be fed on whole bales of hay and cartloads of potato peelings.

Bunyan seems to have then become generally accepted as an occupational folk hero of lumbermen, and even of oil field workers, though folklorists and historians have been suspicious about Bunyan's authenticity, given his apparent print-only existence. Research has suggested that there probably were Bunyan stories in oral circulation among lumbermen in the last part of the nineteenth century, especially in Canada, but that he was not a universally known figure of lumber lore until his legendry, authentic and concocted, was spread through print. The deeds attributed to Bunyan, of course, are similar to those of other occupational heroes, a fact that suggests a folkloric origin, even if Bunyan's rise to popularity came about through written rather than oral processes. While some folklorists consider these processes to be "fakelore," there are many other instances where similar processes have created a folkloric character. As a number of the entries in this encyclopedia illustrate, the interaction of folklore, print, and, latterly, visual and electronic media is an important factor in the creation and perpetuation of many folk heroes and heroines.

Related entries: Crooked Mick; Fink, Mike; Henry, John; Jack-in-the-Green; Mikula; Occupational Heroes; Pecos Bill; Slater, Morris; Stormalong

References and further reading

Dorson, R., *American Folklore*, Chicago: University of Chicago Press, 1960, pp. 3, 44, 128, 199, 201, 208, 214, 216–226.

Dorson, R., *Folklore and Fakelore: Essays toward a Discipline of Folk Studies*, Cambridge: Harvard University Press, 1976, pp. 291–336.

Fowke, E. "In Defence of Paul Bunyan," in Fowke, E. and Carpenter, C. (eds.), *Explorations in Canadian Folklore*, Toronto: McClelland and Stewart, 1985, pp. 189–199.

Greenway, J. (ed.), *Folklore of the Great West: Selections from Eighty-Three Years of the Journal of American Folklore*, Palo Alto, CA: American West Publishing Company, 1969, pp. 347–360.

Hoffman, D., *Paul Bunyan: Last of the Frontier Demigods*, Philadelphia: University of Philadelphia Press, 1952.

C

Calamity Jane
See Women Dressed as Men

Cap o' Rushes
English version of a widespread folktale known throughout Europe and in Indian and Arabic cultures. A young woman is banished by her wealthy father when she tells him that she loves him as much as meat or bread loves salt. She lives in low circumstances, working as a servant wearing a cloak and cap or hood made of rushes. However, she attends dances dressed in her own expensive clothes, and so is not recognized as a humble servant by her master's son, who falls in love with her. Eventually she reveals her true identity through the traditional motif of the finger ring dropped, in this case, into the son's food. The couple is married, and at the wedding feast all the dishes are unsalted. The heroine's father is a guest at the wedding and recognizes both his daughter and the fact that her comparison of love and salt was in fact accurate and expressive of her true love for him. Many of the motifs found in the story relate to those of the Cinderella and Catskin cycles.

> **Related entries:** Assipattle; Catskin; Cinderella; Cinder-Mary; Fairy Tale Heroes; Woodencloak, Katie
> **References and further reading**
> Briggs, K. (ed.), *A Dictionary of British Folk-Tales in the English Language*, 2 vols., London: Routledge and Kegan Paul, 1970–1971, vol. 2, pp. 387–389.
> Dundes, A. (ed.), *Cinderella: A Folklore Casebook*, New York: Garland, 1982.
> Opie, I. and P., *The Classic Fairy Tales*, London: Oxford University Press, 1974.
> Rooth, A., *The Cinderella Cycle*, Lund: C. Gleerup, 1951.

Capone, Al
See Outlaws

Captain Brennan
See Brennan, William

Captain Kidd
See Kidd, William

Caragabi
See Culture Heroes

Carson, Kit
See Frontier Heroes

Cassidy, Butch
See Parker, Robert Leroy

Catskin
Heroine of a number of related European folktales in which she disguises herself in animal skins or other clothing, occasionally revealing herself in magical finery. A prince sees her; a token of some kind is exchanged and later reclaimed; and Catskin marries the prince. These tales are similar in many ways to the Cinderella stories and also use the common motif of the recognition token.

> **Related entries:** Assipattle; Cap o' Rushes; Cinderella; Cinder-Mary; Fairy Tale Heroes; Victims
> **References and further reading**
> Bettelheim, B., *The Uses of Enchantment: The Meaning and Importance of Fairy Tales*, New York: Knopf, 1976, pp. 243–249, 259.
> Cox, M., *Cinderella: Three Hundred and Forty-Five Variants*, London: David Nutt, 1893.

Dundes, A. (ed.), *Cinderella: A Folklore Casebook*, New York: Garland, 1982.

Jacobs, J. (ed.), *English Fairy Tales*, London: The Bodley Head, 1968, pp. 297ff; reprint of *English Fairy Tales* (1890) and *More English Fairy Tales*, 1894.

Rooth, A., *The Cinderella Cycle*, Lund: C. Gleerup, 1951.

Celebrity Heroes

Celebrity is a relatively recent social phenomenon that is largely the product of the mass media, especially those elements concerned with entertainment, notably, film, television, and popular music. The modern age of instant fame and almost as rapid obscurity generates popular heroes and heroines—celebrities of stage, screen, press, music, art, literature, and so on. Many of these celebrities remain within these realms, usually to be succeeded by others who reign in their turn in the relevant pantheons. The Hollywood movie idol Rudolph Valentino (Rodolpho Guglielmi, 1895–1926) is perhaps one of the most familiar, if now fading, examples. Some celebrities, though, do make the transition from popular status to feature in folk expressions of various kinds. More recently, celebrity has extended to other figures, including politicians, artists, writers, thinkers, and scientists.

While the attributed actions of these individuals are rarely heroic in the traditional sense, there is nevertheless an aura of "specialness" about them that generates and regenerates anecdotes, rumors, and beliefs of various kinds, which often take the form of "urban legends" about the supposed activities of film stars like Richard Gere, or popular music figures like Paul McCartney and Michael Jackson. In some cases, a venerable theme of folk heroism may become attached to the image of a dead celebrity. The belief that pop singer Elvis Presley (1935–1977) is still alive is a good example of the refusal to accept the death of the hero that is found in many traditions. A considerable body of other lore about Presley has also developed since his death in 1977.

Sometimes prominent politicians may enter, if briefly, into folklore, as in the case of President Clinton in relation to the Monica Lewinski affair. The events surrounding this affair in the late 1990s generated large numbers of jokes and humorous anecdotes, transmitted rapidly around the world by e-mail and fax machine. While many of these jokes and anecdotes traded on the salacious details of the Clinton-Lewinski liaison, their number and dispersal had the effect of magnifying rather basic human activities into something much more significant. As a result, Monica Lewinski herself attained a level of celebrity, and to many women she was a heroine.

An overwhelming example of popular celebrity was the global outpouring of grief at the death of Lady Diana Spencer, Princess of Wales ("Lady Di" or just "Di," in folk parlance), in 1997. While there was a substantial popular sympathy for Diana and her family, there were also many "sick" jokes circulating by word of mouth, e-mail, and fax machine that satirized the accident. A great deal has been and continues to be written about these events, and while their significance is still uncertain, it is clear that a new kind of popular, global celebrity has been formed, and that this phenomenon will have an impact on the kinds of folk expressions about heroes and heroines that will be commonplace in the twenty-first century and, perhaps, beyond.

While the processes and imperatives that produce popular culture heroes differ in important respects from those of folklore, there are significant overlaps between these expressions of heroism. In the information age, the interactions and cross-influences of folk and popular forms are so extensive and intensive that it is not possible to treat each in isolation. Celebrity heroes tend to be generated by fame, as in entertainment or sporting figures; by notoriety, as in criminals and fraudsters; or through some reported act of survival or endurance, as in solo yacht voyages, mountain rescues, and the like. Some of these figures enter into the folklore of their time and place, though few persist in folk songs, tales, or other forms of folk expression. Those who do tend to take on the familiar characteristics of folk heroes and heroines, and apocryphal stories and beliefs gradually accrete around them. Some examples of this process include baseball players Joe Di Maggio and "Babe" Ruth and the magician Harry Houdini (Ehrich Weiss, 1874–1926). While figures like golfer "Tiger" Woods and basketballer Michael Jordan, as well as stars from other sports, are the objects of intense media adulation at the present moment, it remains to be seen whether they will have any folkloric longevity.

Mass media demand for entertainment content is also a significant element in the perpetuation of certain folk heroes. Figures of tradition, real or mythic, have frequently been the subject of sometimes intensive exploitation in books, popular song, film, and television. Throughout this encyclopedia there are many examples of folk heroes and heroines who have been treated this way, including many fairy tale characters, together with Davy Crockett, Monkey, Robin Hood, Ned Kelly, and Billy the Kid, among others.

Related entries: Fairy Tale Heroes
References and further reading
Bacchilega, C., *Postmodern Fairy Tales: Gender and Narrative Strategies*, Philadelphia: University of Pennsylvania Press, 1997.
Barrick, M., "The Migratory Anecdote and the Folk Concept of Fame," *Mid-South Folklore* 4, 1976, pp. 39–47.
Bluestein, G., *Poplore: Folk and Pop in American Culture*, Amherst: University of Massachusetts Press, 1994.
Boorstin, D., *The Image: A Guide to Pseudo-Events in America*, New York: Atheneum, 1962.
Decker, J., *Made in America: Self-Styled Success from Horatio Alger to Oprah Winfrey*, Minneapolis: University of Minnesota Press, 1997.
Degh, L., *American Folklore and the Mass Media*, Bloomington: Indiana University Press, 1994.
Djupedal, K., "Mass Media, Esoteric Groups, and Folkloristics," *Journal of Popular Culture* 26, no. 4, 1993, pp. 69–78.
Gurko, L., *Heroes, Highbrows, and the Popular Mind*, New York: Bobbs-Merrill, 1953.
Marshall, D., *Celebrity and Power: Fame in Contemporary Culture*, Minneapolis: University of Minnesota Press, 1997.
Narváez, P. and Laba, M. (eds.), *Media Sense: The Folklore-Popular Culture Continuum*, Bowling Green, OH: Bowling Green State University Press, 1986.
Ong, W., *Orality and Literacy: The Technologizing of the Word*, London: Routledge, 1991.
Schechter, H., *The Bosom Serpent: Folklore and Popular Art*, Iowa City: University of Iowa Press, 1988.
Vande Berg, L., "The Sports Hero Meets Mediated Celebrityhood," in Wenner, L. (ed.), *MediaSport*, London: Routledge, 1998, pp. 134–153.

Chang-Hko

Kachin (Burma) heroine of legend who is saved in a boat from a great flood (sometimes in company with her brother, Pawpaw). They take nine cocks and nine needles in the boat with them and, after weathering many stormy days, throw one cock and one needle overboard each day. On the ninth day, the last cock crows and the last needle is heard hitting the bottom, showing that the flood is ebbing. They stay in a cave with two nats, indigenous Burmese spirits, and Chang-Hko gives birth to a son, later killed and dissected by the female nat. The Great Nat then offers the distraught mother the chance to be the mother of all men, but men reject her. In her anger and grief, Chang-Hko swears to "live upon them" forever. As a result, Burmese men must "eat to the nats" by giving an offering of food to these beings whenever they take a meal.

Nats are the spirits and gods of Burmese folk belief, inhabiting sky, rivers, forests, and most other natural features. They are also found in farm fields and buildings and are considered the spirits of the dead. Like supernatural beings in most traditions, nats can be beneficent or malignant and need to be continually propitiated by ceremonies and rituals of all kinds. Nats feature as heroes and heroines in Burmese legendry, with most of these being considered national heroes.

Related entries: Culture Heroes; National Heroes; Religious Heroes
References and further reading
Brockett, E., *Burmese and Thai Fairy Tales*, London: Frederick Muller, 1965.
Cavendish, R. (ed.), *Legends of the World*, London: Orbis, 1982, pp. 72–73.
Leach, M. (ed.), *Funk and Wagnall's Standard Dictionary of Folklore, Mythology, and Legend*, London: New English Library, 1975. Abridged one-volume edition of *Funk and Wagnall's Standard Dictionary of Folklore, Mythology, and Legend*, 2 vols., New York: Funk and Wagnall, 1972, pp. 32–33.

Chapman, John

Known as Johnny Appleseed, John Chapman (1774–1845) traveled throughout the American Midwest, planting apple seeds wherever he went. His ragged, unkempt appearance, his knowledge of plant lore, and his simple philosophy made him a much-loved figure and one around whom various traditions grew up. His love of nature was said to be so great that he would extinguish his campfires rather than have mosquitoes burned in the flames. There may be some truth in this legend, as Chapman died of exposure.

While there is more than a hint of the self-conscious and the manufactured surrounding the Johnny Appleseed story, folklorists have discovered widespread evidence of his persistence in oral tradition, with local orchards often being said to have originated in the passing and casting of Johnny Appleseed. However, it seems likely that these are retrospective traditions

Lithograph of Johnny Appleseed (Library of Congress)

elaborated from the popularization of Johnny Appleseed in children's books, a Disney film, and the verse of popular poets like Carl Sandburg and Vachel Lindsay. Johnny Appleseed has also been commemorated on a U.S. postage stamp, a sure sign of national hero status.

Related entries: Culture Heroes; Frontier Heroes; National Heroes

References and further reading

Botkin, B. (ed.), *A Treasury of American Folklore: Stories, Ballads, and Traditions of the People*, New York: Crown Publishers, 1944, pp. 261–270.

Brunvand, J. (ed.), *American Folklore: An Encyclopedia*, New York: Garland, 1996.

Dorson, R., *America in Legend*, New York: Pantheon Books, 1973.

Charlemagne

King of the Franks and emperor of the west, Charlemagne or Charles the Great (c. 747–814) had a tempestuous reign, much of which is celebrated in courtly song and literature. In addition, there are many folk legends and beliefs about Charlemagne and his less lofty doings, most of which present him as a clever, honest, and generous ruler. In these guises he is usually known as Emperor Karl or, especially to German Catholics, as Karl the Fifth, or just "the Quint."

Like a number of other great leaders, Charlemagne is said not to be dead but only sleeping until his country needs him again. Some legends claim that he sleeps in a deep well in the castle at Nürnberg, where his beard has grown through the stone table on which he slumbers. There is also a well-developed tradition in central Germany involving Karl and Odenberg (Odin's Mountain), near the town of Gudensberg. In Austria, Charlemagne is said to sleep within Untersberg Mountain, crowned and sceptered with his lords all around him. When his beard has flowed to the last corner of the table, the end of the world and the Last Judgment will have arrived.

Related entries: Arthur; Barbarossa; Batradz; Culture Heroes; Danske, Holger; Gearoidh, Iarla; National Heroes; Roderick; Sleepers

References and further reading

Baker, M., *Tales of All the World*, London: Oxford University Press, 1937, pp. 152–155.

Grimm, J. and W. (trans. Ashliman, D.), *Deutsche Sagen* (1816–1818), Folklore and Mythology Electronic Texts, Pittsburgh, PA: University of Pittsburgh, 2000, nos. 22, 28, www.pitt.edu/~dash/folktexts.html#a.

Lyncker, K. (trans. Ashliman, D.), *Deutsche Sagen und Sitten in hessischen Gauen* (1854), Folklore and Mythology Electronic Texts, Pittsburgh, PA: University of Pittsburgh, 2000, pp. 5–7, www.pitt.edu/~dash/folktexts.html#a.

Cheng'er
See Hou Yi

Children's Folk Heroes

Some elements of children's folklore, especially chants, skipping rhymes, and other such expressions, may contain references to legendary or historical heroes and heroines. Because children's lore has a remarkable stability over long periods of time, the heroic characters featured may be quite old, if of unknown authenticity. Counting-out rhymes like "Oranges and Lemons" include characters whose identity is long lost in time. The rhyme "Jack and Jill," in its longer version, has Jill in the role of nurse:

Jack and Jill went up the hill
To fetch a pail of water.
Jack fell down and broke his crown
And Jill came tumbling after.
Up Jack got and home did trot
As fast as he could caper,
While Jill had the job
To plaster his nob
With vinegar and brown paper.

Other nursery rhyme characters with heroic personas include Little Jack Horner and his Christmas pie who: "stuck in his thumb and pulled out a plum / And said 'what a brave boy am I!'"

Children may also adapt heroes and heroines from tale traditions into their own expressions, as in the case of these skipping rhymes:

Cinderella in the cellar
Making love to Rockefeller
Cinderella dressed in yella

Turns around like this.

Or:

Cinderella dressed in yella
Went downstairs to meet her fella
On the way her panties busted
How many people were disgusted?
1, 2, 3, 4 . . .

Children are also skilled at adapting known historical heroes and heroines into their lore. An Australian children's rhyme makes use of the figure of Captain James Cook, who claimed the continent for Britain in 1770:

Captain Cook chased a chook (chicken)
All around Australia
When he got back he caught a smack
For being a naughty sailor.

Another sailor hero features in this widespread skipping rhyme:

Christopher Columbus was a brave man
He sailed to America in an old tin can
The waves got higher, higher, higher, and
  over.
How many miles did he go?
1, 2, 3, 4 . . .

Many versions of these and other children's rhymes (as opposed to nursery rhymes) are scatological or intendedly obscene.

Since the rise of mass media at the start of the twentieth century, children's lore has increasingly appropriated characters from popular fictions, including comics, film, television, and advertising. Frequently such characters are parodied or otherwise satirized, often rudely, as in the case of the popular song and Disney film about Davy Crockett during the 1950s. This early example of "cross-marketing" involved the sale of Crockett items like knives, guns, and the all-important coonskin cap. It also generated a good deal of childhood and young adolescent "Crockett-lore," including jokes (Why does Davy Crockett have three ears? He has a left ear, a right ear, and a wild frontier.) and numerous parodies of the movie's theme song, which became a hit in Britain, America, Australia, and elsewhere. The original lyrics of the song concerned the circumstances of Crockett's birth, his bear-slaying exploits, and his besting of his father, all at the precocious age of three. In children's lore, these lyrics rapidly became the following, recorded in many variants around the English-speaking world:

> Born on a table-top in Joe's cafe
> Greasiest joint in the USA
> Poisoned his mother with DDT
> Shot his father with a .303
> Davy, Davy Crockett
> The man who is no good.

Other media heroes incorporated into children's lore include Hopalong Cassidy, Daniel Boone, Mr. Magoo (who, irresistibly, "did some poo"), Tarzan (who "swings and calls" but meets with a painful accident), and Shirley Temple, among others. More recent heroes and heroines of popular fiction that appear in childlore include Batman and Robin, Wonder Woman, Superman, Superwoman, the Addams Family, the Simpsons, and Mickey Mouse. As with much folklore, characters selected for adaptation in these ways are predominantly male.

It is important to note that the treatment of these characters is an aspect of the folklore of children, as opposed to that for children, like nursery rhymes and "fairy" tales. The former is the genuine, traditional expression of children's culture, a culture often in conflict with the adult world that—tries, at least—to control it, while the latter is what adults, usually in the form of parents and teachers, present to children.

Related entries: Celebrity Heroes; Cinderella; Columbus, Christopher; Crockett, Davy; Fairy Godmother, The; Sandman, The; Santa Claus; Tom the Piper's Son; Tom Thumb; Tooth Fairy, The

References and further reading

Factor, J., *Captain Cook Chased a Chook: Children's Folklore in Australia*, Victoria, Australia: Penguin Books, 1988.

Halliwell, J., *The Nursery Rhymes of England*, London: The Bodley Head, 1970.

Opie, I. and P. (eds.), *The Oxford Dictionary of Nursery Rhymes*, Oxford: Oxford University Press, 1951.

Opie, I. and P., *The Lore and Language of Schoolchildren*, Oxford: Oxford University Press, 1959.

Turner, I., Factor, J., and Lowenstein, W. (comps. and eds.), *Cinderella Dressed in Yella*, 2d. ed., Melbourne: Heinemann, 1978.

Chokanamma

Legendary Indian heroine of the Province of Kerala. She is representative of a frequently encountered type in Indian folklore, a *stya kanni*, often translated as "truth-girl" though having the broader meaning of a young, sexually innocent girl of divine origin and incapable of wickedness. Such characters are usually persecuted in folktales, and this persecution leads to the discovery of the heroine's supernatural abilities.

Chokanamma is born of a deer and is given to a childless Brahman couple to raise. They name her, but she persists in playing in the shrine room, despite repeated orders not to, and so they beat her, and she eventually leaves home. She has a house with seven doors built at a crossroads and lives there until puberty, when her adoptive parents visit her with the traditional milk rice offering. But Chokanamma refuses to allow the couple into the house, and they leave in anger, throwing the rice into a nearby field that subsequently becomes famous for growing red rice. Chokanamma then enters into a palm tree that is cut down by a general, who has twelve bows made from the tree, the largest of which Chokanamma entered. Carried back to the general's house in the form of a bow, Chokanamma causes mischief until a diviner realizes that a goddess is involved and tells the general that he must build a shrine and make annual offerings to Chokanamma. Chokanamma is the focus of cult worship throughout Kerala.

Related entries: Culture Heroes; Fairy Tale Heroes; Helpers; Local Heroes; Religious Heroes; Victims

References and further reading

Beck, B. et al. (eds.), *Folktales of India*, Chicago: University of Chicago Press, 1987, pp. 73–75.

Gray, J., *Indian Tales and Legends*, Oxford: Oxford University Press, 1979 (1961).

Christie, Francis

Francis Christie was the real name of the Australian bushranger known to history and folklore as "Darkie" Gardiner. Gardiner was born near Goulburn (New South Wales) in 1830; his father was a Scots migrant and his mother an Irish-Aboriginal named Clarke. Sentenced to three years hard labor for cattle-stealing in 1850, Clarke, as Gardiner was then known, escaped and left the colony. By 1852 he had returned to New South Wales and was arrested again in February 1854. Thereafter he was in and out of jail on a succession of stock-stealing charges, until 1862 when he masterminded Australia's most spectacular nineteenth-century robbery at Eugowra Rocks. With eleven others (one of whom was probably Ben Hall), Gardiner robbed the Forbes gold escort of 4,000 pounds in cash, over 200 ounces of gold, and the Royal Mail. Most of the loot was recovered fairly soon after the robbery, and in 1864 Gardiner was captured in Queensland, where he was living under an assumed identity. Gardiner was spared the gallows because he had not (as far as could be proven) killed anyone; he was instead sentenced to thirty-two years hard labor. After ten years of constant lobbying by his family, Gardiner was released and exiled, going eventually to the United States, where he is said to have opened a saloon on the San Francisco waterfront and to have been killed there in a gunfight during the 1890s.

Gardiner has survived in Australian folklore as yet another example of the outlaw hero, largely due to his association with the much more folklorically famous Ben Hall and the interconnected group of bushrangers of the Forbes district of New South Wales, who enjoyed extensive support and sympathy from the local population during the 1860s. Many incidents of Gardiner's bushranging career also show him at pains to demonstrate chivalry and courtesy in the tradition of the outlaw hero. Gardiner was reported to be in the habit of returning money to some of his victims for their expenses along the road; he was also known for buying drinks for all present and even for sharing out stolen confectionery. These incidents, along with Gardiner's naming of at least one of his numerous horses "Black Bess" (after Dick Turpin's legendary steed), soon earned him an appropriate outlaw hero reputation. As the editor of the *Sydney Morning Herald* wrote in 1863, some people saw Gardiner and his accomplices as "avengers of the poor and only the robbers of the rich." As well, Gardiner's courtesy to women was renowned. This mixture of folklore and fact is well reflected in Gardiner's ballad, as given by Bradshaw:

FRANK GARDINER
Frank Gardiner he is caught at last and now
    in Sydney gaol,
For wounding Sergeant Middleton and
    robbing the Mudgee Mail;
For plundering of the gold escort, the
    Cargo Mail also;
It was for gold he made so bold, and not
    so long ago.

His daring deeds surprised them all
    throughout the Sydney land,
He gave a call onto his friends and quickly
    raised a band,
Fortune always favored him until the time
    of late,
There were Bourke, the brave O'Meally too,
    met with a dreadful fate.

Young Vane he surrendered, Ben Hall got
    some wounds,
As for Johnny Gilbert, at Binalong was
    found;
Alone he was, he lost his horse, three
    troopers hove in sight,
He fought the three most manfully, got
    slaughtered in the fight.

When lives you take, a warning, boys, a
    woman never trust;
She will turn round, I will be bound,
    Queen's evidence the first.
Two and thirty years he's doomed to slave
    all for the Crown,
And well may he say he cursed the day he
    met Old Mother Brown.

Related entries: Donohoe, Jack; Hall, Ben; Johns, Joseph; Kelly, Edward; Morgan, Daniel "Mad Dog"; Outlaws; Troy, Johnny; Ward, Frederick Wordsworth; Wild Colonial Boy

References and further reading

Bradshaw, J., *The Only True Account of Ned Kelly, Frank Gardiner, Ben Hall, and Morgan*, Sydney: n.p., 1911, p. 6.

Meredith, J. and Anderson, H.(eds.), *Folksongs of Australia*, Sydney: Ure Smith, 1967, p. 30.

Seal, G., *The Outlaw Legend: A Cultural Tradition in Britain, America, and Australia*, Melbourne: Cambridge University Press, 1996, pp. 127–131.

Christmas, Annie

See Occupational Heroes

Cid, El

El Cid, or The Lord, real name Roderigo Diaz de Vivar (c. 1043–1099) was a celebrated soldier during his lifetime and became a rich and powerful ruler of Valencia, the city he wrested from Moorish control in 1094. He was killed in battle against the Moors in 1099.

Legends and beliefs about El Cid were rife during his eventful life and only grew after his death. His tomb had become a popular shrine by the end of the thirteenth century, and it is at this time that one of the most famous and enduring of his legends originated—the story that after he was killed, El Cid's men strapped his body to his horse and sent it into battle. No matter how many Moorish arrows were shot into the corpse, it stayed upright, thus, according to legend, convincing the enemy that El Cid was immortal. A similar tradition is told of the Japanese warrior hero Benkei.

There are said to be about 200 ballads and many legends about El Cid's real and imagined exploits in Spanish. These accounts present El Cid as strong, daring, and able, even after death, to exert supernatural powers. Some ballads, dating from the fifteenth and sixteenth centuries, portray El Cid as a headstrong young man and an enthusiastic, and rude and arrogant, womanizer. These folk songs represent a more down-to-earth, human El Cid, but they nevertheless complement his status as a great warrior and national savior. During the Spanish Civil War (1936–1939), both sides of the conflict claimed to be fighting in the name of El Cid. As well as being the Spanish national hero,

El Cid is well represented in the Spanish-speaking communities of the new world.

Related entries: Culture Heroes; National Heroes; Warriors

References and further reading

Cavendish, R. (ed.), *Legends of the World*, London: Orbis, 1982, pp. 249–253.

Espinosa, A. (ed. Espinosa, M.), *The Folklore of Spain in the American Southwest: Traditional Spanish Folk Literature in Northern New Mexico and Southern Colorado*, Norman: University of Oklahoma Press, 1985, pp. 78–79, 83–84, 127, 131.

Lockhart, J. (ed. and trans.), *The Spanish Ballads*, New York: Century, 1907.

Spence, L., *Spain: Myths and Legends*, London: Harrap, 1920; reprint, New York: Avenel Books, 1986.

Cinderella

Usually said to have been first written down in the ninth century A.D. in China, Cinderella may well be the world's number one fairy tale, though this claim is also made of other widespread tale types such as "Red Riding Hood," "Snow White," and "Sleeping Beauty." The story is, then, perhaps more than 1,000 years old and, like all such stories, has undergone many transformations through time, between cultures, and across distances. Despite much speculation, we can never know what the original story of Cinderella was like, but we can be reasonably sure that it involved a heroine from the bottom of the social order undergoing various tests and tribulations in order to win the love of a hero from the opposite end of the economic scale. These are the timeless and seemingly universal themes of many folk hero narratives.

Modern audiences have taken to the story of the put-upon sister forced to sleep in the grate by her three ugly stepsisters and her nasty stepmother. Cinderella is the classic oppressed innocent and victim. However, in the earliest European literary version, called "The Cat Cinderella" and included in Giambattista Basile's *The Pentamerone* (1634–1636), the heroine is a schemer who meets a just fate. Almost all subsequent versions, though, present Cinderella as the wronged figure who, usually through some recognition device, manages to get her prince.

The most important early publication of Cinderella is that of Charles Perrault in his

1697 *Histoires ou contes du temps passé* (Historical tales from the past), also subtitled *Contes de ma mère l'oie* (Tales of my mother goose), thus beginning the long-standing tradition of nursery rhymes and fairy tales being published under the name of Mother Goose. As with a number of other now classic fairy tales, Perrault was responsible for a considerable refining of the story and for the detail of the glass slipper as a recognition device. In Perrault's version, Cinderella's actions are determined more by the fairy godmother than by Cinderella herself. Mostly she does as the fairy godmother tells her and wins the prince, rather oddly rewarding her unpleasant sisters with marriage to wealthy aristocrats.

Perrault's genteel telling of the tale (that on which the Disney animated feature of 1950 was based), in which the girl is a rather saccharine young innocent, stands in sharp contrast to that of the Grimms, titled "Ashenputtle" or "Ash Girl." In this story, published in 1812, the heroine is much more self-motivated and in control, and it ends with the sisters getting their proper punishment. Birds pluck out their eyes as they make their way to and from Cinderella's wedding. "Thus for their malice and treachery they were punished with blindness for the rest of their lives," ends the Grimms' version, with more than a hint of vengeful sanctimony. The Grimms also included a number of other Cinderella-type tales in their collection, including "Allerleirauh," a "Cap o' Rushes" version, and a "One-eye, Two-eyes, Three-eyes" tale.

The longevity and wide distribution of the Cinderella story and the consistency of many of its motifs from one version to another, notably that of the shoe as a recognition device, has made it one of the most studied of all fairy tales. There is an extensive literature on Cinderella that stretches from the numerous literary rewrites and anthologies, through the mythological speculations of nineteenth-century anthropologists and folklorists, and deep into recent Freudian and Jungian psychology. Folklorists have also devoted considerable time and effort to analyzing and understanding what is perhaps the world's best-known folktale.

Illustration from the cover of an 1897 children's book, Cinderella (Library of Congress)

In a collection entitled *Cinderella: A Casebook*, American folklorist Alan Dundes presents a variety of folkloric approaches to the story of Cinderella, including essays on Russian, Chinese, English, Greek, Indian, and French versions of the Cinderella tale and its distribution in Europe, Africa, and parts of Asia. Other selections in this work deal with a Muslim women's ritual reuse of the story and with spiritual, Jungian, and Freudian interpretations of the story. Further essays cover the actual folkloric rendition of a Tuscan version of the tale and a consideration of the popularization of the Cinderella story in America. Dundes makes it clear that these are but a sampling of the rich variety and diversity of folkloric Cinderella studies, most of which are beholden to the astonishing work of Marian Roalfe Cox, who published her *Cinderella: Three Hundred and Forty-Five Variants of Cinderella, Catskin, and Cap o' Rushes, Abstracted and Tabulated, with a Discussion of Medieval Analogues and Notes* in 1893. In 1951, the Swedish folklorist Anna Birgitta Rooth published her *Cinderella Cycle*, using about 700 different versions of the tale. These are the foundation works of folklore scholarship on this heroine, and, together with the large number of other works on this one story and with its variations and entries in Aarne and Thompson's *The Types of the Folktale* (1910 and 1961), they constitute a convincing case for the antiquity and the persistence of the Cinderella cycle.

The use of the term "cycle" in connection with Cinderella stories is appropriate and advisable. Scholarship has discovered and delineated at least five distinct subtypes of the Cinderella story. One of these is the basic Cinderella story that will be familiar to most western readers; another is the group of tales revolving around a figure called "Catskin"; a third involves a "Cap o' Rushes," and a fourth "One-eyes, Two-eyes, and Three-eyes." In a fifth subtype, the Cinderella role is taken by a male, as in the Native American story of Amala and in some Hungarian stories. Other versions of Cinderella include the Norwegian "Katie Woodencloak," the Georgian "Conkiajgharuna," or "The Little Rag Girl," the Serbian "Pepelyouga," and the Italian "Rosina," to name only a few. Some of these versions combine Cinderella with motifs from other stories.

Related entries: Amala; Assipattle; Cap o' Rushes; Catskin; Cinder-Mary; Fairy Tale Heroes; Woodencloak, Katie; Ye Xian

References and further reading

Argenti, P. and Rose, H., *The Folk-Lore of Chios*, 2 vols., London: Cambridge University Press, 1949, vol. 1, pp. 443–445.

Asbjørnsen, P. and Moe, J. (trans. Dasent, G.), *Popular Tales from the Norse*, Edinburgh: David Douglas, 1888, pp. 357–372.

Bettelheim, B., *The Uses of Enchantment: The Meaning and Importance of Fairy Tales*, New York: Knopf, 1976, pp. 9, 40, 55–56, 62, 64, 72, 103, 105–106, 113, 127, 129, 145–147, 152, 155, 183–184, 199, 236–278, 307, 310.

Calvino, I. (trans. Martin, G.), *Italian Folk Tales: Selected and Retold by Italo Calvino*, New York: Harcourt Brace Jovanovich, Penguin, 1980 (1956), pp. 225–229.

Cox, M., *Cinderella: Three Hundred and Forty-Five Variants*, London: David Nutt, 1893.

Dawkins, R. (comp. and trans.), *Modern Greek Folktales*, Oxford: Clarendon Press, 1953, pp. 115–116; reprint Westport, CT: Greenwood Press, 1974.

Degh, L. (trans. Schossberger, E.), *Folktales and Society: Story-Telling in a Hungarian Peasant Community*, Bloomington/London: Indiana University Press, 1969 (1962).

Dundes, A. (ed.), *Cinderella: A Folklore Casebook*, New York: Garland, 1982.

Eberhard, W. (ed.), *Folktales of China*, London: Routledge and Kegan Paul, 1965, pp. 151–161.

Falassi, A., *Folklore by the Fireside: Text and Context in the Tuscan Veglia*, London: Scolar Press, 1980, pp. 45, 51–68, 185, 324–325.

Hallett, M. and Karasek, B. (eds.), *Folk and Fairy Tales*, Ontario: Broadview Press, 1996, pp. 53–65.

Irizar, L. (ed.), Barandiarán, J. (coll.), White, L. (trans.), *A View from the Witch's Cave: Folktales of the Pyrenees*, Reno: University of Nevada Press, 1988, p. 57.

Lang, A., *The Blue Fairy Book*, London: Longmans, Green, and Co., 1889.

Lüthi, M. (trans. Chadeayne, L. and Gottwald, P.), *Once upon a Time: On the Nature of Fairy Tales*, Bloomington: Indiana University Press, 1976, pp. 59–70.

Massignon, G., *Folktales of France*, London: Routledge and Kegan Paul, 1968, pp. 147–149.

Opie, I. and P., *The Classic Fairy Tales*, London: Oxford University Press, 1974.

Petrovich, W., *Hero Tales and Legends of the Serbians*, London: George G. Harrap, 1917, pp. 224–230.

Rooth, A., *The Cinderella Cycle*, Lund: C. Gleerup, 1951.

Wardrop, M., *Georgian Folk Tales*, London: David Nutt, 1894, pp. 63–67.

Cinder-Mary

Heroine of a Spanish-Mexican version of Cinderella. This story features witches called the "Black Moors" in place of the jealous stepsisters, though one of the witches has a daughter who is jealous of the star placed on Cinder-Mary's head by a fairy godmother figure who also gives Cinder-Mary a magic wand that provides her with whatever she requests. Cinder-Mary is eventually married to the prince, but the witches, feigning friendship, turn her into a bird, a state from which she is freed by the king. Upon learning of the witches and their treachery, the king has them burned to death. Cinder-Mary locks herself in the palace for five days and emerges a virgin.

This version of the Cinderella tale combines elements of the Spanish tradition, such as the villains known as "the Black Moors," with the indigenous figures of the flying witches. The resulting new story is far removed from the reassuring fairy tale versions of Cinderella, though it is recognizable as such. The new tale reflects something of the cultural clash between the invading Spanish who brought the story to South America and the variations and elaborations made by the story's Mexican Indian tellers who incorporated it into their own folklore. This process of cultural transference and adaptation is typical of the means by which hero and heroine traditions were—and are—diffused around the world.

Related entries: Amala; Assipattle; Cap o' Rushes; Catskin; Cinderella; Fairy Tale Heroes; Woodencloak, Katie; Ye Xian

References and further reading
Mason, J., "Four Mexican-Spanish Fairy Tales from Azqueltan, Jalisco," *Journal of American Folklore* 25, 1912, pp. 191–198; reprint, Greenway, J. (ed.), *Folklore of the Great West*, Palo Alto: American West Publishing Company, 1969, pp. 141–143.

Clym of the Clough

Legendary accomplice of English archers William of Cloudesly and Adam Bell. The name "Clym of the Clough" means "Clym of the cliff." He is celebrated with his comrades in a well-known ballad. There are some similarities between the traditions associated with this group of archers and other folk heroes, notably Robin Hood and William Tell, Dunai Ivanovich and Yuriwaka.

Related entries: Bell, Adam; Hood, Robin; William of Cloudesly

References and further reading
Briggs, K. (ed.), *A Dictionary of British Folk-Tales in the English Language*, 4 vols., London: Routledge and Kegan Paul, 1970–1971, vol. 2, 369–374.
Child, F. J., *The English and Scottish Popular Ballads*, 5 vols., New York: Dover, 1965 (1882–1898), vol. 3, pp. 14–39, no. 116.

Columbus, Christopher

Cristoforo Colombo (1451–1506), Spanish-Italian navigator and adventurer long credited as the "discoverer" of North America in 1492 and celebrated as such in a number of Italian immigration songs as well as in popular parlance and in children's folklore. In the United States, Columbus generally has the status of a national hero, especially among Italian-Americans, who often see Columbus Day (October 12) as a legitimation of their status as Americans. But he also has a more ambiguous position, often being associated with the necessities of migration from home to a far and unknown country. According to Luisa del Giudice: "He was sometimes invoked as the first cause of suffering and alienation for Italian immigrants: '*Maledetto Cristoforo Colombo e quando ha scoperto l'America!*' (Damn Christopher Columbus and his discovery of America) is a phrase I have heard on more than one occasion." This ambiguity is a feature of many historical and some nonhistorical folk heroes, including Ned Kelly, Casey Jones, and more than a few tricksters.

Related entries: Children's Folk Heroes; Jones, Casey; Kelly, Edward; National Heroes; Tricksters

References and further reading
Del Giudice, L. (ed.), *Studies in Italian-American Folklore*, Logan: Utah State University Press, 1993, pp. 1–4, 111–112, 120, 127, 135, 141–142, 147, 149.
Mathias, E. and Raspa, R., *Italian Folktales in America: The Verbal Art of an Immigrant Woman*, Detroit: Wayne State University Press, 1988.

Cook, Captain

Captain James Cook (1728–1779), "discoverer" of Australia, features in a number of Aboriginal traditions in which he, his men, and especially his sailing ship, *Endeavour*, return as ghosts of the dead or are interpreted in some other supernatural way. In some areas of the Northern Territory, Captain Cook has become conflated with another Australian folk hero, Ned Kelly.

Cook's voyages also had an impact on the traditions of other indigenous peoples, including the Muchalat people of Nootka Sound on the west coast of Vancouver Island, Canada. Cook spent a month at Nootka Sound in 1778. An account of the first contact between the mariner and the local inhabitants was still in oral tradi-

Captain Cook escaping in a rowboat from natives during a voyage to the Pacific, c. 1750-1779 (Library of Congress)

tion over a century later in the story of Chief Maquinna and Chief Nanaimis who saw a sailing ship for the first time when Cook sailed into the sound. Not knowing what this strange moving object with sticks might be, the Muchalat people speculated that it was a salmon transformed into a strange canoe and that it was being moved by supernatural powers. They became afraid and contemplated hiding. Instead, they launched a canoe with three young warriors and a woman doctor who also believed Cook's ship was a salmon. When they reached the ship she called out "Hello you, you spring salmon. Hello you, dog salmon. Hello, canoe salmon." The first Muchalat canoe was joined by another canoe with another doctor aboard who also hailed Cook's ship in this way. Emboldened, Chief Nanaimis took two beaver skins out to the ship in a canoe paddled by ten young men. When the

chief came near Cook's ship, the chief of the strange boat called out, "What is your name?" Nanaimis identified himself as chief of the Muchalats and asked the stranger his name. "I am Captain Cook," came the reply. Cook then got some blankets and invited the chief aboard. Nanaimis declined but agreed to shake Cook's hand and to accept the gift of two black blankets. Nanaimis then saw that Cook was not an enchanted salmon but a man with fair skin. He gave the two beaver skins to Cook. Chief Maquinna also had his canoe paddled out to the ship, invited Cook to stay in his village the following year, and gave him a sea otter skin. Cook then gave Maquinna his gold-braided hat. Back on the shore, the other people saw that there was nothing to fear and danced a wolf dance. Cook and his crew stayed for some days, trading with the Muchalats and exploring along the coast.

These indigenous traditions concerning Captain Cook provide a good example of the way in which historical incidents become incorporated into oral tradition and of how the heroic figures of one group can appear in the lore of another in quite different roles.

Related entries: Children's Folk Heroes; National Heroes; Nautical Heroes

References and further reading

Clark, E., *Indian Legends of Canada*, Toronto: McClelland and Stewart, 1960, pp. 157–158.

McMillan, C. (coll. and ed.), *Canadian Wonder Tales*, London: The Bodley Head, 1974 (combines two collections published in 1918 and 1922).

Rose, D., *Dingo Makes Us Human: Life and Land in an Aboriginal Australian Culture*, Melbourne: Melbourne University Press, 1992, pp. 198–202, 205, 208, 231.

Cortez, Gregorio

Mexican outlaw hero born in 1875 and dead by 1916. Cortez is the central figure of a strong Mexican-American border tradition of *corrido* (ballad) and legend. As with many such folklorized historical figures, the details of his life and activities are fused with the motifs of outlaw heroism and also of occupational and culture heroes. As Américo Paredes, the chronicler of the Cortez legend, points out, there are hints of the supernatural in his reputedly being the seventh son of a seventh son. Like John Henry and other such types, he is said to have been able to drink more and to work harder than any human. Cortez also takes on some attributes of the warrior hero in his armed struggles against the oppressors. But mostly Cortez is a classic outlaw hero of the Robin Hood type who is celebrated in folklore as a friend of the poor and the powerless who struggles on their behalf and, ultimately, is betrayed and imprisoned, dying in uncertain circumstances. Paredes accurately and poetically describes the interaction between fact and folklore in the legend of Cortez, and in that of other similar folk heroes: "It was as if the Border people had dreamed Gregorio Cortez before producing him, and had sung his life and his deeds before he was born."

Related entries: Bonney, William; Brennan, William; Heroes of Struggle; Hood, Robin; James, Jesse; Kelly, Edward; Outlaws; Turpin, Richard; Warriors

References and further reading

Paredes, A., *With His Pistol in His Hand: A Border Ballad and Its Hero*, Austin: University of Texas Press, 1990 (1958).

Coyote

Main trickster figure and culture hero of much Native American lore. He goes by many names. When Native Americans tell their traditions in English, Coyote is often referred to as "Old Coyote" or in similar fashion, as in the Blackfoot "Old Man Napi," a character identified with Coyote in his trickster roles.

Coyote is in many ways an unattractive character. He bullies people and breaks sexual and other taboos. In this mode, Coyote stories provide teaching devices for the correct moral behavior of young children. However, as with the trickster figures of many cultural groups, Coyote is also often presented as a culture hero who performs the positive functions of bringing fire and craft skills.

In addition to these activities, Coyote may also appear in the role of the numskull, as in the Yurok story of Coyote and the Acorns in which Coyote is fed sour acorns by the people he visits. He likes them so much that he asks how they are made. He is told that the acorns are dampened with water and left for two days. But Coyote thinks this is too easy and continues to bother them for what he thinks must be the real secret of their preparation. Annoyed by this pestering, someone eventually tells him that the secret is to fill a canoe with acorns and tip it into the river, then he has only to walk along the river bank and retrieve the acorns. Stupid Coyote tells his grandmother this wonderful secret and takes all her acorns and throws them into the river, making her very angry. He walks the river bank searching for acorns in vain and becoming very hungry. His grandmother refuses to feed him, telling him to go and eat his own acorns. One day he smells the acorns his grandmother is cooking. She tells him that they are not acorns but excrement. However, he can now tell the difference and eats them, thus avoiding starvation.

Another Coyote tale told among Plains, Plateau, and some California and southwestern Native American groups has Porcupine climb into a buffalo paunch and kill the beast while he is being carried across a river. Coyote then tricks Porcupine out of the buffalo meat. They decide that whichever of them can jump over the body of the buffalo can take all the meat. Coyote succeeds, but Porcupine fails and has his revenge by killing Coyote's children.

The wide diffusion and popularity of Coyote tales is well demonstrated in early ethnographic collections of Native Indian lore, such as that edited by Franz Boas in 1917 and titled *Folk-Tales of Salishan and Sahaptin Tribes*. In this work, a compilation of different fieldwork collections, there appear dozens of Coyote stories from the various language and cultural groups represented. In these traditions, Coyote carries out many deeds, including stealing fire, taming the wind, killing the moon, and introducing salmon to the tribes of the interior. Many of these stories are told in different versions, and Coyote also appears as a subsidiary character in other stories. In some Native American traditions, Coyote tales are single episodes; in others, the tales may be strung together in a loose cycle.

Coyote also plays tricks in Mexican tradition, often using his magic to make a nuisance of himself with poor peasants and their livestock.

Related entries: Culture Heroes; Maui; Tricksters
References and further reading

Boaz, F. (ed.), *Folk-Tales of Salishan and Sahaptin Tribes*, Lancaster, PA: American Folk-Lore Society, 1917.
Clark, E., *Indian Legends of Canada*, Toronto: McClelland and Stewart, 1960, pp. 25–29.
Clarkson, A. and Cross, G. (eds.), *World Folktales*, New York: Charles Scribner's Sons, 1980, pp. 283–284.
Greenway, J. (ed.), *Folklore of the Great West*, Palo Alto: American West Publishing Company, 1969, pp. 147–149, 178, 347.
Radin, P., *The Trickster: A Study in American Indian Mythology*, New York: Philosophical Library, 1956.
Ramsey, J. (comp. and ed.), *Coyote Was Going There: Indian Literature of the Oregon County*, Seattle: University of Washington Press, 1977.
Thompson, S., *The Folktale*, New York: Holt, Rinehart, and Winston, 1946, pp. 316–328.

Crnojevic, Ivan
See Warriors

Crockett, Davy

Davy Crockett (1786–1836) is the center of a large number of American frontier tall tales and legends. In his lifetime, he was a noted "Indian fighter," pioneer, and spinner of tales, both about and against himself. His death at the Alamo, an event itself of considerable mythic significance, only added to his legend, which was burnished by numerous almanacs and other publications. Although he portrayed himself as something of a backwoods hick, he was in reality nothing of the sort and was elected a member of the Tennessee legislature. He was killed, together with another frontier hero, Jim Bowie, at the Alamo during the Texas Revolution of 1835–1836, along with all the other defenders of the garrison.

Crockett tales include his exploits fighting bears, "injuns," and just about anything else. He is able to wield lightning bolts and to accomplish such incredible feats as unfreezing the earth by pouring bear grease over the sun when that heavenly body becomes frozen in its own sweat. Nor is he slow to boast about his many astounding exploits, being the archetypal backwoods and frontier liar. There is also a little of the trickster about Crockett. This combination of attributes led the eminent American folklorist Richard Dorson to hail Crockett as a thoroughly authentic American folk hero, in contrast to those he considered examples of what he labeled "fakelore," such as Paul Bunyan, Febold Feboldson, and numerous other pioneer and occupational figures. Dorson also observed that Crockett was unusual in that he was celebrated both as a teller of tall tales and also featured as the hero in many other tales told about him.

In the 1950s, the continuing interest in the Crockett legend led to a Disney film on the backwoodsman's life and legend. The film was accompanied by a pseudofolk ballad that entered the hit parades of various countries, and by a mass marketing campaign that included the sale of Davy Crockett coonskin caps and

Portrait of Colonel David Crockett by J. G. Chapman (Library of Congress)

other items associated with the hero. Children in America, Britain, Australia, and elsewhere in the world took to the image of Crockett with enthusiasm, producing numerous jokes, games, and parodies of the hit song, most of which were related to the concerns of the youth groups of the period. So, Crockett came to have a second existence as a folk hero of children and adolescents, functioning as a focus for youthful conflict with parents and with society in general. Some of the folk parodies of the Davy Crockett song featured Davy shooting his parents and engaging in knife-fights not with grizzly bears, as in the earlier tradition, but with members of youth gangs. One such song even referred to Crockett as "King of the Universe," another as "King of the Teddy Boys," a male youth group of the period.

Related entries: Chapman, John; Children's Folk Heroes; Frontier Heroes; Liars; Santa Anna, General Antonio López de

References and further reading

Botkin, B. (ed.), *A Treasury of American Folklore: Stories,* Ballads, and Traditions of the People, New York: Crown Publishers, 1944, pp. 5–7, 14–32, 56.

Dorson, R., *American Folklore*, Chicago: University of Chicago Press, 1959, 47, 50, 61–64, 199–214, 235, 270.

Lofaro, M. (ed.), *The Tall Tales of Davy Crockett*, Knoxville: University of Tennessee Press, 1987.

Lomax, J. and A. (colls. and comps.), *American Ballads and Folk Songs*, New York: Macmillan, 1934, p. 251.

Rugoff, M. (ed.), *A Harvest of World Folk Tales*, New York: Viking Press, 1949, pp. 74–79.

Crooked Mick

Legendary occupational hero of Australian shearers and other outback workers. Mick can shear more sheep, cut more trees, and do anything faster than anyone else. He is usually said to reside in a mythical, faraway land called "the Speewah," where everything grows in unnaturally large proportions: the pumpkins are so big that they can be used as houses; the trees are so tall that they have to be hinged to let in the sunlight; the sheep are so large that they cannot be shorn without climbing up a ladder; and so on.

Related entries: Bunyan, Paul; Fink, Mike; Henry, John; Jack-in-the-Green; Jones, Casey; McCaffery; Mikula; Occupational Heroes; Pecos Bill; Slater, Morris; Stormalong

References and further reading

Davey, G. and Seal, G. (eds.), *The Oxford Companion to Australian Folklore*, Melbourne: Oxford University Press, 1993, p. 91.

Wannan, W. (ed.), *Crooked Mick of the Speewah*, Melbourne: Lansdowne, 1965.

Culture Heroes

The term culture hero is often used in the literature of folklore and anthropology to mean a figure of myth who was responsible for the creation of the cosmos, of light, fire, or of humanity itself. These beings are frequently the bringers of essential survival skills such as fishing, weaving, or hunting. Culture heroes are usually male, often warriors, and may be human, animal, supernatural, or any combination of these.

In many cultures, especially African, Native American, and Australian Aboriginal, culture heroes may be identified as trickster figures, though most folk tricksters do not have, or have perhaps lost, their mythological associations. Whatever their form or attributes, culture heroes are considered by those who tell their tales to be the founders and often the keepers of the values, customs, and beliefs of their culture. Some representative examples demonstrate the similarity and diversity of culture heroes around the world.

Caragabi is the culture hero of the Choco Indians of western Colombia. Caragabi created the ancestors and organized the social structure to prevent incest. He also put the heavenly bodies in the sky, gave food-bearing plants to humanity, and was responsible for having the tree of life cut down. Caragabi then went to the sky, to return only when the world has been destroyed by fire. Another South American culture hero is Poseyemu of the Tewa Pueblo. He was conceived through a nut and takes various roles among different groups. Sometimes he is a benefactor dispensing clothing, medicines, and wealth; sometimes he is a liar. In some settings, he has become identified with the snake in the Garden of Eden, and in others he has taken on a Christ-like persona. After living on earth, Poseyemu is said to have either disappeared back into it or to have faded away to the south.

Italapas is the Native American Chinook culture hero and world creator, a version of the widespread Coyote figure. Unlike some Coyote traditions, though, Italapas assists in the creation process rather than hindering it. Italapas is said to have created the land and to have helped the great creator make the first men, teaching them necessary skills, taboos, and social customs.

Another Native American culture hero is Smoking Star, said to have been born of a piece of bison meat. Like a number of heroes from other cultures, Smoking Star almost immediately attains manhood and then performs various heroic deeds to the benefit of his people, including hunting bison and killing dangerous bears and snakes. Smoking Star also rescues captives from the belly of the Great Sucker Fish and kills a giant ogress. He dies, resigned to his fate, pierced by Cree arrows.

Sivirri is the culture hero of the Tjununji people of Cape York, Australia. Inventor of the drum and the wooden canoe, he eventually disappears to the north into the region of the Torres Straits Islands. Anthropologists have traced links between Sivirri and Papuan traditions and also between Sivirri and another culture hero, the Western Islands Torres Strait figure Kwoiam (Kuiama), a noted warrior spear-thrower and the center of an extensive mythology and cult.

Tawhaki is the name the Maori of New Zealand usually give to the mythic hero known elsewhere in Polynesian culture by various names, including Tafa'i in Tahiti and Kaha'i in Hawaii. By whatever local names he is known, this hero is always handsome, brave, and strong. He rescues his parents from hobgoblins, restores lost sight, and eventually ascends to the sky. Tawhaki is a culture hero and also operates to some extent as a healer.

The term culture hero can also designate a figure who may not be credited with the creation of the cosmos but who is nevertheless a significant, perhaps defining, representative of his or her ethnic group. The Irish "King of the Tributes," Brian Boru, was killed in battle against the Danes in 1014. He is the center of many Irish legends and songs, some bawdy, and considered a potent symbol of Irish culture. The legendary peasant strongman of Slovenian culture, Martin Krpan, served the Viennese emperor for many years but eventually requested and was granted the right to return to his farm and to have the right to import salt free of taxes. Although traditionally associated with the region of Istria, he is sometimes considered to be a culture hero of the Slovenian people. In such cases there is often a close correlation between culture heroes and national heroes. However, the terms and the types of heroes they describe should not be confused. National heroes are often culture heroes who have become representative of well-defined nation-states or national groups and who have explicit or implicit government support.

Related entries: Alexander the Great; Alfred the Great; Amala; Anansi; Arthur; Chang-Hko; Chapman, John; Coyote; Danske, Holger; Darcy, Les; Ebbeson, Niels; Gearoidh, Iarla; Haitsi-Aibab;

Havelock the Dane; Hereward the Wake;
Hiawatha; Jolly Swagman, The; Kelly, Edward;
Lemminkäinen; Little Dutch Boy, The;
Lohengrin; Mac Cumhal, Finn; Madoc;
Matthias, King; Mau and Matang; Maui;
Monkey; Mrikanda; Nastasya, Princess; National
Heroes; Nikitich, Dobrynya; O'Malley, Grace;
Shine; Siitakuuyuk; Uncle Sam; Väinämöinen;
Vladimir; Warriors; Yankee Doodle

References and further reading

Alpers, A. (ed.), *Maori Myths and Tribal Legends*, 2d ed.,
Auckland: Addison Wesley Longman New
Zealand, 1964, pp. 106–132.
Baumann, H., *Hero Legends of the World*, trans. S.
Humphries, London: Dent and Sons, 1975
(1972), pp. 133–137.
Green, T. (ed.), *Folklore: An Encyclopedia of Beliefs,
Customs, Tales, Music, and Art*, 2 vols., Santa Barbara:
ABC-CLIO, 1997, pp. 164–167.
Leach, M. (ed.), *Funk and Wagnall's Standard Dictionary
of Folklore, Mythology, and Legend*, London: New
English Library, 1975. Abridged one-volume
edition of *Funk and Wagnall's Standard Dictionary of
Folklore, Mythology, and Legend*, 2 vols., New York:
Funk and Wagnall, 1972, pp. 191, 530, 597,
1016.
O'Sullivan, S., *Legends from Ireland*, Totowa, NJ:
Rowman and Littlefield, 1977, pp. 132–133.
Ó hÓgáin, D., *The Hero in Irish Folk History*, New York:
Gill and Macmillan, 1985, chap. 2.
Poli, B., "The Hero in France and America," *Journal
of American Studies* 2, no. 2, 1968, p. 225.
Segal, R., *Hero Myths: A Reader*, London: Blackwell,
1999.

D

Dad and Dave

Probably an original literary invention of Australian author "Steele Rudd" (Arthur Hoey Davis, 1868–1935), Dad and his idiot son, Dave, first appeared in the *Bulletin* magazine in 1895. Four years later the sketches appeared in book form under the title *On Our Selection*, with various new editions and sequels. The books were best-sellers and appear to have inspired the numerous humorous folktales and jokes told about Dad and Dave. These concentrate on portraying Dad, Dave, and the family as country hicks, as in this brief example:

Mum: Dave's gone and broke his leg, Dad!
Dad: D'yer think we ought to shoot 'im?

The other important aspect of Dad and Dave yarns is the portrayal of Dave as a gormless fool, very much in the tradition of the widely distributed "numskull" stories. In one typical exchange, Dave is leaving home to join the army. Mum, worried about her son in the big city, prevails on Dad to give him a fatherly lecture about the perils of drink, gambling, and women. Dave anxiously and honestly is at pains to let Dad know that he never has any truck with such things. Dad returns to Mum and says: "You needn't worry. I don't think the army will take him anyway, the boy's a half-wit!"

Related entries: Drongo; Kabajan; Knowall, Doctor; Little Moron; Lucky Hans; Numskulls and Noodles; Wise Men of Gotham
References and further reading
Rudd, S., *On Our Selection*, Sydney: Angus and Roberston, 1899.
Wannan, W., *The Australian*, Adelaide: Rigby, 1954, pp. 91–92.

Damien the Leper

See de Veusters, Father Joseph

Danske, Holger

Another name for the Danish national hero also known as Ogier the Dane. He defended his country against Charlemagne (742–814) and features in many ballads. Holger Danske is so large and strong that he requires twelve tailors to make him a new suit of clothes, and they need to climb up ladders to reach his shoulders. When one accidentally clips Holger's ear, Holger thinks he is being bitten by a flea and carelessly brushes at it, crushing the poor tailor to death. Another tradition tells of a witch providing Holger with a pair of spectacles that allow the wearer to see through the ground. Laying down to test them, Holger leaves the mark of the spectacles in the ground outside Copenhagen, where they can still be seen.

According to legend, Holger Danske sleeps with his warriors in a deep, dark cellar under Kronberg Castle. Dressed in armor, his long beard grown through a marble table, he sleeps on and on and in his dreams sees all that happens in Denmark. Like many other such figures, Holger Danske is not dead but only sleeping until the time of his people's need, when he will come again.

Related entries: Arthur; Barbarossa; Culture Heroes; Gearoidh, Iarla; Heroes of Struggle; National Heroes; Sleepers
References and further reading
"CJT," in *Folk-Lore and Legends Scandinavian*, London, 1890, pp. 53–55.
Olrik, A. (ed.), Smith-Dampier, E. (trans.), *A Book of Danish Ballads*, Princeton, NJ: Princeton University Press, 1939.

Darcy, Les

James Leslie Darcy, Australian pugilist (1895–1917) celebrated in song and story for his strength and perseverance. Widely believed to have been murdered in the United States by Americans jealous of his skills and fearful of his effect on American boxing: "He gave up hope, when he got that dope / Way down in Tennessee," as the best-known of his ballads has it. In fact, Darcy died of blood poisoning arising from an injury received in the ring before he left Australia. Darcy was much more than a sporting celebrity and up to and during World War I took on the character of a national hero. Outside boxing circles, his popularity has waned considerably, as the generations that celebrated his exploits and achievements have faded.

Related entries: Celebrity Heroes; National Heroes; Victims
References and further reading
Wannan, W., The Australian, Adelaide: Rigby, 1954, pp. 38–39.

de Veusters, Father Joseph

Father Joseph de Veusters, Belgian missionary of the Order of the Sacred Hearts, also known as "the Picpus fathers" after the location of the early work of the order's founder, who was born in 1840. Upon his ordination, Joseph de Veusters assumed the name of Damien, probably after St. Damien, the selfless fourth-century physician of Cilicia. Damien ministered to the lepers of Molokai and surrounding islands from the early 1870s until his death from leprosy in 1889. His selfless, sometimes controversial, devotion to his calling earned him the stature of hero in the South Pacific during his lifetime. After his death, his legend grew along with attempts to eradicate leprosy that were significantly inspired by his own efforts and achievements.

In 1936, such was Damien's fame that his body was exhumed and returned to Belgium. After the exhumation, his coffin was opened in order to give the local lepers a last look at their hero. They were unhappy that Damien's remains were to be taken away. According to local lore, disturbing the last resting place of a great man will bring retribution. Someone associated with the corpse will die. On the sea journey back to Belgium, after the ship bearing the coffin had left the islands en route for the United States, the captain disappeared; presumably he was washed overboard. His body was never found, and Damien's legend lives on, especially in that part of the world where he carried out his work. A number of books have documented Father Damien's life and legend, and a feature film based on his work was released in 1999 with the title Molokai.

Damien's folklore combines the folk hero types of the helper, the local hero, and the hero of religious belief.

Related entries: Helpers; Local Heroes; Religious Heroes
References and further reading
Clifford, E., Father Damien, New York: Macmillan, 1890.
Farrow, J., Damien the Leper, London: Burns, Oates and Co., 1937.

Deva, Babar

Historical Gujarati outlaw hero of the early twentieth century celebrated in song and story. Born in Goral, near the Gulf of Cambay, India, Babar Deva is said to have been inspired by an earlier outlaw figure named Sayadu Minyano and to have helped ignite Gandhi's protest and resistance movement. His legend is violent; his deeds include the murder of his sister and his wife. However, he also outwits the police who seek to capture him at his daughter's wedding by disguising himself as a woman and giving the bride away under the noses of the authorities. Babar Deva's legendry has an element of resistance to British rule as one of its most appealing local elements. In this aspect, Babar Deva has something of the additional appeal of a hero of struggle, a dimension frequently observed in outlaw heroes.

Related entries: Heroes of Struggle; Hood, Robin; James, Jesse; Kelly, Edward; Local Heroes; Outlaws
References and further reading
Beck, B. et al. (eds.), Folktales of India, Chicago: University of Chicago Press, 1987, pp. 212–219.
Dorson, R. (ed.), Folktales Told around the World, Chicago: University of Chicago Press, 1975, pp. 203–208.

Gray, J., *Indian Tales and Legends*, Oxford: Oxford University Press, 1979 (1961).

Devil, The

The Devil (as opposed to *a* devil) is a figure against which much folk heroism is directed, though in much folklore, the devil often appears as more of a trickster troublemaker than as evil incarnate. This role is generally reserved in Christian cultures for Satan and his various analogues, including "the great beast" and the "Antichrist." In this respect, it is interesting to note that the Book of Revelation 20:1–3 describes Satan in terms reminiscent of common folk villains: "the dragon, that serpent of old, the Devil or Satan." The Devil is often known by alternative folk names such as "Old Nick" or "Clootie" and is widely associated with a supernatural virtuosity on musical instruments—the violin or "fiddle" in Europe, the bagpipes in Scotland, and the banjo or guitar among African-Americans.

In folklore, the Devil will often disguise himself and attempt to trick a human in various ways. A number of ballads, such as "The False Knight on the Road," show such a situation, in which the Devil is invariably outwitted by a streetwise youth or maiden. There are many stories from many traditions about individuals who beat the Devil at his own game. Often these figures are tricksters. Jack o' Kent is a legendary English hero who outwits the Devil, while El Bizarron is a Cuban hero of legend who has similar success. In the traditions of many Christian cultures, this favored theme often shows individuals beating the Devil at his own game and saving their souls in the process.

A common story tells of a hero who is tired of having to continually wade across the ford at a certain spot of a river and wishes aloud for a bridge. The Devil hears this wish and appears to the hero, offering to build the bridge in return for the soul of the first to cross over it. The hero takes the offer, and by the next morning the Devil has magically constructed a fine bridge and waits at the far end for the hero to cross over it and so to fall into his clutches. But the hero is smarter than the Devil and by one or another means arranges for a dog, cat, or

Illustration of a Russian myth telling of wedding guests who foolishly dance in a graveyard and find themselves dancing to the Devil's balalaika; when the music stops they turn into a circle of stones. (Mary Evans Picture Library)

other animal to cross the bridge first, frustrating the Devil's desire for a soul (because in Christian belief animals have no souls) but keeping the bargain and saving his or her soul. This legend is found associated with numerous bridges in Germany, Switzerland, England, and elsewhere in Europe.

Stories in which humans enter into pacts with the Devil are also found in most Christian cultures and include, for example, the "Bearskin" stories of Germany as well as similar tales from Switzerland, Sicily, Russia, Czechoslovakia, Ireland, Finland, Cuba, South America, Norway, the United States, and the Philippines. Other Devil traditions, such as the legends on which the well-known Faust and Dr. Faustus stories are based, have less happy outcomes for the mortals.

Related entries: Baba-Yaga; Jack o' Kent; Ogres; Villains

References and further reading

Blum, R. and E., *The Dangerous Hour: The Lore of Crisis and Mystery in Rural Greece*, London: Chatto and Windus, 1970, pp. 99–100.

Dorson, R., *American Folklore*, Chicago: University of Chicago Press, 1959, pp. 8, 18, 23–24, 27, 35–37, 82–84, 100, 102, 104, 106, 119, 169.

Falassi, A., *Folklore by the Fireside: Text and Context in the Tuscan Veglia*, London: Scolar Press, 1980, pp. 20, 218–220.

Frazer, J., *Folk-Lore in the Old Testament*, 3 vols., London: Macmillan, 1918.

Gaer, J., *The Lore of the Old Testament*, Boston: Little, Brown, 1951.

Hunt, M. (trans. and ed.), *Grimm's Household Tales* (with the author's notes and an introduction by Andrew Lang), 2 vols., London: George Bell and Sons, 1884, pp. 312–324, 440–452.

Dillinger, John

The most notorious of the American criminal heroes of the 1930s, John Dillinger (1902–1934) was named "Public Enemy Number 1" by the FBI. Dillinger attracted—and encouraged—outlaw hero celebrity. Said to have been the recipient of an unjustly harsh prison sentence in his youth, he repeatedly avoided the law, escaped from an "escape-proof" Indiana jail in 1934, and was noted as someone who wanted to rob only the banks, not the poor. He was widely compared—favorably—with Robin Hood, Dick Turpin, and Jesse James, as he successfully robbed bank after bank during the Depression. After he was betrayed by a whorehouse madam and shot by FBI agents in Chicago in July 1934, thousands of people came to the death scene, deliberately soaking up his blood in their garments. Later, thousands viewed Dillinger's coffin, and legends began circulating. According to these legends, Dillinger's penis was unusually large, perhaps a reflection of his fabled ability to avoid capture. There was also a general refusal to believe that Dillinger was dead, and, like other outlaw heroes, he was sighted by many people at many places in the years following his death.

Related entries: Bonney, William; Celebrity Heroes; Fisk, Jim; Floyd, Charles Arthur; James, Jesse; Outlaws; Parker, Robert Leroy

References and further reading

Kooistra, P., *Criminals as Heroes: Structure, Power, and Identity*, Bowling Green, OH: Bowling Green State University Press, 1989, pp. 128–132.

Doctor Knowall

See Knowall, Doctor

Dog-Nyong, General Gim

Legendary Korean warrior hero and strategist who is born in supernatural circumstances and who battles the Japanese at Imzin. Gim Dog-Nyong's grandfather was executed on false charges, and so Gim Dog-Nyong's father prays for twenty years that he might have a son born to him who can avenge this wrongful death. After ten years, a daughter is born, but, disappointed and angry, the father kills the child. Ten years later, as his mother carries another child, she becomes the target of a tiger in the shape of a Buddhist monk. The monk uses many tricks and magic in an attempt to kill Gim Dog-Nyong's mother, but whenever he gets near her, she is protected by flaming swords, and so Gim Dog-Nyong is born.

Like many folk heroes, Gim Dog-Nyong is brave and gifted. He takes the duty of revenging his grandfather seriously and one day goes to a swordsmith and gives him instructions on how to forge a magic sword. When the sword is finished, the smith gives it to Gim Dog-Nyong, saying that he knows that he must die, as he has learned secrets of sword making that mortals should not know. Gim hacks at the smith but succeeds only in cutting off his sleeve, and so spares the man who has helped him. Gim travels to Seoul and takes revenge on the minister who had executed his grandfather on false accusations. The authorities declare that Gim should be punished for this killing. But then, by the magic of his sword, Gim is magically transported the 250 miles back home. When the authorities discover that Gim has this magical ability, the charge against him is quashed.

Gim Dog-Nyong is a good example of the hero who combines fighting abilities with magical powers, attributes found in many hero traditions.

Related entries: Achikar; Ahay; Ahmed; Fereyel;

Habermani; Magicians; Marendenboni; Molo; Nue the Hunter; Shape-Shifters; Warriors

References and further reading

Faurot, J. (ed.), *Asian-Pacific Folktales and Legends*, New York: Simon and Schuster, 1995.

In-Sob, Z., *Folk Tales from Korea*, London: Routledge and Kegan Paul, 1952, pp. 58–59.

Dojrana

Legendary young Serbian woman in love with a youth in the area of Lake Dojrana on the border between Macedonia and Greece. The lake was named in her honor, it is said, because she preferred to drown herself in a deep well rather than to be forced into Turkish concubinage. As she drowned, the well overflowed and its waters flooded the surrounding plain, forming the lake. In common with much of the hero and heroine lore of this region, the theme of outsmarting the Turks or of revenge against them reflects the long and unhappy history of occupation since the fourteenth century that found a modern outcome in the "ethnic cleansing" and civil wars within and around the former Yugoslavia. In addition to her status as a culture hero, Dojrana is also a local hero.

Related entries: Ashma; Green Princess, The; Kraljevic, Marco; Lazar; Local Heroes

References and further reading

Dixon-Kennedy, M., *European Myth and Legend*, London: Blandford, 1997, p. 65.

Mijatovies, C. (ed. and trans.), *Serbian Folklore*, New York: Benjamin Bloom, 1968 (1874).

Rootham, H., *Kossovo: Heroic Songs of the Serbs*, Oxford: Blackwell, 1920.

Donohoe, Jack

Jack Donohoe (Donahoe, Donahue), found guilty of intent to commit an unspecified felony, was transported to New South Wales for life in 1824–1825. Donohoe escaped in 1827, and ballads and some witnesses credit him with many of the attributes of the outlaw hero: he was courteous to women, never robbed "the poor" (in this case the convict and ex-convict population), was heroically daring, and died "game." He enjoyed the sympathy and support of convict society, many of whose members provided Donohoe and his gang with information about trooper movements and with food and shelter. This assistance kept Donohoe alive until 1830, when he was killed in a shoot-out with the trooper police near Sydney.

A number of ballads were composed about Donohoe, though the one that has survived presents the bushranger in unabashed hero terms, drawing explicit comparisons with earlier outlaws, from Robin Hood and Willie Brennan to Captain Freney and Jeremiah Grant. As well, the ballad introduces a strong note of antiauthoritarianism, expressed as antagonism toward the representatives of the English Crown. This element recurs often in subsequent Australian manifestations of the outlaw hero tradition and has also ensured the popularity of the ballad, in various versions, in Ireland.

BOLD JACK DONAHOE

'Twas of a valiant highwayman and outlaw
    of disdain
Who'd scorn to live in slavery or wear a
    convict's chain;
His name it was Jack Donahoe of courage
    and renown—
He'd scorn to live in slavery or humble to
    the Crown.

This bold, undaunted highwayman, as you
    may understand,
Was banished for his natural life from
    Erin's happy land.
In Dublin city of renown, where his first
    breath he drew,
It's there they titled him the brave and bold
    Jack Donahoe.

He scarce had been a twelve-month on the
    Australian shore,
When he took to the highway, as oft he
    had before.
Brave MacNamara, Underwood, Webber
    and Walmsley too,
These were the four associates of bold Jack
    Donahoe.

As Jack and his companions roved out one
    afternoon,
Not thinking that the pains of death would
    overcome so soon,

To their surprise five horse police appeared
all in their view,
And in quick time they did advance to take
Jack Donahoe.

"Come, come, you cowardly rascals, oh, do
not run away!
We'll fight them man to man, my boys,
their number's only three;
For I'd rather range the bush around, like
dingo or kangaroo,
Than work one hour for Government," said
bold Jack Donahoe.

"Oh, no," said cowardly Walmsley, "to that
I won't agree;
I see they're still advancing us—their num-
ber's more than three.
And if we wait we'll be too late, the battle
we will rue."
"Then begone from me, you cowardly
dog," replied Jack Donahoe.

The Sergeant of the horse police discharged
his car-a-bine,
And called aloud to Donahoe, "Will you
fight or resign?"
"Resign, no, no! I never will, until your
cowardly crew,
For today I'll fight with all my might,"
cried bold Jack Donahoe.

The Sergeant then, in a hurry his party to
divide,
Placed one to fire in front of him, and
another on each side;
The Sergeant and the Corporal, they both
fired too,
Till the fatal ball had pierced the heart of
bold Jack Donahoe.

Six rounds he fought those horse police
before the fatal ball,
Which pierced his heart with cruel smart,
caused Donahoe to fall;
And as he closed his mournful eyes he
bade this world adieu,
Saying, "Good people all, pray for the soul
of poor Jack Donahoe."

There were Freincy, Grant, bold Robin
Hood, Brennan and O'Hare:
With Donahoe this highwayman none of
them could compare.
But now he's gone to Heaven, I hope, with
saints and angels too—
May the Lord have mercy on the soul of
Brave Jack Donahoe.

This nineteenth-century rendition is given
by Seal. Other versions of this song tell essentially the same tale in the same sympathetic
manner, and Donohoe is generally acknowl-
edged as the likely progenitor for the later but
much more widely distributed ballad "The
Wild Colonial Boy."

Related entries: Brennan, William; Christie, Francis;
Hall, Ben; Hood, Robin; Johns, Joseph; Kelly,
Edward; Morgan, Daniel "Mad Dog"; Outlaws;
Thunderbolt; Troy, Johnny; Wild Colonial Boy

References and further reading

Butterss, P., "Bold Jack Donahue and the Irish
Outlaw Tradition," *Australian Folklore* 3, 1989,
pp. 3–9.
Meredith, J., *The Wild Colonial Boy: Bushranger Jack
Donahoe, 1806–1830*, Ascot Vale, Victoria: Red
Rooster Press, 1982, pp. 55–56.
Morton, R. (coll.), *Come Day, Go Day, God Send Sunday*,
London: Routledge and Kegan Paul, 1973, pp.
47–49.
Seal, G., *The Outlaw Legend: A Cultural Tradition in Britain,
America and Australia*, Cambridge, UK: Cambridge
University Press, 1996, pp. 121–123.
Zimmermann, G., *Songs of Irish Rebellion: Political Street
Ballads and Rebel Songs, 1780–1900*, Dublin: Allen
Figgis, 1967, pp. 24–25, 76, 101, 103,
269–271.

Doyle, Tom

Historical character who, until the 1960s, was
publican and mayor of the eastern goldfields
town of Kanowna in Western Australia. Tom
was an Irishman whose unusual interpretations
of words and phrases unfamiliar to him provide the humor of the many yarns told about
him in Western Australia. In one of these
gaucheries, the newly married Tom takes his
bride to the city of Melbourne to honeymoon
in a grand hotel. The manager of the hotel asks
the wealthy but unsophisticated Tom if he

Poster for the movie Dragonslayer, 1981 (Kobal Collection/Paramount/Walt Disney Productions)

would like the bridal chamber. Tom replies that while his wife may require it, he will be happy to urinate out the window.

Other Tom Doyle stories concentrate on his embarrassing public outbursts, such as the time he attended a function for a visiting dignitary. For the first time in his life, Tom was confronted with olives. He gingerly picked one up and was concerned to discover that it was moist. Just as the dignitary rose to speak, Tom jumped up and cried out that someone had pissed on the gooseberries. Tom Doyle is a mixture of the numskull and the frontier or bush hero and very much the local "character" hero.

Related entries: Bindieye, Jacky; Crooked Mick; Drongo; Frontier Heroes; Local Heroes; Numskulls and Noodles

References and further reading
Edwards, R., *The Australian Yarn*, Adelaide, SA: Rigby, 1978 (1977), pp. 30–31.
Wannan, W., *Come in Spinner: A Treasury of Popular Australian Humour*, Melbourne: Curry, O'Neill, 1976 (1964), p. 141.

Dragon-Slayers

A major class of heroes and heroines, dragon-slayers and their victims are a constant feature in the traditions of the world. As with many other categories or types of hero, dragon-slayers are predominantly, though not exclusively, male. Closely allied to giant-killers, dragon-slayers often begin life as good-for-nothing layabouts and youngest or only sons, their adventures and misadventures leading to the revelation of unsuspected bravery, strength, and skill. Usually dragon-slayers survive their combats with the scaly fire-breathers and go on to win the gold, the girl, and the kingdom. In one case, at least, that of St. George, a dragon-slayer has become a national and culture hero in a number of different countries and cultures.

Folk heroes generally consider dragons to be in the same general class as serpents, giant worms, sea monsters, and even giant man-eating boars, as in a Papuan tale. Whenever they appear—which is often—dragon-slayers are usually interpreted as culture heroes and/or warrior heroes, such as the princess-rescuing dragon-slayer of Russian folktales, Frolka-Stay-at-Home.

Some scholars consider dragon-slaying motifs and themes in a psychoanalytic light, that is, as projections of our desires to overcome obstacles. Other interpretations see them as survivals of an earlier era in which humans did battle with large, now mostly extinct creatures in a day-to-day battle for survival and mastery, which humans eventually won. From a cultural point of view, dragon-slayers are usually seen as representative of the forces of good over the power of evil, symbolized by loathsome creatures.

Related entries: Baldpate; Boots; Culture Heroes; George, Saint; Giant-Killers; Guy of Warwick; Ivan the Mare's Son; Jack; Li Ji; Lucky Hans; Nikitich, Dobrynya; Ogres; Old Woman's Grandchild; Popovich, Aloisha; Tabagnino the Hunchback; Tardanak; Tsarevich, Ivan; Victims; Villains; Warriors

References and further reading

Bettelheim, B., *The Uses of Enchantment: The Meaning and Importance of Fairy Tales*, New York: Knopf, 1976, pp. 75–76, 111–115, 117–118, 280.

Boyle, J., "Historical Dragon Slayers," in Porter, J. and Russell, W. (eds.), *Animals in Folklore*, London: Brewer/Rowman and Littlefield, The Folklore Society, 1978.

Brown, M. and Rosenberg, B. (eds.), *Encyclopedia of Folklore and Literature*, Santa Barbara: ABC-CLIO, 1998, pp. 167–169.

Daniel, G. et al., *Myth or Legend?* London: Bell and Sons, 1955, pp. 83–85.

Degh, L. (trans. Schossberger, E.), *Folktales and Society: Story-Telling in a Hungarian Peasant Community*, Bloomington: Indiana University Press, 1969 (1962), p. 179.

Ker, A. (coll. and ed.), *Papuan Fairy Tales*, London: Macmillan, 1910, pp. 121–127.

Lüthi, M. (trans. Chadeayne, L. and Gottwald, P.), *Once upon a Time: On the Nature of Fairy Tales*, Bloomington: Indiana University Press, 1976, pp. 47–57.

Seki, K. (ed.), Adams, R. (trans.), *Folktales of Japan*, London: Routledge and Kegan Paul, 1963, p. 33. First published in Japanese in 1956–1957.

Zhao, Q., *A Study of Dragons, East and West*, New York: Peter Lang Publishing, 1992, pp. 119–141.

Drake, Sir Francis

See Magicians; Nautical Heroes

Drongo

The Drongo is the Australian numskull, a heroically stupid figure, usually in a bush setting, who interprets literally whatever he is told. When the boss tells him to "hang a new gate," the Drongo takes the gate out to the nearest tree and hangs it in a noose. When asked to dig some turnips about the size of his head, the Drongo is found pulling up the entire turnip patch and trying his hat on each uprooted turnip for size. The name "Drongo" is said to derive from the name of an Australian racehorse of the 1920s famous for losing races, and is also used as an insult.

Related entries: Dad and Dave; Kabajan; Knowall, Doctor; Little Moron; Lucky Hans; Numskulls and Noodles; Tricksters; Wise Men of Gotham

References and further reading

Wannan, W., *Come in Spinner: A Treasury of Popular Australian Humour*, Melbourne: Curry, O'Neill, 1976 (1964), pp. 131–134.

Dwi-Wozoney

See Villains

E

Earl Gerald
See Gearoidh, Iarla

Ebbeson, Niels
Historical Danish hero of the fourteenth century who, in folklore at least, freed his people from German oppressors. While traditions concerning Ebbeson are clear that he was responsible for the delivery of the country from foreign domination, the historical facts are far murkier. Ebbeson and a company of men murdered Count Gert at Randers on April 1, 1340. War followed, in which Ebbeson took a leading, if brief, role. He was killed in battle at Skanderborg on November 2, 1340. As a consequence of these momentous events compressed into just a few months, Ebbeson was quickly and enduringly honored with the mantle of national hero. His popularity with the people is well expressed in the last verse of his ballad as translated by Gray, in which a woman shares her last loaves of bread with the man who had struck down the country's oppressor:

'Twas a puir auld wife that took him in;
She had only twa loaves o' breid;
But ane she gae to Niels Ebbeson,
For he'd stickit the bald Count dead.

Related entries: Culture Heroes; Heroes of Struggle; National Heroes
References and further reading
Gray, A. (trans.), *Historical Ballads of Denmark*, Edinburgh: Edinburgh University Press, 1958, pp. 138–151.
Simpson, J., *Scandinavian Folktales*, Harmondsworth, Middlesex: Penguin, 1988.

Eight Immortals, The
Figures of an ancient Chinese folk tradition that, like most Chinese folklore, has also been treated widely in literature and art. The eight immortals are:

Tieguao Li (Li Tieguai), usually translated as "Li with the Iron Crutch," is often portrayed as a beggar carrying a gourd of magical medicines.
Han Zhiongli (Zhongli Quan) kills a tiger with a magical flying sword and turns base metals into gold to help the poor.
Zhang Guolao is a hermit and magician who travels on a white donkey able to traverse vast distances in a day.
He Xiang is a young girl who eats powdered mica and so becomes immortal, able to float through the air picking mountain fruit to take home to her mother.
Lan Caihe is sometimes said to be a hermaphrodite and is usually portrayed in blue rags, singing drunken songs.
Lü Dongbin (Lü Zu, or Lü the Patriarch) is an elderly wise man, spiritual guide, magician, and hermit who uses his skills to rid the world of evil.
Han Xiangzi is a clever and emotional character whose sensitivity to nature leads him to try and convince his relative, the Tang writer and statesman Han Yu, to renounce the ways of the world and take up Taoism. He also predicts the future.
Cao You (or Cao Guojui, meaning Cao, the brother of the empress), ashamed that his brother was a criminal, and fearing imperial retribution, distributes his wealth to the poor and travels to the

The Eight Immortals crossing the sea: illustration of a Chinese myth (Mary Evans Picture Library)

mountains in search of enlightenment, which he eventually finds.

Each of these eight figures achieves immortality in a different way, in terms of the Taoist religious beliefs of China. Taoism is usually said to be the indigenous religion of China and has contributed strongly to the diversity and vastness of Chinese belief and folk tradition. The various legends of the Eight Immortals often refer to them as "the wandering immortals," a reference to their many journeys, individually and together. The most widespread of these stories is called "The Eight Immortals Cross the Sea" and tells how, during their wanderings, each of the immortals uses a different object or weapon associated with them as an aid to cross the water. As well as appearing in legend, the Eight Immortals are frequently represented in artworks, furniture, pottery, and other objects, and also in proverbial sayings of the Chinese peoples.

Related entries: Helpers; Magicians; Wise Men and Women

References and further reading

Eberhard, W. (ed.), Parsons, D. (trans.), *Folktales of China*, Chicago: University of Chicago Press, 1965 (1937), pp. 229, 240.

Li, N., *Old Tales of China*, Singapore: Graham Brash, 1983 (1981), pp. 8–11.

Werner, E., *Myths and Legends of China*, New York: Arno Press, 1976 (1922), pp. 214–215, 291–304.

El Cid

See Cid, El

El Khidre

See Khidre, El

Eliezer, Israel ben

See Baal-Shem-Tov

Elijah the Prophet

Perhaps the most frequently encountered and favorite Jewish folk hero. Although Elijah (also called Elias) is a biblical hero, in folklore his activities are usually quite different from those recounted in the Bible. Elijah often appears as a benefactor and helper of the poor, oppressed, and pious. In a Moldavian story, Elijah rewards an impoverished but good old man with a wooden staff. The staff performs many magical and protective acts and ultimately enables the old man to attain his lifelong wish of going to the Holy Land, where the staff is transformed back into a tree. Similar events are told in the legendry of other folk heroes, including Tannhaüser (c. 1200–1270), the German poet whose staff breaks into bud, and Joseph of Arimathea.

In a story collected in Poland in 1906, a poor leper boy is given help by Elijah. Elijah first cures him of leprosy and then asks him what he would like to do in life. The boy says that he would like to be a baker. So Elijah has the boy trained as a baker and some time later comes back to see him. "How do you like being a baker?" Elijah asks. "Not so good," says the boy. "I often burn my hands." "Well, what would you like to be?" Elijah asks him. The boy says that he would like to be a tailor, so Elijah arranges for him to take an apprenticeship in this trade. After some time, the prophet visits the boy and asks him how he is enjoying tailoring. The boy says that he is not enjoying the trade, as he keeps sticking himself with the needles and pins. Elijah asks the boy what else he would like to be. This time he wants to be a shoemaker, so Elijah arranges it. After some time, Elijah visits the boy to see how his shoemaking is going, but again the boy is unhappy with the job and asks to be a surgeon. But the boy is not happy being at everyone's beck and call as a surgeon, and so Elijah makes him a doctor, then merchant, then a soldier, in which capacity he tries every rank but rejects them all.

In the end, the boy says that he wants to be the czar. Elijah agrees but reminds him that he should rule the country well. Once again, when Elijah returns the boy is dissatisfied, as he finds the responsibility of running the whole country to be too heavy. The ever-patient Elijah again asks the boy what he would like to be. The boy answers that he would like to be God. Elijah says that they will have to go up to heaven to find out what God thinks about this request. When they get there, God says to Elijah that perhaps he will now understand that God does sometimes know what he is doing. God tells Elijah to join him and says to the boy, "As for you, you leper, creep back to your box where you belong."

In other traditions, Elijah is not so helpful. In Russian folklore, Elijah is generally known as Il'ia and has a much harsher reputation as a figure of awe and punishment who typically rolls across the fields in thunder and lightning, spreading fear and foreboding.

Related entries: Culture Heroes; Helpers; Joseph of Arimathea, Saint; Khidre, El; Religious Heroes; Wise Men and Women

References and further reading
Ausubel, N. (ed.), A Treasury of Jewish Folklore, London: Vallentine, Mitchell, 1972 (1948), pp. 40, 47, 116, 158, 193, 209, 221, 265, 447, 475, 503.
Ivanits, L., Russian Folk Belief, Armonk and London: M. E. Sharpe Inc., 1989, pp. 12, 17, 26, 29–36, 40, 138–140.
Sabar, Y. (trans. and ed.), The Folk Literature of the Kurdistani Jews: An Anthology, New Haven: Yale University Press, 1982, pp. 68–70.
Weinreich, B. (ed.), Yiddish Folktales, New York: Pantheon, 1988, pp. 107–111, 182–184.

Ero

Yugoslavian peasant trickster who outwits Turks, czars, and kadis (judges). As with all tricksters, there are many tales told of Ero's activities. In one story, Ero tricks a Turkish woman into believing that he has just come from the otherworld and that he knows her dead first husband. Unfortunately, Ero tells her, the husband is poor and therefore unhappy. The woman immediately gives Ero money to take back to the otherworld to make things more pleasant for her dead husband. When her present husband hears what has happened, he is outraged and pursues Ero. Seeing him coming, Ero convinces a miller that the Turk is angry with him rather than with the trickster and offers to take the miller's place. They exchange clothes, which fools the Turk into chasing the miller through the woods. Ero then steals the Turk's horse and rides away. By the time the Turk catches the hapless miller and they both work out that they have been tricked, Ero is long gone. The Turk is forced to return to his wife without the money and, even more shamefully, without his horse. He tells his wife that he did not wish to seem less generous than she in helping her former husband. Just as she sent money, he sent his horse.

Another tale tells of Ero's response when his cow is gored to death by the beast of his master, a kadi. Ero goes to the kadi and tells him what his beast has done. The kadi is unconcerned until Ero reveals that it was actually his own cow that had killed the kadi's animal. Immediately, the judge reaches for the law statutes, but the clever Ero stays his hand, saying, "If you do not look in the law books for my cow, then you will not do so for your own!"

As with many Slavic legends, the stories of Ero often reflect the strained relations between Turkish invaders and those whose country they occupied. A variation of this tale exists in Persian tradition, featuring a hero named Zorab, or Zab for short. The tale presumably reached Yugoslavian folklore through the Turkish invasion in the fourteenth century and the subsequent occupation.

Related entries: Abunuwas; Heroes of Struggle;
Hodja; Tricksters; Zab
References and further reading
Curcija-Prodanovic, N. (comp.), *Yugoslav Folk-Tales*,
Oxford: Oxford University Press, 1957, pp.
1–6, 69–70, 84.
Curtin, J. (ed.), *Myths and Folktales of the Russians, Western
Slavs, and Magyars*, Boston: Little, Brown, 1890.

E-ttool, Zarief

Personification of manhood in the Palestinian
story of Ataba and Zarief E-ttool. The perseverance of Zarief E-ttool in undertaking seemingly
endless and impossible tasks to win the hand of
Ataba is a popular Palestinian heroic theme.
Zarief E-ttool travels to distant countries and
succeeds in many difficult tasks set him by
Ataba's hard-to-please father. Finally, with the
help of a Mukhtar from Egypt, Zarief E-ttool
succeeds in convincing Ataba's father that he is
a worthy son-in-law, and the couple is married
to great rejoicing.

Ataba and Zarief E-ttool are featured in
Palestinian tales, songs, and dances, and elsewhere in the Arabic world. Their story may also
be told to Palestinian children and to young
men and women as a means of transmitting
knowledge of Palestine and the values and attitudes of its culture.

Related entries: Ataba
References and further reading
Abdelhady, T., *Palestinian Folk-Tales*, vol. 3, Beirut:
n.d., p. 136.
Muhawi, I. and Kanaana, S. (eds.), *Speak, Bird, Speak
Again: Palestinian Arab Folktales*, Berkeley: University
of California Press, 1989.

Eulenspiegel, Till (Tyll Ulenspiegel)

Said to be a historical personage named
Thomas Murner, a German peasant who died
in 1350, Till Eulenspiegel is a trickster who carries out often cruel hoaxes on rich, powerful,
but usually stupid publicans, tradesmen, and
burghers. Many trickster tales, often ribald, are
associated with him, beginning with his
youthful japes and ending with his last prank
from beyond the grave.

When he is young, Till Eulenspiegel plays a
prank on his friends and the mean-hearted

*An Austrian actor depicts Till Eulenspiegel in a nineteenth-century
stage version of the traditional tale. (Mary Evans Picture Library)*

people of his town. He develops a great skill at
dancing on a tightrope, collecting money from
the townspeople in appreciation. His young
friends, though, are jealous and sabotage his
rope so that it breaks and drops him in the river
before all the people of the town. Humiliated,
the still dripping young trickster nevertheless
tells his jealous friends to come back next week
when he will dance again and share his takings
with them. With the promise of making some
money, all the young people of the town come
out the next week to help Till Eulenspiegel
dance on the rope. Before mounting the rope,
Till Eulenspiegel says to his friends, "I will
dance in your shoes. Whether they are too big
or too small does not matter. If I fall I will give
you all the money I make from the townspeople." Knowing that they could not lose with
this arrangement, the youth of the town gladly
take off their shoes and give them to Till Eulenspiegel, who puts them all into the leather
apron he is wearing and mixes them up. Then
he mounts the rope, but instead of walking on

it, he begins to throw the shoes up into the air, catching them again in the leather apron. Outraged, the boys claim that they won the bet because Till Eulenspiegel did not kept his side of the bargain. Till Eulenspiegel replies that he did not undertake to dance in their shoes, but with them. And that is exactly what he is doing. Still the boys complain, and Till Eulenspiegel says that he will call off the wager and return their shoes. Then he tosses all the shoes down onto the ground. Because they are all mixed up, the boys cannot find their shoes, and soon arguments and fights break out. Till Eulenspiegel runs home and stays there while the anger of his friends cools and their resolve to pay him back for his trick fades.

In the story usually known as "Till Eulenspiegel's Merry Prank," the king challenges his three jesters, of whom Till Eulenspiegel is one, to a test of cleverness. The king offers money and fine clothing to the jester who can make the greatest wish. The first jester wishes that heaven was paper and the sea ink so that he could write the amount of how much money he would like. The second jester wishes for as many castles as there are stars in the night sky so that he would have room to keep all the money the first jester desires. Till Eulenspiegel's turn comes, and he says that his wish is for the first two jesters to make their will, leaving all their riches to him, and that the king have them both executed immediately. Till Eulenspiegel's cleverness wins him the prize.

Another tale tells of Till Eulenspiegel's final joke, in which, even in death, he outwits and fools those who sought to profit from him in life. As Till Eulenspiegel nears death, he goes to live with an apothecary, who, although he looks after the prankster, plots to gain his fortune when he is gone. Close to the end, Till Eulenspiegel makes his confession, speaks with the town clerk, and then makes out his will, leaving one-third of his estate to the apothecary, one-third to the confessor, and one-third to the town clerk. In return, he is to be buried in holy ground and have masses said for the salvation of his soul. He writes that his possessions are buried in an iron chest, gives the location, and leaves a key for each of his heirs, or-

dering them to open the chest only four weeks after his burial. Then Till Eulenspiegel dies happy. He is buried three days later, with great crowds in attendance. As the coffin is lowered into the grave, one of the ropes breaks, depositing the deceased in an upright, instead of the customary reclining, position. Because he had been such an odd character in his life, the mourners decide to leave him that way. Exactly four weeks later, the apothecary, the confessor, and the town clerk dig up Till Eulenspiegel's iron chest, greedy to have their share of his earthly goods. To their horror, they find nothing but a note and three compartments full of dirt and stones. The note says that the earth and the stones contain all the riches of the world. One-third is for the apothecary, the false friend who kept Till Eulenspiegel only because he wanted to be rewarded. The second third is for the confessor and is to be used to repair the church and plant food for the poor. The final third is for the town clerk— the stones to remind the judges that they are often hard as rock, and the earth to remind them that people need earth to live decently. The three disappointed heirs do not say a word. They and all the people who have come with them to witness the recovery of the chest know that Till Eulenspiegel's last words are true. Even in death, the trickster helped the living to see their follies and to act more wisely, justly, and piously.

In addition to these typical trickster tales, the considerable body of traditions about Till Eulenspiegel includes a number of ribald stories, such as his legendary feats of breaking wind. Heroic farting is also found in other traditions, including those of The 1,001 Nights and the Korean tale of "General Pumpkin," whose explosive powers are used to good effect in destroying stone walls. General Pumpkin also protects his friends from a marauding white tiger by paralyzing the beast with the stench of his flatulence.

The fourteenth-century peasant associated so closely with this extensive German trickster tradition is said to lie buried at Mölln in Schlweswig-Holstein, where his grave has attracted tourists since at least the sixteenth century. Eulenspeigel, in one form or another, became well known throughout western Europe as a consequence of the development of cheap street literature. In England, he was known as "Howleglas" and his misadventures and rude jests were favorites in jest books of the sixteenth century. In the United States, his deeds and misdeeds are also told by German emigrant groups such as the "Pennsylvania Dutch."

Related entries: Abunuwas; Anansi; Ero; Hodja, The; Kabajan; Quevedo; Ramalingadu, Tenali; Tricksters; Urdemales, Pedro de

References and further reading

Christen, K., *Clowns and Tricksters: An Encyclopedia of Tradition and Culture*, Santa Barbara: ABC-CLIO, 1998.

De Coster, C. (trans. Atkisnosn, F.), *The Legend of Eulenspiegel*, 2 vols., London: William Heinemann, 1922.

Harrison, A., *The Irish Trickster*, Sheffield: Sheffield Academic Press, 1988.

In-Sob, Z., *Folk Tales from Korea*, London: Routledge and Kegan Paul, 1952, pp. 66–68.

Michaelis-Jena, R., "Eulenspiegel and Münchhausen: Two German Folk Heroes," *Folklore* 97, no. 1 (1986): 101–108.

Neuberg, V., *Popular Literature: A History and Guide*, Harmondsworth, Middlesex: Penguin, 1977, pp. 41, 43–47.

Oppenheimer, P. (trans.), *A Pleasant Vintage of Till Eulenspiegel, Born in the Country of Brunswick. How He Spent His Life. 95 of His tales*. Translated from the 1515 edition. Middletown, Conn.: Wesleyan University Press, 1972.

Oppenheimer, P. (trans. and ed.), *Till Eulenspiegel: His Adventures*, New York: Garland, 1991.

F

Fairy Godmother, The

Generally said to be derived from the Fates of classical mythology, the Fairy Godmother known widely today is largely the product of the literary fairy tales of Charles Perrault and other authors. The Fairy Godmother looks over her charges and makes sure that nothing bad happens to them. She also rescues them from difficult situations. Both roles are closely akin to those of the helper in many hero and heroine traditions. The tale of Cinderella is probably the best-known version of the theme, which may be related to the idea of a benign "familiar" spirit. Certainly the unfailingly good Fairy Godmother is quite unlike the usually ambivalent fairies—and their equivalents in various folklores—who are just as likely to do ill as good.

Related entries: Cinderella; Fairy Tale Heroes;
  Helpers; Mab, Queen
References and further reading
Briggs, K., *The Fairies in Tradition and Literature*, London:
  Routledge and Kegan Paul, 1967, pp. 176, 193.
Briggs, K., *A Dictionary of Fairies*, London: Allen Lane,
  1976, p. 147.

Fairy Tale Heroes

The "fairy tale" is almost entirely an invention of western literature. Stories involving heroes and heroines, transformations, supernatural beings, and happy endings exist—and presumably have existed—in most of the world's many cultures. But it was in the seventeenth century that the story form we now recognize as the fairy tale began to be given its familiar shape, mainly though not exclusively by the French writers Charles Perrault (1628–1703) and Comtesse d' Aulnoy (1650 or 1651–1705). Perrault published his collection of fairy tales as *Histoires du temps passé: Avec des Moralitez* (1697; first translated into English in 1729). The original edition also contained the additional subtitle *Contes de ma mère l'oie*, giving rise to the widespread marketing of such collections as "Tales of Mother Goose," or variations thereof. Comtesse d'Aulnoy, as Madam Aulnoy, published *Contes de fées* (1697) and *Les Contes nouveaux* (1698). These authors, together with a number of less well-known writers, deliberately set out to create stories and story sequences that would entertain and instruct a growing educated and literate middle class in France, Germany, and elsewhere in Europe.

The narratives these early writers used as the basis for their confabulations and confections were those they had heard from storytellers in childhood and adulthood. Some of these narratives can be traced back to the Italian Giovanni Boccaccio's (1313–1375) reworking of traditional and literary tales in his *Il Decamerone* (*Ten Days' Work*, 1348–1353, first translated into English as *The Decameron* in 1620), and sometimes even farther back to the Greek fables of Aesop (c. 620–560 B.C.) and his many subsequent imitators and expanders. However, the forms the stories took in these earlier works, and the purposes they served, were often transformed by the seventeenth-century inventors of the fairy tale. In these early forms of the genre, we can find the introduction of fairy godmothers and motifs like the glass slipper as a device of recognition. We can also find the beginnings of the happy ending and of everyone—all the good ones, at least—living ever after. By the time the brothers Grimm came to assemble their enormously influential collection of folk tales in the late eighteenth and early nineteenth centuries, the genre—its conventions and its place in civilized society—was already established.

So powerfully was the fairy tale established in the mentality of the Grimms' time and place that they were unable to publish the stories they collected (from a narrow range of informants) in the form in which they received them. As a number of scholars have revealed, the Grimms not only tidied up their collected tales for publication. Wilhelm, especially, also progressively rewrote them for subsequent editions of the *Kinder- und Hausmärchen* (*Children's and Household Tales*, 2 vols., 1812–1815; first translated into English in 1884). This complex work is now widely referred to in English simply as *Grimms' Fairy Tales* and is considered the touchstone of the fairy-tale genre. However, in editing the tales for publication, the Grimms usually excised or ameliorated suggestions of cannibalism, sexuality, and unmotivated evil, all well and truly part of the folkloric versions of these stories. Heroes who appeared in the original stories unnamed were given affectionate names, like Hansel and Gretel. Motives were created to account for the often cruel and evil actions of characters, especially parents. The infamous "wicked stepmother" was introduced as a substitute for the natural mother as the frequent villain of stories. Wicked stepmothers existed in tradition, but the Grimms, apparently unable or unwilling to deal with the notion that a "natural" mother might be capable of abandonment and infanticide (or possibly assuming that their audience would be repelled by such things), used the device of the wicked stepmother to ameliorate or avoid the implications of the tales as collected. Generally, the Grimms also increased the length of the stories from their original tellings. By the time the 1857 edition of *Hausmärchen* appeared, most of the stories were at least twice the length of their originals, with Wilhelm's tinkering progressively shaping the narratives into more fairy-tale like form.

The immense success and influence of the Grimms' work in this field reinforced and confirmed the existing literary form of the fairy tale. Other people, seeing the great commercial success such creations enjoyed, were not slow to follow in the tracks of the Grimms. The last half of the nineteenth century and the early years of the twentieth were filled with "fairy tale" collections and anthologies of both serious scholars like Andrew Lang (1844–1912—author of the famous "colored" fairy book series) and Joseph Jacobs (1854–1916—author/compiler of numerous fairy tale anthologies), and the less specialized and generally less knowledgeable work of children's writers and other popularizers. So prevalent and powerful was the European notion of the fairy tale that it was inflicted on folktales collected from other cultures, thus the publication of books with titles such as "Fairy Tales of Japan" and "Fairy Tales of Burma."

The very category "fairy tale" is itself a limiting concept that inaccurately standardizes elements of folk tradition that circulate in many forms and circumstances. For example, the story most readers will know as "Cinderella" is but one of a great number of existing and possible variations on the same theme. The same can be said of most other "fairy tales." Indeed, different fairy tales are often recovered from folk—as opposed to literary or media—tradition melded together into one story, as in the Bolognese Italian Girricoccola, which is a mixture of "Cinderella" and "Snow White," combined with elements of other folktales.

Jack Zipes and others have shown that the fairy tale was a natural form for the film industry to adopt. The unique capability of film to blend fantasy and apparent actuality made fairy stories an early recruit to the ever-increasing demands of the film business. Especially influential here were animated films, especially those of Disney and imitators. Combined with the incessant flow of children's books that present fairy tales "for young readers," these relatively modern extensions have kept the fairy tale continually before the public. The genre is now an unremarkable element of everyday life and consciousness.

This knowledge of the origins and development of the fairy tale is especially important for an understanding of folk heroes. In the modern world, most of us are shaped by information we receive from media sources rather than from oral sources. The forms of story that played such an important part in earlier periods of history and that in many cultures are still important today no longer form part of the education or everyday knowledge of those born and bred in western industrial societies. We have new forms of storytelling to express our underlying fears and to help us walk in the world. These forms are predominantly involved with the mass media. The Hollywood happy ending, like that of the fairy tale, is a cliché that many of us welcome and seek again and again at the movies. Such stories—their tellings and their endings—are so widespread and popular that they must be seen as an important element of our lives and of modern culture.

As we grow up, we take our heroes and heroines from their representations in the mass media rather than from the stories we are told as children. And even those stories usually come to us from children's books rather than from the folk memories of parents or grandparents. We are used to heroes being the creation of the media, a process that—along with the creation of villains—is integral to the operation of modern media. Many of the historical heroes appearing in these pages have been, to a greater or lesser extent, creations of the popular media of their times. Even as far back as seventeenth-century Europe and second-century A.D. China, the influence of writing, printing, and publishing has played a significant role in the creation and proliferation of "goodies and baddies," heroes and heroines.

The heroes of fairy tales, notably of the variety promulgated by the brothers Grimm and their successors, are an oddly bloodless lot. Indeed, Maria Tatar has pointed out that the predominant characteristic of the fairy tale hero is his humility and naiveté, even stupidity. The heroines of these fictions are also shown by Tatar and other commentators to be relatively passive. Things tend to be done to them, rather than by them. They are frequently victims, at least to begin with. Wicked stepmothers cast them out; they are enchanted; dwarves help them; and, finally, a prince rescues them and marries them. There is nothing clearly heroic in these events and about those who take part in them. It is as though all the characters are being moved through a predetermined script and toward an agreed resolution and closure by some unseen force. It is this secure and knowable aspect of fairy tales, at least the most often retold of them, that perhaps accounts for a good deal of their perennial popularity and wide diffusion.

By contrast to the other vast world of folk narrative outside the genre of the fairy tale, in these stories heroines outnumber heroes. Many fairy tale heroes do not even have a proper name and generally play out their preplotted roles automatically and often without much grasp of what is going on or what is at stake. Nevertheless, either despite or because of their stupidity, and often with the more than magnanimous assistance of bands of helpers, they win through in the end, getting the girl, the gold, and the kingdom. But although the heroine, through the agency of the hero, shares in this good fortune, she rarely does anything heroic. She is generally the object of actions carried out by others, good or bad, and is frequently humiliated in the course of the story, Cinderella being one example of many. Those seeking heroines with greater volition will not often be satisfied by the fairy tale but will seek out the more full-blooded traditions of the folktale.

Related entries: Assipattle; Beauty and the Beast; Cap o' Rushes; Catskin; Celebrity Heroes; Cinderella; Cinder-Mary; Dragon-Slayers; Fairy Godmother, The; Faithful Henry; Faithful John; Frog Prince, The; Giant-Killers; Giricoccola; Goldilocks; Goose Girl, The; Gretel; Halfchick; Hansel; Jack and the Beanstalk; Jack the Giant-Killer; Knowall, Doctor; Little Goose Girl, The; Little Red Riding Hood; Lucky Hans; Lusmore; Mab, Queen; Magicians; Maria, Fenda; Melusine; Monkey Prince; Nou Plai; Ogres; Puss in Boots; Rapunzel; Rashin' Coatie; Sanykisar; Sleeping Beauty; Snow White; Swan Maiden; Victims; Villains; Whuppie, Molly; Woodencloak, Katie; Yannakis; Ye Xian; Zeej Choj Kim; Zelinda

References and further reading

Bacchilega, C., *Postmodern Fairy Tales: Gender and Narrative Strategies*, Philadelphia: University of Pennsylvania Press, 1997.
Bottigheimer, R. (ed.), *Fairy Tales and Society: Illusion, Allusion, and Paradigm*, Philadelphia: University of Pennsylvania Press, 1986.

Dundes, A., "Fairy Tales from a Folkloristic Perspective," in Bottigheimer, R. (ed.), *Fairy Tales and Society: Illusion, Allusion, and Paradigm*, Philadelphia: University of Pennsylvania Press, 1986, pp. 259–270.

Ellis, J., *One Fairy Story Too Many: The Brothers Grimm and Their Tales*, Chicago: University of Chicago Press, 1983.

Hallett, M. and Karasek, B. (eds.), *Folk and Fairy Tales*, Ontario: Broadview Press, 1996.

Lüthi, M. (trans. Erickson, J.), *The Fairytale as Art Form and Portrait of Man*, Bloomington: Indiana University Press, 1984 (1975), chap. 5, "The Fairytale Hero," pp. 135–144.

McGlathery, J. (ed.), *The Brothers Grimm and Folktale*, Urbana and Chicago: University of Illinois Press, 1988.

Tatar, M., "Born Yesterday: Heroes in Grimms' Tales," in Bottigheimer, R. (ed.), *Fairy Tales and Society: Illusion, Allusion, and Paradigm*, Philadelphia: University of Pennsylvania Press, 1986, pp. 95–114.

Tatar, M., *The Hard Facts of the Grimms' Fairy Tales*, Princeton, NJ: Princeton University Press, 1987, pp. 85–105, 106–133, 137–178.

Thomas, J., *Inside the Wolf's Belly: Aspects of the Fairy Tale*, Sheffield: Sheffield Academic Press, 1989.

Warner, M., *From the Beast to the Blonde: On Fairy Tales and Their Tellers*, London: Chatto and Windus, 1994.

Yearsley, M., *The Folklore of the Fairy Tales*, London: Oxford University Press, 1974.

Zipes, J., *Happily Ever After: Fairy Tales, Children, and the Culture Industry*, New York and London: Routledge, 1997.

Zipes, J., *When Dreams Came True: Classical Fairy Tales and Their Tradition*, New York and London: Routledge, 1999, pp. 30–48, 61–79.

Zipes, J. (ed.), *The Oxford Companion to Fairy Tales*, Oxford: Oxford University Press, 2000.

Faithful Henry

Faithful servant of the fairy tale usually known as "The Frog Prince." In the manuscript version of this story, on which the Grimms based their various reworkings, the youngest daughter of a king loses her golden ball down a cool well in a forest. A frog appears and asks her why she is crying. The princess tells the frog, who offers to retrieve the golden ball if she will take him home with her. She agrees, and the frog retrieves the ball. But instead of honoring her promise, the princess runs home to eat with her father. While they are eating there is a knock on the door, the princess answers it to find the ugly frog on the doorstep. She slams the door, but her father asks what is happening, and she tells him about the loss of her ball and the frog's retrieval of it. At this point, the frog entreats entrance, and the king orders the princess to allow the frog in. The frog then asks to be seated next to the reluctant princess, but she will not consent until ordered to do so by her father. After eating, the frog asks to go to bed with the princess. The princess refuses, but again the king commands it so. She goes with the cold, ugly frog to her room and there, in a fit of anger, throws the frog against the wall. He slides down the wall onto her bed and is transformed into a handsome young prince with whom the princess is happy to lie down.

The following morning a magnificent coach arrives bearing the prince's faithful servant (we learn later in the story that his name is Henry), who had been distraught over the previous transformation of the prince into a frog and had to have three iron hoops placed around his heart. The prince and princess board the coach, and while they are traveling to the prince's home they hear a loud cracking sound at which the prince calls out:

Henry, the coach is breaking!
No sir not the coach,
It is a hoop around my heart,
which was in great pain
when you were in the well
when you were a frog. (Grimm 1944)

Subsequent versions of the story elaborate on Henry's role and on the events that led up to the prince being imprisoned in the well as a frog. Henry—or other such helpers, going by many other names—is a frequent feature of such stories.

Related entries: Fairy Tale Heroes; Faithful John; Frog Prince, The; Helpers

References and further reading

Bettelheim, B., *The Uses of Enchantment: The Meaning and Importance of Fairy Tales*, New York: Knopf, 1976, pp. 62, 117, 286–291.

Clarkson, A. and Cross, G. (eds.), *World Folktales*, New York: Charles Scribner's Sons, 1980.

Grimm, J. and W., *The Complete Grimm's Fairy Tales*, New York: Pantheon, 1944.

Faithful John

Figure of European and Asian folktales emphasizing the value of faithful servants, and another example of the heroic helper. In the version provided by the Grimms, a dying king asks his faithful retainer not to allow the king's son to look at the portrait in a locked room of the castle. Eventually the prince does see the portrait, which depicts a beautiful princess, and falls in love, determining to find her regardless of all danger and attempts to dissuade him. The servant, Faithful John, sails with the prince in a ship laden with riches to a strange land. Here Faithful John lures the princess aboard the ship with samples of the treasure it carries, then the ship sails home. The prince reveals his love to the princess, and she falls in love with him. But on the return voyage, John overhears three ravens describing three dangers that will beset the prince: a flying horse that will abduct him, a poisoned bridal robe, and a snake that will fatally bite the bride in the bridal bed. The only way to revive the princess will be to take three drops of blood from her breast. Whoever learns of these dangers cannot reveal them on pain of being turned to stone.

Unable to tell what he knows, Faithful John takes it upon himself to avert the three dangers: he kills the beautiful horse that greets them as the ship docks and snatches away the poisoned robe before the prince can put it on. Finally, in his attempt to protect the princess from the snake in the bridal bed (in some versions to remove the three drops of blood from her breast), Faithful John incurs the prince's enmity and is imprisoned and condemned to death. Just as he is about to die, Faithful John tells the story and, as threatened by the ravens, is immediately turned to stone. Desolate, the prince and princess keep the stone statue until they discover that the blood of their two children can restore Faithful John to life. They happily cut off the children's heads and rub their blood on the statue. Faithful John comes back to life and replaces the two heads on the children's bodies, and they continue their games as if nothing has happened.

Related entries: Baldpate; Fairy Tale Heroes; Faithful Henry; Frog Prince, The; Helpers

References and further reading

Bettelheim, B., *The Uses of Enchantment: The Meaning and Importance of Fairy Tales*, New York: Knopf, 1976.

Dawkins, R. (comp. and trans.), *Modern Greek Folktales*, Oxford: Clarendon Press, 1953, pp. 227–242; reprint Westport, CT: Greenwood Press, 1974.

Grimm, J. and W., *The Complete Grimms' Fairy Tales*, New York: Pantheon, 1944, pp. 43–51.

Fanta-Ghiro'

A legendary female soldier who becomes a general in an Italian tale. Fanta-Ghiro' wins the war and saves her father's kingdom from invasion by an enemy king. The enemy king, seeing Fanta-Ghiro' on the field of battle, instantly falls in love with "him." When her father dies, Fanta-Ghiro' marries the enemy general and becomes queen of both kingdoms. This character is an Italian version of the often encountered female warrior.

Related entries: Female Drummer, The; Mulan; O'Malley, Grace; Warriors; Women Dressed as Men

References and further reading

Calvino, I. (trans. Martin, G.), *Italian Folk Tales: Selected and Retold by Italo Calvino*, New York: Harcourt Brace Jovanovich, Penguin, 1980 (1956), pp. 249–253.

Crane, T., *Italian Popular Tales*, Boston and New York: Houghton Mifflin and Co., 1885; reprint, Detroit: Singing Tree Press, 1968.

Father Christmas

See Santa Claus

Fatima

Last wife of the murdering monster Bluebeard. In some versions of the widespread murderous husband tale type, Fatima is the youngest of four, sometimes seven, sisters. Bluebeard first marries the eldest sister. When she mysteriously disappears, he marries the second sister. When she vanishes, he soon marries the third sister. When this sister is gone, he finally marries Fatima, who discovers the corpses of her three sisters in Bluebeard's chamber. She escapes by various tricks, in some versions by luck, and is instrumental in Bluebeard's downfall. Fatima is similar in many ways to the heroine of *The Arabian Nights*, Scheherazade, who offers herself to a murderous husband but outwits him by her cleverness and skill as a storyteller.

Related entries: Bluebeard; Isabel, Lady; Scheherazade; Wise Men and Women

References and further reading

Briggs, K., *British Folktales*, New York: Pantheon Books, 1977, pp. 87–89.

Hallett, M. and Karasek, B. (eds.), *Folk and Fairy Tales*, Ontario: Broadview Press, 1996, pp. 117–121.

Feboldson, Febold

See Occupational Heroes

Female Cabin Boy, The

Heroine of a number of ballads in which she follows her lover to sea by dressing in man's clothing and successfully impersonating a male. In a version collected by George Gardiner in 1908, the young girl's reason for going to sea is for adventure: "she had a mind of a-roving into some foreign land." The "fair-cheeked impostor" is admired by both the captain and his wife, and a dalliance develops between the captain and the cabin boy. After some time at sea, the cabin boy takes ill and the doctor rushes to the hammock where "he" sleeps only to find the cabin boy in labor:

> The sailors when they heard the joke they all began to stare,
> The child belonged to none of them they solemnly did swear,
> The lady to the captain said "My dear, I wish you joy!
> For 'twas either you or I betrayed the handsome cabin-boy."

Related entries: Fanta-Ghiro'; Female Drummer, The; Female Highwayman, The; Female Smuggler, The; Mulan; O'Malley, Grace; Women Dressed as Men

References and further reading

Purslow, F. (ed.), *Marrow Bones: English Folk Songs from the Hammond and Gardiner Mss*, London: EFDS Publications, 1965, p. 32.

Female Drummer, The

Another of the numerous female warriors of folklore. According to English folklorist Roy Palmer, ballads with titles like "The Gallant She-Souldier," "The Soldier's Delight, or the She Volunteer," and "The Maiden Warrior" became popular from the seventeenth century and lasted well into the nineteenth century. Often these ballads were true stories of women who disguised themselves as men in order to fight with the army or sail to distant locations with the navy. Sometimes the women were inspired by a sense of adventure, as in the case of "a damsel that followed the drum; / For the sake of her true love for a soldier she's gone," the heroine of the eighteenth-century song "The Drum Major." In this fairly typical example of many such ballads cited by Palmer, the heroine is, in all respects but one, a male soldier: "Now she's a drum major and carries the sword, / And appears like a hero, as fierce as a lord." After acquitting herself with courage, the female drummer is eventually discovered and given a bounty, or pension, and then she marries. In other variations on the theme, the female disguises herself as a sailor or soldier to follow her lover, perhaps to war, often as a "Female Soldier" as in the song "William Taylor," or perhaps across the sea, as in "The Female Cabin Boy" and its variants.

Related entries: Fanta-Ghiro'; Female Cabin Boy, The; Female Highwayman, The; Female Smuggler, The; Mulan; O'Malley, Grace; Women Dressed as Men

References and further reading

Doerflinger, W. (coll. and ed.), *Songs of the Sailor and Lumberman*, New York: Macmillan, 1972 (1951), p. 143.

Palmer, R. (ed.), *The Rambling Soldier*, Harmondsworth, Middlesex: Penguin, 1977, pp. 101–103, 137–138, 163–168, 171–172, 226, 253.

Purslow, F. (ed.), *Marrow Bones: English Folk Songs from the Hammond and Gardiner Mss*, London: EFDS Publications, 1965, p. 32.

Female Highwayman, The

A number of female highwaymen appear in balladry and story. The female highwayman is a frequent character in British street balladry from the seventeenth century. One of the most popular of these heroines is usually called Sovay, Shiloh, or Silvy. Her ballad, in the version collected by Vaughan Williams, begins:

Silvy, Silvy all on one day
She dressed herself in man's array
With a sword and pistol all by her side
To meet her true love she did ride.

So disguised, she then robs her true love of his watch and chain and also tries to take a diamond ring from him as well. (Although it is often unstated in the songs, the implication is that Silvy had earlier given the ring to the man as a symbol of their love.) Despite being menaced by a pistol, the true love boldly refuses to give up the precious ring, saying he would rather die. The female highwayman then rides away. Next day, no longer in disguise, she meets her true love, and he recognizes his watch. He is ashamed to have been robbed by a woman, but she tells him:

What makes you flush at so silly a thing,
I fain would have had your diamond ring,
I only did it for to know,
Whether you were a man or no.

As in many folktales, the ring is here used as both a token of true love and a recognition device.

Related entries: Fanta-Ghiro'; Female Cabin Boy, The; Female Drummer, The; Female Smuggler, The; Mulan; O'Malley, Grace; Women Dressed as Men

References and further reading

Lloyd, A., *Folksong in England*, New York: International Publishers, 1970 (1967), pp. 31, 169, 222.

Purslow, F. (ed.), *Marrow Bones: English Folk Songs from the Hammond and Gardiner Mss*, London: EFDS Publications, 1965, p. 32.

Sharp, C. and Vaughan Williams, R., *A Selection of Collected Folk-Songs*, vol. 1, London: Novello, n.d., pp. 62–63.

Female Smuggler, The

Heroine of a number of eighteenth- and nineteenth-century British smuggling ballads. In a version by Whall, "Young Jane," the lady dresses in sailor's clothes; arms herself with pistols, sword, and daggers; and goes aboard ship. The ship is attacked by pirates, and Jane leads the smugglers aboard the pirate ship, slaying them and stealing their cargo of brandy. Back in England, the smugglers are captured and tried, in the course of which Jane's true gender is discovered. Her prosecutor, the "commodore" of the "blockade" or excise men, declines to pursue the case when this is revealed:

He to the judge and jury said,
"I cannot prosecute this maid,
Pardon for her on my knees I crave."

The final verse of the ballad usually has a romantically happy ending:

Then this commodore to her father went,
To gain her hand he asked his consent.
His consent he gained, so the commodore
And the female smuggler are one for evermore.

Related entries: Fanta-Ghiro'; Female Cabin Boy, The; Female Drummer, The; Female Highwayman, The; Mulan; O'Malley, Grace; Women Dressed as Men

References and further reading

Ashton, J., *Modern Street Ballads*, New York and London: Benjamin Blom, 1968 (1888), pp. 245–247.

Coffin, T., *The Female Hero in Folklore and Legend*, New York: Seabury, 1975.

Stanley, J. (ed.), *Bold in Her Breeches: Women Pirates across the Ages*, London: Pandora, 1995.

Whall, W. (coll. and ed.), *Sea Songs and Shanties*, London: Brown, Son, and Ferguson, 1910, pp. 27–30

Fereyel

Strange-born, diminutive eleventh son and legendary hero of an African story. Ten brothers set out to woo the ten beautiful daughters of Debbo Engel, a witch who kills and eats young men attracted by her daughters. As the ten brothers make their fateful way toward Debbo Engel's compound, their worried mother suddenly gives birth to Fereyel, a tiny but fully formed and mature boy who immediately chases after his ten older brothers to warn them of their danger. Unaware that he is their brother, the ten boys spurn him and beat him. As they carry on toward the witch's place, they find a length of fine cloth on the road. One boy picks it up and carries it over his shoulder until it becomes too heavy for him. He then passes it to another brother, who carries it until it becomes too heavy for him, and he passes it to the third brother. This goes on until the cloth reaches the oldest of the ten brothers. When he eventually finds the weight too much, Fereyel's voice cries out from inside the cloth. The boys shake him out and beat him senseless again, returning to their journey.

Some way farther along the road, one of the ten brothers stubs his toe on a silver ring. Rejoicing in his luck, he places the ring on his finger, but after only a few minutes the ring becomes so heavy that he cannot move his arm and can move only with difficulty. He passes the ring to the next brother, to whom the same thing soon happens. As with the cloth, the ring is passed from brother to brother until it reaches the eldest, at which point Fereyel reveals himself from inside the ring. Instead of beating him again, the ten brothers are impressed by his determination and agree to let him follow them to the witch's compound.

When they arrive they are made welcome by Debbo Engel, who takes Fereyel away from the others, leaving them to feast and enjoy the company of her ten beautiful daughters. When darkness falls, the boys are convinced to stay the night by the witch, who lies down beside Fereyel in her own hut, separate from that in which the ten brothers and her own ten daughters are sleeping. Judging that everyone is asleep, Debbo Engel gets up to kill the boys, but she is foiled when Fereyel asks her what she is doing. Eventually the witch falls asleep, and Fereyel sneaks into the other hut and changes the clothes of the boys and the girls. Later, the witch wakes, gets her knife, and slashes the throats of the bodies she believes to be the ten

brothers, saying that they will make a fine breakfast in the morning. She creeps back to her hut where Fereyel is feigning sleep. Waiting until the witch falls asleep again, Fereyel hurries to the hut, wakes his brothers, and shows them what Debbo Engel has done, then he leads them away from the scene as quickly as possible.

When the witch discovers that she has been tricked, she calls up a wind and pursues Fereyel and his ten brothers. Fortunately, Fereyel is able to slow her down by magically turning an egg into a river and a large stone into a mountain, impeding her long enough for them to reach the safety of their own home. But the witch wants revenge and tries various magic stratagems to capture the boys. Three times Fereyel sees through her ploys and saves his brothers. Debbo Engel determines that she will kill Fereyel. She turns herself into a beautiful maiden and entices him into the bush at night. Here she turns herself into an ugly snake and attacks Fereyel. He, knowing all the time that the beautiful young woman was Debbo Engel, immediately transforms himself into a raging fire that consumes the snake. Fereyel returns to his village to be celebrated and feted as a great hero and slayer of the evil witch Debbo Engel.

Fereyel is very much in the mold of the youngest brother who appears to have no heroic qualities but nevertheless turns out to be a hero. We see the same theme in traditions about Jack, Hans, Tom Thumb, and a host of other unpromising figures who end up slaying dragons, rescuing others, and being celebrated as heroes. As in this case, there is often a magical element in such tales. The witch's transformation to a snake is also reminiscent of dragon-slaying hero traditions; scholars such as the Russian Vladimir Propp have argued, for example, that serpents and dragons are structurally identical in folk tradition.

Related entries: Achikar; Ahmed; Boots; Dog-Nyong, General Gim; Dragon-Slayers; Gim; Habermani; Jack; Jack the Giant-Killer; Kihuo; Marendenboni; Molo; No Bigger Than a Finger; Nue the Hunter; Shape-Shifters; Tardanak; Tom Thumb; Wirreenun the Rainmaker

References and further reading

Arnott, K., (ed.), *African Myths and Legends*, London: Oxford University Press, 1962, pp. 200–211.

Dadié, B. (trans. Hatch, C.), *The Black Cloth: A Collection of African Folktales*, Amherst: University of Massachusetts Press, 1987 (1955).

Dorson, R. (ed.), *African Folklore*, Bloomington: Indiana University Press, 1972, 1979.

Propp, V., *Theory and History of Folklore*, Minneapolis: University of Minnesota Press, 1984.

Fink, Mike

Legendary Mississippi River keelboatman who, according to Benjamin Botkin, is referred to as "Snag" on the Mississippi and as the "Snapping Turtle" on the Ohio. Born in the last quarter of the eighteenth century in Pittsburgh, Pennsylvania, Fink died around 1823 after a colorful, though barely documented, life as a boatman on the Mississippi and Ohio Rivers. Although Fink is often cited as an occupational hero of keelboatmen, his folkloric authenticity is somewhat dubious. He first appeared in print in 1821 and rapidly became the focus of a larger-than-life, uncouth, boasting legend. Apart from boasting, Fink's main talent is his ability to shoot accurately; feats of gunmanship feature large in his lore. Fink is often compared with Davy Crockett as an example of the American frontier hero and, indeed, is frequently linked with Crockett in printed almanacs and other works. Like Crockett, and many other heroes and heroines, Fink has been the subject of considerable literary and other reinvention and appropriation. Nonetheless, Fink remains a representative of the type of nineteenth-century hero described by folklorist Richard Dorson as "Ring-tailed Roarers, bullies, brawlers, and daredevils."

Related entries: Bunyan, Paul; Crockett, Davy; Frontier Heroes; Henry, John; Liars; Little Moron; Mikula; Occupational Heroes; Pecos Bill; Stormalong

References and further reading

Botkin, B. (ed.), *A Treasury of American Folklore: Stories, Ballads, and Traditions of the People*, New York: Crown Publishers, 1944, pp. 2–67.

Botkin, B., "Mike Fink," in Leach, M. (ed.), *Funk and Wagnall's Standard Dictionary of Folklore, Mythology, and Legend*, London: New English Library, 1975. Abridged one-volume edition of Funk and

Wagnall's Standard Dictionary of Folklore, Mythology, and Legend, 2 vols., New York: Funk and Wagnall, 1972, p. 724.

Dorson, R., *American Folklore*, Chicago: University of Chicago Press, 1959, pp. 199–243.

Walter, B. and Meine, F. (eds.), *Half Horse, Half Alligator: The Growth of the Mike Fink Legend*, Chicago: University of Chicago Press, 1956.

Fisk, Jim

Entrepreneurial capitalist and scorner of convention, James Fisk is a particularly unlikely folk hero. Fisk began his working life as a peddler, graduated to trading, and earned enough money from the Civil War to start his own business. After various ups and downs Fisk teamed up with Jay Gould in the Erie Railroad venture in 1868, and the two men conducted numerous unscrupulous but mostly profitable business and financial deals. Such was Gould and Fisk's control of the American business world that the eventual collapse of their schemes in September 1869 ruined hundreds of businesses and adversely affected the entire American economy. Fisk died in 1872, shot by Edward Stokes in New York City. The two men were both vying for the attention of a famous actress of the day, Josie Mansfield.

Fisk was an exhibitionist of excessive appetites who was either reviled or adored by the general public, it seems. Fisk's folklore portrays him as a friend to the poor and an enemy of the rich. His ballad (as recorded by Belden) insists that "he never went back on the poor" and shows that it was not necessary to ride a horse and wield a pistol to attain at least some of the attributes of the outlaw hero, in this case a capitalist outlaw. By no stretch of the imagination could Fisk be seen to have represented any oppressed or discontented social group. Nevertheless, his well-known attitude toward the financial establishment and his brief control of that system promoted him in popular media and in folk perception as a hero. In these respects, he anticipates to some extent the usually brief popularity of "gangster heroes," like John Dillinger and "Pretty Boy" Floyd, who colorfully thumbed their noses at the law during the years of the Great Depression.

Related entries: Bass, Sam; Bonney, William; Dillinger, John; Floyd, Charles Arthur; Hood, Robin; James, Jesse; Outlaws; Parker, Robert Leroy; Quantrill, William Clarke; Slater, Morris

References and further reading

Belden, H. (ed.), *Ballads and Songs Collected by the Missouri Folklore Society*, University of Missouri Studies 15, no. 1, 1940, pp. 415–416.

Cohen, N., *Long Steel Rail: The Railroad in American Folksong*, Champaign, IL: University of Illinois Press, 1981, pp. 90–96.

Kooistra, P., *Criminals as Heroes: Structure, Power, and Identity*, Bowling Green, OH: Bowling Green University Press, 1989.

Steckmesser, K. L., *The Western Hero in History and Legend*, Norman: University of Oklahoma Press, 1965.

Floyd, Charles Arthur

Charles Arthur ("Pretty Boy") Floyd, born in 1901, was killed by FBI agents in October 1934, after a career of bank robbery and violence that had made him "Public Enemy Number 1" when John Dillinger was killed three months earlier. His status as a folk hero to the depression-hit working class of Oklahoma is well known, impelled by Woody Guthrie's later ballad. Guthrie was himself an Oklahoman (or "Okie") and based his song on what he was told by sympathizers of Floyd. Like the Australian bushranger Ned Kelly, Floyd is frequently said to have burned the mortgages he found in the safes of banks he robbed. And, as with a number of other American outlaws and gangsters, it is said that Floyd was not the man killed by police. They made a mistake and tried to cover up their incompetence.

Woody Guthrie's famous song about Floyd adroitly manipulates the elements of the outlaw hero tradition in its American permutation. Floyd's wife is abused by a representative of the forces of law and order. Floyd's defense of her honor results in his victory but also in his having to flee "to the trees and timbers," where he is unjustly blamed for all manner of crimes. In true outlaw hero style, however, Floyd has friends and supporters among the poor, whom he aids by leaving gifts of money and paying their mortgages. There is a distinct echo here of traditions that tell of the outlaw hero paying the mortgage only to rob it back from the landlord. Floyd also helps those on relief, and the song points out that one is as likely to be robbed by a fountain pen—that is, by a fast-talking professional or con artist—as by someone like Floyd carrying a gun. In the end, Floyd would never drive a family from their home, as this is not the kind of behavior expected of an outlaw.

This is very much the classic presentation of the outlaw hero, and similar motifs are found in all outlaw hero traditions, whether they refer to historical or folkloric figures.

Related entries: Celebrity Heroes; Dillinger, John; Kelly, Edward; Outlaws

References and further reading

Kooistra, P., *Criminals as Heroes: Structure, Power, and Identity*, Bowling Green, OH: Bowling Green University Press, 1989.

Lingenfelter, R. et al. (eds.), *Songs of the American West*, Los Angeles: 1968, p. 235.

Meyer, R., "The Outlaw: A Distinctive American Folktype," *Journal of the Folklore Institute* 17 (1980): 94–124.

Fox Maiden, The

Form of the Swan Maiden tales especially popular in Asia and among Native Americans, though thought to have originated in China. A man finds all the domestic duties in his home mysteriously carried out. Intrigued, he lies in wait and finds a fox visiting his home. Once inside, the fox takes off its skin and fur and becomes a beautiful young girl. The man hides the fox skin, thus preventing the girl from returning to her fox form, and marries her. They live happily for some time, until the wife rediscovers her fox skin, puts it on, and returns to being a fox (or until the man complains that she has a musty, animal smell, and, insulted, the fox wife takes offense and disappears forever).

The arrival of a mysterious and beautiful young female housekeeper, whether in animal, human, or mixed form, is a recurring element in the traditions of Japan, among Native Americans, and elsewhere. It is related to legends in which an animal takes the shape of a male human and cohabits with a female human, who then gives birth to a child, a well-known example being the "selkie" or seal-man legends of Scotland and the Shetlands. Sometimes this child is misbegotten and grows up to carry out evil deeds. In other cases, the child is blessed with special abilities that are put to positive use, such as an ability to talk with animals.

Another common feature of such traditions is the broken-promise motif, in which the hero is asked by his animal or supernatural bride never to speak her name, refer to her sisters, rebuke her, beat her, and so on. Of course, one day the husband, usually in anger, forgets this promise and speaks the forbidden words or carries out the forbidden deed. The animal, demon, or fairy lover immediately vanishes or otherwise departs, never to be seen again. Often the husband searches in vain for her, usually dying of grief.

Related entries: Bai Suzhen; Kuzonoha; Llyn Y Fan Fach, The Lady of; Magicians; Melusine; Mudjikiwis; Ringkitan; Shape-Shifters; Skorobogaty, Kuzma; Swan Maiden; Tabadiku; Urashima; White Lady; Xiaoqing; Yasuna, Abe No; Yer

References and further reading
Davis, F. Hadland, Myths and Legends of Japan, London: G. G. Harrap and Co., 1913, p. 95.

James, G. (ed.), Japanese Fairy Tales, London: Macmillan, 1923. First published as Green Willow and Other Japanese Fairy Tales, London: Macmillan and Company, 1910, pp. 215–222.

Seki, K. (ed.), Adams, R. (trans.), Folktales of Japan, London: Routledge and Kegan Paul, 1963, pp. 3, 14, 25, 63–104, 107–111. First published in Japanese in 1956–1957.

Tyler, R. (trans. and ed.), Japanese Tales, New York: Pantheon Books, 1987, pp. 114–123.

Werner, E., Myths and Legends of China, New York: Arno Press, 1976 (1922), pp. 370–385.

Wood, J., "The Fairy Bride Legend in Wales," Folklore 103, no. 1, 1992, pp. 56–72.

Franklin, Lord

Lord Franklin (1786–1847) is celebrated in folklore for his ill-fated attempt to find the Northwest Passage, starting in 1845. In 1846 his ships Erebus and Terror were caught in the ice. The party survived for some years while attempts to find and rescue them failed. In 1857 Franklin's second wife, Lady Jane Franklin (1792–1875), organized an expedition to Baf-

fin Bay that discovered some details of the fate of Franklin and his crew. These discoveries caused great excitement in England and elsewhere and led to the creation of a ballad usually known as "Lady Franklin's Lament," which gives a version of events, as they were known at the time, and which is still sung quite widely. As recalled by the author, one of its verses goes:

In Baffin Bay where the whale-fishes blow,
The fate of Franklin no man may know.
The fate of Franklin no tongue can tell,
Lord Franklin along with his sailors dwells.

In the ballad, Franklin and his men appear as tragic heroes of the nation, with Franklin's nautical background investing him with attributes of the military hero. The attention given to the story by the British press of the time also makes Franklin an early example of the celebrity hero.

Related entries: Celebrity Heroes; Culture Heroes; Military Heroes; National Heroes; Nautical Heroes; Victims

References and further reading
Beck, H., Folklore and the Sea, Middletown, CT: Wesleyan University Press, 1973.

Cookman, S., Iceblink: The Tragic Fate of Sir John Franklin's Lost Polar Expedition, New York: John Wiley and Sons, 2000.

Frog Prince, The

Hero of a Grimm fairy tale in which a handsome young prince is transformed into an ugly frog. He is transformed back to his true shape by the kiss of a beautiful young maiden, a king's daughter.

The original story told to the Grimms, like many folktales, was short on details such as the motivation for this act or who had perpetrated it. According to a number of scholars, the Grimms filled in these details in subsequent published editions. The return of the prince to his human shape by the kiss of the young princess has become a well-known image, often used as a representation of the wish fulfillment usually said to be integral to the genre of the fairy tale. Versions of the story, which is related to "Beauty and the Beast," are told throughout western Europe, Scandinavia, the

United States, and Russia. It is also known in a Korean version called "The Toad-Bridegroom."

Related entries: Beauty and the Beast; Fairy Tale
 Heroes; Faithful Henry; Faithful John; Zelinda

References and further reading

Ellis, J., *One Fairy Story Too Many: The Brothers Grimm and
 Their Tales*, Chicago: University of Chicago Press,
 1983.

In-Sob, Z., *Folk Tales from Korea*, London: Routledge
 and Kegan Paul, 1952, pp. 175–178.

Zipes, J., *Breaking the Magic Spell: Radical Theories of Folk
 and Fairy Tales*, Austin: University of Texas Press,
 1979.

Zipes, J., *Fairy Tales and the Art of Subversion*, New York:
 Wildman Press, 1983.

Frontier Heroes

Frontier nations of the New World, including the United States of America, Canada, Australia, and New Zealand, have all developed distinctive folk heroes and heroines that are usually associated with pioneering activities such as exploring, subduing indigenous peoples, stock droving, lumbering, mining, and other forms of mainly rural life and labor. Most of these characters have a larger-than-life quality and are typically braggarts and liars of sometimes astounding audacity. Notable in this respect was the American figure Davy Crockett.

As well as their propensity to exaggeration, pioneer heroes are often credited with a down-to-earth wisdom, usually expressed in pithily humorous form and often collected into books and almanacs sold in great numbers, thus helping to spread the fame and folklore of their subjects. A well-known American example of this type was the frontiersman Daniel Boone (1734–1820). He is credited with the discovery of the Cumberland Gap through the Appalachian Mountains, and over a long and adventurous life he became the center of many legends about his strength, prowess, cunning, and scorn of danger and death. Jim Bowie, best-known as the inventor of the knife that bears his name, was another focus of pioneering legends and traditions in Texas, while Kit (Christopher) Carson (1809–1868), pioneer and backwoodsman, achieved fame for his knowledge of the country and his positive rela-

Lithograph depicting the scout Buffalo Bill (Library of Congress)

tionship with Native Americans. He is the subject of tall tales of backwoods life, many of which are also told of other backwoods and frontier heroes.

A slightly later development usually found in New World societies is the frontier "type." In the United States this person is represented by the cowboy, in Australia by the bushman. Each of these types generates usually mythical characters whose folklore is derived from the circumstances and imperatives of frontier life. Thus Pecos Bill is a cowboy hero in the United States and elsewhere. Crooked Mick is a shearer's hero in Australia. In addition, there are usually historical characters who, to a greater or lesser extent, through their own self-aggrandizement come to be seen in the role of frontier heroes. These figures include William "Buffalo Bill" Cody (1846–1917), army scout, pony express rider, showman, and buffalo hunter, who earned his nickname for shooting almost 5,000 buffalo to supply railway workers with fresh meat. His name and feats became

Daniel Boone fighting with a Native American to protect his family (Library of Congress)

more widely known through his touring with his Wild West Show from 1883. James Butler "Wild Bill" Hickock (1837–1876) was a similar case.

Such masculine activities and images also generate their gender opposites in the form of the cowgirl, perhaps the best-known being American rodeo rider and sharp shooter Annie Oakley (Phoebe Annie Oakley Moses, 1860–1926), who garnered a reputation as a frontier heroine who could equal or outdo men in the male-dominated activities at which she excelled. Oakley is a historical character squarely in the tradition of the female—usually fictional—who dresses in man's attire and operates in a man's world. Annie Oakley was celebrated and romanticized in Irving Berlin's 1946 musical *Annie Get Your Gun*.

As well as their presence in folktales of various forms, frontier heroes may also appear in songs and balladry associated with their deeds, both real and folkloric. All frontier societies have extensive bodies of such traditions. Frequently the images of such characters have been considerably embellished and extended by historians, writers, and filmmakers, often in relation to the development of myths and stereotypes of national identity.

The other side of the frontier also tends to develop heroic characters. These heroes are noted either for the unselfish assistance they give to those who will inevitably invade their land, such as Native American woman Pocahontas, also called Matoaka, who, according to tradition, saved English explorer John Smith's life on two occasions and was an important

A full-length photograph of Annie Oakley (Library of Congress)

mediator between the newcomers and the indigenous people of what is now the state of Virginia. Other figures may be villains to the pioneers they defy but heroes to the indigenous peoples who the pioneers are, usually violently, displacing. Heroes of this type include the Native American Cochise and the indigenous Australians Yagan, Pemulway, and Jandamurra ("Pigeon"), among many others.

Related entries: Bean, Roy; Chapman, John; Crockett, Davy; Donohoe, Jack; Doyle, Tom; Hiawatha; Jones, Galloping; Liars; National Heroes; Outlaws; Wild Colonial Boy

References and further reading

Aiken, R., *Mexican Folktales from the Borderland*, Dallas, TX: Southern Methodist University Press, 1980.

Beatty, B., *A Treasury of Australian Folk Tales and Traditions*, Sydney: Ure Smith, 1960.

Botkin, B. (ed.), *A Treasury of American Folklore: Stories, Ballads, and Traditions of the People*, New York: Crown Publishers, 1944, esp. pp. 150–157 on Buffalo Bill.

Dobie, F. J., *Tales of Old-Time Texas*, London, 1959 (1928), esp. pp. 51–77 on Jim Bowie.

Dorson, R., *America in Legend*, New York: Pantheon Books, 1973.

Edwards, R., *The Overlander Songbook*, St. Lucia, Qld.:University of Queensland Press, 1991.

Finger, C., *Frontier Ballads*, Garden City, NY: Doubleday, Page & Co., 1927.

Fowke, E. (ed.), *Folklore of Canada*, Toronto: McClelland and Stewart, 1976.

Gill, S., *Storytracking: Texts, Stories, and Histories in Central Australia*, New York and Oxford: Oxford University Press, 1998.

Greenway, J. (ed.), *Folklore of the Great West*, Palo Alto, CA: American West Publishing Company, 1969.

Jansen, W., *Abraham "Oregon" Smith: Pioneer, Folk Hero, and Tale-Teller*, New York: Arno, 1977.

Larkin, M., *The Singing Cowboy*, New York: Alfred A. Knopf, 1931.

Lingenfelter, R. et al. (eds.), *Songs of the American West*, Los Angeles: University of California Press, 1968.

Paterson, A. B. (ed.), *The Old Bush Songs*, Sydney: Angus and Robertson, 1905 (various, mostly revised, editions to 1931).

Rose, D., *Dingo Makes Us Human: Life and Land in an Aboriginal Australian Culture*, Melbourne, Australia: Melbourne University Press, 1992.

Steckmesser, K. L., *The Western Hero in History and Legend*, Norman: University of Oklahoma Press, 1965.

Stewart, D. and Keesing, N. (eds.), *Australian Bush Ballads*, Sydney: Angus and Robertson, 1955.

Wannan, W., *The Australian*, Adelaide: Rigby, 1954.

G

Galloping Jones
See Jones, Galloping

Gam-Czan, Marshall Gang
Korean warrior hero of legendary ugliness who wins many battles against the Chinese and conducts various magical and miraculous acts of beneficence for the common people. Gang Gam-Czan is the offspring of a union between a human father and a fox mother, in the assumed shape of a beautiful young woman, and is destined for great heroism from birth. He has a special ability to communicate with animals. In his boyhood, Gang Gam-Czan performs feats of supernatural heroism, including saving a bridegroom when his body is entered by a fox. At age twelve, Gang Gam-Czan passes the civil service examinations and is appointed a magistrate, a position he uses to clear all tigers from the area of Seoul. In another story, he rids a town of a plague of frogs, and in other local traditions, he makes rivers flow silently and rids areas of mosquitoes, all with his magical powers. Gang Gam-Czan's folklore combines the attributes of the warrior, magician, people's friend, and local hero.

> **Related entries:** Androcles; Aniz; Berni, Cesarino Di; Fox Maiden, The; Gim; Local Heroes; Magicians; Military Heroes; Yao Wang
> ***References and further reading***
> In-Sob, Z., *Folk Tales from Korea*, London: Routledge and Kegan Paul, 1952, pp. 56–58.
> Shin-yong, C. and International Cultural Foundation (eds.), *Korean Folk Tales*, Seoul: Si-sa-yong-o-sa Publishers, 1982.

Gardiner, Frank "Darkie"
See Christie, Francis

Gearoidh, Iarla
Earl Gerald, an Irish sleeping hero who is the focus of many legends. According to folk tradition, Gerald was a shape-shifting warrior antagonist of the English occupiers who lived in a castle at Mullaghmast. Gerald is said to be sleeping at a long table, together with his armored warriors and their horses, in a cave beneath Mullaghmast castle. When the time comes, signaled by a blast on a trumpet blown by a miller's son with six-fingers on each hand, Gerald and his warriors will wake, mount their horses, and ride out to do battle. Every seven years, Gerald is said to ride his horse, shod with thick silver shoes, around the Curragh of Kildare. When the horseshoes are worn as thin as a cat's ear he will come back to life, defeat the English, and rule Ireland for twenty years.

The folklore of Earl Gerald endows him with the characteristics of many heroic types, including the shape-shifter, the warrior, the sleeping hero, the national hero, the culture hero, and the hero of struggle.

> **Related entries:** Arthur; Barbarossa; Batradz; Charlemagne; Culture Heroes; Danske, Holger; Heroes of Struggle; Shape-Shifters; Sleepers; Warriors
> ***References and further reading***
> Curtin, J., *Hero-Tales of Ireland*, Boston: Little, Brown and Company, 1911 (1894).
> Kennedy, P., *Legendary Fictions of the Irish Celts*, London: Macmillan, 1866, pp. 172–174.

Gellert
Gellert (Gelert) is an animal hero, a faithful hound. The story seems to date from 1800, when W. R. Spencer privately printed a ballad titled "Beth Gellert, or the Grave of the Greyhound." Spencer claimed that the story was of thirteenth-century Welsh origin, having been

traditional in a village near Mount Snowdon where Llewellyn the Great had once owned a house. However, subsequent research by historian Prys Morgan strongly suggests that this is all romantic nonsense and that Spencer simply reworked elements of a well-known international tale. This may well be so, though versions of this story are still widely told today, especially in its modern incarnation as an "urban legend."

The older story concerns Prince Llewellyn's favorite hound, the bold but gentle Gellert. One day the prince goes out hunting without Gellert, who is not to be found anywhere in the castle. The hunt fails, and Llewellyn returns in great anger. As he approaches the castle, Gellert comes bounding toward him with blood dripping from his fangs. This strange sight causes the Prince to rush to his small son's nursery, where Gellert and the boy often played together. When Llewellyn reaches the nursery he finds blood spattered all around, the cot upturned, and no sign of his son. Believing that the hound has killed and eaten the boy, Llewellyn draws his sword and kills Gellert. Just as he does, there is a small cry from underneath the cot. It is his son, just waking up and unharmed. Lying next to the child are the torn and bloody remains of a wolf. Gellert had defended the sleeping child by slaying the beast. Deep in grief and guilt, Llewellyn buries Gellert with great ceremony, covering the grave with a cairn of stones. The place is called Beth Gellert, meaning "the grave of Gellert."

This sad and affecting tale of the heroic hound has such a hold in folk memory that it also has a contemporary existence as an urban legend. In the modern version, a young married couple needs to go out in a hurry. Unable to find a baby-sitter at such short notice, they decide to leave the family dog—usually said to be a German Shepherd—in the baby's bedroom as protection. They do not expect to be away long and comfort themselves with the thought that the dog has always been a fine family pet. When they return, they enter the child's room to find the cot upturned, blood everywhere, and no sign of the baby. The family pet is in another room, its fangs covered with blood. In a fit of rage, believing the dog has killed his child, the father kills the dog. Just then a whimpering is heard in the hall closet. The parents open it to find a man cowering in the closet, nursing a torn and bleeding arm. "Don't let that dog near me again," the man begs. It turns out that the dog was protecting the child, who is found unharmed beneath the cot, from a possible attack by this man who was burgling the house.

In both the old and new versions of the story, the moral is plain: act in haste and repent at leisure. There are also Indian, Japanese, Russian, German, French, Chinese, Persian, and Jewish versions of this tale, as well as Aesop's fable "The Farmer and His Dog."

Related entries: Tametomo
References and further reading
Baring-Gould, Rev. S., *Curious Myths of the Middle Ages*, London: Green and Co., 1897 (1866), pp. 134–144.
Brunvand, J., *The Mexican Pet*, New York: Norton, 1986, pp. 41–47.
Clouston, W., *Popular Tales and Fictions: Their Migrations and Transformations*, 2 vols., Edinburgh and London: William Blackwood, 1887, vol. 2, pp. 166–186.
Dorson, R., *Folk Legends of Japan*, Rutland, VT: Charles E. Tuttle, 1962, pp. 166–167.
Jacobs, J., *Celtic Fairy Tales*, London: D. Nutt, 1892.
Parry-Jones, D., *Welsh Legends and Fairy Lore*, London: Batsford, 1963 (1953).
Ranelagh, E., *The Past We Share: The Near Eastern Ancestry of Western Folk Literature*, London: Quartet Books, 1979, p. 243.

General Gim Dog-Nyong
See Dog-Nyong, General Gim

General James Wolfe
See Wolfe, General James

Geordie
Name of the probably legendary hero in a popular British ballad, also sung in America. Geordie (sometimes Georgie, as in the eighteenth-century version from Child quoted here), is usually a poacher or outlaw of royal blood who is hanged for his crimes:

He stole fifteen of the King's fat deer
And sent them to Lord Navey.

A usually unnamed woman stands by him, pleading unsuccessfully with the judge to spare Geordie:

And when she came to the good Lord Judge
She fell down upon her knees already,
Saying "My good Lord Judge, come pity me,
Grant me the life of my Georgie."

The judge replies:

"My pretty fair maid you are come too late,
For he is condemned already.
He will be hung in a silken cord
Where there has not been many
For he came of royal blood
And courted a virtuous lady."

The plucky heroine responds:

"I wish I was on yonder hill,
Where times I have been many!
With a sword and buckler by my side
I would fight for the life of my Georgie."

In other versions of the song, the heroine says she would freely give the lives of her two children and the unborn babe that lies within her body in return for the life of Geordie. Although Geordie is the named hero of this ballad tradition, it is clearly the plucky anonymous female who carries out the heroic actions.

Related entries: Heroes of Struggle; Hood, Robin; Victims; Women Dressed as Men

References and further reading

Belden, H. (ed.), Ballads and Songs Collected by the Missouri Folklore Society, University of Missouri Studies 15, no. 1, 1940, pp. 76–78.
Broadwood, L., English Traditional Songs and Carols, London: E. P. Publishing, Rowman and Littlefield, 1974 (1908), pp. 32–33.
Child, F. J., English and Scottish Popular Ballads, 5 vols., New York: Dover, 1965 (1882–1898), vol. 4, pp. 55, 123–142, 351, 370.
Coffin, T., The British Traditional Ballad in North America, rev. ed., Lancaster, PA: American Folklore Society, 1963, pp. 124ff.
Lloyd, A., Folksong in England, New York: International Publishers, 1970 (1967), p. 63.
Vaughan Williams, R. and Lloyd, A. (eds.), The Penguin Book of English Folk Songs, Harmondsworth, Middlesex: Penguin Books, 1959, pp. 42–43.

George, Saint

A most popular saint, George is celebrated not only in England, where he is the patron saint, but also in Portugal, Spain, the Slovenes, Greece, Russia, and throughout the Middle East, where he is often connected with another important folk hero, El Khidre. He is also important in Greek tradition and appears in Rom or Gypsy lore. His slaying of the dragon was not attached to his legend until the twelfth century, by which time he had already been the subject of extensive romanticization by literary chroniclers and in oral tradition.

The historical character on which the legend is based is often said to have been a Christian martyred during the Roman emperor Diocletian's suppression of Christians in 303 A.D. However, this is a far from certain identification. What is known is that a Saint George was popular throughout the Middle East from the third century. His veneration gradually spread and was given a significant impetus during the Crusades, when the cult of St. George was brought back to Europe by returning Crusaders. The Crusades also solidified George's image as a warrior saint and began his steady rise to prominence as England's national hero. "For St. George and England" was a common battle cry from at least as early as the Battle of Agincourt in 1415.

An important aspect of St. George's folklore in English and Scots tradition is as a character in the traditional hero-combat plays usually referred to as "mummer's plays." In these folk dramas performed at Christmas, Easter, or All Hallows, a character called St. George is one of two knights who fight a mortal combat, the other usually known as the Turkish Knight or Turkish Champion. Since 1222, St. George's Day has been April 23 in England. St. George is in many ways an archetypal folk hero, slaying dragons and saving damsels in distress. He is also celebrated for his ability to cure infertility in women.

Italian fifteenth-century painting depicting St. George protecting the princess from the dragon (The Art Archive/Museo Tosio Martinengo Brescia/Dagli Ort)

Related entries: Dragon-Slayers; National Heroes; Religious Heroes; Warriors

References and further reading

Alford, V., *The Singing of the Travels: In Search of Dance and Drama*, London: Max Parrish, 1956, pp. 56, 92, 95.

Barber, R., *Myths and Legends of the British Isles*, Rochester, NY: Boydell Press, 1999, pp. 386–390.

Briggs, K. (ed.), *A Dictionary of British Folk-Tales in the English Language*, 2 vols., London: Routledge and Kegan Paul, 1970–1971, vol. 1, pp. 474–476.

Buchan, D. (ed.), *Scottish Tradition: A Collection of Scottish Folk Literature*, London: Routledge and Kegan Paul, 1984, pp. 213–217.

Cachia, P., *Popular Narrative Ballads of Modern Egypt*, Oxford: Oxford University Press, 1989, pp. 239–246.

Degh, L. (trans. Schossberger, E.), *Folktales and Society: Story-Telling in a Hungarian Peasant Community*, Bloomington: Indiana University Press, 1969 (1962), p. 159.

Downing, C. (trans. and ed.), *Armenian Folk-Tales and Fables*, London: Oxford University Press, 1972, pp. 204–205.

Druts, Y. and Gessler, A. (colls.), Riordan, J. (trans.), *Russian Gypsy Tales*, Edinburgh: Canongate, 1986, pp. 25–27.

Hole, C., *Saints in Folklore*, London: Bell and Sons, 1966, pp. 17–32.

Ivanits, L., *Russian Folk Belief*, Armonk and London: M. E. Sharpe Inc., 1989, pp. 6, 9, 12, 26–29, 31–32, 45, 68, 145–153.

Leach, E., "St. George and the Dragon," in Daniel, G. et al., *Myth or Legend?* London: Bell and Sons, 1955, pp. 79–87.

Riches, S., *St. George: Hero, Martyr, and Myth*, Stroud, UK: Sutton Publishing, 2000.

Tiddy, R., *The Mummer's Play*, Oxford: Oxford University Press, 1972 (1923), p. 78 and passim.

Tong, D., *Gypsy Folktales*, New York: Harcourt Brace Jovanovich, 1989, pp. 183–185.

Giant-Killers

A large and widespread class of heroes, closely related to dragon-slayers. The best-known English-language examples are probably Jack the Giant-Killer and another Jack who chops down a magic beanstalk and kills a giant ogre. But there are many other heroes in all traditions who are credited with such feats. Familiar as the biblical hero and in Jewish tradition, Samson also features in Armenian lore as the slayer of the giant, one-eyed ogre called a *tapagöz*. Samson's great strength and bravery win him the love of the fair Gulinaz (a Persian name meaning "young and tender rose"), and he ultimately becomes the ruler of the kingdom.

Giant-killers are closely related to dragon-slayers, and hero legends often involve the serial slaying of all such beasts encountered. Giants, like dragons, are usually portrayed as fearsome, stupid, and as intimidators of poor or disadvantaged communities, as in the stories of the Punjabi hero, Rasalu. The hero does away with the giants or giantesses, thus restoring normality and security to the grateful populace. As with dragons, ogres, and other villains, giants generally represent the negative principle of evil, the defeat of which is one of the important ways in which heroism is conferred in folklore.

Related entries: Badikan; Guy of Warwick; Haitsi-Aibab; Jack and the Beanstalk; Jack the Giant-Killer; Kihuo; Ogres; Rasalu; Siitakuuyuk; Villains

References and further reading

Ausubel, N. (ed.), *A Treasury of Jewish Folklore*, London: Vallentine, Mitchell, 1972 (1948), pp. 28, 224.

Downing, C. (trans. and ed.), *Armenian Folk-Tales and Fables*, London: Oxford University Press, 1972.

Gim

Young Korean hero of legend whose father, a minister of the king, is killed and whose mother is abducted by robbers. Gim swears to rescue his mother and sets out on his quest to find the robbers. Along the way, he has a number of adventures and encounters. He saves a boy from a bear, and it turns out that this boy has suffered exactly the same fate as Gim. The two become sworn brothers and continue their quest together. While they are crossing a broad river in a boat there is a dreadful storm and the ferry sinks. Gim is washed into the water and regains consciousness on the river bank, being looked after by another boy of his own age. The first boy has disappeared, and it turns out that this second boy has also had his father killed and his mother abducted by robbers. So Gim and the second boy swear loyalty to each other and continue the quest. They come to another river, and this time the second boy is drowned. Gim is rescued by an old woman who lives on an island that, it turns out, is also inhabited by the robbers. But Gim is too feeble to do anything. Soon the robber chief tells the old woman to get rid of Gim, or the robbers will kill her. She hides Gim in a thatched hut by the river. One day a ship sails by in which travels an old man. The old man tells Gim that the boy is the minister's son and that he has come to rescue him. Gim goes with the man, who is a wise man of the mountains, and lives with him for years, learning many magical secrets.

At age sixteen the old man tells Gim that the king is under threat from the robber band and needs Gim's help. The old man tells Gim that he will meet him again exactly three years from this day. Gim sets out for his home and on the way acquires a magic suit of armor and a dragon-horse. He reaches the city, under siege from the robbers, and magically flies over their heads on his steed and into the king's castle. He tells the king he can defeat the robbers, and the grateful ruler makes him a marshall. But it turns out that defeating the robbers is a harder task than Gim anticipates. The robbers are a supernatural group of beings in various forms, including a bear, a fox, a rat, and a tiger. They are assailing the castle with magical means, including fire, flood, and lightning. There is a great battle, during which Gim discovers the body of his childhood betrothed.

Together with the king, Gim escapes to an island, but the supernatural robber band continues to attack them. Gim has a dream in which he sees a butterfly that suggests he should fly after it. He magically turns himself into a swallow and flies off with the butterfly, thousands of miles away to a cave in a mountain. There Gim finds the first boy whom he had saved from the bear. He is studying a book of strategy, and when Gim tells him of the peril he and the king are facing, they join together once again. Transported immediately back to the fighting by magic, they rejoin the battle. But Gim's friend is killed, and the island is submerged by a flood caused by one of the supernatural robbers. Gim and the king are forced to take refuge on another island. Now Gim has another dream of a crow and again turns himself into a swallow to follow the bird's flight. In another cave in another mountain, he finds his second friend and ally. He is practicing the arts of war. When Gim tells him the situation, he allies himself with Gim, and they return to the second island together. But the second boy is slain in the fighting, and Gim and the king are forced to flee to another island, also under threat from the steadily rising flood waters. Fortunately Gim and the king find a ship and set sail. The wise old man who had taught Gim all he knew comes down out of the sky, exactly three years after Gim had first departed to help the king. Acknowledging that Gim's training was insufficient for him to overcome the supernatural robber band, the wise old man tells them he has come to help. He sings a magic song, calling down thunder and lightning that slays all the robbers. Gim and the old man go to the robbers' island where they find Gim's mother and a girl who turns out to be the sister of his second, though now deceased, friend. Gim returns home with the king, his mother, and the girl, whom he soon marries.

This summary of an elaborate version of the legend told by Zong Zin-Il of Yangsan in 1932 would make an excellent fantasy suspense movie. It cleverly weaves together a number of traditional themes and motifs to tell a compelling story that would undoubtedly have held its audience spellbound. The story contains the classical elements of the folktale: the threat to the family; the hero's quest; his attainment of magical powers through encounters with numerous helpers; the magical contest; the ulti-mate attainment of the quest's objective; and the reward of marriage. These elements have been identified and analyzed by various researchers in this field, notably Vladimir Propp, whose *Morphology of the Folktale* contains a formulaic and, he argues, universal folktale structure, of which the tale of young Gim is a fine case study.

Related entries: Achikar; Dog-Nyong, General Gim; Fereyel; Gam-Czan, Marshall Gang; Habermani; Magicians; Marendenboni; Merlin; Molo; Nue the Hunter; Shape-Shifters; Wirreenun the Rainmaker

References and further reading

In-Sob, Z., *Folk Tales from Korea*, London: Routledge and Kegan Paul, 1952, pp. 62–66.

Propp, V., *The Morphology of the Folktale*, Austin: University of Texas Press, 1968.

Shin-yong, C. and International Cultural Foundation (eds.), *Korean Folk Tales*, Seoul: Si-sa-yong-o-sa Publishers, 1982.

Giricoccola

Heroine of a Bolognese Italian tale combining elements of both "Snow White" and "Cinderella." In a version recounted by Calvino, Giricoccola is the youngest and most beautiful of three sisters, envied by the other two. Their father is a merchant who has to leave town on business and who gives his daughters presents of gold, silver, and silk before he goes. After the father departs, the oldest sister takes the gold, and the second oldest takes the silver, leaving Giricoccola with the silk. As the girls sit by the window spinning these materials, the moon rises and says:

> Lovely is the one with gold,
> Lovelier still is the one with silver,
> But the one with silk surpasses them both.
> Good night, lovely girls and ugly girls
>   alike.

The older sisters are enraged, and the next evening they give Giricoccola the silver to spin. This time the moon says that the one spinning the silver is the fairest. The older sisters taunt Giricoccola and the next night give her the gold to spin. But again the moon poetically insists that Giricoccola is the most beautiful. So the older sisters lock the youngest away in a hayloft. The moon sees her crying there and carries her away home. The next afternoon, the two older sisters are spinning when the moon rises and says:

Lovely is the one with gold,
Lovelier still is the one with silver,
But the one at my house surpasses them both.
Good night, lovely girls and ugly girls alike.

The two sisters rush to the hayloft. Finding that Giricoccola is indeed gone, they send for a female astrologer to find her and kill her. The astrologer dresses as a gypsy and goes to the moon's house, where Giricoccola sits spinning at the window. The astrologer says she will sell Giricoccola some handsome hairpins for a very low price. The girl is delighted and asks the astrologer inside. She places one of the pins in Giricoccola's hair, and the girl is immediately transformed into a stone statue. When the moon returns she pulls the pin out and restores Giricoccola to normality but chides the girl for being so careless. Giricoccola promises not to let anyone in again.

The two elder sisters eventually learn from the astrologer that Giricoccola has been restored to life, and so the astrologer performs the same trick as before with the gypsy disguise. This time she offers Giricoccola lovely combs. The young girl cannot resist, and all happens as before. The moon returns to find Giricoccola a statue again and grows angry. She releases Giricoccola once more and makes her promise not to be so silly in the future. The moon says that if it happens again, she will not save Giricoccola. Of course, it happens again. This time the cunning astrologer uses the temptation of a beautiful gown to turn Giricoccola to stone, and the moon sells the statue to a chimney sweep. The sweep carts the statue, still dressed in its beautiful gown, around on a donkey until one day a king's son sees it and falls in love with the image. He buys it for its weight in gold and keeps it in his room. Giricoccola's sisters break into the room to steal the

gown because they want to go to the ball. As soon as they take the gown off the statue, Giricoccola comes back to life. The sisters are afraid, but Giricoccola reassures them, and when the prince returns she surprises him with her story. He marries her immediately, and when the sisters hear about this from the astrologer, they both die of rage.

This story is a good example of the ability of traditional storytellers to weave the various elements of plot into ever-fresh forms. This tale retains aspects of folktale in its details of envy, imprisonment, the supernatural, and the death of the older sisters, but it combines them with the more literary fairy tale elements of the astrologer, the beautiful objects, and the marriage of the heroine to the prince.

Related entries: Cinderella; Fairy Tale Heroes; Snow White

References and further reading
Calvino, I. (trans. Martin, G.), *Italian Folk Tales: Selected and Retold by Italo Calvino,* New York: Harcourt Brace Jovanovich, Penguin, 1980 (1956), pp. 154–156.
Crane, T., *Italian Popular Tales,* Boston and New York: Houghton Mifflin and Co., 1885; reprint, Detroit: Singing Tree Press, 1968.
Mathias, E. and Raspa, R., *Italian Folktales in America: The Verbal Art of an Immigrant Woman,* Detroit: Wayne State University Press, 1988.

Gizo

African Hausa version of the spider trickster usually known as Anansi. Gizo is renowned for his boastfulness, his greed, and his ability to outwit other animals and, occasionally, humans in order to escape from the consequences of his trickery. Like other tricksters in the world's folklore and mythology, Gizo is generally considered to be a culture hero.

Related entries: Anansi; Culture Heroes; Rabbit; Spider; Tortoise; Tricksters

References and further reading
Courlander, H. (comp.), *A Treasury of African Folklore,* New York: Crown, 1975, pp. 60–65.
Dadié, B. (trans. Hatch, C.), *The Black Cloth: A Collection of African Folktales,* Amherst: University of Massachusetts Press, 1987 (1955).
Dorson, R. (ed.), *African Folklore,* Bloomington: Indiana University Press, 1972, 1979.

Godiva, Lady

The historical Godiva was an eleventh-century Anglo-Saxon woman who died in 1080. She was the wife of Leofric, Earl of Mercia. Godiva was intent on performing good works and persuaded her husband to establish a number of monasteries. Her legendary status stems from a thirteenth-century account (in the *Flores Historiarum* or *Flowers of the Historians*) of her continual representations to Leofric about lowering the taxes of the commoners. Leofric eventually agreed to do so, but only on the condition that Godiva ride naked through the streets of Coventry. Godiva took the challenge, wrapping herself in her long hair and asking the townspeople to stay inside their houses to avoid seeing her nudity. The legend goes on to say that Leofric did abolish all taxes, except those on horses.

A seventeenth-century embellishment of this story reports that not all the citizens of Coventry closed their shutters as Godiva rode by. One, a tailor named Tom, opened his window to take a peep at the unprecedented sight and was immediately struck blind for his temerity, thus, in folk etymology at least, giving us the term "Peeping Tom" for a voyeur. In 1678 a festival in honor of Lady Godiva was established as part of the Coventry Fair. While the legend of Lady Godiva's ride has long been promoted by Coventry for purposes of what would now be called "corporate image" and tourism—there is a large statue commemorating the event in the center of Coventry—the origins of the story place Godiva as a folk heroine of social protest.

Related entries: Heroes of Struggle; Local Heroes
References and further reading
Barber, R., *Myths and Legends of the British Isles*, Rochester, NY: Boydell Press, 1999, p. 564.
Briggs, K. (ed.), *A Dictionary of British Folk-Tales in the English Language*, 2 vols., London: Routledge and Kegan Paul, 1970–1971.
Davidson, H., *Patterns of Folklore*, Ipswich, Eng.: Brewer; Totowa, NJ: Rowman and Littlefield, 1960, pp. 80–94.

Lady Godiva riding nude on a horse through the streets of Coventry (Library of Congress)

Goldilocks

In its most widely known version, the tale of the little girl who blunders into the house of the three bears, eating their porridge, sitting in their chairs, and sleeping in their beds, is one of the most unsatisfying of all heroine stories, lacking both motivation and a proper resolution. This has not worried generations of parents, children, and publishers of children's literature or makers of pantomimes in the slightest. Goldilocks is one of the best-loved nursery stories of the modern era, with the heroine's preference for the food or furniture of the baby bear ensuring its popularity with young children.

The origin of what we now know as "Goldilocks and the Three Bears" is usually traced to a Scots story in which three bears are disturbed by a female fox, or vixen, who is then eaten by the bears, but the basic elements of "Goldilocks and the Three Bears" are drawn from the common pool of European folktale. The apparently abandoned house in the woods, the invasion of its privacy, and the insistent three-fold structure of the story are widespread

Goldilocks eating the porridge (Leonard de Selva/Corbis)

motifs and devices of folktale and are adapted to good effect for this much-told tale.

In its modern form, the story of Goldilocks and the three bears can be traced to the early nineteenth century and a book by the English poet Robert Southey (*The Doctor*, 1837). The heroine—a small woman, not a girl called Goldilocks—escapes the wrath of the bears by jumping out the window. Southey's story offers no further information about what might have happened to her. Southey may have based his version on an earlier tradition, known to have been in existence in 1831 (and almost certainly before that), in which an elderly woman takes the Goldilocks role. Joseph Cundall made further changes to the tale between 1849 and 1904, when in his various retellings of the tale, he first made the heroine a small girl and then successively named and renamed her Silver-Hair, Silver-Locks, Golden-Hair, and finally Goldilocks. These changes were complemented by the *Mother Goose's Fairy Tales* anthology of 1878, which changed the Great Huge Bear, Middle Bear, and Little Small Wee Bear into Father Bear, Mother Bear, and Baby Bear. The cumulative effect of these changes was to render what was originally a far more fearsome oral tale into a reasonably comfortable family story that, with its suspense and unrealized hint of menace, made it ideally suited for the nursery, where it remains stubbornly to this day.

Related entries: Baba-Yaga; Children's Folk Heroes; Fairy Tale Heroes; Gretel; Hansel

References and further reading

Bettelheim, B., *The Uses of Enchantment: The Meaning and Importance of Fairy Tales*, New York: Knopf, 1976, pp. 215–224.
Briggs, K. (ed.), *A Dictionary of British Folk-Tales in the English Language*, 2 vols., London: Routledge and Kegan Paul, 1970–1971, vol. 2, pp. 564–566.
Opie, I. and P., *The Classic Fairy Tales*, London: Oxford University Press, 1974, pp. 199–205.
Phillips, E., "The Three Bears," *Man* 54 (1954): 123.
Shamburger, M. and Lachmann, V., "Southey and the Three Bears," *Journal of American Folklore* 59, no. 234, 1946, pp. 400–403.

Golem, The

See Loew, Rabbi Judah

Gongsun Jie

Legendary Chinese hero in the court of Duke Jing of Qi. Gongsun Jie, together with his two companions Guye Zi and Tian Kaijiang, are noisy and bothersome in the court, and the duke is not happy with their behavior, even though they are heroes. The duke asks his wily chancellor, Yän Zi, what to do about these disruptive heroes. The chancellor, knowing that heroes will always value their honor above their lives, has a feast prepared, the centerpiece of which is a dish containing three ripe, full peaches. The duke sits down with the three heroes and says that only the most worthy in the land should eat the peaches. Because he is ruler, he eats one, leaving two. One after the other, the three heroes claim that their heroic deeds make them deserving of a peach. Gongsun Jie claims his first, then Tian Kaijiang, which leaves Guye Zi with no peach. Enraged, he rises and claims that his deeds, which include saving the duke's life on many occasions, are greater than those of his fellows, but, he notes, since no peaches remain he is obviously no longer deserving of his claim to fame. Unable to bear the shame, he draws his sword and kills himself. Gongsun Jie then rises and admits that he and Tian Kaijiang have been excessively rewarded and that, disgraced, they should live no longer. He draws his sword and lops off his own head. Then Tian Kaijiang rises and says that he and his companions have always served the duke as one, but now that they are dead, there is no reason for him to go on and it is his duty to join them. He then kills himself. The duke, pleased at this result, gives them all a magnificent funeral.

In this version of the story, the duke has something of the role of the fatal trickster, and the tale suggests the necessity for even great heroes to cultivate the humility and respect for status traditionally prized in Chinese culture. In another version, known as "Kill Three Warriors with Two Peaches" (appearing in a book titled *Yanzi Chunqiu*, which contains material thought to date from c. 500 B.C.), as translated by Zhang Ye, the three heroes refuse to stand for the duke's chancellor. The chancellor protests at this disrespect and advises that the duke rid himself of the heroes. The duke replies that he is powerless to fight these fierce warriors who dare even to fight tigers. The chancellor says that the heroes do not understand the relationship between superiors and inferiors, and he suggests that the duke reward the heroes with two peaches. This the duke does, saying, "Why don't you eat the peaches according to your deeds?" Gongsun Jie takes the first peach, claiming that he is the only one worthy of such a reward. Tian Kaijiang takes the second peach, making the same claim. Guye Zi says that he is the only one whose deeds merit such a reward and that the other two should give the peaches to him. He then unsheathes his sword, which makes Gongsun Jie and Tian Kaijiang realize that their deeds are no greater than those of their third comrade and that they have been greedy by not sharing the peaches with Guye Zi. Saying "If we do not die, we are no heroes at all," they give their peaches to Guye Zi and behead themselves. Then Guye Zi says that he is now a man without brotherhood (Yi) or benevolence (Ren). "I hate what I have done. If I do not die, I am not a hero." He then gives the peaches back to the duke and kills himself.

Related entries: Tricksters; Warriors
References and further reading
Loewe, M., "Heroes in Chinese Tradition," in Davidson, H. (ed.), *The Hero in Tradition and Folklore*, London: Mistletoe Books, 1985, pp. 142–155.
Osers, E. (trans.), *Chinese Folktales*, London: Bell and Sons, 1971, pp. 188–190. First published in German as Wilhelm, R. (trans.), *Chinesische Märchen*, 1958.
Werner, E., *Myths and Legends of China*, New York: Arno Press, 1976 (1922).

Goose Girl, The

This is the title given by the Grimm brothers to a complex story that contains many ancient and widespread folktale elements, including the swapping of identities, the usurpation of the hero by a pretender, magical powers, the passage from youth to adulthood, retributive justice, and a talking animal.

As the Grimms recount the story from German tradition, a beautiful princess must be sent abroad for her marriage to an elderly king. She carries rich jewelry as the bride-fee and is accompanied by a chambermaid. The princess rides a talking horse named Falada. Just before the princess leaves, her mother cuts her own finger and drips three drops of blood onto a white handkerchief. She gives the blood-stained handkerchief to her daughter, telling her that it will serve her well on her journey. An hour into the journey, the princess and the maid stop by a stream, and the princess hands the maid a golden cup, asking her to fill it. The maid refuses and says that she will no longer be the princess's servant.

They continue the journey until the princess again feels the need for a drink of water. Having now to get the drink herself, the princess leans over the river to drink and in the process drops the blood-speckled white handkerchief into the water. She immediately becomes weak, and the maid overpowers her, steals her dress and horse, and forces her to swear that she will tell no one of the exchange. They then continue to the court of the old king, where the maid passes herself off successfully as the princess and the real princess is assigned to work in the fields, helping a boy to tend the geese.

After a while the false princess asks the old king if the head of the talking horse, Falada, can be chopped off, as she secretly fears the animal will reveal the truth. This is done, and, at the begging of the real princess, the horse's head is nailed above a dark gateway through which she passes each day to her work. Whenever she and the goose boy pass through the gateway, the horse's head repeats the lines:

If this your mother knew,
Her heart would break in two.

Naturally the princess, forced to be a goose girl, is upset, and one day while out with the geese she lets her golden hair down. The goose boy is so entranced by her hair that he tries to pluck a strand, but the princess causes the wind to blow the boy's hat away, forcing him to chase it. For three days, these same events occur. On the third day, the goose boy, now irritated, complains to the king, who secretly observes the same incidents on the fourth day.

That evening the king visits the Goose Girl and asks her what it all means. She tells him that she is bound by a pledge not to reveal her story. Eventually, she agrees to a compromise that the king suggests, which is to tell the truth to the fire hearth. The king, of course, is hiding behind the hearth and so learns her secret. He then gives her proper clothing and invites everyone to a great feast at which the Goose Girl and the false princess are to sit on each side of him.

After eating, the king turns to the false princess and asks what sort of punishment she would give to someone who perpetrated the kind of deception that had been carried out, describing it all in detail, though keeping the fact that he knows the truth concealed. Not realizing that she has been unmasked, the false princess says that the offender should be stripped and placed inside a nail-studded barrel and that the barrel should be dragged around by two white horses until the offender is dead. Then the king reveals that he knows the truth and tells the false princess that she will suffer exactly the fate she has outlined so cruelly. The execution is carried out, and the king weds the Goose Girl, his rightful bride, and they rule the kingdom in peace and holiness.

Versions of this tale, in which the wronged heroine eventually wins her rightful place at the king's side, are told throughout the world. An English version, usually known as "Roswal and Lillian," has the main characters as males and does not feature the marriage element, while an African version can be found in this encyclopedia under the entry "Maria, Fenda."

Related entries: Fairy Tale Heroes; Maria, Fenda; Tabadiku
References and further reading
Bettelheim, B., The Uses of Enchantment: The Meaning and Importance of Fairy Tales, New York: Knopf, 1976, pp. 136–144.
Grimm, J. and W., The Complete Grimm's Fairy Tales, New York: Pantheon Books, 1944, pp. 404–411.

Green Princess, The

Heroine of a Sumatran folktale who unwittingly falls in love with her brother. Rather than enter into an incestuous relationship, she drowns herself in a lake, turning into a large, green-skinned dragon. The lake, in Aceh Province (currently part of Indonesia), is noted for a great abundance of green weed and algae and is the focus of many folk beliefs. As well as being a local legend about the lake, this story is also a cautionary tale, showing that incest is a taboo that must never be broken, even if suicide is the only way to avoid it, a theme and an outcome found in many traditions.

Related entries: Dojrana; Local Heroes; Tricksters
References and further reading
Aman, S., Folk Tales from Indonesia, Jakarta: Djambatan, 1976.
Knappert, J., Myths and Legends of Indonesia, Singapore: Heinnemann, 1977.

Gretel

Heroine of the well-known German folktale of Hansel and Gretel. Hansel and Gretel, brother and sister, are the children of a poor woodcutter who, at the urging of his second wife, the children's stepmother, abandons them in the forest to ensure their own survival. The children overhear this plot, and Hansel collects a pocketful of white pebbles, which he strews on the ground to mark the trail back home. The father and stepmother then abandon the children, unaware that Hansel has marked the trail. By the light of the moon, the children follow the trail of white pebbles back home, where their father joyfully receives them.

All is well until the next famine comes, whereupon the wicked stepmother prevails on the father to try the same strategy again. This time Hansel is unable to get white pebbles and must make a trail with bread crumbs. Unfortunately, after the father and stepmother again desert the children in the depths of the forest, the birds peck up the bread crumbs, leaving Hansel and Gretel alone and lost. After wandering around for some time, usually three days, they are led by a bird into a clearing where there stands a gingerbread house, which they begin to eat. An old lady comes out of the house and invites them inside to rest. It seems as though the children are safe. But the next morning, the old woman throws Hansel into a cage and forces Gretel to cook and clean for her. It turns out that this woman is a witch who plans to fatten Hansel up to the point where she can cook and eat him. Every day she checks how well he is fattening by feeling his finger. Hansel, realizing her plan, capitalizes on the witch's shortsightedness by holding out a chicken bone as a substitute for his finger. The witch cannot understand why the finger does not fatten with all the food she is feeding Hansel, and eventually she becomes impatient and decides to eat him anyway.

At this point she forces Gretel to heat up the stove and tells her to get inside to test the heat. Gretel tricks the witch into getting inside herself and quickly shuts the door on her. She frees Hansel from the cage, and they flee, not forgetting to take the treasure that happens to be stored in the now-cooked witch's house. They are usually helped back to their home by animals. When they arrive, they discover that the wicked stepmother has died, and their father is overjoyed to have them back again.

The numerous motifs and themes of this tale have made it a favorite for analysis and interpretation by folklorists, psychologists, and anyone else with an interest in divining the meaning of folktales. The abandoned child is perhaps the principal motif, followed closely by the wickedness of the stepmother, and by the tricking and burning of the witch on her own fire by the quick-witted Gretel. This is a favorite device of folktale, as in the Russian story of Ivashko, a young hero who tricks the daughter of the witch who plans to eat him into the oven in his stead, causing the witch to unwittingly eat her own child. Ivashko, hiding above the witch in a tree, reveals what she has done and escapes her fury by being carried home courtesy of a flock of swans and geese.

The trails of pebbles and crumbs, the animal helpers, and the apparently welcoming and edible house that turns out to be a trap are also widespread elements of folktale, especially reminiscent of the Russian and Slavic Baba-Yaga. Larger themes include the family, solidarity, bravery, self-help, the primeval fear of forests, and the kindly old lady turning out not to be what she seems. The story and its various forms is well known in northern and western Europe, in Africa, India, Japan, in the Pacific Islands, and among Native Americans.

In most versions of this story, the betrayed and abandoned children save themselves by their own wit and bravery. Hansel deceives the witch with the chicken bone while Gretel awaits the right moment to do away with her so that they can escape and return to their parents—variously a father, mother, or stepmother—who are usually overjoyed to have the children back again. Research has shown that this was largely the form of the original version of the story collected by the Grimms before the 1812 publication of their famous anthology of "fairy" tales. The children were not named in this oral version but were given their names in the first published version, which was also considerably tidied up from the original. Wilhelm Grimm continued to make substantial alterations and additions to the story in subsequent editions of the anthology, sometimes based on his discovery of earlier versions, such as that of Giambattista Basile's *Pentamerone* (1634), according to which Grimm changed the mother from the natural parent into a wicked stepmother. The significance of these alterations has been studied and debated by a number of scholars, most of whom agree that the abandonment motif is the core meaning of the story. However, Jack Zipes, while agreeing that this motif is central to the tale, argues that in effect the Grimms' penultimate version, and its adaptations by others, rationalizes the abandonment of the children and, more widely, the abuse of children that he claims is characteristic of modern society.

Related entries: Fairy Tale Heroes; Fereyel; Hansel; Ogres; Villains

References and further reading

Bettelheim, B., *The Uses of Enchantment: The Meaning and Importance of Fairy Tales*, New York: Knopf, 1976, pp. 11, 14–17, 40, 61–62, 98, 114, 144, 146–147, 151–152, 159–166, 169–172, 179, 201, 205–206, 208, 214, 309.

Bottigheimer, R. (ed.), *Fairy Tales and Society: Illusion, Allusion, and Paradigm*, Philadelphia: University of Pennsylvania Press, 1986.

Hallett, M. and Karasek, B. (eds.), *Folk and Fairy Tales*, Ontario: Broadview Press, 1996, pp. 100–105.

Lüthi, M. (trans. Chadeayne, L. and Gottwald, P.), *Once upon a Time: On the Nature of Fairy Tales*, Bloomington: Indiana University Press, 1976, pp. 59–70.

Zipes, J., "The Rationalization of Abandonment and Abuse in Fairy Tales: The Case of Hansel and Gretel," in Zipes, J., *Happily Ever After: Fairy Tales, Children, and the Culture Industry*, New York and London: Routledge, 1997.

Guiliano, Salvatore
See Outlaws

Guy of Warwick

Legendary Anglo-French romance hero dating from around 1200. Like many heroes, Guy seeks fame in order to win the hand of a woman, in this case Felice, the daughter of the Earl of Warwick. In the process, he accomplishes great feats of arms in the Crusades and slays a Northumbrian dragon. He weds Felice but then repents at his pursuit of love rather than piety and becomes a pilgrim penitent. Later he slays the giant Colbrand near Winchester, England. During his last days, he sends back to Felice the ring she had given him. She rushes to his deathbed, and he dies in her arms. His body gives off a sweet scent that has magical medicinal powers, and he has to be buried in his hermit's cell, as it is impossible to move the body. Guy of Warwick's story was told in France and in England, where it also became the subject of seventeenth-century broadside ballads that further embroidered his already considerable legend. Although now largely forgotten, Guy of Warwick's traditions were once so widespread and potent that he was considered one of the Nine Worthies of the World.

Guy's folklore rather unusually combines a large number of hero types. He is variously, sometimes at once, a great lover, a warrior, a dragon-slayer, a giant-killer, a local hero, and a religious hero. These several accomplishments and attributes perhaps explain his longevity as a hero of romance, popular literature, and folklore.

Related entries: Dragon-Slayers; Giant-Killers; Religious Heroes; Warriors

References and further reading
Barber, R., *Myths and Legends of the British Isles*, Rochester, NY: Boydell Press, 1999, pp. 467–482.

Crane, R., *The Vogue of Guy of Warwick from the Close of the Middle Ages to the Romantic Revival*, Publications of the Modern Languages Association of America, vol. 30, no. 2; New Series, vol. 23, no. 2, 1915.

Westwood, J., *Albion: A Guide to Legendary Britain*, London: Granada, 1985, pp. 269–273.

Guye Zi
See Gongsun Jie

H

Habermani

Hero of an Armenian tale in which he takes the form of a snake. In a version of the story collected in the Alexandropol region around 1880, Habermani's adventures are many and complex. The story begins, as do many others, with a poor old couple. The husband gathers firewood in the forest, and one day he picks up a snake in a pile of twigs and unwittingly carries it home. Once there, the snake "was accepted into the family as though it was their own son." The next day the snake speaks to the old man in a human voice, asking him to go to the king and ask for his daughter's hand on the snake's behalf. After some difficulties with the king's guards, the old man gains an audience with the king, who, thinking the peasant mad, decides to humor him. The king demands what he thinks will be an impossible task from the old man, asking him to build a palace overnight. If he does not succeed, the king threatens to chop off his head.

Despondent, the old man returns home and tells the snake what has happened. The snake tells him to go to a hole in the ground near the place were he gathered brushwood and to call down the hole, "Big lady, little lady, Habermani desires a large palace." The old man does this and on returning home finds his hut transformed into a wonderful palace, even grander than the king's. The king is greatly impressed but now asks the old man to perform two further tasks to secure his daughter's marriage to the old man's son. As before, with the help of the snake-son the old man carries out these tasks, and the king has no option but to give his daughter in marriage. At this point, the old man reveals that his son is a snake, but it is too late for the king to go back on his word. The princess and the snake are married. When they

are finally alone together after the wedding, the snake casts off his snake skin and reveals himself to the princess as a handsome young man. She falls ecstatically in love with him, but the snake swears her to secrecy about his true human nature.

But one day, piqued by the taunts of her peers about her marriage to a snake, the princess reveals the truth. The wonderful castle disappears, and an angry Habermani tells his wife to walk the earth in iron sandals for seven years. Only then will she find him again. The princess sets out on her journey, and Habermani sets off on a journey of his own that takes him into the clutches of a wicked witch who wants to marry her only daughter to him. But Habermani is still in love with his banished princess and refuses, falling into a fever that produces a thirst that cannot be quenched, even by the pitchers of water the witch's daughter brings continually.

Meanwhile, the still-journeying princess comes progressively to a city of clay, a crystal city, a copper city, an iron city, a steel city, and a silver city. At each city she meets a girl carrying pitchers of water from a well, and each girl tells her that Habermani is not there. Finally the princess comes to a golden city and, as before, meets a woman carrying water. Yes, Habermani is inside this city, but he is ill with fever. The princess convinces the witch's daughter to let her use her magic on the water that the witch's daughter takes to Habermani. She agrees, and the princess takes the opportunity secretly to drop her wedding ring into the water. When the snake drinks the water, the ring falls onto his chest and he realizes that the princess has found him at last. But the witch, still wishing to marry her daughter to Habermani, attempts to foil their reunion, setting various impossible tasks for the princess to perform. Just as he had helped the old man, his surrogate father, Habermani now helps the princess perform the tasks, which include fetching five sacks of feathers and twelve ornate dresses.

At the last task, Habermani determines that they must escape the witch. They are pursued by the witch's daughter, and Habermani turns his wife into a windmill and himself into a miller, fooling the witch's daughter, who returns empty-handed to her angry mother. The witch tells her daughter that she has been duped by Habermani's trickery and sends her in pursuit of the couple once again. This time Habermani turns his wife into an orchard and himself into a gardener, again fooling the witch's daughter. Now furious at the news of her daughter's continued stupidity, the witch takes pursuit herself. Habermani causes a forest to grow and turns his wife into a tender green shoot and himself into a small snake, winding himself around the plant. But the witch spots this subterfuge. Habermani pleads with her to let him go and achieve his heart's desire. The witch, having a sudden change of heart, recollects that she had him as a prospective son-in-law for seven years, and she lets the couple go after the snake kisses her lips. Habermani and his wife then change back into human form and journey home. Here Habermani restores the castle, and all is as it was before. Seeing his daughter returned and that Habermani is in fact a handsome son-in-law, the king has the couple remarried in a grand celebration that lasts for seven days and nights.

This summary cannot convey much of the original telling of this tale, from an unknown informant, but it highlights the many common motifs of hero and heroine lore, including the nonhuman disguise and magical powers of the hero, the quest of the (in this case unnamed) heroine, the schemes of the witch, the impossible tasks, and the shape-shifting contest between the hero and the witch, a magical battle that forms the core of many folk ballads and stories. Finally, of course, order is restored, and all returns to the agreeable state it was in until the princess upset the balance by breaking her promise not to reveal the true human nature of her snake-husband. Again, the breaking of a promise, frequently by a female, is a commonly encountered motif of traditional narratives and is often found in relation to nonhuman marriage.

The elaborate and colorful confabulations of this tale echo those of *The 1,001 Nights* and other Middle Eastern traditions, especially the cities constructed of various materials. Also reminiscent of Middle Eastern tale traditions are the journeys undertaken by the characters and the long periods of time that elapse between significant incidents.

Related entries: Fox Maiden, The; Loqman; Magicians; Shape-Shifters; Swan Maiden; Tam Lin; White Lady

References and further reading

Clarkson, A. and Cross, G. (eds.), New York: *World Folktales*, Charles Scribner's Sons, 1980.

Downing, C. (trans. and ed.), *Armenian Folk-Tales and Fables*, London: Oxford University Press, 1972, pp. 157–167.

Haitsi-Aibab

Haitsi-Aibab (Heitsi-eibib) is a Khoikoi (Hottentot) culture hero and shape-shifter. Born in supernatural circumstances, Haitsi-Aibab kills the monster Gã-gorib (Thrower-down) who dares people to throw stones at him. When they do, the stones fly back, killing the thrower and depositing the body in a nearby pit. Haitsi-Aibab goes to see the monster and to take the challenge but cleverly waits until Gã-gorib turns his eyes elsewhere, then throws a rock that hits him beneath the ear, killing him and sending him into his own corpse pit and making the people secure forever. Some versions of the story have a more elaborate combat between the hero and the monster, with Haitsi-Aibab falling into the monster's pit before succeeding in slaying him. Sometimes other Khoikoi heroes take the role of Haitsi-Aibab, including the trickster jackal or the deity Tsi Goab. Haitsi-Aibab is said to have died and been resurrected on various occasions, a belief that may explain the many cairns in South Africa that are identified as his grave.

Related entries: Culture Heroes; Dragon-Slayers; Giant-Killers; Ogres; Shape-Shifters

References and further reading

Arnott, K. (ed.), *African Myths and Legends*, London: Oxford University Press, 1962.

Carey, M., *Myths and Legends of Africa*, London: Paul Hamlyn, 1970.

Leach, M. (ed.), *Funk and Wagnall's Standard Dictionary of Folklore, Mythology, and Legend*, London: New English Library, 1975. Abridged one-volume edition of *Funk and Wagnall's Standard Dictionary of Folklore, Mythology, and Legend*, 2 vols., New York: Funk and Wagnall, 1972, p. 474.

Halfchick

A number of European, Indian, Hispanic, and West Indian folktales feature this legendary character, an underdeveloped chicken or a cock who has been cut up and magically put back together. He goes in search of the king to ask for some grain. Along the way, he befriends a river that accompanies him on his quest. The chicken has various encounters with wolves, robbers, or foxes, and ultimately the king tries to kill him by throwing him on the fire. At this point Halfchick releases the river that he keeps on his person, extinguishing the flames. The king is so impressed that he allows Halfchick to take the grain without paying for it.

A literary version of Spanish origin was popularized in English-speaking countries by Andrew Lang in his *Green Fairy Book* and is probably the most familiar version today. In this telling, against the advice of his mother, Halfchick goes to the king's court in search of a doctor to cure him. But Halfchick fails to help river, wind, and fire when asked, and, upon reaching the court, he is boiled down into a lump by the cooks. The remains are thrown away, and the wind blows Halfchick up to a tower, where he is transformed into a weathercock, forever at the mercy of sun, wind, and rain.

The differences between these versions highlight the almost infinite plot permutations of the folktale and the didactic possibilities of this basic form of narrative. The hero may or may not attain the object of the quest, depending upon his actions in pursuing it, and the outcome can be turned to point a variety of morals. The rather too neatly ironic ending of the Spanish version is an indicator of its literary provenance.

Related entries: Fairy Tale Heroes; Helpers
References and further reading

Creighton, H. (coll.), Taft, M. and Caplan, R. (eds.), *A Folk Tale Journey through the Maritimes*, Nova Scotia: Breton Books, 1993, pp. 138–139.

Klipple, M., *African Folktales with Foreign Analogues*, New York: Garland, 1992, p. 248.

Lee, F. H. (comp.), *Folk Tales of All Nations*, London: Harrap, 1931, pp. 907–909.

Massignon, G. (ed.), Hyland, J. (trans.), *Folktales of France*, Chicago: University of Chicago Press, 1968, pp. 181–185.

Halid

Cunning young beggar of Turkish tradition, whose cleverness brings him the reward of a royal appointment. This story combines elements of the trickster hero with the poor-boy-makes-good motif familiar in many other hero traditions, added to which is an element of wish fulfillment commonly associated with the fairy tale.

Halid and an accomplice hit upon a money-making scheme. Halid lies down in the streets of Istanbul pretending to be dead while his accomplice laments to passers-by how hard a fate it is to die just as one arrives at the fabulous city of Istanbul. This scheme works well for the two fraudsters until the grand vizier comes by and asks why there is a body lying on the ground. Informed that the body is that of a young man who died soon after arrival in the city, the vizier commands an imam, a holy man, to have the body buried at the vizier's expense. Halid, still playing dead, is carried to the mosque and prepared for burial. The imam takes off his cloak and turban while carrying out this task. When he has to leave Halid's body for a moment, the very-much-alive Halid seizes his chance. He dresses himself in the imam's clothes and rushes off to the grand vizier's palace. Here he asks the guards for an audience with the vizier. They tell him that he must first state his business, and he tells them that he is the imam instructed to bury the beggar boy and he has now come for the payment promised by the vizier. This news is conveyed to the vizier, who orders that the impostor be paid five gold pieces. With the money in hand, Halid disappears quickly.

Soon after, the real imam arrives and Halid's ruse is revealed. The vizier orders his chief detective to capture Halid within three days. Failure means the chief detective's death. On the second day, the detective is close behind Halid. With one of the gold pieces he received from the vizier, Halid bribes a druggist and some young men in his shop, saying that his uncle will soon enter the shop. The uncle, says Halid, is mentally unbalanced and will recover his sanity only if subjected to a cold shower. The boy then goes on his way. When the detective enters the shop, he is set upon by the young men and, despite his protestations, held down while the druggist thoroughly drenches him. Halid escapes again. The detective then goes to the vizier and asks to be put to death, as it would be preferable to the fruitless and humiliating task of capturing Halid. Both annoyed and, fortunately, amused, the vizier spares his chief detective and orders all entries to the city guarded night and day.

One night, the guards manage to capture Halid and tie him to a tree, planning to take him to the vizier the following morning. As dawn approaches, the guards are still asleep and Halid sees a hunchback beadle going to the nearby Armenian church to make it ready for the morning service. He calls the beadle over and says, "Beadle, look at my back and see if it is gone." "See if what is gone?" asks the beadle. "Why," says the cunning hero, "my hump." The beadle looks closely and confirms that there is no hump on Halid's back. "Thank you," he says, "now please release me." The beadle unties the ropes and asks Halid how he got rid of his hump. For a small sum, says Halid, and as long as the beadle has not eaten breakfast, he will tell the secret. The beadle agrees, and Halid ties him to the tree, telling him to repeat sixty-one times the words "Esserti, Pesserti, Serspeti." Halid then leaves as the beadle begins intoning these mysterious words. Soon the guards awake and are not pleased to find that they have lost their prisoner, who has been replaced by an apparently raving lunatic, or possibly by a very holy man. They can get nothing out of the man other than the "Esserti, Pesserti, Serspeti" refrain. Eventually, when the beadle has repeated "Es-

serti, Pesserti, Serspeti" sixty-one times, and with the help of the Armenian priest who identifies the beadle as a member of his church, the guards realize how cleverly Halid has tricked them and everyone else. They report all to the chief detective, who tells the grand vizier what has happened. Greatly impressed and amused, the vizier commands a full pardon for the clever beggar-boy on the condition that he confesses to the vizier. Halid does this, kissing the hem of the grand ruler's garment as custom demands. So impressed is the vizier that he immediately appoints Halid to be his chief detective. As in many other traditions, the unpromising but cunning young man is rewarded.

Related entries: Amala; Ashblower, Ivan; Assipattle; Boots; Fereyel; Ilu, Ana; Ivanko the Bear's Son; Jack and the Beanstalk; Jack the Giant-Killer; Kabadaluk; Kapsirko; Kihuo; Knowall, Doctor; Lucky Hans; Marendenboni; Muhammad; Muromets, Ilya; Puuhaara, Antti; Skorobogaty, Kuzma; Tabagnino the Hunchback; Tricksters; Whittington, Dick; Zab

References and further reading

Kúnos, I. (coll.), Bain, R. (trans.), *Turkish Fairy Tales and Folk Tales*, London: Lawrence and Bullen, 1896.

Rugoff, M. (ed.), *A Harvest of World Folk Tales*, New York: Viking Press, 1949, pp. 167–171. Excerpts from Ramsay, A. and McCullagh, F. (trans. and colls.), *Tales from Turkey*, London: Simpkin, Marshall, Hamilton, Kent, and Co., 1914.

Hall, Ben

Australian bushranger. Benjamin Hall (1837–1865) was arrested in 1862 on suspicion of having participated in a minor highway robbery led by another famous bushranger of the time, Frank Gardiner. After spending a month in jail, Hall was acquitted; he then returned home to find that his wife had deserted him, taking their baby son with her. The story goes that Hall then fell in with the Gardiner gang. He was arrested after the notorious Eugowra Rocks gold escort robbery, jailed for two months, and finally released for lack of evidence. On again returning to his property, Hall found that the police had burned his house and left his cattle to die, penned in the mustering yard. From this time, Hall turned to bushranging, joining the many other outlaws operating in this part of the colony. His activities were varied, including highway robbery, raiding wealthier properties, arson, attempted abduction, and raiding towns, including the regional center of Bathurst on October 3, 1863. Financially the raid was a failure, but the fact that these outlaws could attack a major town with impunity panicked the population and also the government of the colony.

In the many ballads and stories about Hall, he is portrayed as the victim of injustice, courteous to women, even-handed, and kind. He robs a squatter (wealthy landowner) but—a common motif in outlaw hero traditions—returns him five pounds to see him to the end of his journey.

The song "Bold Ben Hall," given here in the version gathered by the prominent folk music collector John Meredith from the singing of Mrs. Sally Sloane, contains almost all the motifs of the outlaw hero tradition and is perhaps the most comprehensive example of this tradition in song. A clear and unambiguous line of descent is drawn from the highwaymen heroes of the past, Turpin and Duval:

BOLD BEN HALL
Come all Australian sons with me for a
   hero has been slain,
And cowardly butchered in his sleep upon
   the Lachlan Plain;
Pray do not stay your seemly grief, but let a
   tear-drop fall,
For manly hearts shall always mourn the
   fate of bold Ben Hall.

No brand of Cain e'er stamped his brow,
   nor widows' curse did fall;
When tales are read the squatters dread the
   name of bold Ben Hall.
The records of this hero bold through
   Europe have been heard,
And formed a conversation between many
   an earl and lord.

Ever since the good old days of Dick Turpin
   and Duval,
Knights of the roads were outlaws bold,
   and so was bold Ben Hall.

He never robbed a needy man—his records
   best will show,
Staunch and loyal to his mates, and manly
   to the foe.

Until he left his trusty mates—the cause I
   ne'er did hear,
The bloodhounds of the law heard this and
   after him did steer.
They found his place of ambush and
   cautiously they crept,
Savagely they murdered him whilst the
   victim slept.

Yes, savagely they murdered him, the
   cowardly blue-coat imps,
Who were laid on to where he slept by
   informing peelers' pimps.
No more he'll mount the gallant steed, nor
   range the mountains high;
The widows' friend in poverty, bold Ben
   Hall, good-bye.

Like many such figures, Hall, despite his criminal acts, had the sympathy and the active support of many people who felt they were being poorly treated by the authorities. In this sense he is also a local hero of struggle. As this song makes clear, Hall was betrayed to police by a trusted accomplice and shot dead while he slept at a place called Goobang Creek.

Related entries: Christie, Francis; Donohoe, Jack; Heroes of Struggle; Hood, Robin; Johns, Joseph; Kelly, Edward; Local Heroes; Morgan, Daniel "Mad Dog"; Outlaws; Troy, Johnny; Ward, Frederick Wordsworth; Wild Colonial Boy

References and further reading
Bradshaw, J., The Only True Account of Ned Kelly, Frank Gardiner, Ben Hall, and Morgan, Sydney: n.p., 1911.
Meredith, J. and Anderson, H., Folk Songs of Australia, Melbourne: Sun, 1967, pp. 98–99.
Seal, G., The Outlaw Legend: A Cultural Tradition in Britain, America, and Australia, Melbourne: Cambridge University Press, 1996, pp. 128, 131–139.
Shiel, D. J., Ben Hall: Bushranger, St. Lucia, Qld.: University of Queensland Press, 1983.

Hansel

Brother of the heroine Gretel in the well-known fairy tale of "Hansel and Gretel." Hansel is responsible for laying the trail of white pebbles, or crumbs, that guide him and his sister out of the forest after their parents' first attempt to abandon them. On the next, successful abandonment, Hansel ends up in the witch's cage, being fattened up for her cookpot. Gretel eventually saves him and herself from this fate.

A survey of 2,000 people conducted in then West Germany in the mid-1980s suggested that the story of Hansel and Gretel was known by 94 percent of the population. It is likely that a similarly high percentage of people in other western countries would be familiar with this story of parental abandonment, evil menace, childhood bravery and cunning, and eventual family reunion.

Related entries: Fairy Tale Heroes; Fereyel; Gretel
References and further reading
Bettelheim, B., The Uses of Enchantment: The Meaning and Importance of Fairy Tales, New York: Knopf, 1976, 11, 14–17, 40, 61–62, 98, 114, 144, 146–147, 151–152, 159–166, 169–172, 179, 201, 205–206, 208, 214, 309.
Hallett, M. and Karasek, B. (eds.), Folk and Fairy Tales, Ontario: Broadview Press, 1996, pp. 100–105.
Meredith, J. and Anderson, H. (eds.), Folk Songs of Australia and the Men and Women Who Sang Them, Sydney: Ure Smith, 1967, pp. 98–99.
Mieder, W., "Grim Variations: From Fairy Tales to Modern Anti-Fairy Tales," in Tradition and Innovation in Folk Literature, Hanover, NH, and London: University Press of New England, 1987.

Hare

The hare appears in many traditions around the world. Among Native American groups, the hare may be called Great Hare or White Hare and have the attributes of a creator and culture hero. Some Native American groups identify the Great Hare with the trickster figure, Nanabozho. Known as Little Hare, this animal appears as the main trickster figure in East African tradition and among the Nigerian Jukun and Angass peoples and is generally found throughout African lore, including that of the African diaspora. Perhaps the most familiar hare figure in European lore is found in the well-known fable of the tortoise and the hare, in which the plodding persistence of the tortoise allows him to win the race over the faster

but overconfident hare, a story also told in many other traditions.

Related entries: Anansi; Nanabozho; Rabbit; Ramalingadu, Tenali; Spider; Tortoise; Tricksters
References and further reading
Abrahams, R., African Folktales, New York: Pantheon Books, 1983, pp. 74–75.
Adagala, K. and Kabira, W. (eds.), Kenyan Oral Narratives: A Selection, Nairobi: Heinemann, 1985, pp. 53–55, 61–65, 74–76.
Arnott, K. (ed.), African Myths and Legends, London: Oxford University Press, 1962, pp. 108–111.
Bennett, M., West African Trickster Tales, Oxford: Oxford University Press, 1994, pp. 47–59.
Dorson, R. (ed.), African Folklore, Bloomington: Indiana University Press, 1972, 1979, pp. 36, 38, 76–77, 95–97, 167, 172, 485–494.
Magel, E. (trans. and ed.), Folktales from the Gambia: Wolof Fictional Narratives, Boulder, CO: Three Continents Press, 1984, pp. 179–195.
Smith, A. McCall (coll. and ed.), Children of Wax: African Folk Tales, New York: Interlink Books, 1991 (1989), pp. 18–21, 49–52, 114–116.

Havelock the Dane

Legendary son of the Danish king Birabegn, Havelock is destined to be a great ruler and so becomes the object of a murder plot by his supposed protector, the evil Earl Godard. Havelock escapes to England, in some versions with the help of a fisherman named Grim. He grows up there in lowly and obscure circumstances as Grim's son, marries, and returns to Denmark to take up his rightful position, defeating the pretender Godard and rewarding his foster father, who, it is said, uses the wealth to found the town of Grimsby in Yorkshire, England.

More or less elaborate versions of this basic plot have been in existence since at least the twelfth century. There have been strong local traditions about Havelock and his helper, Grim, in a number of locations in England, including Lincoln and Grimsby. Many of these traditions are commemorated in the existence of stones named after Havelock; also, the ancient seal of the town of Grimsby includes the named figures of Grim and Havelock.

There are clear biblical parallels in the escape from infanticide, and echoes of Arthurian and other legends of great leaders. The occasional helper, Grim, provides an interesting local dimension to the story in its mythic account of the origins of the town of Grimsby.

Related entries: Arthur; Barbarossa; Culture Heroes; Helpers; Jesus; Local Heroes; National Heroes

References and further reading

Barber, R., *Myths and Legends of the British Isles*, Rochester, NY: Boydell Press, 1999, pp. 453–466.

Briggs, K. (ed.), *A Dictionary of British Folk-Tales in the English Language*, 4 vols., London: Routledge and Kegan Paul, 1970–1971.

Westwood, J., *Albion: A Guide to Legendary Britain*, London: Granada, 1985, pp. 232–235.

Hayk

See Warriors

Helpers

Heroes frequently have help from various sources in the pursuit of their quests and in overcoming the obstacles presented to them. The helper may be an older person, as in some versions of Havelock the Dane; a member of the opposite sex, as in Hansel and Gretel; a supernatural or otherwise invisible helper, such as the Fairy Godmother of Cinderella; or one or more magical objects, such as a cloak of invisibility or a magical sword, staff, or other device. The tambourine of Miriam, sister of Moses, for example, enables a rabbi to open the book that confers one Jew from each generation with the knowledge to make him advisor to the king of Babylon. Even a doll may be a helper, as in the Russian story of Vasilisa.

Birds, fish, rabbits, mice, dogs, cats, lions, or other animals are found as helpers of heroes and heroines in the folklores of many nations and cultures, a representative example being Bahram, son of a poor Persian couple who peels silkworm cocoons for their meager living. Bahram rescues a cat, a dog, and a snake from various forms of mistreatment, and these grateful animals help him through a long series of adventures, at the end of which he marries the beautiful princess.

Helpers are also common in the lore of historical figures. The late twelfth-century French minstrel Blondel de Nesle appears in legend as a companion of King Richard I of England (Richard the Lionheart). Blondel, in order to locate Richard after his capture and imprisonment, sings a song he and Richard had composed. He then frees the grateful monarch from his prison and spares the king's subjects from having to raise a massive ransom. Richard is then able to return to England and free his people from oppression.

A small but significant group of heroes are celebrated for their willingness and ability to heal wounds, either physical or supernatural. Healers are a species of helper, constants of hero legendry, and are found in most folk traditions. Healers may also be wise men or women and/or magicians who use their supernatural powers to effect not only cures but also supernatural or physical wounds and ailments. Examples of such healing helpers include the Eight Immortals, Loqman, Tawhaki, and Yao Wang.

Possible helper roles are many, though not unlimited, and helpers appear frequently in most folk hero traditions. So integral is the role of helper that, as the Russian folklorist Vladimir Propp once observed, "when a helper is absent from a tale, this quality is transferred to the hero." In other words, heroes, in the absence of helpers, themselves overcome whatever obstacles may have appeared. So common and important are helpers that all explanatory approaches to folktale devote considerable attention to them and their attributes.

While the helper is a generally positive element, helpers may sometimes have a negative aspect. For example, there are a number of tales in which a hero or heroine defeats a menacing helper by learning his or her name. Rumpelstiltskin is perhaps the most widely known of such "name of the helper" tales, though there are many similar traditions, such as those of Austria (Purzinegele), Hungary (Winterkölbl), and Britain (Tom Tit Tot in England, Whuppity Stoorie in Scotland, Peerifool in the Orkneys). Among the Slavic peoples there is also the tale of Kinkach Martinko.

Related entries: Androcles; Bai Suzhen; Baldpate; Berni, Cesarino Di; Eight Immortals, The; Fairy Godmother, The; Faithful Henry; Faithful John; Havelock the Dane; King of Ireland's Son, The; Little John; Loqman; Macdonald, Flora;

Magicians; Marian, Maid; Momotaro; Nicholas, Saint; Puss in Boots; Rasalu; Reynard the Fox; Sanykisar; Siitakuuyuk; Supparaka; Whittington, Dick; Wirreenun the Rainmaker; Woodencloak, Katie; Yao Wang; Zab

References and further reading

Mehdevi, A., *Persian Folk and Fairy Tales*, London: Chatto and Windus, 1966, pp. 6–21.

Propp, V. (trans. Scott, L.), *Morphology of the Folktale*, Austin: University of Texas Press, 1968, p. 83, passim.

Henry, Faithful

See Faithful Henry

Henry, John

Legendary African-American occupational hero of railroad workers. "John Henry was a steel-drivin' man," as most versions of his ballad put it. The core of John Henry's legend is his contest with a steam drill to lay railroad track, a theme encountered frequently in industrial lore. In John Henry's case, the man wins but dies of exhaustion from the effort.

As well as the contest, there are a number of other elements that appear in most versions of the John Henry legend, including his childhood prophecy of his own death while sitting on his mother's knee and his superhuman strength and matching sexual appetite. Roark Bradford used the figure of John Henry in his *John Henry* (1931), and the story has been frequently reworked in a variety of media. Many attempts to locate a historical "John Henry"—either on the Big Bend Tunnel in West Virginia, where most versions of the story are set, or elsewhere amid the hard-working, nineteenth-century, railroad-building communities—have had the same result as the search for Robin Hood. As well as an occupational hero, John Henry can be seen as a hero of struggle who resists technological threats to his livelihood.

Related entries: Bunyan, Paul; Crooked Mick; Fink, Mike; Heroes of Struggle; Hill, Joe; Jack-in-the-Green; Jones, Casey; Ludd, Ned; Mikula; Mrikanda; Occupational Heroes; Pecos Bill; Slater, Morris

References and further reading

Botkin, B. (ed.), *A Treasury of American Folklore: Stories,*
Ballads, and Traditions of the People, New York: Crown Publishers, 1944, pp. 230–40.

Cohen, N., *Long Steel Rail: The Railroad in American Folksong*, Champaign: University of Illinois, 1981, pp. 61–89.

Dorson, R., *Folklore and Fakelore: Essays toward a Discipline of Folk Studies*, Cambridge: Harvard University Press, 1976, pp. 283–290.

Dorson, R., "The Career of John Henry," in Dundes, A. (ed.), *Mother Wit from the Laughing Barrel: Readings in the Interpretation of Afro-American Folklore*, New York: Garland, 1981 (1973), pp. 568–577.

Green, A., "The Visual John Henry," in *Wobblies, Pile Butts, and Other Heroes*, Urbana and Chicago: University of Illinois Press, 1993, pp. 51–74.

Harris, R., "The Steel Drivin' Man," in Dundes, A. (ed.), *Mother Wit from the Laughing Barrel: Readings in the Interpretation of Afro-American Folklore*, New York: Garland, 1981 (1973), pp. 561–567.

Keats, E., *John Henry: An American Legend*, New York: Pantheon, 1965.

Lomax, J. and A. (colls. and comps.), *American Ballads and Folk Songs*, New York: Macmillan, 1934, p. 3.

Roberts, J., *From Trickster to Badman: The Black Folk Hero in Slavery and Freedom*, Philadelphia: University of Philadelphia Press, 1989.

Hereward the Wake

Historical hero of Anglo-Saxon resistance to the Norman conquest (1066) of what is now England. Hereward the Wake (i.e., Hereward the Wary) is known to have been a landholder under Edward the Confessor, though he appears to have left the country after 1062, returning in 1070 to sack Peterborough Abbey. When his allies surrendered to William the Conqueror, Hereward escaped to lead the fight against the Normans from the marshes of the Isle of Ely, where he sheltered other Anglo-Saxon resisters. These events rapidly gave rise to many legends about Hereward, which continued to evolve into a broad body of hero lore within less than fifty years of his death.

Hereward's legend is, basically, that he is the son of an Anglo-Saxon earl, lives a wild youth, is thus sent abroad, and then returns when he hears that his father's lands have been seized by the Normans. He continually foils the Norman attempts to storm the Isle of Ely. According to one story, also told of other heroes, including King

Alfred the Great, Hereward enters the enemy's camp in disguise, learns their plans, and foils their third and most persistent attempt to build a causeway into the marshes. However, the monks of Ely betray Hereward to the Normans, and he has to escape, eventually making peace with William. Ultimately Hereward is again betrayed by a churchman who is supposed to be guarding him while he sleeps. A large number of Normans break into the house where Hereward is sleeping. Like the great warrior he is, Hereward slays most of them, but he is finally brought down and killed when enemy reinforcements arrive and foully stab the hero in the back.

At one time, Hereward's legend was a powerful one in England. Ballads of his exploits were popular during the twelfth century, and his supposed wooden castle in the fens was a site of pilgrimage in the thirteenth century. From around this time, though, Hereward's status as an outlaw and resister gave way to that of Robin Hood. His legend survives mainly in literature—especially in Charles Kingsley's novel *Hereward the Wake* (1866)—and in the tourism industry.

Related entries: Bell, Adam; Clym of the Clough; Culture Heroes; Heroes of Struggle; Hood, Robin; National Heroes; Outlaws; Turpin, Richard; William of Cloudesly

References and further reading

Barber, R., *Myths and Legends of the British Isles*, Rochester, NY: Boydell Press, 1999, pp. 415–431.

Briggs, K. and Tongue, R. (eds.), *Folktales of England*, London: Routledge and Kegan Paul, 1965.

Westwood, J., *Albion: A Guide to Legendary Britain*, London: Granada, 1985, pp. 181–182.

Heroes of Struggle

Social, political, and economic conflict are the seedbeds for many folk hero traditions. These conflicts are often related to invasion and oppression of one people by another. The folklores of Serbs, Czechs, Slavs, and Russians are especially rich in such tradition as a result of historical circumstances. Many hero traditions from these cultures display a strong antagonism toward the ruling Turks, as in the Croatian legend of Ivo. Similar circumstances lie behind both the invasion of China by Mongols and the Muslim occupation of what is now India. Often slyly subversive tales were, and are, told in these countries about heroes who outsmart the representatives of the despised masters, providing a form of vicarious revenge and also acting as vehicles for the continuation of usually negative folk attitudes toward members of the occupying groups. William Tell is an example of a culture and national hero produced from such circumstances. Others are the Danish Holger Danske (Ogier the Dane), the Armenian warrior hero Hayk, and Daniel O'Connell, perhaps the most illustrious of a great number of such Irish figures. In the new world, colonization led to the development of indigenous folk heroes such as Cochise and Sitting Bull in the United States, and Yagan, Pemulway, and Jandamurra (Pigeon) in Australia.

Since the industrial revolution, struggles between the interests of capital and labor have generated heroes in many cultures. In the cases of agrarian and early-industrial insurrections, we find mythic figures like the English "Ned Ludd," "Captain Swing" of the English rural laborers' revolt of 1830, and the Welsh "Rebecca." In more complex industrial situations, we may also find occupational heroes standing up against the bosses and/or the company, expressing and channeling dissatisfaction and dissent. Joe Hill is one such figure from American labor lore. Helen Gurley Brown is another.

Outlaw heroes, too, are frequently generated in circumstances of struggle and social conflict. Robin Hood, William Brennan, Billy the Kid, and Ned Kelly, among others, have their heroic origins—deserved or otherwise—in the social and political turmoils of their times and places.

Heroes of struggle, apparently paradoxically, may be sometimes derived from figures who normally represent the forces of power and authority. The late eighteenth- and early nineteenth-century British folk image of "Boney"—Napoleon Bonaparte—as a potential liberator of the oppressed classes is one example. The English Lady Godiva, whose husband oppresses the people, is another.

A reenactment of "Song of Hiawatha" by Henry Wadsworth Longfellow, c. 1908 (Library of Congress)

Related entries: Alfred the Great; Armstrong, Johnnie; Bindieye, Jacky; Bonaparte, Napoleon; Brown, John; Culture Heroes; Dojrana; Ebbeson, Niels; Ero; Gearoidh, Iarla; Godiva, Lady; Hereward the Wake; Hill, Joe; Hood, Robin; Jolly Swagman, The; Karagiozis; Kraljevic, Marco; Lazar; Lu Zhishen; Ludd, Ned; Macdonald, Flora; Marian, Maid; McCaffery; Molo; National Heroes; Occupational Heroes; O'Connell, Daniel; O'Malley, Grace; Outlaws; Rákóczi; Rasalu; Rebecca; Santa Anna, General Antonio López de; Shine; Stig, Marsk; Stuart, Prince Charles Edward; Taylor, William; Tell, William

References and further reading

Brown, M. and Rosenberg, B. (eds.), *Encyclopedia of Folklore and Literature*, Santa Barbara: ABC-CLIO, 1998, pp. 367–368.

Darnton, R., *The Great Cat Massacre and Other Episodes in French Cultural History*, New York: Basic Books, 1984.

Green, A., *Only a Miner: Studies in Recorded Coal-Mining Songs*, Urbana: University of Illinois Press, 1972.

Hobsbawm, E. and Rudé, G., *Captain Swing*, London: Lawrence and Wishart, 1969.

Seal, G., "Tradition and Protest in Nineteenth Century England and Wales," *Folklore* 99, no. 2, 1988, pp. 146–169.

Hiawatha (Haiohwatha)

Probably legendary Onondaga (Iroquois) chief of the late sixteenth century, celebrated as shaman and culture hero for uniting into one political unit the usually warring Algonquin, Oneida, Mohawk, Cayuga, and Iroquois peoples. Henry Wadsworth Longfellow, inspired by Algonquin rather than Iroquois traditions, used the meter of the Finnish folk epic *The Kalevala* in his 1855 verse treatment of Hiawatha's story, *The Song of Hiawatha* (1855), bringing this Native American hero to the attention of a broader audience. There is a considerable body of indigenous legendry concerning Hiawatha and his political activities. One of these legends involves his attempts to persuade the magician and tyrant of the Onondaga tribe, Atatarho, to join the League of the Iroquois.

Atatarho is a ruthless and deadly enemy of the league who manages to wreck its attempts to come together. Eventually a meeting of all the chiefs is called near the lodge of the great chief, Hiawatha. All the people attend, but Atatarho, who has already caused the deaths of Hiawatha's wife and two of his three daughters, uses his evil magic to have the people trample the only surviving daughter to death. Grief-stricken, Hiawatha wanders into the wilderness, coming eventually to a lake that he causes the ducks to drain. In the bed of the lake, he finds many colored shells, which he strings in patterns and calls wampum. He travels on until he comes to the cabin of Dekanawida, another Iroquois hero, who offers him hospitality. Hiawatha tells his host his tale of woe and of the madness of Atatarho, and Dekanawida calls the chiefs together and tells them the situation. The chiefs decide to go to Atatarho's home with wampum to heal his sickness. Hiawatha shows them his colored wampum, which they immediately adopt, as it is more beautiful and powerful than the common shells they have been using. They decide that the wampum will always be used in their councils and that it will endure for all time.

Two spies are then sent to Atatarho's place. These men transform into crows and fly over the forest until they spot the rising smoke of Atatarho's lodge. They enter the lodge and find Atatarho with serpents for hair, turtle claws for hands, and feet like bear's claws. Hastily the two spies retreat from the appalling sight and hurry back to the chiefs. They report that Atatarho is a demon, no longer human. The chiefs then travel to Atatarho's house, singing the Six Sacred Songs along the way. When they arrive they invite the local chiefs to come to their fire, explaining their purpose in coming. Then the newcomers begin singing the Six Sacred Songs again. When they finish, they go to Atatarho's lodge to heal him, but when they enter they are as horrified as the spies were. But Dekanawida reminds them that they are chiefs and that they should continue singing and open their wampum. The horrific wizard responds positively to the singing, and Dekanawida is able to sing three more songs to him and to give him a string of wampum. By these means the chiefs heal Atatarho's mind, body, and spirit and make him a natural man again, and he becomes a good leader of his people, ultimately through Hiawatha's discovery of the powerful wampum.

Related entries: Frontier Heroes; Nanabozho; Väinämöinen; Wise Men and Women

References and further reading
Clark, E., *Indian Legends of Canada,* Toronto: McClelland and Stewart, 1960, pp. 138–141.
Thompson, S. (ed.), *Tales of the North American Indians,* Bloomington: Indiana University Press, 1929.

Hill, Joe

A hero of struggle, the Swedish-American Joe Hill (1879–1915) was a noted songwriter and member of the Industrial Workers of the World (IWW), or the "Wobblies," a once powerful industrial trade union centered in the United States. Hill's real name was Joel Hagglund. He was raised in Sweden in humble circumstances and in 1902 migrated to the United States of America accompanied by his brother. He changed his name to Joseph Hillstrom and eventually became widely known in the labor movement as "Joe Hill." He worked at a variety of menial and low-paid jobs, joining the IWW in 1910. The following year he wrote "Casey Jones—the Union Scab," a song that parodied the popular hit of two years earlier and that supported strikers on the South Pacific Line. According to the version of the song published by the IWW, and in direct contradiction of the heroic image of Jones projected in the earlier song, the engineer who had died in the wreck of the Cannonball Express in 1900 had been a scab, a strikebreaker. Jones had betrayed his fellow workers by taking out the train on its last fatal run knowing that it was improperly maintained:

The workers on the S. P. Line
To strike sent out a call;
But Casey Jones the Engineer,
He wouldn't strike at all.
His boiler it was leaking,
And its drivers on the bum,
And his engine and its bearings,
They were all out of plumb.

Hill subsequently became well known as a labor songwriter, but in 1914 he was convicted of murder in Salt Lake City, Utah. The circumstances of the killing and Hill's role in it were ambiguous, but the trial was conducted in a highly charged political atmosphere in which

Hill's activities for the militant IWW probably prejudiced his case. Despite large-scale national protest, including two pleas for clemency from President Woodrow Wilson, Hill was executed by firing squad in November 1915, becoming a working-class martyr. Many of Joe Hill's songs, such as "The Preacher and the Slave" and "Stung Right"—mostly parodies of popular songs of the period and of well-known hymn tunes—are still sung today, and some have passed into oral tradition in other countries where the IWW was once influential.

Joe Hill is a good example of a historical figure who becomes a hero to a well-defined social or cultural group, in his case the radical American left and its international affiliates. He is little remembered outside such circles today.

Related entries: Heroes of Struggle; Jones, Casey; Occupational Heroes
References and further reading
Foner, S. (comp. and ed.), *The Letters of Joe Hill*, New York: Oak Publications, 1965, pp. 7–11, 88–95.
Green, A., "Singing Joe Hill," in *Wobblies, Pile Butts, and Other Heroes*, Urbana and Chicago: University of Illinois Press, 1993, pp. 51–74.
Greenway, J. (ed.), *Folklore of the Great West*, Palo Alto, CA: American West Publishing Company, 1969, pp. 310–327.
Industrial Workers of the World, *Songs to Fan the Flames of Discontent*, Chicago: Industrial Workers of the World, 1912 (and subsequent editions).
Reuss, R., "The Ballad of Joe Hill Revisited," *Western Folklore* 26, 1967, pp. 187–188.
Smith, G., *Joe Hill*, Salt Lake City: University of Utah Press, 1969.

Hind Horn

See Horn, Hind

Hlakanyana

Trickster hero of African traditions who takes various forms, sometimes animal and sometimes human. In Zulu tradition, Hlakanyana is often credited with deeds similar to those told of Hare. In Xhosa folklore, Hlakanyana may take either a male or female form. He/she has a tail like the Devil and a capacity for evil magic and deadly deception.

One tale of Hlakanyana in female form has her deceiving an old woman, her grandmother, into allowing herself to be cooked alive. Hlakanyana arrives at her grandmother's house and suggests that they play at cooking each other. The grandmother agrees, fills a pot, lights the fire, and when the water is warm Hlakanyana gets in. After a while she asks to be taken out of the pot, as it is getting too hot for her. Grandmother takes her out, and then it is her turn to get into the pot. Soon she, too, calls out to be taken from the pot, as it was too hot, but Hlakanyana refuses. Again the grandmother cries out, and again Hlakanyana refuses. Then the grandmother dies.

Hlakanyana puts her into a dish, and when the grandmother's two sons return from hunting they find Hlakanyana wearing the old woman's clothes. She then serves out the meat, and they innocently eat it up, relishing the cannibalistic meal. Hlakanyana goes outside and jeers at the men for eating their own mother. The sons then pursue Hlakanyana with sticks. Hlakanyana runs to a river, where she turns herself into a black rock. The sons arrive soon after but are unable to find the trickster. One son picks up the rock and throws it across the river, saying that if he could find Hlakanyana, he would do the same thing to her. On the other side of the river, Hlakanyana turns herself back into human form, continuing to jeer at the men for eating their mother.

She runs off again and comes to a house where some men are thatching the roof. Hlakanyana goes inside and stitches the foot of the man on the roof to the thatch. Then a huge storm kills the man. Hlakanyana runs on again, coming to another house, where she gets married. One day someone says that since Hlakanyana has been married all the milk in the house has been disappearing; thus a contest is called. A deep hole is dug and filled with milk, and all the people living in the house have to jump across the hole. When it comes to Hlakanyana's turn, she holds back. "Jump," they say, but Hlakanyana will not, saying she is afraid. They continue to call to her to jump, and when she does her devil's tail dips into the milk and the people know who she really is. They beat her and throw her to the dogs, who kill her, thus punishing her for causing the taboo on cannibalism to be broken.

Related entries: Anansi; Hare; Tricksters
References and further reading
Dorson, R. (ed.), *Folktales Told around the World*, Chicago: University of Chicago Press, 1975, pp. 403–404.
Knappert, J., *Myths and Legends of Botswana, Lesotho, and Swaziland*, Leiden: Brill, 1985, pp. 219–222.
Werner, A., *Myths and Legends of the Bantu*, London: Harrap, 1933, pp. 155–171.

Hodja, The

Nasra-ed-Din Hodja, popularly known as "the Hodja," is a familiar trickster hero of Turkish and other Middle- and Near-Eastern countries, who also appears in Yugoslavian folklore, presumably spread to that culture through Turkish invasion and occupation. There exists in Turkey a tombstone to the Hodja, dated to 1284, though, as with many folk heroes, there is little evidence that such a person ever existed.

Many Hodja tales involve proverbial wisdom of the one-upmanship type, as in the story of the borrowed cooking implements, also told of tricksters in other cultures, including the Syrian Djuha. According to the tale, the Hodja needs a cauldron to do some cooking. Not owning one, he borrows one from his neighbor. This cauldron is exactly what the Hodja wants, and he is reluctant to return it to his neighbor. Instead the Hodja takes his neighbor a much smaller cauldron that looks similar to the one he had borrowed. The neighbor is not pleased, but the Hodja tells him that the larger cauldron gave birth to this smaller one and that it is not well enough to be given back yet. Scratching his head, the neighbor nevertheless accepts what the Hodja tells him and gives the smaller cauldron to his wife, who is not pleased. She chastises her husband for being such a fool, but he tells her to be quiet and wait for a few days.

Sure enough, in a few days, the Hodja finishes with the cauldron that he borrowed originally and returns it to his neighbor, saying that it has fully recovered from the strain of giving birth. The husband is vindicated, and his wife is pleased that they now have not only two caul-

drons but a magic cauldron that can apparently give birth to more little cauldrons. They are pleased with the Hodja for bringing this to their attention and tell everyone about it.

Some time later the Hodja needs to borrow the cauldron again. The neighbor is overjoyed. The Hodja might make it give birth to yet another baby cauldron. The neighbor even carries the quite heavy copper pot over to the Hodja's house. Days, and then more days, go by, but the neighbor sees no sign of the cauldron, far less of any baby cauldrons. Eventually, the neighbor goes to see the Hodja and asks him when he intends to return the cauldron.

The Hodja is surprised. Has his neighbor not heard the news? The cauldron died. At hearing this absurdity, even the foolish neighbor realizes that he has been tricked. He begins to yell, attracting a large crowd to the Hodja's house. But the Hodja is unmoved. "The cauldron is dead," he says. "You must return home and give the bad news to the baby cauldron, for anything that is able to give birth to young can also die." The crowd agrees with the Hodja, nodding their heads and saying that he speaks truly. The neighbor can do nothing more than return home to his smaller pot and to the anger of his wife and family.

In another story, the Hodja is shown in the role of a holy man. He asks his congregation if what he is about to say is already known to them. The congregation replies as one that they did not know. The Hodja says that an unknown subject is of no use to them or to him, and he then departs. The next week, facing an even larger congregation anxious to hear whatever it is that the Hodja has to say, he asks the same question. The answer comes, as if prearranged: "Yes, Hodja, we do know." "If that is the case," says the Hodja, "there is no need for you or me to waste our time." And with that he departs again. The following Friday, now with a vast congregation, the Hodja asks again if they know what he is going to say. This time, half the congregation says they do know, while the other half says they do not. Impressed, the Hodja responds: "If the half that knows what I am going to say would tell the other half what it is, I would be very thankful, for it will not be necessary for me to say anything at all." He then steps down and leaves the mosque.

This "fooling" tale is told in many other traditions, usually with a trickster in the role of the preacher or teacher. In common with many trickster stories, its purpose is both to undercut the possible pomposities of religious or other leaders and to indicate that those who mindlessly follow the precepts of such figures are likely to be misled. However, as reference to the numerous other trickster traditions and related entries in this encyclopedia illustrate, the trickster himself is just as likely to be a pompous ass in one or more of his stories. With tricksters, you just never know.

Related entries: Abunuwas; Anansi; *Arabian Nights, The*; Ero; Eulenspiegel, Till; Kabajan; Tricksters; Urdemalas, Pedro de

References and further reading
Barnham, H. (trans.), *The Khoja: Tales of Nasr-ed-Din*, New York: D. Appleton and Co., 1924.
Christen, K., *Clowns and Tricksters: An Encyclopedia of Tradition and Culture*, Santa Barbara: ABC-CLIO, 1998, pp. 153–154.
Curcija-Prodanovic, N. (comp.), *Yugoslav Folk-Tales*, Oxford: Oxford University Press, 1957, pp. 18–19.
Kúnos, I. (coll.), Bain, R. (trans.), *Turkish Fairy Tales and Folk Tales*, London: Lawrence and Bullen, 1896.

Hood, Robin

English outlaw hero and archer who first appears in Langland's *Piers Plowman* (c. 1377). This source is not explicit on Robin's status as a robber of the rich, but by the first half of the following century, his persona as a noble robber and friend of the poor and oppressed is commonplace. The means of Robin Hood's early celebration are a number of early ballads and the major work known as *A Mery Geste of Robyn Hoode*. Although Robin is a commoner in these works (he is not elevated to the aristocracy until the seventeenth century), the world of the *Geste* is that of the rich and powerful. The Sheriff of Nottingham appears in his role of archvillain. There are knights, abbots, nobles, and notables, as well as the king himself. In the end, Robin helps the king and is received into his service. But after a while the expense and

Robin's nostalgia for the greenwood compel him to ask the king for permission to visit his old haunts again. The king grants him a week. Robin returns to the forest, rejoins his band, and his week's holiday extends to twenty-two years, during which time he refuses to accept the monarch's authority. Finally he is betrayed to death by the prioress and Sir Roger. As given by Child, the various versions of the *Geste* present Robin as a heroic figure and usually conclude unequivocally with the verse:

Cryst haue mercy on his soule,
That dyed on the rode!
For he was a good outlaw,
And dyde pore men moch god.

The *Geste* is a literary work of some sophistication, either compiled from existing ballads or using the same materials on which these ballads may have been based. The early ballads of the fifteenth century are certainly less literary (many perhaps being in oral circulation before their capture in print) and also tend to be more proletarian in orientation. While Robin has the scoundrelly but still relatively high-born Sheriff of Nottingham to outwit and corrupt members of the clergy to deal with, he also has encounters with commoners, as in "Robin Hood and the Potter." Here the potter bests Robin, after which Robin symbolically exchanges clothes with him and, in this trickster disguise, goes off to Nottingham for further adventures with the sheriff and, as it turns out, his wife. This story is similar in some ways to the later "Robin Hood and the Pedlar," in which a peddler defeats Robin and Little John in a fight and is incorporated into the "band of merry men." In this ballad, Robin is still a leader of ordinary men, his heroic status dependent on his bravery, courteousness, fairness, and skill. The greenwood hero of the ballads and the *Geste*, then, despite his increasing aristocratic connections, is still quite a way removed from the eighteenth-century identification of Robin Hood as the "Earl of Huntingdon," Robert Fitzooth, supposedly and conveniently descended from both Norman and Saxon forbears. This latter-day fabrication, derived from sixteenth-

and seventeenth-century suggestions that the outlaw was a noble down on his luck, influenced much subsequent thinking about Robin as a wronged aristocrat.

Regardless of the historicity of Robin Hood, his folkloric image is that of the outlaw hero, and he is clearly viewed in such terms from an early period. The courteous archer in Lincoln green, the fabric he allegedly wore, is therefore the archetype against which all subsequent anglophone outlaw heroes are measured. That this is so is made elegantly clear in F. J. Child's account and editing of the Robin Hood ballads, where he presents evidence that these songs celebrating the real or mythical outlaw's exploits were widely sung in England, and beyond, around 1400 and, given the *Piers Plowman* reference, almost certainly earlier. While, according to Child's view, the later balladic treatments of this figure "debase" it in various ways, this "debasement" is in fact a sharpening and refining of the image of Robin Hood. Whereas he is certainly a friend of the poor in the *Geste* and, presumably, in the earlier traditions, by the time of a seventeenth-century treatment titled "The True Tale of Robin Hood" (1632), he is a full-fledged outlaw hero and definitely a morally upright friend of the poor—"all poore men pray for him, / And wish he well might spede." He helps distressed travelers on the road, assists widows and orphans, protects women, generally operates against the established power and corruption of the church, and robs the rich, particularly those who "did the poore oppresse." He does not harm the humble workers nor any man "that him invaded not." He is finally betrayed to death by "a faithlesse fryer."

Much time and learned effort has been devoted to the study of this character—sometimes with the aim of discovering his true identity, sometimes with an interest in the more general mythic significance of the green archer. The conclusions of some research are that Robin remains a figure of uncertain historicity but is a cultural symbol of considerable potency in the English-speaking world. Dobson and Taylor's revised and reissued *Rymes of Robin Hood* discusses Robin Hood place-names, lin-

guistic terms, films, and other evidence of the enduring popularity of the outlaw, as well as a representative selection of mostly literary Robin Hood ballads. Stephen Knight has provided a comprehensive overview of this hero's numerous roles in a variety of cultural forms, old and new. In a comprehensive and careful study, *Robin Hood: A Complete Study of the English Outlaw*, Knight traced the outlaw's career in literature, film, and popular culture up to the present. He showed how the Robin Hood mythology has undergone changes related to social, economic, and ideological pressures. Robin's original folkloric presence is in legends, place-names, proverbs, drama, and, presumably, ballads as a symbolic figure of resistance to authority and of communal solidarity. While these notions have persisted, they have been overlaid and extended by narrative treatments that variously gentrify, politicize, nationalize, and romanticize the hero. At first Robin Hood is a forest fugitive, a common figure in the twelfth and thirteenth centuries. In this guise, Robin is a shadowy opponent of authority and law. These resistant elements, consistent with the image of the outlaw hero, are developed and refined in the ballads of the fourteenth century and after, and also in the widespread Robin Hood plays and games first recorded in the early fifteenth century (at Exeter, 1426–1427). These performances were closely associated with the folk calendar and with traditional activities, including raising funds, sports, competitions, and other festive activities. Records of Robin Hood plays, and of official concern about them, increase throughout the 1500s. By around 1600, most of these plays had quietly faded away or been actively suppressed through a combination of growing Puritanism and civic alarm.

As well as proving his virility in past as well as present popular and high culture, Robin Hood has persisted to some extent in folk song. A few oral versions of Robin Hood ballads were retrieved by English folk song collector Alfred Williams early in the twentieth century and provide evidence, if in somewhat fragmentary form, of the persistence of Robin Hood's image in British tradition. It seems from these partial texts, from Williams's observations on them, and from the age of their singers that Robin Hood may have been in decline as a central figure of rural English folk song by the early part of the twentieth century. As A. L. Lloyd pointed out in *Folksong in England*, only seven or so of the nearly forty Robin Hood ballads noted by Child in the 1880s had been collected in British oral tradition, and a further three in America. These ballads turn up in various states of completeness in the collections of the late and early nineteenth centuries, usually derived from nineteenth-century broadside versions, especially those printed by Such and Catnach. It seems fair to say from the available evidence that while Robin Hood retained a definite niche in oral tradition, he can hardly be said to be a major figure of British, American, or any other English-language folk song.

However, the catalogues of broadside printers of the 1830s show that Robin Hood lived on in printed ballads, and it is in media, literary, and artistic representations that Robin Hood is most alive today. Numerous film versions of Robin Hood continue a Hollywood tradition of regularly celebrating the English outlaw, a tradition dating from 1909 with the film *Robin Hood and His Merry Men* and involving well over thirty productions to date. The outlaw has also had an enduring career in the theater, in dramatic, comic, and musical forms, in a still-remembered television series of the 1950s and 1960s. There are three tourist theme parks and recreations of the Robin Hood myth in and around Nottingham. Robin Hood remains the English-language archetype of the outlaw hero.

A substantial number of other folk heroes—though few heroines—are skilled with bow and arrow. William Tell is perhaps the best known of a number of heroes who shoot apples or other objects from the head of someone close to them, either a family member, close companion, or a lover. Other heroes carry out legendary feats involving bow and arrow, including the Russian Dunai Ivanovich and the Japanese Yuriwaka. Archers generally use their skills to avert catastrophe of some kind, as in the case of the Chinese Hou Yi and his Mongolian counterpart, Erkhii Mergen. Closely related

to archers are spear-throwers, such as the Torres Strait Island hero, Kwoiam. The ability to use such missiles with skill and accuracy is not in itself heroic but, as with Robin Hood, forms a defining element of the archer hero's legendry.

Related entries: Bell, Adam; Clym of the Clough; Geordie; Hereward the Wake; Heroes of Struggle; Kelly, Edward; Outlaws; Tell, William; Turpin, Richard; William of Cloudesly

References and further reading
Chappell, W., *Popular Music of the Olden Time*, 2 vols., New York: Dover Publications, 1965 (1859), pp. 387–400.

Child, F. J., *The English and Scottish Popular Ballads*, 5 vols., New York: Dover, 1965 (1882–1898), vol. 3, pp. 1–132.

Dobson, R. B. and Taylor, J., *Rymes of Robin Hood: An Introduction to the English Outlaw*, 2d. rev. ed. Gloucester: Allan Sutton, 1989 (1976).

Keen, M., *The Outlaws of Medieval Legend*, London: Routledge and Kegan Paul, 1961.

Knight, S., *Robin Hood: A Complete Study of the English Outlaw*, Oxford: Blackwell, 1994.

Lloyd, A., *Folksong in England*, New York: International Publishers, 1970 (1967), pp. 137, 143–145.

Maddicott, J. R., "The Birth and Setting of the Ballads of Robin Hood," *English Historical Review* 93, 1978.

Page, D., *Folktales in Homer's Odyssey*, Cambridge: Harvard University Press, 1973, pp. 104–113.

Purslow, F. (ed.), *Marrow Bones: English Folk Songs from the Hammond and Gardiner Mss*, London: EFDS Publications, 1965, p. 97.

Vaughan Williams, R. and Lloyd, A. (eds.), *The Penguin Book of English Folk Songs*, Harmondsworth, Middlesex: Penguin, 1959, esp. pp. 88–89 for "Robin Hood and the Pedlar."

Williams, A., *Folk Songs of the Upper Thames*, London: Duckworth & Co., 1923, pp. 237, 296.

Hooper, Slappy
See Occupational Heroes

Horn, Hind
The story of Hind Horn, also known as "King Horn" and "Child Horn," seems to derive from exclusively English-language sources, though it has many European parallels. It was first written down in the early thirteenth century as a lengthy romance in which Horn is born of royal parents, grows up with twelve faithful

companions, and has various adventures, including slaying a giant and falling in love with the beautiful Princess Rymenhilde. In the later ballad versions of the story, much of the detail of the earlier *Geste* is pared away and the action concentrates on the seven-year attempt of the hero (now known as Hind Horn) to rescue his beloved from an unhappy union with a foreign lord. Even though he comes to her disguised as a beggar, she recognizes Horn by a ring she had given him many years before, a commonplace recognition device of ballads and folktales. She flees with him, usually to become his wife, or at least to share his bed. Versions of the ballad are known in most European cultures, especially in Scandinavia, and elements of the same story are common in folktales, including the Russian story of Dobrynya Nikitich and Nastasya.

Related entries: Giant-Killers; Moringer, Noble; Nastasya, Princess; Nikitich, Dobrynya; Popovich, Aloisha

References and further reading

Barber, R., *Myths and Legends of the British Isles*, Rochester, NY: Boydell Press, 1999, pp. 441–452.

Child, F. J., *The English and Scottish Popular Ballads*, 5 vols., New York: Dover, 1965 (1882–1898), vol. 1, pp. 187–208, no. 17.

Lloyd, A., *Folksong in England*, New York: International Publishers, 1970 (1967), pp. 162, 198.

Hou Yi

Chinese immortal and archer hero who is asked by the emperor of heaven to shoot down ten suns that are scorching the country, killing the crops, encouraging plagues of snakes and dangerous animals, and making it difficult for the earthly emperor, the legendary Yao, to maintain order. The emperor of heaven gives Hou Yi a red bow and white arrows, with which he travels to earth accompanied by his wife, the beautiful Cheng'er. Hou Yi is greeted as a champion by the people and strides to the center of the square, where he fires his arrows at the suns. He is about to shoot the tenth sun down when Yao stops him, saying that one sun might be useful. Hou Yi also clears the country of snakes and wild beasts, becoming a hero to the people. This part of the legend is similar to the Mongolian story of Erkhii Mergen.

However, Hou Yi's success makes the other immortals in heaven jealous, and they poison the emperor of heaven against him. Hou Yi and Cheng'er are expelled from heaven and must survive by hunting on earth. Hou Yi feels ashamed that his beautiful wife has to endure the life of a mortal because of his fall from grace. He obtains an elixir of immortality, hoping that they can both live together on earth forever. Unfortunately, Cheng'er is not happy with the prospect of living forever the hard life of a mortal. When Hou Yi is away hunting, she swallows all the powerful elixir and flies to the moon, where, according to the Tang Dynasty poet Li Shangyin (c. 813–858), quoted from Faurot:

> Cheng'er, remorseful for having stolen the elixir
> Nightly pines amid the vast sea of the blue sky.

Dating from at least the fourth century B.C., the story of Hou Yi and Cheng'er is said to be known to all Chinese people.

Related entries: Ahay; Bell, Adam; Clym of the Clough; Hood, Robin; Ivanovich, Dunai; Mergen, Erkhii; Patrick, Saint; Tametomo; Tell, William; Warriors; William of Cloudesly; Yuriwaka

References and further reading

Faurot, J. (ed.), *Asian-Pacific Folktales and Legends*, New York: Simon and Schuster, 1995, pp. 76–78.

Li, N., *Old Tales of China*, Singapore: Graham Brash, 1983 (1981), pp. 34–35.

Osers, E. (trans.), *Chinese Folktales*, London: Bell and Sons, 1971. First published in German as Wilhelm, R. (trans.), *Chinesische Märchen*, 1958.

I

Ilu, Ana

Ana Ilu is an orphan boy, legendary hero of the To-Raja people of Celebes-Sulawesi, now part of Indonesia. Ana Ilu's adoptive father is jealous of the boy, and when he finds his own fishing net empty, he tries to steal the fruits of Ana's fishing. But whenever he takes anything from Ana's net, it is magically replaced by something even more valuable. Eventually, increasingly irritated, the adoptive father throws Ana's net into a fig tree. On climbing the tree to retrieve his net, Ana discovers a beautiful shining girl who lives in the sun and has fallen in love with him. She cannot live with him but gives him various magic gifts, including a ring and a basket. The ring saves his life when his wicked stepfather tries to kill him, and the basket provides a never-ending supply of fish and rice with which Ana Ilu is able to feed many of his people. In gratitude they make him king.

This tale features a number of common motifs, including the magical helper and the utensil that provides a never-ending supply of food. The obstacles thrown in the way of the young man achieving his amorous aspirations are also frequently the motivations for heroism and are a structural feature of most folk and fairy tales.

Related entries: Bernèz; Fairy Tale Heroes; Helpers
References and further reading
Knappert, J., *Myths and Legends of Indonesia*, Singapore: Heinnemann, 1977, pp. 91–192.
Terada, A., *The Magic Crocodile and Other Folktales from Indonesia*, Honolulu: University of Hawaii Press, 1994.

Isabel, Lady

Legendary heroine of the English-language version of a widespread European ballad usually titled "Lady Isabel and the Elf-Knight." Lady Isabel is lured away from her home by an elf-knight who plans to murder her along with the previous seven (the exact number varies) king's daughters he has done away with. Lady Isabel foils his plans by various means in different versions, sometimes by drowning him, sometimes by stroking him to sleep. In most versions, she kills the elf-knight, generally interpreted as an incarnation of primal evil, and escapes. In some versions of the ballad, the heroine has other names, such as May Colvin, and the elf-knight may appear as an evil mortal rather than as an otherworldly being. In all cases, however, the knight is evil and the heroine good and resourceful.

Versions of this ballad narrative, which is at least three centuries old, have been found in most European traditions, some of which also include folktale versions of the same story. The tradition continued in nonsupernatural broadside ballads in which young women outwit a man intent on murdering them.

Related entries: Fatima; Scheherazade; Tam Lin; Thomas the Rhymer
References and further reading
Belden, H. (ed.), *Ballads and Songs Collected by the Missouri Folklore Society*, University of Missouri Studies 15, no. 1, 1940, pp. 5–16.
Briggs, K., *The Fairies in Tradition and Literature*, London: Routledge and Kegan Paul, 1967.
Child, F. J., *The English and Scottish Popular Ballads*, 5 vols., New York: Dover, 1965 (1882–1898), vol. 1, pp. 22–62, 485–489, no. 4.

Italapas

See Culture Heroes

Ivan the Mare's Son

One of three brothers, all named Ivan, in the Siberian Tungus people's tradition in which the three brothers, Ivan the Mare's Son, Ivan the

Sun's Son, and Ivan the Moon's Sun, battle a giant serpent and its demon army threatening them and their wives. Eventually the serpent kills the three Ivans and makes off into its underground lair with Marfida, Ivan's wife, and the other two women. Ivan's mother brings the three heroes back to life. Ivan is lowered into the serpent's lair in the underworld and, with Marfida's help, kills the serpent while it sleeps. Ivan then helps the women escape, his two brothers pulling them out of the underworld on ropes.

When they have rescued the three wives, the two brothers turn to treachery, cut the rope, and leave Ivan stranded in the underworld. Here he dies, only to be found again by his mother who restores him to life as before and helps him find his two brothers, their wives, and Marfida, who is being punished for remaining faithful to Ivan. He picks Marfida up, places her on his shoulders, and kills the two brothers. Then, with the magical help of three heron skins he has previously obtained, Ivan the Mare's Son makes a pair of wings with which he and the three wives fly to their homeland, ending their lives in peace and happiness.

Related entries: Avdotya; Dragon-Slayers; Potyk, Mikhail

References and further reading

Afanas'ev, A. (comp.), Guterman, N. (trans.), *Russian Fairy Tales*, New York: Pantheon Books, 1945.
Dixon-Kennedy, M., *European Myth and Legend*, London: Blandford, 1997, pp. 127–129.
Elstob, E. and Barber, R. (trans.), *Russian Folktales*, London: Bell and Sons, 1971. First published as Von Lowis of Menar, A. (trans.) and Olesch, R. (ed.), *Russische Volksmärchen*, 1959.

Ivanko the Bear's Son

Half-man, half-bear hero of Russian tradition. The wife of a wealthy farmer falls into the lair of a bear and is kept there, eventually giving birth to a child who is a man from the waist up and a bear from the waist down. When Ivanko grows up he wants to go to the people of his mother, and together they escape while the bear is out hunting. They return to the woman's farmer husband, and she tells him all

that has happened. He receives Ivanko as a son and asks him to kill a sheep for a homecoming meal. Ivanko asks which sheep he should kill, and his father says, "The first one that looks at you." So Ivanko goes into the yard with the knife, and all the sheep turn their head at once to look at him. He kills them all and skins them, proudly returning to his mother and the farmer. When he discovers that Ivanko has butchered his entire flock, the farmer is furious, saying, "I ordered you to kill one sheep." But Ivanko points out that his father had told him to kill the first one that looked at him, and as they had all looked at him at once, he had done as he was asked.

Thinking that his adoptive son is a sly fellow, the farmer then asks him to guard the storehouse door from the robbers and dogs who often came in the night. Ivanko stands guard over the door until it begins to rain; then he takes the door off its hinges and goes inside. In the morning, the farmer discovers the storehouse door off its hinges and, of course, all the contents of the storehouse stolen. He admonishes Ivanko severely. But Ivanko says that he did as he was told: he stood guard over the storehouse door, and the thieves had not stolen that. Realizing that Ivanko is not sly but an idiot, the farmer plots to get rid of him. He hits upon the idea of sending him down to the lake where the goblins live, in the hope that they will drag him down to a watery grave.

As Ivanko sits by the shore in the pointless task of winding a rope out of sand, as instructed by the farmer, a little goblin jumps out of the water and asks him what he is doing. Ivanko tells him that he is winding a rope to stir up the waters of the lake in order to annoy the goblins because they do not pay rent to the farmer. The goblin disappears beneath the water to consult with his grandfather but soon returns saying that his grandfather declares that if Ivanko can beat the goblin in a race, the goblins will pay rent. However, if Ivanko loses the race, he will be dragged into the lake and drowned. Ivanko wins this first challenge by default, cleverly tricking the goblin into thinking that Ivanko can run faster than a hare. But the goblin returns with his grandfather's iron crutch. He says that the goblins will pay rent if Ivanko can throw the crutch farther than he can.

The goblin goes first and throws the crutch high into the sky, from where it falls to earth embedding itself deep in the ground. Ivanko puts his hand on the crutch to take his turn but realizes that he cannot pull it out of the ground. Instead he cunningly says that he will throw it onto a passing cloud. The goblin, fearing that his grandfather cannot do without the crutch, wrenches it out of the ground and dives back into the lake. He returns shortly to report that his grandfather says that if Ivanko can carry a horse around the lake one more time than the goblin can, the goblins will pay rent. Ivanko accepts the challenge, and the goblin carries a horse around the lake ten times, then collapses, exhausted. Ivanko takes his turn, but instead of carrying the horse, he mounts it and rides around the lake until the horse collapses from exhaustion. Conceding that Ivanko has carried the horse around the lake more times than he, even if carrying it between his legs, the goblin agrees to pay rent. "How much?" he asks. Ivanko says he wants the goblin only to fill his cap with gold and to work for him for one year. The goblin agrees and goes to fetch the gold. While he is away, the wily Ivanko cuts a hole in the top of his hat and, reversing it, places the hat over a deep hole. The goblin has to keep fetching more and more gold to fill the hat, and it is not filled until the evening. Ivanko loads the gold onto a cart and has the goblin haul it to the farmer's house. When he arrives at his adoptive father's house, he says triumphantly, "Now this will please you father! Here you have a workman, and here you have gold as well."

The unpromising hero is here crossed with the numskull and the clever trickster who, despite the unnatural circumstances of his birth, proves himself to the community—in this case his adoptive father and the people he represents—and brings riches and other benefits in the process. These themes are found in many tales, although the resolution is not always positive, as in the case of the African Kihuo. However, many unpromising hero tales have similar happy endings, including the English-language

"Jack and the Beanstalk" and the Scandinavian "Osborn Boots," to name only some examples of this widespread tale type, also known as "John the Bear," and as Juan el Oso in Hispanic tradition.

Related entries: Boots; Drongo; Fairy Tale Heroes; Jack and the Beanstalk; Kihuo

References and further reading

Bain, R. (trans.), *Russian Fairy Tales from the Russian of Polevoi*, London: George Harrap, 1915.

Duddington, N. (trans.), *Russian Folk Tales*, London: Rupert Hart-Davies, 1967.

Elstob, E. and Barber, R. (trans.), *Russian Folktales*, London: Bell and Sons, 1971, pp. 95–99. First published as Von Lowis of Menar, A. (trans.) and Olesch, R. (ed.), *Russische Volksmärchen*, 1959.

Ivanovich, Dunai

Friend of Russian hero Dobrynya Nikitich, Dunai Ivanovich is a legendary knight famed for his archery. At his wedding to Nastasya, he takes her challenge to shoot an arrow through a silver ring on her head, misses, and kills her. The wondrous child Nastasya bears is cut from her womb as she lies dying, and then Dunai Ivanovich kills himself. From the ground where husband and wife lie dead, two rivers spring, that named after Dunai is now known as the Danube. This is both a hero legend and a local legend of a type often associated with heroes who either give their name to a natural feature, such as a river or mountain, or take their name from their (usually fatal) association with such things.

Related entries: Dojrana; Hood, Robin; Local Heroes; Nastasya, Princess; Nikitich, Dobrynya; Tell, William; Warriors

References and further reading

Alexander, A., *Russian Folklore: An Anthology in English Translation*, Belmont, MA: Nordland Publishing Co., 1975, pp. 237–255.

Curtin, J. (ed.), *Myths and Folktales of the Russians, Western Slavs, and Magyars*, Boston: Little, Brown, 1890.

Ivashko

See Gretel

Ivo

See Warriors

J

Jack

A name widely used in English-language tales and songs for the main character. While many tales are told without named protagonists, some tellers will give the name "Jack" to the hero for the sake of convenience and of tradition, "Jack" being a popular name in classic "fairy" tales as well as in less widely known local and regional narratives. An example of this practice is contained in Halpert and Widdowson's *Folktales of Newfoundland* (vol. 1) in the story titled "Jack the Apple Seller," where the narrator, Allan Oake, opens with these words: "Uh . . . Jack, Bill an' Tom now. Jack . . . er . . . not Jack but—whatever—we'll call him Jack anyhow . . . don't make a matter as I know for." Oake then tells a version of "The Three Magic Objects and the Wonderful Fruits," a story often associated with Fortunatus.

Halpert and Widdowson provide a list of international parallels from Canada, the United States, Mexico, the Caribbean and Central and South America, England, Scotland, Ireland, Continental Europe, the Middle East, India, and the Philippines, as well as references to thirteen studies and notes related to this particular tale. While "Jack" is not the hero of all these variants, their number and dispersal highlights the manner in which international tales become attached to favored folk characters and names. Jack has his equivalents in other cultures, including "Jean," sometimes "Jean Sot," in France; "Ti-Jean" in French Canada; "Boots" in Norway; "Ivan" in Russia; and "Hans" in Germany.

Related entries: Boots; Fairy Tale Heroes; Jack and the Beanstalk; Jack Tales; Jack the Giant-Killer; Lucky Hans; Muhammad

References and further reading

Chase, R. (ed.), with notes and contributions by

Halpert, H., *The Jack Tales*, Boston: Houghton Mifflin, 1943.

Halpert, H. and Widdowson, J. (colls. and eds.), *Folktales of Newfoundland: The Resilience of Oral Tradition*, 2 vols., New York: Garland, 1996, vol. 1, esp. pp. 362–369 and the introduction.

Massignon, G., *Folktales of France*, London: Routledge and Kegan Paul, 1968, p. 80.

Jack and the Beanstalk

"Jack and the Beanstalk" is one of the most widespread and most studied of all folktales. In its basic version, the story is that of a boy called Jack who lives on a farm with his widowed mother. They are poor and often have no food. Their only possession is their cow, which, of course, provides them with milk, butter, and cheese. One day Jack's mother tells him that their circumstances are so desperate that they must sell the much-loved and valuable cow. Unhappily, Jack agrees to take the cow to market for sale. Along the way he meets a strange, wizened little man who asks him where he is going. On hearing that Jack is off to market to sell the cow, the little man offers to buy it from Jack for three magic beans. Jack, somewhat spellbound by the man, agrees and returns home with the beans in great excitement.

When he tells his mother what he has done and shows her three beans, she is furious, pointing out in no uncertain terms that Jack has been well and truly taken in by this strange man and has given away their only hope of survival for three worthless beans. In her rage, she throws the beans out the window and into the garden.

Miserably, and hungrily, Jack goes upstairs to bed, berating himself for his foolishness. He goes to sleep and wakes at dawn the next day to see through his bedroom window that an

A WPA project poster depicting Jack climbing the beanstalk and the giant waiting for him (Library of Congress)

enormous beanstalk has sprouted from the discarded beans. The beanstalk is so thick that it is like a tree and so high that it disappears into the clouds.

Full of youthful curiosity, and against his mother's orders, Jack climbs the beanstalk, going up through the clouds and arriving in a strange land ruled over by an ogre and his wife. Jack befriends the ogre's wife, and she hides him when the ogre returns to their castle, hungry as usual, for some small boy to eat and chanting some variant of the famous:

Fee, fie, fo, fum,
I smell the blood of an Englishman.
Be he alive or be he dead,
I'll grind his bones to make my bread.

With the help of the ogre's wife, Jack discovers that the ogre has some useful treasures stored in his castle, including a magic singing harp and a goose that lays golden eggs. Jack resolves to steal these items in order to improve his and his mother's lot.

After a greater or shorter number of adventures and close calls with the ogre, depending on the length of story required by teller and audience, Jack finally escapes down the beanstalk with the golden-egg-laying goose, hotly pursued by an angry ogre. Fortunately, young Jack is fit, which, together with his fright, helps him move quickly. He makes it to the bottom of the beanstalk and into his house as the ogre is still descending through the clouds. Grabbing an axe, Jack rushes out to the garden and desperately chops away at the beanstalk as the ogre gets nearer and nearer. In the nick of time, the beanstalk is felled and the ogre crashes to earth and dies. Jack and his mother now have the golden goose and become enormously wealthy. Jack usually marries a beautiful princess, and they live happily ever after.

Versions of the tale are told throughout the English-speaking world and Europe, and it is also known in Asian tradition. There have been many attempts to explain the popularity and significance of this story and its hero since it first became widely popular in the early eighteenth century. Interpretations include the wilder shores of Freudian analysis represented by Desmonde, in which the beanstalk is treated as a phallic symbol; the therapeutic approach of Bettelheim; the comparison of national stereotypes by Wolfenstein; and the attempt to trace the story to an actual tropical plant by Humphreys. As well, there is a considerable literature about "Jack and the Beanstalk" in the fields of folklore and fairy tale studies.

Related entries: Fairy Tale Heroes; Jack; Jack Tales; Jack the Giant-Killer; Lucky Hans; Ogres; Villains

References and further reading
Bettelheim, B., *The Uses of Enchantment: The Meaning and Importance of Fairy Tales*, New York: Knopf, 1976, pp. 10, 33, 58, 183–195, 226, 309.
Briggs, K. (ed.), *A Dictionary of British Folk-Tales in the English Language*, 2 vols., London: Routledge and Kegan Paul, 1970–1971, vol. 1, pp. 316–322.
Chase, R. (ed.), with notes and contributions by Halpert, H., *The Jack Tales*, Boston: Houghton Mifflin, 1943.
Desmonde, W., "Jack and the Beanstalk," *American Imago* 8, 1951, pp. 287–288.
Hallett, M. and Karasek, B. (eds.), *Folk and Fairy Tales*, Ontario: Broadview Press, 1996, pp. 106–111.

Humphreys, H., "Jack and the Beanstalk," *Antiquity*
22, 1948, pp. 36–38.

Jacobs, J. (ed.), *English Fairy Tales*, London: The
Bodley Head, 1968, pp. 297ff; reprint of *English
Fairy Tales* (1890), pp. 40–45 and *More English
Fairy Tales*, 1894.

Szumsky, B., "The House That Jack Built: Empire
and Ideology in Nineteenth-Century British
Versions of Jack and the Beanstalk," in *Marvels
and Tales: Journal of Fairy-Tale Studies* 13, no. 1, 1999,
pp. 11–30.

Wolfenstein, M., "Jack and the Beanstalk: An American Version," in Mead, M. and Wolfenstein, M.
(eds.), *Childhood in Contemporary Culture*, Chicago:
University of Chicago Press, 1955.

Jack o' Kent

English trickster and deceiver of the Devil in
English-Welsh border tradition, also called
Jack-a-Kent. Jack appears in print for the first
time in a late sixteenth-century play but was
probably already well known in local tradition
by then. A conflation of various historical figures associated with the church and with
magic, Jack features in a considerable number
of tales in which his cleverness allows him to
benefit in various ways. In one tale, he promises to leave his body to the Devil regardless of
whether it is buried inside or outside the
church. Clever Jack has his body interred in the
wall of the church, thus outwitting the Devil
and saving his soul from damnation.

Another tale of Jack's dealings with the Devil
is a well-known international migratory legend
in which Jack one day asks the Devil whether
he would prefer the "tops" or the "butts" (bot-
toms) of the wheat crop about to spring up in
a field. As there was little wheat showing above
ground, the Devil chose the butts, which meant
that when the crop was harvested, the Devil received only the straw while Jack reaped the rewards of the wheat. The next year, Jack again
offered the Devil a choice of the tops or butts;
this time, recalling his previous loss, the Devil
chose the tops. But when the harvest came, the
Devil lost and Jack won again because the field
had been planted with turnips, and so the Devil
was left with the worthless greens while Jack
had the turnips that grew beneath the ground.

In addition to these and other tricks he plays

on the Devil, Jack o' Kent is also credited with
the origins of a number of local landscape features, including a formation caused by a land-
slide and a group of three standing stones, the
latter said to have been thrown there by Jack's
superhuman strength. Jack's supernatural abilities also include traveling rapidly through the
air on a magical steed and his haunting of a
room in Kentchurch Court. He was used as a
bogeyman figure for local children until at
least the start of the twentieth century. The development of the various localized and international traditions surrounding Jack o' Kent,
together with his uncertain status as a figure of
history or folklore, is typical of local heroes in
many cultures.

> *Related entries:* Devil, The; Fairy Tale Heroes; Jack;
> Jack and the Beanstalk; Jack Tales; Jack the
> Giant-Killer; Local Heroes; Tricksters

> **References and further reading**
> Simpson, J. and Roud, S., *A Dictionary of English
> Folklore*, Oxford: Oxford University Press, 2000,
> p. 197.
> Westwood, J., *Albion: A Guide to Legendary Britain*,
> London: Granada, 1985, 341–344, 470.

Jack Tales

Generic name given to the many English-language tales that feature a sometimes comically
bumbling and/or ne'er-do-well character as
their central protagonist. Through various devices, including such things as tricks, devious-
ness, assistance from elsewhere, and sometimes
just luck, Jack overcomes all obstacles and wins
out in the end. In an Irish tale collected by
Kennedy and published in 1866, Jack is a poor
boy who goes to seek his fortune. Along the
way he saves an ass, a dog, a cat, and a cock
from various misfortunes and cruelties, and
they accompany him on his journey. They
come across a group of robbers who have just
robbed Lord Dunlavin's gold and silver. They
frighten the robbers way, recover the loot, and
return it to the grateful lord. Jack is made stew-
ard of Lord Dunlavin's estates, and he then
fetches his poor mother to live in comfort near
the castle. The animals are also looked after for
the rest of their lives.

A Welsh Gypsy tale titled "Jack and his

Golden Snuff-Box" was collected by Francis Hindes Groome in the 1880s from John Roberts. In this story, Jack is an Aladdin-like hero who carries out various impossible tasks set by the father of his beloved. As with the hero of the Irish tale recounted above, this Jack is helped by animals. He succeeds in winning the girl's hand.

American Jack tales often feature a tall-tale element, as in one in which a ne'er-do-well foolishly uses a sign to advertise his success in accidentally killing seven butterflies. The sign reads:

STRONG-MAN-JACK
KILLED-SEVEN-AT-WHACK

A local "king" sees the sign and offers Jack $1,000 if he will kill a boar that has terrorized the area. By luck and stupidity Jack nonchalantly traps and kills the boar, impressing the "king" so much that he gives him another job hunting a unicorn, with similar results. Finally, the king offers Jack $2,000 to kill a lion. Reluctantly Jack accepts and accidentally ends up riding the lion through the area until one of the king's men shoots it dead. All the locals rush toward Jack, amazed at this feat of daring. But Jack is annoyed. "If your men hadn't killed that lion," Jack says, "I would have broken it in for a riding horse." So the king makes his men pay Jack $3,000 compensation, which, together with his previous fees, makes Jack a rich young man—not quite the fool he seems to be at the start of the story.

These anecdotes are characteristic Jack tales in that the hero is often wily, if undeserving, lucky rather than daring, and unscrupulous rather than moral.

Jack has many parallels in other languages, including the Spanish "Juan," the German "Hans," and the French "Jean." A Scandinavian Jack tale involves a character called "Farmer Weathersky," really the devil. Jack triumphs in the end by turning himself into a fox and biting off the head of Weathersky, who has made the tactical error of turning himself into a cockerel.

Related entries: Fairy Tale Heroes; Jack; Jack and the

Beanstalk; Jack the Giant-Killer; Knowall, Doctor; Lucky Hans; Muhammad

References and further reading
Chase, R. (ed.), with notes and contributions by Halpert, H., *The Jack Tales*, Boston: Houghton Mifflin, 1943.
Kennedy, P., *Legendary Fictions of the Irish Celts*, London: Macmillan and Co., 1866, pp. 5–12.
Lee, F. H. (comp.), *Folk Tales of All Nations*, London: Harrap, 1931, pp. 241–242, 252–257.
Rugoff, M. (ed.), *A Harvest of World Folk Tales*, New York: Viking Press, 1949, pp. 47–56.
Tong, D., *Gypsy Folktales*, New York: Harcourt Brace Jovanovich, 1989.

Jack Tar, Jolly

Idealized and often sentimentalized eighteenth century and later image of the typical British sailor and central character of many nautical ballads. Jolly Jack Tar is a rough-and-tumble, hard-living, womanizing character who nevertheless fights valiantly for his country when necessary. He is related to the patriotic stereotype of "the hearts of oak." In a version of a popular Jack Tar ballad collected by Cecil Sharp in 1904, Jack overhears a squire arranging an assignation with a lady. She is to tie a string around her finger and dangle the end out of her window. The squire will come by at the appointed hour and tug on the string, and she will then come downstairs and let him in. Jack gets there before the squire, pulls on the string, and is admitted into the lady's chamber, leaving the squire to fume impotently outside. But the next morning:

The lady woke up and started screaming,
For there's old Jack in his tarry shirt,
And behold his face all streaked with dirt.

Jack reassures the lady that he has not come to rob her, asks forgiveness, and offers to sneak discretely away. But she has fallen victim to the sailor's charms:

"Oh no," says she, "don't stray too far,
For I never will part from my jolly Jack Tar."

Jack Tar is in many ways a nautical version of that other everyday hero, Jack.

Related entries: Jack; Nautical Heroes; Stormalong
References and further reading
Doerflinger, W. (coll. and ed.), *Songs of the Sailor and Lumberman*, New York: Macmillan, 1972 (1951), p. 294.
Hugill, S., *Shanties from the Seven Seas*, London: Routledge and Kegan Paul, 1979 (1961), p. 461.
Lloyd, A., *Folksong in England*, New York: International Publishers, 1970 (1967), p. 169.
Vaughan Williams, R. and Lloyd, A. (eds.), *The Penguin Book of English Folk Songs*, Harmondsworth, Middlesex: Penguin Books, 1959, pp. 54–55.

Jack the Giant-Killer

A close relation of the hero in the well-known tale "Jack and the Beanstalk," Jack the Giant-Killer is an English youth who wins his name and reputation by killing a giant called Cormoran, guardian of the mount of Cornwall. Word of Jack's victory antagonizes another giant, Blunderbore, who is lord of an enchanted castle in a wood near Wales. Blunderbore vows revenge and one day comes across Jack asleep near a fountain outside his wood. He captures Jack, who, nevertheless, soon manages to kill Blunderbore and two other giants who are visiting Blunderbore's castle. Jack then releases three fair ladies imprisoned and starved by Blunderbore and proceeds on his way.

He next encounters a Welsh giant with two heads who, kindly it seems, puts Jack up for the night. But this is only a pretense at kindness. During the night, in Jacobs's version, Jack overhears the two-headed giant muttering:

Though here you lodge with me this night,
You shall not see the morning light:
My club shall dash your brains outright!

Jack gets out of bed and hides. The giant sneaks in late at night and with a large club smashes the bed where he thinks Jack is sleeping. The next morning, Jack appears at breakfast as if nothing has happened, tricking the giant—who like most giants in folklore is not very bright—into killing himself. Jack continues on his merry way, having more encounters with giants, princes, young ladies, and even, in the Joseph Jacobs version at least, with King Arthur, being made a Knight of the Round Table.

Jack meets the giant Galligantua. (Mary Evans Picture Library)

One of Jack's useful skills is invisibility, which he uses to good effect in his giant-killing, which continues unabated, allowing him to rescue various human captives that giants use for food and to obtain vast treasures that most giants seem to have hoarded away.

The last giant Jack disposes of is Galligantua, a monster who abducts lords and ladies and transforms them into various animals. The death of Galligantua changes these victims back to their human shapes. The giant's head is struck off by Jack, in the traditional manner, and dispatched to King Arthur's court, followed the next day by Jack and his retinue of rescued lords and ladies. His reward is to marry the duke's daughter and to be granted a castle and wealthy estate. Jack and his wife live happily for the rest of their lives.

This is how the tale is told by Joseph Jacobs in his well-known *English Fairy Tales* (1893). It would be more accurate to say that this is how Jacobs retells the "tales" of Jack the Giant-Killer.

The episodic structure of this printed version, together with a host of fairy tale motifs, including invisibility, shape-shifting, ogres, damsels in distress, and so on, is a characteristic sign of literary reworking. What Jacobs does here, as in so many other cases of published fairy tales and folktales, is to weave together a number of different Jack the Giant-Killer stories from oral tradition, enhance them with what were by then expected elements of the fairy tale genre, and serve the result up to an enthusiastic Victorian readership. While stories of Jack and other giant-killers are common in British folklore and form part of a large body of stories and ballads that deal with "monsters" of one kind or another, it is unlikely that such elaborately elegant versions of Jack the Giant-Killer were told by those from whom Jacobs and others collected tales.

Nevertheless, such stories were told and retold, if in less elaborate form, among the unlettered classes of the mid-nineteenth century. In a magazine called *Household Words* (vol. 5, no. 124, August 1852, pp. 482ff.), a writer told of his experiences as a convict in Australia, including the manner in which his fellow inmates whiled away the hours when they were locked up at night:

> It was a strange thing, and full of matter
> for reflection, to hear men, in whose rough
> tones I sometimes recognized the most
> stolid and hardened of the prisoners,
> gravely narrating an imperfect version of
> such childish stories as "Jack the Giant-
> Killer," for the amusement of their com-
> panions, who with equal gravity, would
> correct him from their own recollections,
> or enter into a ridiculous discussion on
> some of the facts.

Giants, like ogres, serpents, and the like, usually representing the principle of evil, are bested wherever tales are told and heroes celebrated. The hero of a well-known Grimm folktale known as "The Valiant Little Tailor," for instance, outwits giants by clever ruses and eventually marries a king's daughter. Variations of this theme are common in Africa and else-where, demonstrating a wide preoccupation with the unlikely, even-less-than-ordinary hero who wins out against all the odds. In English-language lore, this hero will often be the prosaic "Jack."

Related entries: Arthur; Dragon-Slayers; Fairy Tale Heroes; Giant-Killers; Jack; Jack and the Beanstalk; Jack Tales; Li Ji; Muhammad

References and further reading

Bettelheim, B., The Uses of Enchantment: The Meaning and Importance of Fairy Tales, New York: Knopf, 1976, pp. 27, 33, 64.

Briggs, K. (ed.), A Dictionary of British Folk-Tales in the English Language, 2 vols., London: Routledge and Kegan Paul, 1970–1971, vol. 1, pp. 329–336.

Calvino, I. (trans. Martin, G.), Italian Folk Tales: Selected and Retold by Italo Calvino, New York: Harcourt Brace Jovanovich, Penguin, 1980 (1956), pp. 357–360.

Chase, R. (ed.), with notes and contributions by Halpert, H., The Jack Tales, Boston: Houghton Mifflin, 1943.

Jacobs, J. (ed.), English Fairy Tales, London: The Bodley Head, 1968, pp. 297ff; reprint of English Fairy Tales (1890), pp. 63–70 and More English Fairy Tales (1894).

Klipple, M., African Folktales with Foreign Analogues, New York: Garland, 1992, p. 308.

Leather, E. (coll.), Folk-Lore of Herefordshire, Hereford and London: Jakeman & Carver, 1912, pp. 174–176.

Jack-in-the-Green

Figure appearing in some forms of English traditional drama, usually said to date from the medieval period. The "Jack" was a male enclosed in a light wooden frame around and through which was wound greenery and ribbons. This figure led the procession through villages, usually collecting money or soliciting drinks. Jack-in-the-Green also appeared in the occupational traditions of British chimney sweeps whose May Day processions were similar in some aspects to much traditional drama, or "mumming." Australian sweeps in Tasmania and New South Wales kept up this tradition until well into the nineteenth century. Similar customs are known throughout western and eastern Europe and Russia, including the Slavic figure of "Green George."

Jack-in-the-Green is often associated with the enigmatic figure usually known as "the Green Man," representations of whom can be found throughout European religious and secular sculpture and art. Despite a great deal of speculation about the pagan, tree-worshipping origins of such figures, there is little evidence to support such theories. The term "green man," for instance, did not exist before 1939. As with other activities and beliefs associated with May Day and other calendar customs, unsupported theorization is the norm, especially in attempts to link such figures with Robin Hood, a character appearing in some forms of traditional English drama.

Related entries: Occupational Heroes
References and further reading
Alford, V., *The Singing of the Travels: In Search of Dance and Drama*, London: Max Parrish, 1956, p. 168.
Judge, R., *The Jack-in-the-Green: A May Day Custom*, Cambridge and Ipswich: D. S. Brewer/Rowman and Littlefield, 1979 (1978 USA).

Jaka Tingkir
See Warriors

James, Jesse
Jesse Woodson James was born in 1847 into relatively comfortable circumstances. Along with other family members and friends, Jesse rode with "Quantrill's Raiders" during the Civil War. Returning to Missouri at the end of hostilities in 1865, he became disillusioned with the nature of society, politics, and economics in western Missouri; probably from 1866, in league with other family members and the related Younger family, he began a career of outlawry rarely equaled.

The Younger-James confederation initially came to public notice in February 1866 with the raid on the bank at Liberty, Missouri. At the time, Jesse James was probably too ill to participate in this raid, but it is widely thought that he planned the details of the robbery, during which an innocent bystander was killed. Three further Missouri banks were robbed by the gang in the period 1866–1867, and in March 1868 the bank in the Kentucky town of Russellville was emptied of $14,000. In December 1869 the gang robbed the bank at Gallatin. Jesse, apparently in cold blood, shot down the cashier in this raid, after which the gang disappeared again until June 1871, when at Corydon, Iowa, they took almost $40,000 from the bank, apparently living off this until robbing the bank at Columbia, Kentucky, in April 1872, shooting the bank clerk in the process. In September that year they were blamed with robbing the cash box of the Kansas City Fair, but they did not return to public view until May 1873, when the gang plundered the bank at Ste. Genevieve. In July 1873 the gang derailed a train on the Chicago, Rock Island, and Pacific Railway, mistakenly expecting it to be laden with gold. Two men were killed in the derailment, which heralded the entry of the James gang into the highly specialized and modern form of highway thieving known as train robbing. Perhaps disillusioned by the paltry takings of this train robbery, the gang next attacked a stagecoach on the way to Hot Springs, Arkansas, in January 1874. Later in the month, the gang successfully robbed the train from St. Louis at Gads Hill, and they followed this with a stagecoach robbery in April. On April 24, Jesse James married his cousin Zerelda Mimms and effectively removed himself from the attention of the authorities and the traveling public for almost nine months, until December, when a gold shipment worth approximately $40,000 was stolen from a train at Muncie, Kansas.

Throughout this period Missouri was in election mode. During the campaign, outlaws in general and the James gang in particular became political issues, with Republicans accusing Democrats of sympathizing with one-time Confederate guerrillas. The election attracted a good deal of interest from newspapers elsewhere in the country, thus spreading the notoriety of Jesse James from the local and state levels to the national level. On January 25, 1875, agents of the Pinkerton detective agency working for the federal government surrounded the home of Jesse's mother and stepfather, Mrs. and Dr. Samuels, in the erroneous belief that Jesse was inside. The agents put an incendiary device

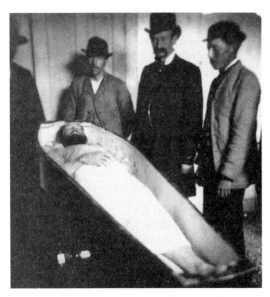

Jesse James in his casket, 1882 (Library of Congress)

depression years of the 1870s, the banks and the railroads were viewed by the general public as the agents of the wealthy and the exploitative. Repossessions by banks and barely controlled financial exploitation by the railroad companies, with consequent economic hardship for many ordinary families, contributed to this negative public image. Those who attacked these interests, for whatever motives, were therefore seen by many people as vicarious avengers of their own disenchantments and difficulties. These attitudes found expression in popular sympathy, and active support for the outlaws and was even manifested in newspapers such as the *Kansas City Times* of August 23, 1876: "The bold highwayman who does not molest the poor or the ordinary traveler, but levies tribute on banks and railroad corporations and express monopolies, is not generally such an object of popular detestation that he cannot secure a fair trial in our courts." In his laudatory *Noted Guerrillas*, the indefatigable J. Edwards described Jesse James as "an outlaw, but he is not a criminal."

After the Northfield fiasco, the James brothers could not be found at all and remained in hiding until October 1879, when, with a new gang, Jesse robbed a train at Glendale, Missouri. The outlaws were widely criticized for this action, even by the Democratic press and by supporters, popular sentiment regarding railroad companies having softened somewhat. In 1880, William Crittenden was elected governor of Missouri. Sympathetic to railroad interests, Crittenden was to engineer the demise of the James gang. But before that happened, the James gang committed a number of further, uncharacteristically brutal crimes. Two railway employees were killed during the gang's next train robbery at Winston in July 1881, and the gang made only a small haul from the train they robbed at Blue Cut, Missouri, in September, mainly by common pilfering of the personal belongings of train passengers.

During this period, the gang was in its final decay. One member was arrested in March 1881 near Nashville, where Jesse had been living. The outlaw leader moved to Kansas City and then to St. Joseph, Missouri, where he lived

through the window of the house, killing Jesse's eight-year-old half brother and severing his mother's right arm. This inept and malicious incident, widely reported and condemned, contributed greatly to the notion that members of the James family were the victims of injustice, always an important element of outlaw hero legends. Public sympathy was such that a bill pardoning the James boys was only narrowly defeated in the Missouri legislature.

Huntington, West Virginia, was the scene of the gang's next bank robbery, probably followed in July 1875 by the Rocky Cut train robbery near Otterville, Missouri. In September, the James gang disastrously mismanaged a raid on the Northfield, Minnesota, bank, during which Jesse murdered the bank clerk who refused to hand over the safe keys; the outlaws themselves were badly shot-up in the ensuing gunfight with some of the citizens of Northfield, who were enraged at this attempt on their savings. The gang split up, and the three Younger brothers—Cole, Jim, and Bob—were captured near Madelia a few weeks later, all badly wounded. They stood trial in due course and were imprisoned. Bob died of tuberculosis after thirteen years, while Cole and Jim were paroled in 1901.

The Northfield raid marks the start of the decline of Jesse James and his gang. During the quietly and respectably as Mr. Thomas Howard. Rewards for Jesse James were now totaling many thousands of dollars, tempting two of the gang's accomplices, Charles and Bob Ford, to plot Jesse's betrayal and death, apparently in complicity with Governor Crittenden. Their chance came on April 3, 1882, when James removed his guns to attend to a household chore and was immediately shot in the back of the head by Bob Ford, who wasted no time in claiming the reward from the governor. Ford (pardoned for the murder of James by the governor) was nevertheless widely reviled for his action, and ten years later he was shot dead in Colorado by a relation of the Youngers. This event is celebrated in the ballad "Jesse James." The lyrics concentrate on the heroic attributes of James, his murder by Ford, and the killer's subsequent—and righteous—end: "as you do you'll get accordin'." Like other outlaw hero ballads, it also identifies its protagonist as a Robin Hood figure:

> Jesse was a man, a friend to the poor
> He'd never see a man suffer pain,
> And with his brother Frank he robbed the
>   Chicago bank,
> And stopped the Glendale train. (Larkin
>   1931)

Jesse James's long and spectacular career as an outlaw established him as a folk hero of the time and place. Oral traditions about Jesse, such as the widow and the landlord story, among others, persisted and spread, aided by the media of the day. But with his death, Jesse James's legend grew in the manner of most outlaw heroes. The essential betrayal was provided by history, while Jesse's hero status was confirmed by rumors and claims that he was not really dead at all, despite the fact that the body of Mr. Howard was identified as that of James by his mother and others who knew him. The most commonly sung Jesse James ballad (a representative example given in Belden) seems to have been composed quite soon after James's death and to have achieved instant sanction and wide circulation.

As with most folk heroes, Jesse's legend-

building was not restricted to the folkloric processes. The popular media and literature industries, sensitive to the currents of hearsay and rumor that flow beneath the surface of society, soon initiated their own stereotyping and representations of Jesse James and his companions. Journalists frequently praised or at least adverted to the Robin Hood characteristics of the James gang. On one occasion, the gang returned the money and belongings of an ex-Confederate soldier, an action that has numerous parallels in the legendry of the outlaw hero.

Other forms and genres of cultural production have been no less fascinated by the James saga. Such productions include various stage dramatizations, including the particularly popular *The James Boys in Missouri*, which was the subject of attempted suppression by an outraged and now respectable Frank James when it played in Kansas City in 1902. The same play, despite Frank's complaints and legal actions, was still drawing large audiences in St. Louis as late as 1911. In 1938, theatrical versions of the story of Jesse James, the noble robber and outlaw hero, reached Broadway in Elizabeth Beall Ginty's *Missouri Legend*, which had a reasonably successful run and was widely staged by amateur theatrical groups.

The James family invested in the first of many feature films about the outlaw. Released in 1921, *Under the Black Flag*, not surprisingly, presented a partisan account of Jesse's activities, though it did little business outside western Missouri. The numerous Hollywood treatments began in 1927 with Paramount's *Jesse James*, a sympathetic portrayal. Tyrone Power played the outlaw hero in the 1939 Twentieth Century Fox production, also titled *Jesse James*. The film was hugely successful, firmly establishing the Jesse James persona as a Hollywood hero and leading man, and ensuring the continued circulation of the popular representation of the outlaw hero. A sequel, *The Return of Frank James*, appeared in the 1940s, followed by two treatments during the 1950s. In 1965, a television series dealing with James was broadcast by ABC television, and the subject has also been treated in radio broadcasts and as a subplot in numerous other movies, including *The Long Rid-*

ers, the *Young Guns* movies, and *The Great Northfield Bank Robbery*, as well as in television shows.

Beginning with the 1875 publication *The Guerrillas of the West; or the Life, Character, and Daring Exploits of the Younger Brothers*, by Augustus C. Appler, Jesse James has been the subject of a great number of books, whether serious, fictional, absurd, opportunistic, or simply entertaining. Appler's book was followed in 1877 by John N. Edwards's *Noted Guerrillas, or the Warfare of the Border*. Both books were partisan accounts and so added to the favorable aspects of the James legend. There were numerous other "serious" accounts of the Jameses in the years before Jesse's death, and there have been over thirty other such titles published since. Some of these accounts have attempted a balanced assessment of the James life and legend, though these attempts are in the minority.

Another widespread and influential form of popular or ephemeral literature in which the James legend was generally celebrated were "dime novels" and other forms of pulp fiction. There were hundreds of titles dealing exclusively, substantially, or tangentially with the characters and events of the James saga. Titles such as *The James Boys and the Mad Sheriff* and *The James Boys at Bay* were capped by other pulp writers anxious to find new twists to an evergreen narrative. These writers produced works titled *Jesse James among the Mormons* and *Jesse James at Coney Island*. Absurd though such titles now sound they had circulations throughout the country in the tens, even hundreds of thousands.

The James legend continues to be celebrated in tourism. Not far from Kansas City, Missouri, Jesse James and his legend still ride along the tourist trail. Jesse's birthplace at Kearney is the site of a museum, gift shop, and audiovisual presentation in the authentically restored James family farmhouse. Jesse's grave can be viewed here (though his body has been moved to the Clay County cemetery to dissuade souvenir hunters from chipping bits off the headstone). And there are the usual accoutrements of outlaw heritage—guns, boots, spurs, remains of his casket, some furniture, and the very table on which his body was embalmed. One of the many James books has been dramatized and performed at the farm as an outdoor spectacle of family theater, involving a cast of twenty actors. In Liberty, Missouri, there is a Jesse James Bank Museum where the curious can see the bank that the James gang robbed, restored to its former glory, together with reenactments of the event.

The history and folklore of Jesse James provide a small example of the complex processes of fact and fiction that combine to produce outlaw heroes and, far less frequently, outlaw heroines. To a significant extent, similar interactions of truth and belief lie behind the legendry of most of the historical figures who are celebrated as heroes of folklore.

Related entries: Bass, Sam; Bonney, William; Cortez, Gregorio; Dillinger, John; Fisk, Jim; Floyd, Charles Arthur; Hood, Robin; Outlaws; Parker, Robert Leroy; Quantrill, William Clarke; Slater, Morris; Troy, Johnny

References and further reading

Belden, H. M. (ed.), *Ballads and Songs Collected by the Missouri Folklore Society*, University of Missouri Studies 15, no. 1, 1940, pp. 403–404.

Larkin, M., *The Singing Cowboy*. New York: Knopf, 1931.

Lomax, J. and A. (colls. and comps.), *American Ballads and Folk Songs*, New York: Macmillan, 1934, p. 128.

Love, R., *The Rise and Fall of Jesse James*, New York: G. P. Putnam's Sons, 1940.

Settle, W. A., Jr., *Jesse James Was His Name, or, Fact and Fiction Concerning the Careers of the Notorious James Brothers of Missouri*, Columbia: University of Missouri Press, 1966.

Steckmesser, K. L., *The Western Hero in History and Legend*, Norman: University of Oklahoma Press, 1965.

Steckmesser, K. L., "Robin Hood and the American Outlaw," *Journal of American Folklore* 79, 1966.

Jane, Calamity

See Women Dressed as Men

Jane, Queen

"Queen Jane was in labour full six weeks and more," begins the ballad of the death of Henry VIII's wife Jane Seymour. It continues, "Until her women grew weary and the midwife gave o'er." King Henry is called and she implores, "Cut my side open and save my baby." "Oh no," replies King Henry, "that's a thing I'll never do / If I lose the flower of England, I'll lose the branch, too." Queen Jane dies, but the baby lives, and although there is "fiddling and dancing" to celebrate the birth, "Poor Queen Jane, beloved, lay cold as a stone."

Jane Seymour gave birth to Prince Edward on October 12, 1537, by natural means, though there was a popular belief, as this ballad suggests, that the birth was assisted by surgery. Jane Seymour died twelve days after the birth. This historical heroine represents a small but significant class of characters whose folkloric celebration is derived from their status as victims of circumstances beyond their control. Queen Jane's bravery in the face of such adversity is also heroic and an appealing subject for commemoration. It is not hard to draw a direct line between this sixteenth-century heroine and the recent treatment of Princess Di.

Related entries: Ahay; Armstrong, Johnny; Ashma; Celebrity Heroes; Franklin, Lord; Halfchick; Isabel, Lady; Ivan the Mare's Son; Judy; Kihachi; Pied Piper, The; Shine; Siung Wanara; Victims

References and further reading
Child, F. J., *The English and Scottish Popular Ballads*, 5 vols., New York: Dover, 1965 (1882–1898), vol. 3, pp. 372–376; vol. 5, pp. 245ff, 298.
Lloyd, A., *Folksong in England*, New York: International Publishers, 1970 (1967), pp. 151–152.
Vaughan Williams, R. and Lloyd, A. L. (eds.), *The Penguin Book of English Folk Songs*, Harmondsworth, Middlesex: Penguin Books, 1959, p. 31.

Jaramillo, Pedro
See Religious Heroes

Jean Sot
See Numskulls and Noodles

Jesus
In common with other biblical figures, Jesus of Nazareth, also known as Jesus Christ and Jesus the Messiah, is the focus of an extensive folklore. Much of this lore is found in various apocryphal books and other writings and usually relates to his childhood or to his last days of earthly life. There are also traditions that relate the characteristics of animals and fish to physical contact with Jesus. Eastern followers of Christianity developed a vast body of lore about Jesus, as did medieval European Christians.

A number of English-language folk songs deal with aspects of the life of Jesus, both legendary and biblical. Many of these songs are folk carols, such as "Christ Was Born in Bethlehem," or briefer ballads like "The Bitter Withy," which is based on the folk belief that the willow tree weeps because Jesus' mother, Mary, whipped the disobedient young Jesus with a willow switch. In the final verse, as recorded by Lloyd, Jesus says:

> Oh, bitter withy, oh bitter withy, you've caused me to smart,
> And the willow shall be the very first tree to perish at the heart.

Much of the folklore of Jesus presents him as a human figure who gets angry, takes revenge, and is delighted or irritated by things. This lore also, as in "Bitter Withy," often credits Jesus with the origins of natural phenomena. In a Hungarian tale, the reason horses are always grazing is that a horse will refuse to carry Jesus until it has eaten its fill. The same story explains the donkey's stamina and resistance to cold as its reward for agreeing to carry Jesus on its back.

There is a considerable amount of other folklore in which plants of one kind or another have characteristics attributed directly to legends of Jesus. In the Hungarian story about the donkey, for example, as the donkey carried Jesus the animal felt great hunger and bit into a reed growing beside the road. "You can still see a gash on every reed stalk to show the bite," the storyteller says.

One well-known, though relatively little-studied, legend is that of Jesus' visit to England, a tale centered mainly around the belief that Joseph of Arimathea brought the boy Jesus to Glastonbury. The same story is also told about a number of other locations in the southwest of England, and it is told in other parts of the world, as well, as in Sicily. Here, as in many other legends, St. Peter is often said to have accompanied Jesus on his travels.

Jesus Christ depicted at the Last Supper with his disciples in a woodcut by Albrecht Dürer (Library of Congress)

The biblical account of the birth, life, and death of Jesus is also similar to the stories of other folk heroes. The extraordinary circumstances of his birth; the wise men bearing gifts; Herod's attempt to have him killed; many of the wonders and miracles he performs; and the circumstances of his death, resurrection, and heavenly persistence, together with the promise of return in the "Second Coming," are all elements found in mythology and folklore around the world.

Related entries: Joseph of Arimathea, Saint; Mary; Religious Heroes

References and further reading

Blum, R. and E., *The Dangerous Hour: The Lore of Crisis and Mystery in Rural Greece*, London: Chatto and Windus, 1970, pp. 80–82.

Briggs, K. (ed.), *A Dictionary of British Folk-Tales in the English Language*, 2 vols., London: Routledge and Kegan Paul, 1970–1971, vol. 1, p. 107.

Broadwood, L., *English Traditional Songs and Carols*, London: Boosey & Co., 1908.

Calvino, I. (trans. Martin, G.), *Italian Folk Tales: Selected and Retold by Italo Calvino*, New York: Harcourt Brace Jovanovich, Penguin, 1980 (1956), pp. 594–598.

Dégh, L., *Folktales of Hungary*, Chicago: University of Chicago Press, 1965, pp. 181–184.

Dundes, A., *Interpreting Folklore*, Bloomington: Indiana University Press, 1980, pp. 223–261.

Hunt, M. (trans. and ed.), *Grimm's Household Tales* (with the author's notes and an introduction by Andrew Lang), 2 vols., London: George Bell and Sons, 1884, pp. 312–324, 440–452.

Ivanits, L., *Russian Folk Belief*, Armonk and London: M. E. Sharpe Inc., 1989, pp. 140–142.

Lloyd, A., *Folksong in England*, New York: International Publishers, 1970 (1967), pp. 127–129.

Paredes, A., *Folktales of Mexico*, Chicago: University of Chicago Press, 1970, pp. 123–124, 178–179, 181.

Potter, C., "Jesus," in Leach, M. (ed.), *Funk and Wagnall's Standard Dictionary of Folklore, Mythology, and Legend*, London: New English Library, 1975. Abridged one-volume edition of *Funk and Wagnall's Standard Dictionary of Folklore, Mythology, and Legend*, 2 vols., New York: Funk and Wagnall, 1972, pp. 548–550.

Ranke, K. (ed.), *Folktales of Germany*, London: Routledge and Kegan Paul, 1966, pp. 154–155.

Rappoport, A., *Medieval Legends of Christ*, London: Ivor Nicholson and Watson, 1934.

Robe, S. (ed.), *Hispanic Folktales from New Mexico: Narratives from the R. D. Jameson Collection*, Mythology and Folktale Studies 30, Berkeley and Los Angeles: University of California Press, 1976, p. 114.

Smith, A. W., "And Did Those Feet . . . ?: The 'Legend' of Christ's Visit to Britain," *Folklore* 100, no. 1, 1989, pp. 63–83.

John, Faithful
See Faithful John

Johnny Appleseed
See Chapman, John

Johns, Joseph
Joseph Johns was transported from England to Western Australia in 1853. He absconded, was captured, and escaped repeatedly throughout the late 1880s, becoming a celebrated identity in the Swan River Colony, later Western Australia, under the folk name "Moondyne Joe." Johns's ability to escape was so marked that he became a local outlaw hero. While the only song extant about Joe is a parody of the nursery rhyme "Pop Goes the Weasel," one can detect in its brevity the set of tensions and conflicts between unpopular authority and those suffering beneath it that typically underlie outlaw heroes. Joe was able to survive so well in the bush due to a network of sympathizers, always a prerequisite for outlaw heroization. Folk traditions about Moondyne Joe include his escapes, his cleverness, and his buried gold. He fits the mold of the outlaw hero through his trickster characteristics.

Related entries: Christie, Francis; Hall, Ben; Kelly, Edward; Local Heroes; Outlaws

References and further reading

Elliot, I., *Moondyne Joe: The Man and the Myth*, Perth: University of Western Australia Press, 1978.

Jolly Swagman, The
Legendary figure of the famous Australian song "Waltzing Matilda," the words of which were written by A. B. "Banjo" Paterson in 1895. The slight story recounted in the song, of which various versions are sung, tells how the jolly swagman (tramp, hobo) steals a sheep. Upon being caught by the squatter, or local land-

owner, and the police, the swagman prefers to drown himself in the water hole rather than be taken alive:

> And his ghost may be heard as you walk
>   past that billabong
> You'll come a-waltzing matilda with me.

"Waltzing Matilda" has become the unofficial national anthem of Australia, and the swagman represents the antiauthoritarian hero common to much Australian folklore. The jolly swagman also has something of the attributes of both a culture hero and a national hero. In his defiance of the squatter, or employer, he also echoes some aspects of the occupational hero and the hero of struggle.

Related entries: Culture Heroes; Heroes of Struggle; National Heroes; Occupational Heroes
References and further reading
Davey, G. and Seal, G. (eds.), *The Oxford Companion to Australian Folklore*, Melbourne: Oxford University Press, 1993, pp. 361–362.

Jones, Casey

Born in 1863 and reared in Cayce, Kentucky— hence his nickname—the Welsh-American John Luther Jones was known as a fast and clever railroad engineer. He was engineer of the Illinois Central Railroad's elite fast passenger train, the Cannonball Express, which ran from Chicago to New Orleans. In 1900 the Cannonball Express was involved in a wreck. Jones was killed, and his body, it is said, was found with one hand on the whistle and the other on the brake. It seems that Jones was celebrated as a hero in a number of songs by African-American railroad workers and was also the subject of a popular song hit of 1909, titled "Casey Jones (The Brave Engineer)," which spread the story far beyond the occupational group of railroad workers.

However, Jones was not considered a hero to all workers. A song by Joe Hill titled "Casey Jones the Union Scab" appeared in the 1912 edition of the Industrial Workers of the World (IWW) songbook. To the tune of the 1909 hit, the gist of the song was that Jones took the engine out while his fellow workers were on strike. He was thus strike-breaking, or "scab-

bing." In the song, Jones goes first to heaven, where, by singing, he scabs on the angels, who are also on strike. The "Angel Union No. 23" then throws Jones out of heaven to hell, where the Devil says:

> Casey Jones, get busy shovelling sulphur—
> That's what you get for scabbing on the
>   S. P. Line.

This contradictory status of Casey Jones in American tradition highlights the frequent ambivalence of folk heroes. While their deeds, real or legendary, may be celebrated by one group, those same deeds may be deplored by others.

Related entries: Bunyan, Paul; Crooked Mick; Fink, Mike; Henry, John; Heroes of Struggle; Hill, Joe; Mikula; Occupational Heroes; Slater, Morris; Stormalong
References and further reading
Botkin, B. (ed.), *A Treasury of American Folklore: Stories, Ballads, and Traditions of the People*, New York: Crown Publishers, 1944, pp. 175–254.
Cohen, N., *Long Steel Rail: The Railroad in American Folksong*, Urbana: University of Illinois Press, 1981, 132–157.
Industrial Workers of the World, *Songs to Fan the Flames of Discontent*, Chicago: Industrial Workers of the World, 1912.
Lomax, J. and A. (colls. and comps.), *American Ballads and Folk Songs*, New York: Macmillan, 1934, p. 36.

Jones, Galloping

Historical figure of Australian, northern Queensland folklore, said to have died in 1960. Galloping Jones was a bush fighter, a drinker, a stock-stealer, and a bank robber. His antics included stealing stock, selling them, and stealing them again the very same night. Once he was arrested by a policeman and an Aboriginal tracker for illegally slaughtering a cow. The evidence was the cow's hide, prominently marked with someone else's brand. On the way back to town, Jones and his captors camped. Jones managed to get the policeman and his assistant drunk, and when they fell asleep, he rode off into the night. However, instead of escaping, he returned a few hours later with a fresh cow hide, which he substituted for the evidence carried by the policeman. The next day, the party arrived in town, where Jones was tried for his crime. When they pulled the evidence from the bag they found the hide bore Jones's brand; the case was dismissed.

In another story, Jones is again captured by a young policeman whom he fools into letting him go behind a bush to relieve himself. Of course, Jones escapes, and the policeman has to return to town without his captive. When he gets to town to report his failure to the sergeant, who is in his usual "office," the pub, there is Jones, washed, and shaved and having a beer. The embarrassed policeman threatens to shoot Jones, but the trickster just says that he felt the need for a cleanup and a drink and that he would now be happy to stroll down to the lockup.

Many stories concerning Galloping Jones are also told of a similar Queensland folk character called Snuffler Oldfield. Galloping Jones traditions are very much in the mold of the larger-than-life pioneer heroes of the American West, with more than a touch of the trickster.

Related entries: Bindieye, Jacky; Crockett, Davy; Crooked Mick; Doyle, Tom; Frontier Heroes; Local Heroes; Tricksters

References and further reading

Edwards, R., *The Australian Yarn*, Adelaide, SA: Rigby, 1978 (1977), pp. 27–29.

Scott, W., *The Long and the Short and the Tall: A Collection of Australian Yarns*, Sydney: Western Plains Publishers, 1985.

Jones, Thomas (Twym Sion Cati)
See Outlaws

Joseph of Arimathea, Saint

According to the Gospels, Joseph was an affluent Jew who had Christ's body taken down from the cross and placed, temporarily, in his own intended tomb. From this sparse information, Joseph has become the focus of a number of legends concerning the visit of the child Jesus to southern England and the later introduction of Christianity to Britain. In the former legend, it is said that Joseph—sometimes said to be the uncle of Jesus—brought the Christ child to southern England, a story also told in and of other countries.

In the latter, better developed story, after the death of Jesus and anywhere between the years 40 and 63 A.D., Joseph and a small band of the faithful travel to Glastonbury carrying the Holy Grail, the chalice used at the Last Supper and into which Christ's blood had been poured at his crucifixion. Joseph reaches the foot of Glastonbury Tor and, tired, stops to pray. He thrusts his wooden staff, usually a hawthorn branch, into the ground, and it immediately roots itself and puts forth buds (a tradition also associated with other religious heroes including Tannhauser and Elijah), the divine sign that this is the place where Joseph should found the Christian faith on these islands. So it is that Christianity came to England and that the Glastonbury area, with its unseasonably flowering thorn bush, its holy well, and its associations with the Arthurian legend and pre-Christian belief, became the holiest spot on the islands. The Holy Grail was eventually buried by Joseph at the foot of the Tor, it is said, though it has never been found, despite many attempts and claims of success. From this basic legend, which has innumerable variations, has grown a complex cycle of belief and story, blending Christianity, pre-Christian belief, Arthurian legend, and New Age celebrations of various kinds. The present complex is the result of interaction between local folk traditions and literary treatments, and mistreatments, over many centuries.

Related entries: Arthur; Jesus; Religious Heroes

References and further reading

Alford, V., *The Singing of the Travels: In Search of Dance and Drama*, London: Max Parrish, 1956, pp. 217–218.

Barber, R., *Myths and Legends of the British Isles*, Rochester, NY: Boydell Press, 1999, pp. 380–385.

Hole, C., *Saints in Folklore*, London: G. Bell and Sons, 1966, chap. 3.

Simpson, J. and Roud, S., *A Dictionary of English Folklore*, Oxford: Oxford University Press, 2000, p. 200.

Westwood, J., *Albion: A Guide to Legendary Britain*, London: Granada, 1985, pp. 21–25, 116.

Judy

Wife of Punch in the English folk puppet play, "Punch and Judy." She is the mother of the baby murdered by Punch's manic brutality.

A Punch and Judy show (Cordaiy Photo Library/Corbis)

When she remonstrates with Punch, he usually beats her to death, going on to perform various other acts of reprehensible but disturbingly appealing violence, in many respects like the classic trickster figure. An old English nursery rhyme also attests to the wide popularity of Punch and Judy's violence:

Punch and Judy
Fought for a pie;
Punch gave Judy
A sad blow in the eye. (Halliwell 1970)

Related entries: Karagiozis; Punch; Tricksters

References and further reading

Byrom, R., *Punch and Judy: Its Origin and Evolution*, Markham, Norfolk: Da Silva Puppet Books, 1988 (1972).

Halliwell, J., *The Nursery Rhymes of England*, London: The Bodley Head, 1970 (1842), p. 26.

Leach, R., "Punch and Judy and Oral Tradition," *Folklore* 94, no. 1, 1983, pp. 75–85.

K

Kabadaluk

Poor Arab beggar boy hero of a long and complicated Yugoslav tale. The czar desires to find a worthy husband for his beautiful and much-loved daughter. He searches everywhere, sending his servants far and wide to find a suitably noble and handsome suitor. Although there are many candidates, none fully please the old czar. Eventually, two of the czar's servants come across a dervish, described as a Muslim monk, on the seashore. He is constantly writing names on scraps of paper and throwing these into the sea. On asking the dervish what he is doing, they are told that he is marrying young men to girls by writing the appropriate names on the scraps of paper. The servants return to the czar, who, seizing this opportunity to discover a suitable suitor for his daughter, sends them back to get a name from the dervish. After a number of return trips to the dervish, he gives them the name Kabadaluk. The servants return to the czar with this welcome news, but no one seems to know anyone called Kabadaluk, and so the czar tells the servants to return to the dervish for the whereabouts of the young man. But this time when the servants reach the seashore, the dervish has disappeared. They return, reluctantly, to the czar with no further news, and so the czar embarks on frenzied efforts to find someone called Kabadaluk. Despite gathering together all the males in his domain, the czar cannot find anyone called Kabadaluk. At the end of this exercise, the czar's Lord Keeper of the Seal comes across an Arab beggar-boy picking blackberries by the road. He turns out to have the name "Kabadaluk." The Lord Keeper of the Seal brings the beggar boy before the czar, but the great man refuses to consider the beggar suitable for his daughter's hand. He tells the Lord Keeper of the Seal to take the boy

into the woods and to kill him, as he wants no such lowborn son-in-law, dervish or no dervish.

The Lord Keeper of the Seal takes the unsuspecting and innocent beggar boy into the woods but cannot bring himself to kill him. Instead he gives him a small box and directs him toward a distant mountain where a dragon lives within a lake. He tells the beggar boy to gather pebbles from the lake, put them in the box, and bring them back to him, and to no one else. Kabadaluk goes innocently off on this quest, unaware that the Lord Keeper of the Seal hopes the dragon will kill him. But the dragon sleeps, and when the boy reaches the lake his skin is magically turned to white and he is made handsome. He takes the pebbles in the box, together with some sand from the lake, and returns toward the city of Constantinople. After a number of adventures, he sells many of the magic pebbles for a great deal of money, becomes a rich man with a large mansion, and lives like a noble. The czar comes to hear of the rich, handsome noble and thinks he might make a suitable match for his still unwed daughter. He sends the Lord Keeper of the Seal off to discover if the young man wishes to marry his daughter. Neither Kabadaluk nor the Lord Keeper of the Seal recognize each other, and the Lord Keeper of the Seal does not ask for Kabadaluk's name. Kabadaluk agrees to marry the czar's daughter. The wedding is held, and at the feast the czar, pleased with himself, is heard to crow that he has outwitted the prophecy of the mysterious dervish.

Bride and groom go off to their new lives together, and it is not until some days later that the czar recalls that he has never asked the name of his daughter's new husband. He sends the Lord Keeper of the Seal to ask the young man's name. When Kabadaluk tells him, the Lord Keeper of the Seal is staggered and finds it difficult to believe. He asks for proof, and, of course, Kabadaluk shows him the box and tells him all the adventures he has had. The Lord Keeper of the Seal is overcome with joy and relieved that the beggar boy was not killed by the dragon. He asks, and is granted, Kabadaluk's forgiveness. Then he travels back to the czar and tells him the whole story, revealing that the dervish's prophecy did come true after all. The czar is not angry, for he has grown fond of his son-in-law, and, after thinking about the situation for a little while, wisely declares that Kabadaluk was fated to marry his daughter and that no one can escape one's fate.

There are numerous parallels in this story with other hero tales. The refusal of the Lord Keeper of the Seal to kill the beggar boy echoes the reluctance of the servant to kill Snow White, while the transformation of the unlikely, lowborn boy into a rich, handsome, and successful hero is also a folktale commonplace, heard in the stories of Jack, Hans, Jean, Ivan, Muhammad, Aladdin, and innumerable other heroes who begin in the most unpromising of ways but who triumph in the end.

Related entries: Aladdin; Jack; Snow White

References and further reading

Curcija-Prodanovic, N. (comp.), *Yugoslav Folk-Tales*, Oxford: Oxford University Press, 1957, pp. 20–26.

Curtin, J. (ed.), *Myths and Folktales of the Russians, Western Slavs, and Magyars*, Boston: Little, Brown, 1890.

Rugoff, M. (ed.), *A Harvest of World Folk Tales*, New York: Viking Press, 1949.

Kabajan

A legendary character featured in many Javanese tales, Kabajan is a combination of the trickster and the numskull. Most stories about Kabajan are located in the domestic and everyday realm and often involve his wife, his father-in-law, and a man called Silah. Kabajan usually manages to outsmart both of the latter. In one story, Kabajan and his father-in-law go hunting for deer. They argue, and the father-in-law decides to go off by himself and set a bird snare, a much easier task than digging the deep pit required to catch a deer. Annoyed, Kabajan tells his father-in-law that he will not be giving him any of the deer meat, as he has not helped prepare the trap. The father-in-law declares that he will not be giving Kabajan any of his catch, either, and both men then go home in a bad mood. The next morning the father-in-law wakes early and goes to see what he has caught.

There is nothing in his bird snare, but in Kabajan's pit is a magnificent deer. The father-in-law is both jealous and angry. He takes the deer and places it in the bird snare. He wakes Kabajan and triumphantly shows him the amazing sight of a deer trapped in a bird snare. When Kabajan finds his own trap empty, he is suspicious but says nothing. At breakfast, Kabajan's wife misses him and asks her father to look for him. The father-in-law finds Kabajan sitting beside the river looking at the water. "What are you doing?" asks the father-in-law. Kabajan tells him to look closely at the river, noting that it is flowing backwards, from downstream to upstream. "Don't be ridiculous," snorts the father-in-law; "that's impossible." "Why is it impossible?" Kabajan replies. "If a deer can get caught in a bird snare, then a river can flow backwards." The father-in-law is then ashamed of himself and confesses. He returns the deer to Kabajan, who, by way of punishment, shares only a few of the bones with him.

In another story, Silah, who is always trying to trick Kabajan, asks him whether he would rather have money or brains. Kabajan chooses brains, much to Silah's incomprehension. "Why?" he asks, scratching his head. "Because," replies Kabajan, "money cannot make brains, but brains can make money." In other Kabajan stories, the trickster appears as something of a numskull. Being too lazy to carry the corn from the garden to the house, Kabajan uses the horse. He gathers all the corn into his arms, mounts the horse, and rides it back to the house. Witnessing this odd behavior, Kabajan's father-in-law asks him why he is sitting on the horse and carrying the corn in his arms. Kabajan replies that he is sparing the horse from getting too tired carrying the corn. In spite of such behavior, Kabajan usually outwits those around him.

Even though Kabajan generally holds his own and better in human exchanges, his folklore shows him bested by the gods. In the story of how Kabajan never became rich, the prayers he and his wife offer on the holy mountain bring forth a god who offers them two wishes. Kabajan and his wife joyfully begin to discuss what they should ask for. He wants money; she wants rice. They are unable to agree, and the conversation develops into a heated argument. After an hour, Kabajan blurts out in frustration, "Oh god, may my wife become ugly like a monkey." Instantly the poor woman is transformed. Kabajan is sorry and wishes for her to be turned back into the woman she was. That was the end of their two wishes, and so they remained poor for the rest of their lives.

Related entries: Numskulls and Noodles; Tricksters
References and further reading
Koutsoukis, A. (trans.), *Indonesian Folk Tales*, Adelaide: Rigby, 1970, pp. 118–124.
Terada, A., *The Magic Crocodile and Other Folktales from Indonesia*, Honolulu: University of Hawaii Press, 1994.

Kandek

Legendary young heroine of an Armenian tale in which she escapes being burnt to death by her mother. Kandek then encounters a werewolf disguised as an old woman who intends to eat the young girl. The werewolf tries various tricks to kill Kandek, who outwits the beast by stratagems reminiscent of Little Red Riding Hood's escape from the wolf. Eventually Kandek cleverly entices the werewolf to its death, first by tricking it into cutting its feet and then by causing it to fall into sacks of salt. The pain kills the werewolf, and so Kandek makes her well-deserved escape.

The escape of the heroine, less often of the hero, by tricking the villain into an oven, bag, or other usually fatal encumbrance is a common device of folktale heroism. It occurs in fairy tales such as "Hansel and Gretel" and in many of the earthier traditions of Europe, Africa, and Asia.

Related entries: Fairy Tale Heroes; Gretel; Little Red Riding Hood; Victims

References and further reading
Downing, C. (trans. and ed.), *Armenian Folk-Tales and Fables*, London: Oxford University Press, 1972, pp. 87–90.

Kapsirko

Kapsirko is a poor Russian peasant of legend who is caught stealing his master's firewood. The penalty for this act is to be banished to Siberia. However, the master decides to give Kapsirko a chance to avoid this fate and sets him the task of stealing a horse from the master's stables. The stables are heavily guarded, but Kapsirko is cunning and succeeds in stealing the horse. The master is still not content and sets Kapsirko what he believes is the even more impossible task of stealing his wife. Kapsirko succeeds in abducting the wife, but in the process of hiding her he loses the woman to a water demon who drags her into a lake. The demon commands its servant to pay Kapsirko for the woman by filling his hat with golden coins. The clever peasant cuts a hole in the hat and holds it over his sled, forcing the servant to keep pouring the money out. Kapsirko returns with his new wealth, no longer a servant, and so no longer under threat of banishment to Siberia. However, the old master misses his wife and begs Kapsirko to get her back for him, in return for half his lands and a great deal of money. Kapsirko agrees and goes back to the lake, where he outwits the water demon in a succession of three contests and wins the woman back. He returns her to his old master, who, true to his word, gives Kapsirko all that he had promised him.

This tale is one of a widespread group of stories in which an unpromising poor hero, less frequently a heroine, uses cunning to outdo, outwit, or otherwise best a wealthy and/or powerful person, becoming wealthy and often powerful in the process. The trick of cutting a hole in the top of the hat in order to receive more gold is encountered in many traditions, including that of Ivanko the Bear's Son. Such tales are often interpreted as a form of lower-class wish fulfillment.

Related entries: Heroes of Struggle; Ivanko the Bear's Son

References and further reading

Afanas'ev, A. (comp.), Guterman, N. (trans.), *Russian Fairy Tales*, New York: Pantheon Books, 1945.

Bain, R. (trans.), *Russian Fairy Tales from the Russian of Polevoi*, London: George Harrap, 1915.

Karagiozis

Comic hero of the Greek shadow puppet theater, which takes its name from him. Karagiozis is a hunchback and is bald and ugly but has a sense of humor and is endowed with cunning of the type associated with trickster figures. He heads a cast of colorful characters drawn from legend and history and is continually getting himself into awkward situations in his attempts to feed himself, usually by pretending to have skills that he does not possess, such as those of a doctor or a dictator. He is assisted by his colleagues, who usually end up bearing the brunt of Karagiozis's antics. Typically the Karagiozis plays have a sharp element of social and political satire, and Karagiozis himself is identified with the poor and oppressed.

Karagiozis has eastern origins and appears to have arrived in Greece via Turkey in the early nineteenth century. However, Karagiozis (the name means "black-eye") is documented in the Ottoman Empire during the seventeenth century. In addition to his great popularity in Greece—which since the 1920s has been aided by the commercial appropriation of Karagiozis into children's literature and, later, television—this hunchback hero has been exported throughout the world in the wake of the Greek diaspora. Karagiozis now has a usually affectionate, though sometimes controversial, place in Australia, New Zealand, Canada, and the United States.

Related entries: Heroes of Struggle; Judy; Punch

References and further reading

Chatzinikolaou, A., "Karagiozis," in Davey, G. and Seal, G. (eds.), *The Oxford Companion to Australian Folklore*, Melbourne: Oxford University Press, 1993, pp. 218–221.

Myrsiades, L. and K., *Karagiozis: Culture and Comedy in Greek Puppet Theatre*, Lexington: University Press of Kentucky, 1992.

Katie Woodencloak

See Woodencloak, Katie

Katya

See Swan Maiden

Kelly, Edward

Australian bushranger Edward "Ned" Kelly (1854–1880) was hanged after a nearly two-year period of outlawry during which he murdered three policemen and, with his gang, robbed banks and stations. The circumstances of Ned Kelly's activities were bound up with his Irish ancestry and the situation regarding land ownership and the administration of justice in northeastern Victoria in the period leading up to the point where the Kelly gang (Ned, his younger brother Dan, Joe Byrne, and Steve Hart) ambushed a group of policemen who were tracking them down in the Wombat Ranges at a place called Stringybark Creek. The Kellys and their many sympathizers and supporters felt that they had been dealt a poor hand in the selection of land suitable for grazing and other agricultural activities. The earlier landholders in the area controlled not only the best land and access to the water and transportation, but also the activities of the police and government administration. A number of historical studies, as well as the royal commission that followed the Kelly outbreak, have shown that these perceptions of injustice were substantially correct.

Although the Kellys were outlawed by legislation and pursued by the police and, eventually, the armed forces, they enjoyed extensive support from members of the local and other similar communities. Kelly played on this support by making speeches and writing letters that cast him in the role of a Robin Hood figure, an image that he fortified by publicly burning the farm mortgages he found in the safes of the banks he robbed. The failure of the police to catch the Kellys led to the offer of an enormous reward for their capture. In June 1880 the gang tried to wreck a train full of police at Glenrowan Station, where they had commandeered the local pub and filled it with hostages. The plan

Ned Kelly, Australian outlaw hero who became a national hero
(Corbis)

failed, and dressed in suits of armor that had been fashioned for them from plowshares, the bushrangers fought a last desperate battle with the police. Three members of the gang were killed, and Ned was badly wounded. He was taken to the capital, Melbourne, nursed back to health, and tried for the murder of Constable Lonigan at Stringybark Creek. He was found guilty and hanged in controversial circumstances on November 11, 1880.

Up to this point, Ned Kelly had been a largely local hero to his supporters and sympathizers. However, such were the sensational and picturesque circumstances of his outlawry, his last stand in armor, and his subsequent trial that 30,000 Victorians petitioned the government for mercy. He had also become a media hero. Glenrowan was accessible from Melbourne by train, and the last stand had been witnessed and photographed by journalists, who were also able to get the news on the newly installed telegraph, ensuring that Kelly made headlines around Australia and through-

out the world. Since his death, Ned Kelly has evolved from a local folk hero to an Australian outlaw hero and, ultimately, to a national hero. In 1980 the federal government produced a postage stamp commemorating the anniversary of Kelly's hanging.

How did a bank robber and murderer become a defining symbol of a nation? Impelled by an incessant media interest, Kelly's historical activities and his folkloric image have combined during the years since 1878 to produce an iconic figure representing many elements of Australian national identity. He was a strong, tough, and resourceful fighter, an excellent bushman, and no respecter of authority, especially in uniform. Many people saw him as an ally of the poor and downtrodden, and he "died game," reputedly saying as he stepped into the noose, "Such is life." Whether he said these words or not, most Australians believe he did, and there is an extensive body of folklore that presents Ned as an outlaw hero of the first order. This lore includes dozens of folk songs and ballads, legends, forms of colloquial speech, and a usually unstated but pervasive view that Ned Kelly is representative of the Australian character and ethos. Australians have even been known to refer to themselves colloquially as "Neds."

Whatever the realities might have been, Ned Kelly features in folk songs, sung during his lifetime and after, as a man who was wronged by the forces of authority: "The governor of Victoria was an enemy of this man," claims a song called "Kelly Was Their Captain." Another song says:

Farewell Dan and Edward Kelly,
Farewell Byrne and Steve Hart too.
With the poor your memory liveth
Those who blame you are but few. (Seal 1980)

Kelly songs also invoke the tradition of the outlaw hero, both in its Australian manifestations (with reference to Jack Donohoe and Ben Hall) and in its English and Irish versions (with reference, by implication, to Turpin and Brennan and even to the archetypal figure of Robin

Hood). In "My Name Is Edward Kelly" as given in Seal (1980), the outlaw speaks some stirring lines of defiance that resonate with an earlier Australian hero, Jack Donohoe, and his later fictional construct "The Wild Colonial Boy":

I'd rather die like Donohoe, that
  bushranger so brave,
Than be taken by the government to be
  treated like a slave.
I'd rather fight with all my might as long as
  I'd eyes to see,
I'd rather die ten thousand deaths than die
  on the gallows tree.

The facts of Ned Kelly's life and bushranging career largely coincided with this widespread folkloric image, ultimately turning him into a national hero. When Australia was threatened by the Japanese advance in World War II, Ned, in a ballad known as "Ned Kelly Was A Gentleman," became a kind of protective culture hero:

Ned Kelly was a gentleman, many hard-
  ships did he endure
He battled to deprive the rich then give it
  to the poor . . .

If Ned and such guerrillas were with us
  here today
The Japs would not be prowling round
  New Guinea and Milne Bay . . .

Poor Ned, he was a gentleman, but never
  understood:
We want men of such mettle now to stem
  the yellow flood. (Seal 1980)

Legends about Kelly, his comrades, and his family members are also plentiful. These legends are of the type usually associated with outlaw heroes around the world and include Ned's activities on behalf of the poor and the fact that his brother, Dan, did not die at Glenrowan but escaped to South Africa or America. The helper appears in the form of his younger sister, Kate. She was credited with various acts of bravery and with helping her brother avoid capture by the police. These traditions usually include the story of Kate dressing as a member of the all-male gang in order to dupe the police. In reality it was Ned's older sister, Maggie, who carried out most of these acts. However, the more romantic Kate has gone down in folklore as heroine of the saga.

Ned Kelly is also a hero to many Aboriginal Australians. In the Northern Territory, Aborigines have adopted Kelly into their cultures, in some cases conflating him with Jesus, other biblical figures, and Captain Cook. Ned's defiance of duly constituted authority and his insistence on the repressive nature of the Victorian government and its police have caused some Western Australian Aborigines to see Kelly as an appropriate representative of their own grievances and struggles against the ongoing consequences of colonization.

Ned Kelly was the subject of Australia's, and the world's, first feature film in 1906, and since then he has been treated in more than a dozen feature films, a television miniseries, books, articles, plays, and art, most notably in the series of paintings by Sidney Nolan. In 2000 the expatriate Australian novelist Peter Carey published a major work on the Kelly story, titled *True History of the Kelly Gang*. The continued interaction of such media and artistic representations with Ned Kelly's extensive folklore has ensured that, like a number of other outlaw heroes, Ned Kelly remains a central element in Australian culture.

Related entries: Christie, Francis; Culture Heroes; Donohoe, Jack; Hall, Ben; Helpers; Heroes of Struggle; Hood, Robin; Morgan, Daniel "Mad Dog"; National Heroes; Outlaws; Ward, Frederick Wordsworth; Wild Colonial Boy; Women Dressed as Men

References and further reading
Jones, I., *Ned Kelly: A Short Life*, Melbourne: Lothian, 1995.
McQuilton, J., *The Kelly Outbreak, 1878–1880: The Geographical Dimension of Social Banditry*, Melbourne: Melbourne University Press, 1979.
Rose, D., *Dingo Makes Us Human: Life and Land in an Aboriginal Australian Culture*, Melbourne: Melbourne University Press, 1992, pp. 198–202, 205, 208, 231.
Seal, G., *Ned Kelly in Popular Tradition*, Melbourne: Hyland House, 1980.
Seal, G., *The Outlaw Legend: A Cultural Tradition in Britain, America, and Australia*, Melbourne: Cambridge University Press, 1996, pp. 147–179.

Kelly, Ned

See Kelly, Edward; National Heroes; Outlaws

Kentigern, Saint (Mungo)

Traditional founder of the Christian church at Glasgow in the sixth century A.D., this Scottish saint is remembered for his boyhood miracles of making a hazel bough catch fire to relight the church lamps and of having life restored to a robin in answer to his prayers. Legends about St. Kentigern's later life include the story of a visit from St. Columba and a tale that is part of the city of Glasgow's coat of arms. According to this story, a migratory legend told elsewhere, a queen betrays her royal spouse and gives her lover her husband's ring. The king finds out, takes the ring from the sleeping lover's finger, throws it into the Clyde, and imprisons the queen. Facing death, the queen sends word to St. Kentigern for help. Kentigern tells the messenger to go fishing in the Clyde. He catches a salmon, opens it, and discovers the ring inside, which he takes back to the queen. She is then able to take the ring to the king, who, forgivingly, releases her.

The folk name of this saint, "Mungo," is thought to derive from an ecclesiastical nickname, "Munghu." St. Kentigern is an example of a religious hero who, in Glasgow, is also celebrated as a local hero. He also has some attributes of the healer and the magician.

> **Related entries:** Helpers; Local Heroes; Magicians; Religious Heroes
> **References and further reading**
> Duckett, E., *The Wandering Saints*, London: Collins, 1959, pp. 88–90.

Khidre, El

"The Green One," El Khidre (also Al-Khadir, El Khudre, and other spellings) is a supernatural and immortal figure of Arabian lore. He appears unnamed in the Koran, and many of the tales attached to him are those told about Elijah and Rabbi Joshua ben Levi in Jewish tradition and St. George in Christian belief. He also makes an appearance in the *1,001 Nights*. El Khidre takes on various functions among the different cultural groups that tell of his doings.

In some stories, for example, he watches over those who travel across water. In Syria, he is known as a dragon-slayer. El Khidre has drunk at the Fountain of Immortal Youth and is often represented as a forever-young man with a long white beard and white hair. He appears also in Indian Muslim traditions, where he is often identified with the river Indus.

El Khidre's legends are bound up with those of other heroic figures of myth and folklore, including Moses, St. George, and Alexander the Great, who unlike El Khidre was not permitted to drink at the water of life. According to a Sufi legend, Moses goes to El Khidre as a pupil. El Khidre is reluctant to take Moses on but eventually does so, warning him that he must not question anything the master does. As the story progresses, El Khidre smashes a hole through a fishing boat, kills a young boy, and, in a village where he and his pupil are denied hospitality, repairs a broken wall. The amazed Moses can no longer keep silent and asks why El Khidre is doing these strange things. El Khidre rebukes him for asking questions and then explains that a wicked king is about to confiscate all seaworthy fishing boats, that the boy was an unbeliever and whose parents would now conceive a more devout child, and that the wall hid a treasure that needed to be kept safe for two orphans to inherit when they came of age. Then El Khidre sends Moses away.

In another of the many folktales about "the green one," a dervish convinces a gullible king that he will bring El Khidre before the king if the king will support the dervish for three years. When the three-year period ends, the dervish cannot produce El Khidre and so runs away. In his flight, he encounters a man dressed in white who agrees to accompany the dervish back to the king and with him to face the royal wrath. The king's ministers are asked to decide what punishment is appropriate. The first minister calls for the dervish to be cut into pieces, the second for him to be boiled in water, the third for him to be burned to death, and the fourth for him to be pardoned. Agreeing with each of the ministers, the man in white points out that the choice of punishments is in accord with the origins of each one: the first minister was the son of a butcher, the second the son of a cook, the third the son of a baker, and the fourth the son of an aristocrat. The king nobly pardons the dervish, and the man in white then reveals himself to be El Khidre. Thus the dervish manages to keep his foolish promise.

In this and similar stories, El Khidre appears in the role of the helper and wise man who reveals the truth, in this case how the social origins of the king's ministers influence their view of the world and how they wield power. Like Elijah, El Khidre also appears in legend as a friend of the poor and oppressed.

Related entries: Alexander the Great; Elijah the Prophet; Helpers; Religious Heroes

References and further reading

Cachia, P., *Popular Narrative Ballads of Modern Egypt*, Oxford: Oxford University Press, 1989, pp. 239–246.

Cavendish, R. (ed.), *Legends of the World*, London: Orbis, 1982, pp. 116–117.

El-Shamy, H. (coll., trans., ed.), *Folktales of Egypt*, Chicago: University of Chicago Press, 1980, pp. 118–132, 137–138.

Hanauer, J. (ed. Pickthall, M.), *Folk-Lore of the Holy Land: Moslem, Christian, and Jewish*, London: Duckworth, 1907, pp. 51–61.

Leach, M. (ed.), *Funk and Wagnall's Standard Dictionary of Folklore, Mythology, and Legend*, 2 vols., New York: Funk and Wagnall, 1972, vol. 1, p. 35.

Kidd, Captain

See Kidd, William

Kidd, William

Scottish buccaneer (c. 1645–1701). William "Captain" Kidd's many piratic exploits, real and imagined, are celebrated in a number of sailor songs and broadside ballads. Along the New England coast there are also tales about his buried, or otherwise secreted, treasure; some of these tales claim that the ghost of Captain Kidd watches over this booty. Kidd is a good example of a villain who, due to the combined influences of folklore and popular romanticization, has attained some positive qualities. He is not regarded in quite as dark a light as Blackbeard.

Related entries: Outlaws; Teach, William; Villains

Captain Kidd burying treasure (Bettmann/Corbis)

References and further reading

Beck, H., *Folklore and the Sea*, Middletown, CT: Wesleyan University Press, 1973, pp. 314–315, 327–330, 337–339, 396, 405.

Dorson, R., "Legends and Tall Tales," in Coffin, T. (ed.), *American Folklore*, Washington, D.C.: Voice of America Forum Lectures, 1968, p. 185.

Hugill, S., *Shanties from the Seven Seas*, London: Routledge & Kegan Paul, 1984 (1961), p. 449.

Lomax, J. and A. (colls. and comps.), *American Ballads and Folk Songs*, New York: Macmillan, 1934, p. 501.

Kihachi

Takeiwatatsu-No-Mikoto, or Lord Takeiwatatsu, is a legendary Japanese individual of exalted rank. His favorite pastime was to sit upon mountain peaks and shoot arrows at local landscape features. One day, seated on Mount Ojo and attended by a strong man named Kihachi, the lord happily fires his arrows at his fancied targets, sometimes successfully, sometimes not. It is Kihachi's job to retrieve the arrows and return them to the lord so that he can continue his target practice. Ninety-nine times, Kihachi races away to collect the arrows without incident. Even for a strong man, however, this task is exhausting, and so when Kihachi returns the hundredth arrow he kicks it toward the lord. This insult greatly angers the lord, and he chases Kihachi with the intention of killing him. The lord catches Kihachi and forces him to the ground, but Kihachi breaks wind, and the lord, confused, lets him go. Recovering, the lord continues his pursuit of Kihachi, and they fight from opposite banks of the Itsugase River, throwing boulders and pine trees at each other. Eventually the lord catches Kihachi and chops off his head. But the head jumps straight back onto the body. So the lord cuts off Kihachi's hand, but it also returns to his arm. The same thing happens when the lord cuts of Kihachi's foot. Embarrassed, the mighty lord finally manages to cut off the arms and legs and head and to bury them and the body in separate places.

When the lord cuts off Kihachi's head the second time, it flies into the sky and soon comes to lay a curse on the lord and the lands of his people, causing frost to blight their crops. Eventually the lord takes pity on his suffering people and beseeches Kihachi's spirit to come down to earth. Kihachi's spirit relents and descends to earth, where the lord duly has it enshrined as Shimomiya, the Frost Shrine in the center of Aso-Dani. The places where the various parts of Kihachi's body were buried are named after him.

This story reflects the importance placed on reciprocity in social relationships in Japanese culture. As Richard Dorson comments in introducing this tale, "This hero-legend has the true folk rawness usually softened by collectors and writers of folk tales."

Related entries: Urashima; Yamato; Yoshitsune; Yuri-waka

References and further reading

Dorson, R., *Folk Legends of Japan*, Rutland, VT: Charles E. Tuttle, 1962, pp. 156–158.
McAlpine, H. and W., *Japanese Tales and Legends*, Oxford: Oxford University Press, 1958.
Redesdale, Lord (ed.), *Tales of Old Japan*, London: Macmillan, 1908.

Kihuo

Legendary African hero of the Vakishamba people. Kihuo is the only male child born to a father who is the chief of his tribe. The chief wishes to remain chief as long as possible and so fears that Kihuo will usurp his power. However, the child is small even as he develops into adolescence, and the chief feels that he has nothing to fear. He even humiliates little Kihuo for his small stature and refuses to let him take the three ordeals that will confirm his initiation into manhood until he has grown large enough to take them. Frustrated, Kihuo goes to another chief and proves to him that he is strong enough, brave enough, and cunning enough to be a man, these being the three tests of manhood. The other chief then initiates him, and from that moment Kihuo starts to grow.

He returns to his own people and excels among them in the manly skills, especially in throwing the club, causing his father increasing concern for his own position. Eventually the young warriors rebel against the aging chief and declare Kihuo their leader, sending Kihuo's father away. Kihuo grows even taller and begins to plot how he can extend his and his people's territory and power. His first step in this direction is to again prove his cunning and to destroy the neighboring people by trickery. Encouraged by this easy victory, Kihuo determines to conquer the powerful people to the west, led by the tyrannical but gigantic Orombo. He challenges Orombo to a duel in which the two chiefs, the gigantic Orombo and the tall but comparatively diminutive Kihuo face off. Orombo taunts Kihuo about his height, calling him a dwarf. Then he throws his great spear but misses Kihuo, who throws his club, killing Orombo at once. Kihuo's men cheer, and so do Orombo's, overjoyed to be rid of the tyrant who had oppressed and abused them for so long.

Kihuo is now the leader of a large tribe, which he uses to conquer other peoples and to extend his territory. Eventually he determines to attack the numerous and powerful Moshi people, led by a chief who is a great and clever leader. Kihuo's men are unhappy about making war on such a tribe, but Kihuo marches them south. As they reach the lands of the Moshi, he commands his men to construct a massive hill of stones, a feat that increases their self-confidence greatly. They call the hill of stones Big Kihuo and march on to fight the Moshi. They are defeated and have to retreat. When they reach the big hill of stones on their way home, Kihuo tells his men to rearrange the stones into another heap. This heap is much smaller and indicates to the men how many of their number have been killed in a vain attempt to attain more territory. Kihuo himself gives the pathetically small pile of stones the name Little Kihuo. He never waged war on anyone again.

This story has parallels with stories of unpromising heroes making good in spectacular ways. In this case, the small stature of Kihuo puts him into a category with Fereyel and Tom Thumb, and his contest with a giant is reminiscent of the familiar story of David and Goliath and of stories about Jack the Giant-Killer. The theme of pride, arrogance, and overconfidence leading to defeat and humiliation of the hero is central to this legend and is also found in other traditions. Although Kihuo is defeated and humiliated through his arrogance, he is still recognized by his people as a great warrior.

Related entries: Fereyel; Giant-Killers; Magicians; No Bigger Than a Finger; Tom Thumb; Warriors

References and further reading

Baumann, H., *Hero Legends of the World*, London: Dent and Sons, 1975 (1972), pp. 49–52.

Courlander, H. (comp.), *A Treasury of African Folklore*, New York: Crown, 1975.

King Horn
See Horn, Hind

King Matthias
See Matthias, King

King of Ireland's Son, The
Hero of an elaborate Irish tale in which the legendary protagonist shoots a raven one winter's day. The raven falls onto the snow, and the King of Ireland's Son is smitten by the sight of the red blood and black feathers against the white snow. He vows to seek a wife with hair as black as a raven, cheeks as red as blood, and skin as

white as snow. He is told of such a woman in the east and journeys forth to find her. On his way, he comes first to a funeral unable to proceed to the burial of the body because the deceased has not paid his debts. The King of Ireland's Son kindly pays these debts, accompanies the corpse to the graveyard, and then proceeds on his way. He falls into the company of a short green man who joins him as his servant in return for being permitted to be the first to kiss the princess when they find her. As they proceed, they are joined by five others, including a skilled marksman who asks for a small home and garden in return for his services on the quest; a man whose hearing is so acute he can hear grass grow; a marvelous runner who stops himself from going too fast by tying one leg up; a mighty breather whose breath is sufficient to blow houses away; and a prodigious breaker of stones. Marked by encounters with giants and the acquisition of various magical objects, including a cap of invisibility, a magic sword, and magic shoes, the quest continues.

When they finally reach the princess, she is enchanted and imprisoned in a castle surrounded by the gory heads of previous suitors placed on spikes. The princess gives the King of Ireland's Son a pair of scissors with the provision that he return them in the morning; she then puts him to sleep. She takes the scissors to the King of Poison and asks him to keep them until morning. The King of Poison falls asleep, and the short green man, wearing the cap of invisibility, comes into the room and, with the help of the magic shoes and sword, takes the scissors back to the King of Ireland's Son, enabling him to return them to the princess as asked.

The next night the princess gives the hero a comb under the same conditions. Much the same events occur, and the short green man gets the comb back to the sleeping hero just in time. On the third night, the princess gives the comb back to the hero with the further stipulation that he must bring it back the next morning along with the head of the man who has used it. Failure to succeed in this task will mean the hero loses his own head. Again the King of Ireland's Son falls asleep, and again the princess takes the comb to the King of Poison, who locks it in a rock and sits guard on it. The short green man, though, uses the magic sword to break into the rock and to cut off the King of Poison's head. The hero then delivers both comb and head to the princess the following morning, as directed.

The princess is angry and sets a further task. She requires three bottles of medicinal balm from the well of the western world. She will send her runner to fetch it, the hero will send his. If her runner returns with the bottles first, then the King of Ireland's Son will lose his head. The hero's extraordinary runner is winning the race when the princess's runner, an old hag, tricks him to sleep, spills his water, and leaves him slumbering with his head on a horse's skull.

At this point, the acute hearer lays his ear on the ground and tells the King of Ireland's Son what has happened and that the hag is winning the race. The marksman shoots an arrow that knocks the horse's skull from under the sleeping runner's head; the breather blows the hag back to the western world; and the hero's runner dashes back to the well, fills his three bottles again, and returns first. The difficult-to-please princess then sets still more tests, all successfully negotiated by the hero's trusty companions. Finally, the princess marries the King of Ireland's Son. However, now the short green man demands the promised first kiss of the bride. It turns out that the princess is in fact filled with serpents that would have killed the hero if the short green man had not killed them all. Now it is safe to return the purified princess to the King of Ireland's Son, and the short green man reveals his true identity as the corpse the hero had so kindly helped on his way to the afterworld at the start of the quest. The short green man and his companions disappear, never to be seen again.

The main motif of this complex tale is revealed at the end. Known as "the grateful dead," it is the basis of, or included in, a number of folktales from many traditions, including European, West Indian, Hispanic, and some traditions of Asia. Generally the story involves a charitable hero who pays for the burial of a corpse. Later, the hero is joined by a strange companion who helps him out in various magical ways, often requiring a share of whatever prize or booty results. Eventually the helper, who may also be in the shape of an animal, assists the hero to attain the love of a princess, and the hero is faced with the possibility of having to cut her in half to honor the condition set by his mysterious helper. At this point the helper reveals his or her identity as the corpse the hero had paid to have buried, and all ends in the traditional happy manner.

The tale of the grateful dead is a version of the helpful companion and the faithful servant type, and the early encounter of the King of Ireland's Son with the burial party is found attached to many stories. This particular tale has an uncommonly large number of folktale motifs embedded within it; so much so that it could even be considered an elaborate tall tale, even by the standards of the wonder tale. There are elements found in many better-known folktales here, including Rumpelstiltskin, Rapunzel, and Snow White.

Related entries: Faithful Henry; Faithful John; Frog Prince, The; Helpers; Rapunzel; Snow White

References and further reading

Behan, B., *Brendan Behan's Ireland: An Irish Sketchbook*, New York: Random House, 1962, pp. 136–141.

Glassie, H., *Irish Folk Tales*, New York: Pantheon, 1985, pp. 39–41.

Gose, E., Jr., *The World of the Irish Wonder Tale: An Introduction to the Study of Fairy Tales*, Toronto: University of Toronto Press, 1985.

Leach, M. (ed.), *Funk and Wagnall's Dictionary of Folklore, Mythology and Legend*, 2 vols., New York: Funk and Wagnall, 1972, pp. 580–581.

McGarry, M. (ed.), *Great Folktales of Old Ireland*, New York: Bell Publishing, 1972.

Ó hÓgáin, D., *The Hero in Irish Folk History*, New York: Gill and Macmillan, 1985.

Knowall, Doctor

Doctor Knowall is the central figure of a widespread folktale told throughout Europe, India, Asia, some parts of Africa, and the New World. In the Grimms' version, perhaps the most familiar, a peasant named Crabb impersonates a doctor and general wise man. A nobleman who has lost a good deal of money requests that

Crabb recover it. The "doctor" and his wife go to the nobleman's castle for a meal, and as each of the sumptuous dishes passes around the table, Crabb says to his wife, "That's the first," "That's the second," and so on. The servants carrying the dishes are responsible for the nobleman's missing money and, in their guilt, assume that Crabb is referring to them as the culprits rather than to the dishes they are carrying. Finally, Crabb is asked to guess what one of the covered dishes contains. Fearing his ruse will be revealed, the "doctor" calls out, "Alas, poor Crabb." This convinces the guilty servants that Crabb is a wise man for, coincidentally, the dish contains crabs. The servants speak with Crabb privately. He is then able to reveal to the nobleman where the missing money is hidden but also shields the servants from retribution. In return, he is rewarded by both the noble and the grateful servants. Most versions of the story, which is probably of Eastern origin, include the pun on the hero's name, which may also be "Cricket" or "Rat," and show that, despite his stupidity, Doctor Knowall does finish by doing the wise thing.

In the Italian version of this story, the "Doctor Knowall" figure is an impoverished peasant named Crab. In India, he may be a poor Brahman named Harisarman, or possibly an unnamed trickster figure, as in a version from the Santal Parganas district north of Calcutta. A Danish rendition, collected in the nineteenth century, shows the narrative similarities between folk hero traditions and highlights the great popularity of the unpromising hero theme.

In the Danish story, the hero is a poor old farmer who makes an unwise sale of land to a doctor in return for the doctor's cloak, pipe, cane, hat, and book of medicines. The farmer's wife is upset when she discovers he has sold their land for these worthless articles. But the farmer says that now he will be able to practice as a doctor and they will soon have all the money they need. Unfortunately, no patients came to see the farmer in his new role as doctor, and so he decides to advertise by placing a sign above his front door. The sign was to say that he was "the greatest doctor in the world,"

but the farmer's spelling skills are poor, and he actually writes on the sign, "Here Lives the Greatest Detective in the World." The oddity of this sign attracts the attention of the king, who makes a mental note that he might one day avail himself of the detective's advertised services.

As it happened, some time later, two of the king's horses are stolen. The horses cannot be found, and so the king sends a servant to the detective for help. The servant arrives at the detective's house and finds him sitting in his doctor's clothes, reading his medicine book. The servant begins to ask for help, but the doctor interrupts him, saying, "I know it already." Taken aback, the servant asks if the doctor can direct him to the horses. The doctor then writes a prescription and tells the servant to have it filled and to take the medicine, saying, "Then you will find them." The messenger does as he is bidden but immediately becomes ill. He manages to get help in a nearby house, but his illness becomes worse. But then he hears a horse neighing outside the house. Going out into the yard, he finds the king's missing steeds and takes them to him. Overjoyed, the king sends the doctor-detective a large sum of money, a fee that pleased the "detective" and his wife very much indeed.

Some time later, the golden ring belonging to the king's daughter is stolen. Again the king calls on the doctor-detective for help and asks him to attend at the palace. The doctor-detective comes to the palace, accompanied by his wife. The king prepares a great feast in their honor, and when the couple sits down to eat, the doctor-detective mutters to his wife to take note of how many fine dishes they eat. As a servant brings in the first dish, the doctor-detective says, "That's the first one." The servant, who is one of the thieves, turns pale and begins to shake. He returns to the kitchens and tells his two companions in crime what happened. The second servant is due to carry in the next dish, and the thieves decide that since the doctor-detective seems to know of their crime, they had better try and get him to come into the kitchen so that they can bribe him to keep quiet. As the second servant brings out the next dish, the doctor-detective says, "This is the second one." As frightened as the first servant, the second servant tries in vain to attract the doctor-detective's attention and then returns to the kitchen. The third servant then comes out carrying the third dish, whereupon the doctor-detective says to his wife, "Here is the third one." So frightened is the third servant that he tugs violently at the doctor-detective's sleeve, gains his attention, and asks him to step in to the kitchen. There, the three servants confess their crime to the cunning doctor-detective, who promises to have them spared from the gallows if they give him a large sum of money and return the ring. They agree, and the doctor-detective asks them to secrete the ring in a cake and serve it to the king's dog the following morning. The thieves agree.

The next morning, the king asks the doctor-detective where the ring and the thief are to be found. Looking around the room, the doctor-detective announces dramatically that both are in that very room. "There is the thief," he proclaims, pointing at the dog. The king is angry at what he takes to be a stupid suggestion, but the doctor-detective asks for the dog to be killed in order for the ring to be found. The dog is dispatched, and the ring is found inside the dead beast's stomach. The amazed and grateful king gives the doctor-detective a great deal of money as a reward, and, in return for his silence, the doctor-detective also receives the money promised by the thieves. So famous does the doctor-detective become, that no one steals anything ever again, and he and his wife live happily on their earnings, honored by all.

The variations on what is essentially the same story are typical of the manner in which folk traditions are adapted to different times and places and to the needs and interests of different social groups.

Related entries: Halid; Numskulls and Noodles
References and further reading
Bay, J., *Danish Folk Tales*, New York: Harper and Brothers, 1899, pp. 111–118.
Bompas, C., *Folklore of the Santal Parganas*, London: David Nutt, 1909, pp. 206–208.
Crane, T., *Italian Popular Tales*, Boston and New York: Houghton Mifflin and Co., 1885; reprint, Detroit: Singing Tree Press, 1968, no. 109.
Jacobs, J. (ed.), *Indian Fairy Tales*, London: David Nutt, 1892; reprint, New York: Dover Publications, 1969, pp. 85–89.
Klipple, M., *African Folktales with Foreign Analogues*, New York: Garland, 1992, pp. 308–309.
Ranke, K. (ed.), Baumann, L. (trans.), *Folktales of Germany*, Chicago: University of Chicago Press, 1966, pp. 142–144.

Kobo Daishi
See Kukai

Koshchei
Usually known as Koshchei the Deathless or Old Bones the Deathless, this Russian monster was unable to be killed because its soul was kept somewhere outside its body. The soul is often said to have been held within an egg or in some remote and secret location. However, Ivan Tsarevich, with the help of Vasilisa Kirbit'evna, succeeds in finding the soul and killing Koshchei. Koshchei also features in other Russian stories, including that of Marya Morevna.

Related entries: Baba-Yaga; Devil, The; Morevna, Marya; Ogres; Tsarevich, Ivan; Villains
References and further reading
Alderson, B. (ed.), *Red Fairy Book: Collected by Andrew Lang*, Harmondsworth, Middlesex: Kestrel Books, 1976, pp. 14–26.
Ralston, W., *Russian Folk-Tales*, London: Smith, Elder, and Co., 1873.

Kraljevic, Marco
Marco the King's Son is the great warrior hero of Serbian and Yugoslav tradition. The historical Marco was a vassal of the Turks and died in 1394, but his folklore takes little account of these difficult facts, and he appears in ballads and folktales as a fierce warrior of great strength who frequently kills large numbers of despotic and villainous Turks. Marco is a great drinker, great lover, and a wise and just ruler who fears the Christian God and defends the faith.

According to one tradition, Marco was the offspring of a *veela*, or fairy queen, and a *zmay*, or dragon. He was an extraordinarily strong man, brave and cunning, a prodigious drinker, and he could be cruel, especially to the hated Turks.

In folklore he is assisted by an alliance with the mountain nymphs and the world's swiftest horse, Sarac or Sharatz (meaning "piebald"), which is also able to talk.

Marco's truthfulness is an important element of his legend, exemplified in the story of how he settles the question of who will inherit the Serbian empire. The contenders are his father, his two uncles, and the young tsarevitch, Ourosho, Marco's godson. They cannot agree on who is to inherit the kingdom and so Marco gets the difficult job of deciding. He consults his mother, who reminds him of the need to tell the truth no matter what, then he rides to Kosovo, where the contenders impatiently await him. Since each contender has a personal connection with Marco, each thinks that he will be chosen. Marco names Ourosho, enraging his father, who tries to kill him. Marco escapes into the church with divine help, and his father curses him roundly, though the new czar, Ourosho, is fulsome in his praise of the hero.

Other elements of Marco's extensive legendry deal with his rescue of a princess from an unwanted marriage to a Moor, or Turk. Marco beheads the unlucky prospective groom with his trademark giant club and thus abolishes wedding taxes imposed by the Moors. He causes the fierce bully Bogdan to be afraid of him, rescues allies and companions, and captures enemy generals, all with the help of his wondrous steed. At the urging of his mother, Marco agrees to marry the daughter of King Shishman of Bulgaria. The wedding procession of the princess is headed by a man who has fallen hopelessly in love with her but nevertheless sells the princess to the doge of Venice for three bootfuls of gold. The princess escapes the doge, makes her way to Marco's tent, and tells the hero what has happened. He visits the doge and takes his predictable revenge. He then carves into two the man who sold the princess.

On another occasion a veela, or fairy, kills Marco's brother with a magic dart. With a characteristic combination of threats and rewards, Marco exhorts his steed Sharatz to pursue the veela. If the horse catches the fairy, Marco promises:

I shall shoe thy hoofs with pure silver and gild them with the finest gold; I shall cover thee with a silken cloak reaching to thy knees, and on it I shall fasten fine silk tassels to hang from thy knees to thy hoofs; thy mane shall I entwine with threads of gold and adorn it with rare pearls. But, woe to thee if thou reachest not the *veela!* Both thy eyes shall I tear out; thy four legs shall I break; and I shall abandon thee here and thou shalt for ever creep from one fir-tree to another (Petrovich 1914).

Spurred on by such blandishments and threats, the wondrous steed does catch up with the fairy, and Marco brings it down with his club, forcing the veela to use magic herbs to return his brother's life. The veela then returns to her sisters and warns them never to shoot at heroes as long as Prince Marco and his Sharatz are alive, as the consequences will be dire. Marco's other adventures are many, though they tend to be similar to these.

Marco's death is heralded by the stumbling of the always sure-footed Sharatz. A veela tells Marco that it is he who is to die and that even his great heroic qualities cannot preserve him from death, "the ancient slayer." Sure of his fate, Marco grieves for himself, bemoaning the fact that even his 300 years of life have not been sufficient. Then, to ensure that no Turk shall ever use his horse, he beheads and buries the faithful Sharatz, breaks his saber and lance, and hurls his great club into the sea saying, "When my club returns from the depths of the ocean, then shall come a hero as great as Marco!" The hero leaves gold for the digging of his grave, for the adornment of churches, and for distribution among the poor. He makes the sign of the cross and, beside a spring, lies down on his cloak to die. His body is passed by many who think he is asleep. After a week, a priest discovers that the hero is dead and has him buried in the white church of Vilindar, in an unmarked grave to keep his remains safe from enemies.

Like a number of other national and culture heroes, Marco is said not to be dead, only sleeping deep inside the mountains near his castle at Prilip and awaiting the next time of his country's need. Every now and then he wakes and looks at the rock where he thrust his sword. When the sword is out of the rock, he will know that it is time to return to help the Serbians regain the empire they lost at the battle of Kosovo.

As these summaries indicate, Marco has parallels with similar figures of other European traditions, and he also appears in Bulgarian and Rumanian lore. He is known as Marco the Plowman from a popular story in which Marco's mother asks him to give up his wild and dangerous ways and to settle into the peaceful life of the farmer. Marco agrees and goes out to plow. Instead of plowing fields, he plows up the Sultan's highway, incurring the wrath of the Turkish overseers, who kill the oxen pulling the plow when Marco refuses to stop. There ensues a great fight in which Marco kills all the overseers and the soldiers sent to help them and takes their weapons home. He throws the bloody blades down at his mother's feet, saying, "This is the harvest I have reaped from my plowing." Marco's mother realizes that there is no point in trying to make Marco change his ways and never again attempts to influence him.

According to Petrovitch, writing around 1914, there are approximately thirty-eight poems and seventy to eighty legends about Marco's exploits, "and there is hardly a Serb or a Bulgar anywhere to be found who cannot recite at least a few of them."

Related entries: Arthur; Culture Heroes; Heroes of Struggle; Moringer, Noble; National Heroes; Sleepers; Warriors

References and further reading
Baumann, H., Hero Legends of the World, London: Dent and Sons, 1975 (1972), pp. 28–30.
Curcija-Prodanovic, N., Heroes of Serbia, London: Oxford University Press, 1963, pp. 67–108.
Lord, A., The Singer of Tales, New York: Athaneum, 1976 (1960), pp. 66–67, 69, 72–75, 99, 113–117, 236–241, 290.
Mijatovies, C. (ed. and trans.), Serbian Folklore, New York: Benjamin Bloom, 1968 (1874).
Petrovich, W., Hero Tales and Legends of the Serbians, London: Harrap, 1914, pp. 59–118.
Rootham, H., Kossovo: Heroic Songs of the Serbs, Oxford: Blackwell, 1920.

Krpan, Martin
See Culture Heroes

Kukai
Kukai (774–835), a historical figure of ninth-century Japan, was given the posthumous name of Kobo Daishi, or "Saint Kobo," by which he is known in folklore. Kukai founded the Ryobu-Shinto sect, a combination of Buddhism and Shinto, the indigenous religion of Japan, after traveling to China to study. He is also credited with the invention of the phonetic script for the Japanese language. Born with his hands in prayer, this holy and wise Japanese figure is known for the various miracles he performs, especially one in which he uses his staff to conjure up a spring. In other tales, the spring is said to possess miraculous healing properties. In some stories, Kobo Daishi is tormented by sea monsters and dragons during his prayers, but he fights these distractions off with magic swords and with the trick of spitting the light of the evening star at them.

Kobo Daishi's most famous temple is the one he had built at Mount Koya. How this came about is the subject of a foundation legend. While still in China wondering where to build his temple in Japan, Kobo Daishi throws a three-pronged wand, or vajra, a holy implement, toward his home country, praying it will come to earth at the place that would be best for his temple. The vajra disappears into the sky, and it is not until Kobo Daishi returns to Japan and establishes his sect that he has the opportunity to go and look for it. He sets out from the capital in the year 816. When he reaches the county of Uchi in the Province of Yamato, he meets a giant, red-faced hunter in a green coat, carrying a bow and arrows and accompanied by two black dogs. Kobo tells the hunter of his purpose, and the hunter replies that he can direct the holy man to the place where his vajra fell to the ground. Kobo follows the directions and reaches a river near the border of Yamato and neighboring Kii Province. There he meets a man who calls himself the Mountain King. The man gives all the land to Kobo. They then go on together and reach a basin surrounded by eight mountain peaks and covered in tall cypress trees. In one of the trees Kobo finds his vajra. He is happy and learns from the Mountain King that he and the hunter Kobo had met earlier were both gods. The Mountain King then vanishes, and Kobo goes to the capital, resigns his offices, and returns to Mount Koya to build the Temple of the Vajra Peak.

Kobo was sixty years old when he died in 835. It is said that he sat in a cave meditating until he passed away, his body sealed inside the cave. Although he was dead, his hair still grew and his disciples eventually shaved it before closing the cave again. It was undisturbed for a long time, until a young student of one of Kobo's disciples opened the cave, shaved the body, and dressed it in new clothes. The cave has not been opened since and is the center of a shrine visited by many pilgrims, even though women have been allowed to participate only since the late nineteenth century. Kobo is also said to be awaiting the coming of the future Buddha known as Minoku. Some of Kobo's miracles, especially those related to water, have counterparts in tales of Christian saints and miracles and in the traditions of other cultures.

Related entries: Elijah the Prophet; Joseph of Arimathea, Saint; Religious Heroes; Wise Men and Women

References and further reading

Cavendish, R. (ed.), *Legends of the World*, London: Orbis, 1982, pp. 66–67.
Dorson, R., *Folk Legends of Japan*, Rutland, VT: Charles E. Tuttle, 1962, pp. 33–36.
McAlpine, H. and W., *Japanese Tales and Legends*, Oxford: Oxford University Press, 1958.
Tyler, R. (trans. and ed.), *Japanese Tales*, New York: Pantheon Books, 1987, no. 26.

Kuzonoha

The white fox bride of Japanese poet-hero Abe No Yasuna. Kuzonoha typifies many of the traits attributed to the fox in Asian traditions, where this animal has a role similar to that of the werewolf of European belief. The fox maiden has the ability to shape-shift from animal to human form, usually at will, and lives with a male human as his wife for a greater or shorter period, eventually disappearing or dying, as in the story of Kuzonoha and Abe No Yasuna.

Related entries: Fox Maiden, The; Shape-Shifters; Swan Maiden; Yasuna, Abe No

References and further reading

Davis, F. H., *Myths and Legends of Japan*, London: G. G. Harrap and Co., 1913, p. 95.
James, G. (ed.), *Japanese Fairy Tales*, London: Macmillan, 1923, pp. 215–222. First published as *Green Willow and Other Japanese Fairy Tales*, London: Macmillan and Company, 1910.
Seki, K. (ed.), Adams, R. (trans.), *Folktales of Japan*, London: Routledge and Kegan Paul, 1963. First published in Japanese in 1956–1957.
Werner, E., *Myths and Legends of China*, New York: Arno Press, 1976 (1922), pp. 370–375.

L

Lady Godiva
See Godiva, Lady

Lady Isabel
See Isabel, Lady

Lazar
Eponymous Serbian founder of the village of Lazaropolje in southern Macedonia. According to legend, Lazar is the sole survivor of a Turkish attack. All the villagers escape to a cave in the hills except one young girl. She taunts the Turks but in the process reveals the whereabouts of the cave. The Turks light fires in the cave's mouth, and all inside are asphyxiated, except Lazar. He crawls through the ground and through the mountain to a valley on the other side, clawing with such power that he carves a furrow through the earth that becomes the bed of a stream. At the point where he emerges from the hill, he establishes the village that bears his name. Lazar is both a local hero and a hero of struggle.

Related entries: Heroes of Struggle; Local Heroes
References and further reading
Curcija-Prodanovic, N., *Heroes of Serbia*, London: Oxford University Press, 1963, pp. 39–45.
Mijatovies, C. (ed. and trans.), *Serbian Folklore*, New York: Benjamin Bloom, 1968 (1874).

Lemminkäinen
Brother of Väinämöinen and hero of the Finno-Ugric epic cycle known as *The Kalevala*. The material of which are thought by some scholars to be 2000 years old. Also known as Ahti, Kaukomieli, or Kauko, Lemminkäinen is a young, happy warrior and lover. After divorcing his first wife, Kylli of Saari, because she broke her promise not to dance again, Lemminkäinen woos the maid of Pohjola, youngest daughter of Louhi, queen of Pohjola, a frozen waste far to the north. Louhi sets Lemminkäinen three tests to prove his worthiness; in the course of the tests, he is killed by an old Lappman and his body is dismembered. His mother reassembles the pieces of the body and, with some heavenly honey, resurrects the hero. Later Lemminkäinen, accompanied by his brothers Väinämöinen and Ilmarinen, steals the Sampo, a magic mill able to turn wastelands into productive farmlands, from Louhi. As they make their escape, the Sampo is broken into three pieces and lost, though enough survives to turn Kalevala into a fruitful and pleasant land. The fate of Pohjola is not told.

Related entries: Culture Heroes; Väinämöinen
References and further reading
Dixon-Kennedy, M., *European Myth and Legend*, London: Blandford, 1997, pp. 145–146.
Lönnrot, E. (comp.), Magoun, F. (trans.), *The Kalevala, or Poems of the Kalevala District*, Cambridge: Harvard University Press, 1963.

Li Ji
Serpent-slaying heroine of Chinese tales and ballads. Li Ji, the youngest of six daughters, offers herself as the tenth annual sacrifice to a giant serpent that terrorizes the people of the Yung Mountains in Fukien. Armed with a snake-hunting dog and a sharp sword, she entices the serpent from its lair with sweetened rice balls and slays it. She enters the cave and recovers the skulls of the previous nine victims, making the point that they died because of their timidity and that she, by implication, has succeeded through her boldness. The king hears of Li Ji's bravery and marries her. He makes her father a magistrate and showers the family with riches in gratitude for Li Ji having rid the country of serpents forever.

In Chinese tradition, serpents often take the role of dragons in hero traditions, since dragons are a symbol of peace, prosperity, and good luck. However, the story of Li Ji is squarely in the tradition of the many dragon-slaying folktales and legends of the world, although women dragon-slayers are much less common than males.

Related entries: Dragon-Slayers; Jack and the Beanstalk; Jack the Giant-Killer; Villains
References and further reading
Roberts, M., *Chinese Fairy Tales and Fantasies,* New York: Pantheon, 1979, pp. 129–131.
Eberhard, W. (ed.), Parsons, D. (trans.), *Folktales of China,* Chicago: University of Chicago Press, 1965 (1937), pp. 6, 51, 65, 78, 111, 170, 186, 234, 236.
Zhao, Q., *A Study of Dragons, East and West,* New York: Peter Lang Publishing, 1992.

Li Kui

Much-loved peasant hero of the Chinese *Water Margin* novel (tenth century A.D., Northern Song Dynasty) about a band of outlaws similar in many ways to Robin Hood's band of merry men. Li Kui's contempt for the repressive elements of society leads him to oppose these elements at every step and to develop a fierce desire to destroy them. These characteristics have given him the nickname of "The Black Whirlwind." Li Kui is simple, sometimes vulgar, but loyal to the poor and the oppressed and committed to the ideals of the outlaws of the marsh.

Related entries: Hood, Robin; Lu Zhishen; Outlaws
References and further reading
Li, N., *Old Tales of China,* Singapore: Graham Brash, 1983 (1981), pp. 165–167.
Osers, E. (trans.), *Chinese Folktales,* London: Bell and Sons, 1971. First published in German as Wilhelm, R. (trans.), *Chinesische Märchen,* 1958.

Liars

Heroic lying is a feature of many folk traditions. It is especially notable in New World frontier societies such as North America and Australia. While these cultures have produced some stupendous liars, boasters, and yarn spinners, including Davy Crockett, Crooked Mick, Mike Fink, and others, great liars are also found elsewhere, most notably in the figure of Baron Münchhausen. Local and regional folk traditions frequently boast celebrated liars or storytellers who can "spin a yarn," as in the example of the American Henry "Len" Lorenzo, tall-tale teller of northern Idaho, whose reputation and repertoire lived on long after his death. Lying, or bending the truth in one way or another, usually for comic effect, is also a feature of many trickster traditions and features prominently in relation to master thieves and their activities.

Related entries: Baba, Ali; Crockett, Davy; Crooked Mick; Frontier Heroes; Local Heroes; Münchhausen; Pepper, Tom; Thieves; Tricksters
References and further reading
Ausubel, N. (ed.), *A Treasury of Jewish Folklore,* London: Vallentine, Mitchell, 1972 (1948), pp. 374–376.
Brunvand, J., "Henry Lorenzo ('Len')," in Brunvand, J. (ed.), *American Folklore: An Encyclopedia,* New York: Garland, 1996, p. 365.
Dorson, R., *American Folklore,* Chicago: University of Chicago Press, 1959, pp. 41–43, 66, 84, 204–205, 211–212.
Jansen, W., *Abraham "Oregon" Smith: Pioneer, Folk Hero, and Tale-Teller,* New York: Arno, 1977.
Mark, V., "Cultural Pastiches: Intertextualities in the Moncrabeau Liars' Festival Narratives," in *Cultural Anthropology* 6, no. 2, 1991, pp. 193–211.
Ranke, K., *Folktales of Germany,* Chicago: University of Chicago Press, 1966, p. 193.

Little Dutch Boy, The

A well-known story in many countries—the legendary tale of the little boy who plugged a leaking dike with his finger long enough for help to arrive and so save Holland from inundation—is little known in the Netherlands. The story is not an authentic piece of Dutch folklore, although many people believe that it is. The Little Dutch Boy and his useful finger originated in the writing of the American author Mary Mapes Dodge, in a book she published in 1865 titled *Hans Brinker, or the Silver Skates.*

This story—its origins and its circulation outside the country of its supposed origin—is a good example of "fakelore," the usually deliberate creation of an item of folklore for a variety of nonfolkloric purposes, sometimes literary, sometimes political, often commercial. While fakelore is usually not of authentic folkloric origins, it may be taken into the folk tradition, as in the case of Paul Bunyan and a number of other heroes and heroines, including, it seems, the Little Dutch Boy.

Related entries: Bunyan, Paul; Children's Folk Heroes; Culture Heroes; Occupational Heroes; Santa Claus

References and further reading
Dodge, M., *Hans Brinker, or the Silver Skates*, n.p., 1865.

Little Goose Girl, The

Heroine of a Scandinavian folktale in which the virginal goose girl weds a handsome prince, saving him from marrying an unchaste princess. Versions of the story are told throughout Europe, and the plot also features in Scots and French ballads. This is a different tale than that best-known in the Grimm brothers' version as "The Goose Girl." Their version is also a bride substitution story but differs in that a wicked servant forces the princess to take on the servant's identity and then impersonates the princess to the prince. Only after the wedding is the truth revealed, when a talking horse's head is placed on the castle wall. As in many other versions of this story, the false princess is duped into describing the manner of her own execution, which, in this case, is to be rolled in a barrel studded with nails. The substituted identity foiled is a feature found in many folktales, including those of heroes.

Related entries: Fairy Tale Heroes; Goose Girl, The; Maria, Fenda; Whuppie, Molly

References and further reading
Leach, M. (ed.), *Funk and Wagnall's Standard Dictionary of Folklore, Mythology, and Legend*, London: New English Library, 1975. Abridged one-volume edition of *Funk and Wagnall's Standard Dictionary of Folklore, Mythology, and Legend*, 2 vols., New York: Funk and Wagnall, 1972, p. 635.

Little John

The large, strong, and skilled companion of Robin Hood. Legend has it that Robin Hood met Little John when both were trying to cross a stream from the opposite sides by way of a narrow log. Each refused to yield to the other, and so they fought with quarterstaves. Little John won, but he was so magnanimous in victory, and his prowess so admired by Robin, that the outlaw immediately invited him to join his band as his second in command. This combat story, in which the person destined to be the hero's helper bests the hero, also features in other Robin Hood lore, including the ballad "Robin Hood and the Peddler," and is often attached to other heroic figures of folklore, such as the Japanese character Benkei.

Related entries: Benkei; Helpers; Hood, Robin; Outlaws

Little Moron

Apparently evolving in the 1920s, Little Moron was an American embodiment of heroic stupidity existing in absurdly humorous anecdotes and school yard jokes. Benjamin Botkin points out that Little Moron stories usually used puns or mistakes to present the Moron as "Superman turned upside down." Sometimes Little Moron anecdotes took the simple form of riddle jokes. For example, "What did Little Moron do when he found out he was dying? He moved into the living room." More elaborate anecdotes had a touch of the occupational hero about them, such as the story in which a group of morons is building a house and one inquires of the boss whether they should build it from the top down or the bottom up. Incredulously, the boss tells them that they must build it from the bottom up, of course. The Little Moron turns to the other morons and says: "Tear 'er down, boys! Gotta start all over!"

Related entries: Dad and Dave; Drongo; Kabajan; Lucky Hans; Numskulls and Noodles; Occupational Heroes; Wise Men of Gotham

References and further reading
Botkin, B, "Little Moron," in Leach, M. (ed.), *Funk and Wagnall's Standard Dictionary of Folklore, Mythology, and Legend*, London: New English Library, 1975. Abridged one-volume edition of *Funk and Wagnall's Standard Dictionary of Folklore, Mythology, and Legend*, 2 vols., New York: Funk and Wagnall, 1972, p. 635.
Dorson, R., *American Folklore*, Chicago: University of Chicago Press, 1959, p. 249.

Little Peachling

See Momotaro

Little Red Riding Hood

Little Red Riding Hood is a multifaceted heroine with a checkered history. The first printed version of the story is that of Charles Perrault, published in Paris in 1697 as "Le petit chaperon rouge" (The Little Red Hat) in his *Histoires du temps passé: Avec des moralitez* (Stories of Times Past: With Morals). As the subtitle of Perrault's work indicates, he was especially concerned to use the stories contained in his work as moral tales, warnings for the young and their adult caretakers of the dangers that lurked in the everyday world. Because of this intent, and because Perrault was very much an upper-middle-class man of his era, he rewrote the orally circulating folktales he selected for an educated, affluent, and discerning audience, excising and ameliorating certain unacceptable elements of the folk versions.

A number of scholars have shown how, and why, Perrault adapted the folk versions of the Little Red Riding Hood story in the way he did. It is now known that tales of ogres, wolves, werewolves, and other monsters threatening to devour small children were commonplaces of European medieval life and that superstitions and beliefs of this sort persisted well into the early modern period. In some parts of France there was endemic dread of walking in the woods alone, and throughout these areas in the fifteenth to the sixteenth centuries, there were innumerable persecutions and trials of individuals believed to be werewolves. Significantly, it is from these areas that many of the folk versions of the Little Red Riding Hood story have been collected by folklorists and others interested in popular traditions. It seems that Perrault, probably through family tradition, had heard some of these stories and used them as the basis for his own moralistic and literary rewrite.

What were the earlier stories like? As far as we are able to tell from oral versions collected in the nineteenth century, they did not mention a "little red riding hood" at all. The version collected by Delarue in Nièvre around 1885 is often put forward as a likely form of the tale. Known simply as "The Story of Grandmother," the story concerns an unnamed little girl who is dispatched to her grandmother's house with bread and milk. On the way she meets a werewolf who asks her which way she is taking—the path of needles or the path of pins. She replies that she is taking the path of needles, and the werewolf says he will take the path of pins. Along the way the little girl collects needles, allowing the werewolf to race ahead along the path of pins to grandmother's house. Here he immediately kills grandmother, puts some of her flesh and a bottle of her blood in the cupboard, and presumably (it is not stated in the text) jumps into grandmother's bed to await the arrival of the little girl.

When she arrives, the girl assumes that the werewolf in the bed is her grandmother, and the werewolf tells her to eat the meat and wine in the cupboard. She does as she is told, and then the murdered woman's cat accuses the girl of being a slut who has eaten the flesh and drunk the blood of her grandmother. The werewolf then tells the little girl to undress and get into bed with him. The little girl, still apparently suspecting nothing amiss, asks where she should put the various items of her clothing. The werewolf replies that she should put them all in the fire, as she will have no further need for them. She does so and then gets into the bed and begins asking the questions that feature in most versions of the story: "Oh, Granny, how hairy you are!" The werewolf replies, "The better to keep myself warm, my child." The girl works her way through the werewolf's nails, shoulders, ears, and nostrils to his mouth, to which the response is, "All the better to eat you with, my child."

Finally realizing her peril, the girl pleads to be let outside the house, as she needs to go to the toilet. The werewolf wants her to defecate in the bed, but she insists on going outside. The werewolf allows her to go only after tying a woolen rope to her foot. When she gets outside, having only feigned her need for relief, the girl ties her end of the rope to a plum tree. When she does not return the wolf calls out,

A nineteenth-century lithograph depicting Little Red Riding Hood (Library of Congress)

"Are you making a load out there?" When there is no reply, he realizes that the girl has tricked him and pursues her. Just in time, the little girl reaches the safety of her own house before the werewolf catches up with her.

Versions similar to this earthy folktale have been collected throughout Europe, the New World, Africa, and Asia. Such stories contain elements that the sophisticated, urban audience Perrault wrote for did not welcome. Thus, the werewolf became a wolf, still dangerous but not as disturbing as a human that transforms into a ravening beast and preys on human beings. The down-to-earth ruse the little girl employs to escape the werewolf's intentions disappears, as does her cannibalistic consumption of grandma's flesh and blood. The paths of pins and needles are lost, and the strong sexual connotations of "grandma's" hairy body are quietly forgotten.

As well as dropping certain motifs, Perrault added some. Few, if any, of the earliest collected versions of this story mention a red riding hood or any other colored hat. Perrault introduced this element and also invented the characterization of the heroine as spoiled, gullible, and ill-prepared to deal with the horrors of the wolf. Because of his strong moralizing aim, Perrault was also compelled to have Red Riding Hood eaten by the wolf instead of saving herself by her own wits as does the much more capable heroine of "The Story of Grandmother" and most of the other folk versions, including an Italian rendition *La Finta Nonna* (The False Grandmother) that features an ogress in the role of the wolf.

Despite, or perhaps because of, these additions and deletions, Perrault's reworking managed to retain much of the flavor and many of the implications of the oral versions, while presenting them in a form acceptable to a growing urban middle-class audience of the kind that would continue to polish Perrault's version of the story for subsequent generations of children.

So appropriate, powerful, and often-reprinted were Perrault's and other literary adaptations of this story, that they generated folk versions of their own. It was probably one of these comparatively sophisticated, urban, middle-class versions that the Grimms heard from their informant, Marie Hassenpflug, an educated and well-bred woman of French and German Huguenot heritage. This version was the basis of their story, first published in 1812 in their *Kinder-und Hausmärchen*, more generally and less accurately called in English "Grimms' Fairy Tales." Research has also shown that various literary and by now folkloric versions of Perrault's "Little Red Riding Hood" were well-known in Germany and that the Grimms would in all likelihood have heard these stories in their own childhood. They were also familiar with a play by Ludwig Tieck titled *Leben und Tod des kleinen Rotkäppchens: eine Tragödie* (1800), in which a woodsman kills the wolf that has eaten Little Red Cap. The Grimms, perhaps following this lead, and also drawing on motifs from other folktales, introduced the happy ending of their heroine, "Rotkäppchen" (Little Red Cap), and her granny, both of whom are saved by a woodsman. The Grimms also introduced an additional sequence, intended to point to a moral, in which Little Red Cap has an encounter with another wolf. She runs to grandma's house and is given advice on how to trick the wolf into death by drowning. This coda ends with the sentence, "But Red-Cap went joyously home, and never did anything to harm any one."

So popular was this version that it has become—usually without the second anticlimactic encounter with a wolf—the standard form of the story. As many scholars have pointed out in relation to this much-studied narrative, in addition to sanitizing the folktale versions and giving them a happy ending, these literary versions profoundly alter the character of the heroine. Thus Little Red Riding Hood, or Little Red Cap, is made into a not very competent and rather silly little girl who has to depend on grandma and the woodsman or hunter to get her out of trouble. In the folk versions, the heroine is duped because of her youth and inexperience, but once she realizes her plight, she uses her own wit and cunning to escape the wolf's or werewolf's jaws. However, so intertwined have the literary, artistic, filmic, mass media, and folkloric representations of Little Red Riding Hood become that it is now difficult, and for practical purposes pointless, to separate them.

"Little Red Riding Hood," with its implicit and explicit suggestions of violence, bestiality, sexuality, and cannibalism has become a near-universal item in the modern popular consciousness. The story and its heroine have been used in advertising, in animated films, in children's storybooks, pantomimes, paintings, and even in pop songs, as in a late 1960s hit that proclaims:

> Hey there Little Red Ridin' Hood,
> You sure are lookin' good;
> You're everythin' a big bad wolf could
> want.

In the song, these words are followed by a high-pitched wolf call—eeoowww!

In addition to this predominantly European tradition of Little Red Riding Hood, an apparently autonomous tradition has been identified in Asia, particularly in China, Japan, and Korea. As with any folktale, versions vary, but the basic Asian type involves a young woman tricking a monster of some kind by threatening to defecate in the bed, by which ruse she saves her brothers and sisters from death. Other versions of the tale are also told in parts of Africa, and it seems likely that it is among the most widespread of all tale types.

Such wide interest in and longevity of one basically simple tale has attracted a never-ending stream of learned, and not-so-learned, speculation about the significance of the story and its heroine. Such speculations include the psychoanalytic approaches of Freud, Jung, Bettelheim, and others; the socio-cultural-sexual interpretations of Jack Zipes; and the cultural historical analysis of Robert Darnton. The psychoanalytic approach tends to concentrate on one or a few versions, either to justify a psychosexual interpretation (Bettelheim, following Freud) or to essentialize motifs and images that recur in many different versions and to impute some universal significance to these (Jung). The main purpose of these interpretations is generally to develop methods of using the story (and other folktales) as a form of psychological and emotional therapy.

Jack Zipes is the most prominent of a number of scholars who have argued at length that "Little Red Riding Hood" represents a significant case of a European (and, by implication, western) cultural expression whose purpose is to regulate sexuality and that the story in its many guises is a symbolic initiation of the young into the "rape culture" of modern times. Robert Darnton, in *The Great Cat Massacre*, uses a version (apparently incomplete) of "Little Red Riding Hood" to suggest that it is a warning of inevitable disaster and is therefore a means of understanding the mental world of the eighteenth-century French peasantry. Anthropologist Mary Douglas, using the fieldwork of Yvonne Verdier, offers a reading that stresses the cannibalistic elements of the rustic French versions of the tale and interprets them as part of the private world of village women.

When considering this story, folklorists generally espouse an intercultural approach that reflects the fundamental comparative basis of folklore studies, and they are often uncomfortable with the many interpretations of the "meaning" of "Little Red Riding Hood" (or any other folktale) that depend on what they see as an inadequate number of often poorly sourced texts, or even on digests and summaries of texts. But even in a coherent field of study with a well-developed ethnographic and conceptual framework, there are many different interpretations. Some folklorists are even inclined toward a Freudian-influenced psychoanalytic approach, as exemplified in the final essay of Alan Dundes's *Little Red Riding Hood: A Casebook*.

While these differences simply reflect the variety of approaches to folktale heroes, they also reinforce the status of "Little Red Riding Hood" as a serious element of the everyday lives of millions of human beings over many hundreds of years. Rather more than just a "fairy tale." But it may be that the tale of Little Red Riding Hood is loosening its strong grip on us. When a fourteen-year-old girl was asked in 1999 what she knew of Little Red Riding Hood, the response was, "She killed a wolf or something, didn't she?"

Related entries: Fairy Tale Heroes; Kandek; Victims
References and further reading

Bettelheim, B., *The Uses of Enchantment: The Meaning and Importance of Fairy Tales*, New York: Knopf, 1976, pp. 13, 23, 61, 66–67, 166–183, 204.

Bottigheimer, R., *Grimms' Bad Girls and Bold Boys: The Moral and Social Vision of the Tales*, New Haven: Yale University Press, 1987.

Bottigheimer, R. (ed.), *Fairy Tales and Society: Illusion, Allusion, and Paradigm*, Philadelphia: University of Pennsylvania Press, 1986.

Darnton, R., *The Great Cat Massacre and Other Episodes in French Cultural History*, New York: Basic Books, 1984.

Douglas, M., "Red Riding Hood: An Interpretation from Anthropology," *Folklore* 106, 1995, pp. 1–7.

Dundes, A. (ed.), *Little Red Riding Hood: A Casebook*, Madison: University of Wisconsin Press, 1989.

Falassi, A., *Folklore by the Fireside: Text and Context in the Tuscan Veglia*, London: Scolar Press, 1980, pp. 68–69.

Hallett, M. and Karasek, B. (eds.), *Folk and Fairy Tales*, Ontario: Broadview Press, 1996, pp. 25–27.

Holbek, B., *Interpretation of Fairy Tales: Danish Folklore in a European Perspective*, Helsinki: Academia Scientarium Fennica, 1987.

Hunt, M. (trans. and ed.), *Grimm's Household Tales* (with the author's notes and an introduction by Andrew Lang), 2 vols., London: George Bell and Sons, 1884, pp. 110–114.

Klipple, M., *African Folktales with Foreign Analogues*, New York: Garland, 1992, pp. 146–147.

Zipes, J., *The Trials and Tribulations of Little Red Riding Hood*, New York: Routledge, 1993 (1983).

Llyn Y Fan Fach, The Lady of

Welsh fairy who marries a poor cowherd after they meet on the shore of the lake of Llyn Y Fan Fach in Carmarthenshire. After overcoming various obstacles and passing a number of tests, the young man is granted the fairy's hand by her father, who warns him that he must never strike her needlessly. They have three sons, and over the course of the marriage the cowherd does indeed strike the fairy wife needlessly on three occasions. After the last occasion, she disappears with the oxen given by her father as her dowry. Later she meets the three sons and teaches them much medical lore.

This story is said to have been collected from oral tradition by Sir John Rhys in the 1880s, though its rather neat use of a variety of folklore motifs such as the demon or fairy lover, tests, obstacles, and the departed mother as a future helper of her offspring suggests at least some literary handling.

Nonetheless, the Lady of Llyn Y Fan Fach is an example of an extensive worldwide tradition, usually referred to as "the fairy bride," in which a supernatural being marries a mortal on condition that a certain taboo never be broken. Eventually, the husband does break the taboo and the bride disappears, leaving the husband brokenhearted and usually with a child or children, offspring of the supernatural union. In some traditions, especially but not exclusively those of Japan and China, the bride may be in the form of an animal. The French stories of Melusine are perhaps the best-known versions of this type. The Lady of Llyn Y Fan Fach is related to Celtic and Scandinavian legends of seal women and mermaids who marry mortal men.

Related entries: Fox Maiden, The; Kuzonoha; Local Heroes; Melusine; Shape-Shifters; Skorobogaty, Kuzma; Swan Maiden

References and further reading

Jones, G., *Welsh Legends and Folk Tales*, London: Oxford University Press, 1955, pp. 182–194.

Wood, J., "The Fairy Bride Legend in Wales," *Folklore* 103, no. 1, 1992, pp. 56–72.

Local Heroes

This category of heroism includes figures, real and imaginary, who are celebrated within a particular community or region. In many cases these heroes are unknown or little known outside their areas of origin. They may be local "characters," celebrated for their eccentricities; they may be men or women who have carried out deeds of special significance to their local communities; or they may simply be figures who, often for unknown reasons, are part of local lore and custom. Sometimes these local figures may be animals, as in the case of the "Red Dog of the Pilbara," a cattle dog famous for its ability to survive and return home in this extremely inhospitable and isolated area of northwest Australia. While Red Dog was alive, his exploits were widely known in the Pilbara region, and after his death in the mid-1990s his legend was even further exaggerated. The legends of the dead dog were featured in a small, illustrated booklet published locally, a typical method of celebrating and perpetuating the folklore of such figures.

Generally, figures of this type have not achieved the national or international recognition of some folk heroes, such as some fairy tale characters, noted outlaws, numskulls, and some occupational heroes, among others that are repeatedly anthologized or are the subjects of various forms of commercialization. Nevertheless, the origins, motivations, and manifestations of local heroes are often similar from culture to culture. Favored types of local heroism include liars or tellers of tall tales; odd or eccentric characters; individuals who carried out feats notable to the locals; individuals who participated in, or sometimes caused, significant local events or processes; and those who gave their name to local places and/or physical features, or who have some other association, often legendary, with local places.

Clearly such figures are, by definition, vast in number and difficult to locate and identify. Some other examples include the English Tyneside heroine, Elsie Marley; the Vermont hero of the American War of Independence, Ethan Allan (1738–1789); and the Serbian Lazar, among others. Heroes of this type are part of the lore of local folk groups and contribute to the sense of place and of belonging that is the center of much community life.

Some heroes who begin their celebrity at the local level may become more widespread, sometimes through word of mouth, though much more powerfully through media networks. The Russian Dobrynya Nikitich is one example. Lady Godiva, naked horse rider of the English city of Coventry, is another, while Paul Bunyan and Febold Feboldson are American occupational heroes who have undergone similar processes. Billy the Kid is an especially useful illustration of the means through which local heroes may attain broader celebration. He was barely known outside the area in which he operated until journalists and dime-novel authors grabbed hold of his image, helping to cast it in the mold of the outlaw hero and also to spread his reputation to a wider audience and, crucially, to other media, such as theater and, ultimately, film. Other outlaw figures, with as good if not better claims to hero status, nevertheless remain largely within the folk knowledge of their local communities, as is the case with Western Australia's bushranger hero, Moondyne Joe. On the other hand, the Italian boy, Giovan Battista Perasso, locally known as "Balilla," is said to have started an insurrection against the occupying Austrians in the city of Genoa in December 1746 by throwing a stone at an imperial officer. According to research by Maria Pia Di Bella, from this act of local heroism Balilla went on to become a national hero, the subject of songs and widespread folkloric, and even official, celebration in later nineteenth-century schoolbooks.

Mythical characters of local notoriety may also achieve a wider fame, as in the example of Uncle Tom Cobleigh, a character in a southwest English song about seven men who borrow Tom Pearce's mare to go to Widdecombe Fair. The song includes the phrase "Uncle Tom Cobleigh and all" in its chorus. This phrase has passed into many varieties of the English language as a catch phrase for complete inclusivity, the equivalent of "everything but the kitchen sink."

Related entries: Ashma; Bonney, William; Bunyan, Paul; de Veusters, Father Joseph; Dojrana; Doyle, Tom; Frontier Heroes; Godiva, Lady; Green Princess, The; Havelock the Dane; Ivanovich, Dunai; Johns, Joseph; Jones, Galloping; Lazar; Liars; Llyn Y Fan Fach, The Lady of; Macdonald, Flora; Marley, Elsie; Nikitich, Dobrynya; Saburo, Koga; Siitakuuyuk; Taylor, William; Whittington, Dick

References and further reading
Baker, R., Hoosier Folk Legends, Bloomington: Indiana University Press, 1982.
Cheney, T., The Golden Legacy: A Folk History of J. Gordon Kimball, Salt Lake City: Peregrine Smith, 1974.
Dorson, R., Johnathan Draws the Long Bow, Cambridge: Harvard University Press, 1946.
Dorson, R., Bloodstoppers and Bearwalkers, Cambridge: Harvard University Press, 1952.
Ioannou, N., Barossa Journeys: Into a Valley of Tradition, Kent Town, SA: Paringa Press, 1997.
Montell, W., The Saga of Coe Ridge, Knoxville: University of Tennessee Press, 1970.

Loew, Rabbi Judah

Creator of the Golem, a living creature of clay and cabalistic magic, having origins in the biblical notion of Adam's "unformed substance." The Golem is given life through Loew's esoteric knowledge and the correct pronunciation of the name of God. In medieval Prague, the Jews were the victims of many pogroms. A man named Thaddeus plots yet another attack on the Jewish community by causing the murder of a Christian child to be blamed on the Jews. The Golem tracks Thaddeus down, reveals his plot, and saves the Jews from yet another pogrom.

Related entries: Adam, Rabbi; Baal-Shem-Tov; Magicians; Religious Heroes
References and further reading
Ausubel, N. (ed.), A Treasury of Jewish Folklore, London: Vallentine, Mitchell, 1972 (1948), pp. 603–612.
Cavendish, R. (ed.), Legends of the World, London: Orbis, 1982, pp. 109–110.
Ginzberg, L. (trans. Szold, H.), The Legends of the Jews, 7 vols., Philadelphia: The Jewish Publication Society of America, 1900.

Lohengrin

Lohengrin is a central figure of medieval German legends. Sometimes said to be the son of Perceval, the innocent knight of the early Arthurian romances, he is known as the "Knight of the Swan." The major part of his story tells how Lohengrin arrives, drawn by a swan, to defend Else of Brabant in a trial of arms against a false charge of parricide. Lohengrin defeats Else's accuser and then marries her. Perceval cautions the hero Lohengrin never to reveal his identity and commands Else never to ask. Eventually she does ask, and Lohengrin answers, only to depart from her, carried by the swan that had first brought him.

Interdictions against revealing names or identities are often associated with Swan Maiden tales, and it seems likely that Lohengrin is a medieval literary enhancement of northern European folktale elements. The tale of Lohengrin was certainly extremely popular throughout Europe in the medieval period and after. Wagner used the story as the basis of his opera Lohengrin, first performed in 1850.

Related entries: Arthur; Culture Heroes; Melusine; Swan Maiden
References and further reading
Leach, M. (ed.), Funk and Wagnall's Standard Dictionary of Folklore, Mythology, and Legend, London: New English Library, 1975. Abridged one-volume edition of Funk and Wagnall's Standard Dictionary of Folklore, Mythology, and Legend, 2 vols., New York: Funk and Wagnall, 1972, p. 642.

Loqman

Loqman, or Luquam, the Wise is a legendary sage and healer of the Middle East. Numerous tales are told about Loqman, and he also appears in tales about other characters. In Armenian versions of his lore, Loqman is said to have originally been a young hunter named Purto who is adopted by the Shah-Mar, king of the snakes, because of his kindness to these animals. Shah-mar gives Purto the secrets of healing, and with this knowledge he is able to cure the king of Adana. Purto is made chief royal physician by a grateful monarch and is thereafter known as Loqman the Wise, the father of medicine.

Related entries: Eight Immortals, The; Habermani; Helpers; Yao Wang
References and further reading
Downing, C. (trans. and ed.), *Armenian Folk-Tales and Fables*, London: Oxford University Press, 1972, pp. 73–80.

Lord Franklin
See Franklin, Lord

Lu Zhishen
Hero of the famous tenth-century *Water Margin* novel of China, also known as *The Outlaws of the Marsh* and *All Men Are Brothers*. Lu Zhishen is a fierce fighter, faithful, a champion of the poor and weak, but also an impetuous and in many ways humorously ridiculous character. Many tales exist about his exploits as a drinker, glutton, a friend of the poor, and also about his ill-judged efforts to become a Buddhist monk, which result in his making a fool and a nuisance of himself.

Related entries: Li Kui; Outlaws
References and further reading
Buck, P. (trans.), *All Men Are Brothers*, New York: The John Day Company, 1968.
Li, N., *Old Tales of China*, Singapore: Graham Brash, 1983 (1981), pp. 157–159, 160–164.

Lucky Hans
Main character in an unusual German story in which the honest but not very clever Hans leaves his apprenticeship with seven years wages in the form of a large gold nugget. Planning to return home to his mother with the fruits of his labor, Hans stupidly bargains the nugget for a horse worth far less than the gold.

Then he swaps the horse for a cow, the cow for a pig, the pig for a goose, and, finally, the goose for a set of grinding wheels, feeling very pleased with himself at the wonderful bargain he believes he has made each time. After a while the grinding wheels become heavy. Hans stops to drink at the river and accidentally drops the stones into the water. Overjoyed, Hans gives thanks that he is now relieved of the burden of the stones and is free to return to his mother completely empty-handed.

This congenital stupidity and incompetence is not uncommon in fairy tales, especially those collected by the brothers Grimm, as noted by Maria Tatar and others. In most cases though, the foolish young man does eventually manage to perform some reasonably heroic action, attaining the gold, the girl, the kingdom and/or other riches. Jack of "Jack and the Beanstalk" is another hero who displays an irritating level of stupidity early in his tale by swapping the family's only asset, a milking cow, for some apparently worthless beans. That the beans later turn out to be magic beans is a matter of luck rather than of judgment or knowledge on Jack's part, and it is only through his subsequent adventures with the giant or ogre that he eventually triumphs.

So spectacularly does the story of "Hans in Luck" flout the usual precepts of the fairy tale that Maria Tatar has argued the audience is meant to read the story as one in which Hans achieves freedom from the need to labor and from any need for the possessions the rewards of such labor may bring. Thus, his loss of everything he has earned represents a return to the basics of human relationships, unhindered by materialism.

Related entries: Jack; Jack and the Beanstalk; Jack Tales; Numskulls and Noodles
References and further reading
Lee, F. H. (comp.), *Folk Tales of All Nations*, London: Harrap, 1931, pp. 511–515.
Tatar, M., "Born Yesterday: Heroes in the Grimms' Fairy Tales," in Bottigheimer, R. (ed.), *Fairy Tales and Society: Illusion, Allusion, and Paradigm*, Philadelphia: University of Pennsylvania Press, 1986.

Ludd, Ned

Also known as "General Ludd," mythic leader of the Luddites, a loosely organized group of English activists who—correctly—feared that increasing use of machinery in the factories of the early industrial revolution would undermine their employability. The Luddites broke industrial and agricultural machines and wrecked factories over an extended period in the nineteenth century. A contemporary ballad titled "General Ludd's Triumph," given by Palmer, begins with Ludd replacing Robin Hood as a hero of folk resistance to perceived oppression and dispossession:

No more chant your old rhymes about
    bold Robin Hood
His feats I do little admire.
I'll sing the achievements of General Ludd,
Now the hero of Nottinghamshire.

Ned Ludd, possibly derived from the name of a Leicestershire laborer, was only one of many names given to mythical or shadowy figures by social protesters in eighteenth- and nineteenth-century Britain. Others were "Captain Swing," said to be the instigator and leader of the Swing riots of the 1830s, and "Rebecca," a gender-ambiguous figure focusing the discontents of the Welsh countryside throughout the nineteenth century, and even into the twentieth. The term "Luddite" persists. The protesters against the World Trade Organization talks in Seattle, Washington, in December 1999, and on subsequent occasions, were labeled Luddites by a number of politicians and commentators.

Related entries: Heroes of Struggle; Occupational Heroes; Rebecca
References and further reading
Palmer, R. (ed.), *A Touch on the Times: Songs of Social Change 1770 to 1914*, Harmondsworth, Middlesex: Penguin, 1974, pp. 286–288.

Lusmore

Hunchback figure in an Irish tale collected by Thomas Crofton Croker. Lusmore is said to mean "great herb" and is a name used for the foxglove plant. The story tells of Lusmore being an outcast because of his deformity. Wandering in the night, he hears the fairies singing and spontaneously adds to their songs. In reward for his joining their harmonies, the fairies rid him of his hump. Another hunchback, hearing of Lusmore's good fortune, tries the same strategy, but it misfires. The fairies add Lusmore's hump to his own, and he dies shortly after. Croker's version of the story even includes an intriguing transcription of the music of the fairy song, complete with countermelody.

The story of Lusmore well illustrates the double-edged nature of fairies in folk tradition. They are capable of beneficent acts as well as malignant ones. For mortals, there is no telling which way things will go, and so it is usually best to have nothing to do with fairies at all; that, at least, is the widespread folk wisdom. The story of Lusmore is contained in the Grimm collection and is also known in Japanese, French, Greek, and Spanish. Traditions in which the fairies bestow gifts or curses upon mortals are also widespread and can be found in Scots, German, Italian, Chinese, and Tibetan lore.

Related entries: Fairy Tale Heroes; Mab, Queen; Tabagnino the Hunchback; Tam Lin; Thomas the Rhymer
References and further reading
Baker, M., *Tales of All the World*, London: Oxford University Press, 1937, pp. 120–123.
Clouston, W., *Popular Tales and Fictions: Their Migrations and Transformations*, 2 vols., Edinburgh and London: William Blackwood, 1887, vol. 2, pp. 352–372.
Croker, T. C. (ed. Wright, T.), *Fairy Legends and Traditions of the South of Ireland*, new and complete edition, London: William Tegg, 1862.
Lee, F. H. (comp.), *Folk Tales of All Nations*, London: Harrap, 1931, pp. 331–335.

M

Mab, Queen

Common English name for the fairy queen of many European folk traditions, usually said to be derived from the Irish Celtic Queen of Connaght, Medb or Maeve. The identification of "Mab" as queen of the fairies is probably from the interest of Elizabethan dramatists and poets in her image. But whether named or not, Mab is no garden fairy and is generally portrayed as a figure of great power who is not to be crossed, especially by humans. She appears in one guise or another in many supernatural ballads, such as Tam Lin, where she casts a spell on the hero, forcing him to live with her in fairyland for seven years. Similarly, Thomas the Rhymer is bewitched by the fairy queen and taken to Elfland. It is likely that the familiar helper of fairy tales, the Fairy Godmother, is in some ways related to this much more fearsome, even primal, figure.

Related entries: Fairy Godmother, The; Fairy Tale Heroes; Magicians; Tam Lin; Thomas the Rhymer

References and further reading
Briggs, K., *The Fairies in Tradition and Literature*, London: Routledge and Kegan Paul, 1967, pp. 46, 169.

Mac Cumhal, Finn

Also known as Finn Mac Cool, this great warrior of Irish mythology and legend is thought to be based on a third-century A.D. leader. His birth is the fulfillment of a prophecy, and he escapes death in a slaughter of the innocents incident of the kind associated with many other heroes, including Jesus of Nazareth and Antti Puuhaara. In his youth, Finn accomplishes feats of strength and speed, is a bard of distinction like all the warriors he leads—a group known as the *Fianna*—and attains vast wisdom through eating salmon that have fed on the nine hazel trees of wisdom. Finn marries a part-animal wife, a deer-woman named Sadb, with whom he conceives the hero Oisin, who is found in the forest and brought to his father by Finn's hunting dog, Bran. Ultimately Finn's own treachery leads to the end of the warrior brotherhood of the *Fianna*, and they are defeated at the Battle of Gabhra.

In a tale about Finn collected in the mid-nineteenth century, the hero is led to the bottom of the Black North by a white doe. She leaves him by a lake, where a beautiful woman appears bemoaning the loss of her ring in the water. Finn gallantly dives to retrieve it, but on his third attempt he suddenly feels the chill of death coming upon him. He finds the ring but has lost his youth and turns into an old man. As he gives the ring back to the woman, she reveals herself as the "king of Greek's daughter." It was she who had disguised herself as a white doe and lured Finn to this place because he had killed her husband and two sons. Finn replies that if he had killed them, it was in fair fight. But she leaves him there to die. His seven companions miss Finn and, minus Finn's grandson Oscar, set out in search of him. They find a fort within which a fine meal is laid out on a table surrounded by seven seats. They sit down to eat and drink, and when they have finished the king of Greek's daughter appears and tells them where Finn is, inviting them to follow her to the lake. But as they try to rise they find that they have been magically stuck to the stone seats. Finn's dog, Bran, then goes to find Oscar and brings him to Finn. Finn manages to tell Oscar to go to the fairy hill and make an enchanter he will find there give him the drink of youth. The enchanter is unwilling to give up the cup, but Oscar forces him to do so and then returns to Finn with the precious liquid. Finn

Flora Macdonald being introduced to Bonnie Prince Charlie (North Wind Picture Archives)

soon recovers his youth and awesome strength, and he and Oscar then free their six comrades by dripping some of the drink of youth on the thighs of each, though there is only a drop left for the grumpy Conan, who has to be forcibly and painfully separated from the rock. They then shouted three times, so loudly they were heard on the Isle of Man, and went home and celebrated for a week.

Finn and his heroic warriors are said to be sleeping in a cave beneath Ireland, awaiting the call to rise again. In Scots tradition, Finn is known as Fingal.

Related entries: Culture Heroes; Jesus; Puuhaara, Antti; Siung Wanara; Sleepers; Warriors
References and further reading
Briggs, K. (ed.), *A Dictionary of British Folk-Tales in the English Language*, 2 vols., London: Routledge and Kegan Paul, 1970–1971, vol. 1, p. 234.
Curtin, J., *Myths and Folk-Lore of Ireland*, Boston: Little,
Brown, 1890; reprint, Detroit: Singing Tree Press, 1968, pp. 204–220.
Glassie, H., *Irish Folk Tales*, New York: Pantheon, 1985, pp. 37–39, 237–244.
Nagy, J., *The Wisdom of the Outlaw: The Boyhood Deeds of Finn in Gaelic Narrative Tradition*, Berkeley: University of California Press, 1985.
O'Sullivan, S. (ed. and trans.), *Folktales of Ireland*, London: Routledge and Kegan Paul, 1966, pp. 23, 42, 57–60.
O'Sullivan, S. (ed.), *Legends from Ireland*, London: Batsford, 1977, p. 154.

Macdonald, Flora

Flora Macdonald (1722–1790) was a heroine of the Scottish Jacobites. She helped Prince Charles Edward Stuart (1720–1788)—"The Young Pretender" or "Bonnie Prince Charlie" in folklore—escape after the battle of Culloden Moor in 1746. Flora agreed to smuggle the prince from the island of Uist to Skye with him disguised as her Irish maid, Betty Burke. Surviving storm and the shots of English soldiers, the plucky Flora, with the help of Jacobite sympathizers, got the prince to safety. She was captured and briefly imprisoned in London, where she was admired rather than reviled by London society.

These events are romantically commemorated in the well-known "Skye Boat Song" or "Speed Bonny Boat," which predicts that "Charlie will come again." Despite numerous attempts and intrigues, he never did, but his hopeless cause and Flora Macdonald's role in it lives on in Scots and English folklore. Flora subsequently married Allan Macdonald and lived in North Carolina between 1774 and 1779. Flora was captured again by the English during the War of Independence and was lucky to escape with her life. The family lost all its possessions and later returned to Skye. Flora died in 1790, bequeathing what were said to be her most precious possessions—a lock of Prince Charlie's hair and his silver shoe buckle, both given to her by him during their flight from the English. Her traditions are still very much part of the folklore of Skye and the surrounding islands.

Related entries: Helpers; Heroes of Struggle; Local
  Heroes; National Heroes; Stuart, Prince Charles
  Edward
References and further reading
Philip, N. (ed.), The Penguin Book of Scottish Folktales,
  Harmondsworth, Middlesex: Penguin, 1995.
Swire, O., Skye: The Island and Its Legends, London:
  Oxford University Press, 1952, pp. 61–67.

MacGregor, Robert

Named "Roy" for his wild red hair, Robert MacGregor (1671–1734) was a noted brigand and leader of Scottish uprisings against the English. Rob Roy's freebooting activities at home and abroad made him the center of some outlaw hero traditions. He was romanticized and popularized far beyond his local notoriety in Walter Scott's Rob Roy (1818) and by Wordsworth and others who turned his relatively commonplace life into the stuff of legend. There is a tourist center dedicated to Rob Roy at Callander.

A ballad called "Rob Roy" exists but is about the less-than-heroic exploits of a son of Rob Roy, known as Robert Oig (the younger) who, in 1750, compelled a Jean Key to marry him in the by-then illegal custom of marriage by rape, a crime for which he was eventually executed in 1754.

Related entries: Heroes of Struggle; Hood, Robin;
  National Heroes; Outlaws
References and further reading
Child, F. J., The English and Scottish Popular Ballads,
  5 vols., New York: Dover, 1965 (1882–1898),
  vol. 4, pp. 243–254, no. 225.

Mad Dog Morgan

See Morgan, Daniel "Mad Dog"

Mademoiselle from Armentieres

Central figure of a widespread song of World War I, the mythical Mademoiselle is something of an occupational heroine to the allied troops, supplying them with food, alcohol, conversation, and other comforts. There were innumerable English-language variants of this song, which, in its World War version, can be dated to 1915 in the familiar rendition beginning: "Mademoiselle from Armentieres, parlez-vous." Most versions of the song range from the ribald to the obscene. The roots of the song and of its obligingly convivial heroine can be traced to the late eighteenth century through sailor folklore and Continental soldier songs.

Related entries: Military Heroes; Occupational
  Heroes
References and further reading
Carey, M. B., Jr., "Mademoiselle from Armentieres,"
  Journal of American Folklore 47, 1934.
Colcord, J., Songs of American Sailormen, New York: Oak
  Publications, 1964 (1938), pp. 106–108.

Madoc

A legendary Welsh hero, Madoc (Madog) first appears in a fifteenth-century poem, although tradition has it that he was the son of the twelfth-century prince of Gwynedd, Owen. Madoc tires of the incessant squabbling between his brothers and sails west in his ship called Gwennan Gorn. Eventually he returns and takes twelve ships back to where he had sailed before. Nothing is ever heard of him again. Somehow, the belief grew that Madoc had discovered the North American continent in or about 1170, landing at what is now Mobile Bay, Alabama. He is said to have interbred with the indigenous inhabitants to form a Welsh-speaking Native American people, the Madon. Nonhistorical though this tradition is, it persists to the present time. In 1953 a group of believers had a commemorative stone placed at Mobile to honor Madoc's legendary achievement.

There are numerous other legends about seafaring adventurers reaching North America long before Christopher Columbus, including stories of the Icelandic adventurer Leif Ericsson (Eiríksson or Erikson), c. 975–1020, who may have established a settlement called Vinland there in or near the year 1000.

Related entries: Columbus, Christopher; Cook, Captain; Culture Heroes; Nautical Heroes

References and further reading

Cavendish, R. (ed.), *Legends of the World*, London: Orbis, 1982, pp. 198–199.

Jones, G., *Welsh Legends and Folk Tales*, London: Oxford University Press, 1955.

Magarac, Joe

See Occupational Heroes

Magicians

The hero with supernatural powers is a figure found frequently in folk tradition. Often these characters employ their magical abilities in contests with similarly endowed villains, as is the case with the diminutive African hero, Fereyel, among many others. Magical powers may also be employed to predict the future, one of Merlin's abilities. They may be employed to immediately transport characters large distances, as in the story of Aladdin. They may enable the magician to cast various spells and charms or to speak with and/or to command animals, as in the Korean story of Marshall Gang Gam-Czan. Heroes with magical powers may also use them to benefit their community, as in the case of the Australian Aboriginal hero, Wirreenun. Magi-

cians may also be healers who use their magic to cure illness, as in the case of the Eight Immortals of China.

Magicians are sometimes cast in the role of national or culture hero, as in the case of Saemund Sigfússon the Wise (1056–1133) of Iceland. A priest-prince of Oddi in southern Iceland renowned during his lifetime for his learning and wisdom, Saemund became by the seventeenth century an Icelandic people's hero, symbol of their dislike of and resistance to Danish rule. He was said to have learned his magic at the Black School and was widely credited with cheating the Devil, an attribute often attached to magicians.

Other national figures sometimes attract magical attributes, including Francis Drake, Walter Raleigh, Owen Glendower, and even Oliver Cromwell. Drake, known to the Spaniards as "El Draco," was widely believed to be in league with the Devil, and there are numerous traditions about his use of this connection to protect the nation against the Armada and to provide his local community with a water supply.

Magicians, depending on their positive or negative status, go by various names in folklore, including sorcerers, wizards, wise men or wise women, magi, witches, warlocks, demons, dervishes, etc. One of the most commonly encountered magical abilities is the skill of shape-shifting, or transmogrification. Being able to turn oneself, or others, into different forms has many applications, including disguise, invisibility, escape, the attainment of power, and so forth. Believed to have lived in the last half century or so before the Christian era commenced, Vikramaditya was the Raja of Ujjayini. He features in numerous folktales as a magician who can send his soul into any other body and is also able to fly. He is a wanderer and wise man with characteristics similar to those attributed to the biblical Solomon.

Magic is one of the relatively few areas of folk tradition in which heroines approach heroes in number. However, magical villainesses are also extremely common, most usually in the form of the witch, such as the Russian Baba Yaga.

Related entries: Achikar; Adam, Rabbi; Ahmed; Culture Heroes; Dog-Nyong, General Gim; Eight Immortals, The; Fereyel; Gim; Habermani; Helpers; Heroes of Struggle; Loew, Rabbi Judah; Marendenboni; Merlin; Molo; Monkey; National Heroes; Nue the Hunter; Pied Piper; Shape-Shifters; Villains; Vseslavevich, Volkh; Wirreenun the Rainmaker; Wise Men and Women

References and further reading

Leach, M. (ed.), *Funk and Wagnall's Standard Dictionary of Folklore, Mythology, and Legend*, London: New English Library, 1975. Abridged one-volume edition of *Funk and Wagnall's Standard Dictionary of Folklore, Mythology, and Legend*, 2 vols., New York: Funk and Wagnall, 1972, pp. 660–663.

Simpson, J. (trans.), Benedikz, B. (intro.), *Legends of Icelandic Magicians*, London: Brewer/Rowan and Littlefield, The Folklore Society, 1975.

Westwood, J., *Albion: A Guide to Legendary Britain*, London: Granada, 1985, pp. 16–18.

Wherry, B., "Wizardry on the Welsh Border," *Folklore* 15, 1904, pp. 75–86.

Maid Marian

See Marian, Maid

Marendenboni

Youngest of eight brothers, this cunning hero of a Soninke (Africa) tale continually outwits a wicked, shape-shifting witch, saving the lives of his brothers and tricking the witch into killing her own children. Marendenboni translates as "child of evil." Similar stories of unpromising heroes appear in other African traditions and in the folklore of many other groups around the world. They can be interpreted as a form of wish fulfillment and retribution in which the villain's homicidal intentions toward the hero or heroine are defeated and, in the killing of the villain's own children, justly punished.

Related entries: Fereyel; Tardanak
References and further reading

Arnott, K. (ed.), *African Myths and Legends*, London: Oxford University Press, 1962.

Rugoff, M. (ed.), *A Harvest of World Folk Tales*, New York: Viking Press, 1949, pp. 29–33.

Marfida

See Ivan the Mare's Son; Victims

Maria, Fenda

Fenda Maria (Lady Maria) is the legendary heroine of an Angolan folktale in which she tries to win the love of the bewitched Lord Vidiji Milanda, who is sleeping beside a distant river. To accomplish this task she must make her way through the dangerous forest, then weep ten jugs of tears. When she has wept eleven jugs, Fenda Maria kindly buys the freedom of a passing slave girl with one jug. She continues to weep, filling ten and one-half jugs with tears. Becoming tired, she asks the slave girl to weep a while but to call her when the tenth jug is almost full so that Fenda Maria can wake the sleeping Vidiji Milanda. But the slave girl fills the jug herself, and when Vidiji Milanda wakens, he marries the slave girl. The betrayed Fenda Maria now becomes the slave of the girl, and they swap names: Fenda Maria becomes Kamaria and Kamaria becomes Fenda Maria.

Before departing on a journey to Portugal, Vidiji Milanda calls his slave girls and asks them what presents they would like. Most want jewelry, but Kamaria, really Fenda Maria, asks for a lamp that lights itself, a razor that sharpens itself, scissors that cut for themselves, and a stone that always tells the truth. With some difficulty Vidiji Milanda obtains these strange requests and gives them to "Kamaria." That night, the heroine throws her magic calabash on the floor and dresses in the fine clothes that come forth. She then tells her story to the four magic objects and asks them to kill her if she does not tell the truth. The lamp lights itself, the razor sharpens itself, the scissors cut, and the stone of truth beats on the floor, but "Kamaria" is unharmed. These events go on for the next three nights. On the last night, an old woman who has witnessed the strange scene brings Vidiji Milanda to see. He hears the story and recognizes "Kamaria" as Fenda Maria, the one destined to be his true wife. They embrace and faint from the joy of the experience. The treacherous slave girl is burned in a barrel of tar, and her remains are coated on the bodies of Fenda Maria and Vidiji Milanda, a custom said to prevent the spirit of the dead person from returning to take revenge on the living.

Fenda Maria's generous nature is highlighted through her freeing the slave girl, even though this means delaying her union with Lord Vidiji Milanda. The slave girl's ungrateful and duplicitous actions identify her as the villain who must, ultimately, suffer appropriate punishment.

This story reverses the gender roles in the European fairy tale complex best known as "Sleeping Beauty" and is reminiscent, especially in the swapping of identity between the heroine and her servant, of the story of "The Goose Girl."

Related entries: Fairy Tale Heroes; Goose Girl, The; Sleeping Beauty

References and further reading

Carey, M., Myths and Legends of Africa, London: Paul Hamlyn, 1970.

Courlander, H. (comp.), A Treasury of African Folklore, New York: Crown, 1975.

Leach, M. (ed.), Funk and Wagnall's Standard Dictionary of Folklore, Mythology, and Legend, London: New English Library, 1975. Abridged one-volume edition of Funk and Wagnall's Standard Dictionary of Folklore, Mythology, and Legend, 2 vols., New York: Funk and Wagnall, 1972, p 375.

Marian, Maid

Legendary female companion of Robin Hood. Like many of the characters in Robin Hood's band of "merry men," Maid Marian is a late addition to the Robin Hood tales and ballads. She is usually said to have been the daughter of a noble, and often she has to be rescued from the clutches of the repulsive and grasping Sheriff of Nottingham, creature of the wicked King John, usurper of the throne of the good King Richard II (Richard the Lionheart), conveniently absent at the Crusades. A figure often named "Maid Marian" also features in traditional May dances in England as Queen of the May, usually wearing a gold crown and holding in her left hand a red pink flower. Much has been made of this heroine's supposed connection with various pre-Christian fertility figures, though, as with almost all such suppositions, there is scant evidence to support such a connection. Her role as helper is one that is paralleled in many hero traditions.

Related entries: Helpers; Hood, Robin

References and further reading

Dobson, R. B. and Taylor, J., Rymes of Robin Hood: An Introduction to the English Outlaw, 2d rev. ed., Gloucester: Allan Sutton, 1989 (1976).

Holt, J., Robin Hood, London: Thames and Hudson, 1989, rev. ed., pp. 37, 48, 160, 162, 166, 186, 192.

Knight, S., Robin Hood: A Complete Study of the English Outlaw, Oxford: Blackwell, 1994.

Marley, Elsie

Historical heroine of a northeastern English folk song who was popular for selling alcohol to a wide variety of customers, including farmers, pitmen, keelmen, and sailors. The historical figure on whom the song is based was a woman named Alice Harrison, born about 1715. She married Ralph Marley, became a famous "alewife" of The Swan public house in the town of Picktree, and was widely know as "Elsie." After a colorful and, some sources claim, loose life and career, Elsie drowned in 1768. Essentially a local heroine, she is still celebrated in Tyneside and elsewhere through the various versions of her song, parts of which also became favorite nursery rhymes.

Related entries: Godiva, Lady; Havelock the Dane; Llyn Y Fan Fach, The Lady of; Local Heroes; Macdonald, Flora; Taylor, William; Whittington, Dick

References and further reading

Halliwell, J., The Nursery Rhymes of England, London: The Bodley Head, 1970 (1842), p. 74.

Marten, Maria

See Victims

Mary

Mother of Jesus, also known as "Mother Mary" and by other honorifics. As God's chosen virgin for the birth of Jesus of Nazareth, Mary has become the object of wide veneration within Christianity, especially in Catholic cultures, where since the medieval period she has been the center of considerable extrabiblical sanctification and cult worship. In Russian and many other traditions she is widely referred to as the "Mother of God." In other folklore, Mary features in stories, songs—especially carols and

An anonymous eighteenth-century Mexican painting, "The Virgin of the Rosary" (Library of Congress)

other religious songs—and beliefs about Jesus. She also appears in folklore in her own right in beliefs about the pink carnation having sprung from her tears as she made her way to Calvary to witness the crucifixion of Jesus.

Related entries: Jesus; Religious Heroes
References and further reading
Gaer, J., *The Lore of the New Testament*, Boston: Little, Brown, 1952.
Ivanits, L., *Russian Folk Belief*, Armonk and London: M. E. Sharpe Inc., 1989, pp. 12, 15–17, 20–21, 23, 25, 32–35, 93, 115, 137, 146–147, 150–152.
Lloyd, A., *Folksong in England*, New York: International Publishers, 1970 (1967), pp. 118–132.

Matthias, King

King of Hungary, King Matthias or Kralj Matjaz (1440–1490) appears as a hero in Bulgarian, Croatian, Hungarian, Ruthenian, Serbian, Slo-

vakian, and Slovenian traditions. A popular ruler, the figure of King Matthias has featured in songs, proverbs, tales, children's lore, and other folk expressions since at least the sixteenth century. He takes a multifaceted role, often combining the attributes of warrior conqueror of the Turks, trickster, and national or ethnic culture hero. Numerous international legends, similar to those told of other great leaders, have become attached to Matthias, but there is also a considerable body of indigenous legendry about his deeds, real and folkloric.

A humorous story collected in the 1950s shows Matthias as a ruler who has the common touch. Puzzled at how the poorly paid hussars of his army are able to spend so much on food and drink, the king disguises himself as a soldier and takes himself to an inn frequented by the soldiers. He passes himself off as a new recruit and is immediately coerced into spending his weekly pay on drinks for the hussars. All the king's money is soon used up this way. One of the hussars, named Jóska, then leaves his sword with the landlord in payment for further drink. By the time the inn closes, the hussars are drunk with brandy, and although they are supposed to return to barracks, they decide to rob the landlord's cellar. They use the king as an accomplice, then return to barracks, taking him with them.

The king is ashamed of himself for taking part in the robbery of a subject's property and also angry at the carefree and slovenly ways of his soldiers. While the drunken hussars snore, he snips off half of Jóska's mustache, then returns to the palace. The elaborate and lengthy mustache is considered a mark of honor by the hussars, and when Jóska wakes in the night and discovers he only has half his magnificent lip hair he is horrified and decides to snip off half the mustaches of his fellow hussars so that he will not look such a fool in the morning. When they wake and discover their half-mustaches, the hussars blame each other and begin fighting. Meanwhile the king, still angry, decides that he will have his revenge on the hussars, and on Jóska in particular. Knowing that the hussar's honored sword is at the inn, he decides to call an inspection of the hussars that will reveal to all that old Jóska has drunk away his sword; thus the king will have him hanged.

When the hussars are informed of the imminent inspection, Jóska is beside himself. He has no sword. He runs around frantically trying to get his sword back or borrow another, but in vain. In desperation, he has a wooden substitute made and rushes to the parade ground with it in his scabbard. The king arrives and hides his amusement at the sight of four half-mustachioed hussars only with difficulty. Keen to discover whether Jóska has his sword, the king commands that a prisoner be brought to the parade ground and that Jóska behead him with his sword. Thinking quickly, Jóska says that he is reluctant to execute the man. But the king flies into a rage and repeats the order. Jóska then asks for a moment to pray, which the king grants. Looking toward heaven he says:

Almighty Lord!
Who art in Heaven
Cast a glance on this poor old hussar,
Into a piece of lath his sword Thou coulds't make
So that his comrade's life he may not take.
(Dégh 1969)

Then he draws his sword, saying, "Look here, sire, your majesty! The Lord has listened to my prayer." Amused and mollified, the king replies, "Well done, old Jóska. I see now that one cannot get the better of a hussar."

Like many warrior and culture heroes, King Matthias is said to be sleeping in a mountain or in caves, guarded by ravens, until the day comes when he will awake and save his people from destruction.

Related entries: Alfred the Great; Arthur; Barbarossa; Batradz; Charlemagne; Cid, El; Culture Heroes; Danske, Holger; Gearoidh, Iarla; National Heroes; Rákóczi; Sleepers; Warrior Heroes

References and further reading

Dégh, L., *Folktales of Hungary*, Chicago: University of Chicago Press, 1965, pp. 161–172, 321–323.

Dégh, L. (trans. Schossberger, E.), *Folktales and Society: Story-Telling in a Hungarian Peasant Community*, Bloomington: Indiana University Press, 1969 (1962).

Mau and Matang

Brother warrior heroes and culture heroes of the island people of Boiogu in the Torres Straits. The brothers are summoned to Arudaru on the mainland of Papua to share food with their friends there. During preparations for the sea voyage there is an ill omen of blood in the canoe. Their sister tells Mau and Matang that this is a warning of great danger and that they should not leave home. They ignore her and sail with their families to Arudaru. During the voyage a canoe is lost and drifts to the sand bank where the spirits of the dead are believed to reside. There is a ghostly manifestation of the brothers each spearing a dugong, then placing their spears in their canoes. The crew of the lost canoe reports these events and their fears that they are evil portents, but Mau and Matang again ignore them and push on to Arudaru. Here they are greeted by the village chief, also called Mau, and made welcome. The next morning, though, they wake and find that all the people have deserted the village except the chief. He gives them breakfast and then declares war upon Mau and Matang. It turns out that Mau and Matang had at some previous time murdered a number of the chief's kinsmen and that he must avenge them. Mau, Matang, and their men make their escape but are ambushed by the Arudaru people as they make their way back through the jungle to the coast. Mau and Matang fight bravely with spear and bow to the end of their last battle. Their enemies, recognizing their heroism, accord them the honor of tying their bodies to trees facing south toward their home and placing the warrior headdress of cassowary and eagle feathers on each of them.

Related entries: Culture Heroes; Victims

References and further reading

Faurot, J. (ed.), *Asian-Pacific Folktales and Legends*, New York: Simon and Schuster, 1995.

Lawrie, M. (coll. and trans.), *Tales from Torres Strait*, St. Lucia: University of Queensland Press, 1972, pp. 31–33.

Maui

Polynesian trickster and culture hero. In some cultures a demigod, in others, such as the

Maori, a human. Whether divine or mortal, Maui features in stories told throughout the South Pacific. Maui performs such feats as catching and imprisoning three of the four winds, capturing fire, and attempting to gain immortality for humankind. The circumstances of his birth are supernatural, and his survival is remarkable. He is often portrayed as the youngest of four or five brothers and, as with many folk heroes in similar circumstances, is constantly attempting to overcome his low status. In Maui's case, these attempts are generally in the form of tricks played on others, many of which involve the transgression of taboo. Often these transgressions are for the good of humankind, as in his stealing of fire. As told in Maori tradition, Maui's conquering of the sun is carried out in order to extend the amount of sunlight in each day. Maui is usually credited with cleverness in crafts and may be said to have invented string games, fishing nets, and other useful items. In some versions of his story, he kills the god Tuna and so wins his wife, Hine. In Maori tradition, Maui attempts to kill Hine, who is the keeper of the dead, and so abolish death. However, he becomes trapped inside her body, and as a result of this failure of his last transgression, human beings now die. In Tongan tradition, Maui is portrayed as a god who fished up many of the South Pacific islands from the sea, forming their mountains and valleys with his bare hands. Here he fulfills the role of the creator and culture hero.

Related entries: Apekura; Culture Heroes; Tricksters
References and further reading
Alpers, A., Maori Myths and Tribal Legends, London: John Murray, 1964, pp. 28–70.
Anderson, J., Myths and Legends of the Polynesians, London: Harrap, 1928, pp. 192–235.
Baumann, H., Hero Legends of the World, London: Dent and Sons, 1975 (1972), pp. 122–127.
Lawrie, M. (coll. and trans.), Myths and Legends of Torres Strait, St. Lucia: University of Queensland Press, 1970, pp. 230–232.
Lee, F. H. (comp.), Folk Tales of All Nations, London: Harrap, 1931, pp. 444–447.
Reed, A., A Treasury of Maori Folklore, Wellington: Reed, 1974 (1963), pp. 116–157.

McCaffery

Central figure of a nineteenth-century British soldier ballad. The probably fictional but typical McCaffery (variously M'Cafferty, M'Caffry, etc.), joins the army at eighteen years of age and fails to take the names of some children playing near the barracks, after being ordered to do so by an officer. As a result he is badly treated. Eventually, goaded beyond endurance, he shoots his commanding officer:

> My loaded rifle I then prepared,
> To shoot my officer on the barrack square.

Depending on different versions of the song, McCaffery is then court-martialed and shot, or tried in a civil court and hanged.

Compared to the generals often celebrated in ballad and tale, McCaffery is a different kind of military hero. He is not a great fighter but rather an everyday person victimized by an inflexible organization. However, the justification for his actions is the ill-treatment he receives at the hands of the military hierarchy. His act of vengeance therefore makes McCaffery a hero to other ordinary soldiers, many of whom also feel themselves oppressed by the officer class. In these respects, McCaffery can be considered a hero of struggle, as well as an occupational hero. It was, and probably still is, believed by many that it is a treasonable offense to sing this song. The singer from whom Fred Hamer collected the version of the song quoted above recounted that she was once told, "If you was found singing that song you'd get ten years in jail."

Related entries: Heroes of Struggle; Military Heroes; Occupational Heroes; Warrior
References and further reading
Green, A., "McCaffery: A Study in the Variation and Function of a Ballad," Lore and Language 3–5, 1970–1971.
Hamer, F. (coll.), Green Groves: More English Folksongs Collected by Fred Hamer, London: EFDS Publications, 1973, pp. 47–48.
Lloyd, A., Folksong in England, New York: International Publishers, 1970 (1967), pp. 222, 263–264.
Palmer, R., What a Lovely War: British Soldiers' Songs from the Boer War to the Present Day, London: Michael Joseph, 1990, pp. 13–14, 56–57.

Melusine

Heroine of French versions of a tradition known throughout Europe and in India and some parts of Asia, especially Japan. The European version of this tradition, telling of a king of Scotland who marries a fairy, first appears in manuscript sources of the twelfth century. The condition of the marriage is what is sometimes referred to as "the lying-in taboo," in which the husband is forbidden to see his wife in her bedroom. Three daughters are born, one of them named Melusine (in some versions, Melusina). After the birth of the third daughter, the king defies the condition of the marriage and looks upon his fairy wife in her bedroom. She immediately returns to the otherworld, often said to be Avalon, a link to the Arthurian romances. When she grows up, Melusine imprisons her father in a mountain. Hearing of this, her fairy mother decrees that Melusine will turn into a snake from the waist down every Saturday. Her only release from this punishment will be if she can find a husband who will avoid seeing Melusine on Saturdays. Melusine marries Count Raymond, who agrees to the condition. They have many sons, though each is born with a defect of some kind. Eventually the count is convinced by a kinsman that Melusine's mysterious Saturday "lying-in" is for the purpose of illicit lovemaking and that these liaisons are the cause of the defects in the children. Raymond breaks down the door of Melusine's bedroom the following Saturday and discovers her half-serpent state. Chastened, he says nothing, but in a subsequent domestic disagreement he refers to Melusine as "a false serpent." Immediately, Melusine takes her leave, and the count never sees her again, even though she returns to nurse her children and to fly mournfully around the castle.

The various motifs in this version of the story, including the eventual departure of the wife due to insult or injury by the mortal husband, exist in the Irish, Japanese, and Hindu traditions, as well as in others. The non- or part-human lover is a common theme of folklore, and stories based upon it invariably end in a manner similar to that of Count Raymond and Melusine.

Related entries: Arthur; Fox Maiden, The; Llyn Y Fan Fach, The Lady of; Lohengrin; Mudjikiwis; Swan Maiden; Yasuna, Abe No

References and further reading

Baring-Gould, Rev. S., *Curious Myths of the Middle Ages*, London: Green and Co., 1897 (1866), pp. 471–523.

Beck, H., *Folklore and the Sea*, Middletown, CT: Wesleyan University Press, 1973, pp. 234–235.

Massignon, G. (ed.), Hyland, J. (trans.), *Folktales of France*, Chicago: University of Chicago Press, 1968.

O'Sullivan, S. (ed.), *Legends from Ireland*, London: Batsford, 1977, pp. 57–59, 155.

Picard, B. (ed.), *French Legends, Tales, and Fairy Stories*, Oxford: Oxford University Press, 1955.

Wood, J., "The Fairy Bride Legend in Wales," *Folklore* 103, no. 1 (1992): 56–72.

Mergen, Erkhii

Mongolian archer hero. Erkhii Mergen promises to shoot down the seven suns scorching the earth. With great confidence in his skills, he undertakes to perform his task using only seven arrows. If he fails, he swears to cut off his thumbs and to become an animal, living in a dark hole drinking dirty water and eating dry grass. The next morning, Erkhii Mergen takes seven arrows and as the suns rise shoots them down one by one. As he looses the seventh arrow at the seventh sun, a swallow flies across the arrow's path. The flight parts the bird's tail feathers, thus giving swallows their forked tail, but misses its target. Seeing how its six brothers have been killed, the seventh sun runs and hides behind a mountain in the west. Shocked and angered, Erkhii Mergen mounts his piebald horse and pursues the swallow. The horse tells him that if its swift legs fail to catch up with the swallow, the archer can cut off its front legs and throw them into the desert. No matter how fast the horse gallops, it cannot catch the swallow. As the seventh sun begins to set, Erkhii Mergen cuts off the horse's front legs and throws them into the desert, whereupon the horse immediately transforms into a jerboa, a jumping mouse that has short front legs. Erkhii Mergen then keeps his boastful promise, cutting off his thumbs and changing into a marmot. This is why the marmot's claws are only four in number. In the marmot's body there is

A movie depiction of Merlin and King Arthur in The Spaceman and King Arthur *(The Kobal Collection)*

a section of flesh called "man's meat." This flesh is believed to be Erkhii Mergen's, and people do not eat it as a mark of respect for the man who saved the world by shooting down six suns. The seventh sun is still afraid of Erkhii Mergen and hides behind the mountains some of the time, creating night and day.

The theme of shooting down a number of suns that are scorching the earth is also found in Chinese tradition, usually attached to the figure of Hou Yi. The dismembering of the gallant steed also echoes the Russian and Serbian traditions of Marco Kraljevic.

Related entries: Ahay; Hood, Robin; Hou Yi; Tametomo; Tell, William; William of Cloudesly; Yuriwaka

References and further reading

Li, N., *Old Tales of China*, Singapore: Graham Brash, 1983 (1981), pp. 34–35.

Metternich, H. (ed.), *Mongolian Folk Tales*, Boulder, CO: Avery Press; Washington, DC: University of Washington Press, 1996, pp. 51–53.

Shah, A., *Folk Tales of Central Asia*, London: The Octagon Press, 1970.

Merlin

Master magician, prophet, and poet first appearing in the Arthurian romances in the twelfth century, though said to have lived many centuries earlier. Merlin's considerable presence in Celtic legend, literature, and popular culture is due to his pivotal roles in the Arthurian romances, which are themselves the products of an extensive intertwining of myth, tradition, and literary refinement. Celtic and medieval traditions, especially those of Wales, Ireland, and Brittany, include stories of a prophetic wild man of the woods. In particular, the Welsh version of this story about an aristocratic poet of the sixth century, Myrddin, is perhaps the most likely source of the name and character of Merlin. In the 1130s, with his fanciful *History of the Kings of Britain*, scholar and early popularizer Geoffrey of Monmouth gave the Arthurian stories the basic shape in which they have continued. Here, Merlin appears as prophet and wizard, a role that Monmouth extended (and to some extent contradicted) in his later *Merlin* (c.

1150). From around 1200, French treatments of Merlin and other aspects of Arthurian romance appeared, often mingled with local traditions and further influencing the development of the romances in Britain. Sir Thomas Malory's *Morte d'Arthur* (1485) presented the defining shape of the English-language versions of the romances, which are the basis for most of the considerable subsequent Arthurian treatments and which establish Merlin in his most familiar modern role, rehearsed in fiction, film, and Broadway musicals.

In addition to—though usually independent of—these many literary treatments, Merlin makes occasional appearances in folklore. In the TomThumb tales, for example, he helps a childless couple bear a child, Tom himself. Merlin also appears in the ballad "Child Rowland" as a magical helper in the quest to rescue the daughter of Arthur from the underworld, or fairyland. There are local legends concerning Merlin in those areas of England that cultivate a connection with the larger Arthurian romances, such as "Merlin's Cave" at Tintagel, and there are some faint echoes of a tradition that Merlin was born on the Ile de Sein off Brittany. Many of these traditions may owe their origins and survival more to the needs of the tourist trade than to the beliefs of local populations. Considerable scholarly and not so scholarly research has been, and continues to be, carried out regarding Merlin and his important roles in the Arthurian romances. From a folkloric point of view, he is generally considered to be a literary refinement of the common folktale character of the magician or wise man. This figure, either male or female, often occupies an ambiguous space between good and evil, helping or hindering in sometimes whimsical ways and also often displaying many of the characteristics of the trickster.

Related entries: Achikar; Arthur; Helpers; Magicians; Tricksters; Wise Men and Women

References and further reading

Barber, R., *Myths and Legends of the British Isles*, Rochester, NY: Boydell Press, 1999, pp. 118–145.

Golnick, J. (ed.), *Comparative Studies in Merlin from the Vedas to C. G. Jung*, Lewiston, NY: The Edwin Mellen Press, 1991.

Stewart, R. J. and Mathews, J. (eds.), *Merlin through the Ages: A Chronological Anthology and Source Book*, London: Blandford, 1995.

Westwood, J., *Albion: A Guide to Legendary Britain*, London: Granada, 1985, pp. 79–80, 340–341, 444–446, 460.

Mikula

Also known as Mikula Selyaninovich, this figure is a Russian plowman hero of the peasantry, celebrated in many ballads and similar in some ways to the American Paul Bunyan and the Australian Crooked Mick of the Speewah. With a huge plow of gold, silver, and maple, and dressed in exotic and colorful clothing, Mikula smashes through massive rocks and huge trees as he plows, and he goes so fast that riders on horseback cannot catch him. He single-handedly defeats vast numbers of robbers, and, impressed by his strength, Volga Svyatoslavovich, nephew and godson of Prince Vladimir of Kiev (Vladimir Bright Sun), makes him the ruler and tax collector of three towns.

Related entries: Bunyan, Paul; Crooked Mick; Henry, John; Kraljevic, Marco; Occupational Heroes; Pecos Bill; Slater, Morris; Stormalong; Vladimir

References and further reading

Elstob, E. and Barber, R. (trans.), *Russian Folktales*, London: Bell and Sons, London: Bell, 1971. First published as Von Lowis of Menar, A. (trans.) and Olesch, R. (ed.), *Russische Volksmärchen*, 1959.

Leach, M. (ed.), *Funk and Wagnall's Standard Dictionary of Folklore, Mythology, and Legend*, London: New English Library, 1975. Abridged one-volume edition of *Funk and Wagnall's Standard Dictionary of Folklore, Mythology, and Legend*, 2 vols., New York: Funk and Wagnall, 1972, p 724.

Military Heroes

Heroes in uniform, or at least in service for warlike purposes, appear in most cultures. Often they are historical figures whose exploits have been celebrated in folklore for any number of reasons, including cleverness, bravery, endurance, victory, and quite often for defeat. Characters of this type include the English Admiral Benbow, the Hungarian Rákóczi, and the many military heroes of Chinese, Japanese, and Korean tradition. Military heroes may also be mythical warriors, such as the Russian Aloisha Popovich. In this last category, and less frequently in the first category, we often find culture heroes or national heroes, such as the Korean Marshall Gang Gam-Czan, the Japanese Benkei, and the Danish Niels Ebbeson, to name only some.

War, or military service, is also one of the arenas in which females dressed as men are found. While there are documented cases of women enlisting and serving in armies or navies as males, in folklore the women who are celebrated tend to be nonhistorical figures who fill a cultural category, such as the female sailor or female soldier of ballads. Often these heroines are motivated by the enlistment or press-ganging of their male lovers and don men's clothing so that they may continue to be close to their object of affection. Some examples of this type include the Chinese Mulan and the Italian Fanta-Ghiro'. In some cases, women have no need to don men's apparel in order to face the world in warlike mode. The Irish Grace O'Malley and the Mongolian Altyn Aryg are some more convincing examples of this heroic group.

Related entries: Aryg, Altyn; Benbow, Admiral; Benkei; Bonaparte, Napoleon; Culture Heroes; Dog-Nyong, General Gim; Ebbeson, Niels; Fanta-Ghiro'; Franklin, Lord; Gam-Czan, Marshall Gang; McCaffery; Mulan; National Heroes; Nautical Heroes; O'Malley, Grace; Rákóczi; Santa Anna, General Antonio López de; Warriors; Wolfe, General James; Women Dressed as Men

References and further reading
Dallas, K., *The Cruel Wars: 100 Soldiers' Songs*, London: Wolfe, n.d.
Palmer, R., *What A Lovely War: British Soldiers' Songs from the Boer War to the Present Day*, London: Michael Joseph, 1990.
Palmer, R. (ed.), *The Rambling Soldier*, Harmondsworth, Middlesex: Penguin, 1977.

Molo

Chinese sword-hero of the Tang dynasty (618–907 A.D.) who helps a young man to free his love, Rose-Red, from slavery in the house of a prince. When the prince finally discovers that Molo masterminded the whole affair, he pardons the young man and Rose-Red but commands his soldiers to kill Molo. A hundred warriors move against Molo, but, even though of advanced years, Molo evades the arrows loosed at him "thick as rain" and disappears. He is seen ten years later selling medicine, not having changed at all in appearance.

Molo is representative of a type of hero, usually referred to as "sword-heroes," found in Chinese tales of this kind. Such heroes are friends of the poor and oppressed and righters of wrongs. As well as having legendary skills with sword and dagger, sword-heroes have magical powers that allow them to move about as if invisible and to fly over and walk up and down walls. They are also said to have the ability to turn human heads into water.

Related entries: Heroes of Struggle; Magicians; Outlaws; Rose-Red; Warriors
References and further reading
Osers, E. (trans.), *Chinese Folktales*, London: Bell and Sons, 1971, pp. 199–203. First published in German as Wilhelm, R. (trans.), *Chinesische Märchen*, 1958.
Werner, E., *Myths and Legends of China*, New York: Arno Press, 1976 (1922).

Momotaro

Little Peachling, or Momotaro, is so-called because he was born from a peach. This Japanese hero, like those of many other cultures, grows strong and brave and goes off to recover treasure stolen by the local ogres, who live on an island. His kindly old foster parents give him some millet dumplings to eat on his journey, and along the way he swaps these dumplings for the services of three helpers, an ape, a pheasant, and a dog. Together the hero and his helpers reach the island, breach the castle, put the ogres to rout, and capture their king. Little Peachling gains the wondrous riches of the ogres and returns home to his foster parents, where he and they live long and prosperous lives.

The parallels with the story "Jack and the Beanstalk" and many other monster-slaying stories are striking. As with many such tales, the hero has an unusual birth, gains the assistance of helpers, in this case animals, defeats the monsters, and gets the treasure. The story also exists in Taiwanese tradition, presumably borrowed from the Japanese, in which culture it is an extremely popular tale.

Related entries: Berni, Cesarino Di; Helpers; Jack and the Beanstalk; Jack the Giant-Killer; Ogres

References and further reading

Eberhard, W., *Studies in Taiwanese Folktales*, Taipei: The Orient Cultural Service, 1971, pp. 104–133.

Faurot, J. (ed.), *Asian-Pacific Folktales and Legends*, New York: Simon and Schuster, 1995, pp. 84–88.

James, G. (ed.), *Japanese Fairy Tales*, London: Macmillan, 1923, pp. 223–227. First published as *Green Willow and Other Japanese Fairy Tales*, London: Macmillan and Company, 1910.

Mitford, A., *Tales of Old Japan*, 2 vols., London: Macmillan and Co., 1871, vol. 1, pp. 267–269.

Seki, K. (ed.), Adams, R. (trans.), *Folktales of Japan*, London: Routledge and Kegan Paul, 1963, pp. 40–43. First published in Japanese in 1956–1957.

Monkey

In Chinese literature and lore, Monkey (Sun Wukong) is the main follower of the historical Buddhist monk, Xuan Zang, who brought back the Buddhist scriptures to China from India in the seventh century. Monkey is a friendly, brave, and energetic character who likes to play tricks, yet he is also a faithful and good-hearted friend. Monkey has become a well-known character in the western world through a television series that features a version of this traditional hero.

One of many stories about Monkey, also known as the Monkey King, is that in which he "borrows" a weapon from the Dragon King. In this tale, Monkey returns to his kingdom from many years of studying spiritual enlightenment. He finds that his subjects are pleased to see him, as they are being terrorized by a monster. Monkey obtains weapons for his people by magical means but cannot find a weapon suitable to his own needs. It is suggested that he obtain a suitable weapon from the Dragon King who lives beneath the sea. The Dragon King shows monkey some massively large and heavy weapons, which Monkey tosses around with ease, saying that they are not sufficient for his needs. Amazed, the Dragon King then suggests, tongue in cheek, that Monkey take the "magic sea-fixing needle," a large and heavy iron pillar

that was stuck into the seabed by the great god Yu to ascertain the correct depths of the seas and the rivers. To the Dragon King's intense annoyance, the cheeky Monkey wishes for the pillar to be a little smaller and it immediately shrinks in size, though still retains its great weight, a perfect weapon. The pillar is even able to shrink down to the size of a needle, small enough to be kept behind Monkey's ear and drawn out whenever the need arises. Monkey makes off with the magic needle without even thanking the Dragon King, who takes his complaint to the Jade Emperor, ruler of all things. Numerous other tales about Monkey follow these events, including how he goes to heaven, where, in accordance with his character, he also causes a great deal of trouble.

Related entries: Culture Heroes; Magicians; Tricksters

References and further reading

Eberhard, W. (ed.), Parsons, D. (trans.), *Folktales of China*, Chicago: University of Chicago Press, 1965 (1937), pp. 68, 128, 206.

Li, N., *Old Tales of China*, Singapore: Graham Brash, 1983 (1981), pp. 176–186.

Werner, E., *Myths and Legends of China*, New York: Arno Press, 1976 (1922), pp. 221–222, 325–369.

Monkey Prince

Central figure of a Philippines tale in which the king's son falls in love with a beautiful young witch who is the daughter of his father's main enemy. The prince refuses to marry the many eligible young women offered to him but, after many years, eventually has to marry at the insistence of his father. On the wedding day, the betrayed young witch angrily turns the prince into a monkey for five hundred years. The spell can be broken only if a young girl falls in love with him. After four hundred years, the monkey prince comes down from the tree where the witch has banished him and tries to find a young girl to love him. His efforts are unsuccessful until he carries off a young girl who has been unlucky in love. After ten days, she falls in love with the monkey prince and he is turned back into his handsome human form. They are married and rule the city together for many long years.

The parallels between this story and European tales such as "Sleeping Beauty" and "Beauty and the Beast" have led to speculation that it is derived from these sources. If so, this is a good example of the ability of people to adapt material from another culture to their own ends, an integral element of the folklore process.

Related entries: Beauty and the Beast; Fairy Tale Heroes; Sleeping Beauty
References and further reading
Fansler, D., *Filipino Popular Tales*, Lancaster and New York: American Folklore Society, 1921.
Faurot, J. (ed.), *Asian-Pacific Folktales and Legends*, New York: Simon and Schuster, 1995.
Leach, M. (ed.), *Funk and Wagnall's Standard Dictionary of Folklore, Mythology, and Legend*, London: New English Library, 1975. Abridged one-volume edition of *Funk and Wagnall's Standard Dictionary of Folklore, Mythology, and Legend*, 2 vols., New York: Funk and Wagnall, 1972, pp. 741–742.

Moondyne Joe
See Johns, Joseph

Morevna, Marya
Legendary heroine of Russian tales involving Aloisha Popovich, Ilya Muromets, Prince Vladimir of Kiev, and Ivan Tsarevich, who has to defeat Koshchei to win Marya's hand. After suffering many defeats, including being cut up by Koshchei the Deathless and restored to life by his avian brothers-in-law, Ivan Tsarevich once again reaches the beautiful Marya, who is in the clutches of the evil old wizard. Koshchei the wizard has a magical talking horse, and Ivan wants a similar steed so that he can rescue Marya. She tricks Koshchei into telling her how to go about getting such a beast. It turns out that magical horses can be had only from another evil entity of Russian lore, the Baba-Yaga. The only way to reach the Baba-Yaga is to cross the river of fire. The only safe way to make such a crossing is to have the magic handkerchief possessed by Koshchei himself. Marya steals the magic handkerchief and gives it to Ivan, who sets off to find the Baba-Yaga. When he gets to her house, it is surrounded by twelve poles, eleven of which have human heads impaled upon them. Unfazed, Ivan tells the witch that

he would like a magic steed like that of Koshchei's. The Baba-Yaga says that he can have one if he successfully looks after her herd of horses for three days. If the horses escape, however, his head will top the twelfth pole. Ivan agrees to the arrangement and begins his three-day task. The horses run away each day, but he is assisted by his bird brothers-in-law and eventually obtains a magic horse. The Baba-Yaga, unhappy at losing Ivan's head, pursues him but falls into the river of fire and drowns. Ivan returns to Marya and escapes with her, but Koshchei comes after them on his magic steed. He overtakes the lovers and is about to smite them when Ivan's magic steed smashes its hooves into Koshchei's head, allowing Ivan to kill him with his battle-ax. Ivan burns Koshchei's body and scatters the ashes on the wind. Marya takes Koshchei's steed for herself, and together the couple rides to visit Ivan's in-laws, where there is great rejoicing. Ivan and Marya return to their kingdom and live a full and happy life together.

Related entries: Baba-Yaga; Muromets, Ilya; Popovich, Aloisha; Tsarevich, Ivan; Vladimir
References and further reading
Alexander, A., *Russian Folklore: An Anthology in English Translation*, Belmont, MA: Nordland Publishing Co., 1975, pp. 154–169.
Curtin, J. (ed.), *Myths and Folktales of the Russians, Western Slavs, and Magyars*, New York: Benjamin Blom, 1971 (1890), pp. 203–217.
Duddington, N. (trans.), *Russian Folk Tales*, London: Rupert Hart-Davies, 1967, pp. 91–102.

Morgan, Daniel "Mad Dog"
Australian bushranger Daniel Morgan operated along the Victoria and New South Wales border between 1863 and 1865, stealing horses, robbing travelers, and occasionally occupying farms and stations. Evidence suggests that he may have been emotionally unbalanced, but he was not the pathological killer painted by the police and the press. In fact, Morgan had considerable support and sympathy, particularly in Victoria, where he was known as "the traveler's friend." The circumstances of Morgan's bushranging were brutal and tragic, ending in his death and disfigurement by police at

Peechelba station (Victoria) in April 1865, as commemorated in "The Death of Morgan." The ballad, as given by Stewart and Keesing, establishes Morgan's heroic stature in its opening verse:

Throughout Australian History no tongue or pen can tell
Of such preconcerted treachery—there is no parallel—
As the tragic deed of Morgan's death; without warning he was shot
On Peechelba station, it will never be forgot.

This fiery ballad of outrage at the manner of Morgan's death is in stark contrast to the image of the bushranger projected in the media of the time, and in literary sources as well. Instead of being the heartless killer, almost an antipodean Frankenstein, Morgan is here represented in full outlaw hero appearance. His death, and its grisly aftermath, are claimed to be the result of treachery, and the blame is squarely laid with the authorities. The second-to-last verse describes Morgan as "the traveler's friend," as the enemy of the squatters, and as a "highwayman" who was able to "do the poor some good." In the final verse Morgan is placed within the pantheon of other notorious New South Wales bushranger heroes, such as John Gilbert, Ben Hall, John Burke, and John O'Meally.

The historian of Morgan, Margaret Carnegie, writes that flowers were placed on Morgan's grave on the day of his death each year until at least the mid-1970s.

Related entries: Christie, Francis; Donohoe, Jack; Hall, Ben; Johns, Joseph; Kelly, Edward; Outlaws; Thunderbolt; Troy, Johnny; Wild Colonial Boy
References and further reading
Bradshaw, J., The Only True Account of Ned Kelly, Frank Gardiner, Ben Hall, and Morgan, Sydney: n.p., 1911.
Carnegie, M., Morgan the Bold Bushranger, Melbourne: Angus and Robertson, 1974, p. 117.
Stewart, D. and Keesing, N. (eds.), Australian Bush Ballads, Sydney: Angus and Robertson, 1955, p. 4.

Morgan, Mad Dog
See Morgan, Daniel "Mad Dog"

Moringer, Noble
German ballad hero of the twelfth century. The ballad of Noble Moringer tells the story of the separation of the married couple on the morning after their wedding and of the bride's promise to wait for seven, sometimes nine, years until Moringer returns. He goes off to war, and the years pass, but still he does not return. Eventually the bride is forced into another marriage. The husband returns on the wedding day, making himself known by the popular device of dropping his wedding ring in his wife's wine cup. The couple is reunited, and the impostor groom is either sent on his way or given a just punishment.

Versions of the story are widespread in European folk balladry, including that of England (Hind Horn), Spain (Count Dirlos), Denmark (Finekonster), Russia (Dobrynya Nikitich and Aloisha Popovich), Serbia, Czechoslovakia, Greece, Rumania, and France.

Related entries: Horn, Hind; Popovich, Aloisha; Nikitich, Dobrynya
References and further reading
Leach, M. (ed.), Funk and Wagnall's Standard Dictionary of Folklore, Mythology, and Legend, London: New English Library, 1975. Abridged one-volume edition of Funk and Wagnall's Standard Dictionary of Folklore, Mythology, and Legend, 2 vols., New York: Funk and Wagnall, 1972, p. 796.

Mrikanda
According to the Koshte, a caste of Indian weavers, Mrikanda was the first to weave cloth from lotus plant fibers. The grateful gods rewarded him with a tiger and a giant. The giant disobeyed Mrikanda, and so he killed it, while the tiger was obedient and respectful of Mrikanda. It is still Koshte belief that if a tiger is encountered in the jungle it is sufficient to speak Mrikanda's name to avoid being attacked. Mrikanda is an interesting case of a figure who combines the attributes of the culture hero and the occupational hero.

Related entries: Culture Heroes; Occupational Heroes

References and further reading

Beck, E. F. et al. (eds.), *Folktales of India*, Chicago: University of Chicago Press, 1987.

Leach, M. (ed.), *Funk and Wagnall's Standard Dictionary of Folklore, Mythology, and Legend*, London: New English Library, 1975. Abridged one-volume edition of *Funk and Wagnall's Standard Dictionary of Folklore, Mythology, and Legend*, 2 vols., New York: Funk and Wagnall, 1972, p. 758.

Mu Lian

Chinese Buddhist monk who rescues his impious and unruly mother from hell, where she has been dragged by two devils. After saving her from the underworld, Mu Lian takes his mother to heaven. The lord of heaven approves this display of filial respect but points out that Mu Lian's actions have also allowed the criminals and evil spirits of hell to escape back into the world. For penance, he must round them up and take them back to hell. Only then will he be allowed back into heaven. It is said that the Hungchow rebellion at the end of the Tang dynasty was the work of Mu Lian, who ensured the deaths of many thousands so that they would go straight back to hell and so that he could discharge his penance.

The descent to the underworld is an ancient and widespread motif of mythology and folklore, in western tradition usually traced back to the Greek figure of Orpheus. Like many heroes who do journey to the underworld, Mu Lian's subsequent activities are ambiguous.

Related entries: Avdotya; Ivan the Mare's Son; Mu-Monto; Nakali; Potyk, Mikhail; Religious Heroes

References and further reading

Eberhard, W. (ed.), Parsons, D. (trans.), *Folktales of China*, Chicago: University of Chicago Press, 1965 (1937), p. 201.

Osers, E. (trans.), *Chinese Folktales*, London: Bell and Sons, 1971, pp. 88–89. First published in German as Wilhelm, R. (trans.), *Chinesische Märchen*, 1958.

Waley, A., *Ballads and Stories from Tun-Huang: An Anthology*, London: George Allen and Unwin, 1960, pp. 216–235.

Mudjikiwis

Hero of certain Plains, Cree, and Ojibwa Native American groups, Mudjikiwis ("Matchikwewis" and other spellings) is the eldest of ten brothers. The brothers mysteriously acquire a beautiful young female housekeeper who marries the fifth brother. But Mudjikiwis secretly desires her and courts her. She rejects him, and he shoots an arrow at her. The housekeeper runs away, and her husband, helped by an old woman with magical powers, pursues her. The fifth brother tracks his wife to the land of the Thunderers and brings her home, together with her nine sisters. The sisters marry the other nine brothers, the eldest marrying Mudjikiwis. The similarities between this story and a number of European tales—the Greek myth of Cupid and Psyche and the tale of the Swan Maiden—have led to suggestions that this is a Native American adaptation of an introduced European tale type. A character named Mudjikiwis appears as the hero's father in Longfellow's *Hiawatha*.

Related entries: Hiawatha; Swan Maiden

References and further reading

Barnouw, V., *Wisconsin Chippewa Myths and Tales*, Madison: University of Wisconsin Press, 1977, pp. 93–119.

Thompson, S. (ed.), *Tales of the North American Indians*, Bloomington: Indiana University Press, 1929.

Muhammad

Common name of the hero in Arabic tales, analogous to "Jack," "Ivan," "Hans," and "Jean" in English, Russian, German, and French traditions, respectively. In one Persian tale, Muhammad is a shepherd boy who outwits the wicked sultan, sending him off along the road to paradise, assuming the throne in his stead, and marrying three beautiful girls. In another Persian tale, Muhammad is a young wastrel known as "Muhammad the Marksman" who nevertheless ends up marrying the king's daughter in the time-honored manner of the wonder tale.

Related entries: Fairy Tale Heroes; Jack; Jack Tales; Jack the Giant-Killer

References and further reading

Kurti, A. (trans.), *Persian Folktales*, London: Bell and Sons, 1971 (1958), pp. 27–39, 90–95.

Mehdevi, A., *Persian Folk and Fairy Tales*, London: Chatto and Windus, 1966.

Mulan

Chinese heroine who dresses as a man to join the army. First recorded in the period 386–581 A.D., she was later given the additional name of Hua as legends about her increased. In the legend given by Li she is the second daughter of Hua Hu, who is too old and infirm to answer the emperor's call for fighters. The message comes first to Mulan, who decides to enlist using her young brother's name, thus satisfying the requirement for one male from the family to join the army. Almost at once Mulan proves her warrior skills by saving a marshall and his men from a dangerous situation. She fights bravely and rises through the ranks, becoming a general after twelve years. Through her sharpness and observation, Mulan is instrumental in winning the Chinese forces a great victory; she is showered with honors by the emperor and is offered the daughter of the marshall in marriage. Mulan has to make up excuse after excuse to avoid the marriage. Eventually, the marshall visits Mulan at home to try and convince the "hero" to marry his son. There he discovers that she is really a woman, a discovery that only increases his admiration for Mulan. According to Li: "Mulan, throughout the ages, has been held up by the Chinese people as a symbol of patriotism, a paragon of filial piety, and a woman of outstanding valour and heroism." This story was treated in the 1998 Disney film.

Related entries: Aryg, Altyn; Fanta-Ghiro'; Female Cabin Boy, The; Female Drummer, The; Female Highwayman, The; Female Smuggler, The; Military Heroes; O'Malley, Grace; Warriors; Women Dressed as Men

References and further reading

Coffin, T., The Female Hero in Folklore and Legend, New York: Seabury, 1975.

Faurot, J. (ed.), Asian-Pacific Folktales and Legends, New York: Simon and Schuster, 1995, pp. 95–98.

Li, N., Old Tales of China, Singapore: Graham Brash, 1983 (1981), pp. 65–67.

Werner, E., Myths and Legends of China, New York: Arno Press, 1976 (1922).

Mu-Monto

Legendary hero of Siberian tradition who travels to the land of the dead to reclaim a horse he had sacrificed on the occasion of his father's fu-

neral. He is led by a black fox to the portals of the underworld and there discovers those who have done wrong in their lives suffering appropriate punishments: the liar's lips are sewn together, thieves are tied up, and a woman wealthy in life must now wear rags. By contrast, the woman who had lived her life in poverty now enjoys great luxury. The theme of the hero's journey through the underworld, where he finds the dead suffering for their earthly sins, is frequently encountered in folklore and also in literature, Dante's Inferno and Milton's Paradise Lost being two notable examples.

Related entries: Avdotya; Ivan the Mare's Son; Nakali; Potyk, Mikhail; Saburo, Koga

References and further reading

Mercatante, A., The Facts on File Encyclopedia of World Mythology, New York: Facts on File, 1968, p. 464.

Riordan, J. (coll. and trans.), The Sun Maiden and the Crescent Moon: Siberian Folk Tales, New York: Interlink Books, 1991.

Münchhausen

Baron Münchhausen is the teller of tall tales and fabulous lies in the book Baron Münchhausen's Narratives of His Marvellous Travels and Campaigns in Russia. First published pseudonymously in 1785 (though written by Rudolph Raspe who may also have contributed some Münchhausen anecdotes to a collection of humorous stories published four years earlier), this book was amended in subsequent additions by various hands, and the character Münchhausen has become a byword for exaggerated stories, many of which have folkloric origins and characteristics.

Münchhausen's stories include that of the hunter who fires a cherry-pip bullet from his rifle, hitting a stag between its horns. He later comes upon the same stag with a cherry tree growing from its head. In another tale, the redoubtable baron, attacked by a ravening beast, thrusts his arm down the beast's throat, grabs its tail, and turns it inside out. In still another tale, the unarmed baron bests a savage Polish bear by throwing a gun-flint down the beast's throat and another into its rear passage. The flints meet in the bear's stomach, explode, and blow the bear to pieces. The baron concludes this story in his typically understated and dead-

Baron Münchhausen flies into a besieged town on a cannonball. (Mary Evans Picture Library)

pan manner: "Though I came off safe that time, yet I should not wish to try it again, or venture against beasts with no other defence." Such tall tales and lies, often delivered in similar manner, are characteristic of many folk heroes (though of few heroines), including Davy Crockett and other heroic braggers and boasters.

Baron Münchhausen is based on the historical figure of Hieronymous Karl Friedrich Freiherr von Münchhausen (1720–1797), a German aristocrat who became renowned for telling tales of his military and other adventures. These tales, it seems, were picked up by Raspe and, with elaborations, turned into the literary yarns associated with "the lying baron," as he became known during his long lifetime. This process of associating a real or imagined individual with a cycle of tall and usually humorous tales is a familiar one in the development of folk characters and can be seen in relation to the occupational heroes Paul Bunyan, Mike Fink, and Joe Magarac; the fron-

tier braggart Davy Crockett; and the trickster figures of the Hodja and Till Eulenspeigel, among others. Like Münchhausen, many of these figures owe a good deal of their popularity to literary and media treatments.

Related entries: Crockett, Davy; Eulenspiegel, Till; Liars

References and further reading

Dorson, R., *American Folklore*, Chicago: University of Chicago Press, 1959, pp. 14, 44, 57, 200–201, 227.

Michaelis-Jena, R., "Eulenspiegel and Münchhausen: Two German Folk Heroes," *Folklore* 97, no. 1, 1986, pp. 101–108.

Raspe, R. et al., *Singular Travels, Campaigns, and Adventures of Baron Münchhausen*, London: Cresset Press, 1948.

Muromets, Ilya

A bedridden peasant who, when in his thirties, is turned into a super-strongman through a drink of magic honey given by two pilgrims. The legendary Ilya Muromets (the name means "from the city of Murom," though he was said to have been born in the nearby village of Karacharovo) appears in numerous folktales and *byliny* (epic ballads). He is the great defender of Christian Russia, aided by his magic bow and flying steed. He becomes the trusted knight of Vladimir Bright Sun (Prince Vladimir of Kiev). Ultimately, though, he becomes arrogant and is turned into a stone statue that is placed inside the Kiev cathedral, a structure he had built with his own hands.

In the *byliny* of "Ilya Muromets and Nightingale" the brigand Ilya, "the fair, fine and handsome lad," sets out to attend mass in the famed city of Kiev. Along the way he almost casually relieves a town under siege from "a force all black, as black as a crow" and then proceeds to capture the feared brigand Nightingale, after putting out his right eye with an arrow. He takes his captive to the great Prince Vladimir at Kiev and tells his story. The prince does not believe one person, a peasant at that, could do such great things and calls Ilya a liar. Ilya has his prisoner whistle like a bird and roar like a beast, his trademark. So loud and horrible is this whistling and roaring that much of the city is destroyed and its people killed. Ilya takes Nightingale into a field and beheads him, saying:

Enough of your bird-like whistle,
Enough of your beastly roar,
You have brought bitter tears to mothers
    and fathers,
Many wives you have turned into widows,
Many children you have left without moth-
    ers. (Alexander 1975)

In many of the legends about his deeds, Ilya is shown defeating the invading Tatars. It has been suggested that one story in which Ilya saves Kiev from invasion is a folklorized version of the battle of 1224, with the actual defeat rendered as a Russian victory through Ilya's great warrior deeds.

Related entries: Nikitich, Dobrynya; Popovich, Aloisha; Tsarevich, Ivan; Vladimir; Warriors

References and further reading

Alexander, A., *Russian Folklore: An Anthology in English Translation*, Belmont, MA: Nordland Publishing Co., 1975, pp. 272–283.
Cavendish, R. (ed.), *Legends of the World*, London: Orbis, 1982, pp. 293–295.
Zheleznova, I. (trans.), *Ukranian Folk Tales*, Kiev: Dnipro Publishers, 1981, pp. 158–164.

N

Nakali

Miskito Indian (Nicaragua and Honduras) hero who journeyed to the underworld in search of a wife. Returning, he told his people of the bridge that is the width of only a single hair and that all who journey to the land of the dead must cross. Beneath the bridge is the cooking pot of the sikla bird. Those who have been uncharitable in their lives, especially in relation to food, will fall into the boiling vessel, while those who have been generous will cross safely to the other side of the one-hair bridge.

A bridge of one-hair's width features in the European story of Molly Whuppie and in other tales in which the hero or heroine journeys to another world beyond the realm of the everyday. In such stories, the bridge of hair may symbolize the fragile barrier between the real world and the underworld, between life and death.

Related entries: Avdotya; Ivan the Mare's Son; Mu-Monto; Potyk, Mikhail; Whuppie, Molly
References and further reading
Leach, M. (ed.), *Funk and Wagnall's Standard Dictionary of Folklore, Mythology, and Legend*, London: New English Library, 1975. Abridged one-volume edition of *Funk and Wagnall's Standard Dictionary of Folklore, Mythology, and Legend*, 2 vols., New York: Funk and Wagnall, 1972, p. 780.

Nanabozho

Also known as Manabozho or Nanabush, the complex trickster, shape-shifter, and culture hero of Algonquin, Cree, Ottawa, Ojibwa, Potawatomi, Fox, Sauk, and Menominee Native Americans and Canadians. Nanabozho generally has a wolf for a brother and is at once the all-powerful creator figure and a trickster buffoon who suffers gross and stupid indignities of many kinds. As is common for such figures, there are varying traditions told about him, with some groups identifying Nanabozho with the Wolverine and the Great Hare. Nanabozho was confused with the Iroquois leader Hiawatha by nineteenth-century collectors and has also been confused in subsequent scholarship with the apparently similar culture heroes of other Native American groups.

Related entries: Coyote; Hare; Hiawatha; Shape-Shifters; Tricksters
References and further reading
Clark, E., *Indian Legends of Canada*, Toronto: McClelland and Stewart, 1960, pp. 25–29.
Dorson, R., *American Folklore*, Chicago: University of Chicago Press, 1959, p. 168.
Leach, M. (ed.), *Funk and Wagnall's Standard Dictionary of Folklore, Mythology, and Legend*, London: New English Library, 1975. Abridged one-volume edition of *Funk and Wagnall's Standard Dictionary of Folklore, Mythology, and Legend*, 2 vols., New York: Funk and Wagnall, 1972, pp. 783–784.

Nanak

Nanak Chand (1469–1538), or Guru Nanak, was founder of the Sikh faith. According to Sikh mythology, he was born to the sounds of heavenly music and early showed himself to be a spiritual being. Something of a real-life ne'er-do-well, Nanak eventually had a vision that led him to become a nomadic preacher promoting a combination of the Muslim and Hindu faiths. In folklore, Nanak features in stories that show him performing miracles of healing and religious belief.

Related entries: Helpers; Religious Heroes
References and further reading
Leach, M. (ed.), *Funk and Wagnall's Standard Dictionary of Folklore, Mythology, and Legend*, London: New English Library, 1975. Abridged one-volume edition of *Funk and Wagnall's Standard Dictionary of Folklore, Mythology, and Legend*, 2 vols., New York: Funk and Wagnall, 1972, p. 784.

Nasra-ed-Din Hodja

See Hodja, The

Nastasya, Princess

Tragic hunting heroine of Russian tradition who, already pregnant, marries the knight Dunai Ivanovich. At the wedding feast, she challenges her boastful husband to a contest in which they might each prove their skill by shooting an arrow across a knife blade and then through a silver ring placed on top of the other's head. Nastasya goes first, successfully shooting three arrows across the knife blade and through the silver ring on top of Dunai's head. Then it is Dunai's turn, but Nastasya begs him not to try, not for her sake but for that of their child. This child, she says, will have golden arms, legs of silver, the moon will shine from his back and the sun from his eyes. He will be the most beautiful and wonderful child ever born. But Dunai ignores these pleas, notches an arrow to his bow, and dips the tip in snake venom. He takes aim and releases the arrow, and it flies straight into Nastasya's heart. The wonderful child is cut from her womb as she dies, and on that spot, it is said, there began to run two rivers, one named for Nastasya and the other for Dunai, now known as the Danube.

Related entries: Culture Heroes; Ivanovich, Dunai; Local Heroes; Muromets, Ilya; National Heroes; Nikitich, Dobrynya; Popovich, Aloisha; Tsarevich, Ivan

References and further reading

Alexander, A., *Russian Folklore: An Anthology in English Translation*, Belmont, MA: Nordland Publishing Co., 1975, pp. 237–255.

Dixon-Kennedy, M., *European Myth and Legend*, London: Blandford, 1997, pp. 167–168.

National Heroes

Often synonymous with culture heroes and heroines, national heroes are those figures who are widely considered by the members and government of a nation-state to be especially outstanding. They tend to have a strong presence in the formal apparatus and activities of government, especially in education, civic observances, and public holidays, and in statues, place-names, and other public memorials. They may also feature in official national projections and expressions, on postage stamps, for instance. While the status of these figures as folk heroes is sometimes uncertain, depending on political and social circumstances, they may have a purchase in the popular consciousness and feature in folk expressions.

In some cases these heroes are historical figures, like the English Alfred the Great (849–899) or the American Betsy Ross (1752–1836), designer and maker of the American flag, the "Stars and Stripes." In other cases, they are legendary figures or icons, such as the American Uncle Sam.

National heroes, historical or not, may be stereotypes of national characteristics, real or imagined. The figure of "the jolly swagman" in Australia, for instance, is representative of the pioneering, antiauthoritarian values many Australians consider to be part of their national identity. Australia is perhaps unique in boasting as a national hero the figure of Ned Kelly, a bushranger or outlaw hero who murdered three policemen and robbed banks. More often, national heroes are associated with resistance to foreign domination. Typically such heroes are warriors who fight valiantly and cleverly, heroes of struggle who represent their people in their hour of need. Some examples of this type include Rákóczi of Hungary, Holger Dankse of Denmark, and El Cid of Spain.

Wars are often the source of national folk hero stereotypes, which include the American "doughboy," the British "tommy," the French "poilu," and the "digger" of Australia and New Zealand. Such generic figures, all male, have a good deal in common with the warrior hero as well as with the culture hero. National heroine types exist in the figure of the nurse, the mother who weeps and waits, and the brave young woman who prefers death to sexual capitulation, as in the story of the Serbian heroine Dojrana.

National heroes are frequently the "discoverers," claimers, and explorers of New World nations. Thus Christopher Columbus has this role in the United States of America, while Captain Cook has it in Australia. Such figures, as well as other types of national hero, are frequently held in high esteem as representatives of national identity, actual or imagined.

Heroes who have been chosen or developed as national figures are often said to be sleeping until their nation needs them once more. The king of Spain who died in 711, Roderick or Roderigo, was the last of the Visigoth monarchs. He was killed by the North African Muslims under Tariq ibn Ziyad and became the center of numerous legends. In some stories, he ends his days as a hermit, devoured by snakes, and in others he is a sleeping monarch, waiting to come again in the time of his country's need.

The processes by which real and mythic folk heroes become national heroes are generally complex and of considerable historical duration. These processes involve an ongoing and often intense interaction between the folk traditions that celebrate such figures and their representation in nonfolkloric form, including formal art, literature, and popular culture.

Related entries: Alexander the Great; Alfred the Great; Arthur; Barbarossa; Bonaparte, Napoleon; Celebrity Heroes; Chang-Hko; Charlemagne; Cid, El; Columbus, Christopher; Cook, Captain; Culture Heroes; Danske, Holger; Darcy, Les; Dojrana; Ebbeson, Niels; Franklin, Lord; Frontier Heroes; Gearoidh, Iarla; Havelock the Dane; Hereward the Wake; Hood, Robin; Jolly Swagman, The; Kelly, Edward; Kraljevic, Marco; Mac Cumhal, Finn; Macdonald, Flora; Matthias, King; Military Heroes; Nikitich, Dobrynya; O'Connell, Daniel; O'Malley, Grace; Rákóczi; Sleepers; Stig, Marsk; Stuart, Prince Charles Edward; Tell, William; Uncle Sam; Väinämöinen; Vladimir; Warriors; Washington, George; Wolfe, General James; Yankee Doodle

References and further reading

Alver, B., "Folklore and National Identity," in Kvideland, R. and Sehmsdorf, H. (eds.), *Nordic Folklore: Recent Studies,* Bloomington and Indianapolis: Indiana University Press, 1989, pp. 12–20.

Botkin, B. (ed.), *A Treasury of American Folklore: Stories, Ballads, and Traditions of the People,* New York: Crown Publishers, 1944.

Clough, B. (ed.), *The American Imagination at Work: Tall Tales and Folk Tales,* New York: Knopf, 1947.

Hosking, G. and Schöpflin, J. (eds.), *Myths and Nationhood,* London: Hurst and Co., 1997.

Nautical Heroes

A large and diverse category of folk heroism. It includes historical figures such as pirates Kidd and Blackbeard, adventurers like Francis Drake, smugglers like Will Watch, admirals like Benbow, together with discoverers Christopher Columbus and Lord Franklin, among others. Also included are fictional voyagers like Sindbad; the occupational heroes of sailors, including Stormalong and Reuben Ranzo; and at least one saint, Nicholas. The exploits of many nautical heroes, real and legendary, are similar to those of their landlocked counterparts in armies and include armed conflicts with enemies, either for defense or offense, and supernatural adventures and encounters of many kinds, ranging from audiences with the sea czar, as in the case of the Russian Sadko, to wondrous feats of navigation and survival, as in the case of the blind Indian navigator, Supparaka.

Related entries: Arabian Nights, The; Benbow, Admiral; Bonaparte, Napoleon; Children's Folk Heroes; Columbus, Christopher; Cook, Captain; Female Cabin Boy, The; Female Smuggler, The; Franklin, Lord; Jack Tar, Jolly; Kidd, William; Madoc; Military Heroes; Nicholas, Saint; O'Malley, Grace; Ranzo, Reuben; Sadko; Santa Anna, General Antonio López de; Stormalong; Supparaka; Teach, Edward; Warriors; Watch, Will

References and further reading

Abrahams, R. et al. (eds.), *By Land and by Sea: Studies in the Folklore of Work and Leisure,* Hatboro, PA: Legacy Books, 1985.

Beck, H., *Folklore and the Sea,* Middletown, CT: Wesleyan University Press, 1973.

Halpert, H., "Tom Pepper: The Biggest Liar on Land or Sea," in Abrahams, R. et al. (eds.), *By Land and by Sea: Studies in the Folklore of Work and Leisure,* Hatboro, PA: Legacy Books, 1985.

Hugill, S., *Shanties from the Seven Seas,* London: Routledge and Kegan Paul, 1979 (1961).

Smith, L. (comp.), *The Music of the Waters: A Collection of the Sailors' Chanties, or Work Songs of the Sea, of all Maritime Nations,* London: K. Paul, Trench and Co., 1888.

Stanley, J. (ed.), *Bold in Her Breeches: Women Pirates across the Ages,* London: Pandora, 1995.

Nicholas, Saint

Said to have lived in Asia Minor during the fourth century, probably as Bishop of Myra,

Nicholas was sainted for his lifetime of charity and for working miracles associated with food and bounty, one of which converted a large group of sailors to Christianity. This is the reason traditionally given for St. Nicholas's status as patron saint of seafarers, an honor that appears to have some cross-fertilization with the legendry of the Russian Saint Nikolai of Mozhaisk. In this role, he is sometimes referred to as "Nicholas the Wet" or "Nicholas of the Sea," and according to Horace Beck, Roman Catholic sailors traditionally wear St. Nicholas amulets for protection against the vagaries of the ocean. He is especially popular in Russian tradition, where he is known as "Nicholas the Wonderworker," "Nikola," or "Mikola." He is known as a healer and protector from evil charms and is generally portrayed as a kind and merciful helper. This multifaceted figure is also the patron saint of Russia, thieves, virgins, and children. In this latter role, he is the basis for the considerable folklore surrounding "Santa Claus" or "Father Christmas."

Related entries: Helpers; Religious Heroes; Sadko; Santa Claus

References and further reading
Beck, H., *Folklore and the Sea*, Middletown, CT: Wesleyan University Press, 1973, p. 304.
Ivanits, L., *Russian Folk Belief*, Armonk and London: M. E. Sharpe Inc., 1989, pp. 12, 23–29, 31–32, 36, 105, 138–140, 145, 151–152.

Nikitich, Dobrynya

Born of a wealthy merchant father, Dobrynya Nikitich (or Kikitich) was skilled in singing, literature, and the strategies of chess. Yet he was also a brave and fierce warrior, second only to the great Ilya Muromets. In folklore, he defeats the dragon or flying serpent Zmei Gorynytch in a river battle but unwisely spares the monster from death. Zmei then abducts Princess Zabava, the niece of Prince Vladimir of Kiev, and Dobrynya goes on a quest to rescue her and, finally, to kill Zmei. After a journey through the underworld he succeeds in both these tasks, killing Zmei's female companion at the same time.

A *bylina*, or Russian epic, titled "Dobrynya and Aloisha" follows the mythic Odysseus and Penelope theme. Dobrynya departs to slay the dragon the morning after his wedding. He tells his bride that he will be gone for seven years and that she must wait for him. Seven years pass, and more, but still Dobrynya does not return, and his wife is forced to wed Aloisha Popovich. Dobrynya returns in the nick of time and, disguised, attends the wedding, revealing himself through the traditional recognition device of dropping his ring into the wedding cup. The ring is recognized, the wedding is halted, and Aloisha is sent packing.

Another byliny, translated in Alexander, is titled "Dobrynya and the Dragon" and tells how the young hero fights the dragon Gorynych, who has three heads and twenty tails. Dobrynya again spares the dragon, who later abducts Prince Vladimir of Kiev's favorite niece, the beautiful Zabava Putiatichna. On the advice of Aloisha Popovich, the prince sends the young Dobrynya in pursuit:

> [He] rode across the wide plain, open field.
> One day followed another like two drops of rain,
> Weeks went by like a rushing stream,
> By day he rode in the glowing sun,
> By night he rode by the silvery moon.

Eventually he smashes his way into the dragon's lair, finding many captives there:

> And at the Dragon's right, next to the vile creature
> Sat the beautiful Zabava Putiatichna.

Dobrynya and Gorynych exchange angry words but do not fight. The hero releases the captives and the princess, returning her safely to Prince Vladimir's "halls of white stone" in the city of Kiev.

In other stories, Dobrynya is dispatched on a quest to find a bride for Prince Vladimir and is also often said to have attacked and killed another Russian hero, Aloisha Popovich, for spreading false stories of his death. He was once said to have been turned into a bull by a witch and to have died at the hands of a giantess. In legend, he is finally beaten by a giant female warrior. Historically, he was killed fighting the Tatars at the battle of Kalka in 1224.

Related entries: Horn, Hind; Moringer, Noble; Muromets, Ilya; Popovich, Aloisha; Tsarevich, Ivan; Vladimir; Warriors
References and further reading
Alexander, A., *Russian Folklore: An Anthology in English Translation*, Belmont, MA: Nordland Publishing Co., 1975, pp. 237–255.
Baumann, H., *Hero Legends of the World*, London: Dent and Sons, 1975 (1972), pp. 20–23.
Cavendish, R. (ed.), *Legends of the World*, London: Orbis, 1982, pp. 294–295.
Curtin, J. (ed.), *Myths and Folktales of the Russians, Western Slavs, and Magyars*, Boston: Little, Brown, 1890.
Elstob, E. and Barber, R. (trans.), *Russian Folktales*, London: Bell and Sons, 1971. First published as Von Lowis of Menar, A. (trans.) and Olesch, R. (ed.), *Russische Volksmärchen*, 1959.

No Bigger Than a Finger

Russian version of the Tom Thumb theme. No Bigger Than a Finger is born when his mother cuts off her little finger while baking a pie. The tiny boy tells his father that if anyone wants to buy him, he must ask for a very large fee. No Bigger Than a Finger then climbs up behind the ear of his father's plow horse and finishes the plowing while his grateful and amazed father looks on and rests.

A wealthy landowner comes by and, not seeing No Bigger Than a Finger on the horse's head, assumes the horse is plowing by itself; the landowner is much impressed by this feat. The tiny boy's father explains what is happening, and the landowner buys No Bigger Than a Finger for a hefty sum. He puts the boy in his pocket, but on the way to the landowner's home No Bigger Than a Finger escapes. As he returns home, he is eaten by a wolf, and every time the wolf tries to kill a sheep, the tiny boy yells out from its stomach to warn the animals. Eventually the wolf can stand this intrusion no longer and asks No Bigger Than a Finger to leave its belly. The boy agrees, as long as the wolf takes him home. This the wolf does. When they reach No Bigger Than a Finger's home village, the boy slithers out of the wolf's innards. Much weakened by hunger, the wolf is easily killed by No Bigger Than a Finger, who then rejoins his parents.

Related entries: Children's Folk Heroes; Fereyel; Kihuo; Magicians; Tom Thumb
References and further reading
Bain, R. (trans.), *Russian Fairy Tales from the Russian of Polevoi*, London: George Harrap, 1915.
Curtin, J. (ed.), *Myths and Folktales of the Russians, Western Slavs, and Magyars*, Boston: Little, Brown, 1890.
Elstob, E. and Barber, R. (trans.), *Russian Folktales*, London: Bell and Sons, 1971, pp. 71–72. First published as Von Lowis of Menar, A. (trans.) and Olesch, R. (ed.), *Russische Volksmärchen*, 1959.

Nou Plai

Hero of a Hmong folktale who, apparently, returns from the dead. He rescues Ntxawm from abduction by tigers and returns to his parents, bringing Ntxawm with him. Ntxawm is a female figure appearing in a number of Hmong traditions. Sometimes she is a shape-shifter, as in the tale of her abduction by tigers and her subsequent rescue by Nou Plai. At other times she may appear as an emperor's daughter, as in the tale of Zeej Choj Kim.

Related entries: Shape-Shifters; Zeej Choj Kim
References and further reading
Livo, N. and Cha, D., *Folk Stories of the Hmong*, Englewood, CO: Libraries Unlimited, 1991, pp. 112–119.

Ntxawm

See Nou Plai

Nue the Hunter

Japanese hunter of supernatural beings and the central figure in a number of legends. Nue is said to have lived at Hatoya in Kamigomura province. According to one of his legends, one day Nue sees his only daughter laughing at the activities of a small snake. Fearful that the snake is tempting his daughter, he kills it and throws the carcass into the stream at the front of his house. The next year, many fish swim in the stream, and Nue catches them with a magic charm. He uses a grass stick to stir up the fish, whereupon they turn into small snakes. Nue takes the snakes to a field and throws them away. The next summer, a strange grass grows on the spot where he had disposed of the snakes; the grass kills any animal that eats it.

Other Nue stories feature his hunting abilities and link these with the supernatural. In one tale, Nue kills a malevolent spirit with a golden bullet. In another, he takes an eye from a white deer he has shot. The eye turns out to be a magic treasure ball that confers perpetual good fortune on all his hunting expeditions.

In discussing these stories derived from Japanese sources, the folklorist Richard Dorson points to the differences between Japanese and American hunter traditions. American frontier heroes such as Davy Crockett and Daniel Boone feature in traditions that humorously exaggerate their abilities to operate in natural environments. The Japanese hunter traditions, of which Nue is representative, feature their heroes in supernatural settings and situations. Although Nue does not seem to use a bow and arrow, his general hunting attributes fit well with those of the archers and spear-throwers who feature in many of the world's hero traditions.

Related entries: Magicians
References and further reading
Dorson, R., Folk Legends of Japan, Rutland, VT: Charles E. Tuttle, 1962, pp. 169–171.
McAlpine, H. and W., Japanese Tales and Legends, Oxford: Oxford University Press, 1958.
Redesdale, L. (ed.), Tales of Old Japan, London: Macmillan, 1908.

Numskulls and Noodles

Heroic stupidity is a feature of many folk traditions. Characters such as the Turkish Hodja, the Australian Drongo, the Italian Bastienelo, the Cambodian Kong, the Chinese Wang, and the Arabic Djuna typify this class of heroism, which seems to be largely restricted to males. Numskulls characteristically perform foolish tasks as a consequence of misunderstanding a verbal communication or of taking it literally. Thus the English Lazy Jack simply does whatever he is told, regardless of the circumstances. The French Jean Sot (Foolish John) puts baby clothes on the chicken he is asked to dress for dinner. Numskull heroes are closely related to complete fools, such as the Wise Men of Gotham (English); the inhabitants of Chelm or Helm (Jewish), where even the intellectually challenged Berel the Beadle seems like a men-

tal giant; the inhabitants of Altstätten (Swiss); the people of Emesa (Persian) and of Schild (German). Similar traditions existed in ancient Greece, where those who lived in the province of Boetia were treated as hopeless hayseeds and hicks. Cognate stories of fooltowns are told in Pakistan, Sri Lanka, and Japan. While foolishness is usually connected with certain towns in most traditions, the same stories may also be told of other places. In Germany, for example, in addition to the fooltown of Schild, folklorists have collected numskull tales about the people of Schwarzenborn and Mutschingen. In other traditions, a number of different towns may be identified as the location of numskull tales, though usually one place predominates.

One of the best-known numskulls-and-noodles tales is that usually titled "The Three Sillies" in English-language traditions and "Clever Elsie" in the Grimm collection. In this story, a young man finds his beloved and her parents hiding and crying down in the cellar because they believe that their daughter will, one day or another, be killed by an ax. The young man travels the world in search of three sillier people, who, of course, he finds. There is the man who tries to jump into his trousers with both his legs, the woman who feeds her cow on the thatched roof of her house, and a town full of fools who are intent on fishing the reflection of the moon out of a pond. Other numskull stories involve the simpleton who chains a wheelbarrow to the wall because it has been attacked by a mad dog and he fears that the barrow might go mad and attack people; the boy who gives hens hot water so they will lay boiled eggs; and the boy who plants a sow so that he can grow pigs.

The numskulls who live in the mythic German town of Schild are so stupid that they built a council house without windows but are unable to understand why it is so dark inside. Eventually they realize that no light can enter the building, but instead of putting in windows, the people of Schild try to carry beams of sunshine into the building, which does not improve the lighting. They then take the advice of a passerby who suggests that they take the roof off. This works well, and they richly re-

Ivan the Ninny sails away with the Princess whom he has won by introducing her father the Tsar to salt, in a Russian tale. (Mary Evans Picture Library)

asked to guard, and sometimes he makes a fortune when he accidentally frightens off the robbers who have stolen it.

There is often a connection between numskulls and tricksters, though the latter have the useful additional characteristic of being smarter than straight-out fools. The Turkish Hodja, for instance, thinking a thief is in his house, fires an arrow into the darkness. It strikes his coat, as he discovers the next morning, when his response is to tell himself that he was lucky not to have been wearing the coat when he shot the arrow at it. Tricksters like Hodja, the German Till Eulenspiegel, and the African Anansi may sometimes, perhaps often, commit such stupidities, but they also successfully play clever or cunning tricks on others. Noodles and numskulls are simply terminally stupid, though they usually come out on top at the end of their tales, if only by pure "dumb luck."

As well as their connection to tricksters, numskull elements and motifs also turn up in other traditions, such as those about the unpromising younger son who does everything wrong, as in the Russian tales of Ivanko the Bear's Son and the German stories of Lucky Hans.

Related entries: Bindieye, Jacky; Dad and Dave; Drongo; Hodja, The; Ivanko the Bear's Son; Kabajan; Knowall, Doctor; Little Moron; Lucky Hans; Ranzo, Reuben; Tricksters; Wise Men of Gotham

References and further reading
Alford, V., *The Singing of the Travels: In Search of Dance and Drama*, London: Max Parrish, 1956, p. 179 and chap. 7, "Swiss Fools and Festivals."
Argenti, P. and Rose, H., *The Folk-Lore of Chios*, 2 vols., London: Cambridge University Press, 1949, vol. 1, pp. 532–533.
Ausubel, N. (ed.), *A Treasury of Jewish Folklore*, London: Vallentine, Mitchell, 1972 (1948), pp. 319–326, 326–342.
Barrick, M., "Numskull Tales in Cumberland County," *Pennsylvania Folklife* 15, no. 4, 1967, pp. 50–52.
Briggs, K., *British Folktales*, New York: Pantheon Books, 1977, pp. 61–63.
Briggs, K. (ed.), *A Dictionary of British Folk-Tales in the English Language*, 2 vols., London: Routledge and Kegan Paul, 1970–1971, vol. 2, pp. 301–308.
Bushnaq, I. (trans. and ed.), *Arab Folktales*, New York: Pantheon Books, 1986, pp. 254–269.

ward the passerby for his assistance. The people of Schild are then very happy—until it rains. After replacing the roof, the people consider what they might do next. Groping around in the darkness of the council house, one of the fools notices a small beam of daylight lancing in through a crack between roof and wall. After looking at the light for a while and giving the matter a good deal of thought, he suggests that it might be possible to light the building by adding some windows. After considering this suggestion for quite a long while, the people of Schild agree that it just might be worth a try.

Jean Sot is a numskull hero in French and French diaspora lore. In the Louisiana French versions, Jean is a fool who usually misunderstands instructions and shoots the cow instead of milking it. Or he may take what he is told literally and throw a dog named Parsley into the broth instead of the herb parsley, as his mother has requested. On other occasions, Jean may remove and take with him a door he has been

Calvino, I. (trans. Martin, G.), *Italian Folk Tales: Selected and Retold by Italo Calvino*, New York: Harcourt Brace Jovanovich, Penguin, 1980 (1956), pp. 60–61.

Clarkson, A. and Cross, G. (eds.), *World Folktales*, New York: Charles Scribner's Sons, 1980, pp. 349–369.

Clouston, W., *The Book of Noodles*, London: Elliot Stock, 1888.

Dorson, R. (coll. and ed.), *American Negro Folktales*, New York: Fawcett World Library, 1967 (1956, 1958), pp. 332–353.

Halliwell, J., *Popular Rhymes and Nursery Tales of England*, London: John Russell Smith, 1849, esp. pp. 37–39 on Lazy Jack.

Halpert, H. (ed.), *A Folklore Sampler from the Maritimes*, with a bibliographical essay on the folktale in English, St. John's: Memorial University of Newfoundland Folklore and Language Publications, 1982, pp. 229–234.

Hasan, A., *The Folklore of Buxar*, Gurgaon, Haryana: The Academic Press, 1978, pp. 104–114.

Jacobs, J. (ed.), *English Fairy Tales*, London: The Bodley Head, 1968, pp. 297ff; reprint of *English Fairy Tales* (1890) and *More English Fairy Tales* (1894), pp. 10–12.

Mayer, F., *Ancient Tales in Modern Japan*, Bloomington: Indiana University Press, 1984, pp. 252–264.

Noy, D. and Baharev, G. (eds. and trans.), *Folktales of Israel*, Chicago: University of Chicago Press, 1963, pp. 179–191.

Ranke, K. (ed.), *Folktales of Germany*, London: Routledge and Kegan Paul, 1966, pp. 177–186.

Weinreich, B. (ed.), *Yiddish Folktales*, New York: Pantheon, 1988, pp. 222–230.

Williams, P. (ed.), *The Fool and the Trickster*, Cambridge: D. S. Brewer; Totowa, NJ: Rowman and Littlefield, 1979.

O

Oakley, Annie
See Frontier Heroes

Occupational Heroes

One of the most prolific fields for the creation of folklore is work. Since the industrial revolution defined work as we know it, trades, professions, and occupations of all kinds have developed. Many of these have long histories and proud traditions of struggle and development. An important aspect of these traditions may be a heroic, larger-than-life figure, usually a male, who represents the skills, values, and beliefs of an industry, trade, or occupation. Typically these figures are superhuman axmen, shearers, train-drivers, sailors, or cowboys about whom numerous tall tales are woven.

In English-language tradition at least, there is sometimes a close connection between occupational folk heroes who are the product of working groups and heroes who are inventions of fiction writers. The controversy about whether Paul Bunyan was an "authentic" folk hero of timberworkers or a literary creation has been echoed in studies of a number of lesser-known American figures. One of these figures is the African-American Annie Christmas, who is said to be almost seven feet tall, to have twelve even taller sons, and to run a floating brothel. Neither her prodigious drinking nor her wild ways ended her days, though. Instead, she is said to have killed herself for the love of one who did not want her. According to folklorist Richard Dorson, Annie was solely the creation of Louisiana writer Lyle Saxon. The legendary Febold Feboldson, occupational hero of Scandinavian-American farmers, is probably based on the stories told about Olof Bergstrom, a Swedish immigrant to America who appears in newspapers and comics of the early twentieth century and about whom many local tales were told around Stromsburg and Gothenburg, Nebraska. Paul Beath put many of these tales in literary form, furthering the Paul Bunyan–like legendry of Febold, which included such widely told tall tales as hitching a bee to a plow to plow a "beeline," along with a host of traditional lies involving giant mosquitoes, hoop-snakes, and the business of cutting and selling frozen postholes. The steel mill worker Joe Magarac, created by writer Owen Francis in the 1930s, is a similar instance of an invented hero. Joe, whose surname means "jackass" in Slovak, is seven feet tall, works all day and night, eats enormous meals, molds molten steel through his fingers, and finally melts himself down into steel to prove that he can, literally, make a higher quality product than iron ore.

A number of other occupational heroes have similarly murky folkloric provenances. Old John was said to be the hero of American printers. All printers knew someone who had seen him, or even spoken with him. Old John was so supernaturally skilled that he could wave his hand across the composing desk and all the type would fall magically into its proper place. He always quit at the most critical moment of a job, when the type was being placed. According to the traditions of the printing trade, when John died he, along with all other printers, would go to compositor's heaven, a print room with all new presses and type. Another example is the occupational hero of American signwriters, Slappy Hooper. Slappy was a larger-than-life character who painted the biggest, best, and fastest signs. He painted on the sky using "sky-hooks" to hold his scaffold, and he once painted a red stove that was so realistic it radiated enough heat to make flowers and weeds bloom in winter. Doubts have been raised from time to time about the authenticity of some occupational heroes of other cultures, such as the Australian figure Crooked Mick, who first came to light in literary rather than folkloric contexts.

Despite the largely, perhaps solely, literary origins of many of these characters, some of them so convincingly echoed the interests and concerns of the occupational groups they purported to represent that they were adopted by those very groups. This was certainly the case with Paul Bunyan and Febold Feboldson and is very much in accord with the processes of folklore, where ideas, characters, and other information originating in nonfolkloric sources may be taken over and adapted by members of folk groups for their own ends and purposes. Broadly distributed themes and story elements of the kind found in most of these occupational hero traditions may be adapted to local places, events, and characters. To describe tales about characters who do not have "authentic" origins within a particular folk group as "fakelore" is to ignore this important aspect of cultural process and implicitly to denigrate those groups who have adopted such characters as occupational heroes.

Occupational heroes should not be confused with the patron saints of many industries and occupations. Such saints are often selected on the basis of the relationship between their skills or attributes and the tasks they perform. So, for example, St. Nikolai is the patron saint of Russian seafarers because he rescues the musician and merchant Sadko of Novgorod from the clutches of the sea czar.

Related entries: Bonaparte, Napoleon; Bunyan, Paul; Crooked Mick; Fink, Mike; Henry, John; Heroes of Struggle; Hill, Joe; Jack-in-the-Green; Jones, Casey; Liars; Little Moron; Mademoiselle from Armentieres; McCaffery; Mikula; Mrikanda; Pecos Bill; Ranzo, Reuben; Slater, Morris; Stormalong

References and further reading
Beath P., *Febold Feboldson: Tall Tales from the Great Plains*, Lincoln: University of Nebraska Press, 1948.
Botkin, B. (ed.), *A Treasury of American Folklore: Stories, Ballads, and Traditions of the People*, New York: Crown Publishers, 1944, pp. 175–254, 546–550.
Dorson, R., *American Folklore*, Chicago: University of Chicago Press, 1959, pp. 199–243.

"Febold Feboldson," in Leach, M. (ed.), *Funk and Wagnall's Standard Dictionary of Folklore, Mythology, and Legend*, London: New English Library, 1975. Abridged one-volume edition of *Funk and Wagnall's Standard Dictionary of Folklore, Mythology, and Legend*, 2 vols., New York: Funk and Wagnall, 1972, pp. 374–375.
Francis, O., "Joe Magarac," *Scribner's Magazine* 90, no. 5, November 1931, pp. 505–511.
Pound, L., *Nebraska Folklore*, Lincoln: University of Nebraska Press, 1987 (1913), pp. 144–155.

O'Connell, Daniel

Daniel O'Connell (1775–1847) was the leader and lawyer who won Catholic emancipation in Ireland. He is the center of numerous legends and appears as a character in other folktales, usually portrayed as a friend of the poor and powerless and also as something of a trickster. In the story of "Daniel O'Connell and the Trickster" a poor man is tricked into selling his two pigs for the price of one at Tralee Fair. The poor man tells the story to Daniel O'Connell, who declares that they will have revenge on the swindler. He asks the poor man to cut off the lobe of his right ear and to put it in an envelope. They then arrange a visit to the swindler at his tobacconist's shop in Tralee. O'Connell tells the poor man that when they get into the shop, he should smoke his pipe. O'Connell will then say to the poor man that he does not smoke very much, and the poor man is to reply that he would smoke seven times as much if he had the tobacco. O'Connell will then say that he will give the poor man all the tobacco he wants. The next day, O'Connell and the poor man go to the tobacconist's shop. The poor man smokes his pipe, and, as agreed, O'Connell promises to give him all the tobacco he wants. O'Connell turns to the tobacconist and orders as much tobacco as will reach from the poor man's toe to the lobe of his right ear. The tobacconist replies that this amount will cost eight shillings, and he then begins to measure the poor man from his toe to the lobe of his right ear. When he reaches the ear, O'Connell says, "We have caught you." He tells the tobacconist that the poor man's right ear lobe is at his home, a considerable distance away. According to the bargain, the tobacconist will have to provide an enormous amount of tobacco for the price of eight shillings. O'Connell then releases the tobacconist from the agreement if he will pay the poor man for the second pig. Stunned, the tobacconist does so, and even pays extra, then goes to his kitchen ashamed. Another version of this tale, involving cows rather than pigs, was collected in 1899 and is given by Glassie.

One story with a political edge to the trickster image of O'Connell tells of him outwitting the English Parliament by wearing his hat for four days running. This made it legal for him to wear a hat in Parliament, even though all other members were required to go bareheaded. The same story also includes O'Connell's success in having one of his English parliamentary opponents commit suicide.

Related entries: Culture Heroes; Heroes of Struggle; National Heroes; Tricksters

References and further reading

Glassie, H., *Irish Folk Tales*, New York: Pantheon, 1985, pp. 93–96.

Sullivan, S. (ed. and trans.), *Folktales of Ireland*, London: Routledge and Kegan Paul, 1966, pp. 231–233.

uí Ógáin, R., *Immortal Dan: Daniel O'Connell in Irish Folk Tradition*, Dublin: Dublin Geography Publications, 1995.

Ogier the Dane

See Danske, Holger

Ogres

Monstrous creatures of great strength, evil, and stupidity who populate the folklores of the world. In Indonesian lore, ogres can be made to believe that a small person is very large and so be frightened away. In eastern European tradition, ogres will try to drink a lake dry to attack the young woman reflected in the waters. Even layabout snippets of boys like Jack, Ivan, Jean, and Hans easily outwit and defeat even many-headed, giant ogres, and just about any other folk hero worth their salt can dispose of these hapless villains in not much more than the twinkling of an eye. Despite their apparent stupidity and the ease with which they are bested, ogres, as a class of

A woodcut depicting the Native American giant ogre, Kloo-Teckl (Library of Congress)

villain, are essential to the existence of heroes and heroines.

As in many other matters connected to folk and fairy tales, the introduction of the term "ogre" is generally attributed to Perrault, though the ogre is a symbol of evil and villainy found almost everywhere by one name or another. Like the heroes they oppose, ogres come in a variety of types, often combined. These include the cannibal, the witch, the ghoul, the animalistic, the gigantic, the one- or many-eyed, and the just plain horrible. Some cultures favor particular forms of ogre. Giants are popular in England, Ireland, Scotland, Sweden, and areas of France. Trolls feature in Norway, while cannibals populate Russian and Slavic lore. The ogre is one of a number of concrete representations of the principle of evil that is an essential opposition in nearly all hero lore.

Related entries: Baba-Yaga; Devil, The; Dragon-
Slayers; Fairy Tale Heroes; Giant-Killers; Villains
References and further reading
Arnold, A. (ed.), *Monsters, Tricksters, and Sacred Cows:
Animal Tales and American Identities*, Charlottesville:
University Press of Virginia, 1996.
Zhao, Q., *A Study of Dragons, East and West*, New York:
Peter Lang Publishing, 1992.

O'Hanlon, Redmond
See Outlaws

Old John
See Occupational Heroes

Old Stormy
See Stormalong

Old Woman's Grandchild

Hero of Plains Native Americans, variously the
son of the sun or of the morning star. According to tradition, this hero leaves the skyworld
in company with his mother. She is killed, but
he manages to reach the earth safely, where he
is taken into the care of an old woman. In
common with many such heroes, he reaches
manhood rapidly and kills a number of monsters, including the dragon-husband of the old
woman. The story ends with the hero becoming the North Star or, in other versions, the
Morning Star, while the old woman becomes
the moon.

Related entries: Dragon-Slayers
References and further reading
Leach, M. (ed.), *Funk and Wagnall's Standard Dictionary
of Folklore, Mythology, and Legend*, London: New
English Library, 1975. Abridged one-volume
edition of *Funk and Wagnall's Standard Dictionary of
Folklore, Mythology, and Legend*, 2 vols., New York:
Funk and Wagnall, 1972, p. 819.
Lowie, R., *The Crow Indians*, New York: Farrar and
Rinehart, 1935, pp. 134–157.

O'Malley, Grace

Grace O'Malley, the anglicized name for Gaelic
Gra'inne Ni' Mha'ille or Granuiale, was born
around 1530 and died around 1600. Historically she was a pirate and sometimes successful

marital opportunist who amassed considerable
property and wealth. She was said to be "the
nurse of all rebellions in the province" (of
Connacht). In folklore she is a swashbuckling
defier of Spaniards, oppressors, and anyone else
who gets in her way. Her exploits are told and
retold in tales that have made her name synonymous with the Irish nation itself.

In *Legends from Ireland*, Sean O'Sullivan relates
two stories that convey the fearsome nature of
the legendary Grace O'Malley. In the first story,
Grace O'Malley's son is abducted by the Flaherties and imprisoned in their castle at Renvyle.
Grace sails into Renvyle harbor, gives birth to a
baby, and on the same day sallies forth against
the Flaherties in their stronghold, threatening
them with dire consequences if they do not
free her son. So frightened are the Flaherties
that they release the son, though in her anger,
Grace still has her cannon do some damage to
their castle.

The second story involves Grace O'Malley's
brother, the Red-Haired Smith. Grace thinks
he is an even finer man than her husband,
Burke. Burke is jealous and tells Grace he will
prove his superiority when the Red-Haired
Smith next comes to visit. Over dinner, Burke
tells the Red-Haired Smith that Grace thinks
he is the better man, an opinion that, Burke
says, he finds insulting. A fight ensues in
which the Red-Haired Smith is killed. Burke
then beheads the body and carries the head to
Grace, inviting her to cry all she wishes. Instead, Grace takes hold of her own rapier, goes
into the garden where her two teenage sons
are playing, and cuts off their heads. She carries these to her husband saying, "'Tis your
turn to cry now! . . . While you weep for your
two sons, I'll weep for my brother, the Red-
Haired Smith."

Grace O'Malley's seagoing exploits, factual
and fictional, also make her a celebrated figure
in sailor lore.

Related entries: Culture Heroes; Heroes of Struggle;
National Heroes; Nautical Heroes; Warriors;
Women Dressed as Men
References and further reading
Beck, H., *Folklore and the Sea*, Middletown, CT:
Wesleyan University Press, 1973, pp. 332–336.

Curtin, J., *Myths and Folk-Lore of Ireland*, Boston: Little, Brown, 1890; reprint, Detroit: Singing Tree Press, 1968.

Grace O'Malley Homepage: http://www.omalley-clan.org/uow/omalley_web/granuaile.htm

McGarry, M. (ed.), *Great Folktales of Old Ireland*, New York: Bell Publishing, 1972.

Ó hÓgáin, D., *The Hero in Irish Folk History*, New York: Gill and Macmillan, 1985.

O'Sullivan, S., *Legends from Ireland*, Totowa, NJ: Rowman and Littlefield, 1977, pp. 122–123.

One Thousand and One Nights

See Arabian Nights, The

Ostropolier, Hershel

Historical figure born in the Ukraine during the second half of the eighteenth century, Hershel Ostropolier has become a Jewish trickster hero of the first order. Hershel worked for some time as a "jester" to the grandson of the Baal-Shem-Tov, founder of Hassidism, and acquired his considerable reputation as a wit and prankster in this role. Hershel's relationship with his employer was a strained one, and a number of his tales turn on incidents involving rabbis. One Sabbath, Hershel was looking through the window of his rabbi's study when he suddenly asked the rabbi what one should do if he sees a cow drowning on the Sabbath—save it or allow it to drown. The rabbi replied that according to the Torah you must let it drown. "What a pity," said Hershel, "there's a cow out in the field drowning. The water is almost up to its head, poor thing." "Well, what can one do?" said the rabbi distractedly. "Nothing, I suppose," replied Hershel. "It does seem a pity though, the water has covered the cow completely now." Irritated, the rabbi asked Hershel why he was carrying on so much about a mere cow. "It's your cow, rabbi."

Hershel also seems to have been unlucky with women, and a good number of his stories involve his usually nagging wife. Someone once asked Hershel if it were true that he beat his wife with a stick and that she hit him over the head with a rolling pin? "That's not completely true," Hershel replied. "Sometimes we change over."

In another of his many tales, Hershel has the best of both his wife and the Jewish community. As usual, Hershel had no money to pay for the Sabbath food. He went to the person in charge of the local treasury, bewailing the death of his wife and asking funds for her burial. With great regret and sympathy, the elders gave Hershel ten rubles. Later they came to Hershel's house to pay their respects to his wife and were stunned to find her alive and happily eating roast chicken. They were outraged and called Hershel a liar and a thief. But Hershel was quite unaffected. "Calm yourselves," he said. "Just think of the ten rubles as an advance—sooner or later she really will be dead."

The theme of the trickster and the honored holy man is often encountered in tradition, with the trickster usually playing on the weaknesses and pretensions of the holy man. A cycle of trickster tales, some 270 stories, recorded in northern Thailand (also told in Burma and among various ethnic groups in the region) concerning a figure named "Sug" includes a good number in which humiliation and physical pain are inflicted on a monk. Tricksters in Jewish tradition also delight in tormenting rabbis and, in a more secular equivalent, often puncture the pomposities of the rulers who employ them as jesters.

Related entries: Baal-Shem-Tov; Religious Heroes; Tricksters
References and further reading
Ausubel, N. (ed.), *A Treasury of Jewish Folklore*, London: Vallentine, Mitchell, 1972 (1948), pp. 286–287, 304–319.
Brun, V., *Sug, the Trickster Who Fooled the Monk: A Northern Thai Tale with Vocabulary*, Scandinavian Institute of Asian Studies Monograph 27, London: Curzon Press, 1976, pp. 10–15, passim.
Weinreich, B. (ed.), *Yiddish Folktales*, New York: Pantheon, 1988.

Outlaws

Most cultures contain heroes or heroines of the outlaw type. Indeed, outlaws are among the most common and most constant heroes and, occasionally, heroines in all the world's folklores. Outlaw heroes are distinguished by their folkloric status as friends of the poor and op-

John Dillinger, notorious outlaw, sits manacled to Sheriff Holley in an Indiana court. His attorney sits next to them. (Bettmann/Corbis)

pressed. Robin Hood is the most familiar and archetypal English-language example of the "noble robber," though all such heroes in whichever language display Robin Hood characteristics to a greater or lesser extent. These characteristics include a forced entry into outlawry because of the unjust actions of an individual or group; the ever-present notion of robbing the rich to give to the poor; kindness and generosity toward the dispossessed and the downtrodden; defiance of the forces of oppression and injustice; bravery; the refusal of unjustified violence; and a general cleverness that allows them, with the help of those social groups who support them, to outwit and outrun their would-be captors. Outlaws and their

gangs have headquarters in forests, mountains, or other places away from everyday tracks where they can hide from pursuit. Robin Hood has the greenwood; Butch Cassidy had "the hole-in-the-wall" hideout; and the Chinese bandits led by Lu Zhishen have the marshes and swamps. There is often more than a touch of the trickster about outlaw heroes, whose folklore frequently includes feats of wonderful escapes from the forces pursuing them or near-supernatural breakouts from jails or ambushes.

Many songs are sung of outlaw heroes, historical and mythic. These songs generally emphasize the extent to which the hero has been driven to outlawry by the evil designs of a lord, a king, or a government, and they provide potted life and death histories—mostly inaccurate—of the individuals they celebrate. The German Schinderhannes, who operated along the Rhine, was renowned for outwitting the wealthy and the forces of authority and was celebrated also for his great generosity to the poor and his courage—typical outlaw hero traits. Schinderhannes and, later, the French Vidocq became the heroes of, as Mackay put it, "many an apocryphal tale," as did the Hungarian outlaw hero Schubry and many of the numerous bandits of Italy.

One of the most common outlaw-hero tales can be found in many parts of the world and involves a poor old widow woman (or other socially vulnerable individual) who cannot pay her rent. Nevertheless, the grasping landlord extracts the last penny she has, leaving her without the means of subsistence. Along comes an outlaw hero who, hearing of the poor woman's distress, rides after the greedy landlord, holds him up along the highway, and robs him of the widow's rent. The outlaw hero then returns to the widow and gives her back the rent money, sometimes along with the other rents collected by the landlord that day.

As this tale illustrates, because outlaw heroes operate on the boundaries between the legal and the extralegal and/or within zones of political, economic, or cultural conflict, they are often ambiguous figures, heroic and admirable to some social groups yet villainous and repulsive to others. Whatever we might think of the grasping landlord, he is within his rights to demand the rent from the tenant of his property. The Australian bushranger Ned Kelly is an excellent example of an ambiguous figure, though there is also ambiguity aplenty surrounding the likes of American outlaws Jesse James and Billy the Kid. A twentieth-century outlaw hero of this kind was the Sicilian Salvatore Guiliano, whose outlaw career balanced precariously between the everyday people who saw him as their friend and helper, the Mafia, the Carabineri, and the government. Similar observations could be made of the many bandit heroes celebrated in the vast folklores of China's numerous ethnic groups.

Outlaw heroes frequently have a relationship to national identity, especially in countries and cultures with histories of oppression and colonization. Thus Redmond O'Hanlon (d. 1861), an Irish outlaw hero, or "Tory," of the Fews Mountains near Newry, is celebrated in tradition as a freedom fighter from British tyranny. Welsh tradition includes stories of Thomas Jones, a sixteenth-century historical figure better known as Twym Sion Cati, a highway robber adept at disguise and escapes. His lore is rich with anti-English themes. In popular tradition, he is said to have retired from his life of Robin Hood–like crime to have married well and ended his life as a wealthy landowner.

Although outlaw hero traditions display a remarkable consistency across time and space, there are cultural differences. In Chinese lore, for instance, the length of Chinese historical experience and the complexity of its social arrangements has led to an institutionalization of banditry in gangs and secret societies. Chinese outlaw heroes are also more likely than most of their western counterparts to be involved in political upheavals and to prosper, or not, depending on the side with which they ally themselves.

Outlaws celebrated in the folklores of some cultures are portrayed as more aggressive and violent, as in the case of many eastern European figures. Others are assigned their heroic status because they represent the desire for revenge of one oppressed group against their oppressors, as in the case of the Indian outlaw Baba Devi.

Outlaw heroes in English-language cultures are overwhelmingly male. In other cultures, notably Hispanic and Indian, there are a number of outlaw heroines, a recent example being Phoolan Devi, the "bandit queen" of India, subject of journalism, books, films, and politics. However, in European tradition at least, the woman who dresses as a man and takes to robbing along the highway is a fairly constant figure, appearing in ballads of the female highwayman type. There is also more than a suggestion of the outlaw about the Irish Grace O'Malley and the American Belle Starr.

As with most heroes, outlaws, whether legendary or historical, are generally endowed with helpers in the stories and songs told about their deeds. Frequently these helpers are members of the outlaws' gangs, whether it be the merry bands of the Chinese *Water Margin* bandits or of Robin Hood, or members of their supporting communities or families, such as "the girl who helped Ned Kelly," allegedly his sister Kate.

A number of modern criminals have attracted the celebration of the folk, especially in America. The figures of John Dillinger, "Public Enemy Number 1" until he was gunned down by federal agents, was one of these, as were Bonny and Clyde, active in the same period and later given posthumous fame in a well-known movie. One of the most notable of such outlaw heroes was Pretty Boy Floyd, whose flamboyant manner, stylish bank robberies, and ability to elude police quickly earned him a modern Robin Hood reputation, especially among members of the social group from which he came, the white, rural poor. Other criminals have attracted a certain degree of ambivalent celebration, including Al Capone and, more recently, Great Train robber Ronald Biggs, who avoided British justice for decades in his highly publicized South American hideaway. Most recently the mantle of outlaw hero has fallen on the virtual brows of computer hackers who use the electronic highways of the internet to commit their allegedly "social" crimes. Mark Abene and "Phiber Optic" are two of the better known of these digital Robin Hoods. Many of these figures owe their folk heroism to the influence of the media, including film, TV, newspapers, magazines, and the Internet itself, as well as to the more traditional channels of oral transmission. They also partake of those qualities attached to celebrities and the heroes of the media.

Related entries: Bass, Sam; Bell, Adam; Bonney, William; Brennan, William; Celebrity Heroes; Christie, Francis; Clym of the Clough; Cortez, Gregorio; Deva, Babar; Dillinger, John; Donohoe, Jack; Fisk, Jim; Floyd, Charles Arthur; Geordie; Hall, Ben; Hereward the Wake; Heroes of Struggle; Hood, Robin; James, Jesse; Johns, Joseph; Kelly, Edward; Li Kui; Little John; Lu Zhishen; MacGregor, Robert; Molo; Morgan, Daniel "Mad Dog"; Parker, Robert Leroy; Quantrill, William Clarke; Slater, Morris; Stig, Marsk; Swift Nicks; Troy, Johnny; Turpin, Richard; Ward, Frederick Wordsworth; Wild Colonial Boy; William of Cloudesly; Women Dressed as Men; Wu Song; Xiao En

References and further reading

Coffin, T., *The Female Hero in Folklore and Legend*, New York: Seabury Press, 1975, esp. pp. 131–139, 191–195 on Belle Starr.

Hobsbawm, E., *Bandits*, London: Weidenfeld and Nicolson, 1969.

Lange, J. de, *The Relation and Development of English and Icelandic Outlaw-Traditions*, Haarlem: H. D. Tjeenk, Willink and Zoon, 1935.

Mackay, C., *Extraordinary Popular Delusions and the Madness of Crowds*, London: R. Bentley, 1841.

Seal, G., *The Outlaw Legend: A Cultural Tradition in Britain, America, and Australia*, Melbourne: Cambridge University Press, 1996.

Zhang, Y., "The Marsh and the Bush: Outlaw Hero Traditions of China and the West," Ph.D. diss., Curtin University of Technology, Perth, Western Australia, 1998.

P

Pak Dungu
See Tricksters

Parker, Robert Leroy
Born in 1866, Robert Leroy Parker came to be, under the name "Butch Cassidy," the leader of "The Wild Bunch," a gang of train and bank robbers that included Harry Longabaugh, known as "The Sundance Kid." After making themselves notorious, Butch Cassidy and the Sundance Kid left the West for New York. Then, after spending some years in Argentina as ranchers, they took up train robbing again. According to one version of the story, they were killed by police in Bolivia in 1909. Other versions of the legend, in common with the stories of most outlaw and many other folk heroes, have it that Butch Cassidy escaped death, living on until the late 1930s in various secluded areas of the United States. There are legends about their lost treasure, and many of the usual outlaw hero tales are told about them. These tales attracted the interest of writers and media professionals, leading eventually to the well-known movie *Butch Cassidy and the Sundance Kid* (1969). This interaction of history, folklore, and the media is characteristic of the ways in which criminals and some other types of hero, such as occupational heroes, are produced and perpetuated.

> *Related entries:* Bass, Sam; Bonney, William; Dillinger, John; Fisk, Jim; Floyd, Charles Arthur; Hood, Robin; James, Jesse; Outlaws; Quantrill, William Clarke; Slater, Morris
> **References and further reading**
> Steckmesser, K. L., "Robin Hood and the American Outlaw," *Journal of American Folklore* 79, 1966, pp. 348–355.
> Steckmesser, K. L., "The Three Butch Cassidys: History, Hollywood, Folklore," in Durer, S. et al.

Paul Newman as Butch Cassidy in Butch Cassidy and the Sundance Kid, 1969 (Kobal Collection/20th Century Fox)

(eds.), *American Renaissance and American West*, Laramie: University of Wyoming Press, 1982, pp. 149–155.

Patrick, Saint
Patron saint and culture hero of Ireland. St. Patrick brought Christianity to Ireland in the fifth century A.D. and is the focus of a number of folk legends and miracles in which, among other things, he rids the country of snakes and informs the people of the curative properties of plants and herbs. In some traditions, such as

A bard with a harp kneels in front of St. Patrick (Library of Congress)

those collected in Mayo early in the twentieth century, and given by O'Sullivan, St. Patrick also takes on the character of a local hero and magician, freeing the people from the tyranny of a loathsome tyrant in league with the powers of evil. St. Patrick bests the villain Crom Dubh—"one of the worst men that could be found" and who "had too much wizardry from the fairy sweetheart," who acted as his familiar and accomplice—and his two equally vicious sons in contests of power. At first St. Patrick quells the vicious mastiffs sent against him by Crom Dubh. Then he extinguishes the fire into which Dubh plans to throw him. St. Patrick and Crom Dubh then engage in a contest of magic in which "there [is] no trick of deviltry, druidism, witchcraft or black art" that Crom Dubh does not use against St. Patrick. But Patrick's holiness prevails. St. Patrick then raises his crosier and causes the cliffs to tumble, trap-

ping Crom Dubh and one of his sons, forcing them to "remain there until the midges and the scaldcrows had eaten the flesh off their bones." The other son is burned alive in a conflagration that he himself sets against Patrick. The victorious saint is honored and celebrated by the local people, and he baptizes them all in the local well, which ever since has been the site of annual pilgrimage and festival on the last Sunday of Lughnas, the seventh month of the Celtic calendar.

Related entries: Local Heroes; Magicians; Religious Heroes

References and further reading

Duckett, E., *The Wandering Saints*, London: Collins, 1959, pp. 30–46.

Glassie, H., *Irish Folk Tales*, New York: Pantheon, 1985, pp. 52–58.

O'Sullivan, S., *Legends from Ireland*, Totowa, NJ: Rowman and Littlefield, 1977, pp. 38–40, 109–113.

Pecos Bill

According to nineteenth-century legend, Pecos Bill was weaned on moonshine and died from drinking nitroglycerin. Pecos Bill is said to be an occupational hero of cowboys in America, Argentina, and Australia. In common with many other such figures, Pecos Bill carries out various remarkable feats associated with his trade. He teaches cowboys songs, stories, and swearwords; he teaches broncos how to buck; and he invents the six-shooter. Traditionally, he is the source of all those things that cowboys know, and some stories tell of Pecos Bill digging the Rio Grande. Like some other American occupational heroes, namely, Febold Feboldson, Joe Magarac, Mike Fink, and Annie Christmas, Pecos Bill has been the subject of debate among folklorists, some of whom claim a literary rather than folkloric origin for the character.

Related entries: Bunyan, Paul; Crooked Mick; Fink, Mike; Frontier Heroes; Henry, John; Jack-in-the-Green; Jones, Casey; McCaffery; Mikula; Mrikanda; Occupational Heroes; Slater, Morris; Stormalong

References and further reading

Botkin, B. (ed.), A Treasury of American Folklore: Stories, Ballads, and Traditions of the People, New York: Crown Publishers, 1944, pp. 175–254.

Dorson, R., American Folklore, Chicago: University of Chicago Press, 1959, pp. 199–243.

Pepper, Tom

A name widely used in English-speaking folklore to refer to a liar, roughly synonymous with Münchhausen. The eminent folklorist Herbert Halpert collected a sailors' song of this title in 1937 and subsequently conducted extensive research into the term for many years. He was unable to discover any folktale or other song traditions concerning Pepper. As he wrote in 1985: "So far as I can determine, Tom Pepper features only in folk speech." Nevertheless, Pepper is the center of a great liar tradition that includes, among other things, the story that he was kicked out of hell for lying. Halpert concluded that the use of the term "Tom Pepper" as an epithet for a liar "is widely but thinly distributed in the English-language tradition, on land and sea."

Related entries: Crockett, Davy; Crooked Mick; Liars; Münchhausen

References and further reading

Halpert, H., "Tom Pepper: The Biggest Liar on Land or Sea," in Abrahams, R. et al. (eds.), By Land and by Sea: Studies in the Folklore of Work and Leisure, Hatboro, PA.: Legacy Books, 1985, pp. 112–120.

Wannan, W., The Australian, Adelaide: Rigby, 1954, p. 67.

Peterkin

Central figure of a Gypsy (Rom) version of a sleeping-hero type tale, often titled "The Red King and the Witch." Peterkin, or "Little Peter," the youngest of the Red King's three sons, discovers that his sister is a witch. He begs money from his father, buries it in a secret place, and goes on a supernatural quest that lasts for an indeterminate but lengthy period (twenty, one hundred, perhaps a million years). During his journeys, he has many encounters with Death and Old Age, but they are unable to take him. On his return, he discovers that because so much time has passed all that once stood has vanished except for the well. He goes to the well but finds his evil sister waiting there to destroy him. He makes the sign of the cross and kills her, then speaks with an old man who faintly remembers being told of the Red King by his father's father. Peterkin then digs up the treasure he had buried, now deep within the ground. He opens it, only to discover Death and Old Age waiting there for him. They both lay hold of him, and he dies. The old man buries him, taking the treasure and Peterkin's horse.

First published in a Rumanian version in 1878, this story has been claimed as a uniquely Gypsy tale. Certainly the rather bleak conclusion is a reflection of the fatalism often found in Gypsy traditions, though elements such as the testing of the hero, his quest, and the long sleep or elapsing of a great period of time while the hero is away are found in many folk hero traditions.

Related entries: Baldpate; Seven Sleepers, The; Sleepers; Urashima; Van Winkle, Rip

References and further reading

Groome, F. H., Gypsy Folk Tales, London: Hutchinson, 1899.

Lee, F. H. (comp.), *Folk Tales of All Nations*, London: Harrap, 1931, pp. 528–531.

Tong, D., *Gypsy Folktales*, New York: Harcourt Brace Jovanovich, 1989, pp. 152–156.

Pied Piper, The

A hero turned villain, the Pied Piper of Hamelin is the ambiguous focus of an enduring medieval legend. In 1284 the town of Hamelin in Saxony is disturbed by a plague of rats. The piper, dressed in motley, hence the term "pied," pipes the rats into the River Weser, where they drown. But the people of the town refuse to pay him, and so he pipes their children inside Koppenberg Hill, from where they have never emerged. Only one lame child, too slow to keep up with the others, survives.

This is the most familiar version of this enigmatic legend today, though its original form, as far as can be known, was a little different. One of the earliest and most significant accounts of the event is the fourteenth-century version appearing in the Latin chronicle *Catena Aurea* (The golden chain) and written by a monk known as Heinrich of Hereford. This account says nothing about a plague of rats but simply tells of a handsome and well-dressed young man appearing in the city on the Feast of Saints John and Paul (June 26). He goes through the streets playing a magnificent silver pipe, attracting about 130 children, who follow him out of the city to the execution ground known as Calvary. There they all vanish without trace. Heinrich gives an earlier written source for this information and also refers to the testimony of an eyewitness relayed to him through the witness's son. In this version of the story, the piper is not "pied," there are no rats and no reluctant townspeople who refuse to pay a fee, and no children return.

By the mid-1550s, an account written in Bamberg has added such details as the return of two naked children, one blind and one mute, and the threat of the piper to return for more children in 300 years. Another account from around the same period identifies the piper as the Devil and the fate of the children as a result of God's retribution for human sin. The return of the one lame child seems to appear first in

A German illustration of the Brothers Grimm fairy tale "The Pied Piper of Hamlin" (Bettmann/Corbis)

the English translation made by Richard Verstegan in 1605.

The detail of the rat plague first appears in the Swabian *Zimmer Chronicle* of 1565. However, by this time there were other legends involving rat- and mouse-catchers elsewhere in Europe, and it may be that these legends became mixed with the basic Hamelin story. By whatever and various ways the story evolved, it was already a popular item of print entertainment by the early seventeenth century and, in one version or another, continued to attract the interest of poets like Robert Browning ("The Pied Piper of Hamelin," 1842) and folklorists like the Grimm brothers. It also carried on a busy life in oral tradition, being the subject, for example, of a number of German folk songs.

This disturbing legend has attracted a good deal of scholarly speculation through the succeeding centuries. Some scholars suggest that the legend is derived from the eastward migrations of young Germanic peoples during the thirteenth century. Others relate the story to the disastrous Children's Crusade, in which many children left their homes never to return. There are also suggestions that the story is related to the medieval dance epidemic known as "St. John's Dance" or "St. Vitus' Dance," or to a major bubonic plague outbreak. Others have looked to mythological and historical sources for enlightenment and explanation.

Whatever its source, the tale has been continually in oral tradition and, later, in literature, theater, children's books, advertising, cartoons, political propaganda, films, and, of course, in the tourism industry of the city of Hamelin. The multifaceted character of the legend of the Pied Piper is due largely to the ambiguity of the piper's character. In addition to the many uses to which the tradition has been put, in the end it is perhaps primarily an appealing moral tale about just rewards ("you must pay the piper's fee") and about being careful which processions you follow.

Related entries: Local Heroes; Magicians; Villains

References and further reading

Baring-Gould, Rev. S., *Curious Myths of the Middle Ages*, London: Green and Co., 1897 (1866), pp. 417–446.

Briggs, K. (ed.), *A Dictionary of British Folk-Tales in the English Language*, 2 vols., London: Routledge and Kegan Paul, 1970–1971, vol. 1, pp. 564–565.

Jacobs, J. (ed.), *English Fairy Tales*, London: The Bodley Head, 1968, pp. 297ff; reprint of *English Fairy Tales* (1890) and *More English Fairy Tales*, 1894.

Mieder, W., "The Pied Piper of Hamelin: Origin, History, and Survival of the Legend," in Mieder, W., *Tradition and Innovation in Folk Literature*, Hanover, NH, and London: University Press of New England, 1987.

Ranke, K. (ed.), Baumann, L. (trans.), *Folktales of Germany*, Chicago: University of Chicago Press, 1966.

Piercala

See Tricksters

Pocahontas

See Frontier Heroes

Popovich, Aloisha

Born under rumbling thunder, the legendary Russian warrior and trickster hero Aloisha Popovich ("priest's son") rides out to take on the world the very next day. His major triumph is to slay a villain named Tugarin (historically, probably the eleventh-century Polovcy chieftain Tugorhan, sometimes represented as a fiery dragon) and to dismember his body. Aloisha's other attributes are his ability to win by cleverness, often through pranks. He meets his end when one such prank goes badly wrong. When another Russian hero, Dobrynya Nikitich, goes away, leaving his wife Nastasya behind, Aloisha goes to her and tells her that Dobrynya is dead and that she should marry him. Nastasya wisely rejects this approach, but Prince Vladimir compels her to marry another man. Dobrynya returns during the wedding, stops it, and attacks Aloisha, whom he beats convincingly. In some versions of the story, Dobrynya beats Aloisha to death.

The *byliny*, or epic song, of "Aloisha Popovich and Tugarin Zmeevich," one of many such epic songs, begins in ringing style:

From Rostov, the glorious, the beautiful city,
Like two bright falcons soaring into the sky,
Two young and mighty heroes set out to travel far.
One of them was Aloisha Popovich.

The song goes on to describe Tugarin Zmeevich—He is:

tall, indeed he is a giant,
His shoulders are as broad as a barrel,
At an arrow's length is his right eye from his left;
He rides a steed—a vile and vicious beast,
From its nostrils fire blazes,
Pillars of smoke pour from its ears.

Disguised as a pilgrim, Aloisha kills Tugarin:

Young Aloisha Popovich turned,
He turned and faced young Tugarin,

With the club he struck him on his daring
  head,
He cracked young Tugarin's skull;
Tugarin fell upon the damp earth,
And Aloisha jumped on his black chest.

The hero then beheads Tugarin and steals his
clothes, making his companions think that he
is Tugarin pursuing them. Ekim Ivanovich mistakenly kills Aloisha, his "dearest friend." However, with the help of "drinks from beyond the
sea," Aloisha is brought back to life, and the heroes continue on their journey to the city of
Kiev, where they are received by "the kindest of
princes—Vladimir." Just as Aloisha is magically
resurrected, so Tugarin comes back to life and
joins the heroes at Prince Vladimir's table, dis-
gracing himself with his foul manners and obscene behavior. Aloisha vows to kill Tugarin
again. A fight is arranged and:

Young Tugarin turned around to look,
Young Aloisha attacked, cut his daring head.
Tugarin's head fell upon the damp earth
  like a beer barrel;
Aloisha dismounted, untied a leather
  strap,
He pierced the ears on Tugarin's head,
He tied the head through the ears to his
  steed,
He brought the head to Kiev, into the
  princely court,
He cast the head into the center of the
  princely court.
Prince Vladimir saw Aloisha Popovich,
He led him into his splendid halls,
He seated Aloisha behind a table set for a
  feast,
And indeed a feast was held in Aloisha's
  honor.

Then Vladimir asks Aloisha to stay and serve
him in return for a handsome reward, to which
the hero agrees, serving "faithfully and earnestly."
  In history, Aloisha Popovich was one of the
heroes slain at the battle of Kalka in 1224.

Related entries: Horn, Hind; Moringer, Noble;
  Muromets, Ilya; Nikitich, Dobrynya; Tricksters;
  Tsarevich, Ivan; Vladimir; Warriors

References and further reading
Alexander, A., Russian Folklore: An Anthology in English
  Translation, Belmont, MA: Nordland Publishing
  Co., 1975, pp. 256–271.
Cavendish, R. (ed.), Legends of the World, London:
  Orbis, 1982, pp. 294–295.
Elstob, E. and Barber, R. (trans.), Russian Folktales,
  London: Bell and Sons, 1971. First published as
  Von Lowis of Menar, A. (trans.) and Olesch, R.
  (ed.), Russische Volksmärchen, 1959.

Poseyemu
See Culture Heroes

Potyk, Mikhail
In Russian lore, Mikhail Potyk and his wife, Avdotya, agree that if one of them dies the survivor will join the dead partner in the grave. Avdotya dies first and is buried in a deep tomb.
Mikhail then goes into the tomb, taking a rope
with him, one end of which is tied to the
church bell so that he can summon help and be
pulled out of the tomb if his nerve fails him.
He reaches Avdotya's corpse and lies down beside it, lighting a candle he has brought with
him to cast a little light into the burial chamber. At midnight, the tomb is invaded by a large
number of snakes and a fiery dragon. Mikhail
slays the dragon, cuts off its head, and rubs it
against Avdotya's body. This act of bravery and
the magic in the dragon's head brings her back
to life. Mikhail hauls on the rope and rings the
church bell. He and Avdotya are hauled back
among the living and live happily together for
many more years.
  The descent of the hero into the underworld
is found in many traditions, such as the Siberian story of Ivan the Mare's Son. Sometimes the
quest results in success, as in the case of
Mikhail Potyk and Avdotya. In other stories, the
hero may return empty-handed yet in some
way strengthened by the experience, if not always for the better, as in the tradition of the
Chinese underworld visitor Mu Lian.

Related entries: Avdotya; Ivan the Mare's Son; Mu
  Lian; Mu-Monto; Nakali
References and further reading
Curtin, J. (ed.), Myths and Folktales of the Russians, Western
  Slavs, and Magyars, Boston: Little, Brown, 1890.

Dixon-Kennedy, M., *European Myths and Legends*, London: Blandford, 1997, p. 189.

Pretty Boy Floyd
See Floyd, Charles Arthur

Pretty Polly
See Victims

Prince Charles Edward Stuart
(The Young Pretender)
See Stuart, Prince Charles Edward

Princess Nastasya
See Nastasya, Princess

Punch
Main male character of the English folk puppet play "Punch and Judy," first published in 1828, though in existence at least fifty years earlier. While displaying aggression and violence toward other characters in the play, especially to his baby and wife, Judy, the hunchbacked and ugly Punch is nevertheless something of a hero in the trickster mold. Although he usually beats Judy to death, his subsequent escapes from the law in the shape of the Policeman and his defeats of the Doctor, Death, and the Devil have the quality of heroic transgression. These feats have ensured the survival of, and even a sneaking affection for, this brutally antisocial figure. In some versions of the play, Punch even tricks Jack Ketch, the hangman, into hanging himself, once again escaping retribution for his acts, and demonstrating a trick often encountered in folktales, where the hero fools the villain into killing himself or herself.

The character of Punch, also known as "Mr. Punch," is usually said to derive from the Italian *Pulcinello* (Punchinello in English) and, via the commedia dell'arte, ultimately from the Roman comedy. Punch also owes something to the French tradition of the hunchbacked fool. An old English nursery rhyme given by Halliwell makes this connection explicit:

Oh! mother,
I shall be married to Mr. Punchinello

A poster for a presentation of a Punch and Judy show, Iowa, 1940 (Library of Congress)

To Mr. Punch,
To Mr. Joe,
To Mr. Nell,
To Mr. Lo,
Mr. Punch, Mr. Joe,
Mr. Nell, Mr. Lo,
To Mr. Punchinello.

Like many trickster figures, Punch represents the defiance of regulation and authority that is a feature of much folklore. A still common colloquial expression is to be "as pleased as Punch," a reference to the regrettable but oddly appealing gloating that Punch displays after each of his violent acts.

Related entries: Judy; Karagiozis; Tricksters; Villains
References and further reading
Byrom, M., *Punch and Judy: Its Origin and Evolution*, Aberdeen: Shiva Publications, 1972.
Fraser, P., *Punch and Judy*, London: Batsford; New York: Van Nostrand Reinhold, 1970.

Halliwell, J., *The Nursery Rhymes of England*, London: The Bodley Head, 1970 (1842), p. 189.

Leach, R., "Punch and Judy and Oral Tradition," *Folklore* 94, no. 1, 1983, pp. 75–85.

Puss in Boots

Best-known European version of a widely distributed tale in which a cat, or other animal such as a fox, monkey, or jackal, helps a young man achieve wealth and the hand of a beautiful princess. The theme of the animal helper is frequently encountered in all the world's folk traditions, though the tale of "Puss in Boots" and versions related to it are especially common, being found in the oral traditions of Mongolia and other Central Asian regions, in the Caucasus, Armenia, Greece, and throughout Asia Minor and Europe. As a consequence of Perrault's literary refinement of the tale into "Puss in Boots" in 1697 and the subsequent popularity of his work, and of other literary and mass media reworkings of the tale, the story and the figure of the fierce but helpful booted cat is now known throughout the world.

In Perrault's telling, titled "The Master Cat or Puss in Boots," the three sons of a miller are bequeathed a mill, an ass, and a cat. The youngest son receives the apparently much less valuable and less useful cat and decides to eat it and use the skin for a fur muff or hand warmer. Alarmed, the cat, amazingly, speaks to the boy, saying that if the boy gives him some boots and a bag he will go into the woods, and the boy will discover that he is not as bad off as he thinks. The cat catches game and takes his catch to the king, saying that the game is a present from a Marquis de Carrabas. Later, knowing the king is coming by, the cat tells his master to take off his clothes, get into a river, and pretend that he has been robbed. The king gives the naked hero royal garments to wear and allows him to ride in the royal coach, where the king's daughter falls immediately in love with the young man, who, through the cat's suggestions, everyone assumes to be the fabulously wealthy Marquis de Carrabas. The cat then runs ahead, threatening the local peasants into saying that the lands the royal coach will pass through are those of the Marquis de Carrabas.

The cat then comes to a shape-shifting ogre in a magnificent castle. The cat soon dispatches this unpleasant obstacle by cunning, fooling the ogre into transforming himself into a mouse, which the cat promptly eats. The king, his smitten daughter, and the young man arrive and are overwhelmed at the castle's splendor. After a few cups of wine, the king suggests that the "Marquis" marry the princess, an offer the young hero quickly accepts. The cat is made a lord and needs to chase mice only for fun.

Although Perrault is the source of the most common modern version of "Puss in Boots," earlier writers also utilized the theme, including Giovan Straparola in his *Le Piacevoli Notta* (The pleasant nights), published in two parts in 1550 to 1553, and Giambattista Basile in his *Lo Cunti de li Cunti* (The tale of tales, known from the 1674 edition as *Il Pentamerone*), published between 1634 and 1636. These writers made different uses of the theme according to their eras, the kind of society they inhabited, and the audiences for whom they wrote. The Grimm brothers included a version similar to Perrault's in their 1812 *Kinder- und Hausmärchen* (Children's and household tales). However, the theme of a cunning animal helping a young hero to success is much older than even the earliest of these reuses of the plot and its variants.

Folklorists have identified two main strands of the tale that eventually became Perrault's "Puss in Boots." An extensive Central Asian tradition has a fox helping a hunter who spares its life. The tale then proceeds similarly to that told by Perrault, with the fox securing wealth and a palace by killing a Mangus, a common demon figure of Central Asian tradition. More recent versions involve the fox promising the young hunter the daughter of the king of birds in marriage and then cunningly killing the king of birds as well as a rich man and giving their wealth to the young man as his reward for sparing the life of the fox.

As we move closer to Europe, the hero tends to become a miller or, especially in Greece, a grape-grower. Another feature of tales from this area is the inclusion of the gold-weighing scales. In this motif, the fox borrows a set of scales from the king to weigh its master's gold.

Returning the scales, the fox cleverly leaves a gold coin on them. The king wishes to return the coin, but the fox says there is no need; the king should give it to his servants, as the fox's master has so many more.

Armenian, Caucasian, Turkish, Greek, and some European versions also include an episode in which the animal helper feigns death in order to test the gratitude and sincerity of the hero being helped. Often, though by no means always, the hero takes the opportunity to rid himself of the helper. Sometimes the helper simply disappears; sometimes it seeks revenge by revealing the truth about the hero's humble origins or even by seeking to have the hero killed by those whose castle or palace the hero has acquired as a result of the helper's devoted trickery. It seems that it is the western European versions of the tale that change the helper from a fox to a cat, a fact that has led a number of folklorists to suggest that the story originated in the east, possibly in India, and was transmitted to Europe through Arabic, North African, Greek, Balkan, and southern Italian contacts.

Whatever the course, or courses, of the tale's development it became firmly established in western folklore and literary tradition from the seventeenth century. It was featured in chapbooks and other street literature and, later, in children's books. In the twentieth-century, it made its way into film, including an early treatment of Walt Disney in 1922. The moral ambiguity of the story (after all, the young hero succeeds through the animal helper's deceit and violence) and the exceptionally passive role of the hero—who barely lifts a finger, compared with the almost manic activity of the fox or cat on his behalf—perhaps accounts for some of the tale's appeal and its continual refinements and adaptations through many centuries of eastern and western culture.

Related entries: Fairy Tale Heroes; Helpers; Skorobogaty, Kuzma; Whittington, Dick

References and further reading

Briggs, K., *Nine Lives: The Folklore of Cats*, New York: Pantheon, 1980.

De Caro, F. (ed.), *The Folktale Cat*, Little Rock, AR: August House, 1992.

Hallett, M. and Karasek, B. (eds.), *Folk and Fairy Tales*, Ontario: Broadview Press, 1996, pp. 94–97.

Kaplanoglou, M., "Puss in Boots and The Fox-Matchmaker: From the Central Asian to the European Tradition," *Folklore* 110, 1999, pp. 57–62.

Massignon, G. (ed.), Hyland, J. (trans.), *Folktales of France*, Chicago: University of Chicago Press, 1968, pp. 96–97.

Zipes, J., "Of Cats and Men: Framing the Civilizing Discourse of the Fairy Tale," in *Happily Ever After: Fairy Tales, Children, and the Culture Industry*, New York: Routledge, 1997.

Puuhaara, Antti

Legendary Finnish hero whose birth to a humble farming couple is accompanied by a seer's prediction that he will inherit the great wealth of a fox-skin merchant who happens to be staying at the couple's house on the night of the birth. The merchant overhears this prediction and decides that to prevent it from coming true he will have to kill the baby. He convinces the parents to let him adopt the boy, and when he is far enough away from the farm, he hangs the child in the forest. Fortunately, a hunter comes by shortly, hears the child's cries, and releases him. The hunter takes the boy home and raises him as his own, giving him the name Antti. When the other villagers learn of the circumstances in which the hunter found Antti, they nickname him "Puuhaara," meaning a branch or the fork of a tree. Antti grows into a strong and handsome man.

One day, the wealthy fox-skin merchant happens to come to the village again. He hears the locals talking about this strangely named young man and asks how he came by it. When he is told, he realizes that Antti Puuhaara is the baby he had tried to murder so many years before. Still desperate to stop the seer's prediction from coming true, the merchant has Antti deliver a letter to the merchant's home. The obliging young man has no idea that the letter contains instructions to the merchant's employees to capture Antti and hang him from a birch tree. Along the way toward his fate, Antti becomes tired and lies down to sleep, holding the letter in his hand. As he sleeps two students come by, read the letter, and decide to change it. While the exhausted Antti sleeps on, they rewrite the letter to command the merchant's retainers to marry his daughter to Antti and, instead of hanging the young man, to string the merchant's old dog up to the birch tree. The students then continue on their way, congratulating each other on the cleverness of their trick. Antti wakes up, knowing nothing of all this, and continues on to the merchant's home, where he is received in accordance with the rewritten instructions in the letter.

The students were good forgers and, despite the strangeness of the requests, Antti is married to the merchant's daughter and the merchant's dog is hung. When the merchant returns home some weeks later he is thunderstruck to discover how his evil plans have gone awry. Nevertheless, he manages to hide his anger and plots to get rid of Antti, now so close to fulfilling the seer's prediction. He sends Antti to see Louhi, the Witch of the North, ruler of the cold kingdom of Pohjola. Antti is to ask the question "What makes man happy?" and to return with the answer. Stick in hand, Antti dutifully strides off to do as his father-in-law requests.

Along the way he meets a Hiisi, a giant nature being. The Hiisi asks him where he is going, and when he tells the giant of his quest, the Hiisi asks him also to find out from Louhi how to improve his failing orchard. Antti agrees to return with the answer to this question as well, and the giant gives Antti a white stallion to help him on his journey. Antti then comes across another giant who has lost the keys to his castle. Upon hearing of the young hero's quest, this giant asks him to find out from Louhi where his keys have gone. If Antti brings back the answer, he will give him his best treasure in payment. Antti agrees and goes on his way, soon encountering a third Hiisi. This one is sitting on top of a pine tree roasting elk meat. He invites the hungry young man to join him and, on hearing that he is traveling to Louhi, asks him to find out from the witch why he has to spend his life sitting in a pine tree, as this makes it difficult for him to hunt food. Antti agrees to ask this question and rides on to a river, where an old hag takes him across the water in a small boat. When the hag learns

of Antti's quest, she asks him to find out from Louhi why it is that she must spend her life ferrying travelers across the river. Antti agrees and gets out on the far bank, continuing his journey on foot as the boat had been too small to accommodate the white stallion. Fortunately it is not far to Louhi's house, though when Antti gets there he finds that she is out and only her daughter is at home.

The handsome young man and the witch's daughter get on very well, and Antti tells her that he has come to ask her mother a number of important questions. He tells the girl what they are, and she says that she doubts that her mother will be willing to give the answers. She then suggests that she put the questions to her mother while Antti hides behind the stove. He can then overhear the answers and make his escape. Cleverly, the daughter tricks her mother into revealing the answer to each of the five questions. In answer to the query of Antti's father-in-law as to how man can find happiness, Louhi says, "Man is happiest when digging earth; trees have to be pulled by the roots from the ground, rocks shifted into piles, and the ground cleared for a field instead." In answer to the first giant's question about his orchard failing to thrive, Louhi says that there is a giant worm in the orchard and its breath is drying out the fruit. The orchard will fruit fully once the worm has been killed between two stones. The Witch of the North then reveals the whereabouts of the second giant's lost castle keys— under the top step—and how the tree-sitting giant can get down—by pushing an alder staff into the roots of the tree, which will then tumble down in a mass of gold. As for the old hag, she could escape, Louhi says, quite easily. All she needs to do the next time she ferries a traveler over the water is to jump out onto the bank first and to push the boat back with her left heel, saying, "I will be off now, you stay behind in the boat." That will condemn the traveler to take her place forever.

Antti overhears these answers and makes off the way he had come. At the river, the hag asks for the answer to her question, but Antti, wisely, will not give it until she has ferried him over the water. When he is safely on shore, he tells her, much to her delight, then mounts the white stallion still waiting there and rides off to where the tree-sitting Hiisi awaits his return. When he gets there, Antti plunges an alder stick into the roots, as Louhi had said, and the tree comes down in a heap of gold, freeing the giant. He is so delighted that he gives Antti a reward of golden branches. When Antti reaches the giant outside the locked castle, he is able to tell him where the keys are, and the giant gives Antti yet more gold. Then he rides to the Hiisi with the orchard and tells him how to get rid of the worm that is harming his fruit. The giant allows Antti to keep the white stallion as his reward, and the young hero then rides back to his father-in-law's house. Amazed and annoyed that Antti has survived, the father-in-law demands the answer to his question. Antti tells him, though his father-in-law is not impressed. Rather, he is depressed that Antti is alive and envious of all the wealth he has acquired during his adventures.

The merchant then decides to take the same journey in search of even more riches than he already possesses. After traveling for some time, the merchant comes to the same river Antti had crossed and is eagerly ferried across by the old hag. As the boat approaches the far bank, the hag does as Louhi had advised, jumping onto the bank first and pushing the boat and the merchant in it back into the river with her left heel, saying, "I will be off now, you stay here." And so the hag is freed and the merchant becomes the ferryman forever and ever because there are no more visitors for Louhi, as Antti had gained all her knowledge. Thus it is that every Finn found out how to be happy. Antti becomes master of the merchant's household, living happily with his wife and inheriting all the merchant's wealth, exactly as the seer had predicted at his birth.

This summary of a lengthy story, given in Henderson and collected in 1850, reveals the differences between the mythological cycle of narratives contained in the *Kalevala* and the folkloric treatment of similar themes. While Louhi,

the giant Hiisi, and the cold, dead world of Pohjola are common to both the *Kalevala* and folklore, the oral telling of this tale emphasizes the everyday status of the characters and the relative mundanity of their concerns—home, family, wealth, and happiness. In this case, the story also has the characteristic happy ending associated with the fairy tale, along with a number of morals—that innocence and honesty bring rewards, that greed will be punished, and that happiness does not depend on wealth but on the simple necessities of everyday life. Antti is also related to the considerable number of unprepossessing heroes who achieve their success by little more than luck, such as the German "Lucky Hans" and a good many of the "Jack" and similar characters of English-language lore. The structure and many of the events in this story parallel those in a tale usually known in the German version as "The Devil with the Three Golden Hairs." In one form or another, it is an extremely widespread tale type, known in North America, South America, China, and Africa.

Related entries: Culture Heroes; Jack Tales; Lemminkäinen; Lucky Hans; Väinämöinen

References and further reading

Booss, C., *Scandinavian Folk and Fairy Tales*, New York: Crown Publishers, Avenel Books, 1984.

Fillmore, P., *Mighty Mikko: A Book of Finnish Fairy Tales and Folk Tales*, New York: Harcourt Brace and Co., 1920.

Grimm, J. and W., *The Complete Grimm's Fairy Tales*, New York: Pantheon Books, 1944, pp. 151–158.

Henderson, H. (ed. and trans.), *The Maiden Who Rose from the Sea and Other Finnish Folktales*, Enfield Lock: Hisarlik Press, 1992, pp. 63–77.

Kvideland, R. and Sehmsdorf, H. (eds.), *Scandinavian Folk Belief and Legend*, Minneapolis: University of Minnesota Press, 1988.

Lönnrot, E. (comp.), Magoun, F. (trans.), *The Kalevala, or Poems of the Kalevala District*, Cambridge: Harvard University Press, 1963.

Pentikäinen, J. (trans. and ed. Poom, R.), *Kalevala Mythology*, Bloomington: Indiana University Press, 1989 (1987).

Q

Quantrell
See Quantrill, William Clarke

Quantrill, William Clarke
Historical outlaw hero, William Clarke Quantrill was born in Ohio in 1837, the first of eight children. From 1860 he attracted official attention for murder and horse stealing. Quantrill fought with the Confederate forces at Lexington and then became known as the leader of an irregular guerrilla force, widely mispronounced as "Quantrell's Raiders," that operated in Missouri and Kansas, nominally on the side of the Confederacy. Quantrill and his men were formally declared outlaws by the Union in 1862, took part in the capture of Independence, Missouri, in August that year, and thereafter became part of the regular Confederate forces, where Quantrill had the rank of captain. In August 1863, Quantrill led a large group of men on a raid on the town of Lawrence, Kansas, during which many civilians were butchered and much of the town burned. This was a revenge raid for what the supporters of the Confederacy believed to be the effective murder of female supporters of their cause, who had been arrested by the Union and imprisoned in what was probably an unsafe building. In retaliation for the raid on Lawrence, Union forces ransacked and burned the properties of everyone living beyond the towns in Jackson, Bates, Cass, and Vernon counties. This "burnt district," one of the numberless vengeance grievances of the Civil War, was to become the home area of the James gang. Quantrill also appears to have been responsible for the murder of a number of federal noncombatants. In May 1865, the guerrilla leader was fatally wounded in an encounter with federal forces in Kentucky.

In the version of Quantrill's ballad reprinted here (from Lingenfelter, with the common misspelling/mispronunciation of his name) he is described as a hero in relation to his attack on Lawrence, an act that could become heroic only through the processes of partisan folklore:

QUANTRELL
Come all you bold robbers and open your
    ears;
Of Quantrell the lion heart you quickly
    shall hear.
With his band of bold raiders in double
    quick time,
He came to lay Lawrence low, over the line.

Chorus:
All routing and shouting and giving the
    yell,
Like so many demons raised up from hell,
The boys were so drunken with powder
    and wine,
And come to burn Lawrence just over the
    line.

They came to burn Lawrence; they came
    not to stay.
They rode in one morning at breaking of
    day
With guns all a-waving and horses all
    foam,
And Quantrell a-riding his famous big
    roan.

They came to burn Lawrence; they came
    not to stay.
Jim Lane he was up at the break of the day;
He saw them a-coming and got in a fright,
Then crawled in a corn crib to get out of
    sight.

Oh, Quantrell's a fighter, a brave-hearted
  boy:
A brave man or woman he'd never annoy.
He'd take from the wealthy and give to the
  poor,
For brave men there's never a bolt to his
  door.

Like Billy the Kid and some other historical
characters whose careers were extremely violent, Quantrill was an unlikely folk hero. Nevertheless, the interaction of history and folklore
has produced "Quantrell," who, like a number
of figures, was a hero to some but a villain to
others.

Related entries: Bass, Sam; Bonney, William; Fisk,
  Jim; Floyd, Charles Arthur; James, Jesse;
  Outlaws; Parker, Robert Leroy; Slater, Morris
References and further reading
Finger, C., Frontier Ballads, Garden City, NY:
  Doubleday, Page and Company, 1927.
Kooistra, P., Criminals as Heroes: Structure, Power, and
  Identity, Bowling Green, OH: Bowling Green
  University Press, 1989.
Lingenfelter, R. et al. (eds.), Songs of the American West,
  Berkeley: University of California Press, 1968,
  pp. 314–315 (quoting Finger).
Lomax, J. and A. (colls. and comps.), American Ballads
  and Folk Songs, New York: Macmillan, 1934, p.
  133.

Queen Jane
See Jane, Queen

Queen Mab
See Mab, Queen

Quevedo
Quevedo is a popular trickster hero of Mexican
and much Latin American culture. Like some
other trickster figures, such as Germany's Till
Eulenspiegel, Quevedo is a great traveler, as in
this Mexican story given by Paredes. Once, in
France, the king hears many complaints about
Quevedo's obscenity and impolite tricks. The
king banishes Quevedo from the country, on
pain of hanging. Quevedo begs to be given another chance; the king agrees, as long as
Quevedo plays a trick on him that involves
Quevedo making an apology even grosser than
the trick itself. He gives Quevedo three days to
carry out this trick. Quevedo agrees but is unable to think of a trick that will comply with
the king's directions. On the third day, faced
with execution or expulsion, Quevedo goes
gloomily to the king's court to face his fate. He
hides behind some curtains, and as the king
comes along the corridor with all the nobles
and notables of the city, he passes right by
Quevedo's hiding place. Suddenly, Quevedo has
a brilliant idea. Just as the king passes by the
curtains, Quevedo reaches out and grabs the
king by his private parts. Shocked and outraged, the king demands to know what
Quevedo is doing. "I beg your pardon, your
majesty," he says, "I thought it was the queen."

This mildly bawdy story is characteristic of
Quevedo lore, much of which is concerned
with sexuality and anality. According to folklorist Jean MacLaughlin, quoted by Dorson, the
stories she collected in Peru are of a "characteristically obscene nature." MacLaughlin also
notes that many of the stories told about
Quevedo in Peru are those associated with another trickster of Hispanic culture, Pedro de
Urdemalas.

Quevedo is thought to be based on the historical figure of the Spanish poet Don Francisco
de Quevedo y Villegas (1580–1645).

Related entries: Eulenspiegel, Till; Hodja, The; Jack o'
  Kent; Kabajan; Ostropolier, Hershel; Tricksters;
  Urdemalas, Pedro de
References and further reading
Dorson, R. (ed.), Folktales Told around the World,
  Chicago: University of Chicago Press, 1975,
  pp. 541–545.
Paredes, A., Folktales of Mexico, Chicago: University of
  Chicago Press, 1970, pp. 33–34.
Toor, F., Mexican Folkways, New York: Crown
  Publishers, 1947.

R

Rabbi Adam

See Adam, Rabbi

Rabbit

Trickster figure among southeastern Native American groups. A similar character is known variously as "Hare" and "Cottontail" in other Native American traditions. Sometimes Rabbit is also a culture hero, the bringer of fire or stealer of the sun. Rabbit is also featured as a character in Native American adaptations of European tales.

A figure called Rabbit is also found in African tradition, mainly Nigerian and Dahomean, in which guise he came to America with African slaves. The Rabbit tales told by this group formed the basis for the Joel Chandler Harris (1848–1908) Brer Rabbit stories, told by Uncle Remus, the first collection of which was published in 1880.

Related entries: Abunuwas; Anansi; Coyote; Gizo; Hare; Hlakanyana; Spider; Tortoise; Tricksters
References and further reading
Adagala, K. and Kabira, W. (eds.), *Kenyan Oral Narratives: A Selection*, Nairobi: Heinemann, 1985, pp. 59–61.
Dorson, R. (ed.), *African Folklore*, Bloomington: Indiana University Press, 1972, 1979, pp. 36, 38, 76–77, 95–97, 167, 172, 485–494.
Robe, S. (ed.), *Hispanic Folktales from New Mexico: Narratives from the R. D. Jameson Collection*, Mythology and Folktale Studies 30, Berkeley and Los Angeles: University of California Press, 1976, pp. 41, 53.

Railroad Bill

See Slater, Morris

Rákóczi

A famed resister of Austrian domination in Hungary. The historical Prince Rákóczi, Ferenc II (1676–1735), organized a largely successful rebellion against the occupying Austrian forces in 1703. However, the insurrection was betrayed and suppressed in 1711, and Rákóczi went into exile, ending his life in Turkey. These events have generated an extensive and significant body of Hungarian folklore about Rákóczi, his battles, capture, and escape. As with many such heroes of struggle, there is a refusal to believe that he is dead. According to tradition, when foals are born with teeth and the crucifix turns over by itself, Rákóczi will return and lead his people from oppression once again. In one tale of Rákóczi, the prince takes some time off for hunting during his siege of the fortress of Szatmár. He goes to a farmhouse for the night, but Austrian soldiers see him, surround the house, attack it, and set it alight. The prince and his two huntsmen are outnumbered, as the bodyguard had gone in search of food. Rákóczi and the huntsmen make a gallant stand but are about to be overwhelmed or burned to death when the bodyguard rides back. Angrily they attack the Austrian attackers, slaying them to a man. The prince is saved and rewards his valiant soldiers. Rákóczi is considered a national hero in Hungary.

Related entries: Heroes of Struggle; Military Heroes; National Heroes; Warriors
References and further reading
Dégh, L., *Folktales of Hungary*, Chicago: University of Chicago Press, 1965, pp. 218–220, 330.
Dégh, L. (trans. Schossberger, E.), *Folktales and Society: Story-Telling in a Hungarian Peasant Community*, Bloomington: Indiana University Press, 1969 (1962).

Ramalingadu, Tenali

Also known as Tenali Ramakrishna and, in Tamil lore, as the court jester Tenali Rama, this legendary trickster hero is famous in the traditions of India's Andhra province. Like other tricksters, this one's tales often concern the deflation of pomposity, power, and wealth.

In one story, Tenali Ramalingadu hears that the king will give the Brahmans a solid gold mango each to atone for his inability to provide these fruits to his mother, who had requested them as she lay dying. On the day appointed for the giving of the gold mangoes, the trickster sets himself up outside the palace gates with a brazier in which he heats iron rods to red. As the Brahmans arrive, he tells them that they will receive as many gold mangoes as the number of burns each will consent to suffer. Eagerly the Brahmans agree to be burned, some as many as ten times. When they ask for that number of gold mangoes, though, they are disappointed and complain to the king. He orders Tenali Ramalingadu brought before him to explain his actions. Ramalingadu says that just as the king's mother had died craving mangoes, so his mother had died of rheumatism, the treatment for which is cauterization of the joints. Since Ramalingadu was unable to supply this treatment, he decided that, just as the Brahmans were willing to receive the gold mangoes, so they should be willing to receive cauterization.

> **Related entries:** Abunuwas; Hodja, The; Kabajan; Tricksters
> **References and further reading**
> Beck, E. F. et al. (eds.), *Folktales of India*, Chicago: University of Chicago Press, 1987, pp. 236–238.
> Gray, J., *Indian Tales and Legends*, Oxford: Oxford University Press, 1961.

Ranzo, Reuben

Featured in a number of sea chanteys, Reuben is in some ways a nautical version of a "numskull." "Ranzo was no sailor," goes the most coherent of the songs about him, and he usually has to be flogged to his duty. The captain takes pity on him and teaches him how to be a sailor so successfully that Reuben eventually becomes captain or chief mate of a whaling ship. There are a number of crude variations on this basic theme, most of which depict the not very heroic hero as an inept scapegrace. However, Reuben's antics did provide sailors with a cover from which to criticize their own officers.

> **Related entries:** Heroes of Struggle; Jack Tar, Jolly; Nautical Heroes; Occupational Heroes; Santa Anna, General Antonio López de; Stormalong
> **References and further reading**
> Doerflinger, W. (coll. and ed.), *Songs of the Sailor and Lumberman*, New York: Macmillan, 1972 (1951), p. 23.
> Hugill, S., *Shanties from the Seven Seas*, London: Routledge and Kegan Paul, 1979 (1961), pp. 240–243.
> Smith, L. (comp.), *The Music of the Waters: A Collection of the Sailors' Chanties, or Work Songs of the Sea, of all Maritime Nations*, London: K. Paul, Trench and Co., 1888, pp. 19, 32–33.
> Whall, W. (coll. and ed.), *Sea Songs and Shanties*, London: Brown, Son, and Ferguson, 1910, pp. 63–64.

Rapunzel

Long-haired heroine of a well-known folktale. Versions of this story are told throughout Europe, the Americas, and the West Indies, though the best-known version is probably the much-embellished fairy tale popularized by the Grimm brothers in 1812. In their telling, a man and wife wish for a child but have long been unable to have one. They live in a house overlooking a beautiful garden that belongs to a fearsome witch. One day, the woman looks into the fine garden and wishes for some radishes. Her obliging husband overcomes his fear of the witch, climbs over the high wall of the witch's garden, and helps himself to some radishes. He takes these home to his wife, who enjoys them so much that she desires more and cannot rest until she has them. Once again screwing up all his courage, her husband climbs into the witch's garden. But this time the witch is waiting for him. She is angry and threatens to cast an evil spell on the man. Hastily he explains his wife's desire for the radishes. The witch has an apparent change of heart and says that she can have all the radishes she wants on condition that the man and his wife allow the witch to have their child. In return, the witch promises she will care for the child. The man, in fear and confusion, agrees, probably thinking that as they have no child there is no need for concern.

However, a child is born to the man and his wife. They named her Rapunzel and "she grew to be the most beautiful child under the sun." On her twelfth birthday, the witch claims her according to the agreement with her father and locks her in a tower deep in the forest. The tower has no door and no stairs, only a small window at the top. When the witch wants to enter the tower she stands down below and calls out, "Rapunzel, Rapunzel, let down your hair." Rapunzel then throws her long, golden tresses through the small window. Reaching down to the ground, Rapunzel's hair forms a silken ladder the witch can use to climb in and out of the tower.

After a few years, a king's son happens to go near the tower and hears Rapunzel's lovely voice in song. He finds the tower but cannot enter and so rides home again. But every day he comes back and hides in the forest, listening to the entrancing melodies of Rapunzel's singing. One day he sees the witch approach the tower and call out to Rapunzel to throw her hair down; in this way he learns the secret of entry to the tower. The next day, he goes to the foot of the tower and calls out, "Rapunzel, Rapunzel, let down your hair." She does, and he climbs up. At first Rapunzel is frightened because apart from her father she has never seen a man before. The prince then seduces Rapunzel—though the Grimm tale says simply that he "talked in a loving way to her"—and the lovers plot Rapunzel's escape. She tells the prince that each evening when he comes to her, he should bring a skein of silk, which she will then weave into a ladder that will allow her to escape with the prince. This plan proceeds happily until Rapunzel lets slip to the witch that the prince makes a visit on the day the witch is elsewhere. In a fury, the witch hits Rapunzel, cuts off her hair, and takes the girl to a desert, leaving her "to die in great misery and grief."

Back at the tower the witch ties the tresses to the window, and when the prince returns in

The witch climbing up Rapunzel's hair. (Mary Evans Picture Library)

search of his love, the witch throws the hair down as if all is well. When the prince reaches the top, he finds the witch waiting for him, and she tells him that his beloved is lost. In grief and fear he throws himself out the window, falling into thorns that break his fall but blind him. He then wanders the wild wood in mourning, living off berries and roots for many years, until one day he arrives at the desert where the witch had left Rapunzel to die. Hearing a familiar voice, he makes his way toward it. By some miracle, Rapunzel has survived and given birth to twins, a boy and a girl. Rapunzel recognizes her prince and embraces him, weeping for joy. Her tears fall upon his eyes, freeing him of blindness. The prince then takes Rapunzel (and, presumably, the twins) back to his kingdom "where he was received with great demonstrations of joy."

In the usual manner of the fairy tale, events

in this story occur with little or no motivation, preparation, or even logic. Rapunzel is unexplainedly born to a previously barren couple for no good reason other than to fulfill the witch's condition that she should have the couple's child. The witch then locks Rapunzel away for no apparent purpose, in an isolated tower to which entry and exit is unnecessarily difficult. Rapunzel and the prince's escape plan is annoyingly long-winded. Why can't he simply bring back a rope on his next visit? Rapunzel, who shows no other signs of idiocy, blurts out the secret of her lover to the witch and then somehow survives in the desert, giving birth to twins and keeping them alive until the prince miraculously stumbles across his new family some years later. Her tears magically cure the prince's blindness, and he is free to take her back to his kingdom in the traditional fairy tale manner, though in the Grimms' version we are not told whether he also takes his two children or leaves them to perish in the desert.

Of course, in collusion with the genre of the fairy tale we suspend our disbelief for the reward of having the tension resolved in the happy ending, which, after all, is what these narratives are all about. The means by which the hero and heroine reach the end of the story are less important than the fact that they reach it and that things conclude with smiles all around. Even the defeat of the villain has not anywhere near the same importance as reaching the happy ending. In the fairy tale of Rapunzel, the pointlessly malevolent witch suffers no punishment for her actions.

We are, it seems, meant to interpret these stories and the often odd events that constitute them as metaphors. In the story of Rapunzel, the common motifs of the promised (usually female) child, the imprisonment to preserve the heroine's virginity, the rescue by the handsome prince (well, almost), the mutilation of the hero, his wandering in the wilderness, the abandonment in the desert, the healing power of the heroine's tears, and the inevitable happy closure are all classic elements of fairy tale fantasy—even though there is not a fairy in, or out, of sight.

Our need for such narratives has ensured their perpetual popularity. In the form we call the "fairy" tale, such stories date from the seventeenth century, and the earthier folktales on which many of the fairy tale encounters of princes, beautiful singing maidens, and the like are based date from some considerable number of centuries earlier. Scholars will continue to offer new interpretations of the significance of such fairy tales ("Rapunzel" being an obvious favorite for psychoanalytic approaches), while we continue to read them, turn them into films, and, sometimes, tell them to our children.

Related entries: Fairy Tale Heroes

References and further reading

Bettelheim, B., The Uses of Enchantment: The Meaning and Importance of Fairy Tales, New York: Knopf, 1976, pp. 16–17, 58, 113, 131–132, 145, 148–150, 199.

Bottigheimer, R. (ed.), Fairy Tales and Society: Illusion, Allusion, and Paradigm, Philadelphia: University of Pennsylvania Press, 1986.

Hallett, M. and Karasek, B. (eds.), Folk and Fairy Tales, Ontario: Broadview Press, 1996, pp. 73–76.

Hunt, M. (trans. and ed.), Grimm's Household Tales (with the author's notes and an introduction by Andrew Lang), 2 vols., London: George Bell and Sons, 1884, pp. 50–54.

Lüthi, M. (trans. Chadeayne, L. and Gottwald, P.), Once upon a Time: On the Nature of Fairy Tales, Bloomington: Indiana University Press, 1976, pp. 109–120.

Minard, R., Womenfolk and Fairy Tales, Boston: Houghton Mifflin, 1975.

Opie, I. and P., The Classic Fairy Tales, London: Oxford University Press, 1974.

Rasalu

Famed legendary hero of the Punjab. Raja Rasalu's considerable legendry, like much Indian folklore, has been subject to long and intensive literary elaboration that coexists with a robust oral tradition. Rasalu, like many heroes, is born in magical circumstances. In fulfillment of the awesome prophecies of holy men, Rasalu is taken at birth to an underground palace, together with a colt born on the same day and destined to become his faithful magical steed, a sword, a spear, and a shield. According to the prophecies, Rasalu is to remain in the underground palace for twelve years, during which time his parents, the king and queen, are not allowed to look upon him, on pain of death. Rasalu grows tall and strong and acquires all the skills and knowledge fitting for a prince. He also acquires a parrot, destined to be a companion in his later adventures, to whom he talks. In his twelfth year, Rasalu grows restless and, against the advice of his caretakers, saddles his wondrous steed, dons his armor, and rides forth into the world toward the city of his father. However, upon his arrival, the king and queen are afraid to look on their son, knowing that the twelve years have not fully passed. Unaware of the twelve-year ban, Rasalu interprets his parents' reticence as rejection and storms out into the world. From this point Rasalu's life is one of questing, adventure, fighting, generosity, and occasional arrogance.

Rasalu is at first accompanied by the traditional companions, a carpenter and goldsmith's son, who vow to protect the prince. They are successful at this until a "dreadful unspeakable horror" comes upon them in the night. Rasalu slays the creature, and when the two companions see what kind of fearsome beasts they are likely to encounter in Rasalu's company, they fear for their lives and forsake him. Rasalu travels on with only his arms, his steed, and his parrot for company. With his sword and his bow and arrow he kills giants who are intimidating the city of Nila. Later he becomes a poor holy man in order to see the fabulously beautiful Queen Sundran. When she sees Rasalu, she is smitten with his youthful beauty and eventually throws herself on a sacred fire for love of him.

After other adventures, Rasalu ultimately comes to the city of King Sarkap, notorious for beheading people, including his brother, whose headless corpse gives Rasalu useful advice about taking his own dice, made of human bones, to play chaupar (an ancient game played with dice on a board in the shape of a cross) with Sarkap. On the way to play Sarkap, Rasalu encounters seventy fair maidens, daughters of King Sarkap. The hero indulges in some more or less playful flirting with these women, in the course of which his eye falls upon one of the youngest, who warns him against playing against Sarkap. The ever-confident Rasalu replies, in Steel's translation:

Fair maiden, I come from afar,
Sworn conqueror in love and war!
King Sarkap my coming will rue,
His head in four pieces I'll hew;
Then forth as a bridegroom I'll ride.
With you, little maid, as my bride!

As he comes close to Sarkap's city, the generous Rasalu rescues a cat's kittens from some potters' kilns, and the grateful mother cat gives him one of the kittens, saying it will be helpful if he meets with difficulties. Sarkap and Rasalu agree to play three games of chaupar. Sarkap wagers his kingdom on the first game, his worldly wealth on the second, and his head on the third. Rasalu bets his arms on the first game, his horse on the second, and his head on the third. With the help of his pet rat, Sarkap wins the first two games. Rasalu then remembers the kitten and the bone dice and insists that they play now with his dice rather than those of Sarkap. The king becomes afraid and summons all the women of his palace to parade in their finery, hoping that this sight will distract Rasalu from his game. However, this ploy is unsuccessful, and the kitten helps Rasalu by preventing the rat from upsetting the playing pieces, as the animal had done in the previous two games, to Sarkap's advantage. Now Rasalu wins back his arms and his horse and finally beats Sarkap at his own game. Just as the hero is triumphant, a servant rushes in to announce that a daughter has been born to Sarkap. Angry and humiliated at his loss, Sarkap orders the child killed, saying she has brought him bad luck. But Rasalu, according to Steel, rises "up in his shining armour, tender-hearted and strong, saying 'Not so, O king! She has done no evil. Give me this child to wife; and if you will vow, by all you hold sacred, never again to play chaupar for another's head, I will spare yours now!'" Sarkap agrees and gives the baby to Rasalu on a golden dish, together with a fresh mango branch. Rasalu goes to the Murti Hills, having Sarkap's many prisoners released on the way, places the baby in an underground palace, and plants the mango branch at the door, promising that the tree will blossom in twelve years and that he will then return to marry the princess, whose name is Kokilan. When twelve years have passed, Rasalu fulfills his promise.

Rasalu's cycle, given here only in summary, bears all the elements of the traditional hero. Although his tales have been worked and re-worked to form a literary narrative cycle, they can also be told as individual stories, many of which include motifs found in other traditions. In his encounter with the seventy fair maidens, for instance, Rasalu is aided by a cricket he has saved from a burning forest. One of the challenges set by the maidens, in response to Rasalu's rash boast that he will perform any task, requires him to separate millet from a huge pile of sand, an impossible task found in many traditions. The cricket brings its fellows to help, and they succeed in separating the millet from the sand in just one night. Like other heroes, Rasalu receives further assistance from many other helpers along the way, facilitating his successful accomplishments of slaying monsters and giants and, finally, besting the notorious Sarkap, himself a considerable figure of Punjab folklore.

Speculation about the origins of Rasalu place him as a non-Aryan resister of invasion, probably between 300 and 900 A.D. In tradition, he is often identified with the Scythian hero Sali-vahana of the late first century A.D. There are also considerable parallels between Rasalu's lore and that of the southern Aryan conqueror Vikramaditya, of the last half of the first century B.C. Rasalu combines a number of hero types, including the warrior, the giant-killer, the dragon-slayer, and the hero of struggle.

Related entries: Dragon-Slayers; Giant-Killers; Heroes of Struggle; Warriors

References and further reading

Beck, B. et al. (eds.), *Folktales of India*, Chicago: University of Chicago Press, 1987.

Deva, I., *Folk Culture and Peasant Society in India*, Jaipur: Rawat Publications, 1989.

Mohanti, P. (ed.), *Indian Village Tales*, London: Davis-Poynter, 1975.

Steel, F. (coll.), *Tales of the Punjab Told by the People*, London: The Bodley Head, 1973 (1894), pp. 159–183, 224–233.

Rashin' Coatie

Heroine of a Scottish dialect (Morayshire) version of Cinderella collected from Miss Margaret Craig of Darliston, Elgin, by English folklorist Andrew Lang and published in *Revue Celtique 3*, 1876–1878. Lang also collected and published other versions of Cinderella, writing a number of detailed studies of the story as well as essays on the work of Charles Perrault.

Related entries: Amala; Assipattle; Cap o' Rushes; Catskin; Cinderella; Cinder-Mary; Fairy Tale Heroes; Woodencloak, Katie; Ye Xian

References and further reading

Bettelheim, B., *The Uses of Enchantment: The Meaning and Importance of Fairy Tales*, New York: Knopf, 1976, pp. 251, 257–258, 267.

Jacobs, J. (ed.), *English Fairy Tales*, London: The Bodley Head, 1968, pp. 297ff; reprint of *English Fairy Tales* (1890) and *More English Fairy Tales*, 1894.

Lang, A., *Perrault's Popular Tales*, Oxford: Clarendon Press, 1888.

Lang, A., "Cinderella and the Diffusion of Tales," *Folk-Lore 4*, 1893.

Rebecca

Mythic female and symbolic leader of Welsh Rebecca rioters from the 1830s to the early twentieth century. "Rebecca" would appear at the head of a group of rioters dressed as a woman (many of the male Rebecca rioters dressed in women's clothes), often riding a white horse. The Rebecca riots were generally in support of common rights and other perquisites that the rural laborers of Wales considered their traditional due, such as the right to fish for salmon in streams and rivers. Other popular targets of Rebecca were the tollgates that entrepreneurial landholders set up across public roads, turning previously free transportation and access routes into private businesses. Rebecca rioters were also protesting against the Poor Laws, rents, taxes, and the general administration of justice.

The figure of Rebecca is a personification of the spirit of struggle that is found in some aspects of folk tradition, embodying the aspirations and discontents of local, regional, and sometimes national social groups.

Related entries: Culture Heroes; Heroes of Struggle; Local Heroes; Ludd, Ned; National Heroes;

Occupational Heroes; Outlaws; Shine; Taylor, William

References and further reading
Jones, D., *Rebecca's Children: A Study of Rural Society, Crime, and Protest*, Oxford: Clarendon Press, 1989.
Seal, G., "Tradition and Protest in Nineteenth-Century England and Wales," *Folklore* 100, no. 2 (1988):146–169.

Red Cap, Little
See Little Red Riding Hood

Red Riding Hood, Little
See Little Red Riding Hood

Religious Heroes
This large category includes heroes of all kinds: founders of faiths, martyrs, saints, the pious, the brave, the compassionate, and the wise. The religious traditions of most cultures and peoples, whether written or oral, are full of heroic stories, many of which appear as discrete narratives in other cultures, usually disassociated from their religious significance. The Christian Bible, notably the Old Testament, the Koran, the Torah, and many other such holy books are vast repositories of folk heroism. As is well known, many of these works share common characters and incidents, even though these may be interpreted in different ways according to the various belief systems in which they appear. In addition to such authorized works, there usually exist considerable bodies of apocryphal material that contain even more lore.

Religious belief is a fertile ground for the creation of folk heroes. Those who are celebrated may be founders of their religions (Nanak Chand, founder of Sikhism; Jesus of Nazareth, founder of Christianity), helpers of the founder (Mary, the Apostles), or those who are martyred to its creed—a large group in all religious systems—or any combination of these. Frequently such individuals, real and mythic, receive the official approbation of their belief system, sainthood in one form or another. Around many such figures form folk traditions, beliefs, and customs that in the case of the major religions have become the foundations of complex social and cultural systems. In the generally more humble realms of the folkloric, religious heroes are celebrated in down-to-earth ways, with the stories of their deeds often being humorous, ridiculous, or even irreverent. Tales told of many Jewish holy men, for example, often emphasize their shortcomings as well as their virtues.

The spread of some religious belief systems, especially Christianity, around the world has led many religious figures to take on folkloric roles in different cultures. St. George is one such example, while Saint James, known as Santiago, is the patron saint of Spain and also identified by some South American Indian groups who experienced Spanish colonization as the thunder god. In the New World, the legendary doings of saints are told among immigrant groups and their descendants, in part as a means of continuing their links with the homeland where the stories are located. Other groups, such as Mexicans of Spanish descent, locate the traditions of their saints and holy people in the New World itself. Such legends tend to concentrate on the spiritual or supernatural powers of the saint or holy man. One example given by Dorson is the south Texas folk healer Pedro Jaramillo of Los Olmos, celebrated as a miraculous healer among Mexican families from the 1880s. Stories of Jaramillo emphasize his magical ability to effect cures, often involving prescribed actions being performed nine times.

Christian religious figures often have a role in folk drama, especially in Latin cultures. Jesus, Mary, and Joseph, for example, are found in the Nativity and also in other forms of traditional theater. God is also featured in some traditions, often those of a humorous nature.

Religious heroes are frequently found in folklore as helpers, sometimes as healers, and generally combine their status as official figures of veneration with the unofficial tales and beliefs that are popularly held or told about them. Like most folk heroes, they straddle the boundaries between different, often oppositional, cultural spaces, in these cases between the spiritual and the mundane.

Related entries: Adam, Rabbi; Baal-Shem-Tov; Brigid (Brigit), Saint; Chokanamma; de Veusters, Father Joseph; Elijah the Prophet; George, Saint; Guy of Warwick; Helpers; Jesus; Joseph of Arimathea, Saint; Kentigern, Saint; Khidre, El; Kukai; Loew, Rabbi Judah; Magicians; Mary; Nanak; Nicholas, Saint; Patrick, Saint; Seven Sleepers, The; Valentine, Saint

References and further reading

Ausubel, N. (ed.), *A Treasury of Jewish Folklore*, London: Vallentine, Mitchell, 1972 (1948), pp. 104–223.

Blum, R. and E., *The Dangerous Hour: The Lore of Crisis and Mystery in Rural Greece*, London: Chatto and Windus, 1970, pp. 88–94.

Dorson, R., *Buying the Wind: Regional Folklore in the United States*, Chicago: University of Chicago Press, 1964, pp. 500–508.

El-Shamy, H. (coll., trans., ed.), *Folktales of Egypt*, Chicago: University of Chicago Press, 1980, pp. 149–169.

Espinosa, A. (ed. Espinosa, M.), *The Folklore of Spain in the American Southwest: Traditional Spanish Folk Literature in Northern New Mexico and Southern Colorado*, Norman: University of Oklahoma Press, 1985, pp. 201–213.

Frazer, Sir J., *Folk-Lore in the Old Testament*, 3 vols., London: Macmillan, 1918.

Gaer, J., *The Lore of the Old Testament*, Boston: Little, Brown, 1951.

Gaer, J., *The Lore of the New Testament*, Boston: Little, Brown, 1952.

Heath-Stubbs, J., "The Hero as a Saint: St. George," in Simpson, J. (trans.), *Legends of Icelandic Magicians* (with an introduction by B. Benedikz), London: Brewer/Rowman and Littlefield, The Folklore Society, 1975, pp. 1–15.

Hunt, M. (trans. and ed.), *Grimm's Household Tales* (with the author's notes and an introduction by Andrew Lang), 2 vols., London: George Bell and Sons, 1884, pp. 312–324, 440–452.

Ivanits, L., *Russian Folk Belief*, Armonk and London: M. E. Sharpe Inc., 1989, pp. 136–153.

Lüthi, M. (trans. Chadeayne, L. and Gottwald, P.), *Once upon a Time: On the Nature of Fairy Tales*, Bloomington: Indiana University Press, 1976, pp. 35–46.

Paredes, A., *Folktales of Mexico*, Chicago: University of Chicago Press, 1970, pp. 176–177.

Porter, R., "Heroes in the Old Testament: The Hero as Seen in the Book of Judges," in Simpson, J. (trans.), *Legends of Icelandic Magicians* (with an introduction by B. Benedikz), London: Brewer/Rowman and Littlefield, The Folklore Society, 1975, pp. 90–111.

Sabar, Y. (trans. and ed.), *The Folk Literature of the Kurdistani Jews: An Anthology*, New Haven/London: Yale University Press, 1982, pp. 104–134.

Reynard the Fox

French animal figure of great cunning and guile, also known as "Reynardine" in some traditions. He is a rebellious coward, a liar, and a seducer, the role he takes in a well-known British ballad in which the protagonist is described as "that sly, bold Reynardine." All in all, he is not a very promising character for a hero, yet Reynard, in one guise or another, has survived as a popular figure of European folklore, helped greatly by his frequent appearances in print. Medieval literary satires featuring "Renard" were popular in France, Germany, and elsewhere in Europe, while Caxton translated the tales into English (from Flemish) in 1481. The image of the fox as a wily survivor is much older than the medieval period and can be traced to Aesop's fables, which include a number of stories in which foxes display a ruthless but effective will to live, sometimes at the expense of others.

A popular trickster story involving Reynard is one in which a fool is convinced by the fox that a horse can be caught if the dupe ties himself to the animal's tail. Versions of this story are told widely, in such countries as Germany, Norway, the Netherlands, China, as well as in African-American tradition. The wide spread of such folktales reflects the natural attributes of foxes, especially their cunning and bravery.

Foxes also appear frequently as helpers of human heroes in European and Central Asian folktales, displaying their characteristics to good effect. They feature recurrently in ballad traditions, often as deceivers and, especially in African and Africa-American traditions, as shape-shifters and tricksters. In eastern traditions, foxes are often portrayed as having the power to transform themselves from animals into humans, usually females, engaging in sexual activity with human males and even becoming their wives for shorter or longer periods.

Related entries: Bluebeard; Fox Maiden, The; Helpers; Kuzonoha; Puss in Boots; Skorobogaty, Kuzma; Yasuna, Abe No

References and further reading

Baker, M., *Tales of All the World*, London: Oxford University Press, 1937, pp. 83–90.

Delarue, P. (ed.), Fife, A. (trans.), *The Borzoi Book of French Folk Tales*, New York: Knopf, 1956.

Guerber, H., *Myths and Legends of the Middle Ages: Their Origin and Influence on Literature and Art*, London: Harrap, 1909, pp. 35–58.

Jacobs, J. (ed.), *English Fairy Tales*, London: The Bodley Head, 1968, pp. 297ff; reprint of *English Fairy Tales* (1890) and *More English Fairy Tales* (1894).

Osers, E. (trans.), *Chinese Folktales*, London: Bell and Sons, 1971, pp. 21, 23, 131–146. First published in German as Wilhelm, R. (trans.), *Chinesische Märchen*, 1958.

Picard, B. (ed.), *French Legends, Tales, and Fairy Stories*, Oxford: Oxford University Press, 1955.

Rugoff, M. (ed.), *A Harvest of World Folk Tales*, New York: Viking Press, 1949, pp. 304–314.

Ringkitan

Legendary heroine of a Sulawesi (Celebes, now Indonesia) story who is forced by her parents to marry a cuscus (a monkey-like marsupial). Her eight sisters and other locals tease her about this all the time, especially about the fact that no one knows what the cuscus does for a living. One day Ringkitan secretly follows the cuscus to work and sees him transform into a handsome young man. Keeping this to herself, she works out a way of tricking her husband into revealing his true human form, which he does, telling her his name is Kusoi.

Their marriage is even happier after this, but Ringkitan's eight sisters grow jealous of her good fortune in marrying such an eligible catch, and they plot a way to get rid of her by hanging her from a tree with her own hair. Kusoi, in the shape of a sailor, rescues her and takes her back to the village, where, eventually, he reveals her to the eight wicked sisters in beautiful, rich clothes. Kusoi points out that he knows who the guilty ones are, but that their guilt alone is sufficient punishment for them. That night each sister comes to Ringkitan to ask forgiveness. They never bother her again, and Ringkitan lives a life of wealth and happiness with her love, Kusoi. In the variant name of Rangkatin, this hero is also known in Sabah tradition.

Related entries: Bai Suzhen; Fox Maiden, The; Kuzonoha; Llyn Y Fan Fach, The Lady of; Magicians; Melusine; Mudjikiwis; Shape-Shifters; Swan Maiden; Tabadiku; Urashima; White Lady; Xiaoqing; Yasuna, Abe No; Yer

References and further reading

Aman, S., *Folk Tales from Indonesia*, Jakarta: Djambatan, 1976.

Knappert, J., *Myths and Legends of Indonesia*, Singapore: Heinnemann, 1977.

Marsh, I. (comp. and ed.), *Tales and Traditions from Sabah*, rev. ed., The Sabah Society, 1988, 1989, pp. 24–26.

Robin Hood

See Hood, Robin

Roderick (Roderigo)

See National Heroes; Sleepers

Rose-Red

Heroine of a Chinese Tang dynasty tale in which she is a slave-girl seeking to escape. She charms a young man into falling in love with her, and he then enlists the help of his servant, the aging but still effective sword-hero Molo, in effecting her escape and her marriage to the lovestruck young man.

Related entries: Molo

References and further reading

Osers, E. (trans.), *Chinese Folktales*, London: Bell and Sons, 1971, pp. 199–203. First published in German as Wilhelm, R. (trans.), *Chinesische Märchen*, 1958.

Werner, E., *Myths and Legends of China*, New York: Arno Press, 1976 (1922).

Roy, Rob

See MacGregor, Robert

S

Saburo, Koga

Japanese hero who rescues a princess from the otherworld. Saburo and his two older brothers, together with Princess Tokioyo, go hunting one day. Near a lake, the princess suddenly disappears, and she is eventually discovered at the bottom of a cavern, standing near a palace. The brothers make a rope and basket from vine leaves, lower it down into the cavern, and retrieve the princess. But when she is safely on solid ground again, she remembers that she has left the book of sutras her parents gave her down in the cavern. Saburo goes back down into the cavern, but in the palace there is a *tengu*, or evil spirit, and Saburo does not return. Distraught, the princess throws herself into Lake Suwa.

In the meantime, Saburo continues to live underground, being treated as a samurai by those who live there, marrying and having a son. One day, after nine years, his underworld wife finds Saburo in tears and asks him why he cries. He tells her what happened many years before. She sympathizes and gives him leave to search for the princess he still loves. She asks him to take nine rice bowls with him on his quest. Appearing to the villagers of the overworld as a snake, Saburo nevertheless finds the princess in Lake Suwa and joins her there.

Years pass, and Saburo's son grows. One day he finds his mother crying. When he inquires why she weeps, she tells him the story of his father. The boy makes nine rice bowls for his mother and sends her to find Saburo. After much searching, she eventually comes to Lake Suwa. Legend has it that a slab of ice, known as "God crossing the Lake," appears on the lake's surface and marks Saburo's journey as he travels incessantly between the homes of the princess and his wife. The motif of rescue from a deep well or cave is widespread in the folk traditions of the world, and this story is a good example of the localization of an international element of hero tales.

> **Related entries:** Avdotya; Ivan the Mare's Son; Local Heroes; Mu Lian; Mu-Monto; Nakali; Potyk, Mikhail; Sadko; Tam Lin; Thomas the Rhymer
>
> **References and further reading**
> Dorson, R., *Folk Legends of Japan*, Rutland, VT: Charles E. Tuttle, 1962, pp. 158–160.
> McAlpine, H. and W., *Japanese Tales and Legends*, Oxford: Oxford University Press, 1958.
> Ozaki, Y., *The Japanese Fairy Book*, Tokyo: Fuzanbo Pub. Co., 1909; reprint New York: Dover Publications, 1967.

Sadko

A legendary poor musician of Novgorod whose playing pleases the sea czar, who, in return, helps him outwit the wealthy merchants of the city and become rich himself. But Sadko gets more arrogant as he grows richer and forgets to thank the sea czar or to offer him tribute. On a voyage back from a trading trip, his ship stuffed with riches, Sadko is compelled to return to the sea czar and to play for him forever. His playing is so exciting that the sea czar dances furiously, causing the waves to rise and the sea to be riven with great storms. Many sailors drown, and people pray to St. Nikolai for help. In the guise of an old man, St. Nikolai helps Sadko escape, and in gratitude, Sadko, never sailing the seas again, builds the cathedral in Novgorod, in honor of Nikolai.

> **Related entries:** Arabian Nights, The; Nicholas, Saint; Supparaka; Thomas the Rhymer
>
> **References and further reading**
> Bailey, J. and Ivanova, T. (trans.), *An Anthology of Russian Folk Epics*, Armonk and London: M. E. Sharpe, 1998, pp. 296–306.

Cavendish, R. (ed.), *Legends of the World*, London:
Orbis, 1982, pp. 295–296.

Elstob, E. and Barber, R. (trans.), *Russian Folktales*,
London: Bell and Sons, 1971. First published as
Von Lowis of Menar, A. (trans.) and Olesch, R.
(ed.), *Russische Volksmärchen*, 1959.

Sahin

The legendary Sahin is the youngest of forty
brothers in a number of Palestinian Arabic tales
in which the brothers are continually outwitted
by forty women, led by a vizier's daughter
(who is also Sahin's cousin in the Palestinian
version). The vizier's daughter discovers Sahin
preparing food for his thirty-nine brothers,
who are out hunting. She offers herself as a
wife to Sahin, and her thirty-nine companions
to his brothers, an offer that the young Sahin
willingly accepts. They sit together as Sahin
prepares his brothers' dinner, and then the girl
asks him to climb a ladder to retrieve some nuts
from a high shelf. When he reaches the shelf,
the girl pulls the ladder away, steals the food,
and returns to her companions. Sahin, looking
a fool, is still up on the shelf when his hungry
brothers return from the hunt; he looks even
more a fool when he discovers that the food is
gone. He tells his brothers that the cats have
eaten it, and he then prepares a makeshift meal
from the results of their day's hunting.

The next morning, the brothers ride out
hunting again, warning Sahin not to let the cats
eat their dinner again. That evening, as Sahin prepares the food, the vizier's daughter comes
again. Sahin admonishes her for tricking him,
but only lightly, as he is in love with her. This
time she asks to use the bathroom and wonders
if Sahin will help her, since she does not know
how to use it. The gullible Sahin ends up head
down in the toilet, and the vizier's daughter
once again gets away with the dinner. When the
brothers return, they miss Sahin and their dinner
and make a meal for themselves. As they prepare
for sleep one of the brothers goes into the bathroom and discovers Sahin in his embarrassing
position. The brothers lift him out and ask how
he managed to get into such a mess. He tells
them that he slipped on the bathroom floor and
that the cats must have eaten the dinner again.

The following morning, the brothers again
mock Sahin about the dinner and the cats, and
again he assures them that all will be well on
their return that evening. Off ride the brothers,
and Sahin again goes about his household
chores until the evening, when the vizier's
daughter, after gathering her thirty-nine female
cronies, visits him yet again. Once more Sahin
complains of his treatment at her hands, but
she speaks lovingly and soothes him, eventually
convincing him to bring something to drink.
She gets him so drunk that he passes out, and
she then makes a concoction of sugar that removes all his body hair, dresses him in
women's clothes, and makes up his face to look
like that of a woman. Then she steals the dinner
yet again, leaving the insensible Sahin in his
bed. The brothers return, find Sahin missing,
and prepare their own meal. One of them says
he suspects that Sahin has a girlfriend, which is
why he keeps disappearing. Not until bedtime
do they find the body on the bed. At first they
think it is Sahin's girlfriend and cry out,
"Sahin's bride." But then they unwrap the
scarves and find that it is their brother. They
throw cold water on him and, when he awakes,
demand an explanation.

Sahin tells them about the forty women for
the forty brothers, and his eldest brother decides
that he will sort things out. The next day, he stays
with Sahin while the other brothers go hunting.
As usual, the vizier's daughter arrives and begins
talking sweetly to Sahin. Before she gets too far,
though, the elder brother rushes out of hiding
and threatens her with his sword, asking her if it
is true about the forty wives for the forty brothers. She assures him that it is and, as she had with
Sahin, sweet-talks him into her wiles. The eldest
brother pays her the bride-price and arranges for
the forty brothers and the forty wives-to-be to
meet the next evening at the public baths. The
vizier's daughter returns to her girlfriends with
the money and distributes it. Sahin tells his
brother that he is a bigger fool than Sahin himself, who lost only a few dinners not their
money. But Sahin's brother is certain that all will
be well, and the next evening all the brothers go
to the baths as planned. Sure enough, the forty
girls appear and go in one by one.

The brothers wait at the gates for them to come out so that each might claim his bride. They wait and wait, but the women do not come out. Finally, the brothers go into the baths and discover that the girls escaped through a back door. The brothers realize that they have been fooled even more than Sahin but cannot work out what to do. At this point, Sahin steps in and volunteers to do something. He disguises himself as a woman and visits the vizier's daughter and her friends in their home. They realize who he is but pretend to think that Sahin is their aunty. The women make "aunty" wash their clothes and then bathe each one of them. Then they expose Sahin as a man by compelling him to take a bath. They beat him with their towels, and he runs naked into the street and back to his astonished brothers.

Now thoroughly humiliated, the brothers decide that their only recourse is to ask the king for the hands of the girls in marriage, in the usual manner. The king grants the request to all the brothers except Sahin. Guessing that the brothers would place this request before the king, the vizier's daughter had asked the king to give her to Sahin only after a waiting period of one month. Sahin, who is plotting to kill the vizier's daughter as soon as he gets hold of her, agrees. In the meantime, the vizier's daughter has a life-size doll made out of halvah in her own image. She dresses the doll in her clothes and jewels, attaches a string to it, and sits it on her bed. When Sahin arrives with murderous intent, he does not notice that the figure on the bed is a doll. Thinking that it is the vizier's daughter, he vents his rage at the humiliations he has suffered at her hands. Under the bed, the vizier's daughter pulls the string to make it seem that the doll is agreeing with Sahin's ranting. Sahin assumes that the nodding head is a further insult, and so, as he finishes his rant, he chops off the doll's head. A slice of the halvah flies into his mouth, and it is so sweet that he cries out in amazement and regret, "If in death you're so sweet, what would it have been like if you were still alive?" Hearing these words, the vizier's daughter comes out from under the bed and embraces Sahin, saying, "I'm alive." The couple consummates

their marriage and lives together happily as man and wife.

This unusual and involved love story is characteristic of many Middle Eastern stories in its exaggeration of number and elaboration of detail. Although Sahin is the nominal hero of the tale, it is the cleverness of the vizier's daughter that provides most of the interest and also the narrative energy. It is not so much that Sahin eventually wins the object of his desire as it is that the vizier's daughter succeeds in catching him. This is a victory for the attractions of the flesh, it seems, as Sahin and his brothers do not appear to be very intelligent and are certainly no match for the wily vizier's daughter, a very clever heroine.

Related entries: Arabian Nights, The; Ataba; Bernèz; E-ttool, Zarief; Guy of Warwick; Horn, Hind; Moringer, Noble; Wise Men and Women

References and further reading
Abdelhady, T., *Palestinian Folk-Tales*, vol. 3, Beirut: Ibenrashed Publishing Company, n.d.
Muhawi, I. and Kanaana, S. (eds.), *Speak, Bird, Speak Again: Palestinian Arab Folktales*, Berkeley: University of California Press, 1989, pp. 130–144.

Saint Bride
See Brigid (Brigit), Saint

Saint George
See George, Saint

Saint Joseph of Arimathea
See Joseph of Arimathea, Saint

Saint Kentigern
See Kentigern, Saint (Mungo)

Saint Patrick
See Patrick, Saint

Sandman, The
Mythical character of a widespread European nursery story for children (as opposed to that of children) who sprinkles magical sand into the eyes of children to make them go to sleep. The flakes of "sleep" that are sometimes in the eyes

of children the next morning may be greeted with the words "The sandman came to see you last night" or something similar. The Sandman seems to have remained a largely European and American tradition, one that has been commercialized in songs, children's books, and other forms of popular entertainment. The first recorded use of the term appears in an 1861 translation of Hans Christian Anderson's folk-like stories. However, spirits and suchlike folk figures that are said to assist children to sleep have been traced in English lore to the early nineteenth century. A "Dustman" performing the same function as the Sandman appeared as early as 1821.

Related entries: Children's Folk Heroes; Santa Claus; Tooth Fairy

References and further reading

Leach, M. (ed.), *Funk and Wagnall's Standard Dictionary of Folklore, Mythology, and Legend*, London: New English Library, 1975. Abridged one-volume edition of *Funk and Wagnall's Standard Dictionary of Folklore, Mythology, and Legend*, 2 vols., New York: Funk and Wagnall, 1972, p. 970.

Simpson, J. and Roud, S., *A Dictionary of English Folklore*, Oxford: Oxford University Press, 2000, pp. 313–314.

Santa Anna, General Antonio López de

General Antonio López de Santa Anna (1794–1876) was a Mexican general, president, and dictator. He commanded the Mexican army that defeated the defenders of the Alamo during the Texas Revolution of 1835–1836. The defenders included the famous frontier heroes Jim Bowie and Davy Crockett. Santa Anna had the six survivors of the attack executed, engendering a legend of bloodthirstiness and military success that has been the basis of his folkloric presence, assisted by a long, stormy, and often brutal career in Mexican politics and the military.

In folklore, Santa Anna (Santana, Santyanna) features in a number of sea chanteys involving voyages to Mexico, and also in sailor songs, mostly variants of one known as "The Plains of Mexico." Like a somewhat similar figure, Napoleon Bonaparte or "Boney," Santa Anna is sometimes portrayed in folklore as a loser, sometimes as a winner, and not usually with much historical accuracy.

Related entries: Bonaparte, Napoleon; Crockett, Davy; Military Heroes; Nautical Heroes

References and further reading

Botkin, B. (ed.), *A Treasury of American Folklore: Stories, Ballads, and Traditions of the People*, New York: Crown Publishers, 1944, p. 835.

Doerflinger, W. (coll. and ed.), *Songs of the Sailor and Lumberman*, New York: Macmillan, 1972 (1951), p. 78.

Hugill, S., *Shanties from the Seven Seas*, London: Routledge and Kegan Paul, 1979 (1961), pp. 82–86.

Smith, L. (comp.), *The Music of the Waters: A Collection of the Sailors' Chanties, or Work Songs of the Sea, of all Maritime Nations*, London: K. Paul, Trench and Co., 1888, p. 47.

Santa Claus

The modern folk hero of Christmas consumerism originally went by various names in different countries and has a long and complex history that probably began with the Norse winter god, Odin. The Christian version is based on St. Nicholas ("St. Nick"), said to have been a fourth-century bishop of the city of Myra in Asia Minor. "Santa Claus"—increasingly just "Santa"—is an American term that began to influence British usage from the 1870s. However, in the English form of "Father Christmas," the figure was known in the fifteenth century, when houses were opened up at Christmas time with the cry, "Welcome, old Father Christmas." He went underground during the Cromwellian period, along with many other folk customs, but was brought back to life in the Restoration of 1660. He has been with us ever since, receiving various boosts to his image, such as the ballad "'Twas the Night before Christmas," composed in 1822 by the American clergyman Clement Clark Moore. In 1863, Thomas Nast drew an illustration for *Harpers Bazaar* magazine that portrayed "Santa" as a jolly, tubby man in white whiskers, wearing red, with a wide leather belt, smoking a pipe, and carrying gifts. The modern Father Christmas had arrived. In the 1930s an advertising campaign for the Coca Cola company further developed these essentials into the jolly, round figure we know today, a figure spread around the world by the ever-more-influential channels of the mass media and its commercial imperatives.

There are numerous other similar folk figures, including the French Père Fouettard, who accompanies the Bonhomme Noël, and the German Knecht Ruprecht. Dutch tradition supports the figure of Sinter or Sante Klaas, who rides a white horse and is accompanied by two "Black Peters," young boys with blackened skin dressed in page uniforms.

Related entries: Children's Folk Heroes; Nicholas, Saint; Religious Heroes

References and further reading

Baker, M., *Discovering Christmas Customs and Folklore*, rev. ed., Princes Risborough, Bucks. Buckinghamshire, Eng.: Shire Publications, 1992 (1968).

Leach, M. (ed.), *Funk and Wagnall's Standard Dictionary of Folklore, Mythology, and Legend*, London: New English Library, 1975. Abridged one-volume edition of *Funk and Wagnall's Standard Dictionary of Folklore, Mythology, and Legend*, 2 vols., New York: Funk and Wagnall, 1972, p. 971.

Simpson, J. and Roud, S., *A Dictionary of English Folklore*, Oxford: Oxford University Press, 2000, pp. 61–66, 119–120, 314.

Santiago

See Religious Heroes

Sanykisar

Heroine of Kashmiri tradition about whom various tales are told, some dealing with brother-sister incest. Many of these tales concern Sanykisar's adoption by a crow, who provides all her needs. One day a king rides by the crow's nest where Sanykisar lives. He is beguiled by her beauty, but she refuses his entreaties. The king has the tree in which she nests cut down, and she is taken to his palace, where the king's other six wives live. Later the king issues a command to all his wives, saying that whoever husks rice the fastest shall be his chief queen. Sanykisar does not know how to husk the rice, but fortunately her crow-father, who has been searching for her, finds her just then and brings a flock of birds to carry out the husking. Consequently, Sanykisar finishes first. The other wives ask her how she managed to husk the rice so quickly. She tells them that she put the rice paddy in a mortar and pestle in the river and that the husks floated away, leaving clean rice floating to the surface of the waters. The other wives immediately go to the river to copy this technique and, of course, spend many fruitless hours waiting for their rice to rise to the surface.

The next day the king sets another task for his wives. They must all decorate their rooms, and whoever does the best job will be his chief queen. Once again Sanykisar receives help from her crow-father and his bird friends, who bring sweet-smelling herbs and flowers from afar so that the girl can decorate her room long before the other wives. Again the other wives want to know how Sanykisar has been so successful, and so quickly. Again she lies, telling them that she smeared the walls with human and cow waste. And again the other six wives do what Sanykisar has described. The resulting stench repels the king, who is pleasantly relieved on stepping into the heroine's room to find it so fresh and fine.

On the third day, the king asks his wives to make some tasty dishes and says that the cook of the finest dish will be his chief queen. As usual, Sanykisar is at a disadvantage and sits near the window of her room, sighing and sobbing. The ever-obliging crow-father and his flock of birds help out once more, preparing choice foods quickly. The stupid other wives yet again ask Sanykisar her secret and believe her when she tells them that she cooked the food in an inedible herb, cow dung, and cow urine. They do likewise and offer their foul dishes to the king, who becomes ill after sampling them. Furious, he recovers sufficiently to go to Sanykisar's room, where he enjoys delightful dishes, the likes of which he has never tasted before. He then makes Sanykisar his chief queen, divorces the other six wives, and rules happily with Sanykisar for many years.

Animals who assist heroes are common in fairy tales and can be found in many traditions, though in this case there is a particularly close connection between the crow-parent and the hapless heroine.

Related entries: Berni, Cesarino Di; Fairy Tale Heroes; Helpers

References and further reading

Beck, E. F. et al. (eds.), *Folktales of India*, Chicago: University of Chicago Press, 1987, pp. 49–56.

Dhar, S., *Kashmir Folk Tales*, Bombay: Hind Kitabs Publishers, 1949.

Gray, J., *Indian Tales and Legends*, Oxford: Oxford University Press, 1961.

Satan

See Devil, The

Scheherazade

Scheherazade is the narrator of *The Arabian Nights' Entertainments* or *1001 Nights* and the heroine of the story that frames this famous compilation of tenth-century Indian-Persian folktales. She agrees to marry King Shahryar, a Bluebeard-like figure who, having been betrayed by his wife, conceives a great hatred of women. He gives vent to this hatred by marrying the young virgins of the kingdom and killing them the following morning. After the king has killed all the other virgins only Scheherazade, daughter of the king's vizier, remains. Against her father's wishes, she agrees to marry the king, saying she will be the means of deliverance. To escape the fate of those who went before her, Scheherazade keeps the king amused by telling him stories that end before the climax, making him anxious to hear the endings and causing him to spare her for another day and night. The tales Scheherazade tells occupy "the thousand and one nights" of the book's title. At the end of the cycle, a child is born to Scheherazade and the king, and his love for the child puts an end to his monstrosity.

Related entries: Arabian Nights, The; Bluebeard; Fairy Tale Heroes; Fatima; Villains; Wise Men and Women

References and further reading

Burton, R., *The Arabian Nights' Entertainments*, 13 vols., London: H. Nichols, 1894–1897.

Jurich, M., *Scheherazade's Sisters: Trickster Heroines and Their Stories in World Literature*, Westport and London: Greenwood Press, 1998.

Lee, F. H. (comp.), *Folk Tales of All Nations*, London: Harrap, 1931, pp. 121–124.

Schinderhannes

See Outlaws

Seven Sleepers, The

The Germanic tradition of the "Seven Sleepers," or *Seibenschlaefer*, is based on the Christian story of the "Seven Sleepers of Ephesus," versions of which are also found in Islamic tradition. The legend recounts that seven brothers of Ephesus refused the Roman Emperor Decius's order to renounce their faith. He had the brothers entombed in a cave for their defiance, and they all entered into a sleep that lasted 196 years. A passing shepherd then discovered the cave, and the seven sleepers awoke to find that in the intervening years the Roman Empire, under the Emperor Theodosius, now allowed Christians to follow their beliefs. After appearing to all Christians as examples of courage and fortitude, the seven sleepers returned to their cave and went to sleep forever.

Related entries: Religious Heroes; Sleepers; Van Winkle, Rip

References and further reading

Baring-Gould, Rev. S., *Curious Myths of the Middle Ages*, London: Green and Co., 1897 (1866), pp. 93–112.

Hole, C., *Saints in Folklore*, London: G. Bell and Sons, 1966, chap. 10.

Lüthi, M. (trans. Chadeayne, L. and Gottwald, P.), *Once upon a Time: On the Nature of Fairy Tales*, Bloomington: Indiana University Press, 1976, pp. 35–46.

Ranke, K. (ed.), Baumann, L. (trans.), *Folktales of Germany*, Chicago: University of Chicago Press, 1966.

Shape-Shifters

Also known as transmogrification or transforming, shape-shifting involves characters with the ability to change themselves into animal, vegetable, mineral, and supernatural forms. Such characters are commonly encountered in hero traditions. Shape-shifting may occur in many ways and for a variety of purposes. A common situation involves a man's attempts to win a woman. Tales and songs of this type often involve a contest, as in the ballad usually known as "Twa Magicians," in which the "lusty smith" eventually wins the woman's maidenhead when she turns herself into a bed and he shape-shifts into a green coverlet or eiderdown. The ability of a hero or heroine to maintain a hold on the beloved while he or she is being changed into all manner of usually loathly or uncomfortable things is also met with quite often, as in the ballad of "Tam Lin."

Another frequent use of shape-shifting occurs in the form of contests between sorcerers or between the hero and the villain, as in the Scandinavian tale of Farmer Weathersky, in which Weathersky—in reality the Devil—is out-shifted by a young hero named, in English translation, Jack. In ballads such as "The False Knight" and its variants, the Devil, in the form of a knight, appears to a small boy on the road and asks questions that the young boy artfully parries, thus, it is implied, escaping damnation.

Shape-shifting may also be used for disguise in order to escape from bondage, elude pursuers, or enter otherwise impenetrable castles. The wicked queen in "Snow White" uses a number of disguises in her attempts to kill the heroine. Often a human will take animal form as a disguise, a theme that is well attested in classical and other mythologies, as well as in folklore.

Shape-shifting is a standard element in trickster traditions around the world. In Native American traditions, the ability of heroes to shape-shift, or transform, is extremely widespread and usually associated with trickster figures such as Coyote, Hare, and Rabbit. The African Anansi, or Spider, is a great shape-shifter. In Chinese and Japanese tradition, shape-shifting is common, especially in relation to the fox.

Related entries: Barleycorn, John; Fereyel; Fox Maiden, The; Frog Prince, The; Habermani; Hodja, The; Jack; Magicians; Melusine; Nanabozho; Nou Plai; Ringkitan; Snow White; Stagolee; Swan Maiden; Tabadiku; Tam Lin; Tricksters; Vseslavevich, Volkh; White Lady; Xiaoqing

References and further reading

Green, T. (ed.), *Folklore: An Encyclopedia of Beliefs, Customs, Tales, Music, and Art*, 2 vols., Santa Barbara: ABC-CLIO, 1997, pp. 803–805.
Porter, J. and Russell, W. (eds.), *Animals in Folklore*, London: Brewer/Rowman and Littlefield, The Folklore Society, 1978, pp. 113–182.
Radin, P., *The Trickster: A Study in American Indian Mythology*, New York: Philosophical Library, 1956.
Seki, K. (ed.), Adams, R. (trans.), *Folktales of Japan*, London: Routledge and Kegan Paul, 1963, pp. 78, 89, 95, 97–98, 108–110, 112, 114, 144, 178. First published in Japanese in 1956–1957.

Shine

Fictional character of African-American lore, especially of toasts and songs. According to tradition, Shine was a stoker and the only black person aboard the *Titanic*. He warned the captain of the ship's danger, but he was ignored. He managed to survive the sinking by feats of physical strength, cleverness, and good sense, mainly by jumping overboard and swimming to safety. In some versions of the legend, existing primarily in the form of toasts, Shine refuses the bribes, including money and sexual favors, and pleas of passengers in order to save himself. "Get your ass in the water and swim like me," Shine advises the captain. These words are said to be one of the most popular toasts in African-American tradition. The racial one-upmanship displayed by Shine makes him an apt hero of struggle and also a culture hero whose survival is all the sweeter since "Negroes" were denied passage on the *Titanic*'s maiden voyage as a result of the racial prejudices of the period. As well as racial tension, this folk hero also displays an element of class antagonism and has something of the trickster in his attitudes and actions.

Related entries: Culture Heroes; Heroes of Struggle; Tricksters

References and further reading

Abrahams, R., *Afro-American Folktales*, New York: Pantheon Books, 1985, pp. 282–283.
Hancock, S., "Shine," in Brunvand, J. (ed.), *American Folklore: An Encyclopedia*, New York: Garland, 1996, p. 665.
Jackson, B., *"Get Your Ass in the Water and Swim Like Me": Narrative Poetry from Black Oral Tradition*, Cambridge: Harvard University Press, 1974.
Roberts, J., *From Trickster to Badman: The Black Folk Hero in Slavery and Freedom*, Philadelphia: University of Pennsylvania Press, 1989.

Shiruyeh

See Victims

Sigfússon, Saemund

See Magicians

Siitakuuyuk

Mythic hero of Inuit (previously "Eskimo") tradition. Siitakuuyuk is said to have been raised by a brown bear, and various tales are told about him. In most of them he appears as a protector of his people and family in the Point Barrow region of Alaska. In one tale, Siitakuuyuk investigates the disappearance of Point Barrow men who have not returned from hunting. He comes upon a man who has been killing the hunters, for no apparent reason. Siitakuuyuk enters into contests with the murderer, including a foot race, which Siitakuuyuk wins. The man then tries to kill Siitakuuyuk with a dagger, but Siitakuuyuk manages to wound him fatally with the same knife. As he is dying, the man asks Siitakuuyuk to cut off his head and place it on a rock and to bury his body. He also asks Siitakuuyuk to tell his family that he will not be coming home again. Siitakuuyuk eventually finds the man's family and marries his widow, becoming stepfather of his two sons, who plot to kill him.

In other stories, Siitakuuyuk slays a giant polar bear and a great fish that have been killing Point Barrow hunters. On another occasion, one of Siitakuuyuk's sons goes out hunting caribou but keeps returning empty-handed. Puzzled at this sudden failure of his son's competence, Siitakuuyuk follows him on a hunting trip and finds that the son is catching caribou but that some other men from Point Barrow are stealing his prizes. Siitakuuyuk warns the men off, and they take heed for some days, but soon they are back to their stealing, and Siitakuuyuk eventually spears one of the men, twirling the body around in the air like an impaled salmon for all to see. After that the son has no more trouble when caribou hunting.

In his cycle of tales, Siitakuuyuk is very much a localized culture hero whose actions relate to the values and beliefs of the traditional Inuit lifestyle. Although his activities take place in a restricted geographical area and among local communities, Siitakuuyuk nevertheless displays the qualities of the epic hero.

Related entries: Culture Heroes; Dragon-Slayers;
  Giant-Killers; Local Heroes
References and further reading
Hall, S. Jr., *The Eskimo Storyteller: Folktales from Noatak,
  Alaska,* Knoxville: University of Tennessee Press,
  1975, nos. PM 102, PM 131.

Sindbad the Sailor

See *Arabian Nights, The*

Siung (Tiung) Wanara

First-born son of a Sundanese (West Java) king. The father commands a servant to drown the boy in fear of a prophecy that he will grow up and kill the king. The servant only pretends that he has killed the child, who is then fostered by a poor and childless fisher couple. He grows up, calls himself Siung Wanara (monkey-tusk), and becomes a famous blacksmith. The king visits the smith to look at his famous work and recognizes the features of Siung Wanara's mother. Wishing to get rid of the son, the king plots to capture Siung Wanara in a metal cage of his own making. His plan is foiled by Siung Wanara and his foster father, who reveal to the people the true identity of Siung Wanara and the cruelty of the king in trying to murder him. The people depose the king and make Siung Wanara their new king, under the name Tiung Wanara.

Many elements of this tradition are also found in European, Middle Eastern, and African folklore and literature. The birth of a child who is prophesied to rule is a feature of biblical stories, as is the attempt of the ruler, in this case the child's father, to have the child murdered. The inability or unwillingness of the servant to kill the child is found in a number of fairy tales, notably Snow White. And, of course, the eventual fulfillment of the prophecy, unmasking of the villain, and ascension of the hero to the throne are the stock conclusions of many fairy tales.

Related entries: Fairy Tale Heroes; Jesus; Mac
  Cumhal, Finn; Snow White; Victims

References and further reading

Knappert, J., Myths and Legends of Indonesia, Singapore: Heinnemann, 1977, pp. 24–30.

Terada, A., The Magic Crocodile and Other Folktales from Indonesia, Honolulu: University of Hawaii Press, 1994.

Sivirri

See Culture Heroes

Skorobogaty, Kuzma

"Kuzma" means "quick-rich" in Russian, and the legendary figure is the not very promising, lazy son of poor but honest peasants. Exasperated at his uselessness, the parents send Kuzma away to live alone in the woods looking after the chickens. A female fox attacks the chickens, and Kuzma catches it, but he spares its life when the fox promises to help him marry the beautiful and wealthy daughter of the local czar. Through various deceptions and tricks, the fox convinces the czar that Kuzma, whom the czar has never seen, would be an appropriate, and wealthy, groom for his daughter.

Finally, the day when Kuzma must make an appearance at court arrives. Kuzma tells the fox that he cannot go, as he has no fine clothes or anything else. But the fox has one more trick to play. She takes Kuzma to a small bridge over a river near the czar's palace and, oddly, asks him to saw it down. She then tells Kuzma to strip off his rags and throw them into the river, along with his broken-down old horse. Kuzma is then to roll around in the sand at the water's edge until the fox returns. The fox rushes to the palace screaming that the czar's bridge must be of poor quality, as it has broken under the weight of Kuzma and the treasure he is bringing with him. Alarmed at the potential loss of this wealthy future son-in-law, the czar rushes with his servants to Kuzma's rescue and brings him to the palace, dressing him in fine robes and quickly marrying him to the beautiful princess. Kuzma lives in the court doing nothing but singing songs, and the fox also lives there in great honor.

The animal helper, in this case a trickster-like one, has parallels in many traditions, as does the upward social mobility of the poor, indolent, and apparently incompetent young man.

Related entries: Androcles; Berni, Cesarino Di; Fox Maiden, The; Helpers; Jack and the Beanstalk; Puss in Boots; Tricksters; Whittington, Dick; Yao Wang; Yasuna, Abe No

References and further reading

Afanas'ev, A. (comp.), Guterman, N. (trans.), Russian Fairy Tales, New York: Pantheon Books, 1945.

Bain, R. (trans.), Russian Fairy Tales from the Russian of Polevoi, London: George Harrap, 1915, pp. 85–93.

Duddington, N. (trans.), Russian Folk Tales, London: Rupert Hart-Davies, 1967, pp. 29–34.

Lee, F. H. (comp.), Folk Tales of All Nations, London: Harrap, 1931, pp. 858–862.

Slappy Hooper

See Occupational Heroes

Slater, Morris (Railroad Bill)

"He never worked and he never will," claims Railroad Bill's ballad. African-American Morris Slater was an Alabama turpentine still worker who became an outlaw hero from 1892. His specialty was robbing freight trains and, it is said, distributing the loot to the poor and needy. His folklore includes his trickster ability to turn himself into an animal, usually a black dog, in order to escape capture, a skill he shares with another black American hero, Stagolee. On one occasion, with the sheriff, posse, and dogs in hot pursuit, Bill changed into a dog and accompanied the pack to the house of his lover, staying behind to do some courting when the pursuers departed. In this story, Bill takes on the added dimensions of the shape-shifter and legendary lover. The historical railroad Bill was shot dead by Sheriff Leonard McGowan on March 7, 1896.

Related entries: Bonney, William; Henry, John; James, Jesse; Jones, Casey; Occupational Heroes; Outlaws; Stagolee

References and further reading

Cohen, N., Long Steel Rail: The Railroad in American Folksong, Urbana: University of Illinois Press, 1981, pp. 122–131.

Lomax, J. and A. (colls. and comps.), American Ballads and Folk Songs, New York: Macmillan, 1934, p. 118.

Roberts, J., "'Railroad Bill' and the American Outlaw Tradition," *Western Folklore* 40 (1981): 315–328.

Sleepers

Heroes sent to sleep for shorter or longer periods are plentiful in the folklore of the world. There are three main types of sleeping hero.

The first is the warrior who sleeps to come again in the time of his people's need. In the English-language warrior hero tradition King Arthur—the "once and future king" who sleeps until England, or Britain, is threatened by invasion—is the most familiar and popular example. There are, however, similar traditions about other sleeping heroes in the British Isles, including one in Castle Rushen in the Isle of Man and one at Craig-y-Dinas in Wales. In German tradition there are similar stories about Barbarossa (Emperor Frederick I). In Switzerland there are stories about the Three Tells, and in Denmark about Holger Danske. Gearoidh provides an Irish version of these migratory legends, while the Swedes have the twelve knights of Ållaberg to rescue them when the time comes. Slovenian lore celebrates Kralj Matjaz (King Matthias); the Serbs tell of the deeds done by Ivan Crnojevic; and the Spanish have Roderick or Roderigo as their sleeping king. The location of these sleeping heroes is almost always in caves beneath castles or in deep mountain caverns.

The second variety of sleeping hero involves the man who wanders off from human companionship to a place where he encounters supernatural figures who, it seems, cause him to sleep for many years. Eventually he wakes and returns home only to find that one or more generations have passed and that everyone he knew is long gone. Rip Van Winkle is perhaps the most familiar sleeper, created by Washington Irving in 1819–1820 and almost certainly based on folk traditions familiar to the author. Although Rip is a literary invention, he has passed into folklore to some extent, aided by his popular representations in books, films, and other media. Wang Chi is a Chinese hero who witnesses a ghostly game of chess and then falls into a magical sleep that lasts for many years. Urashima is a Japanese equivalent. Peter Klaus is the German Rip, while Peterkin is a Gypsy (Rom) version of the same figure. The Seven Sleepers are another variation on this theme. Most of these heroes do their sleeping in or on mountains.

The third type of sleeper is the fairy tale heroine who is put to sleep by a magic spell and awakened only by the kiss or other attentions of the hero, whom she usually marries. "Sleeping Beauty" is the best-known example of this tradition, though similar tales may be found in many folklores.

Related entries: Arthur; Barbarossa; Batradz; Charlemagne; Culture Heroes; Danske, Holger; Gearoidh, Iarla; Kraljevic, Marco; Mac Cumhal, Finn; Matthias, King; Merlin; National Heroes; Peterkin; Roderick; Seven Sleepers, The; Sleeping Beauty; Thomas the Rhymer; Urashima; Van Winkle, Rip; Warriors

References and further reading
Hardy, J. (ed.), *The Denham Tracts*, London: The Folklore Society, 1892, vol. 1, pp. 197–198.
Hofberg, H. (trans. Myers, W.), *Swedish Fairy Tales*, Chicago: W. B. Conkey, 1893, pp. 109–110.
Kennedy, P., *Legendary Fictions of the Irish Celts*, London: Macmillan and Co., 1866, pp. 171–174.
MacDougall, J., *Folk and Hero Tales: Waifs and Strays of Celtic Tradition*, London: David Nutt, 1891, pp. 73–75.
Simpson, J., *Scandinavian Folktales*, Harmondsworth, Middlesex: Penguin, 1988, pp. 55–56.

Sleeping Beauty

Usually titled in books of fairy tales "The Sleeping Beauty," this widespread, ancient, and well-known folktale is almost always told in English simply as "Sleeping Beauty." Known in one version or another since at least the fourteenth century, "Sleeping Beauty" has had a long literary as well as folkloric life. Successive tellers of the tale, such as Perrault ("La Belle au Bois Dormant") and the Grimms (in English, "Little Briar Rose"), have added to it or subtracted from it in various ways, leaving us with the modern version as more-or-less solidified in the Disney animated feature film.

Most readers will be familiar with the Grimm plot, in which a queen, after many years of unsuccessful attempts, finally gives birth. Overjoyed, the king and queen invite

The prince discovers Sleeping Beauty. (Bettmann/Corbis)

everyone in the kingdom to come to the palace to celebrate the birth of their daughter. There are thirteen wise women in the kingdom, and all must be invited. Unfortunately, the king has only twelve gold plates and so, to avoid embarrassment, invites only twelve. While these women bestow gifts of beauty and happiness on the royal baby, the offended thirteenth wise woman angrily curses the child, saying that she will die at fifteen years of age through a prick in her finger. One of the invited wise women is able to lighten the curse from death to one hundred years of sleep.

Spinning machines and their sharp spindles are immediately banned in the kingdom, but in her fifteenth year, the princess comes across an old woman spinning in a castle tower. The princess picks up the spindle and pricks herself, bringing the prophetic curse into effect. She falls asleep, and so does everyone else in the palace, from the king and queen down to the lowliest servant and even the flies on the wall. A great thorn hedge grows around the palace, cutting it off from the world. The legend of the sleeping beauty attracts many young men to the palace, but despite their skill, strength, and determination they all fail to break through and waken the sleeping beauty with a kiss. Eventually, one hundred years pass, and a prince does succeed in breaking through. He kisses the sleeping princess, and she wakes, along with everyone and everything else in the palace. Life returns to normal, and the young prince and Sleeping Beauty marry.

Some elements of the story can be traced to Greek myth, though the motifs of a sleeping princess and magic sleep in general are widely distributed in the world's folktale traditions. The popularity and wide spread of this story and its variants have attracted extensive comment and analysis. Psychological and psychoanalytic approaches generally interpret the story as a metaphor of the sexual awakening of young women that, whatever the parents may think or do about it, is bound to occur sooner or later. In Bettelheim's *The Uses of Enchantment*, for example, there is an extended discussion of the Sleeping Beauty stories along these lines, stressing that the theme of the futility of trying to prevent the child's sexual maturity is common to all versions of the story.

Folklorists would perhaps be more inclined to argue that it is unlikely that every version of "The Sleeping Beauty," past and present, revolves around this theme or that the story was or is told with such intentions. While Bettelheim and other psychoanalysts may be right about some, even many, tellings of this tale, it is not likely to have the same significance in all the societies and in all the periods in which it has been told, a notion akin to the Jungian "one-symbol-does-for-all" archetype. Only on-the-ground fieldwork can determine the significance of any particular telling of "The Sleeping Beauty," or any other folktale. The fact that there have been and continue to be so many differing interpretations of the story is a testament to its popularity, longevity, and wide distribution. That so many meanings can be found within it is due to that peculiar magic we continue to find in those reworked folktales known as "fairy tales."

Related entries: Beauty and the Beast; Fairy Tale Heroes; Sleepers; Snow White

References and further reading

Bettelheim, B., The Uses of Enchantment: The Meaning and Importance of Fairy Tales, New York: Knopf, 1976, pp. 139, 145, 180, 225–236, 277, 309.

Bottigheimer, R. (ed.), Fairy Tales and Society: Illusion, Allusion, and Paradigm, Philadelphia: University of Pennsylvania Press, 1986.

Calvino, I. (trans. Martin, G.), Italian Folk Tales: Selected and Retold by Italo Calvino, New York: Harcourt Brace Jovanovich, Penguin, 1980 (1956), pp. 485–489.

Lüthi, M. (trans. Chadeayne, L. and Gottwald, P.), Once upon a Time: On the Nature of Fairy Tales, Bloomington: Indiana University Press, 1976. pp. 21–34.

Massignon, G. (ed.), (trans. Hyland, J.), Folktales of France, Chicago: University of Chicago Press, 1968, pp. 133–135.

Tatar, M., The Hard Facts of the Grimms' Fairy Tales, Princeton, NJ: Princeton University Press, 1987.

Smoking Star

See Culture Heroes

Snow White

In their version of this favorite and widely known fairy tale, "Little Snow White" (no. 53), the Grimms begin like this: "Once upon a time, in the middle of winter when the snow flakes fell like feathers from the sky, a queen sat at a window which had a frame of black ebony. And as she was sewing while looking at the snow, she pricked her finger with the needle and three drops of blood fell on the snow. The red looked so beautiful on the white snow that she thought to herself, 'I wish I had a child as white as snow, as red as the blood, and with hair as black as the wood of the window frame'"

Thus the scene is set for the birth of Snow White, the death of her mother, and the taking of a new wife by the king, Snow White's father, one year later. All goes well until Snow White turns seven. Then the trouble begins. The stepmother turns out to be of the wicked variety and is insanely envious of Snow White's beauty, imploring the magic "mirror, mirror on the wall" to tell her "who is the fairest of them all" and receiving the answer she does not wish to hear.

As most children know from either the Disney animated feature (the first version of which was released in 1937) or from any number of children's books, Snow White is expelled from the castle. The wicked queen orders a woodsman to murder the young girl in the forest, but the man cannot bring himself to commit this cold-blooded deed and instead leaves Snow White alone in the wilderness. Here she is found and looked after by seven dwarfs. But the wicked queen discovers that Snow White is not dead and disguises herself in various forms in attempts to kill her. At her third attempt, the queen tricks Snow White into eating a poisoned apple, and the girl dies. She is laid out in a crystal coffin and mourned over by the dwarfs and birds until a handsome prince arrives. He kisses her and, bumping the coffin in the process, wakens her from what was only a deeply drugged sleep after all. She marries the prince, and the wicked stepmother is punished by being made to wear red-hot shoes in which she must dance until her death. The young couple lives happily ever after and, in the manner of most fairy tales and folktales, the cultural equilibrium is reestablished with the defeat of evil and the succession of the generations.

This version of Snow White is satisfyingly complete, with its elaborated narrative structure, its deployment of many ancient and widespread motifs of myth and legend (including the helpers, the wicked stepmother, the narcissistic streak of the queen, the sleep of the heroine, and her awakening with a kiss), and its just rewards and deserts for heroine, hero, and villainess. Most of the many other versions of the tale are less refined and extended, though they tend to retain the symbolic elements of blood, whiteness, and black hair and the motivations of the wicked stepmother as essentially sexual jealousy.

Differences between various versions of Snow White–type tales are highlighted in a number of analyses undertaken from various perspectives. Steven Swann Jones, for instance, shows how the pattern of action varies in three different versions of "Snow White." Nevertheless, comparison of the versions reveals an underlying structure. The heroine may be killed by a poisoned apple in one version, by a raisin in another, or by a poisoned needle in yet another; nonetheless, she is killed, and the narrative proceeds to the next significant action. In comparing the Grimms' version of Snow White with French and Italian versions, Jones points to the quite different ways in which each of the significant actions within the story is accomplished.

In the Grimms' opening situation a queen learns from a magical mirror that the heroine is more beautiful than she. In the Italian version, it is a stepmother who resents her new stepdaughter. In the French version, the stepmother is jealous of her husband's apparent preference for the stepdaughter. In the second significant action, the Grimms' version has the queen ordering a servant to kill the heroine, but instead the servant leaves her in the forest. In the Italian version, the stepmother commands the stepdaughter to tend a dangerously located basil plant. In the French version the stepmother asks her husband to abandon the heroine on a distant mountain.

Snow White discovered by the seven dwarfs (Mary Evans Picture Library)

The third significant action in the Grimms' version involves the dwarfs taking in the heroine. In the Italian version an eagle carries her to a fairy palace. In the French version, the heroine surreptitiously performs domestic chores in the palace of forty giants until they find her out and adopt her. In the fourth significant action the Grimms have the wicked queen discover her location by the magic mirror. In the Italian version, the eagle tells the stepmother the heroine's whereabouts. The French story has the stepmother consulting the sun about any woman more beautiful than herself and discovering the heroine's whereabouts accordingly. In the fifth significant action the Grimms' persecuting queen attempts to murder the heroine, first with a poisoned staylace and comb; eventually she succeeds with the poisoned apple. In the Italian tale, the stepmother enlists the aid of a witch, who fails to kill the heroine with poisoned sweetmeats but succeeds with a poisoned dress. Finally, in the Grimms' version a prince obtains the heroine's body. He bumps her coffin, and Snow White revives and marries him. In the Italian version, the prince obtains the heroine's body, and his mother then removes the poisoned dress in order to wash it, thus causing the heroine to return to life. Heroine and hero are married. In the French conclusion, the father of the prince who discovers the body presses the heroine's chest, causing her to regurgitate the raisin and to breath again. Prince and heroine then marry.

Jones's purpose in carrying out this enlightening analysis is to pursue a larger argument about narrative structure in folktales, but his analysis also usefully reveals the extent to which all versions of a particular tale are essentially different ways of telling the same story. The means by which the significant actions that make up the core story are brought about is not as important as the carrying out of the actions themselves. The actions, usually strung together in the same sequence, lead inexorably to the climax of the story and to its resolution in the traditional happy ending in which hero and heroine are united in marriage. This narrative structure and its culmination are a symbolic parallelism of the male and female principles that motivate many folktales, especially those of the fairy tale variety. Similar comparisons are possible between different versions of most folktales.

Like most fairy tales, Snow White has numerous international parallels, including the Jewish story of Romana. In her tale, of Middle Eastern origin and perhaps the archetype of "Snow White and the Seven Dwarves," Romana falls in with forty thieves rather than the seven dwarves. The rest of the story is remarkably similar to that of Snow White, with much the same happy ending. Likewise, the theme of the mother, or stepmother, attempting to harm her children or stepchildren is found in many tra-

ditions. The brothers S'ad and Sa'id, the sons of a poor woodworker, feature in Persian and Middle Eastern tradition. Their mother falls in love with a wealthy man and, in order to please him, plots to kill her two sons. They escape and after many adventures become rich and honored rulers.

Related entries: Fairy Tale Heroes; King of Ireland's Son, The; Shape-Shifters; Sleepers; Sleeping Beauty

References and further reading
Bettelheim, B., The Uses of Enchantment: The Meaning and Importance of Fairy Tales, New York: Knopf, 1976, pp. 9, 16, 72, 98, 113, 115, 127, 139, 145, 147, 194–215, 217–219, 222, 226, 232, 274, 277–278, 283, 285–286.
Briggs, K. (ed.), A Dictionary of British Folk-Tales in the English Language, 2 vols., London: Routledge and Kegan Paul, 1970–1971, vol. 1, p. 494.
Dawkins, R. (comp. and trans.), Modern Greek Folktales, Oxford: Clarendon Press, 1953; reprint Westport, CT: Greenwood Press, 1974.
Hallett, M. and Karasek, B. (eds.), Folk and Fairy Tales, Ontario: Broadview Press, 1996, pp. 65–73.
Jones, S., "The Structure of 'Snow White,'" in Bottigheimer, R. (ed.), Fairy Tales and Society: Illusion, Allusion, and Paradigm, Philadelphia: University of Pennsylvania Press, 1986, pp. 165–186.
Klipple, M., African Folktales with Foreign Analogues, New York: Garland, 1992, pp. 244–248.
Kurti, A. (trans.), Persian Folktales, London: Bell and Sons, 1971 (1958), pp. 96–108.
Zipes, J., Happily Ever After: Fairy Tales, Children, and the Culture Industry, New York and London: Routledge, 1997.

Sot, Jean

See Numskulls and Noodles

Spider

See Anansi; Tricksters

Spiewna

Heroine of a Polish tale in which a king named Bartek has his clown, Pies, impersonate the king to his potential bride, Bialka. The purpose of the deception is to determine how virtuous Bialka will be as a future queen. Pies dresses in the regal finery of his master, and Bialka treats him as king, while also treating the disguised Bartek with contempt. Bialka's sister, Spiewna, does not treat the disguised king with contempt but accepts him as an equal. Bartek decides that Spiewna is the really virtuous one of the two sisters and marries her instead, leaving Bialka to content herself with an aging musician for a husband. The point of this tale seems to be that those who are great, or who aspire to greatness, must treat the not-so-great with respect. The tale can be interpreted as a moral allegory about the appropriate relationships between different social classes, as well as a reminder that arrogance is an ugly failing.

The theme of disguise and changed identities is often found in folk traditions of romantic love.

Related entries: Goose Girl, The; Maria, Fenda
References and further reading
Jones, A., *Larousse Dictionary of World Folklore*, Edinburgh and New York: Larousse, 1995, p. 52.

Stagolee

An African-American badman hero of almost Faustian proportions. His name is sometimes spelled "Stagalee" or "Stackerlee" or in some similar fashion. Stagolee's legendry is complex and diffuse, existing in story, folk ballad, popular song, and in verbal folklore forms such as the toast. In the basic story, Stagolee is born with supernatural abilities and tries to enhance these by selling his soul to the Devil. The Devil gives him a magical Stetson hat, which allows him to perform various supernatural feats, including changing his shape and size. Stagolee is also a notorious gunman who, in most versions of his ballad, "tote[s] a stack-barrelled blow gun and a blue steel forty-four," weapons he uses to shoot the professional gambler Billy Lyon (also "Lyons," "O'Lyons," or other variation, and sometimes "Galion"), who the Devil uses to steal back the Stetson after becoming irritated by Stagolee's misuse of his powers, which includes such things as causing the San Francisco earthquake. Stagolee executes Lyon and is then arrested, tried, and eventually hanged, despite the rope's failing to crack his neck. Stagolee goes to hell and, in some ver-

sions of the story and in some songs, takes over running the place from the Devil himself.

In common with many folk heroes, there is more than a little ambiguity in Stagolee's legend. In some of the songs about his exploits, he is described as a good man and his killing of the bullying Lyon is an act of community service. There is also a strong male bawdy tradition involving Stagolee toasts, many of which emphasize his sexual prowess. There have been numerous attempts to trace a historical origin for Stagolee, but his birth, life, and death remain firmly fixed in legend.

Related entries: Devil, The; Outlaws; Slater, Morris (Railroad Bill); Villains
References and further reading
Abrahams, R., *Afro-American Folktales*, New York: Pantheon Books, 1985, pp. 238–240.
Botkin, B. (ed.), *A Treasury of American Folklore: Stories, Ballads, and Traditions of the People*, New York: Crown Publishers, 1944, pp. 120–131.
Brunvand, J. (ed.), *American Folklore: An Encyclopedia*, New York: Garland, 1996, pp. 684–686.
Jackson, B., "*Get Your Ass in the Water and Swim Like Me*": *Narrative Poetry from Black Oral Tradition*, Cambridge: Harvard University Press, 1974.
Lomax, J. and A. (colls. and comps.), *American Ballads and Folk Songs*, New York: Macmillan, 1934, p. 93.
Roberts, J., *From Trickster to Badman: The Black Folk Hero in Slavery and Freedom*, Philadelphia: University of Philadelphia Press, 1989.

Stig, Marsk

Hero of a Danish ballad sequence in which he champions the rights of the people against the oppressions and impositions of the king, Eric. The name "Marsk Stig" (also spelled "Marstig") means "Marshall Stig," and the legends are based on a historical personage named Stig Anderson, the leader of nine men banished in 1287 in connection with the murder of King Eric Klipping the previous year. The men went to the island of Hjaelm and, with the assistance of the Norwegians, pursued a guerrilla war against Denmark. The historical reasons for these events are murky and are related to the political imperatives of the period. In folklore though, Marsk Stig has become an outlaw hero in the mold of Robin Hood and the many other such noble robbers who people the world's folk traditions.

According to the ballads, Marsk Stig is wronged by the king, who seduces his wife while the hero is away fighting battles on the king's behalf. This event becomes the justification for the considerable body of ballads combining historical facts and folkloric speculations.

Related entries: Heroes of Struggle; Hood, Robin; Outlaws

References and further reading

Gray, A. (trans.), *Historical Ballads of Denmark*, Edinburgh: Edinburgh University Press, 1958, pp. 85–128.

Stormalong

Also known as "Stormy" and "Old Stormy," Stormalong was an occupational hero of sailors in the days of sail. He is featured in a number of chanteys, or sailors' work songs, and is the main character of one usually titled simply "Stormalong," as given by Whall:

> O Stormy he is dead and gone,
> To my way you Stormalong
> O Stormy was a good old man
> Ay, ay, ay Mister Stormalong.

Subsequent verses tell of Stormalong's reverential burial:

> We'll dig his grave with a silver spade,
> And lower him down with a golden chain.

And of how the singer wishes he was Old Stormy's son so that he could build a ship of a thousand ton and "fill her up with New England rum." The chantey ends with Stormalong's legacy to those who follow the sea:

> O Stormy's dead and gone to rest,
> Of all the sailors he was best.

Stormalong is also the subject of tall tales, such as the one in which his gigantic ship is blown onto the Isthmus of Panama. So great is the hurricane and so large the ship that it is forced to cleave through the ground instead of the waves, thus creating the Panama Canal. Other tales and songs emphasize this occupational hero's strength, boldness, and general manliness, a fondly sardonic projection of the working seaman's self-image.

Related entries: Bunyan, Paul; Crooked Mick; Fink, Mike; Henry, John; Jack-in-the-Green; Mikula; Nautical Heroes; Occupational Heroes; Pecos Bill; Slater, Morris (Railroad Bill)

References and further reading

Beck, H., *Folklore and the Sea*, Middletown, CT: Wesleyan University Press, 1973, p. 148.

Doerflinger, W. (coll. and ed.), *Songs of the Sailor and Lumberman*, New York: Macmillan, 1972 (1951), p. 83.

Hugill, S., *Shanties from the Seven Seas*, London: Routledge and Kegan Paul, 1979 (1961), pp. 72, 75–76.

Smith, L. (comp.), *The Music of the Waters: A Collection of the Sailors' Chanties, or Work Songs of the Sea, of all Maritime Nations*, London: K. Paul, Trench and Co., 1888, pp. 16–17.

Whall, W. (coll. and ed.), *Sea Songs and Shanties*, London: Brown, Son, and Ferguson, 1910.

Stuart, Prince Charles Edward

Prince Charles Edward Stuart, the Young Pretender (1720–1788), was celebrated by rebellious Scots in song, verse, and tale and is still an important figure of Scots history and lore. "Bonnie Prince Charlie," as he was widely known to friend and foe alike, escaped the En-

Prince Charles Edward Stuart from the portrait by Le Tocque, Paris, 1748 (North Wind Picture Archives)

glish after the battle of Culloden Moor in 1746, assisted by Flora Macdonald. This event is remembered—and romanticized—in the "Skye Boat Song" or "Speed Bonny Boat." Bonnie Prince Charlie also appears in Irish folklore in the tradition that he once took refuge in Donegal to escape his pursuers. Bonny Prince Charlie has become a Scots national hero, representing the long antagonisms between England and Scotland.

Related entries: Culture Heroes; Macdonald, Flora; National Heroes

References and further reading

Buchan, D., *Scottish Tradition: A Collection of Scottish Folk Literature*, London: Routledge and Kegan Paul, 1984.

Ford, R., *Vagabond Songs and Ballads of Scotland*, Paisley: A. Gardner, 1899.

Swire, O., *Skye: The Island and Its Legends*, London: Oxford University Press, 1952, pp. 61–67.

Sun Wukong

See Monkey

Supparaka

Supparaka is a blind but wise master mariner of Indian tradition. He is asked by a group of merchants to pilot their ship on a long and dangerous voyage. During the four months of the journey, Supparaka's great knowledge nets the merchants vast wealth in precious stones and other valuables from the various mythical oceans they pass through. Finally, threatened by a deadly sea, Supparaka saves all by getting the merchants to perform an act of religious faith. Magically the ship and all aboard are transported home in one day, flying through the air. Supparaka distributes the wealth among the merchants, telling them that now they have no further need to risk their lives undertaking dangerous sea voyages. He continues to do good things for the rest of his life, and after his death he is received into heaven. An outstanding example of the heroic helper.

Related entries: Helpers; Nautical Heroes; Wise Men and Women

References and further reading

Beck, E. F. et al. (eds.), *Folktales of India*, Chicago: University of Chicago Press, 1987.

Gray, J. E. B. (ed.), *Indian Tales and Legends*, London: Oxford University Press, 1961, pp. 13–18.

Swan Maiden

The most familiar version of a widely dispersed folktale in which a half-human, half-supernatural maiden in the shape of a swan marries a young man, who holds the secret of her swan form, variously a robe of feathers, a ring, a crown, or a gold chain. Depending on the version of the tale, the hero either hides the enchantment device, ensuring the continued human form of his wife, or breaks a condition of the marriage agreement, thus turning the maiden back into a swan, losing her forever. Research has revealed the existence of this powerful story in Slavic, Scandinavian, and Arabian traditions, in western and southern Europe, in South America, and throughout Asia, in Britain and Ireland, in Australia, Polynesia, Melanesia, Indonesia, Africa, India, Sri Lanka, Burma, the Philippines, and among Native Americans.

Narrative examples of this tradition include the story of the Russian seal hunter from Archangel, Ivan Savelevich, who falls in love with a *rusalka*, or seal woman. He follows her into the water but, realizing his mistake in the nick of time, makes the sign of the cross, whereupon he is magically transported back to the safety of his home. Another example is the story of Katya, an orphaned peasant girl of Slavonian legend who attracts the affections of a spirit, or *dvorovoi*. The dvorovoi plaits her hair and warns her never to take the plaits out. When Katya eventually realizes that the dvorovoi is unable to engage in physical lovemaking, she becomes engaged to a human youth named Stefan. In her bedroom the night before the wedding, she lets down her hair. The next morning the neighbors find her strangled in her own hair. The moral of this chilling tale and of many others like it seems to be that humans should avoid involvement with the unpredictable members of the otherworld, a widespread and venerable piece of folk wisdom echoed in traditions about the fairy folk, the little people, jinn, and other such supernatural beings.

Swan Maiden traditions are closely related to other tale types involving animal grooms and relationships between humans and animals or between humans and part animal, part supernatural beings, such as selkies (man-seal), mermaids and mermen, woman-snakes, frog-princes, and so forth. Beast marriages, as such liaisons are often called, are among the most widespread and consistent motifs of mythology and folklore. Considerable speculation has gone into the significance of such traditions, which also exist in ballad and song form.

Related entries: Bai Suzhen; Beauty and the Beast; Fox Maiden, The; Frog Prince, The; Kuzonoha; Llyn Y Fan Fach, The Lady of; Melusine; Mudjikiwis; Ringkitan; Tabadiku; Urashima; White Lady; Xiaoqing; Yannakis; Yasuna, Abe No; Yer

References and further reading

Booss, C., *Scandinavian Folk and Fairy Tales*, New York: Crown Publishers, Avenel Books, 1984, pp. 248–250.

Leavy, B., *In Search for the Swan Maiden: A Narrative on Folklore and Gender*, New York: New York University Press, 1994.

Swift Nicks

The English highwayman William Nevison was popularly known as "Swift Nicks" because he was said to have made the famous one-day ride from London to York usually attributed to Dick Turpin. The historical Nevison was born in 1639 and hanged on March 15, 1684. Active in and around York, Derby, Nottingham, and Lincoln, Nevison had quite a long career of highway robbery. A large reward of twenty pounds was offered for his arrest on a charge of murder. A female member of Nevison's gang apparently informed against the highwayman, and he was captured near Wakefield, imprisoned, tried, and hanged at York.

Nevison's longevity in folk memory is at least partly related to the nineteenth- and early-twentieth-century literary romanticizations of the highwayman, but he is also described in glowing terms in a broadside ballad:

Did you ever hear tell of that hero
Bold Nevison it was his name
And he rode about like a brave hero
And by that he gained a great fame

Nevison's ballads insist that he robs only the rich to benefit the poor, offers no unjustified violence, and is self-righteously defiant of the forces of authority when captured. An oral version of a broadside ballad about Nevison was collected by Percy Grainger in 1908 from Mr. Joseph Taylor, Brigg, Lincolnshire. It concludes with the defiant lines:

I have never robbed no man of tuppence,
And I've never done murder nor killed.
Though guilty I've been all my lifetime,
So gentlemen do as you please.

Related entries: Brennan, William; Hood, Robin; Outlaws; Turpin, Richard

References and further reading

Grainger, P., coll., *Unto Brigg Fair*, lp disk, Leader Records LEA 4050-B, 1972.

Hayward, A. L., *Lives of the Most Remarkable Criminals*, London: Reeves and Turner, 1735, pp. 57, 111–112, 425–427, 513.

Hindley, C., *Curiosities of Street Literature*, London: Reeves and Turner, 1871, p. 169.

Seal, G., *The Outlaw Legend: A Cultural Tradition in Britain, America, and Australia*, Melbourne and Cambridge: Cambridge University Press, 1996, pp. 8, 49–52, 201.

T

Tabadiku

"Tabadiku" means a length of bamboo in the language spoken by the Tabarus on the island of Halmahera, now part of Indonesia. Tabadiku, whose voice is as melodious as a bamboo flute, is the son of a poor woman. When grown, he asks to marry one of the chief's seven daughters. Six of the daughters refuse to marry a length of bamboo, but the youngest daughter consents to live with a bamboo stick of a husband, as the six older sisters contemptuously describe Tabadiku.

Some time later, the younger sister joins the other six picking fruit. While they are picking, a handsome prince rides up. The six elder sisters pelt him with fruit, but the younger sister offers him the best of the fruit. The six elder sisters go to Tabadiku that evening and tell him that his wife is apparently courting the favors of the handsome prince. Tabadiku answers that he does not care and that she may go with him if that is her wish, as he is only a piece of bamboo.

A similar event occurs two more times, but on the third time the handsome prince, who is Tabadiku in disguise, takes his wife home. There he tells her to burn a length of bamboo in the fire. She throws it in, and it explodes, forming a large and grand stone house complete with servants. Tabadiku and his wife live here happily, causing great jealousy among the elder sisters. In their envy, the older sisters plot to kill the youngest by burying her in a snake hole. Tabadiku finds her there and revives her. She then kills the six eldest sisters. Eventually Tabadiku becomes king, and his wife bears a son.

This fairy-tale-like story is one of many such stories found around the world in which a hero or heroine makes an apparently poor marriage match but is ultimately rewarded for humility and constancy. The fate of the six jealous and scheming elder sisters is an echo of Cinderella's horrid stepsisters and of similar characters in many other traditions. In the story of Tabadiku, these characters suffer a dire punishment for their wrongdoing, while in the more sanitized tradition of the European fairy tale, punishment is usually the less drastic banishment from the kingdom or perhaps marriage to a lowly or otherwise undesirable suitor.

Related entries: Cinderella; Fairy Tale Heroes; Goose Girl, The; Spiewna

References and further reading

Aman, S., *Folk Tales from Indonesia*, Jakarta: Djambatan, 1976.
Knappert, J., *Myths and Legends of Indonesia*, Singapore: Heinnemann, 1977, pp. 168–170.

Tabagnino the Hunchback

Italian Bolognese version of an ancient tale in which the hunchbacked hero outwits an ogre, thus saving the kingdom and receiving a reward from the grateful king. Once again, this is a variation on the theme of the unlikely or unpromising hero or heroine, a motif met with throughout the world. The unlikeliness may take various forms, such as youth and indolence (Jack the Giant-Killer, Osborn Boots), apparent stupidity (the Jack of "Jack and the Beanstalk"), lowly social position (Cinderella), physical form, including size, or lack of it (Tom Thumb), or physical deformity, as in the case of Tabagnino. In all cases, the hero or heroine displays unsuspected qualities that may include bravery, cleverness, kindness, strength, and so on, and that allow him or her to overcome whatever obstacles appear and to succeed. Importantly, success of this kind is always rewarded in folklore, usually by wealth, position, marriage, or by all three. Tabagnino is appointed secretary to the king, who holds him always in high esteem.

Related entries: Boots; Cinderella; Fairy Tale Heroes; Jack; Jack and the Beanstalk; Jack the Giant-Killer; Lusmore; Tom Thumb

References and further reading

Calvino, I. (trans. Martin, G.), *Italian Folk Tales: Selected and Retold by Italo Calvino*, New York: Harcourt Brace Jovanovich, 1980 (1956), pp. 157–162.

Crane, T., *Italian Popular Tales*, Boston and New York: Houghton Mifflin and Co., 1885; reprint, Detroit: Singing Tree Press, 1968.

Tam Lin

The legendary Tam Lin is a central figure in a famous Scots and English ballad of that name. One day he meets a spirited young woman, Janet (in some versions Lady Margaret), fathering a child upon her. In response to her father's concern to learn the name of her lover, Janet says he is not "an earthly knight" but "he's an elfin grey"; moreover, as a version given by Child (anglicized here) puts it:

The steed that my true-love rides on
Is lighter than the wind;
With silver he is shod before,
With burning gold behind.

The ballad moves on in like poetic style to recount how Janet returns to the place she had met Tam Lin, usually Carterhaugh, with the intent of killing the unborn baby because of its nonhuman fathering. Tam Lin appears and assures her that he is indeed an earthly knight, having been captured by the queen of the fairies seven years before and held in thrall by her and her court ever since. What is more, he says, the coming night is Halloween, the seventh anniversary of his capture, and the fairies pay a tithe to hell at the end of every seven years. "I am so fair and full of flesh," he says to Janet, "I fear it be myself." Tam Lin asks Janet to rescue him from the fairy court when he rides with them at the midnight hour. He tells her how to recognize him in the host. He will ride a milk-white steed and be dressed in a certain manner. He also tells her what will happen. In their efforts to stop him from returning to his own kind, the fairy folk will turn Tam Lin into many unpleasant things. He tells Janet that no matter how horrible he appears, she must hold onto him, and in the end she will win him back.

That night Janet goes to Miles Cross, the appointed place, to await the passing of the fairy court. "About the middle of the night she hear[s] the bridles ring" and waits until the rider on the milk-white steed approaches, whereupon she runs over, pulls him down, and covers him with her green mantle, as Tam Lin had bidden her to do. Observing this, the fairy queen is furious. She turns Tam Lin into a snake, a lion, a bear, a burning brand, and other loathsome creatures and objects. But true to her promise, Janet holds tight through all these trials until the queen finally turns Tam Lin into a naked man and Janet wins the battle and her lover. The fairy queen then curses Janet and Tam Lin:

Had I known, Tam Lin, she said,
What this night I would see,
I'd have taken out your two grey eyes
And turned you to a tree.

As with many ballads, although the male is nominally the hero it is often the female who displays the most courage in pursuing, holding, or otherwise helping her true love. While names, places, and the exact details of these events change from version to version, Tam Lin is a well-known ballad. The basic story of the ballad has been traced back to the Greek legend of the forced marriage of Thetis and Peleus appearing in the *Iliad*, traditionally dated to c. 750–725 B.C., versions of which have been recovered in story form from Cretan oral tradition. Variations on the theme of the human in fairyland are also widespread in folklore.

Related entries: Fairy Tale Heroes; Mab, Queen; Shape-Shifters; Thomas the Rhymer

References and further reading

Briggs, K., *The Fairies in Tradition and Literature*, London: Routledge and Kegan Paul, 1967.

Buchan, D., *Scottish Tradition: A Collection of Scottish Folk Literature*, London: Routledge and Kegan Paul, 1984, pp. 159–164.

Child, F. J., *The English and Scottish Popular Ballads*,

5 vols., New York: Dover, 1965 (1882–1898), vol. 1, pp. 335–358, no. 39.

Jacobs, J. (ed.), *English Fairy Tales*, London: The Bodley Head, 1968, pp. 297ff; reprint of *English Fairy Tales* (1890) and *More English Fairy Tales*, 1894.

Wilson, B., *Scottish Folk Tales and Legends*, Oxford: Oxford University Press, 1960 (1954), pp. 41–45.

Tametomo

Minamoto Tametomo is a twelfth-century Japanese warrior and archer of legend. Strong and violent, even in youth, during a fit of anger he cuts the head off his favorite dog. The head flies up into a tree overhanging Tametomo and his samurai servant and kills a large snake about to attack the men below. Seeing this, Tametomo regrets his act and, together with the servant, buries the dog. Similar stories are told of other Japanese heroes, and faithful animal legends are well known throughout the world, for example in India (the faithful mongoose) and Wales (Gellert). Tametomo is the uncle of Yoshitsune, another celebrated Japanese folk hero.

Related entries: Ahay; Gellert; Hood, Robin; Hou Yi; Ivanovich, Dunai; Warriors; Yoshitsune; Yuriwaka

References and further reading

Dorson, R., *Folk Legends of Japan*, Rutland, VT: Charles E. Tuttle, 1962, pp. 166–167.

McAlpine, H. and W., *Japanese Tales and Legends*, Oxford: Oxford University Press, 1958.

Tar, Jolly Jack

See Jack Tar, Jolly

Tardanak

Legendary Russian peasant hero who outwits and kills the seven-headed monster, Yelbeggen. One day Tardanak is working in the fields when Yelbeggen comes past and commands Tardanak to jump into the sack he is carrying. Knowing what fate is in store for him, yet also knowing that it is pointless to resist, Tardanak does as the monster tells him. Some time later, Yelbeggen grows tired and goes to sleep. Tardanak seizes his chance to escape, refilling the monster's sack with flowers and shrubs and escaping back home. The monster awakes but, not realizing that his prey has escaped, goes home to his brood of seven-headed monster children, thinking that he has plenty for them to eat. When they open the sack they discover that Tardanak has escaped, and Yelbeggen then returns to the farm and commands him to jump into the sack again, which Tardanak does reluctantly. Yelbeggen does not sleep on the way home this time. As soon as he gets there, he hangs the sack from the ceiling and leaves to collect firewood so that he can cook Tardanak.

While Yelbeggen is away, the little monsters are curious about the sack and come close to it. Tardanak asks them if they would like to play, but they refuse. He tempts them further by promising to make them some feathered arrows, and they untie the sack and release him. He immediately cuts off all the little monsters' heads, hides them behind the kitchen bench, and throws their bodies into the cauldron. Then he digs a hole in the ground and hides in a corner until Yelbeggen returns with the firewood. The monster sees the remains of his children in the pot but assumes that these are Tardanak's grisly bits, so he lights the fire and calls the children in to supper. But, of course, they do not answer, despite repeated calling. The monster then goes to the kitchen bench and discovers the severed heads of his children. Realizing that Tardanak has done this, he steps outside and roars out from his seven heads, "Where are you, Tardanak?" Tardanak replies that he is inside the house stoking the fire. Yelbeggen rushes back inside but cannot see Tardanak. In a rage, Yelbeggen rushes round searching for Tardanak. Eventually, he sees the hole Tardanak has dug in the ground. Sure that he can now wreak a terrible revenge on Tardanak, Yelbeggen thrusts his seven heads into the hole, deeper and deeper, his slashing teeth in search of Tardanak, until his heads are so deep they are stuck inside the hole. Then Tardanak rushes out of his hiding place and pours the boiling mixture from the pot all over Yelbeggen, killing the monster. Tardanak returns home and continues plowing his fields.

The slaying of the monster's (or other form of villain) progeny by the hero, usually followed by the slaying of the monster itself, is a frequently encountered theme in folklore. In this story, the ordinary hero displays unexpected cleverness and courage in defeating Yelbeggen and in ridding the world of his brood. After performing this service for humanity, Tardanak returns to his lowly job of plowing as if nothing untoward has occurred—an everyday hero.

Related entries: Dragon-Slayers; Fereyel; Marendenboni; Villains
References and further reading
Baumann, H., Hero Legends of the World, London: Dent and Sons, 1975 (1972), pp. 39–42.
Elstob, E. and Barber, R. (trans.), Russian Folktales, London: Bell and Sons, 1971. First published as Von Lowis of Menar, A. (trans.) and Olesch, R. (ed.), Russische Volksmärchen, 1959.

Tawhaki
See Culture Heroes

Taylor, William
Probably fictional hero of an English poaching song: "There's none like young Taylor . . ." While out poaching one winter night, Taylor and his companions are discovered by a group of gamekeepers. All the poachers run away, except William Taylor, who fights the keepers, leaving five of them dead. He is captured only when another keeper hits him over the head from behind. William Taylor is tried and hung, having refused to name his companions.

Poachers feature as heroic figures in many British folk songs and tales of the eighteenth and nineteenth centuries, though they are rarely named. Instead, they are presented as representatives of their type. Because of beliefs about common rights and the usurpation of those rights over centuries, the rural poor rarely considered poaching to be a crime, at least not morally. Poachers, like many outlaws, are thus generally presented in heroic manner. A poacher prosaically named "Bill Brown," killed by the keepers, is the hero of another poaching song in which the purpose of his being identified is to commemorate the circumstances of his death, presented as murder at the hands of vicious keepers. Folk heroes of this mundane, essentially localized type are ex-

tremely common in the world's traditions and are often associated with resistance to perceived oppression.

Related entries: Heroes of Struggle; Local Heroes; Ludd, Ned; Outlaws; Rebecca
References and further reading
Hamer, F. (comp.), Garner's Gay, London:EFDS Publications, 1967, p. 34.
Ives, E. D., George Magoon and the Down East Game War: History, Folklore, and the Law, Urbana and Chicago: University of Illinois Press, 1988.
Lloyd, A., Folksong in England, New York: International Publishers, 1970 (1967), pp. 245–246.

Teach, Edward
So-called from his luxuriant dark whiskers, Blackbeard (Edward Teach, ?–1718) terrorized America's Atlantic and Caribbean waters early in the eighteenth century. His piracy and brutality eventually led to his capture and hanging in 1718. Legends about Blackbeard include the inevitable lost treasure stories and the stories that his skull was made into a drinking cup and that his headless corpse swam around his ship three times. Blackbeard was hardly heroic, but a representative of the type of the great villain

"Death of Blackbeard the Pirate," a print sent from Virginia in 1791 showing Blackbeard fighting with sailors. (Corbis)

whose deeds are so outrageous that they acquire a kind of manufactured heroism. And, of course, to the fraternity of pirates and their ilk, Blackbeard was a hero.

Related entries: Bluebeard; Kidd, Captain; Outlaws; Villains; Warriors
References and further reading
Beck, H., *Folklore and the Sea*, Middletown, CT: Wesleyan University Press, 1973, p. 53.
Mullen, P., *I Heard the Old Fisherman Say: Folklore of the Texas Gulf Coast*, Logan: Utah State University Press, 1978, p. 111.

Tell, William

Like the English Robin Hood, the fourteenth-century Swiss William Tell remains a figure of myth rather than history. Like many such figures, though, his legend has great staying power, not only in the folk legends and ballads of his home country but in literature, film, television, and children's literature and theater, as well as in Schiller's famous play *Wilhelm Tell* (1804).

In the basic story, the Austrian occupiers of Switzerland in the province of Uri are commanded by a despotic individual named Herman Gessler. Wishing to further humiliate the Swiss, Gessler orders a pole set up in the village square. He has his hat nailed to the top of the pole and commands that all the Swiss must bow to it. Tell, a noted archer, refuses, and so Gessler has Tell's son tied to a tree with an apple upon his head. Tell is told to split the apple in two with an arrow or bolt (some versions speak of bows, others of crossbows). Tell takes two bolts and with the first performs this near-miraculous feat. Gessler then asks why Tell had taken two bolts. The hero replies that if he had killed his own son he would have used the second bolt to kill Gessler. Doubly embarrassed, the outraged Gessler has Tell arrested and placed aboard a ship for prison. In a storm, Tell escapes from the ship by leaping onto a rock still known as "Tell's Leap." He returns to his home region and kills Gessler, providing the spark that ignites a general Swiss uprising, the eventual expulsion of the Austrians, and the establishment of the Helvetian Confederation.

These events are not recorded before the late fifteenth century, nearly two hundred years

William Tell tries to shoot an apple off the top of the boy's head. (Bettmann/Corbis)

after they are supposed to have occurred. Nor is there any other evidence for the existence of a historical figure named William Tell. There is also little consistency in the dates and other details of the Tell legend. Although sources sometimes give a precise date for Tell's archery feat (1307), there is little or no evidence that such an event ever took place.

The apple-shooting incident is found in mythology and folklore around the world, including that of ancient Greece, Denmark, England, northern Europe, Russia, Persia, Turkey, Mongolia, and India. Like Robin Hood, Tell inhabits the shady area between the outlaw hero and the national hero.

Related entries: Culture Heroes; Heroes of Struggle; Hood, Robin; National Heroes
References and further reading
Fiske, J., *Myths and Mythmakers*, London: Trubner, 1873, chap. 1, "The Origins of Folk-Lore."
Lee, F. H. (comp.), *Folk Tales of All Nations*, London: Harrap, 1931, pp. 910–912.

Thieves

Thieving is not an obvious subject for celebration, but there are many heroic thieves in folklore, including outlaw heroes, some tricksters, and, most well-defined perhaps, the "master thief." Master thieves feature in a group of folktales distributed widely throughout European and Asian cultures. The core of all master thief stories is the lazy, good-for-nothing hero, often the youngest of three brothers, who trumpets his belief that he is a master thief. A king, or other usually aristocratic authority figure, hears of this claim and sets the young boaster the task of stealing the king's horse or other belongings. Through one or more ruses, the master thief succeeds in this basic task. He is then set the more difficult task of perhaps stealing linen from the bed of the king's wife and also stealing her finger ring. Despite the cleverness with which he goes about this task, usually tricking the king out of the bedroom so that he can enter and accomplish the feat, the master thief is generally caught at this point and sentenced to death. However, again with his cleverness, the master thief escapes by duping someone else to take his place.

Master thief motifs are old and often found in literary and mythological sources, most obviously in stories of the Greek figure Autolycus, son of Hermes and stealer of his neighbors' flocks. Around 450 B.C., the historian Herodotus included a master thief story in his historical writing. Master thief motifs are often attached to characters, such as Ali Baba. They may also be combined with other tale types, such as those involving ogres, as in "Jack and the Beanstalk," and tricksters. There are variations on this basic theme in many cultures, including the Irish, Indian, Native American, Scots, Afro-American, Mexican (Ite'que), French, Turkish, and Middle Eastern.

Related entries: Baba, Ali; Halid; Jack the Giant-Killer;
Jones, Galloping; Liars; Outlaws; Tricksters

References and further reading

Briggs, K. (ed.), A Dictionary of British Folk-Tales in the
English Language, 2 vols., London: Routledge and
Kegan Paul, 1970–1971, vol. 2, pp. 408–410.

Hunt, M. (trans. and ed.), Grimm's Household Tales
(with the author's notes and an introduction
by Andrew Lang), 2 vols., London: George Bell
and Sons, 1884, pp. 324–331.

Thomas the Rhymer

Thomas Rymour of Erceldoune (c. 1220–1297), was also known as "True Thomas" for his prophetic abilities. Thomas the Rhymer features in Scots ballads as a man who was bewitched by the fairy queen (sometimes called the queen of heaven). In most versions of the ballad including the excerpts from Child given here, the fairy queen takes Thomas up onto her horse and rides with him:

> For forty days and forty nights
> They rode through red blood to the knee,
> And he saw neither sun or moon,
> But heard the roaring of the sea.

The fairy queen gives Thomas bread and wine, and he falls asleep, his head in her lap. While he sleeps, she shows him a vision of two roads. One is narrow and "thick beset with thorns and briers." This is the path of righteousness, though few care to take it. The other road is broad and easy to travel, but it is the path of wickedness and leads men straight into the gates of hell. She takes Thomas on into Elfland itself, swearing him to secrecy about what he might see there on pain of never returning to his "ain countrie." Thomas is then dressed in elfin clothes and "shoes of velvet green," then

> Till seven years were past and gone
> True Thomas on earth was never seen.

Thomas the Rhymer is closely related to the various traditions of sleeping heroes, and he was still commonly spoken of in Scotland at least as late as the middle of the nineteenth century.

Related entries: Isabel, Lady; Mab, Queen; Magicians;
Sleepers; Tam Lin

References and further reading

Briggs, K., The Fairies in Tradition and Literature, London:
Routledge and Kegan Paul, 1967.

Briggs, K. and Tongue, R. (eds.) Folktales of England,
London: Routledge and Kegan Paul, 1965.

Buchan, D., Scottish Tradition: A Collection of Scottish Folk
Literature, London: Routledge and Kegan Paul,
1984, pp. 143–146.

Child, F. J., The English and Scottish Popular Ballads, 5

vols., New York: Dover, 1965 (1882–1898), vol. 1, pp. 317–329, no. 37.

Lloyd, A., *Folksong in England*, New York: International Publishers, 1970 (1967), p. 145.

Wilson, B., *Scottish Folk Tales and Legends*, Oxford: Oxford University Press, 1960 (1954), pp. 8–17.

Thousand and One Nights

See Arabian Nights, The

Thunderbolt

See Ward, Frederick Wordsworth

Tian Kaijiang

See Gongsun Jie

Tingkir, Jaka

See Warriors

Tom the Piper's Son

English nursery rhyme character. His well-known ditty, as given by Halliwell, goes:

Tom he was a piper's son,
He learnt to play when he was young,
And all the tune that he could play
Was "Over the Hills and Far Away";
Over the hills and great way off,
The wind shall blow my top-knot off.

So begins a famous English nursery rhyme featuring the doings of this legendary young piper whose music made people, pigs, and cows dance. Probably derived from an earlier tale usually known as "The Friar and the Boy," this nursery rhyme is perhaps an echo of the Pied Piper of Hamelin.

Related entries: Children's Folk Heroes; Pied Piper, The; Tom Thumb

References and further reading

Halliwell, J., *The Nursery Rhymes of England*, London: The Bodley Head, 1970 (1842), pp. 32, 75.

Opie, I. and P. (eds.), *The Oxford Dictionary of Nursery Rhymes*, Oxford: Oxford University Press, 1951, pp. 408–412.

Tom Thumb

English-language children's folklore hero. The theme of the midget hero is well known in the folklore of Europe, Japan, and India. The English version, first in print in 1621 but undoubtedly existing in oral tradition for some time before, involves Tom Thumb. In his often extensive stories, Tom generally gets involved in hoax and similar situations appropriate to his diminutive stature, such as falling into a pudding mixture and almost being baked. He is also looked after by fairies, and he arrives at King Arthur's court after being swallowed by a salmon. In some versions, Tom Thumb dies in a fight with a spider.

Related entries: Arthur; Children's Folk Heroes; Fereyel; Kihuo; No Bigger Than a Finger

References and further reading

Briggs, K. (ed.), *A Dictionary of British Folk-Tales in the English Language*, 2 vols., London: Routledge and Kegan Paul, 1970–1971, vol. 1, pp. 531–533.

Hallett, M. and Karasek, B. (eds.), *Folk and Fairy Tales*, Ontario: Broadview Press, 1996, pp. 85–93.

Halliwell, J., *The Nursery Rhymes of England*, London: The Bodley Head, 1970 (1842), pp. 32–41.

Klipple, M., *African Folktales with Foreign Analogues*, New York: Garland, 1992, pp. 237–238.

Massignon, G. (ed.), Hyland, J. (trans.), *Folktales of France*, Chicago: University of Chicago Press, 1968, p. 80.

Tooth Fairy, The

Fictional children's heroine, a fairy who is said to take away the milk teeth of children when they fall out, often leaving a small payment. The Tooth Fairy tradition has been little studied and only reached the literature in the late 1950s. However, many people have recollections of this custom, and of its heroine, going back to at least the 1920s. There are numerous variations on the tradition, which has become increasingly commercialized in recent years and which, despite the existence of folk traditions concerning the disposal of teeth, may well have a commercial origin. The basic elements involve taking a milk tooth after it has fallen out and leaving it under a pillow or in a glass of water when the child goes to sleep at night. In the morning, the tooth has disappeared, and a small coin may be found in its place, "payment" from the tooth fairy. While there is some linking of fairies and children's teeth in Robert Herrick's *Hesperides* (1648), there appears to be no such thing as a "tooth fairy" before the twentieth century. Nonetheless, there is an extensive body of world folklore dealing with the disposal of baby teeth. In his 1928 work *Folklore of the Teeth*, L. Kanner surveyed the various customs involving the casting away of milk teeth. These customs include such things as crushing the teeth, in which state they may be ingested by the parent, usually the mother, or, as in Macedonia, the teeth may be thrown to the crows. There is a wide and frequent association of milk teeth disposal with mice, which may have biblical origins. In his otherwise wide-ranging and comprehensive survey, Kanner makes no mention of a "tooth fairy."

Related entries: Children's Folk Heroes
References and further reading
Kanner, L., *Folklore of the Teeth*, New York: Macmillan, 1928, pp. 47–53, passim.
Opie, I. and P., *The Lore and Language of Schoolchildren*, Oxford: Oxford University Press, 1959, p. 305.
Opie, I. and Tatum, M. (eds.), *A Dictionary of Superstitions*, Oxford: Oxford University Press, 1989, p. 394.
Simpson, J. and Roud, S., *A Dictionary of English Folklore*, Oxford: Oxford University Press, 2000, pp. 364–365.

Tortoise

Main trickster figure among Nigerian Yoruba, Edo, and Ibo peoples, also found in West and East African traditions as a less significant figure. Tortoise is also the main trickster figure in Cuba. Tortoise tales invariably show the hero using his wits to win out, usually by escaping from certain death and, in the process, killing those who would bring about his demise. However, as with most tricksters, Tortoise also falls foul of the trickery of others, as in the story of the Tar Baby, also told of Anansi and many other African and African-American tricksters.

Related entries: Anansi; Hare; Rabbit; Spider; Tricksters
References and further reading
Arnott, K. (ed.), *African Myths and Legends*, London: Oxford University Press, 1962, pp. 13–15, 22–24.
Dadié, B. (trans. Hatch, C.), *The Black Cloth: A Collection of African Folktales*, Amherst: University of Massachusetts Press, 1987 (1955), pp. 52–61.
Knappert, J., *Myths and Legends of Botswana, Lesotho, and Swaziland*, Leiden: Brill, 1985, pp. 238–240.
Smith, A. M. (coll. and ed.), *Children of Wax: African Folk Tales*, New York: Interlink Books, 1991 (1989), pp. 75–78.
Todd, L., *Tortoise the Trickster and Other Folktales from Cameroon*, London: Routledge and Kegan Paul, 1979.

Tricksters

Tricksters form one of the largest groups of all hero types and are found in most folk traditions. They are identified by their propensity to play tricks upon their fellows, to engage in buffoonery, and, in many cases, to break taboos. Whatever the exact nature of their activities, mild or serious, tricksters continually transgress the boundaries of what is considered proper, normal, or simply sensible. They have a more than passing relationship to the fool or clown of literary and dramatic traditions and display a similar capacity to get away with outrageous acts that would land ordinary folk in deep, perhaps terminal, trouble.

Tricksters are especially important in Native American and African traditions, where they may also have the roles of culture/creator figures. In these traditions, the essential ambiguity of the trickster is perhaps best displayed. In the lore of the African Ashanti, for instance, Anansi is a culture hero, the creator of the moon and of significant customs, yet there are tales in which Anansi is responsible for bringing debt to the Ashanti and even for human greed. Yo, a Dahomean (West Africa) trickster depicted as a human rather than as an animal, displays gross and undisciplined behavior.

Similar apparent contradictions and paradoxes can be found in the trickster figures of most cultures. Bamapana, the trickster hero of the Australian Murngin people (Arnhem Land), is usually presented as a merry but stupid figure, often referred to as the "crazy man" who violates many cultural taboos, including that of incest.

Tricksters may also be related to numskulls and so act in stupid ways, though they usually manage to redress any damage done to them. Pak Dungu is the simple but honest hero of a Javanese tale in which he is tricked into selling the family buffalo for a mere 50 rupiah, its real worth being 250 rupiah. After his wife angrily commands him to get the money back, the not-so-stupid Pak Dungu tricks the three men who took advantage of him into believing that a small bell can magically pay for any food they buy at eating houses. He gets his 250 rupiah and his revenge on the three men.

Trickster traditions are among the oldest traditions of folklore, with tricksters and trickster motifs easily identified in myth cycles and in early folklore and literary sources. Tales about the major Arabic trickster Goha, related to the Turkish Hodja, date earlier than the eleventh century, and the frequency with which trickster figures are found in indigenous myth suggests a considerable longevity of this heroic type. The Syrian trickster is named Djuha; the Afghani equivalent is Abu Khan; and Compair Lapin is the Louisiana African-American name for the character more widely known as Brer Rabbit. Piercala is the Flemish trickster, similar to the German Till Eulenspiegel, and appears in seventeenth-century ballads and other lore, often with a moralistic conclusion.

Trickster characteristics may also be observed in heroes of other types, such as outlaws, magicians, and warriors, an indication of the profound significance of trickster figures and their actions in cultures of all times and places.

Related entries: Abunuwas; Anansi; Bertoldo; Coyote; Culture Heroes; Ero; Eulenspiegel, Till; Gearoidh, Iarla; Gizo; Hare; Hlakanyana; Hodja, The; Jack o' Kent; Jones, Galloping; Kabajan; Magicians; Maui; Monkey; Nanabozho; Numskulls and Noodles; O'Connell, Daniel; Ostropolier, Hershel; Popovich, Aloisha; Quevedo; Rabbit; Ramalingadu, Tenali; Shape-Shifters; Shine; Skorobogaty, Kuzma; Tortoise; Urdemalas, Pedro de

References and further reading

Babcock, B., "A Tolerated Margin of Mess: The Trickster and His Tales Reconsidered," *Journal of the Folklore Institute* 11, no. 3, 1975, pp. 147–186.
Barker, W. and Sinclair, C. (colls.), *West African Folk Tales*, London: Harrap and Co., 1917.
Brun, V., *Sug, the Trickster Who Fooled the Monk: A Northern Thai Tale with Vocabulary*, Scandinavian Institute of Asian Studies Monograph 27, London: Curzon Press, 1976, pp. 10–15, passim.
Christen, K., *Clowns and Tricksters: An Encyclopedia of Tradition and Culture*, Santa Barbara: ABC-CLIO, 1998.
Dhar, A., *Folk Tales of Afghanistan*, New Delhi: Sterling Publishers, 1982, pp. 114–128.
El-Shamy, H., *Folktales of Egypt*, Chicago: University of Chicago Press, 1980, pp. 224–225.
Green, T. (ed.), *Folklore: An Encyclopedia of Beliefs, Customs, Tales, Music, and Art*, 2 vols., Santa Barbara: ABC-CLIO, 1997, pp. 811–814.
Harrison, A., *The Irish Trickster*, Sheffield: Sheffield Academic Press, 1988.
Jurich, M., *Scheherazade's Sisters: Trickster Heroines and Their Stories in World Literature*, Westport and London: Greenwood Press, 1998.
Koutsoukis, A. (trans.), *Indonesian Folk Tales*, Adelaide: Rigby, 1970, pp. 118–124.
Newall, V., "The Hero as a Trickster: The West Indian Anansi," in Davidson, H. (ed.), *The Hero in Tradition and Folklore*, The Folklore Society Mistletoe Series 19, London: The Folklore Society, 1984, pp. 46–89.
Radin, P., *The Trickster: A Study in American Indian Mythology*, New York: Philosophical Library, 1956.

Troy, Johnny

Known only through a song, Johnny Troy is especially interesting as an example of an Australian hero who has a busy life in American tradition, while having apparently dropped from Australian folklore altogether. In his ballad, excerpted below, Troy is brave, defiant, and altogether a fine specimen of the noble convict and outlaw hero. Troy is also mentioned in company with other convict and bushranger heroes in Francis (Frank the Poet) MacNamara's "The Convict's Tour of (or 'to') Hell," composed in 1839, as well as in the best-known of the ballads about convict bushranger Jack Donohoe. Johnny Troy's lengthy ballad resonates with many of the characteristics of the outlaw hero and begins with an unequivocal assertion of his heroism, continuing in like vein to his fearless death on the scaffold when:

His friends and all that knew him,
Wept for this fearless boy:

"There goes our brave young hero
By the name of Johnny Troy!"

Why this fine hero ballad retains a hold in American tradition but has not taken hold in Australia or been found in British lore is a mystery that is still as intriguing as it was when Kenneth Porter first drew attention to it in 1965.

Related entries: Christie, Francis; Donohoe, Jack; Hall, Ben; Johns, Joseph; Kelly, Edward; Morgan, Daniel "Mad Dog"; Outlaws; Thunderbolt; Wild Colonial Boy

References and further reading

Porter, K., "'Johnny Troy': A 'Lost' Australian Bushranger Ballad in the United States," *Meanjin Quarterly* 24, June 1965.

Seal, G., *The Outlaw Legend: A Cultural Tradition in Britain, America, and Australia*, Melbourne: Cambridge University Press, 1996, pp. 82–85.

Tsarevich, Ivan

Ivan Tsarevich, or Ivan the Prince, was the third son of Czar Vyslav of Gorokh and Vasilisa Prekrasnaya. He is generally considered to be a major figure of Russian heroic folklore, winning numerous victories over monsters and assorted enemies. His most famous legendary doings are his quest to catch the fire bird Zhar-Ptitsa, notorious for stealing golden apples from the Czar's garden, and his battles against Koshchei in order to win the hand of Marya Morevna.

Related entries: Culture Heroes; Dragon-Slayers; Koshchei; Morevna, Marya; Muromets, Ilya; Popovich, Aloisha; Vladimir; Warriors

References and further reading

Alexander, A., *Russian Folklore: An Anthology in English Translation*, Belmont, MA: Nordland Publishing Co., 1975, pp. 154–169.

Curtin, J. (ed.), *Myths and Folktales of the Russians, Western Slavs, and Magyars*, New York: Benjamin Blom, 1971 (1890), pp. 203–217.

Duddington, N. (trans.), *Russian Folk Tales*, London: Rupert Hart-Davies, 1967, pp. 91–102.

Turpin, Richard

Born in either 1705 or 1706 (sources differ on the date), Richard ("Dick") Turpin was the son of an Essex innkeeper or farmer. He became a butcher and, when his business declined, took to stealing cattle to stock his shop. Discovered in this illegal sideline, Turpin joined a gang of smugglers and deer poachers, taking part in unpleasant crimes of violence, rape, and robbery. A reward of 100 guineas was eventually offered for members of the gang, who were soon betrayed and mostly captured. Turpin escaped this time and many times thereafter. From early 1735 he embarked on a career as a highwayman, mostly in and around Epping Forest.

It is from this period that the Turpin legend originates. While his previous activities had been largely submerged in the relative anonymity of the criminal gang, his appearance in official records of various kinds as a notorious individual established a basis for his later heroization. The interaction of the official and the unofficial that characterizes the creation and continuation of most folk legends can be seen operating here.

After shooting his accomplice, Tom King, Turpin was obliged to escape from the London area. Turpin eventually traveled to Yorkshire, going under the assumed maiden name of his mother, Palmer, and living as a horse stealer and dealer. Turpin's sudden disappearance was no doubt the cause of popular and official speculation, a fact that further contributed toward the development of his legend. Turpin's popularity and his growth as folk legend at this time is attested in the writings of Abbe le Blanc, who tells us that in 1737 stories about Turpin's valor, generosity, and general good bearing were being told wherever he went while living in England.

In 1739 "Palmer" was arrested, according to tradition, following an argument that led him to shoot a publican's gamecock. Palmer's true identity was discovered when he wrote from jail to his friends and relations in Essex. His handwriting was recognized, and someone informed on him. Eventually he was tried and convicted to hang for the stealing of a mare and foal. He paid five men to follow the cart transporting him to the York gallows on April 7, 1739, where he died bravely in heroic fashion. The "mob" then rescued Turpin's body from the officials in order to save it from the humiliation of dissection by the surgeons. They buried the highwayman in a proper grave filled with quicklime to foil any attempt at exhumation. Immediately the belief arose that Turpin had been restored to life and, in accordance with many hero traditions, lived on.

As was the custom of the period, the chapbook publishers had their wares already printed and on sale even before the unfortunate suffered. Turpin was commemorated immediately in *The Trial of Turpin*, an often reprinted account of his legend, and in many subsequent works, remaining a stock character of popular literature. The ballad "Turpin's Appeal to the Judge," given by Humphreys, contains lines echoed throughout Turpin's legend as the Robin Hood of his day: "The Poor I fed, the Rich likewise / I empty sent away." The broadside version of the song usually known as "Dick Turpin and the Lawyer" tells the story of Turpin outwitting a lawyer, robbing an excise man (customs officer), a judge, and a Palmer. A nineteenth-century addition to the Turpin legend was the story of the faithful, powerful, and, in folk tradition, magical steed "Black Bess." On this mount Turpin was supposed to have made the famous one-day ride to York. This sentimental tearjerker was issued around 1865 and is a good example of subsequent media romanticization of Turpin. The song was popular in the United States in oral versions mostly derived from the broadside.

Turpin's popularity and, even if less markedly, that of other highwayman heroes was not restricted to the ballad mongers, the tellers of tales, and those forced to the depths and margins of society, like the "Gypsies" who frequently honored their children with Turpin's name. Richard Turpin's doings, real and imagined, were exploited in respectable forums like Harrison Ainsworth's *Rookwood* (1834), a work that molded the well-known highwayman hero into the figure of romance.

As far as folklore is concerned, Turpin was an escaper and disguiser, was betrayed by accomplices on two occasions, and mostly conducted himself with appropriate highwayman aplomb and dignity up to and including his public execution, where he died "game," behaving, as *The Gentleman's Magazine* of April 7, 1739, described the highwayman's final performance:

> in an undaunted Manner; as he mounted the ladder, feeling his right Leg tremble, he stamp'd it down, and looking round about him with an unconcerned Air, he spoke a few Words to the Topsman, then threw himself off, and expir'd in five Minutes.

Since this appropriate if heroic death, or at least its appropriate reporting, the legend of Turpin has proliferated in place-names, local legends, and beliefs. There are inns, jails, castles, hills, and valleys all over England where Dick Turpin is alleged to have slept, stayed, hidden, robbed, or simply to have ridden by, through, or over.

Related entries: Bonney, William; Brennan, William; Hood, Robin; James, Jesse; Kelly, Edward; Outlaws; Swift Nicks

References and further reading
Barlow, D. *Dick Turpin and the Gregory Gang*, London: Phillimore, 1973.
Humphreys, A. L., "The Highwayman and His Chap-Book," *Notes and Queries*, 4 May 1940–8 June 1940.
Neuberg, V., *Popular Literature: A History and Guide*, Harmondsworth, Middlesex: Penguin, 1977.
Seal, G., *The Outlaw Legend: A Cultural Tradition in Britain, America, and Australia*, Melbourne: Cambridge University Press, 1996, pp. 8, 52–62, 155.
Smith, Captain A., *A Complete History of the Lives and Robberies of the Most Notorious Highwaymen*, 1719.

u

Uncle Sam

A name said to have originated from a man who supplied beef to the United States Army during the War of 1812, one Samuel ("Uncle Sam") Wilson (1766–1854). By the 1850s, Uncle Sam, with his thin frame, long hair, whiskers, striped pants, and swallowtail jacket, had replaced the earlier Brother Jonathan as the established symbol of the United States of America. The initials "U.S." are said, in folklore, to be those of Uncle Sam, who is a good example of a patriotic, national folk hero.

Related entries: Chapman, John; National Heroes; Washington, George

References and further reading

Alver, B., "Folklore and National Identity," in

Uncle Sam— "I Want You" by James Montgomery Flagg (Library of Congress)

Kvideland, R. and Sehmsdorf, H. (eds.), *Nordic Folklore: Recent Studies*, Bloomington and Indianapolis: Indiana University Press, 1989, pp. 12–20.

Leach, M. (ed.), *Funk and Wagnall's Standard Dictionary of Folklore, Mythology, and Legend*, London: New English Library, 1975. Abridged one-volume edition of *Funk and Wagnall's Standard Dictionary of Folklore, Mythology, and Legend*, 2 vols., New York: Funk and Wagnall, 1972, p. 1149.

Urashima

Japanese fisherman hero who marries the daughter of the Dragon King of the Sea. Urashima lives in their undersea kingdom for what seems to him a short time and then wishes to return to his home for a visit. His wife gives him a box or bottle and tells him not to open it if he hopes to see her again. When he returns home, he finds that three hundred years have passed and that everything and everyone he knew have long disappeared. In shock, he opens the bottle or box. A puff of smoke issues forth, and he dies on the beach between the sea and the land. The smoke was his life spirit. In some versions of the story, Urashima turns into dust. This story is popular in Japan and is said to date from at least the eighth century A.D.

The theme of a great deal of time passing in the real world while the hero, less frequently the heroine, sleeps or is otherwise detained in another place, as in this case, is found in the traditions of many cultures. Despite this wide diffusion, though, there is little similarity of meaning or moral derived from such incidents.

Related entries: Peterkin; Sleepers; Thomas the Rhymer; Van Winkle, Rip

References and further reading

James, G. (ed.), *Japanese Fairy Tales*, London:

Macmillan, 1923, pp. 209–214. First published as *Green Willow and Other Japanese Fairy Tales*, London: Macmillan and Company, 1910, pp. 209–214.

Lee, F. H. (comp.), *Folk Tales of All Nations*, London: Harrap, 1931, pp. 690–696.

Seki, K. (ed.), Adams, R. (trans.), *Folktales of Japan*, London: Routledge and Kegan Paul, 1963, pp. 111–114. First published in Japanese in 1956–1957.

Tyler, R., *Japanese Tales*, New York: Pantheon Books, 1987, pp. 154–156, 283–284.

Urdemalas, Pedro de

Also known as Pedro el de Malas, Pedro de Urdemales, Peter the Mischief-Maker, or simply Pedro, this hero is a Spanish trickster popular in Mexico and Latin America. He is often a young rogue who has various adventures and escapades in his travels, outwitting those who try to take advantage of him, in the great tradition of the tricksters of all cultures. In one of his stories, Pedro appears as the younger brother of Juan, both sons of a poor man. Juan decides to leave home to seek his fortune, and as he leaves his father advises him never to trust a jagged stone, a lapdog, or a blond man. On his travels Juan has some minor misfortunes with a jagged stone and a lapdog and then comes to the house of a blond man. Forgetting his father's advice, he contracts with the man to work as his servant, with an arrangement that the first party to become angry will have three strips of flesh ripped from the back of his neck to his backside. Also, Juan will be paid when the cuckoo sings. Juan's first chore is to fetch wood, and in the process he becomes angry with his blond master, who then takes the three strips of flesh to which he is entitled, whereupon Juan dies.

Back home, Pedro and his father wonder what has become of Juan, and so Pedro sets out to find him, armed with the same advice his father had given Juan. Like Juan, Pedro comes to a stream with jagged stones. But instead of trying to use them as stepping-stones, he crosses without touching the stones, and so avoids the injuries they had inflicted upon Juan. Then he meets a lapdog, but instead of letting it bite him, as Juan had, Pedro kills it. Finally, Pedro comes to the home of the blond man who had

killed Juan, and he makes the same bargain. However, unlike the unfortunate Juan, Pedro remembers his father's words and warns himself to be careful. The blond man gives Pedro the same task he had given Juan. But instead of getting angry at being unable to bring the cartload of wood through either of the two gates, Pedro uses a pickax to smash a new gateway in the blond man's wall. Seeing the damage, the blond man grumbles, whereupon Pedro asks if he is angry. The master replies that he is not angry, although he does not like what he has seen.

As the story continues, the blond man gives Pedro further impossible tasks, including killing a giant, all of which Pedro succeeds in accomplishing, much to the disgruntlement of the master. The result of all these incidents is financial disaster for the blond man and his wife. Accordingly, they decide that they must get rid of Pedro because he is eventually going to ruin them. The blond man tells his wife to stand at the window and sing like a cuckoo so that Pedro will know that his wages are due and will then go away. Early the next morning, the wife stands at the window and sings like a cuckoo. Pedro gets his shotgun and shoots her dead, an act that finally causes the blond man to lose his temper. Pedro then takes the three stripes of flesh from his back, and like Juan, the man dies, at which point Pedro sends for his father, and they take over the house and property of the blond man and his wife.

Some migratory legends have become attached to the figure of Pedro, producing relatively lengthy and complex stories, as in the above example and in "Pedro Urdemales Cheats Two Horsemen," given by Pino-Saavedra. Another lengthy Pedro tale is the version of the frequently collected "The Smith Outwits the Devil"—given in Dorson's selection of regional American folklore, *Buying the Wind*—in which the role of the blacksmith is taken by "Pedro de Ordimalas." But there are also many shorter, usually single-episode tales in which Pedro robs priests, inadvertently kills his mother, and outwits gringos and murderous *arrieros* (mule drivers). In another story, Pedro slyly alerts the villagers to their own ignorance by setting up a school for the children. The only thing Pedro teaches the children is to say "You can't, and I can't either." After a while, the parents, wanting to know what their children have learned at school, ask them to read something to them. The children answer as Pedro has taught them: "It says you can't, and I can't either." The villagers soon realize that their children are saying that neither they nor their parents can read. Enraged, the parents go to have it out with the schoolteacher, only to find that Pedro has disappeared in a cloud of dust, together with his wife.

In some stories Pedro dies, and in one of these he goes to purgatory, where he annoys the demons by, perversely, doing good. Pedro eventually desires to see or visit heaven and manages to sneak in, only to have God turn him to stone, making him the doorstep of heaven.

As with many folk figures, the origins of Pedro are at best murky. The most common version of the name is composed of the Spanish words urdir, meaning "to warp," and mal, meaning "evil." Cervantes (1547–1616) wrote a play titled Pedro de Urdemalas, based on preexisting tales, and a not very heroic, but similar character named Juan de Urdimales appeared in mid-nineteenth century popular Mexican literature.

Related entries: Abunuwas; Ero; Eulenspiegel, Till; Gearoidh, Iarla; Hodja, The; Jack o' Kent; Ostropolier, Hershel; Quevedo; Tricksters

References and further reading
Clarkson, A. and Cross, G. (eds.), World Folktales, New York: Charles Scribner's Sons, 1980, pp. 293–297.
Dorson, R., Buying the Wind: Regional Folklore in the United States, Chicago: University of Chicago Press, 1964, pp. 429–434.
Dorson, R. (ed.), Folktales Told around the World, Chicago: University of Chicago Press, 1975, pp. 558–563.
Espinosa, A. (coll.), Cuentos populares espanoles, 3 vols., Buenos Aires, Argentina: Espasa-Calpe, 1946–1947, vol. 3, pp. 158–159.
Hansen, T., The Types of the Folktale in Cuba, Puerto Rico, the Dominican Republic, and Spanish South America, Berkeley: University of California Press, 1957.
Miller, E., Mexican Folk Narrative from the Los Angeles Area, Austin: University of Texas Press, 1973, pp. 333–335.
Paredes, A., Folktales of Mexico, Chicago: University of Chicago Press, 1970, pp. 155–160.
Pino-Saavedra, P., Folktales of Chile, Chicago: University of Chicago Press, 1967, pp. 219–233.
Robe, S. (ed.), Hispanic Folktales from New Mexico: Narratives from the R. D. Jameson Collection, Mythology and Folktale Studies 30, Berkeley and Los Angeles: University of California Press, 1976, pp. 73–76, 119–120, 185–187, 200.
Toor, F., A Treasury of Mexican Folkways, New York: Crown Publishers, 1947, pp. 529–531.

V

Väinämöinen

Main hero of the *Kalevala*, the Finnish epic of verse, song, and ballad. Väinämöinen and his brothers Ilmarinen and Lemminkäinen are the sons of Kaleva, a misty mythical character identified with Finland itself. Kalevala is also the name of the land in which this hero and his offspring live. Väinämöinen is a culture hero who sows barley and fells trees. He journeys through the world, encountering many other characters with whom he frequently enters into magical contests. In a dream, his mother tells him to journey north in search of a bride. He travels to the distant northern land of Pohjola, pursued by the evil Joukahainen, who attacks him, causing Väinämöinen to fall into the sea. He is rescued by Louhi, mistress of Pohjola. In gratitude, Väinämöinen undertakes to have his brother, Ilmarinen the smith, fabricate the Sampo, a magical mill that produces plenty. In return, Louhi pledges her daughter, the maid of Pohjola, to Ilmarinen. However, Väinämöinen himself falls in love with the maid and undertakes various magical quests and impossible tasks—including an expedition to the home of the dead, Tuonela—in order to win her. Barely escaping from Tuonela, the hero is then eaten by a giant, whom he also escapes. In the course of these adventures, he learns many magical songs and much wisdom about the creation of all things. Thus armed, he returns to Pohjola in his magical boat and voyages back to Kalevala with the maid.

On the way, they catch a large pike, and from its jaws Väinämöinen fashions a *kantele*, a Finnish dulcimer, and plays it, bringing all living things to the spot to better appreciate the music and to weep at its beauty. The first kantele is lost, but Väinämöinen makes another of birch wood. However, the mistress of Pohjola is not impressed with the hero's command of magic and sends disease and a bear against Kalevala. Väinämöinen protects the land from these threats and also recovers the sun and moon stolen by Louhi. After various further adventures, he becomes leader of the region of Karelia but is displaced by a child born to the virgin Marjatta. Väinämöinen leaves the country, declaring that he will return to help his people. He sails away to another world between heaven and earth, leaving behind his kantele and his songs.

The numerous stories that make up the *Kalevala* were partly collected and entirely assembled in 1835 by Elias Lönnrot. There are many elements that appear to be unique to Finnish tradition, and many others that are shared with other cultural traditions, notably those of the other Scandinavian countries as well as Russia, Lithuania, and, especially, Estonia, where Kaleva, or Kalevi, is also the first hero. His son is named Kalevipoeg and is portrayed as a friendly giant. He was the central object of F. R. Kreutzwald's epic assemblage of legends in *Kalevipoeg* (1857–1861).

Related entries: Culture Heroes; Lemminkäinen; Musicians; National Heroes; Puuhaara, Antti

References and further reading

Aarne, A. and Thompson, S., *The Types of the Folktale: A Classification and Bibliography*, Folklore Fellows Communication 184, Helsinki: Academia Scientiarum Fennica, 1961. Translated and enlarged from the 1928 edition written by S. Thompson.

Kirby, W. F., *The Hero of Estonia*, 2 vols., London: n.p., 1895.

Kvideland, R. and Sehmsdorf, H. (eds.), *Scandinavian Folk Belief and Legend*, Minneapolis: University of Minnesota Press, 1988.

Lönnrot, E. (comp.), Magoun, F. (trans.), *The Kalevala, or Poems of the Kalevala District*, Cambridge: Harvard University Press, 1963.

Valentine, Saint

Famous as the patron saint of lovers, the historical St. Valentine is an uncertain figure. He may have been a Roman doctor and priest who was martyred in the reign of Claudius II. Or he may have been a bishop of Turni executed in Rome about 273 A.D. Or both these persons may have been one. In any case, long before the existence of such a saint, the ancient Greeks are said to have celebrated February 14—or the equivalent on their calendar—as the day of the goddess Hera, symbolic of femininity and marriage, and the Romans continued the custom in relation to their deity Juno. The day, then, already had associations with love and marriage when the historical Valentine was martyred, although the association between his feast day and young love appears to date only from the fourteenth century.

St. Valentine has a long history of commemoration within the Christian church, although the "Saint" is often dropped nowadays, a reflection of the day's secular and almost totally folkloric significance for young—and not so young—lovers. Cards bearing traditional messages (often insulting) are exchanged, printed in the newspapers, or published on the Internet. Gifts of flowers and sweets are exchanged. St. Valentine's Day is a popular one for folkloric predictions about the future of one's love life. The day is also widely observed by the wearing of a yellow crocus, the flower of St. Valentine. Yellow birds seen flying on St. Valentine's day are also believed to be a good omen. St. Valentine is the patron saint of travelers, of the young in general, and of beekeepers, and his name is believed to be efficacious when invoked against the plague, fainting, and epilepsy. This belief places the enigmatic but useful figure of St. Valentine in the category of healer and also emphasizes his status as an everyday religious folk hero, similar to St. Christopher, also a patron saint of travelers, or to St. Nicholas, in his other folk identity as Santa Claus.

Related entries: Helpers; Religious Heroes
References and further reading
Knowlson, T., *The Origins of Popular Superstitions and Customs*, Hollywood: Newcastle Publishing Co., 1972 (1910), pp. 17–19.
Opie, I. and Tatum, M. (eds.), *A Dictionary of Superstitions*, Oxford: Oxford University Press, 1989, pp. 419–420.
Simpson, J. and Roud, S., *A Dictionary of English Folklore*, Oxford: Oxford University Press, 2000, pp. 373–374.

Van Winkle, Rip

The hero of Washington Irving's 1819–1820 literary reworking of an ancient and widespread folklore theme, the sleeper or sleepers who snooze through time. Rip is a happy-go-lucky, unassuming Dutch-American peasant from the Catskill Mountains. One day Rip meets a strangely dressed traveler carrying a keg up a mountain. Rip kindly helps the traveler with his task. When they reach the mountaintop, they come upon a group of people dressed in the same odd way as the traveler and playing ninepin. Rip drinks from the keg and falls asleep. When he wakes, everything around him seems strange. He returns to the village in fear of his wife's scolding—she is known for her sharp tongue—only to discover that he has been asleep for twenty years. His wife is now dead and his children grown. Rip then lives the rest of his life in comfortable indolence. It turns out that the strangely dressed people Rip met on the mountain were the ghosts of the explorer Henrik Hudson and his men.

There are many tales from many traditions that use the themes of a sleeping hero and of strange games being played by unusual people in distant and elevated areas. The Chinese Wang Chih and the German Peter Klaus are two examples, and Irving almost certainly based his reworking on the German story in which the Thuringian goatherd chases one of his goats into a cave where twelve ancient knights are playing skittles. He watches the game and drinks from a tankard of wonderful-tasting liquid and then goes to sleep. He wakes twenty years later with a long beard and, on returning to the village, finds that the members of his generation have all died. He then discovers his daughter, now a grown woman with a child of her own. She recognizes him; he kisses his grandchild; and the villagers welcome him back after his long sleep.

Related entries: Merlin; Peterkin; Seven Sleepers, The;
  Sleepers; Thomas the Rhymer; Urashima
References and further reading
Baker, M., *Tales of All the World*, London: Oxford
  University Press, 1937, pp. 208–218.
Irving, W., *The Sketch Book*, New York: C. S. Van
  Winkle, 1819–1820.

Vasilisa

Legendary heroine of a popular Russian story.
In some versions of the story Vasilisa is from a
wealthy background, in others she is poor.
Nevertheless, the initial situation is the same.
The beautiful Vasilisa's mother dies, giving her
daughter the deathbed gift of a small doll. Vasilisa's father remarries a woman who has two
daughters of her own, whom she favors over
Vasilisa. Mother and daughters force Vasilisa to
do all the chores—chop the wood, lay the fire,
light the fire, cook the meals, clean the floors,
and so on, in a never-ending round of menial
tasks aimed at destroying the good looks that
the stepmother and stepsisters envy. But despite
their worst efforts, Vasilisa gets more beautiful
every day. Vasilisa's secret is the doll, which
magically accomplishes most of her many tasks.

One day, Vasilisa's father has to leave home
for an extended period. Left alone, the four
women must fend for themselves. One night in
a howling storm, the stepsisters and Vasilisa
find that they have run out of light for their
weaving, knitting, and spinning. The only way
to get light is to go to the Baba-Yaga's house.
The Baba-Yaga is an evil witch who lives in the
forest and eats people. The stepsisters are afraid
to go, so they force Vasilisa to undertake the
dangerous journey. She is distraught, but the
doll says that she will look after Vasilisa and tells
her not to worry.

On her way through the forest, Vasilisa sees
three strange horsemen, the first is dressed in
white, the second in red, and the third all in
black. The Baba-Yaga's hut is fenced with
human skulls whose eye sockets glow in the
darkness, and the gates and locks are bones and
teeth. The Baba-Yaga appears flying in a mortar,
swinging a pestle, and sweeping her way with
a broom. "I smell Russian flesh," she cries,
sniffing the air. Then she asks Vasilisa what she

wants. Vasilisa says that she has come for a light,
and the Baba-Yaga takes her into the hut, telling
Vasilisa that she must work. As she enters the
house, Vasilisa is menaced by a birch tree, a
dog, and a cat, but the witch orders them not
to touch her. Then the witch asks her maid for
food and eats a gluttonous meal, giving Vasilisa
only a lump of bread. The Baba-Yaga then sets
Vasilisa the task of picking out the black bits
from a sack of millet, saying that if she misses
even one black fragment, she will be gobbled
up. Then the witch goes to sleep. Vasilisa is distraught, but again her doll comforts her, telling
her to go to sleep and that when she wakes in
the morning everything will be done. While
Vasilisa sleeps, the doll calls upon birds to pick
over the millet and put the good seed into a
sack. Just as the task is completed, day breaks
and the white horseman rides by the gate.
When the Baba-Yaga wakes, she is angry that
the apparently impossible task had been completed. She then tells Vasilisa to separate a sack
of peas and poppy seeds and flies off in her
pestle just as the sun rises.

At this moment, the red horseman rides by.
This time the doll accomplishes the task by
calling up all the local mice. As night falls, the
household waits for the Baba-Yaga to return
and the black horseman rides by. When the
Baba-Yaga returns and finds that Vasilisa has
again completed the task, she is angry and tells
Vasilisa to go to bed. From her bed Vasilisa
overhears the witch telling the maid to light
the fire because she is going to roast the young
girl in the morning. Again the doll tells Vasilisa
what to do. Vasilisa goes to the maid and gives
her a silk handkerchief, asking her for help. The
maid agrees, saying that she will make the
witch sleep longer than usual while Vasilisa
makes her escape. The maid also tells Vasilisa
not to be afraid of the three horsemen: the
white one represents day; the red one, sunrise;
and the black one, night. Vasilisa makes her way
past the cat, which she pacifies by throwing it
a pie; past the dog, which she calms with a
piece of bread; and then past the birch tree,
which she ties with ribbon. She runs out
through the gate of bones, first greasing the
creaky hinges. As she begins to run into the

dark forest, the black horseman rides by, and, despite what the maid had told her, she is frightened. She asks her doll what to do, and the doll tells her to take one of the skulls from the fence and to find her way by the glowing light of its eye socket.

Back at the Baba-Yaga's house, the witch finally awakens and discovers that Vasilisa has escaped. She asks the cat why it did not stop Vasilisa, and the cat replies that in all the years she has served the Baba-Yaga the witch has never given her pie. When she asks the dog why it did not bite Vasilisa, the dog says that it has never had more than a bone and that the girl gave him bread, and so he let her pass. The birch says that it has never before had its branches bound, and the gate says that the Baba-Yaga has never bothered to grease its hinges. Enraged, the Baba-Yaga beats the cat, the dog, the tree, and the gate so much that she forgets all about Vasilisa, who by now has made her way home. When she gets inside, her stepsisters are angry that she has been gone so long, leaving them with little or no light. They grab the skull and place it in the house for a light. But the skull's eye sockets fix on the stepsisters and their wicked mother and burn them wherever they go. By morning, all three have been burned to cinders. Vasilisa buries the skull, and on that spot red roses grow. Then she goes into town and lives with an old woman.

One day she asks the woman to bring her flax, and with it Vasilisa weaves a wonderfully fine garment. The old woman takes it to the palace and sells it to the prince, who is so impressed that he orders two shirts to be made from it. Amazed by the skill and beauty of the shirts, the prince sends for their maker. When he sees the beautiful Vasilisa, he falls in love with her and makes her his wife. When Vasilisa's father returns, he and the old woman also go to live in the palace, along with the doll that Vasilisa always carries with her. There they all live happily together.

This horror story with a happy ending contains elements of "Snow White," "Hansel and Gretel," and "Cinderella" and features the classic villain of Russian folklore, the cannibalistic witch Baba-Yaga. The impossible tasks of separating such things as wheat and chaff, grains of sand, and so on are often met with in hero lore, especially when the hero or heroine is assisted by animals, often birds, as in the case of Sanykisar. Vasilisa is blessed with a good many helpers in her story, especially the doll, whose wisdom and magic—the gift of the heroine's mother—save Vasilisa from the Baba-Yaga and, in telling her what to do with the skull, bring about her release from the domination of the wicked stepmother and stepsisters. From that point, Vasilisa is free to link up with her prince charming, and all the good characters of this wonder tale live happily ever after in the traditional manner. Vasilisa's lack of a family is resolved by her marriage and the return of her father. The evil characters get their justly fatal deserts. The Baba-Yaga is outwitted and faces mutiny from her helpers. At the end of the tale, the rightful order of things is restored, albeit at a higher level, as Vasilisa is elevated to the aristocracy through winning the love of the prince.

Related entries: Baba-Yaga; Cinderella; Fairy Tale Heroes; Helpers; Snow White; Victims; Villains
References and further reading
Afanas'ev, A. (comp.), Guterman, N. (trans.), *Russian Fairy Tales*, New York: Pantheon Books, 1945, pp. 439–447.
Alexander, A., *Russian Folklore: An Anthology in English Translation*, Belmont, MA: Nordland Publishing Co., 1975, pp. 141–153.
Baumann, H., *Hero Legends of the World*, London: Dent and Sons, 1975 (1972), pp. 11–16.
Curtin, J. (ed.), *Myths and Folktales of the Russians, Western Slavs, and Magyars*, New York: Benjamin Blom, 1971 (1890), pp. 124–136.
Duddington, N. (trans.), *Russian Folk Tales*, London: Rupert Hart-Davies, 1967, pp. 112–120.

Veusters, Father Joseph de

See de Veusters, Father Joseph

Victims

A group of heroes, real and mythic, best known for their status as the usually tragic victims of violence, intrigue, oppression, or other malevolence. These figures include the usually female protagonists of murder ballads, such as the American "Pretty Polly," in which Polly is foully murdered by her lover "young Willie" so that he can avoid responsibility for her pregnancy. Willie lures Polly to a lonely spot one dark night and murders her, a common plot of many such stories. A similar character from British balladry is Maria Marten, central figure of a nineteenth-century murder case known as the Red Barn murder. The culprit was finally tracked down, tried, and hanged. These events were the subject of a sensational ballad that reflected the tremendous public interest in the case and that reportedly sold over a million copies. Versions of the song are still collected in Britain, America, and Australia.

Further afield, the child dervish Shiruyeh is the hero of an Iranian cycle of tales in which he is cast into a well by his brothers, jealous of their father's affection for him. Shiruyeh is rescued and travels to distant lands, having various adventures along the way, including the slaying of lions and dragons. Shiruyeh is another of the widely distributed class of heroes who suffer at the hands of their jealous siblings, natural or otherwise.

Some victims of political intrigue have become celebrated in folklore, including Mary Queen of Scots and the Chinese brother and sister duo Ahay and Ashma. Victim heroes may also be the result of usually high-profile disasters, such as Lord Franklin's ill-fated expedition to find the Northwest Passage. Sometimes, usually in wonder tales, the central characters are just unlucky, as in the widespread "Halfchick."

Heroes may also begin their stories as victims but, due to their own efforts, make good, as in the case of many Jack, Jean, Hans, and Ivan stories. Or they may come out on top through help from others, as do Siung Wanara and Cinderella. In these instances, the victimization of the later-to-be hero provides the basis for the narrative force of the tale and for the interest of the audience in seeing if and how the hero overcomes such obstacles.

Related entries: Ahay; Amala; Aniz; Apekura; Armstrong, Johnnie; Ashma; Barleycorn, John; Bindieye, Jacky; Cap o' Rushes; Catskin; Chokanamma; Cinderella; Darcy, Les; Dojrana; Fairy Tale Heroes; Fatima; Franklin, Lord; Geordie; Gongsun Jie; Green Princess, The; Gretel; Halfchick; Hansel; Isabel, Lady; Ivan the Mare's Son; Jane, Queen; Judy; Kandek; Kihachi; Mau and Matang; Pied Piper, The; Scheherazade; Shine; Siung Wanara; Tam Lin; Thomas the Rhymer; Xishi; Ye Xian

Villains

Heroes cannot exist without villains. Generally these figures represent evil or wrongdoing of some kind and span an amazing array of types, including magicians, sorcerers, ogres, giants, fairies, elves, dwarves, witches, demons, the Devil, temptresses, dragons, giant worms, and snakes. The purpose of such characters is to oppose, obstruct, or undermine the hero and in many cases to personify the principle of evil. As such, villains represent a force that is out of kilter with the rightful order of things, and accordingly, in folklore at least, they must be overcome so that the natural balance can be restored.

The Baba-Yaga (Iaga) of Russian and Slavic tradition exemplifies most of the characteristics of folk villains. She is an evil, often cannibalistic witch figure, similar in many respects to the witch who plans to eat Hansel and Gretel. She lives away from humankind, deep in remote forests, and has great magical powers that she uses to attain her usually wicked ends, although like some other villains of the supernatural type, the Baba-Yaga is occasionally helpful to heroes.

Similar in many ways are the tall, big-bosomed wild women of Polish tradition known as Dwi-Wozoney, and as the Diva-ta-Zena in Bulgarian belief. Despite their frigid hearts, these women are passionate lovers, often enslaving younger humans. They may tickle humans to death, and, like the fairies, they are said to substitute changelings for human children. They are symbolic of the villainy that heroes must overcome in all traditions.

The principle of evil may be present in anything and anywhere and, in a wide range of possibilities and permutations, is a constant feature of world folklores. It is most vividly and consistently a principal component of folktales, though it may also be important in ballads and other forms of folk expression, such as traditional drama, proverbial sayings, folk belief and customs.

Related entries: Baba-Yaga; Bluebeard; Devil, The;
    Dragon-Slayers; Giant-Killers; Kidd, William;
    Koshchei; Magicians; Ogres; Outlaws; Pied
    Piper, The; Punch; Stuart, Prince Charles
    Edward; Teach, Edward; Thieves; Wulgaru

Vladimir

Also known as Vladimir Bright Sun or Fair Sun,
the legendary Prince Vladimir of Kiev is a powerful figure closely associated with the greatest
Russian folk heroes Aloisha Popovich, Ilya
Muromets, Dobrynya Nikitich, and Ivan Tsarevich. Prince Vladimir of Kiev is usually said to
be a composite of two historical figures, the
tenth-century Vladimir I and the twelfth-
century Vladimir II, both noted rulers and
Russian empire builders. Prince Vladimir is an
unusual hero whose behavior is not that generally associated with heroism. He treats people
unfairly and is something of a coward. He
throws the great hero Ilya Muromets into a
dungeon. When the dragon Tugarin publicly
outrages the prince's wife, it is Aloisha, not
Vladimir, who faces up to the beast. Despite
these serious failings, the various Russian heroes, or *bogatyrs*, respect Vladimir's position as
ruler and, despite revolts and aggressions of
various kinds, continue to support him.

Vladimir, his bogatyrs, and their deeds are all
represented in the *byliny*, the epic verse legends
chanted by peasants over many centuries, embroidered from one generation and one per-
former to the next in the manner of the oral
epics of many nations and cultures. The Russian
byliny represent an idealized golden past in
which Russian heroes defend their country and
its highest ideals. As with most traditions of this
sort, historical accuracy is not the point of the
exercise. Rather it is the celebration of the legendary deeds of arms, love, and ethnic preser-
vation that matter. While the byliny are fading as
a living art form, the stories they tell have been
recycled in literary and other forms and are still
well known among contemporary Russians.

Related entries: Culture Heroes; Muromets, Ilya;
    National Heroes; Nikitich, Dobrynya; Popovich,
    Aloisha; Tsarevich, Ivan
References and further reading
Cavendish, R. (ed.), *Legends of the World*, London:
    Orbis, 1982, pp. 291–292.
Elstob, E. and Barber, R. (trans.), *Russian Folktales*,
    London: Bell and Sons, 1971. First published as
    Von Lowis of Menar, A. (trans.) and Olesch, R.
    (ed.), *Russische Volksmärchen*, 1959.
Ivanits, L., *Russian Folk Belief*, Armonk/London: M. E.
    Sharpe Inc., 1989, pp. 13, 17, 19, 29.

Vseslavevich, Volkh

Also known as "Volga," this legendary Russian
shape-shifter and strongman features in folktale
and ballad. His mother, Marfa Vseslavevna, is
impregnated by a serpent. When Volkh is born
there are earthquakes and the brightest moon
ever seen in the sky. When only an hour and a
half old, he asks his mother to dress him in
armor, and by the age of fifteen he has an army
of 300, some versions say 7,000, youths. He
takes his army to India, using his various magical powers, including turning his soldiers into
ants, to make them victorious and to feed
them. His army slaughters all resistance in
India, apart from 300, some versions say
7,000, beautiful maidens whom his soldiers,
having settled in the new land, take as wives.
Volkh takes the queen of the maidens as his
wife and rules wisely over all. It has been suggested that Volkh is to some extent based upon
the historical personage Prince Vseslav of
Polotsk, who attacked and captured Kiev in
1068.

Related entries: Shape-Shifters; Warriors
References and further reading
Cavendish, R. (ed.), *Legends of the World*, London:
    Orbis, 1982, pp. 292–293.
Elstob, E. and Barber, R. (trans.), *Russian Folktales*,
    London: Bell and Sons, 1971. First published as
    Von Lowis of Menar, A. (trans.) and Olesch, R.
    (ed.), *Russische Volksmärchen*, 1959.

W

Ward, Frederick Wordsworth

Frederick Wordsworth Ward, "Thunderbolt," was born in Windsor, News South Wales, in or around 1836. An Australian bushman and stockman of high caliber, Ward was imprisoned for horse-stealing in 1856 and sentenced to prison on Cockatoo Island, the jail from which no one had been able to escape. In company with another inmate, highway robber Fred Britten (with whom "Thunderbolt" is often confused in folklore), Ward escaped the island in September. The escapees stole clothing and headed north toward the New England area, where Ward officially began his career as a bushranger.

Between the time of his escape and the day he was shot and killed by a trooper policeman in May 1870, "Thunderbolt," "Captain Thunderbolt," and "Captain Ward," as he was variously known, managed to pursue a career of intermittent robbery, becoming a celebrated local hero. He is said to have handed money back to those who needed it more than he did, and, as his ballads indicate, he was perceived by many to operate in a style and manner befitting the bushranging and highwayman heroes of the past. One version of a toast or poetic introduction said to have been composed and used by Ward himself goes:

My name is Frederick Ward, I am a native
   of this isle;
I rob the rich to feed the poor and make
   the children smile.

Folk traditions regarding "Thunderbolt" are well in keeping with the general run of those attached to outlaw heroes and include the stories of his alleged return of gold to a number of children at Moonbi and of his hidden trea-sure. Most importantly, the traditions also include the belief that Ward was not really killed in 1870 and that he lived on in Australia, New Zealand, America, or Canada.

> *Related entries:* Christie, Francis; Donohoe, Jack; Hall, Ben; Johns, Joseph; Kelly, Edward; Local Heroes; Morgan, Daniel "Mad Dog"; Outlaws; Wild Colonial Boy
>
> **References and further reading**
> Rixon, A., *The Truth about Captain Thunderbolt, Australia's Robin Hood*, Sydney: G. M. Dash, 1940 (and various subsequent editions).
> Williams, S., *A Ghost Called Thunderbolt*, Woden, ACT: Poppinjay Press, 1987.

Warriors

Warriors are perhaps the most obvious folk heroes and are the type most frequently included in hero anthologies. The individual who bears arms against enemies either human, animal, or supernatural is found in all cultures, in all times, and in all places. The essential attribute of the warrior is bravery, though this attribute is usually accompanied by other skills and abilities, including great strength, prowess with one or more weapons, leadership, and the use of magical powers, including shape-shifting and sometimes the helpful intercession of the supernatural. These features, in one combination or another, allow heroes to perform magnificent deeds of a usually gory kind.

Mighty warriors often have roles as heroes of other types. Figures such as Arthur or Ogier the Dane share some similarities with military heroes. A great number of warrior heroes are also culture or national heroes credited with the establishment and/or the defense of a culture, ethnicity, or nation against outside threats of invasion and enslavement, as is the case with the legendary Armenian Hayk, the handsome hero of the Armenian people. Hayk is a giant who delivers his people from the Babylonians and organizes them to fight against subsequent invaders of their mountainous homeland. Hayk is symbolized by a bow and a triangular arrow, a reference to his military success with such a formation of his forces. The Armenian people call themselves Hay in his honor and call their country Hayastan. Some warrior heroes have trickster abilities, as in the case of the Russian Aloisha Popovich. Despite these other attributes, however, it is their warlike abilities that are uppermost in the lore of warrior heroes, and whatever their other roles warrior heroes are a distinctive group with their own special claims to celebration.

Warriors also often become rulers. Jaka Tingkir, son of Kebo Kananga II of Java, is a central figure in a group of legends in which he performs many feats of bravery and eventually becomes sultan of Java. Warrior heroes who are also culture heroes can develop legends of "the once and future king" type associated with Arthur. The Serbian Ivan Crnojevic resisted the Turkish advance and is said to be sleeping in the embrace of the mountain nymphs in a cave near Obod, southern Montenegro, awaiting the need to awaken for his people's defense. It is popularly said that thunder is a product of his anger. Warriors almost always meet heroic deaths. The Croatian Ivo, for instance, is said in song and tale to have defeated 50,000 Turks with a force of only 800 soldiers. Ivo dies in his mother's arms, and with a priest's blessing, just as he finishes telling her of his glorious battles against the Turks.

Warriors are predominantly males, though women may sometimes be found participating in war through the subterfuge of dressing as men, as in the case of the Italian Fanta-Ghiro', the Chinese Mulan, and the female drummers and other women who don the soldier's uniform in English-language traditions. The probably mythic women warriors usually referred to as "Amazons" are an exception, as is the Siberian heroine Altyn Aryg, to the otherwise almost total domination of this category of the heroic by males.

Related entries: Alexander the Great; Alfred the Great;

Arthur; Aryg, Altyn; Barbarossa; Batradz; Benbow, Admiral; Benkei; Bonaparte, Napoleon; Cid, El; Culture Heroes; Danske, Holger; Dog-Nyong, General Gim; Gam-Czan, Marshall Gang; Gearoidh, Iarla; Gongsun Jie; Guy of Warwick; Havelock the Dane; Ivanovich, Dunai; Kihuo; Kraljevic, Marco; Mac Cumhal, Finn; Matthias, King; Mergen, Erkhii; Military Heroes; Molo; Muromets, Ilya; Nikitich, Dobrynya; O'Malley, Grace; Outlaws; Popovich, Aloisha; Rákóczi; Rasalu; Santa Anna, General Antonio López de; Tametomo; Tsarevich, Ivan; Väinämöinen; Vseslavevich, Volkh; Warriors; Washington, George; Wolfe, General James; Women Dressed as Men; Xiang Yu; Yamato; Yoshitsune; Yuriwaka

References and further reading

Cavendish, R. (ed.), *Legends of the World*, London: Orbis, 1982.

Curcija-Prodanovic, N., *Heroes of Serbia*, London: Oxford University Press, 1963.

Downing, C. (trans. and ed.), *Armenian Folk-Tales and Fables*, London: Oxford University Press, 1972.

Mijatovies, C. (ed. and trans.), *Serbian Folklore*, New York: Benjamin Bloom, 1968 (1874).

Petrovich, W., *Hero Tales and Legends of the Serbians*, London: Harrap, 1914.

Talbot, A., "The Hero as a Warrior: Sigfrid," in Simpson, J. (trans.), *Legends of Icelandic Magicians* (with an introduction by B. Benedikz), London: Brewer/Rowman and Littlefield, The Folklore Society, 1975, pp. 16–29.

Washington, George

Historical hero of the United States of America. George Washington (1732–1799) was commander in chief of the Continental army during the American Revolution, then the first president of the United States of America. Washington's generalship was the subject of considerable celebration at the time, through his subsequent political career, and after his death. "Lady Washington's Lament," a popular ballad on the themes of Washington's death, begins (as recorded in Jackson):

> When Columbia's brave sons called my
>   hero to lead 'em,
> To vanquish their foes and establish their
>   freedom,
> I rejoiced at his honours, my fears I
>   dissembled,

President George Washington depicted on horseback with sword drawn (Library of Congress)

At the thought of his danger, my heart how
    it trembled!
O my Washington! O my Washington!
O my Washington! all was hazardous!

While this song has, fortunately perhaps, not found a place in folk tradition, Washington's heroic image is alive and well and is probably best known from the apocryphal story in which a young George chops down a cherry tree. When asked by his father if he has done the deed, George is unable to tell a lie and confesses. The story reflects the popular need to believe in the moral superiority of the leader. This folk legend grew up after Washington achieved his status as a national and military hero. It is a good example of the process in which the historical deeds of a real person are retrospectively given additional desired qualities through folk inventions. Such traditions are often referred to as "invented traditions," and so they are. The fact that they are invented, though, does not preclude them from being taken up and widely believed, if they fulfill one or more communal needs. With the national heroes of many countries and peoples, as with Washington, there is

a strong popular desire to see the leader as a figure who embodies whatever moral virtues his—less often her—people espouse.

Related entries: Celebrity Heroes; Military Heroes; National Heroes

References and further reading

Hobsbawm, E. and Ranger, T. (eds.), *The Invention of Tradition*, Cambridge: Cambridge University Press, 1984.

Jackson, G., *Early Songs of Uncle Sam*, Boston: Bruce Humphries, 1933, pp. 79, 95–97.

Watch, Will

English smuggling hero of an early nineteenth-century sentimental sea ballad. Watch is mortally wounded in battle but returns to his darling Susan to be buried where the billows dash and the sea winds loudly blow. The illegal trade of smuggling has generated numerous, highly romanticized heroes, though most of these are criminals and so celebrated only by the communities who support smuggling. Will Watch is a commercialized version of such local characters. Like Jolly Jack Tar and other similar idealized representations, Watch is a consequence of mass media stereotyping designed—usually successfully—to appeal to growing market segments. In the case of Will Watch and the like, such markets were those of the eighteenth and nineteenth centuries, though essentially the same processes can be seen in the way modern media such as newspapers, magazines, radio, television, and film create and sustain idealized figures.

Related entries: Celebrity Heroes; Heroes of Struggle; Nautical Heroes; Outlaws

References and further reading

Whall, W. (coll. and ed.), *Sea Songs and Shanties*, London: Brown, Son, and Ferguson, 1910, pp. 39–41.

White Lady

Also known as Bai Suzhen, this Chinese heroine is an ancient white snake that has acquired the power to change herself into a beautiful young woman. She has a faithful green snake maidservant named Xiaoqing, also able to transform herself into human form. Suzhen falls in love with an apothecary named Xu Xian in the city of Hangzhou. Suzhen and Xu Xian marry and live happily for some months, until the Abbot of Jinshan Monastery, Fahai, an evil man jealous of the couple's happiness, informs Xu Xian that his wife is a demon and that he is in mortal danger. Xu Xian then gets Suzhen drunk, whereupon she returns to her snake form before his eyes. He falls into a deep shock.

Recovering from her drunkenness, White Lady risks her life to steal a divine medication to restore her beloved husband's health. After months of nursing him with the assistance of Xiaoqing, Suzhen restores Xu Xian to his senses. But the wicked Fahia then kidnaps him and holds him in the monastery. White Lady lays siege to the monastery but, as she is heavily pregnant, loses the battle and has to flee with Xiaoqing. In the confusion of battle, Xu Xian escapes from the monastery and later is reunited with Suzhen at the spot where they had first met, Broken Bridge. Not surprisingly, White Lady is unhappy with her husband's earlier betrayal, and Xiaoqing wants to punish him. However, eventually Suzhen and Xu Xian make up and resume life as a married couple. But Fahai has not given up, and after the baby is born, he finds them and uses magic to trap White Lady in Leifeng Pagoda, where she languishes until many years later when the faithful Xiaoqing returns, burning the Pagoda and freeing her mistress.

Related entries: Magicians; Shape-Shifters; Swan
    Maiden; Xiaoqing

References and further reading

Ding Wangdao, *Chinese Myths and Fantasies*, Beijing: China Translation Publishing Company, 1991.
Eberhard, W. (ed.), Parsons, D. (trans.), *Folktales of China*, Chicago: University of Chicago Press, 1965.
Li, N., *Old Tales of China*, Singapore: Graham Brash, 1983 (1981), pp. 12–14.

Whittington, Dick

Perhaps most familiar today as a pantomime figure, the English historical personage Richard Whittington (c. 1358–1423) is a folk symbol of perseverance. From humble origins and assisted by his faithful cat, Dick searches for his fortune on the streets of London, which he has heard are paved with gold. But he can find work only as a lowly domestic servant in the home of a wealthy merchant. Here he is poorly treated by the cook and also plagued by mice in his humble quarters, so he buys a cat for one penny. Dick's master organizes a ship to sail to Barbary on a trading voyage, and he offers his servants a chance to take a share in the enterprise. Dick has only his cat, which he advances as his small contribution to the voyage, while he stays behind. The ship arrives at its destination to find that the local king's palace is infested with rats. Dick's cat is brought to the palace and rapidly eradicates the problem. The grateful monarch buys the ship's cargo for a vast sum, and Dick's cat for ten times more.

While the cat is having these profitable adventures abroad, poor Dick is still suffering the oppressions and humiliations of the cook back in London. Eventually he decides that he has had enough and runs away. He gets as far as Holloway, where he sits down to rest. He then hears the bells of the Church of St. Mary-le-Bow, known colloquially since the seventeenth century as "Bow Bells," ringing, and they seem to be saying: "Turn Again, Dick Whittington, Lord Mayor of London."

Dick decides to go back, and shortly after his return the ship arrives with the earnings of the voyage, making Dick wealthy. He marries his master's daughter and does indeed become lord mayor of London—three times.

The historical Sir Richard Whittington was a mercer from a wealthy family who loaned Henry V large sums of money to pursue his French wars. Undoubtedly assisted by such largesse, Sir Richard was three times lord mayor of London, in 1397–1398, 1406–1407, and 1419–1420. He died without children in 1423, leaving much of his wealth to charity. Sir Richard probably became connected with the widespread folktale motif of the helpful animal, in this case a cat, during the late sixteenth century. There are numerous carvings, stones, and places associated with Dick Whittington all around London and in Gloucestershire, the birthplace of the historical Sir Richard Whittington. The detail of Bow Bells is a seventeenth-century addition to the legend that was perhaps established through his reputation as a friend of the poor. Whatever the reasons for the origins of the Dick Whittington traditions, they provide an excellent example of the local hero gradually accreting appropriate motifs drawn from the international pool of hero folktales.

Related entries: Helpers; Jack o' Kent; Local Heroes; Puss in Boots

References and further reading
Briggs, K., Nine Lives: The Folklore of Cats, New York: Pantheon, 1980.
Clouston, W., Popular Tales and Fictions: Their Migrations and Transformations, 2 vols., Edinburgh and London: William Blackwood, 1887, vol. 2, pp. 65–78.
De Caro, F. (ed.), The Folktale Cat, Little Rock, AR: August House, 1992.
Jacobs, J. (ed.), English Fairy Tales, London: The Bodley Head, 1968, pp. 297ff; reprint of English Fairy Tales (1890) and More English Fairy Tales (1894).

Whuppie, Molly

Heroine of an English tale closely related to "Jack and the Beanstalk." In the extended version published by Joseph Jacobs in 1898, Molly and her two older sisters are abandoned by their parents at a giant's house in the woods because there is not enough food for the whole family. The giant is out, but the giant's wife takes the three sisters in and feeds them. But then the giant returns, roaring, in the traditional manner:

Fee, fie, fo, fum,
I smell the blood of some earthly one

The giant orders the three sisters to stay the night but insists that they all sleep together with his own three daughters in the same bed. The giant puts straw ropes around the necks of Molly Whuppie and her sisters but puts gold chains around the necks of his own children. Molly takes notice of this, and as soon as everyone else has fallen asleep she switches the ropes and the chains. Later, the giant returns with his club and feels for the necks of the children. In the darkness, he assumes that the children with the ropes are Molly and her sisters, and he batters them to death. When he leaves, well

pleased with himself, Molly wakes her own sisters, and they escape, coming eventually to a king's grand home.

The king is mightily impressed with their story and says to Molly that if she can go back and steal the giant's sword, he will give his eldest son in marriage to her eldest sister. Molly agrees and succeeds in stealing the sword. But as she makes her escape the sword rattles, waking the giant, who pursues her to the "bridge of one hair," which Molly can cross but the giant cannot. The giant angrily threatens her never to come again, and Molly takes the sword back to the king, who keeps his promise to wed his son to Molly's oldest sister.

After the wedding, the king says to Molly that he will give his second-oldest son in marriage to Molly's second-oldest sister if she will steal the giant's purse. Again, the obliging Molly agrees and steals his purse. Again the giant awakens and pursues her, and again she escapes across the "bridge of one hair," returning with the purse to the king. The second sister and king's second son are duly married. Then the king says that he will give his youngest son to Molly if she will steal the giant's finger ring. Yet again Molly agrees and goes off to the giant's house. The giant is asleep, and she gets the ring off his finger, but he wakes and catches her. "Now I have caught you, Molly Whuppie, and, if I had done as much ill to you as ye have done to me, what would ye do to me?"

Molly says that she would put herself in a sack with a cat, a dog, a needle and thread, and some shears and then hang the sack on the wall while she went to the woods and got a very thick stick with which to beat her to death. The giant does exactly what the ever-obliging Molly suggests. While he is away getting the stick, Molly cries out: "Oh, if ye saw what I see." The giant's wife, intrigued, asks what she sees. But Molly just keeps on crying out, "Oh, if ye saw what I see." Eventually, curiosity gets the better of the giant's wife and she asks to be taken into the sack so that she can see whatever it is that Molly sees. Molly cuts a hole in the sack with the shears and, taking the needle and thread with her, jumps down onto the floor. She then helps the inquisitive giant's wife inside the sack and quickly sews up the hole.

Of course, the giant's wife sees nothing and begins to cry out to be released, but Molly ignores her and hides behind a door. The giant returns with a large tree and begins to batter the sack on the wall, his wife's cries of protest drowned by the barking of the dog and mewing of the cat. Molly takes this opportunity to run out the back door. The giant sees her and pursues her once again to the "bridge of one hair" over which she escapes. "Woe worth you, Molly Whuppie! Never you come again," he says to her. She replies, as she had on the previous two occasions, rather cryptically: "Never more, carle, will I come again to Spain." Molly takes the ring to the king, is duly married to the king's youngest son, and never sees the giant again.

The complexity of this version of the story is matched by the large number of traditional motifs woven through it, including those associated with other tales, such as the abandonment of the children ("Hansel and Gretel"), the "fee, fie, fo, fum"–chanting giant and his wife ("Jack and the Beanstalk"), the unwitting infanticide of the giant occasioned by Molly's sharpness and bravery (the story of Marendenboni), the return for more ("Jack and the Beanstalk"), the giant's adoption of Molly's own suggestion for her murder ("The Little Goose Girl"), and the tricking of the giant's wife into the sack and her death ("Hansel and Gretel"). As well, there are a number of other traditional motifs here that are found in tales and ballads around the world, including the sword that rattles to warn its owner it is being stolen, the three sisters, the giant's three children, the king's three sons, and the escape over the "bridge of one hair" that is too frail for the giant to cross, which is found in the Miskito Indian tale of Nakali.

Related entries: Fairy Tale Heroes; Gretel; Hansel; Jack and the Beanstalk; Little Goose Girl, The; Marendenboni; Nakali

References and further reading

Briggs, K. (ed.), *A Dictionary of British Folk-Tales in the English Language*, 2 vols., London: Routledge and Kegan Paul, 1970–1971, vol. 1, pp. 400–403.

Jacobs, J. (ed.), *English Fairy Tales*, London: The

Bodley Head, 1968, pp. 297ff; reprint of *English Fairy Tales* (1890) and *More English Fairy Tales* (1894), pp. 79–81.

Yolen, J. (ed.), *Favourite Folktales from around the World*, New York: Pantheon Books, 1986.

Wild Colonial Boy

Main fictional character of an Australian ballad of the 1860s celebrating the activities of a historical bushranger named Jack Doolan (Duggan, Dowling, etc.). The Wild Colonial Boy is a type of the outlaw hero. His defiance and bravery are reflected in the lines from his ballad that claim that he would rather die than "live in slavery, bound down with iron chains." His ballad is based to a considerable extent on the earlier traditions surrounding the historical Jack Donohoe and is widely sung outside Australia—in New Zealand, the United States, Canada, Ireland, England, Scotland, and Wales.

Related entries: Brennan, William; Christie, Francis; Donohoe, Jack; Hall, Ben; Johns, Joseph; Kelly, Edward; Morgan, Daniel "Mad Dog"; Outlaws; Ward, Frederick Wordsworth

References and further reading

Meredith, J., *The Wild Colonial Boy: Bushranger Jack Donohoe, 1806–1830*, Ascot Vale: Red Rooster Press, 1982.

Seal, G., "The Wild Colonial Boy Rides Again: An Australian Legend Abroad," in Craven, I. (ed.), *Australian Popular Culture*, Cambridge: Cambridge University Press, 1994.

William of Cloudesly

Archer hero of sixteenth-century English balladry who, like William Tell, shoots an arrow through an apple on the head of his son. The story of the ballad titled "Adam Bell, Clim of the Clough, and William of Cloudesly" is that the three protagonists are outlawed for crimes against the game laws and take refuge in the forest. William is married and one day decides to visit his wife and family at Carlisle. He is betrayed to the authorities by an old woman to whom he has provided charity for seven years. The sheriff arrives with a large force, surrounds the house, and burns it down. The family escapes, but William is taken. He is on his way to be hung in Carlisle when Adam Bell and Clim of the Clough rescue him. After killing virtually all the authorities in Carlisle, the outlaws escape to the forest, where William is reunited with his family.

The outlaws now decide that they must approach the king for a pardon, and they travel to London. William takes his eldest son and leaves his wife and other two boys in the care of nuns. The outlaws approach the king, who refuses them a pardon; however, the queen obtains their escape from the gallows. As soon as this arrangement is confirmed, the news of the massacre at Carlisle arrives, and the king is greatly saddened and angered. He wants to see how well the men who wreaked such devastation upon his authorities can shoot a bow. An archery contest ensues in which the three men show off their almost supernatural skills. The king declares Cloudesly the best archer he has ever seen. William claims to be even better than that and offers to split an apple laid on his son's head at a distance of sixty paces. The king commands him to attempt the feat, on pain of death if he fails, and also death for his two companions if the child is struck. Fortunately William is successful, and the king and queen reward him well and press him into their service. His son is likewise provided for, and his companions travel to Rome to be absolved of sin. All three then live the remainder of their lives happily serving the king.

In his discussion of this ballad, Child notes the long and widespread existence of the arrow-shot-from-the-head motif throughout European folklore—north, south, east, and west—and also in the literature of Persia, Turkey, and elsewhere, as well as its occurrence in the Tell legend. The connection to the Robin Hood legends is also clear.

Related entries: Armstrong, Johnnie; Bell, Adam; Clym of the Clough; Hood, Robin; Victims

References and further reading

Briggs, K. (ed.), *A Dictionary of British Folk-Tales in the English Language*, 2 vols., London: Routledge and Kegan Paul, 1970–1971, vol. 1, 369–374.

Child, F. J., *The English and Scottish Popular Ballads*, 5 vols., New York: Dover, 1965 (1882–1898), vol. 3, pp. 15–39, including ballad no. 116.

Wirreenun the Rainmaker

Rainmaking magician and hero of a tradition recorded by K. Langloh Parker in the mid-1890s from the Noongahburra people of the Narran River area in New South Wales, Australia. In this story the people are much in need of rain, and they begin to doubt the magic of their rainmaker, the aging Wirreenun. Their discontent comes to the old man's attention, and on three successive days he goes to the much depleted water hole and places a number of sacred and secret objects into it. After the third day, Wirreenun tells the young men to build raised houses for all the tribe. Then he tells everyone to come with him to the water hole. Wirreenun jumps into the water and commands the others to do likewise. As they splash in the water, Wirreenun goes round behind each man and appears to suck out a lump of charcoal from his head. He spits these lumps into the water. When Wirreenun tries to leave the water, a young man grabs him and throws him back in a number of times, until Wirreenun is cold and shivering. This is a signal for all to leave the water hole. Wirreenun then makes all the people go and sleep in a large bough shed while he and two elderly men and two elderly women wait outside, dressed in all their clothes and walking round and round the shed.

Eventually a large storm appears and begins to throw down lightning accompanied by the vast rumble of thunder. The people are frightened, but Wirreenun says that he will go out into the storm and calm the tempest. The magician sings to the storm until the thunder and lightning fade and are replaced by showers of rain. It rains for some days, after which the drought-stricken country is green again and a great corroboree is held in Wirreenun's name. But the old man is unimpressed by this celebration. Instead, he joins with the rainmakers of a neighboring tribe and together they cause a great rain to fall and fill a plain with water, turning it into a giant lake. Then Wirreenun tells his people to fish in the lake. At first they refuse, saying that it is pointless, as there is only rainwater in the lake. But Wirreenun insists, and, to humor him, they do as they are asked. To their surprise and delight they are rewarded with great hauls of fish, with plenty for all. The elders declare that such a great occasion should be marked by a *borah*, or initiation of the young men, an event that became part of the legendry of the Noongahburra people and that acknowledges the triumph of Wirreenun the Rainmaker.

Wirreenun is a culture hero who uses his magical abilities to benefit his people, despite their lapse of belief in his powers. His control over the element most important to the survival of the people is exemplified in his rainmaking success.

Related entries: Achikar; Culture Heroes; Magicians; Merlin; Wise Men and Women

References and further reading

Berndt, R. and C., *The Speaking Land: Myth and Story in Aboriginal Australia*, Ringwood: Penguin, 1989.

Parker, K. L. (coll. and ed.), *Australian Legendary Tales*, Twickenham: Senate, 1978 (1896), pp. 120–124.

Wise Men and Women

Like many other positive and some negative attributes, wisdom may be a source of heroism. Wise heroes, such as the Assyrian Achikar, may have magic powers that assist their wisdom or that they use wisely and for good. Wisdom is often an attribute of religious figures, such as the Jewish Baal-Shem-Tov and the Muslim El Khidre. While wise heroes may have magical powers, magicians or "wizards" are not necessarily wise, and these figures constitute another, if closely related, category of folk heroes.

Wisdom of a kind may also be displayed by folk heroes who use their native wit in clever, cunning, or otherwise intelligent ways to save themselves or their companions or to triumph against villainy of various kinds. Frequently these figures are women, including such outwitters as Scheherazade, Fatima, Lady Isabel, and Wungala. One widespread tale of this type is related to "The Peasant's Wise Daughter" (no. 94 in the Grimms' collection), in which a young woman successfully negotiates a set of impossible tasks, such as appearing neither naked nor clothed, a theme also treated in folk balladry. Sometimes known as "The Sly Country Girl" or by a similar title, the tale is also well known in Italy, Czechoslovakia, and Russia.

Related entries: Achikar; Amaradevi; Baal-Shem-Tov; Eight Immortals, The; Elijah the Prophet; Fatima; Helpers; Hiawatha; Isabel, Lady; Khidre, El; Magicians; Scheherazade; Supparaka; Wungala

References and further reading

Afanas'ev, A. (comp.), Guterman, N. (trans.), *Russian Fairy Tales*, New York: Pantheon Books, 1945, pp. 252–255.

Calvino, I. (trans. Martin, G.), *Italian Folk Tales: Selected and Retold by Italo Calvino*, New York: Harcourt Brace Jovanovich, Penguin, 1980 (1956), pp. 261–266.

Lüthi, M. (trans. Chadeayne, L. and Gottwald, P.), *Once upon a Time: On the Nature of Fairy Tales*, Bloomington: Indiana University Press, 1976, pp. 121–134.

Wise Men of Gotham

Known since at least the late medieval period as the home of fools, the English town of Gotham in Nottinghamshire is the focus of numerous legends and numskull tales, including one that tells of the supposed origins of the town's stupidity. One version of the story has it that King John (infamous in the later Robin Hood tradition) is on his way to Nottingham and wishes to take a short cut through the lands of the Gothamites. The villagers are afraid that if this happens it will establish a precedent for a right-of-way through which anyone can walk or ride, threatening their crops and other farming activities. They bar the king's way and then, when the king sends soldiers to punish them, pretend that they are all mad and so not responsible for their highly dangerous defiance of the monarch. When the soldiers arrive at Gotham, they find the inhabitants rolling cheeses along the ground to get them to market, trying to catch cuckoos so that they can keep their song and have spring forever, and drowning eels in buckets of water.

According to Halliwell, the "foles of Gotham" were already renowned in the fifteenth century, and there were sufficient stories about them extant for a collection to be made in the early sixteenth century. Halliwell quotes an example:

Illustration of the nursery rhyme "Three Wise Men of Gotham" (Mary Evans Picture Library)

man tale of the "Five Journeyman Travelers," the Pakistani "Seven Wise Men of Buneyr," and the Sri Lankan men of Kadambawa, as well as Finnish and Japanese versions.

> **Related entries:** Dad and Dave; Drongo; Kabajan; Knowall, Doctor; Little Moron; Lucky Hans; Numskulls and Noodles

References and further reading

Briggs, K. (ed.), *A Dictionary of British Folk-Tales in the English Language*, 2 vols., London: Routledge and Kegan Paul, 1970–1971, vol. 2, pp. 67, 287, 349–336.

Clouston, W., *The Book of Noodles*, London: Elliot Stock, 1888, pp. 28–29.

Halliwell, J., *The Nursery Rhymes of England*, London: The Bodley Head, 1970 (1842), p. 43 (no. 65).

Henderson, H. (ed. and trans.), *The Maiden Who Rose from the Sea and Other Finnish Folktales*, Enfield Lock: Hisarlik Press, 1992, pp. 138, 146.

Jacobs, J. (ed.), *English Fairy Tales*, London: The Bodley Head, 1968, pp. 297ff; reprint of *English Fairy Tales* (1890) and *More English Fairy Tales* (1894).

Parker, H., *Village Folk-Tales of Ceylon*, London: Luzac and Co., 1910, vol. 1, p. 258.

Swynnerton, C., *Indian Nights' Entertainment; or, Folk-Tales from the Upper Indus*, London: Elliot Stock, 1892, p. 305.

Three wise men of Gotham
Went to sea in a bowl:
And if the bowl had been stronger,
My song would have been longer.

Bywords for stupidity and obduracy, the numskull men of Gotham have their heroically dim-witted counterparts in many other traditions, including the Jewish people of Helm in Poland, the German burghers of Schild, and the Biellese of Italy. As with the story of King John, though, there is often an element of cleverness in the apparent stupidity of such people, though this is not an infallible aspect of these traditions. Another story told of the Wise Men of Gotham is that twelve of them went fishing in a boat but returned in a state of great despair, believing that one of them had drowned. Each man, forgetting to count himself, could count only eleven fishermen in the boat. Variations of this tale are widespread and include the Ger-

Wolfe, General James

James Wolfe (1727–1759) was an English general who, after a distinguished military career, commanded a British force of 9,000 men in the French and Indian War. In June 1759 he and his army laid siege to the city of Quebec. Unable to take the city and its French defenders by frontal assault, Wolfe took a large part of his army up the cliffs above the city to The Plains of Abraham, also known as The Heights of Abraham, forcing the defenders into an open battle that Wolfe's forces won decisively. Wolfe was killed in the fighting. The combination of a British victory and the tragic end of the commander in the field made the story ideal for ballad celebration, and Wolfe's heroism is commemorated in a number of songs and ballads that emphasize his bravery and ability to inspire his men, as in the opening of this contemporary song titled "Brave Wolfe," given by Jackson:

Cheer up my young men all,
Let nothing fright you;

An engraved version of a painting by Benjamin West, "The Death of General Wolfe" (Library of Congress)

Though oft objections rise;
Let it delight you.
Let not your fancy move,
Whene'er it comes to trial;
Nor let your courage fail,
At the first denial.

As with Lord Nelson almost half a century later, Wolfe's death at the moment of victory opened a deep well of public sympathy, and numerous ballads were composed about his exploits, which was also the case with Nelson. However, while few, if any, of Nelson's ballads have lasted well in the mouths of singers, Wolfe seems to have been more fortunate, perhaps because of the handsome melodies to which his ballads are usually sung. Two versions of a song titled "Bold General Wolfe" were collected in Dorset by English folklorist Henry Hammond early this century. Wolfe is portrayed as a gallant leader, exhorting his men to feats of valor, even in death:

Now here's a hundred guineas in bright
    gold,
Take it and part it for my blood runs cold,
And use your soldiers as you did before,
Your soldiers own, your soldiers own,
And they will fight for evermore.

Related entries: Benbow, Admiral; Benkei; Bonaparte, Napoleon; Franklin, Lord; Gam-Czan, Marshall Gang; McCaffery; Military Heroes; National Heroes; Santa Anna, General Antonio López de

References and further reading

Jackson, G., *Early Songs of Uncle Sam*, Boston: Bruce Humphries, 1933, pp. 174–177.

Lloyd, A., *Folksong in England*, New York: International Publishers, 1970 (1967), p. 252.

Purslow, F. (ed.), *Marrow Bones: English Folk Songs from the Hammond and Gardiner Mss*, London: EFDS Publications, 1965, p. 4.

Women Dressed as Men

Women who dress in men's clothes and pursue activities usually associated with males appear with some frequency in folklore. These plucky girls—they are almost always young—appear in ballads as female highwaymen, female soldiers, female smugglers, and female sailors. They don men's clothes either out of a sense of adventure, such as wishing to fight in wars, or in order to follow a lover in his journeys as sailor or soldier. In folktales, too, a woman sometimes dresses as a man in order to follow a lover, as in the Chinese story of Mulan.

Western traditions support a number of masculinized folk heroines, including Martha Jane Burke (c. 1852–1903), who, as "Calamity Jane," became a legend in and around Dakota in the 1870s for her riding and shooting skills. She was an associate of Wild Bill Hickock and is said to have gained her folk name because she promised "calamity" for any man who courted her. Nevertheless, she married in 1885 to a man named Canary. Calamity Jane's legend is related to that of other historical and fictional women who act as men and has been the subject of Broadway and Hollywood romanticization.

A similar example is Myra Belle Shirley (1848?–1889), or Belle Starr, the leader of a group of rustlers and outlaws and a paramour of Cole Younger, a member of the Jesse James gang. She was known in her day by various journalistic epithets, including the "Queen of the Bandits" and "Petticoat of the Plains." Ambushed and killed in 1889, her legend continued, fueled mainly by dime novels, popular journalism, and Hollywood movies. Belle Starr is a good example of a local or regional folk heroine who owes much of her glory to the attentions of the mass media.

Masculinized female figures like those described above and like those mentioned elsewhere in this encyclopedia are often found in circumstances where the rules of everyday behavior do not apply or are in some way suspended. This circumvention of rules may be due to a frontier situation, as was the case with Calamity Jane and Belle Starr, or to situations of military combat, as in the cases of Mulan, the Italian Fanta-Ghiro', and the many female sol-

A full-length portrait of Martha Canary (Calamity Jane) playing to the camera, c. 1895 (Library of Congress)

diers and sailors who appear in folklore, as, for example, in the British broadside ballad "William Taylor" (not to be confused with the poaching song of the same name), also sung in America.

Related entries: Aryg, Altyn; Fanta-Ghiro'; Female Cabin Boy, The; Female Drummer, The; Female Highwayman, The; Female Smuggler, The; Geordie; Magicians; Mulan; O'Malley, Grace; Outlaws

References and further reading

Belden, H. (ed.), *Ballads and Songs Collected by the Missouri Folklore Society*, University of Missouri Studies 15, no. 1, 1940, esp. pp. 182–183 for "William Taylor."

Coffin, T., *The Female Hero in Folklore and Legend*, New York: Seabury, 1975.

Simpson, J., "'Be bold, but not too bold': Female Courage in Some British and Scandinavian Legends," *Folklore* 102, no. 1(1991): 16–30.

Stanley, J. (ed.), *Bold in Her Breeches: Women Pirates across the Ages*, London: Pandora, 1995.

Woodencloak, Katie

Norwegian version of Cinderella in which a king's wife dies, leaving him with a beautiful young girl. The king marries a widowed woman who also has a daughter. But the stepmother is wicked, and her daughter is as ugly as the princess is beautiful. Both women are jealous of the princess, and when the king is called away to war, they starve and beat the princess and eventually turn her out of the house to herd the cattle. She makes friends with a large dun-colored bull who asks her why she is weeping. She refuses to say, but the bull knows her unhappy and hungry situation. He tells her to take a cloth from his ear and to spread it on the ground. The princess does this, and the cloth magically produces all the food she could ever want. After eating this wonderful food for some time, the princess is restored to her full health and beauty, much to the anger of the wicked stepmother and her daughter. They send their maid to spy on the princess, and the maid returns with the secret of the princess's continuing health and beauty. At this point, the king returns victorious from the wars, and the princess is pleased to see him, expecting to be restored to her rightful position. But the wicked stepmother pretends to be ill and says that she can be cured only by eating the flesh of the dun-colored bull. The king decrees that the bull must be slaughtered. Distraught, the princess visits the bull and tells him of his fate. The bull says that once they have killed him, she will be next, and so he proposes that they escape together. Reluctantly, for she loves her father, the princess agrees, and they leave that night. The king sends out search parties, but the bull and the princess have too much of a start and, with her mounted on his back, the young girl and the magical bull travel on through many lands.

One day they come to a copper wood. The bull tells the princess that whatever she does as they pass through the wood she must not touch a single leaf or they will both be in mortal danger from the three-headed troll who owns the wood. The princess does her best to avoid touching a leaf but accidentally rips one from a tree. Dismayed, the bull tells her to keep

the copper leaf in her possession. When they reach the edge of the wood, the three-headed troll appears and has a terrible fight with the bull. The bull manages to win but is sorely wounded. He is restored with ointment that the troll holds in a pouch at his belt and is soon able to continue the journey. After a long time, the bull and the princess come to a silver wood. This time the bull gives the same warning, but adds that this wood is guarded by an even fiercer six-headed troll. Once again the princess is unable to avoid tearing a leaf, and again the bull reminds her to keep it in her possession. At the far end of the wood, the bull does battle with the six-headed troll and manages to best him, once again being cured of his wounds by the dead troll's magic ointment. Though now much weakened, eventually the bull is well enough to continue, and the couple travels on through many more lands for a long time, until they come to a gold wood. This wood is even thicker and deeper than the previous two forests and, the bull says, is guarded by a nine-headed troll. This time, despite her best efforts, the princess tears a golden apple from a tree, and again, the bull instructs her to keep it safe. The bull again manages to kill the nine-headed troll and is restored to reasonable health by the troll's stock of magic ointment. Eventually the bull is well enough to continue. The duo continues slowly, until they come near to a great castle. The bull tells the princess that she must go to the castle and live in a pigsty. In the sty she will find a wooden cloak that she must wear, and she must also take the name "Katie Woodencloak." Then she must ask for employment in the castle scullery, the lowliest of positions. But before she leaves, the princess must kill the bull, flay his hide, and lay it under a nearby rock wall, covering the copper and silver leaves and the golden apple. By the wall is a stick that she must use to knock on the rock wall if she ever needs anything. The princess at first refuses to kill the bull, but eventually she does kill him, and then she goes to the pigsty, dons the wooden cloak, and obtains employment in the castle scullery.

The next Sunday, after performing all the hardest and most menial tasks available in the castle, Katie Woodencloak asks the cook if she can take the prince's bath water up to his room. Incredulous, the cook laughs at her and says that the prince would not care to look at such an ugly girl. But Katie persists, and eventually she is allowed to take the prince's bath water. As she climbs the stone steps to the prince's chamber, her wooden cloak clatters so loudly that the prince comes out to see what all the noise is about. As the cook predicted, the prince is disgusted at the sight of Katie and throws the bath water over her, saying that he would not use any water such an ugly girl might bring him.

After this incident, Katie gets permission to go to church. On the way, she goes to the rock wall and knocks on it with the stick, as instructed by the bull. A man magically appears out of the wall and asks her what she wants. Katie explains that she is off to church but has no decent clothes to wear. The man magically produces a bright copper dress and a horse and saddle, so Katie rides to church decked out as a fine lady. The prince also happens to be at worship, and when he sees this copper girl he falls deeply in love with her. After the service, the prince rushes to open the door for the copper girl and obtains one of her gloves. Asking where she is from, he receives the odd answer, "Bath." Katie then rides off, and the prince spends the next week going through the land, asking for the proud lady who rode off from church without her glove and for the whereabouts of a place called "Bath." But all his efforts are to no avail.

The next Sunday Katie asks to take the prince his bath towel; as before, she is eventually allowed to do so. When the prince sees the ugly girl in the black wooden cloak, he is disgusted and throws the towel in her face, refusing to use a fabric touched by such smutty hands. Again Katie gets leave to go to church, even though the cook and maids cannot understand why such an ugly, dirty, and insignificant girl would want to go there. Katie tells them that she finds the priest's sermons do her good. On the way, she again detours to the rock wall, knocks upon it with the stick, and this time obtains an even more magnificent dress of silver from the magical man. At church, all happens as it had the previous Sunday. This time, in answer to the prince's desire to know where she lives, Katie replies "Towel-land" and drops her riding whip. The prince stoops to pick it up, and Katie is away again. The prince then spends another futile week trying to locate both Katie and mysterious "Towel-Land."

On the following Sunday, the prince calls down to the servants for a comb. Katie obtains permission to take it to him, with the usual result. Katie again visits the rock wall, and this time the magical man gives her a magnificent gold and diamond dress with matching shoes, and her steed is likewise equipped with rich saddlery and cloth. At church, the smitten prince tries again to impress the golden woman, this time by pouring pitch onto the doorstep so he can gallantly help her across the black, sticky mass. She spurns his help and plants her foot in the middle of the pitch as she makes her way back to her glowing steed. One of her golden shoes sticks in the pitch, and the prince picks it up. This time, when the prince asks where she is from, she answers, "From Comb-land." Before the prince can return the golden shoe, the woman rides off. The prince then goes all over the world with the golden shoe, trying to find "Comb-land." Failing in this endeavor, he lets it be known far and wide that he will wed the woman whose foot fits the shoe.

Women come from everywhere, but the shoe fits none of them perfectly—except for one, the ugly daughter of Katie's wicked stepmother. Reluctantly, the prince is forced to keep his word, and the wedding feast is prepared. The ugly stepsister is dressed in finery, though when she puts on the golden shoe it gushes blood. As a last resort, when they reach the castle the prince has the maids and servants try on the golden shoe, but it fits none of them. Eventually the prince says that since everyone else in the land has tried on the shoe, even the ugly Katie Woodencloak should try. Everyone laughs, but the prince insists, and Katie is called. She clatters into view, wearing her dirty wooden cloak, and everyone present derides her. But when she puts her foot into the shoe, it fits perfectly and she is transformed into the beautiful lady the prince has desired, wearing her golden finery, glowing like the sun, and wearing on her other foot the pair of the golden shoe. The prince clasps her to him, kisses her, and is overjoyed when he hears that she really is a princess. Then they are married.

This long and complex story, given here only in the barest outline, well illustrates the richness of oral storytelling and the relative poverty of those fairy tale versions such as Cinderella. In this story, the Cinderella character is the focus of a large number of supernatural events, which are told in the classic triple movement of the folktale: she is helped by a talking bull and a magic man who lives in a rock; she obtains the magic objects of copper and silver leaves and the golden apple, as well as the bull's hide and use of the magic stick; these items allow her to appear in magnificent finery. At the same time, and this is the essential Cinderella element, she is the dirtiest and most despised of the low, clattering around the palace in her strange wooden cloak, the symbol of her degradation. Eventually, of course, her role is reversed and she retains her rightful place as a princess at the side of the snooty prince, who, we assume, has been humbled by his quest to find the one whose foot will fit the golden shoe.

The slaying of the faithful animal helper, almost always excised from fairy tale versions, is a commonplace of traditional folktale. In the Scandinavian tale of "Lord Peter," for example, the family cat turns out to be a princess bewitched by a troll. After making Peter appear to the king as if he is a wealthy young lord, the cat asks Peter to cut off its head. Reluctantly Peter does as requested. In this case, the cat turns into a beautiful princess and is married to the low-born boy, who becomes "Lord" Peter.

Despite the differing gender of the protagonists, the role reversals of hero and heroine in the stories of Peter and Katie are structurally identical elements. As a classic folk heroine, Katie Woodencloak displays courage, determination, cleverness, and not a little wit. The initial dirtiness and humiliation of the central character, reversed and resolved in the ultimate happy ending, are the recurring elements of such Cinderella-type stories recorded from many of the world's folk traditions.

Related entries: Amala; Assipattle; Cap o' Rushes; Catskin; Cinderella; Cinder-Mary; Fairy Tale Heroes; Ye Xian

References and further reading
Asbjørnsen, P. and Moe, J. (trans. Dasent, G.), *Popular Tales from the Norse*, Edinburgh: David Douglas, 1888, pp. 357–372.
Cox, M., *Cinderella: Three Hundred and Forty-Five Variants*, London: David Nutt, 1893.
Dundes, A. (ed.), *Cinderella: A Folklore Casebook*, New York: Garland, 1982.
Rooth, A., *The Cinderella Cycle*, Lund: C. Gleerup, 1951.

Wu Song

Legendary Chinese outlaw hero of the Robin Hood type. Wu Song is brave, strong, a fierce fighter able to kill tigers, an avenger of wrongs, and a friend of the poor and dispossessed. As with heroes in many traditions, Wu Song early establishes his heroic abilities, in this case his great strength. In one tale of his early life, Wu Song has been away from home for many years when he decides to return to see his elder brother. After a long journey, he nears home, and on the last mountain before he arrives he finds a wine shop, where he stops for a rest and a meal. Before eating and drinking, he notices a sign that says "Three Bowls and You Cannot Top the Ridge." Nevertheless, he eats well and drinks three bowls of wine. Ignoring the sign, he asks the landlord for another bowl, but the landlord refuses, claiming that the local wine is so powerful it has acquired the name "Wine That Knocks You Down Outside the Door." But Wu Song insists, and so the landlord serves him another bowl, and another, until Wu Song has incautiously consumed eighteen bowls of wine. Wu Song then continues his journey, despite being warned by the landlord of a fierce tiger roaming the area and eating people.

He does not get far before the effects of the wine cause him to sit down on a rock for a rest. Almost immediately, the fierce tiger springs from its nearby hiding place. The tipsy Wu Song only just manages to dodge aside and to grab the club he always carries. He takes a swing at the tiger but misses and breaks the club against a tree trunk. Then the tiger is upon him again, and he fights for his life with only bare hands. Eventually, Wu Song manages to force the tiger's muzzle into the ground, and the tiger shows signs of weakening. Wu Song is then able to grip the tiger's neck in his left hand and form his right fist into an iron-like hammer. He smashes this down on the tiger's body again and again, perhaps fifty titanic blows in all. Eventually blood flows from the tiger's mouth, eyes, nose, and ears, and the beast dies. News of how Wu Song killed the tiger with his bare hands spreads quickly, and he is given a hero's welcome when he arrives in his home town.

Related entries: Hood, Robin; Li Kui; Lu Zhishen;
    Outlaws; Warriors
References and further reading
Børdahl, V. (ed.), *The Eternal Storyteller: Oral Literature in Modern China*, Richmond, UK: Curzon Press, 1999, pp. 255–281.
Eberhard, W. (ed.), Parsons, D. (trans.), *Folktales of China*, Chicago: University of Chicago Press, 1965 (1937).
Li, N., *Old Tales of China*, Singapore: Graham Brash, 1983 (1981), pp. 168–170.

Wulgaru

A being, or beings, created through an attempt by a Waddaman Aboriginal man named Djarapa to make a man from wood, stone, red-ochre paint, and magic songs. The resulting creature is a shambling mess of twisted limbs and uncoordinated movements and eyes that blaze like stars. Ever since its misbegotten creation, the Wulgaru has menaced the Waddaman (Northern Territory, Australia) people as keeper and judge of the dead and guardian of tribal law, appearing in their oral traditions as a principle of evil.

The similarities between this story and that of the Golem and, in literature, of Frankenstein are echoed in other traditions in which the inanimate are given life or the dead are made to walk again. However, such structural and narrative similarities do not mean that such narratives have the same meanings in different cultures. While the Golem operates as an avenger of the oppression suffered by the Jews, the

Wulgaru has a more fundamental role for Waddaman culture, appearing as the caretaker of the spirits and regulator of the rules governing everyday life. As with all forms of folklore, it is necessary to ascertain the significance of stories, songs, and other expressions and practices according to their provenance among the people or peoples who maintain them. The remarkable similarities and parallels observed between many folk traditions strongly suggest some universal need to balance opposition and contradictions of life and belief. On the other hand, the way in which these balances are articulated from culture to culture and the specific meanings that arise from those articulations are specific to the folk groups among whom they are found.

Related entries: Baba-Yaga; Ogres; Villains; Wirreenun
    the Rainmaker; Wungala
References and further reading
Berndt, R. and C., *The Speaking Land: Myth and Story in Aboriginal Australia*, Ringwood: Penguin, 1989.
Harney, W., *Tales from the Aborigines*, Adelaide, SA: Rigby, 1959, pp. 90–101, 103–106.

Wungala

Heroine of the Waddaman people whose traditional country was southeast of the Katherine River in Australia's Northern Territory. As the tale was told to collector Bill Harney around the mid-twentieth century, Wungala takes her young son, Bulla, seed-gathering after the wet season. Excited, Bulla runs around finding the best mounds of seeds, but when a dark cloud passes across the sun, Wungala tells him to be quiet. She tells him that when the shadows come, so might the evil-big-eyed-one who lives in a cave in the nearby hills. If the evil-big-eyed-one, known as a Wulgaru, hears Bulla, he will come out of his cave, find them, and cause evil to befall them. Undeterred, Bulla keeps up his chatter until an evil Wulgaru does appear. Terrified, he runs to his mother, pointing at a Wulgaru creeping toward them through the shadows.

Wungala knows that the only way to avoid the evil of a Wulgaru is to ignore it, to go about her business and to show no fear. Responding to Bulla's cries, she speaks to him as if nothing has happened, saying that he is mistaken, it is only the shadows of the swaying bushes. Trusting his mother, Bulla calms down and goes on gathering seeds. This apparent nonchalance enrages the Wulgaru, who gives a fierce yell, alarming a wallaby, which, in turn, gives Bulla another fright. He runs to his mother again, saying that as well as seeing the Wulgaru he has also heard it and that they should run away. But Wungala, knowing that no matter what happens she must not show fear, calms his fears again by saying that it is just a cockatoo.

Wungala then begins grinding the seeds on a large flat stone to make flour for bread, as if nothing has happened. This continued indifference only further angers the Wulgaru, who begins to jump around, even going so far as to thrust his evil face into Wungala's as she calmly continues her baking. Still he elicits no response. When the damper, or bush bread, is baked nice and hot, Bulla, who had gone to sleep, awakens and tells his mother that the Wulgaru is still there. "No," said his mother,

"that is just the smoke from the fire." Hearing this, the monster pounces at Wungala, its claws ready to tear her apart. But she jumps straight at him, pushing the hot and sticky damper into the Wulgaru's face. The creature screams in pain as it tries to claw the hot and sticky dough from its mouth and eyes, giving Wungala her chance to snatch up Bulla and to run back to her camp and the shelter of her people.

Related entries: Wirreenun the Rainmaker; Wise Men and Women; Wulgaru

References and further reading

Gill, S., *Storytracking: Texts, Stories, and Histories in Central Australia*, Oxford: Oxford University Press, 1998.

Harney, W., *Tales from the Aborigines*, Adelaide, SA: Rigby, 1959, pp. 98–101.

Mathews, J. (comp.), White, I. (ed.), *The Opal That Turned into Fire and Other Stories from the Wangkumara*, Broome: Magabala Books, 1994.

Rose, D., *Dingo Makes Us Human: Life and Land in an Aboriginal Australian Culture*, Melbourne: Melbourne University Press, 1992.

Xiang Yu

Historical Chinese warrior hero of the early second century B.C., between the Qin and Han dynasties. Xiang Yu was a thirty-one-year-old commander of an army contending for the control of China. Braver than he was wise, Xiang Yu was tricked into making a disastrous attack against an opposing force led by Han Xin. Xiang Yu's army was ambushed, pinned down, and surrounded, and Xiang Yu became increasingly demoralized by Han Xin's psychological warfare. Xiang Yu's consort, Lady Chu, attempted to divert and console him by performing a graceful double-sword dance. With his men deserting and the enemy encroaching, Xiang Yu realized that the only hope of survival was to break through the encircling army. He mounted his black horse, and to it confided his worries, especially in regard to the fate of Lady Chu after his inevitable extermination. Meanwhile, fearing that she would only hinder Xiang Wu's escape, Lady Chu killed herself. Xiang Yu then fought his way through the enemy forces and finally reached the Wujiang River with only twenty-six of his men surviving. A ferryman offered to take them across to the east side of the river to escape the pursuing soldiers of Han Xin. But the possibility of escape reminded Xiang Yu of his home and of how, having lost his army, he would be unable to face his venerable leaders, should he succeed in returning. He then took his own life, and over the next four centuries (206 B.C. to 220 A.D.), the Han dynasty reunified the country.

Related entries: National Heroes; Warrior Heroes
References and further reading
Li, N., *Old Tales of China*, Singapore: Graham Brash, 1983 (1981), pp. 5–7.
Werner, E., *Myths and Legends of China*, New York: Arno Press, 1976 (1922).

Xiao En

Legendary Chinese Robin Hood figure who, having retired to lead a simple life as a fisherman with his daughter, Guiying, resists the local landlord's imposition of a fishing tax. Xiao En is whipped by a corrupt magistrate and made to kowtow to the landlord. Ashamed and enraged, he decides to seek revenge against the landlord. Guiying, concerned for his safety, accompanies him on his mission of vengeance, helps him kill the landlord, and then flees with him back to the greenwood.

Related entries: Hood, Robin; Outlaws; Wu Song
References and further reading
Eberhard, W. (ed.), Parsons, D. (trans.), *Folktales of China*, Chicago: University of Chicago Press, 1965 (1937).
Li, N., *Old Tales of China*, Singapore: Graham Brash, 1983 (1981), pp. 18–19.

Xiaoqing

Legendary Chinese heroine of the faithful maidservant type in the story of the White Lady, also called Bai Suzhen. As her mistress is in reality an ancient white snake who has managed to transform herself into female human form, so Xiaoqing is a green snake who has transformed into a human being.

Related entries: Bai Suzhen; Helpers; Shape-Shifters; White Lady
References and further reading
Li, N., *Old Tales of China*, Singapore: Graham Brash, 1983 (1981), pp. 12–14.

Xishi

Chinese heroine of legend, a silk-washer who sacrifices herself to the vengeful and imperial ambitions of Goujian, prince of Yue. Goujian wants revenge on the man who has been his captor for three years, Fuchai, prince of Wu. Goujian's minister, one Fan Li, is ordered to find a beautiful maiden willing to sacrifice herself. Fan Li finds Xishi, and Goujian has her sent to Fuchai, who falls in love with her so deeply that he neglects his kingdom. Eventually he even consults with Xishi about matters of state, and her advice is always in favor of Goujian. Xishi also brings about the death by suicide of Fuchai's best general, leaving the way open for Goujian's forces to defeat Fuchai and take over his kingdom. Fuchai then commits suicide.

There are various accounts of the fate of Xishi. Some say she simply vanished; others say she drowned. Perhaps the most satisfying account holds that she was reunited with Fan Li, who discovered her washing silk, and that they sailed away together.

Related entries: Fairy Tale Heroes; Victims
References and further reading

Eberhard, W. (ed.), Parsons, D. (trans.), *Folktales of China*, Chicago: University of Chicago Press, 1965.
Li, N., *Old Tales of China*, Singapore: Graham Brash, 1983 (1981), pp. 102–104.

Y

Yamato

Second-century Japanese warrior hero whose exploits are a blend of the legendary and the historical. Yamato was the father of Emperor Chai, who ruled from 192–200 A.D., and the early versions of his traditions show him as a violent, almost trickster-like figure who slays his own brother and his enemies. He was said to have been given a magical sword, named "Cloud Cluster," by his aunt, a high priestess. However, early Yamato traditions have him defeating enemies by his cleverness rather than by the magic sword. In one such story, he tricks his enemy into a friendly fight after he has switched the enemy's real sword for a wooden copy.

During his subsequent exploits, Yamato makes greater use of the sword. In one tale he uses it as a means of escape from burning vegetation that has been set afire by his enemies, who hope to burn him alive. In another story, he falls in love with the beautiful Iwato-hime and ultimately leaves the great sword in her safekeeping. Going once more on his travels, Yamato meets again the great serpent he had once ignored. According to legend, Cloud Cluster had been fashioned from the monster's tale, and it is angered at Yamato's use of the sword. Although Yamato tries to ignore the monster, his foot accidentally touches it as he passes, and he falls fatally ill. Iwato-hime then comforts him in death and has him buried. A white bird flies out of his grave. In some versions of the story, Yamato's body turns into a white bird that flies away, presumably to heaven. In other legends, Yamato marries different princesses, disguises himself as a woman, kills numerous other foes, and slays at least one serpent. There are some apparent parallels with the Arthurian legend in this tradition.

Related entries: Arthur; Dragon-Slayers; Warriors
References and further reading
Cavendish, R. (ed.), *Legends of the World*, London: Orbis, 1982, pp. 61–63.
Davis, F. H., *Myths and Legends of Japan*, London: G. G. Harrap and Co., 1913, pp. 51–57.

Yankee Doodle

The earliest reference to the well-known ditty and its eponymous hero seems to be in a Boston periodical, *Journal of the Times*, in September 1768, though the tune, at least, was apparently well known for some time before this date. Various claims for the origins of the catchy tune (which was used by both the British and American sides during the War of Independence) and words have been made, and there are many different versions of the lyrics. Yankee Doodle's reported exploits, the best known of which is to "stick a feather in his hat and call it macaroni," are whimsical rather than heroic.

The term itself originally referred to a person from the New England states and was used by the Confederate forces in the Civil War as a slur against the Union side. As often happens in such cases, the Yankees took up the insult and wore it as a badge of pride, further developing the character into something of a roguish trickster figure. As is usual with such widely known and culturally significant names, its origins are the subject of considerable folk etymologizing. There are claims for a Native American origin and, perhaps more likely, for an origin in the nicknames Dutch settlers gave their English neighbors in the New England region. Over time, the name "Yankee Doodle" became synonymous with the national spirit and identity of the United States and came to personify the American way, both at home and abroad.

Related entries: Culture Heroes; National Heroes; Uncle Sam; Washington, George

References and further reading

Dorson, R., *American Folklore*, Chicago: University of Chicago Press, 1959, pp. 41, 47.

Leach, M. (ed.), *Funk and Wagnall's Standard Dictionary of Folklore, Mythology, and Legend*, London: New English Library, 1975. Abridged one-volume edition of *Funk and Wagnall's Standard Dictionary of Folklore, Mythology, and Legend*, 2 vols., New York: Funk and Wagnall, 1972, p. 1187.

Yannakis

Hero of a Greek Gypsy tale, a comical version of the Grimms' "The Boy Who Wanted to Learn What Fear Is," a popular story throughout Europe. The story begins with a poor orphan, Yannakis, who is unable to understand what his sister means when she says she is afraid of the dark. He beats her for what seems to him a delusion, but she persists in her fears, and so Yannakis packs up and leaves. He comes first to a town where the inhabitants are terrified of ghosts. Yannakis cannot understand their fear and asks to be locked up for the night in a haunted inn. There he is visited by three fairies, all beautiful women, who attempt to lure him into their harmful embraces. But Yannakis, not knowing what fear is, remains unimpressed by their advances and unafraid. In this way he defeats the three hosts, taking from each a token—from the first, a bracelet; from the second, a ring; and from the third, a handkerchief. The villagers are overjoyed to be released from their fear of the ghostly fairies and shower the hero with gifts and money. He continues on his way.

He comes to a river where a boat full of people is trying to cross over. Unfortunately, to pass across the water the passengers have to sacrifice one of their number to the demon that lives in the water. They are about to throw an old man over the side when Yannakis, saying that he will go himself, jumps into the water. Yannakis finds a mermaid hanging to the side of the boat, and he demands to know why she is terrorizing people. As were the three fairies, the mermaid is stunned by the young man's lack of fear and wishes to kiss him, but he refuses, slapping her and making her swear on her mother's milk that she will stop terrorizing

travelers. The mermaid takes Yannakis from the water and back to her cave on dry land, where she kisses him, believing he must be one of her kind, as he has shown no fear of her. Then she brings him precious gifts, telling him to take whatever he wants. Yannakis says he wants nothing but eventually takes a bracelet for his sister. The mermaid then magically transports Yannakis to the city, since the boat on which he was traveling is long gone.

In the city, Yannakis inquires at a rich man's house for lodging. The man can only suggest that he stay in the graveyard. It seems that the king and his vizier have made a wager that no one can go there at the dead of night and cook halvah on one of the graves. Ninety people have tried for the prize, but all have been found dead in the morning. If someone can best the demonic creature in the cemetery, he or she will receive half the king's treasury. Yannakis cannot understand what all the fuss is about, and the rich man tells him that everyone is now too afraid to try for the prize. Not knowing what fear is, Yannakis goes to the cemetery. When he gets there, he builds a fire on top of the grave with some old, broken wooden crosses and starts to cook the halvah. Just before it is ready, a loathsome corpse arises from the grave demanding halvah. Yannakis hits the thing with the cooking spoon, telling it to wait until the halvah is ready. The corpse tries to intimidate Yannakis, all the time demanding halvah, but the young man keeps hitting it with the spoon. As soon as the halvah is ready, Yannakis pours it over the corpse, thus defeating it. The people are so pleased to be rid of the corpse that they make Yannakis rich, and he begins his journey home.

When he gets to the river and begins the boat crossing, the mermaid swims up and invites him to dinner. Still not afraid of anything, Yannakis accepts. In her cave are the three fairies he had first defeated and the loathsome corpse. They all toast the young man and dance with him until dawn, when he leaves for home. When he gets there, he embraces his sister and gives her all the treasure he has collected, saying that although they are now rich, he never did find out what it felt like to be afraid. Just then he needs to go to the toilet. He goes behind some trees and pulls down his pants, and a stork comes up and bites him on the backside. Yannakis runs home, trembling: "Sister, I'm afraid," he cries. And that's how Yannakis learns what fear is. The hero and his sister thereafter live richly and well—"and we're still telling their story."

Although this Gypsy version of the tale as given by Tong is elaborate and lengthy, Yannakis is the equivalent of the hero of a shorter Italian story known as "Dauntless Little John," in which the young John outwits a giant ogre and wins fame and fortune for his fearlessness. But one day John looks behind himself and, seeing his own shadow for the first time, dies of fright. These tales are examples of the ill-deserving hero whose often imprudent or misguided actions bring about worldly success and, sometimes, personal enlightenment.

Related entries: Fairy Tale Heroes; Jack Tales; Ogres; Swan Maiden

References and further reading

Calvino, I. (trans. Martin, G.), *Italian Folk Tales: Selected and Retold by Italo Calvino*, New York: Harcourt Brace Jovanovich, 1956; Penguin, 1980, pp. 3–4.

Grimm, J. and W., *The Complete Grimm's Fairy Tales*, New York: Pantheon Books, 1944, pp. 29–39.

Irizar, L. (ed.), Barandiarán, J. (coll.), White, L. (trans.), *A View from the Witch's Cave: Folktales of the Pyrenees*, Reno and Las Vegas: University of Nevada Press, 1988, p. 115.

Tong, D., *Gypsy Folktales*, New York: Harcourt Brace Jovanovich, 1989, pp. 145–151.

Yao Wang

Celebrated healer of Chinese tradition and subject of numerous legends, including the story of his removal of a bone from the throat of a tiger. In gratitude, the tiger undertakes to guard the healer's house. In another legend, Yao Wang saves the life of a snake that turns out to be the daughter of Ching Yang, the dragon king. Yao Wang is magically transported to the dragon kingdom, where the king offers him a great feast. But the hero declines, saying that he lives only on air and wine.

Yao Wang is one of the great cast of folk characters whose heroism depends on their relationship with animals. In his case, as with Androcles and many other heroes, Yao Wang's willingness to assist dangerous animals gains him their loyalty and protection.

Related entries: Androcles; Berni, Cesarino Di; Eight Immortals, The; Helpers; Loqman

References and further reading

Leach, M. (ed.), *Funk and Wagnall's Standard Dictionary of Folklore, Mythology, and Legend*, London: New English Library, 1975. Abridged one-volume edition of *Funk and Wagnall's Standard Dictionary of Folklore, Mythology, and Legend*, 2 vols., New York: Funk and Wagnall, 1972, p. 1188.

Minford, J., *Favourite Folktales of China*, Beijing: New World Press, 1983.

Roberts, M. (ed. and trans.), *Chinese Fairy Tales and Fantasies*, New York: Pantheon Books, 1979.

Yasuna, Abe No

Japanese poet who saves a white fox from being hunted down by a group of nobles. He later marries a woman called Kuzonoha, who dies giving birth to a son. Three days after her death, Kuzonoha reappears to Abe No Yasuna in a dream and tells him that she was the white fox he had saved from the nobles.

The animal bride is a widespread folktale motif, as is that of the animal groom. Also common is the dream in which the beloved deceased—usually the female—appears to the lover. In Japanese and other eastern traditions, the fox appears frequently as a female shape-shifter, and, according to folk belief, she can be identified by a tongue of flame flickering above her human head.

Related entries: Bai Suzhen; Fox Maiden, The; Kuzonoha; Llyn Y Fan Fach, The Lady of; Magicians; Melusine; Mudjikiwis; Ringkitan; Shape-Shifters; Skorobogaty, Kuzma; Swan Maiden; Tabadiku; Urashima; White Lady; Xiaoqing; Yer

References and further reading

Seki, K. (ed.), Adams, R. (trans.), *Folktales of Japan*, London: Routledge and Kegan Paul, 1963, pp. 3, 14, 25, 107–111. First published in Japanese in 1956–1957.

Werner, E., *Myths and Legends of China*, New York: Arno Press, 1976 (1922), pp. 370–375.

Ye Xian

A Chinese heroine of the Cinderella type. Her story first appears in a ninth-century work by

Duan Chengshi. Ye Xian is broadly similar to the European Cinderella; she is mistreated but eventually attains a rich and happy life through magical intervention. However, the Chinese story concentrates on the wicked stepmother's mistreatment of Ye Xian. The stepmother cruelly attempts to spoil Ye Xian's rapport with animals and forbids her to participate in festive occasions. Ye Xian loses a golden shoe instead of a glass slipper, though the king who comes to possess it seeks her out and marries her in much the same way as occurs in the European Cinderella tales. Versions of the story of Ye Xian are still in oral circulation in China after eleven centuries.

Related entries: Assipattle; Cap o' Rushes; Catskin; Cinderella; Cinder-Mary; Fairy Tale Heroes; Woodencloak, Katie

References and further reading

Anon., *The Peacock Maiden: Folk Tales from China*, 3d ser., Beijing: Foreign Languages Press, 1981 (1958).

Ding Wangdao, *Chinese Myths and Fantasies*, Beijing: China Translation Publishing Company, 1991.

Eberhard, W. (ed.), Parsons, D. (trans.), *Folktales of China*, Chicago: University of Chicago Press, 1965 (1937), pp. 156–161.

Yer

Heroine of a Hmong (Laos, Thailand, and Vietnam) tale in which she, her sister-in-law, and her three children are almost the victims of a tiger dressed as Yer's brother-in-law. Yer fights off the ravening tiger dressed in her brother-in-law's clothes, using red pepper, salt, and ashes. During these encounters, a crow friendly to Yer arrives and is dispatched to take word of her plight to her family. Armed to the teeth, the family arrives to rescue Yer, only to find that the tiger is down at the river washing salt, ashes, and pepper out of his sore eyes. Yer's eldest brother tells her to call the tiger and offer to marry him. The tiger agrees, and while wedding arrangements are being made, Yer's other brothers dig a large pit covered with leaves. They offer to take the tiger back to the river for more eye bathing. Seemingly in kindly fashion, they escort him to the river, guiding the tiger over the pit. He falls in; they spear him to death; and Yer goes home with her family.

In this tale, the widespread theme of the beast marriage is implicated, though frustrated, as a means of preserving the family structure, a frequent feature of folktales.

Related entries: Fox Maiden, The; Nou Plai; Swan Maiden; Zeej Choj Kim

References and further reading

Faurot, J. (ed.), *Asian-Pacific Folktales and Legends*, New York: Simon and Schuster, 1995.

Livo, N. and Cha, D., *Folk Stories of the Hmong*, Englewood, CO: Libraries Unlimited, 1991, pp. 69–72.

Yoshitsune

Historical Japanese figure (1159–1189) and member of the famous Minamoto clan. In 1174 Yoshitsune joined his brother Yoshinaka in a revolt and became a great military figure, occupying Kyoto and defeating the Taira in 1184–1185. He later fell out with his powerful brother and was defeated by him in an attempted revolt. Yoshitsune fled and disappeared for some years, pursued by his enemies. He was betrayed by a friend and committed suicide. On these historical facts folklore has erected a considerable legendry surrounding Yoshitsune. He appears in this lore as a mighty warrior. He was served by other warriors almost as mighty, notably Benkei, and is the nephew of the warrior Tametomo.

Related entries: Benkei; Tametomo; Warriors; Yuriwaka

References and further reading

Anesaki, M., "Japanese Mythology," in Grey, L. and MacCulloch, J. (eds.), *The Mythology of All Races*, 30 vols., Boston: Marshall Jones Company, 1916–1932, vol. 8, pp. 207–387.

Davis, F. H., *Myths and Legends of Japan*, London: G. G. Harrap and Co., 1913, pp. 39, 41–44.

Dorson, R., *Folk Legends of Japan*, Rutland, VT: Charles E. Tuttle, 1962, pp. 163, 166.

Yuriwaka

Japanese warrior hero of great strength and bravery who fights a sea battle against the Mongols, making good use of his great archery skills. Victorious, he makes for home with his fleet, but he is betrayed by two brothers, Beppo Taro and Beppo Jiru, who strand Yuriwaka on an island. The brothers return home and tell everyone that Yuriwaka has been killed in battle, and they consequently inherit all his wealth. As well, Beppo Taro harbors a great lust for Yuriwaka's wife. She, however, resists his insolent and aggressive advances, clinging to the hope that Yuriwaka is alive. But Beppo Taro decides that if he cannot have her he will drown her. A faithful servant substitutes his daughter, Lady Manju, for Yuriwaka's wife, and the girl is killed instead.

Now desperate, Yuriwaka's wife writes a note and sends it off, tied to the leg of the great warrior's pet falcon. The falcon eventually finds Yuriwaka, who is still on the island. He reads the note, is enraged at what has happened, and writes a note to his wife in his blood, swearing revenge. The falcon takes the note back to Yuriwaka's wife, and she writes another in reply. The faithful bird just manages to get back to the island with the note when, exhausted, it dies. Yuriwaka is then rescued by a passing fishing boat and returns home in disguise. He takes a lowly job as a servant in the Beppo castle, only revealing his true identity at the New Year archery competition, where he proves who he is by being the only one able to bend the great iron bow of Yuriwaka. He then kills Beppo Taro and is restored to his rightful standing, property, and wife. In gratitude for the sacrifice of Lady Manju and his falcon, Yuriwaka builds

temples to each. It is said that his body lies beneath the mound of Yuriwaka in Bungo Province.

According to folklorist Richard Dorson, this tale of treachery, loyalty, revenge, and reward is essentially a Japanese reworking of Homer's *Odyssey*, which probably reached Japan toward the end of the sixteenth century. With Yuriwaka taking the role of Ulysses, the story includes motifs found in many other hero traditions, including the faithful servant, the animal helper, and the righting of wrongs. However, Japan has an extensive folklore of warrior heroes that precedes contact with the west and that includes such notable figures as the mighty Yoshitsune, said to have led the Minamoto clan against the Taira, and Minamoto Yorimitsu, known poetically as "Raiku," who was a celebrated warrior of eleventh-century Japan.

Related entries: Benkei; Hou Yi; Mergen, Erkhii; Warriors; Yoshitsune

References and further reading

Davis, F. H., *Myths and Legends of Japan*, London: G. G. Harrap and Co., 1913, pp. 368–369.
Dorson, R., *Folk Legends of Japan*, Rutland, VT: Charles E. Tuttle, 1962, pp. 154–156.
Mayer, F., *Ancient Tales in Modern Japan*, Bloomington: Indiana University Press, 1984, no. 331.
McAlpine, H. and W., *Japanese Tales and Legends*, Oxford: Oxford University Press, 1958.
Tyler, R. (trans. and ed.), *Japanese Tales*, New York: Pantheon Books, 1987.

Z

Zab

Persian legendary hero whose full name is
Zorab. Zab is the son of a poor widow. He
works hard for the few pennies that sustain
him and his mother, but he has one large
fault—Zab cannot resist telling untrue tales.
One day, when he comes home from gathering
wood in the forest, his mother asks him what
he has done that day. Zab claims to have visited
a great house and to have sold a sack of silk to
a princess for ten pieces of gold. He then takes
ten copper pennies out of his pocket. His
mother despairs, telling him that his story-
telling will get him into trouble. But Zab just
laughs and goes on with his fantasies.

Some time later, the young tale-teller meets
a man who asks him what he has in his sack. In
his usual fantastical manner, Zab tells him that
the sack is full of silk and spice and that he
wants ten pieces of gold for it. The man gives
Zab the gold, and Zab goes on his way until he
comes across a child begging for money. Zab
gives the child the ten gold pieces. By now the
man has discovered that the sack he bought for
ten pieces of gold contains only twigs. He
searches out Zab, accuses him of fraud, and begins beating him. Surprised, Zab says he will be
happy to return the man's gold, but then he remembers he has given it away to the boy. The
man flies into a rage, beats Zab senseless, and
steals his horse. When Zab returns home, his
mother asks him what has become of the
horse. Unable to restrain himself, Zab tells her
that it turned into a dragon and flew into the
sky. When she asks where the money for the
wood is, Zab tells her that he was given ten
pieces of gold for the wood and that he gave
these to a child begging for bread. His mother
is distraught. They have no money and no
horse. Zab tells his mother not to worry. He
will go out into the world, and his stories will
make both their fortunes.

He wanders for many days, growing dirtier
and wilder, until he comes to an oasis. Here he
meets a maidservant who, taken aback by his
appearance, asks him who he might be. As
usual, Zab cannot tell the truth. He says that he
is the gatekeeper of the Land of Ghosts. It tran-
spires that the first husband of the maidservant's mistress had died the year before and, although since remarried, the mistress would
like to have news of her former husband. Zab
pretends that he has seen the man in the afterlife and that he is in trouble because he has
fallen into debt. The mistress asks Zab to take
him gold. Zab agrees but says he needs transport to the Land of Ghosts. He is given a horse
that turns out to be his own, and he realizes
that the woman's new husband must be the
man who beat him and stole his horse. He tells
the woman that he will need to take the dead
man a kiss from his wife, and Zab thus receives
a long, sweet kiss before riding away with the
gold, laughing to himself.

The woman's second husband returns home
shortly, and after hearing the story from his
wife, realizes she has been deceived. He pursues Zab to a mill, where the boy has convinced
the miller that the king has sent a horseman to
tear the skin from his bald head to make a
drum because the monarch is dissatisfied with
the quality of his flour. Pretending to be helpful, Zab convinces the miller to change clothes
with him. When the pursuer arrives, he does
not recognize Zab in the miller's clothes. Zab
tells him where the miller is hiding and escapes
with his horse and with the husband's. The
miller, in fear of his life, is punching metal pins
into his head. Amazed at this sight, the man
asks him what he is doing, and the miller tells

him that his scalp will be no good for the king's drum as it is now full of holes. Eventually the man convinces the miller that he is not from the king and that they have both been fooled. He then walks back home.

When he reaches the house, his wife, still angry at his refusal to believe her story, berates him. Realizing that she will never be convinced that Zab was not from the Land of Ghosts he decides to enter into the confabulation. He tells her that he gave the gatekeeper of the Land of Ghosts his horse to give to her husband so that he could ride around and enjoy the view in the afterlife. Mollified, the wife gives her husband a long, sweet kiss. Meanwhile, Zab returns to his mother wearing the miller's fine clothes, carrying a purse of gold, and with two horses. His mother wants to know where he has been and what he has been doing. He tells her truthfully all the things that have happened to him. She does not believe one word of it and asks to see the gold. He shows it to her, and she says, "My son, your stories have come true at last, and now you will never have to tell another story." Zab told the truth for ever after.

A similar, if less involved, version of this story features the Yugoslavian trickster hero Ero. The point of that story is to show a member of the oppressor group being outsmarted by native wit and cleverness. In the story of Zab, the point is rather to tell a version of the "Jack and the Beanstalk" theme in which the unlikely young man eventually succeeds in securing the future of his mother and himself. Zab also attains a measure of wisdom, a common theme of folktales. As this story demonstrates, Persian folktales have long been the object of both literary and oral reworking and refinement.

Related entries: Ero; Jack and the Beanstalk
References and further reading
Kurti, A. (trans.), Persian Folktales, London: Bell and Sons, 1971 (1958).
Lee, F. H. (comp.), Folk Tales of All Nations, London: Harrap, 1931, pp. 807–820.
Mehdevi, A., Persian Folk and Fairy Tales, London: Chatto and Windus, 1966, pp. 51–61.

Zeej Choj Kim

A lazy man of Hmong (Laos, Thailand, and Vietnam) legend who is accused of making the emperor's daughter, Ntxawm, pregnant. The emperor orders his sons to kill both Zeej Choj Kim and Ntxawm, but the brothers cannot bring themselves to do it. They leave the couple by the river, but tell their father that they have done his bidding. Beside the river, Zeej Choj Kim and Ntxawm encounter a black and a white crow. In an uncharacteristically rapid move, Zeej Choj Kim captures the white crow, and, as the price of its freedom, he extracts from the black crow a magic ball that, among other things, can prepare all kinds of food and drink.

Meanwhile, the emperor and his sons are losing a great battle. The sons suggest that the emperor ask Zeej Choj Kim for help. The emperor is furious to find that they have disobeyed his orders to kill Zeej Choj Kim, but eventually he concedes that any help is better than none. Zeej Choj Kim agrees to help but asks that enormous amounts of food be cooked in preparation for his arrival on the battlefield. Despite their father's scoffing, the emperor's sons do as Zeej Choj Kim asks. When he finally does arrive, Zeej Choj Kim causes vast numbers of soldiers to march out of his magic ball. As each group emerges, they eat their share of the food that has been prepared and then go off to fight the emperor's enemies. By the time the emperor returns to the scene of battle there are only three of the enemy left alive. The emperor is so pleased that he immediately hails Zeej Choj Kim as his rightful son-in-law, inviting him and Ntxawm back to the palace for a feast. The couple is invited to stay in the town with the emperor and his family, and Zeej Choj Kim and Ntxawm live happily ever after, greatly honored by all the people.

Related entries: Fairy Tale Heroes; Nou Plai; Yer
References and further reading
Faurot, J. (ed.), Asian-Pacific Folktales and Legends, New York: Simon and Schuster, 1995.
Livo, N. and Cha, D., Folk Stories of the Hmong, Englewood, CO: Libraries Unlimited, 1991, pp. 73–78.

Zelinda

The heroine of an Italian Beauty and the Beast story that begins in much the same way as the better-known versions but has a dreadful dragon as the beast. The three daughters each ask for a present—one wants a dress; another wants a shawl; but Zelinda is happy for her father simply to bring her home a handsome rose. The father quickly obtains the shawl and the dress but has to search farther for the rose, it being out of season. He eventually comes upon an imposing walled garden filled with beautiful flowers. The gate is slightly open, and he goes inside, finding a fine rose bush in flower. There is no one to be seen, and so he plucks a rose from the bush. As soon as he does so, a fire-breathing dragon appears, threatening to kill him. Begging for mercy, he is presented with the usual choice of saving himself or giving the monster one of his daughters.

When the father returns home with this choice, the two older sisters turn on Zelinda and blame her for their predicament because she wanted a rose. Zelinda meekly bows to this intimidation and agrees to be taken to the monster. Once there, they are well looked after, and the father is allowed to go, leaving Zelinda to her fate. But instead of eating her, the monster tries to woo her. She refuses his attentions and blandishments until one day the monster tells her that her father is dying, showing her an image of him on his deathbed in a magic mirror. Zelinda begs the monster to save her father and promises to marry the monster in return. As soon as these words are out, the monster transforms into a handsome young man. He tells Zelinda that he is the son of the king of oranges and that a witch had turned him into the monster until such time as a beautiful girl broke the spell by agreeing to become his wife.

Related entries: Beauty and the Beast; Cinderella; Fairy Tale Heroes; Faithful Henry; Frog Prince, The

References and further reading

Calvino, I. (trans. Martin, G.), *Italian Folk Tales: Selected and Retold by Italo Calvino*, New York: Harcourt Brace Jovanovich, Penguin, 1980 (1956).

Crane, T., *Italian Popular Tales*, Boston and New York: Houghton Mifflin and Co., 1885; reprint, Detroit: Singing Tree Press, 1968, pp. 7–11.

INDEX OF HEROIC TYPES

This index lists heroes in accordance with their main attributes. A number of figures appear under more than one category, as they display the attributes of one or more folk hero types. Readers may find this index useful for tracking heroes with similar traits, such as magical abilities, archers, lovers, and so on, or those whose traditions are thematically related, such as outlaws or victims.

Animals and Animal-Related

Anansi
Androcles
Aniz
Apekura
Beauty and the Beast
Berni, Cesarino Di
Coyote
Fox Maiden, The
Frog Prince, The
Gam-Czan, Marshall Gang
Gellert
Goldilocks
Goose Girl, The
Habermani
Halfchick
Hare
Kraljevic, Marco
Kuzonoha
Melusine
Monkey
Monkey Prince
Nanabohzo
Puss in Boots
Rabbit
Reynard the Fox
Skorobogaty, Kuzma
Spider
Swan Maiden

Tametomo
Tortoise
Whittington, Dick
Yao Wang
Yasuna, Abe No
See also Fairy Tale Heroes; Shape-Shifters

Arabian Nights Characters

Ahmed
Aladdin
Baba, Ali
Scheherazade
See also Arabian Nights, The; Fairy Tale Heroes;
    Magicians

Archers

Ahay
Bell, Adam
Clym of the Clough
Hood, Robin
Hou Yi
Ivanovich, Dunai
Kihachi
Mergen, Erkhii
Mudjikiwis
Nue the Hunter
Rasalu
Tametomo
Tell, William
William of Cloudesly
Yuriwaka
See also Magicians; Warriors

Beauties

Allen, Barbara
Amaradevi
Ataba
Beauty and the Beast
Fatima

Morevna, Marya
Nastasya, Princess
Rapunzel
Rose-Red
Scheherazade
Sleeping Beauty
Snow White
Vasilisa
Zelinda
See also Fairy Tale Heroes; Women Dressed
    as Men

Children and Children's Heroes
Cook, Captain
Fairy Godmother, The
Goldilocks
Little Dutch Boy, The
Pied Piper, The
Sandman, The
Santa Claus
Tom Thumb
Tom the Piper's Son
Tooth Fairy
See also Children's Folk Heroes

Culture Heroes
Alexander the Great
Alfred the Great
Amala
Anansi
Arthur
Chang-Hko
Chapman, John
Coyote
Danske, Holger
Darcy, Les
Ebbeson, Niels
Gearoidh, Iarla
Haitsi-Aibab
Havelock the Dane
Hereward the Wake
Hiawatha
Jolly Swagman, The
Kelly, Edward
Kraljevic, Marco
Lemminkäinen
Little Dutch Boy, The
Lohengrin
Mac Cumhal, Finn

Madoc
Matthias, King
Mau and Matang
Maui
Monkey
Mrikanda
Nastasya, Princess
Nikitich, Dobrynya
O'Malley, Grace
Shine
Siitakuuyuk
Uncle Sam
Väinämöinen
Vladimir
Yankee Doodle
See also National Heroes; Warriors

Diminutive Beings
Fereyel
Kihuo
No Bigger Than A Finger
Tom Thumb
See also Children's Folk Heroes; Magicians

Dragon-Slayers
Baldpate
Boots
George, Saint
Guy of Warwick
Ivan the Mare's Son
Li Ji
Nikitich, Dobrynya
Old Woman's Grandchild
Popovich, Aloisha
Tabagnino the Hunchback
Tardanak
Tsarevich, Ivan
See also Giant-Killers; Ogres; Villains

Fairies and Fairy Tales
Assipattle
Beauty and the Beast
Cap o' Rushes
Catskin
Cinderella
Cinder-Mary
Fairy Godmother, The
Faithful Henry
Faithful John

Frog Prince, The
Giricoccola
Goldilocks
Goose Girl, The
Gretel
Halfchick
Hansel
Jack and the Beanstalk
Jack the Giant-Killer
Knowall, Doctor
Little Goose Girl, The
Little Red Riding Hood
Lucky Hans
Lusmore
Mab, Queen
Maria, Fenda
Melusine
Monkey Prince
Puss in Boots
Rapunzel
Rashin' Coatie
Sanykisar
Sleeping Beauty
Snow White
Swan Maiden
Whuppie, Molly
Woodencloak, Katie
Yannakis
Ye Xian
Zeej Choj Kim
Zelinda
See also Dragon-Slayers; Fairy Tale Heroes;
    Giant-Killers; Magicians; Ogres; Villains

Frontier Heroes
Bean, Roy
Chapman, John
Crockett, Davy
Donohoe, Jack
Doyle, Tom
Hiawatha
Jones, Galloping
Wild Colonial Boy
See also Liars; National Heroes; Outlaws

Giant-Killers
Badikan
Guy of Warwick
Haitsi-Aibab

Horn, Hind
Jack and the Beanstalk
Jack the Giant-Killer
Kihuo
Rasalu
Siitakuuyuk
See also Dragon-Slayers; Ogres; Villains

Healers
Eight Immortals, The
Loqman
Yao Wang
See also Helpers; Magicians; Wise Men and
    Women

Helpers
Androcles
Bai Suzhen
Baldpate
Eight Immortals, The
Fairy Godmother, The
Faithful Henry
Faithful John
Havelock the Dane
King of Ireland's Son, The
Little John
Loqman
Macdonald, Flora
Marian, Maid
Momotaro
Nicholas, Saint
Puss in Boots
Rasalu
Reynard the Fox
Sanykisar
Siitakuuyuk
Supparaka
Whittington, Dick
Wirreenun the Rainmaker
Woodencloak, Katie
Yao Wang
See also Magicians

Heroes of Struggle
Alfred the Great
Armstrong, Johnnie
Bindieye, Jacky
Bonaparte, Napoleon
Brown, John

Dojrana
Ebbeson, Niels
Ero
Gearoidh, Iarla
Godiva, Lady
Hereward the Wake
Hill, Joe
Hood, Robin
Jolly Swagman, The
Karagiozis
Kraljevic, Marco
Lazar
Lu Zhishen
Ludd, Ned
Macdonald, Flora
Marian, Maid
McCaffery
Molo
O'Connell, Daniel
O'Malley, Grace
Rákóczi
Rasalu
Rebecca
Santa Anna, General Antonio López de
Shine
Stig, Marsk
Stuart, Prince Charles Edward
Taylor, William
Tell, William
See also Culture Heroes; National Heroes;
    Occupational Heroes; Outlaws

Liars
Crockett, Davy
Crooked Mick
Münchhausen
Pepper, Tom
See also Frontier Heroes; Thieves; Tricksters

Local Heroes
Ashma
Bonney, William
Bunyan, Paul
de Veusters, Father Joseph
Dojrana
Doyle, Tom
Godiva, Lady
Green Princess, The
Havelock the Dane

Ivanovich, Dunai
Johns, Joseph
Jones, Galloping
Lazar
Llyn Y Fan Fach, The Lady of
Macdonald, Flora
Marley, Elsie
Nikitich, Dobrynya
Saburo, Koga
Siitakuuyuk
Taylor, William
Whittington, Dick
See also Frontier Heroes

Lovers
Allen, Barbara
Ataba
Beauty and the Beast
Bernèz
E-ttool, Zarief
Frog Prince, The
Guy of Warwick
Horn, Hind
Little Goose Girl, The
Morevna, Marya
Moringer, Noble
Mudjikiwis
Nou Plai
Rapunzel
Rose-Red
Sahin
Snow White
Spiewna
Väinämöinen
Valentine, Saint
Vasilisa
Xishi
Zeej Choj Kim
Zelinda
See also Fairy Tale Heroes

Magicians
Achikar
Adam, Rabbi
Ahmed
Dog-Nyong, General Gim
Eight Immortals, The
Fereyel
Gim

Habermani
Loew, Rabbi Judah
Marendenboni
Merlin
Molo
Monkey
Nue the Hunter
Pied Piper, The
Vseslavevich, Volkh
Wirreenun the Rainmaker
See also Culture Heroes; Heroes of Struggle;
    Magicians; National Heroes; Shape-Shifters;
    Villains; Wise Men and Women

Military Heroes
Benbow, Admiral
Benkei
Bonaparte, Napoleon
Dog-Nyong, General Gim
Ebbeson, Niels
Fanta-Ghiro'
Franklin, Lord
Gam-Czan, Marshall Gang
McCaffery
Mulan
O'Malley, Grace
Rákóczi
Santa Anna, General Antonio López de
Wolfe, General James
See also Culture Heroes; National Heroes;
    Nautical Heroes; Warriors; Women Dressed
    as Men

National Heroes
Alexander the Great
Alfred the Great
Arthur
Barbarossa
Bonaparte, Napoleon
Chang-Hko
Charlemagne
Cid, El
Columbus, Christopher
Cook, Captain
Danske, Holger
Darcy, Les
Ebbeson, Niels
Franklin, Lord
Gearoidh, Iarla

Havelock the Dane
Hereward the Wake
Hood, Robin
Jolly Swagman, The
Kelly, Edward
Kraljevic, Marco
Mac Cumhal, Finn
Macdonald, Flora
Matthias, King
Nikitich, Dobrynya
O'Connell, Daniel
O'Malley, Grace
Rákóczi
Stig, Marsk
Stuart, Prince Charles Edward
Tell, William
Uncle Sam
Väinämöinen
Vladimir
Washington, George
Wolfe, General James
Yankee Doodle
See also Culture Heroes; Frontier Heroes;
    Military Heroes; Sleepers; Warriors

Nautical Heroes
Benbow, Admiral
Bonaparte, Napoleon
Columbus, Christopher
Cook, Captain
Female Cabin Boy, The
Franklin, Lord
Jack Tar, Jolly
Kidd, William
Madoc
Nicholas, Saint
O'Malley, Grace
Ranzo, Reuben
Sadko
Santa Anna, General Antonio López de
Stormalong
Supparaka
Teach, William
Watch, Will
See also Children's Folk Heroes; Warriors

Nonhuman Lovers
Bai Suzhen
Kuzonoha

Llyn Y Fan Fach, The Lady of
Melusine
Mudjikiwis
Ringkitan
Tabadiku
Urashima
White Lady
Xiaoqing
Yasuna, Abe No
Yer
See also Fox Maiden, The; Magicians;
    Shape-Shifters; Swan Maiden

Numskulls and Noodles
Bertoldo
Bindieye, Jacky
Dad and Dave
Drongo
Ivanko the Bear's Son
Kabajan
Knowall, Doctor
Little Moron
Lucky Hans
Ranzo, Reuben
Wise Men of Gotham
See also Tricksters

Occupational Heroes
Bonaparte, Napoleon
Bunyan, Paul
Crooked Mick
Fink, Mike
Henry, John
Hill, Joe
Jack-in-the-Green
Jones, Casey
Little Moron
Mademoiselle from Armentieres
McCaffery
Mikula
Mrikanda
Pecos Bill
Ranzo, Reuben
Slater, Morris (Railroad Bill)
Stormalong
See also Heroes of Struggle; Liars

Outlaws
Bass, Sam

Bell, Adam
Bonney, William
Brennan, William
Christie, Francis
Clym of the Clough
Cortez, Gregorio
Deva, Babar
Dillinger, John
Donohoe, Jack
Fisk, Jim
Floyd, Charles Arthur
Geordie
Hall, Ben
Hereward the Wake
Hood, Robin
James, Jesse
Johns, Joseph
Kelly, Edward
Li Kui
Little John
Lu Zhishen
Molo
Morgan, Daniel "Mad Dog"
Parker, Robert Leroy
Quantrill, William Clarke
Slater, Morris (Railroad Bill)
Stig, Marsk
Swift Nicks
Troy, Johnny
Turpin, Richard
Ward, Frederick Wordsworth
Wild Colonial Boy
William of Cloudesly
Wu Song
Xiao En
See also Celebrity Heroes; Heroes of Struggle;
    Women Dressed as Men

Religious Heroes
Adam, Rabbi
Baal-Shem-Tov
Brigid (Brigit), Saint
Chokanamma
de Veusters, Father Joseph
Elijah the Prophet
George, Saint
Guy of Warwick
Jesus
Joseph of Arimathea, Saint

Kentigern, Saint
Khidre, El
Kukai
Lowe, Rabbi Judah
Mary
Nanak
Nicholas, Saint
Patrick, Saint
Seven Sleepers, The
Valentine, Saint
See also Helpers; Magicians

Shape-Shifters
Barleycorn, John
Fereyel
Fox Maiden, The
Frog Prince, The
Habermani
Hodja, The
Jack
Melusine
Nanabozho
Ringkitan
Snow White
Stagolee
Swan Maiden
Tabadiku
Tam Lin
Vseslavevich, Volkh
White Lady
Xiaoqing
See also Magicians; Tricksters

Sleepers
Arthur
Barbarossa
Batradz
Charlemagne
Danske, Holger
Gearoidh, Iarla
Kraljevic, Marco
Mac Cumhal, Finn
Matthias, King
Merlin
Peterkin
Seven Sleepers, The
Sleeping Beauty
Thomas the Rhymer
Urashima

Van Winkle, Rip
See also Culture Heroes; National Heroes;
    Warriors

Thieves
Baba, Ali
Halid
Jones, Galloping
See also Outlaws; Shape-Shifters; Tricksters

Tricksters
Abunuwas
Anansi
Bertoldo
Coyote
Ero
Eulenspiegel, Till
Gearoidh, Iarla
Gizo
Hare
Hlakanyana
Hodja, The
Jack o' Kent
Jones, Galloping
Kabajan
Maui
Monkey
Nanabozho
O'Connell, Daniel
Ostropolier, Hershel
Popovich, Aloisha
Quevedo
Rabbit
Ramalingadu, Tenali
Shine
Skorobogaty, Kuzma
Spider
Tortoise
Urdemalas, Pedro de
See also Magicians; Shape-Shifters

Under/Otherworld Visitors
Avdotya
Ivan the Mare's Son
Mu Lian
Mu-Monto
Nakali
Potyk, Mikhail
Saburo, Koga

Sadko
Tam Lin
Thomas the Rhymer
See also Magicians; Shape-Shifters; Sleepers

Unpromising Heroes
Amala
Ashblower, Ivan
Assipattle
Boots
Fereyel
Halid
Ilu, Ana
Ivanko the Bear's Son
Jack and the Beanstalk
Jack the Giant-Killer
Kabadaluk
Kapsirko
Kihuo
Knowall, Doctor
Lucky Hans
Marendenboni
Muhammad
Muromets, Ilya
Puuhaara, Antti
Skorobogaty, Kuzma
Tabagnino the Hunchback
Whittington, Dick
Zab
See also Fairy Tale Heroes; Jack Tales; Victims

Victims
Ahay
Amala
Aniz
Apekura
Armstrong, Johnnie
Ashma
Barleycorn, John
Bindieye, Jacky
Cap o' Rushes
Catskin
Chokanamma
Cinderella
Darcy, Les
Dojrana
Fatima
Franklin, Lord
Geordie

Green Princess, The
Gretel
Halfchick
Hansel
Isabel, Lady
Jane, Queen
Judy
Kandek
Kihachi
Mau and Matang
Pied Piper, The
Scheherazade
Shine
Tam Lin
Thomas the Rhymer
Wanara, Siung (Tiung)
Xishi
Ye Xian

Villains
Baba-Yaga
Bluebeard
Devil, The
Kidd, William
Koshchei
Pied Piper, The
Punch
Stuart, Prince Charles Edward
Teach, William
Wulgaru
See also Magicians; Monsters; Ogres; Outlaws;
    Thieves

Warriors
Alexander the Great
Alfred the Great
Arthur
Aryg, Altyn
Barbarossa
Batradz
Benbow, Admiral
Benkei
Bonaparte, Napoleon
Dog-Nyong, General Gim
Gam-Czan, Marshall Gang
Gearoidh, Iarla
Gongsun Jie
Guy of Warwick
Havelock the Dane

Ivanovich, Dunai
Kihuo
Kraljevic, Marco
Mac Cumhal, Finn
Matthias, King
Mergen, Erkhii
Molo
Muromets, Ilya
Nikitich, Dobrynya
O'Malley, Grace
Popovich, Aloisha
Rákóczi
Rasalu
Santa Anna, General Antonio López de
Tametomo
Tsarevich, Ivan
Väinämöinen
Vseslavevich, Volkh
Washington, George
Wolfe, General James
Xiang Yu
Yamato
Yoshitsune
Yuriwaka
See also Culture Heroes; Military Heroes;
    Outlaws; Women Dressed as Men

Wise Men and Women
Achikar
Amaradevi
Baal-Shem-Tov
Eight Immortals, The
Elijah the Prophet
Fatima
Hiawatha
Isabel, Lady
Khidre, El
Scheherazade
Supparaka
Wungala
See also Helpers; Magicians

Women Dressed as Men
Aryg, Altyn
Fanta-Ghiro'
Female Cabin Boy, The
Female Drummer, The
Female Highwayman, The
Female Smuggler, The
Geordie
Mulan
O'Malley, Grace
See also Magicians; Outlaws

COUNTRY/CULTURE INDEX

This index gives an approximate indication of the origins and spread of hero folk traditions. As this encyclopedia amply demonstrates, many of these traditions are found in different nationalities and among different language, ethnic, religious, and cultural groups. Consequently, it is rarely possible to say that a particular hero belongs exclusively to a particular nation or culture. However, certain heroes and/or heroic types are often associated with a particular country or cultural group. It is these dominant, rather than exclusive, associations that this index highlights. Because of the wide diffusion of some traditions, a good number of heroes will be found in more than one country/culture category.

Aboriginal Australian
Bindieye, Jacky
Cook, Captain
Kelly, Edward
Mau and Matang
Wirreenun the Rainmaker
Wulgaru
Wungala
See also Culture Heroes

African
Abunuwas
Anansi
Fereyel
Gizo
Haitsi-Aibab
Hare
Hlakanyana
Kihuo
Marendenboni
Maria, Fenda
Rabbit

Spider
Tortoise

African-American
Anansi
Henry, John
Shine
Slater, Morris (Railroad Bill)
Stagolee

Arabic
Ahmed
Aladdin
Arabian Nights, The
Baba, Ali
Khidre, El
Muhammad
Scheherazade

Armenian
Badikan
Habermani
Kandek
Loqman

Assyrian (Iraq)
Achikar

Australian
Bindieye, Jacky
Christie, Francis
Crooked Mick
Dad and Dave
Darcy, Les
Donohoe, Jack
Doyle, Tom
Drongo
Hall, Ben

Australian (cont.)
Johns, Joseph (Moondyne Joe)
Jolly Swagman, The
Jones, Galloping
Kelly, Edward
Morgan, Daniel "Mad Dog"
Troy, Johnny
Ward, Frederick Wordsworth (Thunderbolt)

Belgian
de Veusters, Father Joseph
Tricksters

Breton
Bernèz

Buddhist
Kukai

Burmese
Chang-Hko

Cambodian
Amaradevi

Canadian
Bunyan, Paul
Jack
Mademoiselle from Armentieres
Siitakuuyuk (Inuit)

Chilean
Urdemalas, Pedro de

Chinese
Ahay
Ashma
Bai Suzhen
Eight Immortals, The
Gongsun Jie
Hou Yi
Li Ji
Li Kui
Lu Zhishen
Molo
Monkey
Mu Lian
Mulan
Nou Plai

Rose-Red
White Lady
Wu Song
Xiang Yu
Xiao En
Xiaoqing
Xishi
Yao Wang
Ye Xian
Yer

Christian
Androcles
Devil, The
Fairy Godmother, The
George, Saint
Jesus
Joseph of Arimathea, Saint
Kentigern, Saint (Mungo)
Mary
Santa Claus
Seven Sleepers, The
Valentine, Saint

Danish
Danske, Holger
Ebbeson, Niels
Havelock the Dane
Stig, Marsk

Dutch
Little Dutch Boy, The

English
Alfred the Great
Allen, Barbara
Arthur
Barleycorn, John
Bell, Adam
Benbow, Admiral
Bonaparte, Napoleon
Clym of the Clough
Female Cabin Boy, The
Female Drummer, The
Female Highwayman, The
Female Smuggler, The
Franklin, Lord
George, Saint
Godiva, Lady

Greek
George, Saint
Karagiozis
Yannakis

Gypsy (Rom, Roma, or Romany)
Baldpate
Peterkin
Yannakis

Halmahera (Indonesia)
Tabadiku

Hindu
Rasalu

Hungarian
Matthias, King
Rákóczi

Indian
Chokanamma
Deva, Babar
Halfchick
Mrikanda
Nanak
Ramalingadu, Tenali
Rasalu
Sanykisar
Supparaka

Irish
Brennan, William
Brigid (Brigit), Saint
Gearoidh, Iarla
King of Ireland's Son, The
Lusmore
Mac Cumhal, Finn
O'Connell, Daniel
O'Malley, Grace
Patrick, Saint
See also Culture Heroes

Italian
Berni, Cesarino Di
Bertoldo
Columbus, Christopher
Fanta-Ghiro'
Giricoccola

Tabagnino the Hunchback
Zelinda

Japanese
Benkei
Fox Maiden, The
Kihachi
Kukai
Kuzonoha
Momotaro
Nue the Hunter
Sabura, Kogo
Tametomo
Urashima
Yamato
Yasuna, Abe No
Yoshitsune
Yuriwaka

Java (Indonesia)
Kabajan
Siung (Tiung) Wanara
See also Tricksters; Warriors

Jewish
Adam, Rabbi
Baal-Shem-Tov
Elijah the Prophet
Loew, Rabbi Judah
Ostropolier, Hershel

Korean
Dog-Nyong, General Gim
Gam-Czan, Marshall Gang
Gim
Zeej Choj Kim

Mexican
Cinder-Mary
Cortez, Gregorio
Coyote
Quevedo
Santa Anna, General Antonio López de
Urdemalas, Pedro de

Mongolian
Aryg, Altyn
Mergen, Erkhii

Muslim
George, Saint
Halid
Khidre, El

Native American
Amala
Coyote
Hiawatha
Mudjikiwis
Nanabohzo
Old Woman's Grandchild
See also Culture Heroes; Frontier Heroes

New Zealand Maori
Apekura
Maui
See also Culture Heroes

North American
Bass, Sam
Bean, Roy
Bonney, William
Brown, John
Bunyan, Paul
Chapman, John
Columbus, Christopher
Crockett, Davy
Dillinger, John
Fink, Mike
Fisk, Jim
Floyd, Charles Arthur
Henry, John
Hiawatha
Hill, Joe
Jack
James, Jesse
Jones, Casey
Kidd, William
Little Dutch Boy, The
Little Moron
Parker, Robert Leroy
Pecos Bill
Pepper, Tom
Quantrill, William Clarke
Sandman, The
Santa Anna, General Antonio López de
Santa Claus
Shine

Slater, Morris (Railroad Bill)
Stagolee
Stormalong
Teach, William
Tooth Fairy
Troy, Johnny
Uncle Sam
Van Winkle, Rip
Washington, George
Yankee Doodle

Norwegian
Boots
Goose Girl, The
Woodencloak, Katie

Pacific Islands
Apekura
de Veusters, Father Joseph
Maui

Palestinian
Ataba
E-ttool, Zarief
Sahin

Persian
Zab
See also Helpers; Victims

Philippines
Monkey Prince

Polish
Spiewna
See also Villains

Russian
Ashblower, Ivan
Avdotya
Baba-Yaga
Batradz
Elijah the Prophet
Ivanko the Bear's Son
Ivanovich, Dunai
Kapsirko
Koshchei
Mikula
Morevna, Marya

Russian (cont.)
Muromets, Ilya
Nastasya, Princess
Nikitich, Dobrynya
No Bigger Than a Finger
Popovich, Aloisha
Potyk, Mikhail
Sadko
Skorobogaty, Kuzma
Tardanak
Tsarevich, Ivan
Vasilisa
Vladimir
Vseslavevich, Volkh

Scots
Armstrong, Johnnie
Assipattle
Geordie
Macdonald, Flora
Rashin' Coatie
Rob Roy
Stuart, Prince Charles Edward
Tam Lin

Serbian
Dojrana
Kraljevic, Marco
Lazar

Siberian
Ivan the Mare's Son
Mu-Monto

Sikh
Nanak

Slovenian
See Culture Heroes

South American
Nakali
Quevedo
Urdemalas, Pedro de
See also Culture Heroes

Spanish
Cid, El
Urdemalas, Pedro de

Sulawesi (Indonesian)
Ilu, Ana
Ringkitan

Sumatra (Indonesian)
Green Princess, The

Swiss
Tell, William

Turkish
Halid
Hodja, The

Uygar (China)
Aniz

Yugoslavian
Ero
Kabadaluk
Kraljevic, Marco

Welsh
Gellert
Llyn Y Fan Fach, The Lady of
Madoc
Rebecca

CHRONOLOGY OF FOLK HEROES

This chronology has been provided for readers who wish to search for heroes from a particular historical period. It includes both legendary and historical figures. Legendary figures are entered at the date they were earliest recorded in recognizable form.

The chronology is arranged by centuries, although the names of the heroes within each century are arranged alphabetically.

Names included in this chronology are not only headword entries but also characters mentioned in passing.

The chronology also includes important collections containing stories and/or songs about heroes.

It is not possible to provide definitive dates for all the heroes who appear in the encyclopedia, and the chronology should be treated only as a general guide.

Ninth Century B.C.
Elijah the Prophet

Seventh Century B.C.
Khidre, El

Sixth–Fifth Centuries B.C.
Aesop's fables (c. 620–560 B.C.). Many of Aesop's fables were rewritten in verse by the Greek poet Babrius, probably in the first or second century A.D., and in Latin verse by the Roman poet Phaedrus (c. 15 B.C.–50 A.D.) in the first century A.D. The collection that now bears Aesop's name consists for the most part of later prose paraphrases of the fables of Babrius.

Fourth Century B.C.
Alexander the Great

Hayk
Hou Yi and Cheng'er
Master Thief (Herodotus)

Third Century B.C.
Second Century B.C.
Xiang Yu

First Century A.D.
Jesus
Joseph of Arimathea, Saint
Mary
Seven Sleepers, The

Second Century
Xiang Yu
Yamato

Third Century
Mac Cumhal, Finn
Mulan
Valentine, Saint

Fourth Century
George, Saint
Nicholas, Saint
Sadko
Santa Claus

Fifth Century
Achikar
Arthur
Brigid (Brigit), Saint
Patrick, Saint

Sixth Century
Kentigern, Saint (Mungo)
Merlin

Seventh Century
Charlemagne
Molo
Monkey
Rose-Red

Eighth Century
Abunuwas
Roderick
Urashima

Ninth Century
Alfred the Great
Cinderella
Kobo Daishi (Kukai)
Ye Xian

Tenth Century
Ahmed
Aladdin
Boru, Brian
Hasan
Morgiana
1001 (or *Arabian*) *Nights*
Scheherazade
Sindbad
Vladimir

Eleventh Century
Boru, Brian
Cid, El
Gellert
Godiva, Lady
Hereward the Wake
Vseslavevich, Volkh
Yuriwaka

Twelfth Century
Barbarossa (Frederick I)
Benkei
Blondel
Guy of Warwick
Havelock the Dane
Madoc
Moringer, Noble
Tametomo
Yoshitsune

Thirteenth Century
Hodja, The
Horn, Hind (Child Horn)
Nikitich, Dobrynya
Pied Piper, The
Popovich, Aloisha
Stig, Marsk
Thomas the Rhymer

Fourteenth Century
Bell, Adam
Boccaccio, Giovanni, reworked traditional and
    literary tales in his *Il Decamerone*
Ebbeson, Niels
Eulenspiegel, Till
Hood, Robin, as portrayed in Langland's *The
    Vision of William Concerning Piers the Plowman*,
    better known as *Piers the Plowman* (written
    c. 1360–1400)
Kraljevic, Marco
Sleeping Beauty
Tell, William
Whittington, Dick

Fifteenth Century
Columbus, Christopher
Madoc
Matthias, King (Kralj Matjaz)
Wise Men of Gotham

Sixteenth Century
Amala
Armstrong, Johnnie
Bell, Adam
Bertoldo
Clym of the Clough
Hiawatha
Jack o' Kent
Jane, Queen
Judy
Nanak
O'Malley, Grace
Punch
Straparola, Giovan, *Le Piacevoli Notta* (The pleas-
    ant nights, 1550–1553)
Teach, William
Urdemalas, Pedro de
William of Cloudesly
Yuriwaka

Seventeenth Century

Aulnoy, Madam, *Contes de fées* (1697) and *Les Contes nouveaux* (1698)

Basile, Giambattista, his *Lo Cunti de li Cunti* (The tale of tales, known from the 1674 edition as *Il Pentamerone*) was published between 1634 and 1636

Benbow, Admiral

Boccaccio, Giovanni, his *Il Decamerone* was translated into English as *The Decameron* in 1620

Fairy Godmother, The

Female Cabin Boy, The

Female Drummer, The

Female Highwayman, The

Female Smuggler, The

Karagiozis

Kidd, William

Perrault, Charles, *Histoires ou Contes du Temps Passé* (Historical tales from the past, 1697)

Quevedo

Swift Nicks

Tom Thumb

Eighteenth Century

Allen, Barbara

Baal-Shem-Tov

Baba, Ali

Beauty and the Beast

Bonaparte, Napoleon

Boone, Daniel

Cook, Captain

Crockett, Davy

Fairy Godmother, The

Macdonald, Flora

Marley, Elsie

Münchhausen

O'Connell, Daniel

Ostropolier, Hershel

Rákóczi

Ross, Betsy

Stuart, Prince Charles Edward

Tam Lin

Teach, William

Turpin, Richard

Washington, George

Wolfe, General James

Yankee Doodle

Nineteenth Century

Bass, Sam

Bean, Roy

Bindieye, Jacky

Bonney, William (Billy the Kid)

Brennan, William

Brer Rabbit

Brown, John

Bunyan, Paul

Burke, Martha Jane (Calamity Jane)

Burton, R., *The Arabian Nights' Entertainments* (1894–1897)

Chapman, John (Johnny Appleseed)

Christie, Francis

Cody, William Frederick (Buffalo Bill)

Cortez, Gregorio

Crooked Mick

Dad and Dave

de Veusters, Father Joseph

Dillinger, John

Drongo

Fink, Mike

Fisk, Jim

Franklin, Lord

Gatiloke (collected, contents much older)

Gellert

Goldilocks

Grimm, Jacob and Wilhelm, authors of *Kinder- und Hausmärchen* (Children's and household tales), 2 vols. (1812–1815; translated into English, 1884)

Hall, Ben

Hooper, Slappy

James, Jesse

Johns, Joseph (Moondyne Joe)

Jones, Casey (John Luther Jones)

Kelly, Edward (Ned)

Lusmore

McCaffery

Morgan, Daniel "Mad Dog"

Nanak

Parker, Robert Leroy (Butch Cassidy)

Pecos Bill

Pemulway

Pepper, Tom

Pigeon

Quantrill, William Clarke (Quantrell)

Rebecca

Santa Anna, General Antonio López de

Shirley, Myra Belle (Belle Starr)
Slater, Morris (Railroad Bill)
Stagolee
Swing, Captain
Taylor, William
Troy, Johnny
Uncle Sam
Ward, Frederick Wordsworth (Thunderbolt)
Watch, Will
Wild Colonial Boy
Wirreenun the Rainmaker (collected)
Yagan

Twentieth Century
Darcy, Les
Deva, Babar
Di, Princess
Dillinger, John
Doyle, Tom
Floyd, Charles Arthur (Pretty Boy)
Goldilocks (under this name)
Hill, Joe
Jones, Galloping
Mademoiselle from Armentieres
Magarac, Joe
Shine
Tooth Fairy

BIBLIOGRAPHY

This bibliography consists of both the sources used for the entries in the encyclopedia, and additional works, especially collections of folktales and songs, that may be useful to readers wishing to pursue interests in folk heroes and other aspects of folklore. It also contains a number of important classificatory and bibliographical works.

Aarne, A. and Thompson, S., *The Types of the Folktale: A Classification and Bibliography*, Folklore Fellows Communication 184, Helsinki: Academia Scientiarum Fennica, 1961. Translated and enlarged from the 1928 edition written by S. Thompson.

Abbott, G., *Macedonian Folklore*, Cambridge: Cambridge University Press, 1903.

Abdelhady, T., *Palestinian Folk-Tales*, vol. 3, Beirut: Ibenrashed Publishing Company, n.d.

Abrahams, R., *African Folktales*, New York: Pantheon Books, 1983.

———, *Afro-American Folktales*, New York: Pantheon Books, 1985.

———, "Some Varieties of Heroes in North America," *Journal of the Folklore Institute* 3 (1966).

Abrahams, R. et al. (eds.), *By Land and by Sea: Studies in the Folklore of Work and Leisure*, Hatboro, PA: Legacy Books, 1985.

Adagala, K. and Kabira, W. (eds.), *Kenyan Oral Narratives: A Selection*, Nairobi: Heinemann, 1985.

Addy, S., *Household Tales and Other Traditional Remains*, London: Sheffield, 1895.

Afanas'ev, A. (comp.), Guterman, N. (trans.), *Russian Fairy Tales*, New York: Pantheon Books, 1945.

Aiken, R., *Mexican Folktales from the Borderland*, Dallas: Southern Methodist University Press, 1980.

Alderson, B. (ed.), *Red Fairy Book: Collected by Andrew Lang*, Harmondsworth, Middlesex: Kestrel Books, 1976.

Alexander, A., *Russian Folklore: An Anthology in English Translation*, Belmont, MA: Nordland Publishing Co., 1975.

Alford, V., *The Singing of the Travels: In Search of Dance and Drama*, London: Max Parrish, 1956.

Algarin, J., *Japanese Folk Literature: A Core Collection and Reference Guide*, New York: Bowker and Co., 1982.

Alpers, A., *Legends of the South Sea*, London: John Murray, 1970.

Alpers, A. (ed.), *Maori Myths and Tribal Legends*, 2d ed., Auckland: Addison Wesley Longman New Zealand, 1964.

Aman, S., *Folk Tales from Indonesia*, Jakarta: Djambatan, 1976.

Anderson, H., *Time out of Mind: Simon McDonald of Creswick*, Melbourne: National Press, 1974.

Anderson, J., *Myths and Legends of the Polynesians*, London: Harrap, 1928.

Anon., *The Peacock Maiden: Folk Tales from China*, 3d ser., Beijing: Foreign Languages Press, 1981 (1958).

Argenti, P. and Rose, H., *The Folk-Lore of Chios*, 2 vols. London: Cambridge University Press, 1949.

Arnold, A. (ed.), *Monsters, Tricksters, and Sacred Cows: Animal Tales and American Identities*, Charlottesville: University Press of Virginia, 1996.

Arnott, K., *Animal Folk Tales from Around the World*, London and Glasgow: Blackie and Son, 1970.

Arnott, K. (ed.), *African Myths and Legends*, London: Oxford University Press, 1962.

Asbjørnsen, P. and Moe, J. (trans. Dasent, G.), *Popular Tales from the Norse*, Edinburgh: David Douglas, 1888.

Ashliman, D., Folklore and Mythology Electronic Texts, Pittsburgh, PA: University of Pittsburgh, 2000, www.pitt.edu/~dash/folktexts.html#a.

Ashton, J., Modern Street Ballads, New York and London: Benjamin Blom, 1968 (1888).

Ausubel, N. (ed.), A Treasury of Jewish Folklore, London: Vallentine, Mitchell, 1972 (1948).

Babcock, B., "A Tolerated Margin of Mess: The Trickster and His Tales Reconsidered," Journal of the Folklore Institute 11, no. 3: 1975.

Bacchilega, C., Postmodern Fairy Tales: Gender and Narrative Strategies, Philadelphia: University of Pennsylvania Press, 1997.

Bailey, J. and Ivanova, T. (trans.), An Anthology of Russian Folk Epics, Armonk and London: M. E. Sharpe, 1998.

Bain, R. (trans.), Russian Fairy Tales from the Russian of Polevoi, London: George Harrap, 1915.

Baker, M., Tales of All the World, London: Oxford University Press, 1937.

———, Folklore of the Sea, London and North Pomfret, VT: David and Charles, 1979.

———, Discovering Christmas Customs and Folklore, rev. ed., Buckinghamshire, Eng.: Shire Publications, 1992 (1968).

Barbeau, M., The Golden Phoenix and Other French-Canadian Fairy Tales (retold by Michael Hornyansky), New York: Scholastic Book Services, 1965 (1959).

Barber, R., Myths and Legends of the British Isles, Rochester, NY: Boydell Press, 1999.

Baring-Gould, S. (comp.), Folk Songs of the West Country. Annotated from the mss. at Plymouth Library with additional material by Gordon Hitchcock. Newton Abbot, Devon: David and Charles, 1974.

Baring-Gould, S., Curious Myths of the Middle Ages, London: Green and Co., 1897 (1866).

Barkataki, S. (comp.), Tribal Folk-Tales of Assam (Hills), Asam, Gauhati: Publication Board, 1970.

Barker, W. and Sinclair, C. (colls.), West African Folk Tales, London: Harrap and Co., 1917.

Barlow, D., Dick Turpin and the Gregory Gang, London: Phillimore, 1973.

Barnham, H. (trans.), The Khoja: Tales of Nasr-ed-Din, New York: D. Appleton and Co., 1924.

Barnouw, V., Wisconsin Chippewa Myths and Tales, Madison: University of Wisconsin Press, 1977.

Barrick, M., "Numskull Tales in Cumberland County," Pennsylvania Folklife 15, no. 4 (summer 1967).

———, "The Migratory Anecdote and the Folk Concept of Fame," Mid-South Folklore 4 (1976).

Bascom, W., African Folktales in the New World, Bloomington: Indiana University Press, 1992.

Baumann, H., Hero Legends of the World, London: Dent and Sons, 1975 (1972).

Bay, J., Danish Folk Tales, New York and London: Harper and Brothers Publishers, 1899.

Beatty, B., A Treasury of Australian Folk Tales and Traditions, Sydney: Ure Smith, 1960.

Beck, B. et al. (eds.), Folktales of India, Chicago: University of Chicago Press, 1987.

Beck, H., Folklore and the Sea, Middletown, CT: Wesleyan University Press, 1973.

Belden, H. (ed.), Ballads and Songs Collected by the Missouri Folklore Society, University of Missouri Studies 15, no. 1, 1940.

Belden, H. and Hudson, A. (eds.), The Frank C. Brown Collection of North Carolina Folklore, 7 vols., Durham, NC: Duke University Press, 1952.

Bennett, M., West African Trickster Tales, Oxford: Oxford University Press, 1994.

Berndt, R. and C., The Speaking Land: Myth and Story in Aboriginal Australia, Ringwood, Vic.: Penguin, 1989.

Bettelheim, B., The Uses of Enchantment: The Meaning and Importance of Fairy Tales, New York: Knopf, 1976.

Bin Gorion, M. (coll.), Ben-Amos, D. (trans.), Mimekor Yisrael: Classical Jewish Folktales, 3 vols., Bloomington: Indiana University Press, 1976.

Bluestein, G., Poplore: Folk and Pop in American Culture, Amherst: University of Massachusetts Press, 1994.

Blum, R. and E., The Dangerous Hour: The Lore of Crisis and Mystery in Rural Greece, London: Chatto and Windus, 1970.

Boaz, F. (ed.), Folk-Tales of Salishan and Sahaptin Tribes, Lancaster, PA: American Folk-Lore Society, 1917.

Boccaccio, G., *The Decameron*, New York: The Heritage Press, 1940 (1620).

Bødker, L., Hole, C., and d'Aronco, G. (eds.), *European Folk Tales*, Hatboro, PA: Rosenkilde and Bager; Copenhagen: Folklore Associates, 1963.

Bompas, C., *Folklore of the Santal Parganas*, London: David Nutt, 1909.

Boorstin, D., *The Image: A Guide to Pseudo-events in America*, New York: Athaneum, 1962 (1961).

Booss, C., *Scandinavian Folk and Fairy Tales*, New York: Crown Publishers, Avenel Books, 1984.

Børdahl, V. (ed.), *The Eternal Storyteller: Oral Literature in Modern China*, Richmond, UK: Curzon Press, 1999.

Botkin, B. (ed.), *A Treasury of American Folklore: Stories, Ballads, and Traditions of the People*, New York: Crown, 1944.

Botkin, B. (ed.), *A Treasury of American Anecdotes*, New York: Random House, 1957.

Botkin, B. (ed.), *A Treasury of Western Folklore*, New York: Crown, 1964.

Bottigheimer, R., *Grimms' Bad Girls and Bold Boys: The Moral and Social Vision of the Tales*, New Haven and London: Yale University Press, 1987.

Bottigheimer, R. (ed.), *Fairy Tales and Society: Illusion, Allusion, and Paradigm*, Philadelphia: University of Pennsylvania Press, 1986.

Boyle, J., "Historical Dragon Slayers," in Porter, J., and Russell, W. (eds.), *Animals in Folklore*, Ipswich, Eng.: Brewer/Rowman and Littlefield, The Folklore Society, 1978.

Brice, D., *The Folk-Carol of England*, London: Herbert Jenkins, 1967.

Briggs, K., *The Fairies in Tradition and Literature*, London: Routledge and Kegan Paul, 1967.

———, *British Folktales*, New York: Pantheon, 1977.

———, *Nine Lives: The Folklore of Cats*, New York: Pantheon, 1980.

Briggs, K. (ed.), *A Dictionary of British Folk-Tales in the English Language*, 2 vols., London: Routledge and Kegan Paul, 1970–1971.

Briggs, K. and Tongue, R. (eds.), *Folktales of England*, London: Routledge and Kegan Paul, 1965.

Broadwood, L., *English Traditional Songs and Carols*, London: E. P. Publishing, Rowman and Littlefield, 1974 (1908).

Brockett, E., *Burmese and Thai Fairy Tales*, London: Frederick Muller, 1965.

Brown, M. and Rosenberg, B. (eds.), *Encyclopedia of Folklore and Literature*, Santa Barbara, CA: ABC-CLIO, 1998.

Brownlee, F., *Lion and Jackal and Other Native Folk Tales from South Africa*, London: George Allen and Unwin, 1938.

Brun, V., *Sug, the Trickster Who Fooled the Monk: A Northern Thai Tale with Vocabulary*, Scandinavian Institute of Asian Studies Monograph 27, London: Curzon Press, 1976.

Brunvand, J., *The Mexican Pet*, New York: Norton, 1986.

Brunvand, J. (ed.), *American Folklore: An Encyclopedia*, New York: Garland, 1996.

Buchan, D., *Scottish Tradition: A Collection of Scottish Folk Literature*, London: Routledge and Kegan Paul, 1984.

Burrison, L. (ed.), *Storytellers: Folk Tales and Legends from the South*, Athens: University of Georgia Press, 1989.

Burton, R., *The Arabian Nights' Entertainments*, 13 vols., London: H. Nichols, 1894–1897.

Bushnaq, I. (trans. and ed.), *Arab Folktales*, New York: Pantheon Books, 1986.

Butler, B., *The Myth of the Hero*, London: Rider and Co., 1979.

Butterss, P., "Bold Jack Donahue and the Irish Outlaw Tradition," *Australian Folklore* 3(1989): 3–9.

Byrom, M., *Punch and Judy: Its Origin and Evolution*, Aberdeen: Shiva Publications, 1972.

Cachia, P., *Popular Narrative Ballads of Modern Egypt*, Oxford: Oxford University Press, 1989.

Calvino, I. (trans. Martin, G.), *Italian Folk Tales: Selected and Retold by Italo Calvino*, New York: Harcourt Brace Jovanovich, 1980 (1956).

Campbell, C. (trans. and ed.), *Tales from the Arab Tribes*, London: Lindsay Drummond, 1949.

Campbell, J., *The Hero with a Thousand Faces*, Princeton, NJ: Princeton University Press, 1968.

Campbell, J. F., *Popular Tales of the West Highlands*, London: Alexander Gardiner, 1890.

Capp, B., "Popular Literature," in Reay, B.

(ed.), *Popular Culture in Seventeenth Century England*, London: Croom Helm, 1988 (1985).

Carey, M. B., Jr., "Mademoiselle from Armentieres," *Journal of American Folklore 47*, 1934.

Carey, M., *Myths and Legends of Africa*, London: Paul Hamlyn, 1970.

Carnegie, M., *Morgan the Bold Bushranger*, Melbourne: Angus and Robertson, 1974.

Carrison, M. and Chhean, K., *Cambodian Folk Stories from the Gatiloke*, Rutland, VT and Tokyo: C. E. Tuttle Co., 1987.

Carter, A. (ed.), *The Second Virago Book of Fairy Tales*, London: Virago Press, 1992.

Cashdan, S., *The Witch Must Die: How Fairy Tales Shape Our Lives*, New York: Basic Books, 1999.

Cashman, R., "The Heroic Outlaw in Irish Folklore and Popular Tradition," *Folklore* 111, no. 2 (2000): 191–215.

Cave, C. et al. (eds.), *Ned Kelly: Man and Myth*, Melbourne: Cassell Australia, 1968.

Cavendish, R. (ed.), *Legends of the World*, London: Orbis, 1982.

Chappell, W., *Popular Music of the Olden Time*, 2 vols., New York: Dover, 1965 (1859).

Chase, R. (ed.), with notes and contributions by Halpert, H., *The Jack Tales*, Boston: Houghton Mifflin, 1943.

Chaudury, I. (ed.), *Folk Tales of Haryana*, New Delhi: Sterling Publishers, 1974.

Cheng Quiang, *Zhongguo Minjian Chuanshuo* (Chinese folk legends), Hangzhou: Zhejiang Educational Publishing House, 1995.

Child, F. J., *The English and Scottish Popular Ballads*, 5 vols., New York: Dover, 1965 (1882–1898).

Christen, K., *Clowns and Tricksters: An Encyclopedia of Tradition and Culture*, Santa Barbara, CA: ABC-CLIO, 1998.

Christensen, A. (ed.), Kurti, A. (trans.), *Persian Folktales*, London: Bell and Sons, 1971.

Christiansen, R. (ed.), *Folktales of Norway*, London: Routledge and Kegan Paul, 1964.

"CJT," *Folk-Lore and Legends Scandinavian*, London, 1890.

Clark, E., *Indian Legends of Canada*, Toronto: McClelland and Stewart, 1960.

Clarkson, A. and Cross, G. (eds.), *World Folktales*, New York: Charles Scribner's Sons, 1980.

Clifford, E., *Father Damien*, New York: Macmillan, 1890.

Clough, B. (ed.), *The American Imagination at Work: Tall Tales and Folk Tales*, New York: Knopf, 1947.

Clouston, W., *Popular Tales and Fictions: Their Migrations and Transformations*, 2 vols., Edinburgh and London: William Blackwood, 1887.

———, *The Book of Noodles*, London: Elliot Stock, 1888.

Coffin, T., *The British Traditional Ballad in North America*, rev. ed., Philadelphia: American Folklore Society, 1963.

———, *The Female Hero in Folklore and Legend*, New York: Seabury Press, 1975.

Coffin, T. (ed.), *American Folklore*, Washington, D.C.: Voice of America Forum Lectures, 1968.

Coffin, T. and Cohen, H. (eds.), *The Parade of Heroes: Legendary Figures in American Lore*, Garden City: Doubleday, Anchor Press, 1978.

Cohen, N., *Long Steel Rail: The Railroad in American Folksong*, Champaign, IL: University of Illinois Press, 1981.

Colcord, J., *Songs of American Sailormen*, New York: Oak Publications, 1964 (1938).

Cole, J. (ed.), *Best-Loved Folktales of the World*, Garden City: Doubleday, 1982.

Collison, R., *The Story of Street Literature*, Santa Barbara, CA: ABC-CLIO, Inc., 1973.

Combs, J. H. (ed. D. K. Wilgus), *Folksongs of the Southern United States*, Austin: University of Texas Press, American Folklore Society Reprint, 1967 (1925).

Copper, B., *A Song for Every Season*, Frogmore: Paladin, 1975 (1971).

Courlander, H., *Tales of Yoruba Gods and Heroes*, New York: Fawcett Publications, 1974.

Courlander, H. (ed.), *Ride with the Sun: An Anthology of Folk Tales and Stories from the United Nations*, New York: McGraw-Hill Book Company, 1955.

Courlander, H. (comp.), *A Treasury of African Folklore*, New York: Crown, 1975.

Cowan, J., *Legends of the Maori*, vol. 1, Wellington: Harry H. Tombs, 1930.

Cowan, J. (ed.), *Fairy Folk Tales of the Maori*, 2d.

ed., Auckland: Whitcombe and Tombs, 1930.

Cox, M., Cinderella: Three Hundred and Forty-Five Variants, London: David Nutt, 1893.

Coxwell, C., Siberian and Other Folk-Tales, London: C. W. Daniel, 1925.

Crane, T., Italian Popular Tales, Boston and New York: Houghton Mifflin and Co., 1885; reprint, Detroit: Singing Tree Press, 1968.

Creanga, I. (trans. Nandris, M.), Folk Tales from Roumania, London: Routledge and Kegan Paul, 1952.

Creighton, H. (coll.), (ed. Taft, M. and Caplan, R.), A Folk Tale Journey through the Maritimes, Nova Scotia: Breton Books, 1993.

Croker, T. C. (ed. Wright, T.), Fairy Legends and Traditions of the South of Ireland, new and complete edition, London: William Tegg, 1862.

Curcija-Prodanovic, N., Heroes of Serbia, London: Oxford University Press, 1963.

Curcija-Prodanovic, N. (comp.), Yugoslav Folk-Tales, Oxford: Oxford University Press, 1957.

Curtin, J., Myths and Folk-Lore of Ireland, Boston: Little, Brown, 1890; reprint, Detroit: Singing Tree Press, 1968.

———, Hero-Tales of Ireland, Boston: Little, Brown, 1911 (1894).

Curtin, J. (ed.), Myths and Folktales of the Russians, Western Slavs, and Magyars, New York: Benjamin Blom, 1971 (1890).

Dadié, B. (trans. Hatch, C.), The Black Cloth: A Collection of African Folktales, Amherst: University of Massachusetts Press, 1987 (1955).

Danaher, K., Folktales of the Irish Countryside, Cork: Mercier Press, 1967.

Daniel, G. et al., Myth or Legend? London: Bell and Sons, 1955.

Darnton, R., The Great Cat Massacre and Other Episodes in French Cultural History, New York: Basic Books, 1984.

Dasent, G. (comp.), Popular Tales from the Norse, Edinburgh: David Douglas, 1888; reprint, Detroit: Grand River Books, 1971; and also as East o' the Sun and West o' the Moon, New York: Dover Publications, 1970.

Davey, G. and Seal, G. (eds.), The Oxford Companion to Australian Folklore, Melbourne: Oxford University Press, 1993.

David, G., Female Heroism in the Pastoral, New York: Garland Publishing, 1991.

Davidson, H., Patterns of Folklore, Ipswich, Eng.: Brewer; Totowa, NJ: Rowman and Littlefield, 1960.

Davidson, H. (ed.), The Hero in Tradition and Folklore, London: Mistletoe Books, 1985.

Davis, F. H., Myths and Legends of Japan, London: G. G. Harrap and Co., 1913.

Dawkins, R. (comp. and trans.), Modern Greek Folktales, Oxford: Clarendon Press, 1953; reprint Westport, CT: Greenwood Press, 1974.

Day, L., Folk-Tales of Bengal, London: Macmillan and Co., 1883.

de Bosschére, J., Folk Tales of Flanders, New York: Dodd, Mead, and Co., 1918.

de Caro, F. (ed.), The Folktale Cat, Little Rock, AR: August House, 1992.

De Coster, C. (trans. Atkinson, F.), The Legend of Eulenspiegel, 2 vols., London: William Heinnemann, 1922.

De Larrabeiti, M., The Provencal Tales, New York: St. Martin's Press, 1988.

de Vries, J. (trans. Timmer, B.), Heroic Song and Heroic Legend, London and New York: Oxford University Press, 1963 (1959).

Decker, J., Made in America: Self-Styled Success from Horatio Alger to Oprah Winfrey, Minneapolis: University of Minnesota Press, 1997.

Dégh, L., Folktales of Hungary, Chicago: University of Chicago Press, 1965.

———, American Folklore and the Mass Media, Bloomington: Indiana University Press, 1994.

Dégh, L. (trans. Schossberger, E.), Folktales and Society: Story-Telling in a Hungarian Peasant Community, Bloomington: Indiana University Press, 1969 (1962).

Del Guidice, L. (ed.), Studies in Italian-American Folklore, Logan: Utah State University Press, 1993.

Delarue, P. (ed.), Fife, A. (trans.), The Borzoi Book of French Folk Tales, New York: Knopf, 1956.

Deva, I., Folk Culture and Peasant Society in India, Jaipur: Rawat Publications, 1989.

Dhar, A., Folk Tales of Afghanistan, New Delhi: Sterling Publishers, 1982.

Dhar, S., *Kashmir Folk Tales*, Bombay: Hind Kitabs Publishers, 1949.

Ding Wangdao, *Chinese Myths and Fantasies*, Beijing: China Translation Publishing Company, 1991.

Dixon-Kennedy, M., *European Myth and Legend*, London: Blandford, 1997.

Dobie, F. J., *Tales of Old-Time Texas*, London, 1959 (1928).

Dobson, R. B. and Taylor, J., *Rymes of Robin Hood: An Introduction to the English Outlaw*, 2d rev. ed., Gloucester: Allan Sutton, 1989 (1976).

Doerflinger, W. (coll. and ed.), *Songs of the Sailor and Lumberman*, New York: Macmillan, 1972 (1951).

Dorson, R., *American Folklore*, Chicago: University of Chicago Press, 1959.

———, *Folk Legends of Japan*, Rutland, VT: Charles E. Tuttle, 1962.

———, *Buying the Wind: Regional Folklore in the United States*, Chicago: University of Chicago Press, 1964.

———, *America in Legend*, New York: Pantheon Books, 1973.

———, *Folklore and Fakelore: Essays toward a Discipline of Folk Studies*, Cambridge, MA: Harvard University Press, 1976.

———, "The Debate over the Trustworthiness of Oral Traditional History," in Dorson, R., *Folklore*, Bloomington: Indiana University Press, 1972.

———, "The Career of John Henry," in Dundes, A. (ed.), *Mother Wit from the Laughing Barrel: Readings in the Interpretation of Afro-American Folklore*, New York: Garland, 1981 (1973).

Dorson, R. (coll. and ed.), *American Negro Folktales*, New York: Fawcett World Library, 1967 (1956, 1958).

Dorson, R. (ed.), *Folktales Told around the World*, Chicago: University of Chicago Press, 1975.

Dorson, R. (ed.), *African Folklore*, Bloomington: Indiana University Press, 1979 (1972).

Douglas, G., *Scottish Fairy and Folk Tales*, Edinburgh: Walter Scott Publishing Co., 1901.

Downing, C. (trans. and ed.), *Armenian Folk-Tales and Fables*, London: Oxford University Press, 1972.

Druts, Y. and Gessler, A. (colls.), Riordan, J. (trans.), *Russian Gypsy Tales*, Edinburgh: Canongate, 1986.

Duckett, E., *The Wandering Saints*, London: Collins, 1959.

Duddington, N. (trans.), *Russian Folk Tales*, London: Rupert Hart-Davies, 1967.

Dundes, A., *Interpreting Folklore*, Bloomington: Indiana University Press, 1980.

———, "Fairy Tales from a Folkloristic Perspective," in Bottigheimer, R. (ed.), *Fairy Tales and Society: Illusion, Allusion, and Paradigm*, Philadelphia: University of Pennsylvania Press, 1986.

Dundes, A. (ed.), *Mother Wit from the Laughing Barrel: Readings in the Interpretation of Afro-American Folklore*, New York: Garland, 1981 (1973).

Dundes, A. (ed.), *Cinderella: A Folklore Casebook*, New York: Garland, 1982.

Dundes, A. (ed.), *Little Red Riding Hood: A Casebook*, Madison: University of Wisconsin Press, 1989.

Dykes, J. C., *Billy the Kid: The Bibliography of a Legend*, Norman: Oklahoma University Press, 1952.

Eberhard, W., *Studies in Taiwanese Folktales*, Taipei: The Orient Cultural Service, 1971.

Eberhard, W. (ed.), Parsons, D. (trans.), *Folktales of China*, Chicago: University of Chicago Press, 1965 (1937).

Edmondson, M., *Lore: An Introduction to the Science of Folklore and Literature*, New York: Holt, Rinehart, and Winston, 1971.

Edwards, R., *The Big Book of Australian Folk Songs*, Adelaide, SA: Rigby, 1976.

———, *The Australian Yarn*, Adelaide, SA: Rigby, 1978 (1977).

———, *200 Years of Australian Folk Song Index*, Kuranda, Qld: Rams Skull Press, 1988.

———, *The Overlander Songbook*, St. Lucia, Qld.: University of Queensland Press, 1991.

Elliot, I., *Moondyne Joe: The Man and the Myth*, Perth: University of Western Australia Press, 1978.

Ellis, J., *One Fairy Story Too Many: The Brothers Grimm and Their Tales*, Chicago: University of Chicago Press, 1983.

El-Shamy, H. (coll., trans., ed.), *Folktales of Egypt*, Chicago: University of Chicago Press, 1980.

Elstob, E. and Barber, R. (trans.), *Russian Folktales*, London: Bell and Sons, 1971. First published as Von Lowis of Menar, A. (trans.) and Olesch, R. (ed.), *Russische Volksmärchen*, 1959.

Engelke, V. (trans. Lindow, J.), *Swedish Legends and Folktales*, Berkeley: University of California Press, 1978 (1892).

Erdoes, R. and Ortiz, A., *American Indian Myths and Legends*, New York: Pantheon Books, 1984.

Espinosa, A. (Espinosa, M. ed.), *The Folklore of Spain in the American Southwest: Traditional Spanish Folk Literature in Northern New Mexico and Southern Colorado*, Norman: University of Oklahoma Press, 1985.

Evans-Pritchard, E. (ed.), *The Zande Trickster*, Oxford: Oxford University Press, 1967.

Factor, J., *Captain Cook Chased a Chook: Children's Folklore in Australia*, Ringwood: Penguin, 1988.

Falassi, A., *Folklore by the Fireside: Text and Context in the Tuscan Veglia*, London: Scolar Press, 1980.

Fansler, D., *Filipino Popular Tales*, Lancaster and New York: American Folklore Society, 1921.

Farrow, J., *Damien the Leper*, London: Burns, Oates and Co., 1937.

Faurot, J. (ed.), *Asian-Pacific Folktales and Legends*, New York: Simon and Schuster, 1995.

Fife, A. E., Fife, A. S., and Gardner, N. (eds.), *Songs of the Cowboys*, New York: Clarkson N. Potter, Bramhall House, 1966.

Fillmore, P., *Czechoslovak Fairy Tales*, New York: Harcourt Brace and Howe, 1919.

———, *Mighty Mikko: A Book of Finnish Fairy Tales and Folk Tales*, New York: Harcourt Brace and Co., 1920.

———, *The Shoemaker's Apron: A Second Book of Czechoslovak Fairy Tales*, New York: Harcourt Brace and Howe, 1920.

Finger, C., *Bushrangers*, New York: McBridge and Co., 1924.

———, *Frontier Ballads*, New York: Doubleday, Page and Co., 1927.

Fiske, J., *Myths and Mythmakers*, London: Trubner, 1873.

Foner, S. (comp. and ed.), *The Letters of Joe Hill*, New York: Oak Publications, 1965.

Ford, R., *Vagabond Songs and Ballads of Scotland*, Paisley: A. Gardner, 1899.

Foster, J. (ed.), *The World's Great Folktales*, New York: Harper and Brothers, 1953.

Fowke, E., *Folktales of French Canada*, Toronto: NC Press, 1979.

———, *Lumbering Songs from the Northern Woods*, Toronto: NC Press, 1985 (1870).

———, *Tales Told in Canada*, Toronto: Doubleday Canada, 1986.

———, "In Defence of Paul Bunyan," in Fowke, E. and Carpenter, C. (eds.), *Explorations in Canadian Folklore*, Toronto: McClelland and Stewart, 1985.

Fowke, E. (ed.), *Folklore of Canada*, Toronto: McClelland and Stewart, 1976.

Fraser, P., *Punch and Judy*, London and New York: Batsford, Van Nostrand Reinhold, 1970.

Frazer, J., *Folk-Lore in the Old Testament*, 3 vols., London: Macmillan, 1918.

Gaer, J., *The Lore of the Old Testament*, Boston: Little, Brown, 1951.

———, *The Lore of the New Testament*, Boston: Little, Brown, 1952.

Garner, A., *The Guizer*, New York: Greenwillow Books, 1976.

Geldart, E. (ed.), *Folk-Lore of Modern Greece: The Tales of the People*, London: W. Swan Sonnenschein and Co., 1884.

Gill, S., *Storytracking: Texts, Stories, and Histories in Central Australia*, Oxford: Oxford University Press, 1998.

Ginzberg, L. (trans. Szold, H.), *The Legends of the Jews*, 7 vols., Philadelphia: The Jewish Publication Society of America, 1900.

Glassie, H., *Irish Folk Tales*, New York: Pantheon, 1985.

Glassie, H. (ed.), *Irish Folk History: Texts from the North*, Philadelphia: University of Pennsylvania Press, 1982.

Goetinck, G., *Peredur: A Study of Welsh Traditions in the Grail Legends*, Cardiff: University of Wales Press, 1975.

Golnick, J. (ed.), *Comparative Studies in Merlin from the Vedas to C. G. Jung*, Lewiston, NY: Edwin Mellen Press, 1991.

Goody, J., *The Interface between the Written and the Oral*, Cambridge: Cambridge University Press, 1987.

Gose, E., Jr., *The World of the Irish Wonder Tale: An Introduction to the Study of Fairy Tales*, Toronto: University of Toronto Press, 1985.

Gray, A. (trans.), *Historical Ballads of Denmark*,

Edinburgh: Edinburgh University Press, 1958.

Gray, J., *Indian Tales and Legends*, Oxford: Oxford University Press, 1979 (1961).

Green, A., *Wobblies, Pile Butts, and Other Heroes*, Urbana and Chicago: University of Illinois Press, 1993.

Green, A. E. "McCaffery: A Study in the Variation and Function of a Ballad," *Lore and Language* 3 through 5, 1970–1971.

Green, T. (ed.), *Folklore: An Encyclopedia of Beliefs, Customs, Tales, Music, and Art*, 2 vols., Santa Barbara: ABC-CLIO, 1997.

Greenway, J. (ed.), *Folklore of the Great West: Selections from Eighty-Three Years of the Journal of American Folklore*, Palo Alto, CA: American West Publishing Company, 1969.

Grey, L. and MacCulloch, J. (eds.), *The Mythology of All Races*, 30 vols., Boston: Marshall Jones Company, 1916–1932.

Grimm, J. and W., *The Complete Grimm's Fairy Tales*, New York: Pantheon Books, 1944.

Grimms' Fairy Tales, Electronic Text Project, Carnegie-Mellon University, 2000.

Grinnell, G. B., *Pawnee Hero Stories and Folk-Tales*, Lincoln: University of Nebraska Press, 1961.

Groome, F. H., *Gypsy Folk Tales*, London: Hutchinson, 1899.

Guerber, H., *Myths and Legends of the Middle Ages: Their Origin and Influence on Literature and Art*, London: Harrap, 1909.

Gunkell, H. (trans. Rutter, M.), *The Folktale in the Old Testament*, Sheffield: Sheffield Academic Press, 1987.

Gurko, L., *Heroes, Highbrows, and the Popular Mind*, New York: Bobbs-Merrill, 1953.

Gutch, J. M., *A Lytell Geste of Robin Hood*, 2 vols., London: John Russell Smith, Joseph Lilly, 1850.

Hafner, K. and Markoff, J., *Cyberpunk: Outlaws and Hackers on the Computer Frontier*, London: Fourth Estate, 1991.

Hall, S., Jr., *The Eskimo Storyteller: Folktales from Noatak, Alaska*, Knoxville: University of Tennessee Press, 1975, nos. PM 102, PM 131.

Hallett, M. and Karasek, B. (eds.), *Folk and Fairy Tales*, Ontario: Broadview Press, 1996.

Halliwell, J., *The Nursery Rhymes of England*, London: The Bodley Head, 1970 (1842).

———, *Popular Rhymes and Nursery Tales of England*, London: The Bodley Head, 1970 (1849).

Halpert, H., "Truth in Folk-Songs: Some Observations on the Folk-Singer's Attitude," in Halpert, H. and Herzog, G., *Traditional Ballads from West Virginia*, New York: National Service Bureau, WPA, 1939.

———, "Tom Pepper: The Biggest Liar on Land or Sea," in Abrahams, R. et al. (eds.), *By Land and by Sea: Studies in the Folklore of Work and Leisure*, Hatboro, PA: Legacy Books, 1985.

Halpert, H. (ed.), *A Folklore Sampler from the Maritimes*, with a bibliographical essay on the folktale in English, St. John's: Memorial University of Newfoundland Folklore and Language Publications, 1982.

Halpert, H. and Widdowson, J. (eds.), *Folktales of Newfoundland: The Resilience of Oral Tradition*, 2 vols., New York: Garland, 1996.

Hamer, F. (coll.), *Garner's Gay*, London: EFDS Publications, 1967.

Hamer, F. (coll.), *Green Groves: More English Folksongs Collected by Fred Hamer*, London: EFDS Publications, 1973.

Hanauer, J. (ed. M. Pickthall), *Folk-Lore of the Holy Land: Moslem, Christian, and Jewish*, London: Duckworth, 1907.

Hanghe, A. (coll. and trans.), *Folktales from Somalia*, Uppsala: Scandinavian Institute of African Studies, 1988.

Hardy, J. (ed.), *The Denham Tracts*, London: The Folklore Society, 1892.

Harlan, L., "Rajasthani Hero Legends," in MacDonald, M. (ed.), *Traditional Storytelling Today: An International Sourcebook*, Chicago: Fitzroy Dearborn, 1999.

Harney, W., *Tales from the Aborigines*, Adelaide, SA: Rigby, 1959.

Harris, R., "The Steel Drivin' Man," in Dundes, A. (ed.), *Mother Wit from the Laughing Barrel: Readings in the Interpretation of Afro-American Folklore*, New York: Garland, 1981 (1973).

Harrison, A., *The Irish Trickster*, Sheffield: Sheffield Academic Press, 1988.

Hasan, A., *The Folklore of Buxar*, Gurgaon, Haryana: The Academic Press, 1978.

Haswell, G. (coll.), *Ten Shanties Sung on the Australian Run, 1879*, Perth: The Antipodes Press, 1992.

Hayward, A., *Lives of the Most Remarkable Criminals*, London: Reeves and Turner, 1735.

Hearne, B., *Beauty and the Beast:Visions and Revisions of an Old Tale*, Chicago: University of Chicago Press, 1989.

———, "Booking the Brothers Grimm: Art, Adaptations, and Economics," in McGlathery, J. (ed.), *The Brothers Grimm and Folktale*, Urbana and Chicago: University of Illinois Press, 1988.

Henderson, H. (ed. and trans.), *The Maiden Who Rose from the Sea and Other Finnish Folktales*, Enfield Lock: Hisarlik Press, 1992.

Hendricks, G., *The Bad Man of the West*, San Antonio, TX: Naylor, 1941.

Herd, D. (coll. and ed.), *Ancient and Modern Scottish Songs, Heroic Ballads, etc.*, 2 vols., Edinburgh: Scottish Academic Press, 1973(1776).

Hilton, R. H., "The Origins of Robin Hood," *Past and Present* 14, 1958.

Hindley, C., *Curiosities of Street Literature*, London: Reeves and Turner, 1871.

Hitchcock, G. (ed.), *Folksongs of the West Country*, Sabine Baring-Gould MS collection, London, 1977.

Hla, L. (trans. Tun, T. and Forbes, K.), *Prince of Rubies and Other Tales from Burma*, n.p., 1980.

Hobsbawm, E., *Bandits*, London: Weidenfeld and Nicolson, 1969.

Hobsbawm, E. and Rudé, G., *Captain Swing*, London: Lawrence and Wishart, 1969.

Hobsbawm, E. and Ranger, T. (eds.) *The Invention of Tradition*, Cambridge: Cambridge University Press, 1984.

Hodgetts, E. (trans.), *Tales and Legends from the Land of the Tsar*, 2d. ed., 1891; reprint, New York: Krauss Reprint Co., 1972.

Hofberg, H. (trans. Myers, W.), *Swedish Fairy Tales*, Chicago: W. B. Conkey, 1893.

Hoffman, D., *Paul Bunyan, Last of the Frontier Demigods*, Philadelphia: University of Philadelphia Press, 1952.

Hole, C., *English Folk-Heroes*, London: Batsford, 1948.

———, *Saints in Folklore*, London: G. Bell and Sons, 1966.

Holloway, J. and Black, J., (eds.), *Later English Broadside Ballads*, London: Routledge and Kegan Paul, 1975, vol. 1.

Holt, J., *Robin Hood*, rev. ed., London: Thames and Hudson, 1989.

———, "The Origins and the Audience of the Ballads of Robin Hood," *Past and Present* 18, 1960.

Hook, S., *The Hero in History:A Study in Limitation and Possibility*, London: Secker and Warbyrg, 1945(1943).

Hugill, S., *Shanties from the Seven Seas*, London: Routledge and Kegan Paul, 1979 (1961).

Hunt, M. (trans. and ed.), *Grimm's Household Tales*, with the author's notes and an introduction by Andrew Lang, 2 vols., London: George Bell and Sons, 1884.

Ingledew, C. J., *The Ballads and Songs of Yorkshire*, London: n.p., 1860.

In-Sob, Z., *Folk Tales from Korea*, London: Routledge and Kegan Paul, 1952.

Ioannou, N., *Barossa Journeys: Into a Valley of Tradition*, Kent Town: Paringa Press, 1997.

Irizar, L. (ed.), Barandiarán, J. (coll.), White, L. (trans.), *A View from the Witch's Cave: Folktales of the Pyrenees*, Reno and Las Vegas: University of Nevada Press, 1988.

Irwin, R., *The Arabian Nights: A Companion*, London: Allen Lane, 1994.

Ivanits, L., *Russian Folk Belief*, Armonk and London: M. E. Sharpe Inc., 1989.

Ives, E. D., *George Magoon and the Down East Game War: History, Folklore, and the Law*, Urbana and Chicago: University of Illinois Press, 1988.

Jackson, B., *"Get Your Ass in the Water and Swim Like Me": Narrative Poetry from Black Oral Tradition*, Cambridge: Harvard University Press, 1974.

Jackson, G., *Early Songs of Uncle Sam*, Boston: Bruce Humphries, 1933.

Jacobs, J. (ed.), *Celtic Fairy Tales*, London: David Nutt, 1892.

Jacobs, J. (ed.), *English Fairy Tales*, London: David Nutt, 1893.

Jacobs, J. (ed.), *More Celtic Fairy Tales*, London: David Nutt, 1894.

Jacobs, J. (ed.), *More English Fairy Tales*, London: David Nutt, 1894.

Jacobs, J. (ed.), *Indian Fairy Tales*, London: David Nutt, 1892; reprint, New York: Dover Publications, 1969.

James, G. (ed.), *Japanese Fairy Tales*, London: Macmillan, 1923. First published as *Green Willow and Other Japanese Fairy Tales*, London: Macmillan and Company, 1910.

James, L., *Print and the People 1819–1851*, London: Allen Lane, 1976.

Jansen, W., *Abraham "Oregon" Smith: Pioneer, Folk Hero, and Tale-Teller*, New York: Arno, 1977.

Jekyll, W. (coll. and ed.), *Jamaican Song and Story*, New York: Dover, 1966 (1907).

Jones, A., *Larousse Dictionary of World Folklore*, Edinburgh and New York: Larousse, 1995.

Jones, D., *Rebecca's Children: A Study of Rural Society, Crime, and Protest*, Oxford: Clarendon Press, 1989.

Jones, D. E., "Clenched Teeth and Curses: Revenge and the Dime Novel Outlaws," *Journal of Popular Culture* 7, no. 3, 1973.

Jones, G., *Welsh Legends and Folk Tales*, London: Oxford University Press, 1955.

Jones, I., *Ned Kelly: A Short Life*, Melbourne: Lothian, 1995.

Jones, M., "(PC+CB) X SD (R+I+E) = Hero," *New York Folklore Quarterly* 27, 1971.

Judge, R., *The Jack-in-the-Green: A May Day Custom*, Cambridge: D. S. Brewer; Ipswich, Eng.: Rowman and Littlefield, 1979 (1978 USA).

Junne, I., *Floating Clouds, Floating Dreams: Favorite Asian Folktales*, Garden City, NY: Doubleday, 1974.

Jurich, M., *Scheherazade's Sisters: Trickster Heroines and Their Stories in World Literature*, Westport and London: Greenwood Press, 1998.

Kanner, L., *Folklore of the Teeth*, New York: Macmillan, 1928.

Karpeles, M. (ed.), *Cecil Sharp's Collection of English Folk Songs*, 2 vols., London: Oxford University Press, 1974.

Keats, E., *John Henry: An American Legend*, New York: Pantheon, 1965.

Keen, M., *The Outlaws of Medieval Legend*, London: Routledge and Kegan Paul, 1961.

———, "Robin Hood: A Peasant Hero," *History Today*, October 1958.

Kennedy, P., *Legendary Fictions of the Irish Celts*, London: Macmillan and Co., 1866.

———, *Folksong of Britain and Ireland*, London: Cassel, 1975.

Ker, A. (coll. and ed.), *Papuan Fairy Tales*, London: Macmillan, 1910.

Kidson, F., *A Garland of English Folk-Songs*, London: Ascherberg, Hopwood and Crew, 1926.

———, *Traditional Tunes*, East Ardsley: S. R. Publishers, 1970 (1891).

Kinsley, J. (ed.), *The Oxford Book of Ballads*, Oxford: Clarendon Press, 1969.

Klapp, O., *Heroes, Villains, and Fools: Reflections of the American Character*, Englewood Cliffs, NJ: Prentice-Hall, 1962.

———, "The Folk Hero," *Journal of American Folklore* 62, no. 243, 1949.

Klipple, M., *African Folktales with Foreign Analogues*, New York: Garland, 1992.

Knappert, J., *Myths and Legends of Indonesia*, Singapore: Heinnemann, 1977.

———, *Myths and Legends of Botswana, Lesotho, and Swaziland*, Leiden: Brill, 1985.

Knight, S., *Robin Hood: A Complete Study of the English Outlaw*, Oxford: Blackwell, 1994.

Kooistra, P., *Criminals as Heroes: Structure, Power, and Identity*, Bowling Green, OH: Bowling Green State University Press, 1989.

Koutsoukis, A. (trans.), *Indonesian Folk Tales*, Adelaide: Rigby, 1970.

Kruse, H. H., "Myth in the Making: The James Brothers at Northfield, Minnesota, and the Dime Novel," *Journal of Popular Culture* 10, no. 2, 1976.

Kúnos, I. (coll.), Bain, R. (trans.), *Turkish Fairy Tales and Folk Tales*, London: Lawrence and Bullen, 1896.

Kvideland, R. and Sehmsdorf, H. (eds.), *Scandinavian Folk Belief and Legend*, Minneapolis: University of Minnesota Press, 1988.

Kvideland, R. and Sehmsdorf, H. (eds.), *Nordic Folklore: Recent Studies*, Bloomington and Indianapolis: Indiana University Press, 1989.

Landtman, G., *The Kiwai Papuans of British New Guinea*, London: Macmillan and Co., 1927.

Lang, A., *The Blue Fairy Book*, London: Longman, Greens, and Co., 1889.

———, *The Red Fairy Book*, London: 1890.

———, *The Yellow Fairy Book*, London: 1894.

———, *The Violet Fairy Book*, London: 1901.

Lange, J. de, *The Relation and Development of English and Icelandic Outlaw-Traditions*, Haarlem: H. D. Tjeenk, Willink and Zoon, 1935.

Larkin, M., *The Singing Cowboy*, New York: Alfred A. Knopf, 1931.

Lawrie, M. (coll. and trans.), *Myths and Legends of Torres Strait*, St. Lucia: University of Queensland Press, 1970.

Laws, G., *American Balladry from British Broadsides*, Philadelphia: American Folklore Society, 1957.

———, *Native American Balladry: A Descriptive Study and a Bibliographical Syllabus*, rev. ed., Philadelphia: American Folklore Society, 1964 (1950).

Leach, M. (ed.), *Funk and Wagnall's Standard Dictionary of Folklore, Mythology, and Legend*, London: New English Library, 1975. Abridged one-volume edition of *Funk and Wagnall's Standard Dictionary of Folklore, Mythology, and Legend*, 2 vols., New York: Funk and Wagnall, 1972.

Leach, M. (ed.), *The Ballad Book*, New York: Harper and Brothers, 1955.

Leavy, B., *In Search for the Swan Maiden: A Narrative on Folklore and Gender*, New York: New York University Press, 1994.

Lee, F. H. (comp.), *Folk Tales of All Nations*, London: Harrap, 1931.

Leodas, N. S., *Thistle and Thyme: Tales and Legends from Scotland*, London: The Bodley Head, 1965.

Li, N., *Old Tales of China*, Singapore: Graham Brash, 1983 (1981).

Lingenfelter, R. et al. (eds.), *Songs of the American West*, Berkeley: University of California Press, 1968.

Livo, N., *Who's Afraid? Facing Children's Fears with Folktales*, Englewood, CO: Teacher Ideas Press, 1994.

Livo, N. and Cha, D., *Folk Stories of the Hmong*, Englewood, CO: Libraries Unlimited, 1991.

Lloyd, A., *Folksong in England*, New York: International Publishers, 1970 (1967).

Lockhart, J. (ed. and trans.), *The Spanish Ballads*, New York: Century, 1907.

Lofaro, M. (ed.), *The Tall Tales of Davy Crockett*, Knoxville: University of Tennessee Press, 1987.

Logan, H., *A Pedlar's Pack of Ballads and Songs*, Edinburgh: n.p., 1869.

Lomax, J. *Our Singing Country*, New York: Macmillan, 1949.

Lomax, J. and A. (colls. and comps.), *American Ballads and Folk Songs*, New York: Macmillan, 1934.

Lönnrot, E. (comp.), Magoun, F. (trans.), *The Kalevala, or Poems of the Kalevala District*, Cambridge: Harvard University Press, 1963.

Loomis, R. (ed.), *The Grail: From Celtic Myth to Christian Symbol*, London: Constable, 1993.

Lord, A., *The Singer of Tales*, New York: Athaneum, 1976 (1960).

Lüthi, M. (trans. Chadeayne, L. and Gottwald, P.), *Once upon a Time: On the Nature of Fairy Tales*, Bloomington: Indiana University Press, 1976.

Lüthi, M. (trans. Niles, J.), *The European Folktale: Form and Nature*, Bloomington: Indiana University Press, 1982 (1947).

Lüthi, M. (trans. Erickson, J.), *The Fairytale as Art Form and Portrait of Man*, Bloomington: Indiana University Press, 1984 (1975).

MacDonald, M. (ed.), *Traditional Storytelling Today: An International Sourcebook*, Chicago: Fitzroy Dearborn, 1999.

MacDougall, J., *Folk and Hero Tales: Waifs and Strays of Celtic Tradition*, London: David Nutt, 1891.

Mackay, C., *Extraordinary Popular Delusions and the Madness of Crowds*, London: R. Bentley, 1841.

Maddicott, J. R., "The Birth and Setting of the Ballads of Robin Hood," *English Historical Review* 93, 1978.

Magel, E. (trans. and ed.), *Folktales from the Gambia: Wolof Fictional Narratives*, Boulder, CO: Three Continents Press, 1984.

Maranda P. (ed.), *Mythology: Selected Readings*, Harmondsworth, Middlesex: Penguin, 1972.

Mark, V., "Cultural Pastiches: Intertextualities in the Moncrabeau Liars' Festival Narratives," *Cultural Anthropology* 6, no. 2, 1991.

Marsh, I. (comp. and ed.), *Tales and Traditions from Sabah*, rev. ed., Kota Kinabalu: The Sabah Society, 1989 (1988).

Marshall, D., *Celebrity and Power: Fame in*

Contemporary Culture, Minneapolis: University of Minnesota Press, 1997.

Marshall, J. J., Irish Tories, Rapparees, and Robbers, Dungannon: Tyrone Printing Co., 1927.

Martin, Charles L., A Sketch of Sam Bass, the Bandit, Dallas, TX: Worley & Co., 1880.

Maspero, G. (trans. Johns, A.), Popular Stories of Ancient Egypt, New Hyde Park: University Books, 1969. First published in English in 1915.

Massignon, G. (ed.), Hyland, J. (trans.), Folktales of France, Chicago: University of Chicago Press, 1968.

Massola, A., Bunjil's Cave: Myths, Legends, and Superstitions of the Aborigines of Southeast Australia, Melbourne: Landsdowne Press, 1968.

Mathews, J. (comp.), White, I. (ed.), The Opal That Turned into Fire and Other Stories from the Wangkumara, Broome: Magabala Books, 1994.

Mathias, E. and Raspa, R., Italian Folktales in America: The Verbal Art of an Immigrant Woman, Detroit: Wayne State University Press, 1988.

Mayer, F., Ancient Tales in Modern Japan, Bloomington: Indiana University Press, 1984.

Mayer, F. (trans. and ed.), The Yanagita Kunio Guide to the Japanese Folk Tale, Bloomington: Indiana University Press, 1986 (1948).

Mayor, A., "Bibliography of Classical Folklore Scholarship: Myths, Legends, and Popular Beliefs of Ancient Greece and Rome," Folklore 111, no. 1, (2000): 123–138.

McAlpine, H. and W., Japanese Tales and Legends, Oxford: Oxford University Press, 1958.

McColl, E. and Seeger, P., Traveller's Songs from England and Scotland, London: Routledge and Kegan Paul, 1977.

McCulloch, W. (coll. and trans.), Bengali Household Tales, London: Hodder and Stoughton, 1912.

McGarry, M. (ed.), Great Folktales of Old Ireland, New York: Bell Publishing, 1972.

McGlathery, J. (ed.), The Brothers Grimm and Folktale, Urbana and Chicago: University of Illinois Press, 1988.

McMillan, C. (coll. and ed.), Canadian Wonder Tales, London: The Bodley Head, 1974 (combines two collections published in 1918 and 1922).

McQuilton, J., The Kelly Outbreak, 1878–1880: The Geographical Dimension of Social Banditry, Melbourne: Melbourne University Press, 1979.

Megas, G., Folktales of Greece, Chicago: University of Chicago Press, 1970.

Mercatante, A., The Facts on File Encyclopedia of World Mythology, New York: Facts on File, 1968.

Meredith, J., The Wild Colonial Boy: Bushranger Jack Donahoe, 1806–1830, Ascot Vale: Red Rooster Press, 1982.

Meredith, J. and Anderson, H. (eds.), Folksongs of Australia, Melbourne: Sun, 1967.

Meredith, J. and Whalan, R., Frank the Poet, Melbourne: Red Rooster Press, 1979.

Meredith, J., Covell, R., and Brown, P., Folksongs of Australia, vol. 2, Sydney: University of New South Wales Press, 1987.

Metternich, H. (ed.), Mongolian Folk Tales, Boulder, CO: Avery Press; Washington, DC: University of Washington Press, 1996.

Meyer, R., "The Outlaw: A Distinctive American Folktype," Journal of the Folklore Institute 17 (1980): 94–124.

Michaelis-Jena, R., "Eulenspiegel and Münchhausen: Two German Folk Heroes," Folklore 97, no. 1 (1986): 101–108.

Mieder, W., "Grim Variations: From Fairy Tales to Modern Anti-Fairy Tales," in Tradition and Innovation in Folk Literature, Hanover and London: University Press of New England, 1987, chap. 1.

———, "The Pied Piper of Hamelin: Origin, History, and Survival of the Legend," Tradition and Innovation in Folk Literature, Hanover and London: University Press of New England, 1987, chap. 2.

Mijatovies, C. (ed. and trans.), Serbian Folklore, New York: Benjamin Bloom, 1968 (1874).

Minard, R., Womenfolk and Fairy Tales, Boston: Houghton Mifflin, 1975.

Minford, J., Favourite Folktales of China, Beijing: New World Press, 1983.

Mohanti, P. (ed.), Indian Village Tales, London: Davis-Poynter, 1975.

Montell, W., The Saga of Coe Ridge, Knoxville: University of Tennessee Press, 1970.

Morton, R. (coll.), Come Day, Go Day, God Send

Sunday, London: Routledge and Kegan Paul, 1973.

Muhawi, I. and Kanaana, S. (eds.), *Speak, Bird, Speak Again: Palestinian Arab Folktales*, Berkeley: University of California Press, 1989.

Myrsiades, L. and K., *Karagiozis: Culture and Comedy in Greek Puppet Theatre*, Lexington: University Press of Kentucky, 1992.

Nagy, J., *The Wisdom of the Outlaw: The Boyhood Deeds of Finn in Gaelic Narrative Tradition*, Berkeley: University of California Press, 1985.

Narvaéz, P. and Laba, M. (eds.), *Media Sense: The Folklore-Popular Culture Continuum*, Bowling Green, OH: Bowling Green State University Press, 1986.

Nassau, R., *Where Animals Talk: West African Folk Lore Tales*, Boston: Four Seas Company, 1919.

Neuberg, V., *Popular Literature: A History and Guide*, Harmondsworth, Middlesex: Penguin, 1977.

Newall, V., "The Hero as a Trickster: The West Indian Anansi," in Davidson, H. (ed.), *The Hero in Tradition and Folklore*, The Folklore Society Mistletoe Series 19, London: The Folklore Society, 1984.

Noy, D. and Baharev, G. (eds. and trans.), *Folktales of Israel*, Chicago: University of Chicago Press, 1963.

O'Connor, W. (coll. and trans.), *Folk-Tales from Tibet*, London: Hurst and Blackett, 1906.

Ó hÓgáin, D., *The Hero in Irish Folk History*, New York: Gill and Macmillan, 1985.

———, *Myth, Legend, and Romance: An Encyclopedia of the Irish Folk Tradition*, London: Ryan Publishing, 1990.

uí Ógáin, R., *Immortal Dan: Daniel O'Connel in Irish Folk Tradition*, Dublin: Dublin Geography Publications, n.d.

Olrik, A., "Epic Laws of Folk Narrative," in Dundes, A. (ed.), *The Study of Folklore*, Englewood Cliffs, N.J.: Prentice-Hall, 1965, pp. 129–141.

Olrik, A. (ed.), Smith-Dampier, E. (trans.), *A Book of Danish Ballads*, Princeton: Princeton University Press, 1939.

Ong, W., *Orality and Literacy: The Technologizing of the Word*, London: Routledge, 1991 (1982).

Opie, I. and Opie, P., *The Lore and Language of Schoolchildren*, Oxford: Oxford University Press, 1959.

———, *The Classic Fairy Tales*, London: Oxford University Press, 1974.

Opie, I. and Opie, P. (eds.), *The Oxford Dictionary of Nursery Rhymes*, Oxford: Oxford University Press, 1951.

Opie, I. and Tatum, M. (eds.), *A Dictionary of Superstitions*, Oxford: Oxford University Press, 1989.

Oppenheimer, P. (trans.), *A Pleasant Vintage of Till Eulenspiegel, Born in the Country of Brunswick. How He Spent His Life. 95 of His tales*. Translated from the 1515 edition. Middletown, CT: Wesleyan University Press, 1972.

Oppenheimer, P. (trans. and ed.), *Till Eulenspiegel: His Adventures*, New York and London: Garland, 1991.

Orbell, M., *Maori Folktales*, Auckland: Blackwood and Janet Paul, 1968.

———, *The Illustrated Encyclopedia of Maori Myth and Legend*, Christchurch: Canterbury University Press, 1995.

Ortutay, G. (ed.), *Hungarian Folk Tales*, Budapest: Corvina, 1962.

Osers, E. (trans.), *Chinese Folktales*, London: Bell and Sons, 1971. First published in German as Wilhelm, R. (trans.), *Chinesische Märchen*, 1958.

O'Shaughnessy, P. (ed.), *Yellowbelly Ballads*, pt. 1, Lincoln: Lincolnshire and Humberside Arts, 1975.

O'Sullivan, S. (ed. and trans.), *Folktales of Ireland*, London: Routledge and Kegan Paul, 1966.

O'Sullivan, S. (ed.), *Legends from Ireland*, London: Batsford, 1977.

Ozaki, Y., *The Japanese Fairy Book*, Tokyo: Fuzanbo Pub. Co., 1909; reprint, New York: Dover Publications, 1967.

Page, D., *Folktales in Homer's Odyssey*, Cambridge: Harvard University Press, 1973.

Palmer, K., *Oral Folk-Tales of Essex*, Newton Abbot: David and Charles, 1973.

Palmer, R., *What a Lovely War: British Soldiers' Songs from the Boer War to the Present Day*, London: Michael Joseph, 1990.

Palmer, R. (ed.), *A Touch on the Times: Songs of Social Change 1770 to 1914*, Harmondsworth, Middlesex: Penguin, 1974.

Palmer, R. (ed.), *Everyman's Book of British Ballads*, London: Everyman, 1981.

Paredes, A., *Folktales of Mexico*, Chicago: University of Chicago Press, 1970.

———, *With His Pistol in His Hand: A Border Ballad and Its Hero*, Austin: University of Texas Press, 1990 (1958).

Parker, H., *Village Folk-Tales of Ceylon*, London: Luzac and Co., 1910.

Parker, K. L. (coll.), *Australian Legendary Tales*, Twickenham: Senate, 1978 (1896).

Parry-Jones, D., *Welsh Legends and Fairy Lore*, London: Batsford, 1963 (1953).

Paterson, A. B. (ed.), *The Old Bush Songs*, Sydney: Angus and Robertson, 1905 (various, mostly revised, editions to 1931).

Pentikäinen, J. (trans. and ed. Poom, R.), *Kalevala Mythology*, expanded ed., Bloomington: Indiana University Press, 1999 (1987).

Percy, T. (ed. Prichard, V.), *Reliques of Ancient English Poetry*, New York: Crowell, and Co., 1875.

Petrovich, W., *Hero Tales and Legends of the Serbians*, London: Harrap, 1914.

Phelps, E., *The Maid of the North: Feminist Folk Tales from Around the World*, New York: Holt, Rinehart, and Winston, 1981.

Philip, N. (ed.), *The Penguin Book of Scottish Folktales*, Harmondsworth, Middlesex: Penguin, 1995.

Picard, B. (ed.), *French Legends, Tales, and Fairy Stories*, Oxford: Oxford University Press, 1955.

Pike, R., "The Reality and Legend of the Spanish Bandit Diego Corrientes," *Folklore* 99, no. 2 (1988): 242–247.

Pino-Saavedra, P., *Folktales of Chile*, Chicago: University of Chicago Press, 1967.

Pinto, V. de Sola and Rodway, A. (eds.), *The Common Muse: An Anthology of Popular British Ballad Poetry, Fifteenth–Twentieth Century*, London: Chatto and Windus, 1957.

Poignant, R., *Myths and Legends of the South Seas*, London: Hamlyn, 1970.

Poli, B., "The Hero in France and America," *Journal of American Studies* 2, no. 2, 1968.

Polster, M., *Eve's Daughters: The Forbidden Heroism of Women*, San Francisco: Jossey-Bass Publishers, 1992.

Pomare, M. (ed. Cowan, J.), *Legends of the Maori*, vol. 2, Wellington: Harry H. Tombs, 1934.

Porter, J. and Russell, W. (eds.), *Animals in Folklore*, Ipswich, Eng.: Brewer; Totowa, NJ: Rowman and Littlefield, The Folklore Society, 1978.

Porter, K., "'Johnny Troy': A 'Lost' Australian Bushranger Ballad in the United States," *Meanjin Quarterly* 24, June 1965.

Posselt, F., *Fables of the Veld*, London: Oxford University Press, 1929.

Pound, L., *Nebraska Folklore*, Lincoln: University of Nebraska Press, 1987 (1913).

Pourrat, H. (ed.), *A Treasury of French Tales*, London: George Allen and Unwin, 1953.

Propp, V., *The Morphology of the Folktale*, Austin: University of Texas Press, 1968.

———, *Theory and History of Folklore*, with an exchange with Claude Lévi-Strauss, Minneapolis: University of Minnesota Press, 1984.

Purslow, F., *The Constant Lovers*, London: EFDS Publications, 1972.

Purslow, F. (ed.), *Marrow Bones: English Folk Songs from the Hammond and Gardiner Mss*, London: EFDS Publications, 1965.

Purslow, F. (ed.), *The Wanton Seed: More English Folk Songs from the Hammond and Gardiner Mss*, London: EFDS Publications, 1968.

Rackham, A., *Fairy Tales from Many Lands*, London: Piccolo, 1978 (1916).

Radin, P., *The Trickster: A Study in American Indian Mythology*, New York: Philosophical Library, 1956.

Raglan, Lord, *The Hero: A Study in Tradition, Myth, and Drama*, London: Methuen and Co., 1936.

Ralph Vaughan Williams Broadside Scrapbook, Ralph Vaughan Williams Memorial Library, Cecil Sharp House, English Folk Dance and Song Society, London.

Ralston, W., *Russian Folk-Tales*, London: Smith, Elder, and Co., 1873.

Ramsay, A. and McCullagh, F., *Tales from Turkey*, London: Simpkin, Marshall, Hamilton, Kent, 1914.

Ramsey, J. (comp. and ed.), *Coyote Was Going There: Indian Literature of the Oregon Country*, Seattle: University of Washington Press, 1977.

Randall, B., "The Cinderella Theme in North-West Indian Folklore," in Smith, M. (ed.), *Indians of the Urban North-West*, New York: Columbia University Press, 1949.

Randolph, V., *Ozark Folk Songs*, 4 vols., Columbia: The State Historical Society of Missouri, 1946–1950.

Ranelagh, E., *The Past We Share: The Near Eastern Ancestry of Western Folk Literature*, London: Quartet Books, 1979.

Rank, O., *The Myth of the Birth of the Hero*, New York: The Journal of Nervous and Mental Diseases Publishing Company, 1914.

Ranke, K. (ed.), *Folktales of Germany*, London: Routledge and Kegan Paul, 1966.

Rappoport, A., *Myth and Legend of Ancient Israel*, 2 vols., London: Gresham Publishing Co., 1928.

———, *Medieval Legends of Christ*, London: Ivor Nicholson and Watson, 1934.

Raspe, R. et al., *Singular Travels, Campaigns, and Adventures of Baron Münchhausen*, London: Cresset Press, 1948.

Rattray, R., *Akan-Ashanti Folk Tales*, Oxford: Oxford University Press, 1930.

Reay, B. (ed.), *Popular Culture in Seventeenth-Century England*, London: Routledge, 1988 (1985).

Red, H., *Spanish Legends and Traditions*, Boston: Richard G. Badger, 1914.

Redesdale, L. (ed.), *Tales of Old Japan*, London: Macmillan, 1908.

Reed, A., *Myths and Legends of Maoriland*, Wellington: Reed, 1961 (1946).

———, *A Treasury of Maori Folklore*, Wellington: Reed, 1974 (1963).

Reed, A. and Hames, I. (eds.), *Myths and Legends of Fiji and Rotuma*, Auckland: Reed, 1967.

Reuss, R., "The Ballad of Joe Hill Revisited," *Western Folklore* 26, 1967.

Riches, S., *St George: Hero, Martyr, and Myth*, Stroud, UK: Sutton Publishing, 2000.

Riordan, J. (coll. and trans.), *The Sun Maiden and the Crescent Moon: Siberian Folk Tales*, New York: Interlink Books, 1991.

Ritson, J., *Robin Hood*, 2 vol., London: n.p., 1795.

Robe, S. (ed.), *Hispanic Folktales from New Mexico: Narratives from the R. D. Jameson Collection*, Mythology and Folktale Studies 30, Berkeley and Los Angeles: University of California Press, 1976.

Robe, S. (ed.), *Hispanic Folktales from New Mexico: Narratives from the R. D. Jameson Collection*, Mythology and Folktale Studies 31, Berkeley and Los Angeles: University of California Press, 1980.

Roberts, J., *From Trickster to Badman: The Black Folk Hero in Slavery and Freedom*, Philadelphia: University of Pennsylvania Press, 1989.

———, "'Railroad Bill' and the American Outlaw Tradition," *Western Folklore* 40(1981): 315–328.

Roberts, M. (ed. and trans.), *Chinese Fairy Tales and Fantasies*, New York: Pantheon Books, 1979.

Rollins, H. E. (ed.), *The Pepys Ballads*, Cambridge: Cambridge University Press, 1929–1931.

Rooth, A., *The Cinderella Cycle*, Lund: C. Gleerup, 1951.

Rootham, H., *Kossovo: Heroic Songs of the Serbs*, Oxford: Blackwell, 1920.

Rose, D., *Dingo Makes Us Human: Life and Land in an Aboriginal Australian Culture*, Melbourne: Melbourne University Press, 1992.

Rowe, K., "To Spin a Yarn: The Female Voice in Folklore and Fairy Tale," in Bottigheimer, R. (ed.), *Fairy Tales and Society: Illusion, Allusion, and Paradigm*, Philadelphia: University of Pennsylvania Press, 1986.

Rugoff, M., (ed.), *A Harvest of World Folk Tales*, New York: Viking Press, 1949.

Sabar, Y. (trans. and ed.), *The Folk Literature of the Kurdistani Jews: An Anthology*, New Haven: Yale University Press, 1982.

Sadhu, S., *Folk Tales from Kashmir*, London: Asia Publishing House, 1962.

Sandburg, C., *The American Songbag*, New York: Harcourt Brace and Co, 1927.

Saxon, L. et al. (eds.), *Gumbo Ya-Ya: A Collection of Louisiana Folk Tales*, New York: Bonanza Books, 1965.

Schechter, H., *The Bosom Serpent: Folklore and Popular Art*, Iowa City: University of Iowa Press, 1988.

Schwartz, H., *Elijah's Violin and Other Jewish Fairy Tales*, New York: Harper and Row, 1983.

———, *Miriam's Tambourine: Jewish Folktales from Around the World*, New York: Seth Press, 1986.

Scott, Bill, *The Long and the Short and the Tall: A Collection of Australian Yarns*, Sydney: Western Plains Publishers, 1985.

————, *Pelicans and Chihuahuas and Other Urban Legends: Bill Scott Talking about Folklore*, St. Lucia: University of Queensland Press, 1995.

Scott, Bill (ed.), *The Second Penguin Australian Songbook*, Ringwood, Vic.: Penguin, 1980.

Seal, G., *Ned Kelly in Popular Tradition*, Melbourne: Hyland House, 1980.

————, *The Hidden Culture: Folklore in Australian Society*, Melbourne: Oxford University Press, 1989; reprint, Perth: Black Swan Press, 1998.

————, *The Outlaw Legend: A Cultural Tradition in Britain, America, and Australia*, Melbourne and Cambridge: Cambridge University Press, 1996.

————, "Tradition and Protest in Nineteenth-Century England and Wales," *Folklore* 100, no. 2, (1988): 146–169.

————, "Deep Continuities and Discontinuities in the Outlaw Hero Traditions of Britain, Australia, and America," *Lore and Language* 10, no. 1, (1993): 27–46.

————, "The Wild Colonial Boy Rides Again: An Australian Legend Abroad," in Craven, I. (ed.), *Australian Popular Culture*, Cambridge: Cambridge University Press, 1994.

Segal, D. "The Connections Between the Semantics and the Formal Structure of a Text" in Maranda, P. (ed.), *Mythology*, Harmondsworth, Middlesex: Penguin, 1972. Translated from Italian by R. Vitello. Originally published in Russian in *Peotika II*, Varsovie, 1966, pp. 15–44.

Segal, R., *Hero Myths: A Reader*, London: Blackwell, 1999.

Segal, R. (ed.), *Anthropology, Folklore, and Myth*, New York: Garland, 1966.

Segal, R. (ed.), *In Quest of the Hero*, Princeton: Princeton University Press, 1990.

Seki, K. (ed.), Adams, R. (trans.), *Folktales of Japan*, London: Routledge and Kegan Paul, 1963. First published in Japanese in 1956–1957.

Settle, W. A., Jr., *Jesse James Was His Name, or, Fact and Fiction Concerning the Careers of the Notorious James Brothers of Missouri*, Columbia: University of Missouri Press, 1966.

Shack, W. and Marcos, H. (trans. and eds.), *Gods and Heroes: Oral Traditions of the Gurage of Ethiopia*, London: Oxford University Press, 1974.

Shah, A., *Folk Tales of Central Asia*, London: The Octagon Press, 1970.

Sharp, C., *A Book of British Song for Home and School*, London: John Murray, 1902.

Shartse, O. (ed.), Bilenko, A. (trans.), *Ukrainian Folk Tales*, Kiev: Dnipro Publishers, 1974.

Shepard, L., *The History of Street Literature*, Newton Abbot: David and Charles, 1973.

Sherlock, P. (ed.), *West Indian Folk-Tales*, Oxford: Oxford University Press, 1966.

Shiel, D. J., *Ben Hall: Bushranger*, St. Lucia, Qld.: University of Queensland Press, 1983.

Shin-yong, C. and International Cultural Foundation (eds.), *Korean Folk Tales*, Seoul: Si-sa-yong-o-sa Publishers, 1982.

Sideman, B., (ed.), *The World's Best Fairy Tales*, Pleasantville: Reader's Digest Association, 1967.

Simeone, W. E., "Robin Hood and Some Other American Outlaws," *Journal of American Folklore* 71, 1958.

Simpson, C., *The British Broadside Ballad and Its Music*, New Brunswick: Rutgers University Press, 1966.

Simpson, J., *Scandinavian Folktales*, Harmondsworth, Middlesex: Penguin, 1988.

Simpson, J. (trans.), *Legends of Icelandic Magicians*, with an introduction by B. Benedikz, London: Brewer/Rowman and Littlefield, The Folklore Society, 1975.

Simpson, J. and Roud, S., *A Dictionary of English Folklore*, Oxford: Oxford University Press, 2000.

Sjoestedt, M., *Gods and Heroes of the Celts*, Blackrock and Portland: Four Courts Press, 1994 (1940).

Smith, A. M. (coll. and ed.), *Children of Wax: African Folk Tales*, New York: Interlink Books, 1991 (1989).

Smith, Captain A., *A Complete History of the Lives and Robberies of the Most Notorious Highwaymen*, 1719.

Smith, G., *Joe Hill*, Salt Lake City: University of Utah Press, 1969.

Smith, L. (comp.), *The Music of the Waters: A Collection of the Sailors' Chanties, or Work Songs of the Sea, of all Maritime Nations*, London: Kegan and Paul Co., 1888.

Spence, L., *Spain: Myths and Legends*, London: Harrap, 1920; reprint, New York: Avenel Books, 1986.

Spufford, M., *Small Books and Pleasant Histories: Popular Fiction and Its Readership in Seventeenth-Century England*, London: Methuen, 1981.

Stanley, J. (ed.), *Bold in Her Breeches: Women Pirates across the Ages*, London: Pandora, 1995.

Stapleton, A., *Robin Hood: The Question of His Existence*, Worksop: Sissons and Son, 1899.

Steckmesser, K. L., *The Western Hero in History and Legend*, Norman: University of Oklahoma Press, 1965.

———, "Robin Hood and the American Outlaw," *Journal of American Folklore* 79, 1966.

———, "The Three Butch Cassidys: History, Hollywood, Folklore," in Durer, S. et al. (eds.), *American Renaissance and American West*, Laramie: University of Wyoming Press, 1982.

Steel, F. (coll.), *Tales of the Punjab Told by the People*, London: The Bodley Head, 1973 (1894).

Stenbock-Fermor, E., "The Story of Van'ka Kain," in Lord, A. (ed.), *Slavic Folklore: A Symposium*, Philadelphia: American Folklore Society, 1956.

Stevens, E. (coll. and trans.), *Folk-Tales of Iraq*, London: Oxford University Press, 1931.

Stewart, D. and Keesing, N. (eds.), *Australian Bush Ballads*, Sydney: Angus and Robertson, 1955.

Stewart, R. J. and Mathews, J. (eds.), *Merlin through the Ages: A Chronological Anthology and Source Book*, London: Blandford, 1995.

Stone, K., "Things Walt Disney Never Told Us," *Journal of American Folklore* 88, 1975.

———, "Feminist Approaches to the Interpretation of Fairy Tales," in Bottigheimer, R. (ed.), *Fairy Tales and Society: Illusion, Allusion, and Paradigm*, Philadelphia: University of Pennsylvania Press, 1986.

Stoneman, R. (trans. and ed.), *Legends of Alexander the Great*, London: J. M. Dent, 1994.

Straparola, G. (trans. Waters, W.), *The Nights of Straparola*, London: Lawrence and Bullen, 1894.

———, *The Facetious Nights*, London: Society of Bibliophiles, 1901 (1550–1553).

Stubbes, K., *The Life of a Man*, London: EFDS Publications, 1970.

Studza, I. et al. (trans.), *Fairy Tales and Legends from Romania*, New York: Twayne Publishers, 1972.

Surmelian, L., *Apples of Immortality: Folktales of Armenia*, Berkeley and Los Angeles: University of California Press, 1968.

Swire, O., *Skye: The Island and Its Legends*, London: Oxford University Press, 1952.

Swynnerton, C., *Indian Nights' Entertainment; or, Folk-Tales from the Upper Indus*, London: Elliot Stock, 1892.

Szumsky, B., "The House That Jack Built: Empire and Ideology in Nineteenth-Century British Versions of 'Jack and the Beanstalk,'" in *Marvels and Tales: Journal of Fairy-Tale Studies* 13, no. 1, 1999.

Tatar, M., *The Hard Facts of the Grimms' Fairy Tales*, Princeton: Princeton University Press, 1987.

———, "Born Yesterday: Heroes in the Grimms' Fairy Tales," in Bottigheimer, R. (ed.), *Fairy Tales and Society: Illusion, Allusion, and Paradigm*, Philadelphia: University of Pennsylvania Press, 1986.

Tatum, S., *Inventing Billy the Kid: Visions of the Outlaw in America, 1881–1981*, Albuquerque: University of New Mexico Press, 1982.

Terada, A., *The Magic Crocodile and Other Folktales from Indonesia*, Honolulu: University of Hawaii Press, 1994.

Thomas, J., *Inside the Wolf's Belly: Aspects of the Fairy Tale*, Sheffield: Sheffield Academic Press, 1989.

Thompson, S., *The Folktale*, New York: Holt, Rinehart, and Winston, 1946.

Thompson, S., (ed.), *Tales of the North American Indians*, Bloomington: Indiana University Press, 1929.

Thorp, N. H. et al. (eds.), *Songs of the Cowboys*, New York: Clarkson N. Potter, Bramhall House, 1966.

Todd, L., *Tortoise the Trickster and Other Folktales from Cameroon*, London: Routledge and Kegan Paul, 1979.

Tong, D., *Gypsy Folktales*, New York: Harcourt Brace Jovanovich, 1989.

Toor, F., *A Treasury of Mexican Folkways*, New York: Crown Publishers, 1947.

Topsfield, L., *Chrétien de Troyes: A Study of the Arthurian Romances*, Cambridge: Cambridge

University Press, 1981.

Treharne, R., *The Glastonbury Legends*, London: Sphere, 1971 (1967).

Turner, I., Factor, J., Lowenstein, W. (comps. and eds.), *Cinderella Dressed in Yella*, 2d. ed., Melbourne: Heinemann, 1978.

Tyler, R. (trans. and ed.), *Japanese Tales*, New York: Pantheon Books, 1987.

Vande Berg, L., "The Sports Hero Meets Mediated Celebrityhood," in Wenner, L. (ed.), *MediaSport*, London: Routledge, 1998.

Vaughan Williams, R. and Lloyd, A. L. (eds.), *The Penguin Book of English Folk Songs*, Harmondsworth, Middlesex: Penguin, 1959.

Von Franz, M., *The Feminine in Fairy Tales*, Boston: Shambhala Publications, 1993 (1972).

Waley, A., *Ballads and Stories from Tun-Huang: An Anthology*, London: George Allen and Unwin, 1960.

Walker, B. and W. (colls. and eds.), *Nigerian Folk Tales*, New Brunswick, NJ: Rutgers University Press, 1961.

Walker, B. and Ahmet, E., *Tales Alive in Turkey*, Cambridge: Harvard University Press, 1966.

Walter, B. and Meine, F. (eds.), *Half Horse, Half Alligator: The Growth of the Mike Fink Legend*, Chicago: University of Chicago Press, 1956.

Wannan, W., *The Australian*, Adelaide: Rigby, 1954.

———, *Come in Spinner: A Treasury of Popular Australian Humour*, Melbourne: John Currey, O'Neill Publishers, 1976 (1964).

———, *A Dictionary of Australian Folklore*, Sydney: Lansdowne Press, 1981 (c.1970).

Wannan, W. (ed.), *Crooked Mick of the Speewah*, Melbourne: Lansdowne Press, 1965.

Ward, D. (ed. and trans.), *The German Legends of the Brothers Grimm*, New York: Institute for the Study of Human Issues; London: Millington Books, 1981.

Ward, R. (ed.), *The Penguin Book of Australian Ballads*, Ringwood, Vic.: Penguin, 1964.

Wardrop, M., *Georgian Folk Tales*, London: David Nutt, 1894.

Warner, M., *From the Beast to the Blonde: On Fairy Tales and Their Tellers*, London: Chatto and Windus, 1994.

Waters, G. W. (ed.), *The Facetious Nights of Giovanni Francesco Straparola*, London: Society of Bibliophiles, 1894.

Waters, G. W. (ed.), *The Nights of Straparola*, 2 vols., London: Lawrence and Bullen, 1894.

Webster, W., *Basque Legends: Collected, Chiefly in the Labourd*, London: Griffith and Farran, and Walbrook and Co., 1877.

Weinreich, B. (ed.), *Yiddish Folktales*, New York: Pantheon, 1988.

Welsford, E., *The Fool: His Social and Literary History*, London: Faber, 1935.

Werner, A., *Myths and Legends of the Bantu*, London: Harrap, 1933.

Werner, E., *Myths and Legends of China*, New York: Arno Press, 1976 (1922).

West, J. (comp. and trans.), *Faroese Folk-Tales and Legends*, Lerwick: Shetland Publishing Co., 1980.

Westwood, J., *Albion: A Guide to Legendary Britain*, London: Granada, 1985.

Whall, W. (coll. and ed.), *Sea Songs and Shanties*, London: Brown, Son, and Ferguson, 1910.

Wheeler, P., *Albanian Wonder Tales*, New York: Doubleday, Doran, and Co., Junior Literary Guild, 1936.

White, C., *History of Australian Bushranging*, 2 vols., Melbourne: Rigby, 1893.

White, J., *Git Along Little Dogies: Songs and Songmakers of the American West*, Urbana: University of Illinois Press, 1975.

White, R., "Outlaw Gangs of the Middle Border: American Social Bandits," *Western Historical Quarterly* 12, no. 4, 1981.

Wilgus, D. K., *Anglo-American Folksong Scholarship Since 1898*, New Brunswick, NJ: Rutgers University Press, 1959.

Wilhelm, R. (ed.), Osers, E. (trans.), *Chinese Folktales*, London: G. Bell and Sons, 1971.

Williams, A., *Folk Songs of the Upper Thames*, London: Duckworth and Co., 1923.

Williams, P. (ed.), *The Fool and the Trickster*, Cambridge: Brewer; Ipswich, Eng.: Rowman and Littlefield, 1979.

Williams, S., *A Ghost Called "Thunderbolt,"* Woden, ACT: Poppinjay Press, 1987.

Wilson, B., *Scottish Folk Tales and Legends*, Oxford: Oxford University Press, 1960 (1954).

Winslow, C., "Sussex Smugglers," in Hay, D. et

al. (eds.), *Albion's Fatal Tree: Crime and Society in Eighteenth-Century England*, London: Allen Lane, 1975.

Wolkenstein, D., *The Magic Orange Tree and Other Haitian Folktales*, New York: Alfred A. Knopf, 1978.

Yates, D., *A Book of Gypsy Folk-Tales*, London: Phoenix House, 1948.

Yearsley, M., *The Folklore of the Fairy Tales*, London: Oxford University Press, 1974.

Yeats, W. B. (ed.), *Fairy and Folk Tales of Ireland*, Gerrards Cross: Colin Smythe, 1988 (1888, 1892).

Yolen, J. (ed.), *Favourite Folktales from around the World*, New York: Pantheon Books, 1986.

Zhang, Y., "The Marsh and the Bush: Outlaw Hero Traditions of China and the West," Ph.D. diss., Curtin University of Technology, Perth, Western Australia, 1998.

Zhao, Q., *A Study of Dragons, East and West*, New York: Peter Lang Publishing, 1992.

Zheleznova, I. (trans.), *Ukrainian Folk Tales*, Kiev: Dnipro Publishers, 1981.

Zimmermann, G., *Songs of Irish Rebellion: Political Street Ballads and Rebel Songs, 1780–1900*, Dublin: Allen Figgis, 1967.

Zipes, J., *Breaking the Magic Spell: Radical Theories of Folk and Fairy Tales*, Austin: University of Texas Press, 1979.

———, *Fairy Tales and the Art of Subversion*, New York: Wildman Press, 1983.

———, *Don't Bet on the Prince: Contemporary Feminist Fairy Tales in North America and England*, Aldershot: Gower, 1986.

———, *Fairy Tale as Myth, Myth as Fairy Tale*, Lexington: University Press of Kentucky, 1994.

———, *Happily Ever After: Fairy Tales, Children, and the Culture Industry*, New York and London: Routledge, 1997.

———, *When Dreams Came True: Classical Fairy Tales and Their Tradition*, New York and London: Routledge, 1999.

Zipes, J. (ed.), *The Trials and Tribulations of Little Red Riding Hood*, New York: Routledge, 1993.

Zipes, J. (ed.), *The Oxford Companion to Fairy Tales*, Oxford: Oxford University Press, 2000.

INDEX

Jing of Qi, 92
"John Brown's Body" (song), 34
John Henry (Bradford), 104
John, King, 168, 272, 273
"John the Bear," 117
Johnny Appleseed. *See* Chapman, John
Johns, Joseph, 131, 158
Jolly Swagman, The, 131–132, 184
Jones, Casey, 47, 107, 132
Jones, Galloping, 132–133
Jones, S.: Snow White and, 235, 237
Jordan, Michael, 39
Joseph, 219
Joseph of Arimathea, Saint, 64, 129, 133
Jóska, 169, 170
Joukahainen, 259
Journal of the Times, Yankee Doodle and, 283
Juan, 122, 256
Judy, 133–134, 205
Jung, Carl, 156
Juno, 260

Kabadaluk, 135–136
Kabajan, 136–137
Kadambawa, 273
Kadi, Ero and, 65
Kaha'i, 52
Kaleva, 259
Kalevala, The, 106, 151, 209, 259
Kalevi, 259
Kalevipoeg, 259
Kalevipoeg (Kreutzwald), 259
Kamaria, Maria and, 167
Kandek, 137
Kanner, L., 250
Kanowna, 60
Kansas City Times, 126
Kapsirko, 137–138
Kara Khan, Aryg and, 13
Karacharovo, 181
Karagiozis, xii, 138
"Katie Woodencloak," 46
Katya, 240
Kauko, 151
Kaukomieli, 151
Kebo Kananga II, 266
Keesing, N.: Morgan and, 178
Kelly, Dan, 138, 139, 140
Kelly, Edward "Ned," xix, 39, 47, 78, 105, 138–140, 139, 184, 197, 198
Kelly gang, 138

Kelly, Kate, 140, 198
Kelly, Maggie, 140
"Kelly Was Their Captain," 139
Kennedy, Sergeant: murder of, 139
Kentchurch Court, 121
Kentigern, Saint, 141
Kerala, 42
Ketch, Jack, 205
Key, Jean, 165
Khalil, 15
Khan Bogu, Badikan and, 19
Khidre, El, 4, 85, 141–142, 272
Kidd, William, xviii, 142, 142, 185
Kihachi, 142–143
Kihuo, 32, 117, 143–144
Kikitich, Dobrynya. *See* Nikitich, Dobrynya
"Kill Three Warriors with Two Peaches," 92
Kinder- und Hausmärchen (Grimm brothers), xiv, 70, 155, 206
King of Ireland's Son, The, 144–145
King of Poison, 144, 145
"King of the Teddy Boys," Crockett and, 51
"King of the Tributes," 52
"King of the Universe," Crockett and, 51
King, Tom, 252
Kingsley, Charles, 105
Kinkach Martinko, 103
Kirbit'evna, Vasilisa, 147
Kirby, Captain, 24
Klaus, Peter, 232, 260
Kloo-Teckl, 193
"Knight of the Swan," 159
Knight, Stephen, 111
Knights of the Round Table, 13, 123
Knowall, Doctor, 145–147
Kobo Daishi. *See* Kukai
Kokilan, 218
Kong, 188
Koppenberg Hill, 202
Koran, 219
Koshchei, 147, 177, 252
Koshte, Mrikanda and, 178
Kozenitz, Preacher of, 17
Kraljevic, Marco, 147–149, 173
Kreutzwald, F. R., 259
Krpan, Martin, 52
Kukai, xii, 149–150
Kusoi, Ringkitan and, 221
Kuzonoha, 150, 285
Kwoiam (Kuiama), 52, 112

Kylli of Saari, 151

"La Belle au Bois Dormant" (Perrault), 232
La Finta Nonna, 155
"Lady Franklin's Lament," 79
"Lady Isabel and the Elf-Knight," 115
Lady of the Lake, 13, 22
"Lady Washington's Lament" (ballad), text of, 266–267
Lan Caihe, 63
Lancelot, 13
Land of Ghosts, Zab and, 289, 290
Lang, Andrew, xiv, 70, 218
  on Ahmed, 3
  Halfchick and, 99
Langtry, Lily, 22
Lapin, Compair, 251
Last Supper, 130, 133
Laughead, W. B., 34
Lazar, 151, 158
Lazaropolje, 151
Lazy Jack, 188
Le Blanc, Abbe, 252
"Le petit chaperon rouge" (Perrault), 154
Le Piacevoli Notta (Straparola), 206
League of the Iroquois, 106
Leben und Tod des kleinen Rotkäppchens: eine Tragödie (Tieck), 155
Legends from Ireland (O'Sullivan), 194
Leifeng Pagoda, 19, 268
Lemminkäinen, 151, 259
Leofric, Earl of Mercia, 90
Leprince de Beaumont, Mme, 22
Les Contes nouveaux (d'Aulnoy), 69
Lévi-Strauss, Claude, xv, xvi
Lewinski, Monica, 38
Li, 180
Li Ji, 151–252
Li Kui, 152
Li Shangyin, 113
Liars, 152
Lincoln, 102, 111
Lindsay, Vachel: Appleseed and, 40
Lingenfelter, R., 21, 211
"Little Briar Rose" (Grimms), 232
Little Dutch Boy, The, 152–153
Little Goose Girl, The, 153
"Little Goose Girl, The," 270
Little Hare, 102
Little John, 110, 153
Little Kihuo, 144
Little Moron, 153
Little Peachling, 175

Witch of the North, 208–209
Wobblies. *See* Industrial Workers of the World
Wolfe, James, 273–274, 274
Wolfenstein, M., 120
Wolverine, 183
Wombat Ranges, 138
Women dressed as men, 275
Wonder Woman, 42
Woodencloak, Katie, 276–278
Woods, "Tiger," 39
Wordsworth, William, 165
World Trade Organization, Luddites and, 161
Wu Song, 278–279
Wulgaru, 279
Wungala, 272, 279–280

Xiang Yu, 281
Xiaoqing, 267, 268, 281
Xiao En, 281
Xiaqing, 19
Xishi, 281–282

Xu Xian, 19, 267–268
Xuan Zang, Monkey and, 176

Yagan, 82, 105
Yamato, 283
Yan Zi, 92
Yankee Doodle, 283–284
Yannakis, 284–285
Yan/zi Chunqiu, 92
Yao, 113
Yao Wang, 103, 285
Yasuna, Abe No, 150, 285
Ye Xian, 285–286
Yelbeggen, Tardanak and, 245, 246
Yer, 286
Yo, 250
Yorimitsu, Minamoto, 287
Yoshitsune, 24, 245, 286, 287
Young Guns (film), 31, 128
Young Guns II (film), 31
"Young Jane" (Whall), 75
Young Pretender, The. *See* Stuart, Charles Edward

Young Willie, Pretty Polly and, 263
Younger, Bob, 126, 127
Younger, Cole, 126, 127, 275
Younger, Jim, 126, 127
Younger-James confederation, 125
Yuriwaka, xx, 47, 112, 286–287

Zab, 65, 289–290
Zabava, Princess: Nikitich and, 186
Zarief E-ttool, Ataba and, 15
Zeej Choj Kim, 187, 290
Zelinda, 23, 291
Zeus, 5
Zhang Guolao, 63
Zhang Ye, 93
Zhar-Ptitsa, 252
Zimmer Chronicle, 202
Zipes, Jack, xv, 70
    on Hansel and Gretel, 95
    on Little Red Riding Hood, 156
Zmay, 147
Zong Zin-Il, 88

ABOUT THE AUTHOR

Graham Seal is an Australian folklorist and the author of a number of books, including *The Hidden Culture: Folklore in Australian Society*, *The Oxford Companion to Australian Folklore* (jointly edited with Gwenda Beed Davey), and *The Outlaw Legend: A Cultural Tradition in Britain, America and Australia*. He teaches at Curtin University of Technology, Perth, Western Australia.